CANADIAN DUALISM

LA DUALITÉ CANADIENNE

LA DUALITÉ CANADIENNE

Essais sur les relations entre Canadiens français et Canadiens anglais

Ouvrage réalisé par

MASON WADE

en collaboration avec un Comité du Conseil de Recherche en Sciences sociales du Canada sous la direction de

JEAN-C. FALARDEAU

PRESSES UNIVERSITAIRES LAVAL

UNIVERSITY OF TORONTO PRESS

CANADIAN DUALISM

Studies of French-English Relations

Edited by

MASON WADE

for a Committee of the Social Science Research Council of Canada under the chairmanship of

JEAN-C. FALARDEAU

UNIVERSITY OF TORONTO PRESS

PRESSES UNIVERSITAIRES LAVAL

Printed in Canada
London: Oxford University Press

Reprinted in 2018
ISBN 978-1-4875-8551-8 (paper)

Avant-propos

LE LIVRE que voici est l'épilogue d'une longue histoire. S'il fallait raconter au long cette histoire, c'est tout un autre livre qu'il faudrait écrire. Cette histoire nous reporterait plus de quinze ans en arrière, à un moment où quelques Canadiens de bonne volonté, enthousiasmés par le dynamisme de la vie académique et la maturité croissante de notre pays, conçurent un vaste plan de recherche sur la dualité culturelle dans le Canada contemporain. Mais cette histoire aux débuts enthousiastes serait aussi celle d'une longue persévérance, de beaucoup d'efforts, d'échecs, de rebondissements. Elle ressemblerait à celle des Rois Mages dont la patience fut telle que, malgré toutes les adversités, une étoile apparue au-dessus de l'horizon vint, comme une récompense, confirmer leur foi initiale. Cette histoire serait surtout celle de la patience de la Fondation Carnegie qui a permis à notre aventure de se mettre en marche, de se poursuivre, et, finalement, de déboucher à la périphérie de la terre promise.

D'abord, un mot de la pré-histoire de notre entreprise. Comme je viens de le rappeler, un certain nombre d'universitaires canadiens, dans les années d'après-guerre, avaient le sentiment que notre pays était entré dans une période nouvelle de sa vie adulte. Le moment était venu d'étudier objectivement les facteurs de tout ordre grâce auxquels les deux grands partenaires de la nation canadienne, les Canadiens de langue française et les Canadiens de langue anglaise, étaient parvenus à accepter un *modus vivendi* relativement stable. Il serait important et bienfaisant de faire affleurer le vécu au niveau de la conscience, de façon à permettre une plus grande franchise et une plus grande liberté dans les conduites à venir. Au printemps de 1945, le Conseil de Recherche en Sciences sociales du Canada demanda à un comité spécial de déterminer, après enquête, si une telle étude était réalisable. Ce comité donna une réponse affirmative et un nouveau comité de trois membres, les professeurs B. S. Keirstead, A. R. M. Lower et moi-même, fut constitué avec mandat de discuter et de préparer un plan d'enquête.

Au printemps de 1948, la Fondation Carnegie accorda au Conseil de Recherche en Sciences sociales du Canada une généreuse subvention pour permettre l'exécution du plan de recherche que nous avions proposé. L'objectif essentiel de cette recherche était de dégager les caractères dominants de la dualité de cultures au Canada et de déterminer par quels moyens la nation canadienne avait dominé ses tensions internes. Notre ambition était de déceler les forces d'association et de dissociation dans la vie nationale. Dans ce but, nous avions circonscrit un certain nombre de champs d'enquête dont chacun semblait correspondre à une étape ou à un domaine caractéristique de l'évolution des relations entre Canadiens français et Canadiens anglais : l'histoire récente du « mariage de raison » canadien; les conditionnements écologiques et démographiques des relations sociales; les institutions et les partis politiques en tant que cadres d'affrontement, de discussion et de compromis; les processus de la vie économique; les échanges socio-culturels et les conséquences psychologiques résultant de la distance sociale, des contacts et des tentatives de communication.

Tel était notre espoir. Mais nous avons constaté, pour notre compte, qu'il y a loin de la coupe aux lèvres. Ce qui se passa durant les mois, durant les années qui suivirent, ressembla davantage à une comédie italienne qu'à la symphonie minutieusement prévue. Quiconque a déjà tenté, surtout au Canada, d'amorcer une recherche sociale associant des spécialistes appartenant à des disciplines diverses imaginera facilement ce que furent nos avatars. Au surplus, notre tâche n'était pas simple car nous abordions de vastes domaines relativement inexplorés par la recherche sociale canadienne. Avec patience et diligence, nous sollicitâmes tous ceux dont nous jugions la collaboration nécessaire. Plusieurs répondirent à notre invitation. Un certain nombre de chercheurs se mirent au travail à notre appel. Avec d'autres, il fallut composer et accepter des compromis. Mais un trop grand nombre de ceux que nous avions souhaités comme collaborateurs étaient déjà absorbés par d'autres soucis ou d'autres champs de recherche. Le Canada académique, après tout, n'est pas si vaste, et le nombre des chercheurs n'est pas si élevé. Aussi nos archives contiennent-elles plus de compte-rendus de colloques et de discussions, plus de correspondance inquiète que de manuscrits achevés...

Malgré tous les obstacles, nous avons la satisfaction d'avoir inspiré plusieurs études originales de haute qualité, comme les monographies du professeur Nathan Keyfitz sur les tendances démographiques en milieux urbains, du professeur E. F. Beach sur les revenus des Canadiens de langue anglaise et de langue française, du professeur F. W. Gibson, sur l'histoire politique du Canada entre 1911 et 1930, l'excellente bibliographie de Monique Lortie sur les études ethniques au Canada. Durant ce temps, notre comité s'était adjoint de nouveaux membres : le regretté professeur H. A. Innis qui, depuis les débuts, avait joué pour nous le rôle de mentor; M. John-E. Robbins, le discret magicien du Conseil de Recherche en Sciences sociales du Canada; le R.P. Bernard Mailhiot o.p. et le professeur J. A. Corry. Celui-ci fut, par la suite, remplacé par deux nouveaux membres, le professeur Alexander Brady et le directeur des Archives nationales, M. W. Kaye Lamb. Six années s'écoulèrent ainsi, ponctuées d'arrivées et de départs, de démarrages et de retraites. A l'hiver de 1954, nour dûmes reconnaître que notre plan original était téméraire dans l'état actuel de la vie académique canadienne. Il fallait renoncer à notre vaste plan d'enquête et restreindre notre effort à une tentative plus modeste et plus immédiatement réalisable.

Nous décidâmes à ce moment de préparer un volume. Nous demanderions à des collaborateurs reconnus pour leur compétence de présenter, en de brèves synthèses, l'opinion qu'ils se font, à partir de leur expérience et des recherches existantes, des relations entre Canadiens anglais et Canadiens français. Une telle synthèse panoramique apporterait un éclairage nouveau sur le Canada contemporain. Elle clarifierait les données de la vie nationale. Elle mettrait à jour des questions nouvelles et, ce faisant, elle provoquerait peut-être, à plus ou moins brève échéance, les recherches en profondeur que nous avions en vue au point de départ. Nous eûmes la bonne fortune d'associer à ce nouveau projet l'un des plus érudits observateurs de la vie canadienne, le professeur Mason Wade. A notre demande, il accepta de diriger la préparation du volume. Ensemble, nous discutâmes le plan de l'ouvrage, le choix des collaborateurs, et il se mit à la tâche. Voici enfin, après quatre autres années, le résultat de notre effort commun.

Dira-t-on que la montagne a enfanté d'une souris ? Avant de juger l'ensemble de notre activité, il faudra tenir compte d'un autre fait. C'est grâce à l'influence directe ou indirecte de notre comité qu'ont été entrepris, dans plusieurs universités, dans plusieurs centres de recherche canadiens, des travaux d'un type nouveau portant sur un aspect ou l'autre de la dualité de cultures au Canada. Je veux mentionner seulement, parmi les plus importants : les recherches sur les composantes psycho-sociales des relations inter-ethniques poursuivies sous la direction du P. Noël Mailloux o.p. par l'Institut de Recherches en Relations humaines de Montréal; l'enquête sur les perspectives culturelles de l'enseignement élémentaire canadien-français entreprise, depuis quelques années, par l'Ecole de Pédagogie de l'Université Laval. A ces travaux de longue haleine il faut ajouter de nombreuses études subventionnées par le Comité psychologique et sociologique du Conseil de Recherche pour la Défense, en particulier celles des professeurs J. M. Blackburn et Andrew Kapos de l'Université Queen's, et les travaux exécutés pour le compte des Laboratoires médicaux du Conseil de Recherche pour la Défense par le professeur David N. Solomon et J. Jacques Brazeau. Ces recherches, à elles seules, justifient *a posteriori* l'existence de notre comité. Déjà, nous pouvons nous réjouir des ces résultats. Et peut-être aurons-nous encore de nouveaux motifs de satisfaction, dans l'avenir, au fur et à mesure que nous connaîtrons d'autres travaux qui nous doivent leur inspiration.

* * *

Je tiens, en dernier lieu, à souligner certaines remarques de l'excellente Préface de Mason Wade. Le sujet de chaque chapitre de ce volume est traité par deux auteurs, l'un de langue française, l'autre de langue anglaise. Nous avons estimé que la meilleure façon d'illustrer les similitudes et les différences entre les attitudes, les opinions et les idéologies des deux groupes culturels était de les faire analyser simultanément par des observateurs de chaque groupe. Chaque auteur s'est exprimé dans la langue de son choix et son essai est publié tel quel, sans traduction. Le lecteur canadien cultivé, d'où qu'il soit, est de plus en plus soucieux de bien connaître les deux langues officielles de son pays. Nous lui présentons un livre bilingue au vrai sens du terme.

L'image du Canada que nous présentons dans ces essais est celle d'un pays qui, dans la définition officielle qu'il donne de lui-même, inclut la dualité de cultures. Cette conception n'est peut-être pas encore partagée par un certain nombre de Canadiens qui rêvent d'un canadianisme intégral. Mais il faut être réaliste. Malgré la subdivision de notre pays en dix états provinciaux distincts, malgré la diversité de ses régions géographiques et économiques, malgré la diversité ethnique de sa population, malgré enfin la solidité de ses structures politiques transcontinentales, le grand fait de la vie canadienne est la coexistence de deux univers culturels, l'un français, l'autre anglais. Comme l'a écrit après beaucoup d'autres Malcolm Ross, « nous sommes depuis les débuts, et sans possibilité d'échapper à notre destin, une nation à double foyer ». Cette dualité a déterminé la nature même du gouvernement canadien et les caractères de notre constitution. Elle sous-tend la vie nationale. Elle dessine les traits du visage sous lequel les autres peuples nous connaissent et nous reconnaissent. Nous souhaitons que dans ce livre, comme dans un miroir fidèle, on retrouve l'image de notre identité profonde.

En 1949, dans son discour présidentiel à la Société royale du Canada, M. Gustave Lanctôt distinguait trois périodes caractéristiques dans l'histoire de la coexistence des groupes français et anglais au Canada depuis deux siècles : la période du rapprochement social et de la separation politique, de 1760 à 1791; l'étape de l'influence mutuelle dans la vie politique, de 1791 à 1867; enfin, depuis la Confédération, la phase de l'interaction proprement dite, accentuée par la détente qui a suivi les années 1914–18 et par une communication plus intense entre les « élites » de chaque groupe. Il souhaitait que le Canada cessât d'être le pays de « deux solitudes » pour devenir, en exemple au monde, le pays de « deux fortitudes ». Peut-être sommes-nous déjà engagés dans cette nouvelle étape. Est-il téméraire d'espérer que ce livre, à sa façon, éclairera la route dans cette direction ?

JEAN-C. FALARDEAU
président, 1952–8
Comité pour l'étude des deux cultures
Conseil de Recherche en Sciences sociales du Canada

Université Laval
1958

Foreword

THIS BOOK is the result of a long story. To recapitulate the contrapuntal, often painful chapters of this story would, alone, fill another book. Not unlike the story of the Magi, it would illustrate how constancy of purpose and determination in the course of a collective undertaking can measure up against misfortune and, after endless uncertainties, eventually stimulate the reappearance, on the horizon, of the long-expected star. Let it suffice to mention here some of the essential stages of this research expedition which may help to convey its full meaning as well as to record the patience of the Carnegie Corporation which has made it possible.

The pre-history of the book can be traced to the summer of 1945 when a committee was nominated by the Social Science Research Council of Canada to explore the possibilities of initiating a study of French-English relations in Canada. It was felt that the time had come in Canada for a frank and objective appraisal of the historical and contemporary factors which have determined, through conflict, accommodation and co-operation, the formal and informal patterns of relations between the two major component groups of our increasingly mature nation. As a result of the discussions of this nucleus of social scientists, a clearer vision of the project was attained and a smaller committee, consisting of Professors B. S. Keirstead, A. R. M. Lower, and the writer, was instructed to draft a more definite outline.

The spring of 1948 marks the beginning of the proper history of this book, when a generous grant was made by the Carnegie Corporation for the contemplated study. The specific aim of the project, as it was then formulated, was to reveal the nature of biculturalism in Canada and to ascertain the various social techniques which the Canadian people have worked out for the resolution or containment of the inner tensions of their country. It was to be a study of the balance of the centripetal and centrifugal social forces within the Canadian nation. A few specific areas of investigation were carefully delineated as representing the more meaningful stages or levels of relations between French and English in Canada: the historical highlights of the Canadian *mariage de raison* up to the present time; the demographic and ecological substratum of social coexistence; the political techniques and institutions of mutual adjustment; the dynamics of economic life; the psycho-sociological implications of communication and reciprocal recognition.

Such was the ambition, such was the hope. What actually occurred in the course of the following months and years might look, from the outside, like a breath-taking succession of plays within the play. Those who have had experience with inter-disciplinary research projects will easily picture the inevitable ups and downs; particularly those who have had experience with social research in Canada. Actually, our own experience has been unique in that our committee was venturing into relatively unexplored domain where very little basic research had yet been done by Canadian scholars. Numerous contributors were sought and invited; some answered; a few started investigations in the direction which we proposed to them. The lines of approach of the study were modified in order to meet the preferences of potential collaborators. The organizational and inspirational formula of the project was left flexible enough to permit any individual researcher or team of researchers to become associated with it. But most of those whom we had originally hoped to attract were already committed to other preoccupations and other fields of research. Our files thus include the records of more discussion seminars, of more suggestions, of more hopeful or distressed correspondence than of completed studies.

Yet, despite all shortcomings, we rejoice in having inspired and sponsored a varied range of highly valuable studies such as those of Dr. Nathan Keyfitz on demographic problems and urban influences on the size of families in French Canada, of Professor E. F. Beach on income differentials, of Professor F. W. Gibson on political accommodation in Canada between 1911 and 1930, as well as Miss Monique Lortie's critical bibliography on bicultural relations in Canada. To our committee were added new members, who included the late Professor H. A. Innis, our periodic adviser since the very first days; Dr. John E. Robbins, the untiringly helpful Secretary of the S.S.R.C.C.; Father Bernard Mailhiot, o.p., and Professor J. A. Corry, who was later replaced by two new members, Professor Alexander Brady and Dr. W. Kaye Lamb. Six years, punctuated by enthusiastic entrances and uncontrollable exits, had now elapsed. In the winter of 1954, it was unanimously felt that the project should be redesigned on a more immediately workable, less ambitious plan. The most sensible alternative seemed to be to shape our final effort into the form of a book of essays on biculturalism. Such a book would have a dual purpose: it would set forth, on the basis of past research and recent observation, what is now known about the main aspects of French-English in Canada; in so doing, it would raise questions and uncover with precision the areas where further research is necessary and thus stimulate, in a more direct, perhaps provocative manner, the sort of fundamental exploration which we had initially in mind. We were fortunate enough to induce the best-qualified scholar, Professor Mason Wade, to act as editor of such a book. We agreed on an outline and on a choice of potential contributors. And here, at the end of four more years, is the outcome of our journey.

Shall it be said that the mountain in labour has brought forth a mouse? I suggest that one cannot pass judgment on our endeavour without taking into account a fascinating, still prolonged series of chain reactions which it has originated in the field of social research in Canada. Many projects bearing on one aspect or the other of biculturalism, which have been undertaken or are still under way in Canadian universities and research institutions, have directly or indirectly been inspired by our committee's work and stimulus. I want to mention here only a few of the most outstanding, such as the studies on the dynamics of inter-ethnic relations conducted by the Centre de Recherches en Relations humaines of Montreal, under the guidance of Father Noël Mailloux, o.p., and the long-range study on the cultural outlook of teaching in Quebec undertaken by Laval University's School of Pedagogy. To these must be added various studies sponsored by the Defence Research Board's Committee on Sociological and Social Psychological Problems, for example the surveys of Dr. J. M. Blackburn and Dr. Andrew Kapos of Queen's University, or those initiated by the Defence Research Medical Laboratories itself, and I refer particularly to the contributions of Dr. D. N. Solomon and Mr. J. Jacques Brazeau. This sketchy enumeration is far from exhaustive. Already, our reasons for satisfaction are not negligible. Our surprise may very well be increased when we learn, in years to come, of all the pioneering studies which will have grown out of our efforts. Time will tell.

Nothing needs to be added to the candid sociological Introduction of the editor. One or two aspects of it, though, deserve re-emphasis. First, the fact that this book on biculturalism reports the labour of two groups of contributors: for each topic under scrutiny we have selected two authors, one English, one French. It has seemed that the most eloquent way of illustrating the similarities or the differences in attitudes, opinions, and ideologies between the French and the English was to have them exposed through the respective eyes of each group. Moreover, each author has expressed himself in the language of his choice. We are thus offering a truly bilingual book to the alert Canadian reader who is more and more willing and expected to be at home with his country's two main languages.

Secondly, the picture presented here is that of a Canada which is now officially defining itself in terms of its cultural dualism. This view may not correspond to the conception which many Canadians have of themselves or of all Canadians as unhyphenated social beings. Yet, notwithstanding Canada's regional and provincial diversities and varied ethnic distribution, notwithstanding its increasing political equilibrium and social strength, the dominant fact of Canadian life is the coexistence of two major cultural groups, the French- and the English-speaking social universes. "We are," as Malcolm Ross has written, "inescapably, and almost from the first, the bifocal people." It is this biculturalism which has determined the very nature of our government and of our constitution, the texture of our national life, the true face which we present to others and which they see. Our hope is that this book is a not too unfaithfully mirrored image of our deeper, real self.

In his presidential address to the Royal Society of Canada in 1949, Dr. Gustave Lanctôt recapitulated what, in his opinion, had been the three characteristic stages in the history of French-English coexistence and cultural cross-fertilization in Canada for the last two centuries: social *rapprochement* and political separation, between 1760 and 1791; reciprocal political influence between 1791 and 1867; the modern phase of greater rapport and co-operation, accelerated by a healthy easing of the situation after 1914–18 and subsequent wider cultural communication between the *élites*. His confidence was that we might have reached the stage when the former "two solitudes" were becoming "two fortitudes." Perhaps we are living this new historical phase. Is it presumptuous to fancy that our book, in its fashion, may serve as a beacon?

JEAN-C. FALARDEAU

Chairman, 1952–8
Committee on Biculturalism
Social Science Research Council of Canada

Laval University
1958

Contents / Table des matières

Introduction

THE PURPOSE OF THIS BOOK is to analyse and interpret the present state of biculturalism in Canada. This is an examination of the way in which English-speaking and French-speaking Canadians behave toward each other as parts of the same national whole, and the way in which the ideas of one group have been affected by those of the other. The underlying assumption of these studies is that these two groups constitute the foundation of the Canadian nation, and that the behaviour of each can only be understood in the context of its relationship with the other. The basic question raised in these studies is whether there has been communication, adjustment, and co-operation between the two cultural groups, or misunderstanding, friction, and conflict. Inevitably, since Canada has been created on the basis of compromises, the answers do not fall neatly into either category, but partly under both. This book is intended to shed some light on the questions "What is Canada?" and "How much have English-speaking Canadians and French-speaking Canadians contributed to the Canadian whole?"

Since the answers inevitably vary greatly in different areas of national life, it has seemed useful to limit this book to such basic fields as social outlook, religion and philosophy, the law, demography, economics, labour, and politics. Because the situation varies so much in Quebec and in other parts of Canada where there are significant French-Canadian groups, there are special studies of the Maritimes, Ontario, and the west. A section on New England, where more than a third of the French-Canadian people in North America have found homes away from home, is included for the useful comparisons it affords. Since the time is not yet in Canada when a Canadian of either group can speak with confidence for both English and French Canadians, each topic is dealt with by both an English Canadian and a French Canadian. One of the best ways of getting a better understanding of a complicated situation is to see it through the eyes of another person, and in these fundamental matters even the difference of approach can be suggestive of the different ideologies involved.

If this book should be found useful, it is hoped that it may be supplemented by another concerned with the more humanistic aspects of biculturalism, such as education, literature, art, music, radio, and television. In these fields until very recently there has been little contact between English and French Canada; there were two cultures rather than biculturalism, a situation recalling that described by Pierre Chauveau in 1876 when he likened the Canada of that day to the famous staircase of the Château de Chambord, so constructed that two persons could mount it without meeting and without seeing each other except at intervals: "English and French, we climb by a double flight of stairs toward the destinies reserved for us on this continent, without knowing each other, without meeting each other, and without even seeing each other, except on the landing of politics. In social and literary terms, we are far more foreign to each other than the English and French of Europe."[1] But with the official recognition of biculturalism by the Report of the Massey Commission, the former "Two Solitudes" have been drawing closer to each other, the process expedited by a general recognition that if Canadian culture is not to be swamped by American culture, it must be both French and English.

Obviously these brief essays do not pretend to be definitive studies. The intention is to state the situation, suggest tentative hypotheses on the basis of present knowledge, and indicate the areas where further research is most urgently needed. The book will serve its purpose if it stimulates further study of these matters. In the past there has been a curious reluctance on the part of both English and French Canadians to examine the fundamentals of their national relationship, presumably for fear of disturbing it, and in a desire to let well enough alone. But now that the diplomatic tradition of the *bonne entente*, with its formal exchanges of polite compliments, has been outmoded by the rapid national development of Canada, both English and French Canadians appear willing to join in frank and searching examinations of their attitudes in the interest of true mutual understanding. It is probably unfortunate that thus far so much of the research has been done on French Canada by English-speaking scholars. There is no reason why French Canada should be the only Canadian guinea-pig, and French-Canadian studies of English Canada would certainly be enlightening and valuable. With the growth of exchanges of professors and students between the English and French universities, the prospects for a better-balanced mutual examination of the Canadian heritage are much brighter.

Such an examination need not be mere contemplation of one's navel,

[1]P.-J.-O. Chauveau, *L'Instruction publique au Canada* (Québec, 1876), p. 335.

as some criticism of the Canadian tendency toward self-examination has suggested. Findings of international significance have been achieved by such group efforts as the Laval symposium on the social effects of industrialization in the province of Quebec, the Canadian Westinghouse conference on Canada's future, and the Laval symposium on renewable natural resources.[2] The device used at the latter Laval symposium of examining a major problem successively from the world, North American, Canadian, and provincial points of view proved very rewarding, as did the pooling of the talents of French-Canadian, English-Canadian, and American scholars in studying the impact of industrialization in Quebec. It would appear that many cooks do not necessarily spoil a bicultural broth.

A word should be said about how this volume was put together. The editor was asked by the Committee on Biculturalism of the Social Science Research Council of Canada to prepare an outline of topics and to suggest authors. Both this outline and the list of contributors were modified by the committee and by the hazards attendant upon all collaborative scholarly enterprises. The authors were selected both for their expertness in their fields and for their acquaintance with the situation on the other side of the ethnic fence which still exists in some areas of Canadian life. Since many of the older generation of Canadian scholars have frequently put their views on these matters on record, an effort was made to select younger men whose views were not so well known. It is the editor's belief that there is a significant difference in the attitudes of the older and younger generation, reflecting the recent rapid growth of Canadian national feeling and the coming together of French- and English-Canadian nationalism in a common Canadian nationalism. The focus of this volume is on the present, although there must necessarily be some consideration of the historical development of contemporary attitudes. The general reader will probably regret that not much is said about the future, but the scholar is understandably reluctant to engage in crystal-ball gazing. And then, if the present situation is well understood, the future may confidently be left to take care of itself. Finally, it should be noted that the individual contributions are dated as of the time of writing, since the completion and publication of this book have been postponed by the delays inevitably attendant upon collective scholarly enterprises.

The editor has not attempted to offer any guidance to the con-

[2]J.-C. Falardeau, éd., *Essais sur le Québec contemporain* (Québec, 1953); G. P. Gilmour, ed., *Canada's Tomorrow* (Toronto, 1954); G. Maheux, éd., *Conservation des richesses naturelles renouvelables* (Québec, 1953).

tributors, other than to try to keep the French and English writers on each topic within shouting distance of each other. It was his feeling that each contributor should be left free to formulate and analyse the particular problem as he saw fit, since the varying approaches would in themselves be revealing. The editor's principal function has been the ungrateful one of prodding busy people to fulfil the promises which he wrung from them in unguarded moments. In the final section entitled "Conclusions" he attempts to sum up the symposium, to bring out the differences and analogies of English and French attitudes, and to suggest the most urgent areas for further investigation. He has sought to be a neutral arbitrator, looking at a domestic situation from outside the family, but with sympathy for both English and French points of view acquired from his residence in and study of both parts of Canada.

The editor wishes to express his indebtedness to Professor Jean-C. Falardeau for preparing French translations of the preliminary pages and for checking the French texts at various stages. He is also most grateful to Miss Francess G. Halpenny and Miss Jean C. Jamieson of the University of Toronto Press for their unfailing helpfulness with the problems that arose during the course of publication.

MASON WADE

Director, Canadian Studies Program
University of Rochester

Préface

L'OBJET DE CE VOLUME est d'étudier la coexistence des deux groupes culturels dominants dans le Canada d'aujourd'hui et, plus précisément, d'observer la manière dont les Canadiens anglais et les Canadiens français se comportent les uns envers les autres en tant qu'éléments d'un même ensemble national, et la manière dont les attitudes et les idéologies des deux groupes se sont réciproquement influencées. Le postulat sur lequel reposent ces essais est que ces deux groupes constituent la substance de la nation canadienne. D'autre part, on ne peut comprendre les comportements de chacun que si on les perçoit dans la perspective des relations d'un groupe avec l'autre. Notre préoccupation principale a été de déterminer jusqu'à quel point, dans l'histoire récente de la coexistence canadienne, il y a eu communication, adaptation réciproque, coopération, ou inversement, mésentente, friction, conflit, entre les deux groupes. Comme le Canada a été le résultat d'incessants compromis, le jugement ne peut pas être nettement tranché. La réalité canadienne a un caractère antinomique. En définitive, les deux questions fondamentales que nous tentons d'éclairer sont les suivantes : « Qu'est-ce que le Canada ? » — « Dans quelle mesure les Canadiens anglais et les Canadiens français ont-ils respectivement contribué à l'édification d'un Canada commun ? »

Les réponses à ces questions varient grandement selon les divers paliers de la vie nationale. C'est pourquoi nous avons cru sage de restreindre nos analyses aux domaines suivants qui nous ont semblé les plus significatifs: attitudes et idéologies collectives; religion et philosophie; droit; phénomènes démographiques; vie économique; vie ouvrière; vie politique. Par ailleurs, les données de la coexistence sont fort différentes dans la province de Québec et dans les autres régions canadiennes où vivent des groupes francophones. Nous avons donc consacré des études spéciales aux provinces maritimes, à l'Ontario et aux provinces de l'ouest. Pour fins de comparaison et de contraste, nous avons aussi inclus une monographie sur la Nouvelle-Angleterre où plus d'un tiers da la population d'origine canadienne-française d'Amérique du Nord vit loin du foyer ancestral. Enfin, le moment ne semble pas encore tout à fait venu, au Canada, où quiconque puisse parler avec également de compétence et d'assurance du groupe anglais *et* du groupe français. Sur chacun des sujects fondamentaux, il existe deux modes différents de voir et de penser, l'un français, l'autre anglais. Nous avons cru réfléter fidèlement l'état de la pensée canadienne en faisant traiter chaque sujet par deux auteurs, l'un de langue anglaise, l'autre de langue française. Sur chaque problème on aura ainsi une double optique. Ces différences d'optiques elles-mêmes sont révélatrices des différences dans les idéologies en présence.

Si ce volume a le succès désiré, nous voudrions qu'il soit complété plus tard par un second volume qui traiterait, celui-là, des formes d'expression intellectuelle et artistique des deux cultures : éducation, littérature, beaux-arts, musique, radio et télévision. Jusqu'a une époque récente, il n'y a eu que très peu de communication réelle, en ces domaines, entre Canadiens français et Canadiens anglais. Il y avait des remparts plutôt que des rencontres entre les deux cultures. La situation contemporaine n'est guère différente de celle que décrivait Pierre Chauveau, en 1876, lorsqu'il comparaît le Canada au fameux escalier du château de Chambord, construit de telle manière que deux personnes puissent monter en même temps sans se rencontrer et en ne s'apercevant que par intervalles. « Anglais et français, écrivait-il, nous montons comme par une double rampe vers les destinées qui nous sont réservées sur ce continent, sans nous connaître, nous rencontrer, ni même nous voir ailleurs que sur le palier de la politique. Socialement et littérairement parlant, nous sommes plus étrangers les uns aux autres de beaucoup que ne le sont les Anglais et les Français d'Europe[1] ». Mais, depuis la reconnaissance officielle de la dualité culturelle canadienne par le Rapport de la Commission Massey, les « deux solitudes » de jadis se sont davantage rapprochées l'une de l'autre. On reconnaît de plus en plus que si la culture canadienne doit résister à l'envahissement culturel américain, elle doit manifester son identité française et anglaise.

Ces essais n'ont pas la prétention de dire le dernier mot. Notre but a été de décrire un état social, de formuler de nouvelles hypothèses pour interpréter celui-ci à la lumière de nos connaissances actuelles, et enfin d'indiquer les secteurs où il faut poursuivre la recherche. Notre livre aura atteint son but si, justement, il stimule une étude plus approfondie des questions qu'il soulève. Dans le passé, tant les Cana-

[1]P.-J.-O. Chauveau, *L'Instruction publique au Canada* (Québec, 1876), p. 335.

diens français que les Canadiens anglais se sont étrangement abstenus d'observer de près la nature des rapports qui les unissent dans une symbiose nationale. Crainte de rompre un fragile équilibre ou conviction que le mieux est l'ennemi du bien ? Mais on a maintenant dépassé le stade de la traditionnelle « bonne entente » et de la politesse conventionnelle. Dans un Canada revigoré, les deux groupes semblent également désireux de se connaître d'une façon réaliste en vue d'une compréhension mutuelle authentique. Il est peut-être regrettable que, jusqu'à maintenant, ce soit le Canada français qui ait davantage été l'objet d'étude de la part d'observateurs anglophones. Mais il n'y a aucune raison pour que le Canada français soit l'unique objet canadien de curiosité scientifique. Des études par des Canadiens français sur le Canada anglais seraient fascinantes et enrichissantes. Grâce à l'échange accru de professeurs et d'élèves entre universités françaises et anglaises, on peut prévoir que, dans un avenir prochain, l'héritage canadien sera l'objet d'enquêtes plus judicieuses et mieux équilibrées.

De telles enquêtes devront éviter la tentation de narcissisme à laquelle entraîne souvent une certaine tendance canadienne à l'examen de conscience stérile. D'ailleurs, il existe d'excellents modèles à imiter. Je songe en particulier à des études collectives récentes dont l'intérêt dépasse de beaucoup les frontières nationales, tels le symposium organisé en 1953 par la Canadian Westinghouse sur l'avenir du Canada et les deux symposia tenus en 1952 à l'Université Laval, l'un sur les répercussions sociales de l'industrialisation, l'autre sur les ressources naturelles[2]. Dans le dernier cas, on a retiré un immense profit d'un tour d'horizon permettant d'observer un même phénomène successivement dans ses perspectives mondiales, nord-américaines, canadiennes et régionales. Dans le cas précédent, pour évaluer les effets de l'industrialisation dans la province de Québec, on a fait appel aux lumières conjuguées de spécialistes canadiens-français, canadiens-anglais et américains. Lorsqu'il s'agit d'échanges culturels, beaucoup de cuisiniers ne gâtent pas nécessairement la sauce...

Un mot de la façon dont ce livre a vu le jour. Un comité spécial du Conseil de Recherche en Sciences sociales du Canada intéressé à l'étude de la dualité culturelle au Canada, ayant décidé de publier un volume d'essais, m'invita à en assumer la réalisation. Il fallut mettre au point un plan général et une liste de collaborateurs. Ce plan et cette

[2]G. P. Gilmour, ed., *Canada's Tomorrow* (Toronto, 1954); Jean-C. Falardeau, éd., *Essais sur le Québec contemporain* (Québec, 1953); G. Maheux, éd., *Conservation des richesses naturelles renouvelables* (Québec, 1953).

liste durent être plusieurs fois modifiés, tant par le comité lui-même que par suite des aléas qui guettent toute entreprise de cette nature. Les collaborateurs furent choisis à la fois pour leur compétence et pour leur faculté de vision au delà des frontières de leurs milieux respectifs. Etant donné que plusieurs professeurs et spécialistes canadiens de la génération qui nous précède ont souvent eu, dans le passé, l'occasion d'exprimer leurs vues sur les sujets que nous traitons, nous avons préféré choisir des collaborateurs plus jeunes dont les vues sont moins connues. Pour ma part, j'ai la conviction qu'il existe une différence marquée entre les attitudes de la génération précédente et celles de la génération actuelle. Cette différence réflète l'évolution rapide du sentiment canadien tout autant que la fusion graduelle du nationalisme canadien-français et du nationalisme canadien-anglais en une forme nouvelle de patriotisme canadien global. En outre, ce livre porte principalement sur le présent bien que, nécessairement, on ait fait appel au passé dans tous les cas où il fallait récapituler la genèse des attitudes contemporaines. Le lecteur déplorera peut-être que nous parlions peu de l'avenir. Il comprendra cependant que l'observateur scientifique se refuse à jouer le rôle de devin. D'ailleurs, si l'on comprend bien le présent, on a toutes les raisons de laisser l'avenir à lui-même. On notera enfin que chaque essai porte la date de sa composition. Cette façon de procéder tient au fait que la publication de ce volume a été différée par des retards inévitables dans une entreprise collective comme celle-ci. Elle permettra au lecteur d'évaluer chaque essai de manière équitable.

Les auteurs de ces essais n'ont reçu aucune directive. On a seulement demandé que chaque couple d'auteurs français et anglais se situe dans une même perspective. Chaque collaborateur a été libre de présenter et d'analyser son sujet comme il l'entendait. L'optique de chacun, en effet, est en elle-même révélatrice. La principale tâche du soussigné a été d'aiguillonner les collaborateurs, professionnellement absorbés par des tâches multiples, et de leur rappeler les échéances auxquelles, dans un moment de faiblesse, ils avaient librement consenti...Il a aussi tenté, comme son mandat le demandait, de faire le bilan des essais, de dégager les analogies et les différences caractéristiques dans les attitudes des Canadiens anglais et des Canadiens français, et enfin d'indiquer dans quels domaines il faudrait poursuivre la recherche. Il a voulu jouer le rôle d'arbitre impartial, observant et jugeant de l'extérieur une scène de famille. Mais il a aussi voulu remplir ce rôle avec toute la sympathie que, à la suite de ses travaux et de ses séjours dans les deux univers culturels canadiens, il continue d'éprouver pour les attitudes des Canadiens des deux groupes.

A M. Jean-C. Falardeau revient le mérite d'avoir fait les versions françaises des pages préliminaires et d'avoir revisé les textes français. Mlles Francess G. Halpenny et Jean C. Jamieson des Presses de l'Université de Toronto n'ont pas cessé de rendre d'utiles services au cours de la publication.

MASON WADE

Directeur, Institut d'Etudes canadiennes
Université de Rochester

I. ABSTRACT FACTORS

A. Social Outlook

I. PERSPECTIVES GÉNÉRALES

A. Attitudes et idéologies

The English-Canadian Outlook

G. V. FERGUSON
Editor-in-Chief, The Montreal Star

THIS IS ABOUT the twelve million Canadians who, regardless of racial origin, use the English tongue in common speech and who—most of them—know no other. They are predominantly Protestant in religion; and their culture and traditions, their moral, social and political outlook flow in the main from Anglo-Saxon sources—either direct from Great Britain, or from the American colonies in their revolutionary days.

Of these twelve million souls, between three and four million have little British or American blood in their veins. They or their ancestors came to Canada direct from the Europe that lies west of the Urals. They used to be called "New Canadians," an expression now falling into disuse as the process of Canadianization gathers strength. Stephen Leacock once remarked of the Ukrainian immigrant to Canada that, if he were just left long enough alone, he would in due course glow with pride over Nelson's victory at Trafalgar. His prophecy has not been fulfilled. The descendant of the Ukrainian peasant has, to be sure, learned some British history in school. He has become, however, not British but Canadian. When he thinks of the past, he chiefly thinks—more and more fitfully as time goes on—of the cultural heritage and nationalist ambitions of his own forbears. Of these he is vastly proud and keeps them in high remembrance. Leacock, when he devised his wisecrack, was thinking in terms of a British-Canadian ideal which, even by the time he coined it, was rapidly losing strength.

Nevertheless it is true that the mark and pattern of the life of the English-speaking Canadian is more British than it is anything else. These influences came to bear upon him in distinctive ways, the chief of which was the early settlement of Ontario and New Brunswick by the Loyalists who fled the Thirteen Colonies after the American Revolution. The intensity of their convictions and their emotions has been admirably set out in Kenneth Roberts' novel, *Oliver Wiswell.*

Its pages provide an important clue to those bewildered persons who, to this day, cannot understand why the obvious economic unity of North America with its vast complementary resources should be so irrevocably divided politically. The United Empire Loyalists, only a few thousands in number, laid an indelible mark on the basic thinking of those who joined them or came after them. They imprinted a pattern which, after 165 years, remains strong.

They created Ontario, richest and most populous of the Canadian provinces. They reinforced the loyalties of the Atlantic provinces. The major political and social pressures upon the three prairie provinces and British Columbia were imposed by this stock which, for a century now, has been more or less steadily reinforced by successive waves of immigration direct from Britain and from Ulster. That pattern is a curious blend of deep affection for Great Britain and of a latent but tenacious undercurrent of anti-Americanism. It was the chief influence, most directly felt and expressed in Canada's colonial days. There have been groups and occasions when the English Canadian has been even more vociferously loyal to the Crown than the British have been themselves. Walter Bagehot's candid analysis of the decline of the monarchy and the growth of republicanism in England ninety years ago would have been impossible for a Canadian. As late as 1914, it is reported that Col. Sam Hughes, Canadian Minister of Militia, hauled down the Union Jack from his headquarters in disgust that a British Liberal Government should delay its declaration of war against Germany until four days after the first shots had been fired.

History's hand is heavy but not remorseless. Other influences now chiefly weigh upon a mid-twentieth-century English Canada which, for the first time in its history, has developed a national sense and an independence which bear only slight resemblances to the thinking of its colonial days. Of these the biggest single factor is the impact of modern technology and the industrial revolution. These have chiefly come to Canada not from Great Britain but from the United States. With them have come the recognition that Canada has stopped being a British colony and has become an American nation, a part of North America dominated by its huge neighbour. American technicians and managers, American money, American ideas, songs, books, radio and movies, styles and fashions, American goods of all kinds, material and spiritual, flow increasingly across the Canadian border. A stranger on brief passage might mistake Vancouver for Seattle, Winnipeg for Des Moines, Toronto for Buffalo or Cleveland. It would be only on closer examination that the marked differences would become manifest: the slightly slower tempo of life, the less volatile reaction to events, the more sober, more conservative attitudes of mind, the higher degree of sabbatarianism, the greater gift for compromise and the middle way, the stricter disciplines of a parliamentary as against a congressional democracy, the respect for law and for order, the modesty which flows as much from a long history of colonial dependence as from a realistic sense of the place of a small nation in a big-power world.

It is only of late that Canadians have come to know that their own scholars, their own artists, their own musicians, their own engineers, doctors, and athletes—or the best of them—are as good as the best in the world; and pride has joined with satisfaction in the discovery. But, typically, Canadians also recognize that most of them can find outside the national borders greater opportunities for the exercise of their skills, that older and richer countries provide greater facilities for development and for emulation. But this is something very different from the old feeling of innate inferiority which afflicts the colonial mind.

There is much to be said for the breaking of the colonial tie with spectacular speed or with violence, just as there is much to be said for learning to swim by being cast without warning into deep water. Canada's slow movement to political autonomy, by spaced stages, most of them effected by prior arrangement with the metropolitan power, has played its own part in the formation of the Canadian character and outlook. The special factors in play here affect, or have affected, English Canada in the way described. Their effect on French Canada has probably been in many respects quite different. The British colonial by deliberate choice stands in a category quite other than that of the French colonial whose land became a British dependency by the accident of arms.

The influences described up to now have been largely historical and traditional. Consider now the effect of the efforts of the English Canadians to settle and to develop a land whose area, Alaska apart, exceeds that of the United States. There were, to begin with, not very many of them. They had their own difficult tasks to maintain and to enlarge their lives in Ontario. Fifteen hundred miles beyond them to the west there lay the empty prairie lands. Generation after generation of frontier settlers made their appearance on the Canadian scene, each one pushing the limits of settlement further west and further north. The communities they formed were primitive, precisely like those which settled the American West, save for one important fact. The climate was much more against them. The winter is longer and much more severe; the rainfall, more uncertain. The hazards of settlement and of life were, and are, more difficult: the farmer who does not know the risks of untimely frosts and utter failure should not attempt the task of Canadian settlement. Before long another factor supervened. The western pioneers learned that their products—the chief one was wheat—had to find foreign markets. The domestic market, unlike the United States market for the American pioneers, was far too small to buy all they grew. From the beginning western Canada had to export or perish. There grew up, on this economic basis, an attitude of mind different from that of the rest of the continent, apart from the cotton-exporting areas of the southern United States.

This brought an awareness of the outside world not only to western Canada but to all English Canada. It used often to be said of the American western farmer that the world ended for him at Chicago. For his Canadian counterpart, the world ended in Liverpool, centre of the British wheat trade and a great re-exporting centre for the rest of Europe. The western Canadian became a free trader, a thing the American farmer never was. It was a factor which broadened his outlook, made him aware of the outside world, brought and kept him in touch with the thinking of Europe to an extent new and strange to the North American continent. One of the immediate effects of this was to strengthen the old traditional British sentiment in the newer parts of Canada. Britain was the market, and where the markets were, there the heart lay also.

The cross-currents, however, never failed. Across the strong, dominant, Ontario-British tradition, across the great, foreign, inarticulate mass of European settlers, there swept also the important influence of the American settlers who, attracted by the prospect of free land, flowed into the Prairies in substantial numbers. They brought with them various strong religious strains, none of which was very much different from the Presbyterianism and Methodism of the dominant, eastern Canadian stock: all were Protestant, all strongly evangelical. This evangelical missionary fervour, coupled with the Puritanism of New England and the austerity of English Methodism, deeply affected the outlook of the people as a whole. As time went on the evangels changed their content. They became as much social, economic, and political as religious. It is no accident that the political protest movements on the Prairies, between 1915 and 1935, were all highly seasoned with a moral or quasi-evangelical fervour: from the Single Taxers and the Prohibitionists to the Social Crediters. Like all fighting minority creeds, these determined to impose their zealotry on the passive, unreflective majorities which sought only to be left alone, but were too lethargic to organize themselves effectively in opposition.

This spirit of independence and protest on the Prairies had interesting social and political consequences. Imbued with a strong regional spirit, the prairie peoples regarded themselves as the most vigorous and the most enlightened of all Canadian groups. The western settlers, with cash in their pockets, the result of a good crop or two, would return to visit their old homes in Ontario and the Atlantic provinces, leaving no doubt in the minds of their relatives and former cronies that "the East" was a dreary, dull, unprogressive part of the country, lacking the western enterprise and initiative so amply evidenced by their big fur coats and travelled talk. They pointed out too that "the East" was fit only to fasten itself like a leech on the hardy pioneers, its banks, its mortgage and trust companies squeezing money out of the aggressive prairie dwellers for the sake of the do-nothing *rentiers* and the Big Interests which ran the railroads, making pots of money for eastern and foreign shareholders. Against this soft and, to their minds, immoral way of life, they set their own hard work, their pioneering, their aggressive, free and easy ways, the purity of their austerity.

Thus regional differences became accentuated, but out of that spirit of prairie independence there flowed also a firm rejection of whatever remained in Canada of the old spirit of colonial subordination and inferiority. Recall the remark in Hugh MacLennan's novel *Barometer Rising* from one of its colonial maritime characters, "I've wasted a whole lifetime in this hole of a town. Everything in this country is second-rate. It always is in a colony."

It would be pleasant in such circumstances to record that, as the Prairies threw off this yoke and asserted themselves through the mouths of such spokesmen as John S. Ewart and John W. Dafoe, there blossomed a myriad harvest of creative work in the arts and letters. The facts, however, are otherwise. Canada's artists, musicians, and men and women of letters have come mainly from the "effete East." The fact is, as E. K. Brown has written in his essay *On Canadian Poetry*:

> A . . . powerful obstacle at present to the growth of a great literature is the spirit of the frontier, or its afterglow. Most Canadians live at some distance from anything that could even in the loosest terms be known as a material frontier; but the standards which the frontier-life applied are still current, if disguised. Books are a luxury on the frontier; and writers are an anomaly. On the frontier a man is mainly judged by what he can do to bring his immediate environment quickly and visibly under the control of society. No nation is more practical than ours; admiration is readily stirred,

even more readily than south of the border, by the man who can run a factory, or invent a gadget or save a life by surgical genius. This kind of admiration is a disguised form of the frontier's set of values. No such admiration goes out to any form of the aesthetic or contemplative life. The uneasiness in the presence of the contemplative or aesthetic is to be ascribed to the frontier feeling that these are luxuries which should not be sought at a time when there is a tacit contract that everyone should be doing his share in the common effort to build the material structure of a nation. That a poem or a statue or a metaphysic could contribute to the fabric of a nation is not believed. In a gathering of ruminative historians and economists, speaking their mind one evening in Winnipeg years before the war was imminent, the unanimous opinion was that a destroyer or two would do more than a whole corpus of literature to establish a Canadian nationality. The dissent of two students of literature was heard in awkward silence. If there were any belief in the national value of art or pure thought, the strong desire of the frontiersman that what is being built should eclipse all that was ever built before would make a milieu for art and thought that would at the root be propitious.

In a disguised form of frontier life what function can the arts hold? They are at best recreative. They may be alternatives to the hockey match, or the whiskey bottle, or the frivolous sexual adventure as means of clearing the mind from the worries of business and enabling it to go back to business refreshed. The arts' value as interpretation is lost in the exclusive emphasis on their value as diversion, and even their value as diversion is simplified to the lowest possible form—a work of art must divert strongly and completely. It must divert as a thriller or a smashing jest diverts, not as an elaborate and subtle romance or a complicated argument diverts. In a word, Canada is a nation where the best-seller is king, as it is on the frontier.[1]

If this is true of all Canada, as Brown believed, it was particularly true of the Prairies where the frontier itself was seldom out of either mind or sight. With it too went a deep sense of conformity. If in politics and economics fresh currents of thought often blew, in matters of social outlook the maverick was frowned on. Frontiersmen and their descendants develop a deep sense of the need to work together. To do so they must be "regular," undeviating from a common pattern of behaviour, reacting all together in the same way to external stimuli. This solidarity yields rich dividends in the material sense, but the price it exacts from rebels and nonconformists is heavy indeed. Hence perhaps a cause of the country's deep conservatism, notable in the English-speaking and Jewish minorities in Montreal. To preserve the values they have in the presence of a large majority owning to a different culture and tradition, the degree of their conformity and even of their church-going is greater than elsewhere. It is not that they are

[1] Revised ed., Toronto: Ryerson, 1944, pp. 20–2.

more religious than their fellow citizens: it is "the thing to do." Otherwise, anchors may drag.

This spirit of conformity can be seen too in the vast proliferation of service clubs and organizations. Many of them, to be sure, reflect the need for intensive urban organization, for the frontier demands community co-operation above all else. But it also is a symptom of the Canadian's deep need to behave as his fellows behave. Sharing identical material ambitions—and having few others—they nourish each other by constant communal gatherings. Their unwritten law is that each shall behave as do his comrades, a recipe which provides the basis of the highway to promotion, to greater earnings and security.

Up to now this essay has sedulously avoided the subject of French Canada. It may be remembered, however, that in describing the kind of people English-speaking Canadians are, their gift for moderation and for compromise was noted. This results, more than anything else, from the existence of the biracial, bicultural state, the existence as fellow citizens of at least four million men and women whom the twelve million English-speaking Canadians understand hardly at all. The statement is a bald one, subject to sundry qualifications. The main fact, however, stood until the beginning of the Second World War. English Canada recognized the existence of French Canada, taking it into rational account in most, if not all, its political judgments. But, because of differences of race and language, culture and tradition, and, to some extent, religion, Quebec remained a *terra incognita* to almost all English Canadians.

There was in many minds an unhappy identification of French Canadian and Roman Catholic—the result of the activities of the Orange Lodge of Ontario two generations before. Many English Canadians knew personally a few French Canadians but when they put two and two together, and found that the French Canadian was also a Catholic, the combination proved, certainly in most impersonal relations, just a little too much. They preferred more comfortably to forget about Quebec.

When they were forced to think about it, as, for instance, when Canon Groulx, in the thirties, came to the edge of advocating a separate French-Canadian state, or when a convinced nationalist like Maurice Duplessis became Premier of Quebec in 1936, English Canada stirred uneasily, and said it was as it had always suspected. The passage by Premier Duplessis in 1937 of the Padlock Law confirmed English Canada's fears. Was it not true, as had often been whispered, that

French Canada was fascist at heart, totalitarian, authoritarian, and had no real instinct for North American democracy or for the Anglo-Saxon tradition? Such remarks were often heard, and they were not offset by any real intermingling of the races at any social, scholarly, or political level. Contacts of that kind were rare.

The average English Canadian knew nothing at all about Quebec except what he happened to read in his own newspaper or hear on the radio. His newspapers were edited and managed by men who could not speak French at all and who, save in very rare instances, could not even read it. They were dependent on scanty Canadian Press dispatches for their knowledge of what was going on in Quebec. Often these dispatches did not even appear. When they did, they helped little to dissipate the firm conviction of most English Canadians that a Catholic society is a monolithic structure, dominated by its hierarchy; that there is no great turmoil of conflicting views and opinion within it; and, hence, that the brief dispatches represented the rounded and convinced opinion of all their fellow citizens of French blood and tradition.

Ever since the general election of 1911 when Quebec nationalists, under Henri Bourassa, joined hands with the Conservative party to defeat the Liberals under Sir Wilfrid Laurier, English Canada has paid some attention to the views of *Le Devoir*, then Bourassa's organ. *Le Devoir* then became, so far as English Canada was concerned, the voice of Quebec. It is testimony to the inertia of mankind and to the stereotypes of modern mass communications that, at least up to the Second World War, this conviction remained. This imperfect view did little to remove the prejudices of the average English Protestant against the average French Catholic.

A misunderstanding based both on race and on language is not easy to overcome. It cannot be said that English Canada made any great effort to do so. Quebec was a part of Canada. Children knew, were familiar with, and greatly admired the great figures that strode through the early pages of Canadian history—Champlain, Maisonneuve, Dollard, La Salle, Frontenac, Talon, La Vérendrye, Joliet, Marquette, and Montcalm. They did not even regard the Battle of the Plains of Abraham as the symbol of a "conquest" which left the French Canadians an inferior and subject race. It had happened too long ago. They also regarded Papineau and the Rebellion of 1837 in Lower Canada as a glorious chapter in the national annals, for they equated Papineau with William Lyon Mackenzie: both doughty fighters against privilege and the Family Compact, both of them glorious symbols of the march toward self-government. The complexities of that situation, the score of fascinating cross-currents in Quebec, the actual ambitions, for instance, of Lafontaine, eluded them—and their teachers—completely. Nor was this surprising, for it is only in the last few decades that English-Canadian historians have plunged into the task of adequate interpretation.

This broad statement of basic goodwill is true enough, but it overlooks the existence of a minority—no more than a minority—of the English Canadians whose memories and whose stereotypes were steeped in the two wars in which Canada had participated and against which strong opposition had been raised in French Canada. In this group there was both distrust and suspicion, even a degree of hostility. The French Canadians were not "regular" in the sense in which that word was used a few pages back. There was something wrong with them. They had to be watched. They would, if they got a chance, "put something over on us." Let it be emphasized that this group was always a minority, its members mainly to be found in Ontario and the Atlantic provinces with a handful in British Columbia in so far as the people of that pleasant but distant province ever thought of Canada at all. The membership was, in the main, composed of that class of people known a generation ago as "imperialists," men and women who believed that, when Britain called, the Canadian answer must be "Ready, aye ready." Relatively few in numbers they were powerful in business ability, wealth, privilege, and position. Some day somebody will call them the lineal descendants of the members of the Family Compact—but not the present author, who has learned enough of the complexities of social and political problems to avoid, when he can, too great simplification of them.

But this small group shared with most of the rest of English Canada the greatest, single, abiding fault of the Anglo-Saxon race, a broad term which in this context includes very large numbers of the American people as well. They believed that they were innately superior to all "foreigners," and particularly to foreigners who did not speak English or spoke it with an accent unfamiliar to them. This sense of social and political superiority has been directly responsible for many of the major events in international affairs in our lifetime. Forster's *A Passage to India* portrays the essence of a problem which afflicts Anglo-American policies in Asia to this day, and which will afflict them for generations to come. Returning to Canada however, it is as clear as can be that this instinct—or defect?—has afflicted and plagued Canada ever since 1763.

There has been, and there still is, far too little effort by English Canadians to recognize that French Canada possesses and cherishes ideals which are at least equal to the values the English Canadian prizes. The fact that they are different from those English Canada takes for granted is virtually enough to convince the latter that they are foreign, strange, and inferior. It could be seen in the hopeless misunderstanding which followed the efforts of the Quebec Church to implement in a fashion the great papal encyclicals *Rerum novarum* and *Quadragesimo anno.* These efforts were promptly denounced in English Canada as the manifestation of fascist tendencies in Quebec. When Adrien Arcand and his Blue Shirts raised a positive fascist banner in Quebec, English Canada regarded it as a natural development of what it had all along suspected. When Maurice Duplessis assumed the mantle of Honoré Mercier as the spokesman of what is so imperfectly called Quebec nationalism, English Canada took it for granted that he believed holus-bolus in the writings of Canon Groulx and in the even more extreme writings of various ultra-nationalist groups. It was always this kind of writing which received currency in English Canada. The voice of the moderate, middle-of-the-road groups was seldom heard.

Besides this there were, of course, more genuine difficulties which resulted from the basically different approach of the English Protestant and the French Catholic to public problems. The passage of the famous Padlock Law by Premier Duplessis is a case in point. It was—and indeed it is—a law which genuinely outrages anyone brought up in the strict, liberal, Anglo-Saxon Protestant tradition. There can be little doubt that the emotions it arouses in French-Catholic minds are very different. To many of these it represents a sensible, orthodox approach to the problem of the containment of communism. It is, however, an authoritarian law; and the politically conscious English Canadian resents and protests its implications, the injustices to which it may give rise, and the assumption that the executive can properly assume functions which in the English-speaking provinces are left, as a matter of course, to the courts.

The Padlock Law confirmed the judgment of the extremists in English Canada that the French, when it came to democratic procedures and instincts, did not have the heart of the matter in them. There was a great *brouhaha* in English Canada for the disallowance of the law by the federal Government. When Ottawa refused to disallow it, English Canadians, recalling Prime Minister Mackenzie King's anti-conscriptionism in the First World War, and the solidarity of his support from Quebec, nodded their heads wisely and sadly. The refusal was widely interpreted as token of the fact that Mr. King had "sold out to Quebec." These fears were reinforced by the unintelligent predictions of academics that nothing could prevent the emergence in Canada of a French-Canadian over-all majority by 1973. Distrust increased. There was perhaps reasonable ground for the finding made, it is said, in a pre-war survey by the United States State Department, that, of all the biracial, bicultural nations in the world, Canada was the least likely to survive the strains and stresses of another world war.

How then, ten years after the end of the war which was supposed to bring division and destruction to the Canadian state, has it happened that the condition of the nation, in its vital biracial and bicultural aspects, is better than it has ever been since the Treaty of Paris was signed? The answer cannot be a simple one. The most obvious, the most apparent one is that, in the years between the wars, with the exception of a five-year interregnum, Canada was governed by a statesman whose prime objective was to heal the deep and festering sores left by the conscription crisis of 1917. He achieved his purpose mainly by the steady use of Burke's guiding principle—that of salutary neglect. If there was an issue likely to exacerbate racial relations, he resolutely refused to take action. The Padlock Law is a case in point.

Mr. Mackenzie King had learned in 1917 the effects upon national unity of the always latent determination of the English majority to have its own way, in accordance with the democratic principle that a minority has only one real right—the right to become a majority. So far as it was consistent with his determination to maintain the Liberal party in power, he was determined to do nothing which would make racial and cultural relations either uneasy or difficult. He was, at almost any cost, determined to avoid strife. In this determination he was greatly assisted by other factors. One was his own instinct against the centralization of power in federal hands. Another was to be found in a series of judgments by the Judicial Committee of the Privy Council, then Canada's final court of appeal, which strengthened provincial jurisdiction. This suited Mr. King very well. It not only decreased the difficulty of his own immediate tasks. It accorded well with his recognition of the fact that, when an English Canadian talked about the government he meant the federal authority, whereas when a French Canadian thought of *le gouvernement* he meant his own government at Quebec.

Few of Mr. King's major measures appreciably increased federal control if there was any way out of it. Several of them were deliberately designed to enlarge provincial jurisdiction. This was hardly perceived in English Canada, where provincial rights are more a historical phrase than a living reality. Yet his years in office almost imperceptibly met the minimum needs of the majority in the English-speaking provinces while they did nothing to arouse the sensibilities and the jealousies of the French minority basically determined to preserve their own special place in Confederation.

In his second volume on Sir John A. Macdonald, Donald Creighton cites a letter written to Campbell, Macdonald's bosom friend, about the proposed extension of the boundaries of Ontario and Quebec to Hudson Bay:

> I look to the future in this matter. . . . farther ahead, perhaps than I should. But are we not founding a nation? Now just consider for yourself—what a country of millions, lying between English Canada and the Atlantic will be. I have no objections to the French as French or as Catholics, but the block caused by the introduction of French law and the Civil Code would be very great.[2]

The guess may be made that no letter, written in such a vein, can be found in all the vast accumulation of the Mackenzie King Papers.

Indeed, to digress for a moment from the major theme of this essay, it may be said that the real union between French and English Canada, though initially forged by the short-lived Macdonald-Cartier partnership, was made into living reality first by Laurier and a galaxy of able English-speaking colleagues, and finally and for all time by the partnership between Mackenzie King and Ernest Lapointe. This is not supposed to be a political dissertation. But the influence of men of state upon the national *mores* is not to be disregarded: in the years between the wars, it was fortunate that the right foundations were laid, despite the strains of the depression, despite the writings of Quebec extremists, despite the partial reincarnation of the Mercier doctrines by a flamboyant government in Quebec.

There was still another factor involved in the change and one with which Mackenzie King's cautious major policies had little to do. The force that, in a brief period of time, swung English Canada out of its former semi-colonial ways of thinking and into a broad and genuine nationalism was the influence (mostly outside Quebec) of the veterans of the Canadian Expeditionary Force of the First World War. These men had in the main enlisted as soldiers as a result of emotional states of mind: the feeling of loyalty to the metropolitan power, the sense of excitement, the love of doing things together with their fellow men.

[2]*John A. Macdonald: The Old Chieftain* (Toronto: Macmillan, 1955), p. 485.

But their service meant that, for the very first time in Canadian history, hundreds of thousands of men wore the magic name "Canada" on their uniformed shoulders. They spoke for two years, three years, or four years for "Canada" as against "the Blimeys," the "Aussies," and the rest. They fought as a team fights for its own side, and their pride in their own team created a feeling among them which had nothing to do with region or race. They could, if they wanted to, criticize this province or that, this race or that (but outsiders could not). They were for Canada, and their many triumphs were Canadian victories. They were better, man for man—so they believed—than any other part of the Allied forces on the Western Front. They would fight the enemy to prove it. They were also to fight their Allies, as they sometimes did in off moments, to prove it again.

When these men came home, they had, through some strange half-emotional alchemy, sloughed off many of the ideas with which they had gone to war. They had become Canadians, fierce and proud in their defence of it. As they grew older, spending their off hours talking old battles over again, the sense of nationalism deepened. It is perhaps one of the tragedies of the time that French Canada neither shared to any great extent in this devoted comradeship nor understood the revolution it had effected in the minds of English Canadians.

It is clear today that this intense development went far to create the Canadian nation we know. It would still shock many English Canadians to learn—though the facts are available in Mason Wade's penetrating study *The French Canadians*—that the ideal toward which the nation was moving at breakneck speed was the ideal explicitly set forth by Henri Bourassa a good many years before. There had been, in fact, a vast maturing of the English-Canadian mind. The old colonialism, the old "imperialism," had practically gone.

This became clear quite soon after the outbreak of the Second World War, even though it was aided by other factors. There was in 1939 in the English-speaking provinces nothing like the unbridled, emotional enthusiasm manifest in 1914. There was a good deal of continental isolationism in Canada, and, to young and old alike, the chief feeling was that this was where they had come in before. There was therefore little or nothing of the expected racial tension. Canada did not put itself on a war footing, starting in where the tension of 1917–18 had left off. There was in fact a mood of unity of the most encouraging kind.

If there was no recognition of the impressive and penetrating thought of Bourassa as an individual, a yeast had been working in the minds of the English-speaking intelligentzia which had, apparently, worked through society as a whole. Some part of this change had been effected by the repeated meetings, for more than ten years, of the Canadian Institute of International Affairs which, though largely composed of English-speaking Canadians, had always contained members of the relatively new English-Canadian nationalist group. Apart from that, more and more Canadians had lost their immediate ties with the land either of their ancestors or their birth. They were thinking naturally in Canadian terms. If their conclusions about the war were not dissimilar from that of their fathers, they were differently based. As part of that process there was a readiness to understand the attitudes and aspirations of French Canada.

While actual contacts, socially and politically, remained as scarce as ever, there had been built into the English-Canadian mind an understanding of the fact that Quebec thought and behaved differently from the rest of Canada, that the problem was there, and that it was a practical business for the country to get along together. English Canada had no urge, it had certainly no desire, to stumble blindly into the violent and bloody misunderstandings that had marked and marred Anglo-French relations in 1917–18. Looking back at it, it seems likely that this state of mind in 1939 laid the foundation for the *rapprochement* which in the ten years after the war began to yield rich fruit. Politically brought forth and nurtured, it now begins to yield a harvest in every field of human endeavour.

This account jumps over the actual crises which afflicted the course of racial and cultural relations during the war. At least from an English-Canadian point of view, they seemed to leave no permanent scars, no deep rifts. This writer travelled repeatedly over at least six of the English-speaking provinces during the war, and maintained contacts with wider circles by correspondence. It is a fact to be noted that it was not until the so-called conscription crisis of 1944 that there seemed to be any real recrudescence of the kind of feeling which permeated English Canada twenty-five years before.

There were, to be sure, editorials in the English-speaking press which reflected the old sentiments, the old misunderstandings, and the old hates. What was significant was the large number of abstentions in that field of opinion. The case for and against the proposals of Mr. Ralston, Minister of Defence, and later of the Government as a whole, was argued on a different and far more rational plane. In private conversations and in social contacts in English Canada, the same phenomenon could be observed. It was the exception rather than the rule that racial presuppositions came to the front in argument. In the old traditional circles of imperialism there were some signs that the distrust and the dislike of the French had again come to the fore, but these were notably modified by the passage of time. On the whole, the change from a quarter-century before was marked.

Older Canadians are still surprised, though not unpleasantly surprised, that this crisis was surmounted as well as it was. Outside Quebec, few people knew that the English managerial class in that province had, either through wisdom or the necessities of maintaining war production, been forced to use every means in their power to encourage French-Canadian management, from executive roles down to the foreman level. There was, for almost the first time, a conscious effort to remove from French Canadians the stigma of being hewers of wood and drawers of water for their English-speaking managers. The experiment worked well. The same process was to be seen in the civil service at Ottawa, where similar efforts were noted. It became widely known in English Canada, moreover, that positive efforts were being made in Quebec itself to create in its educational system studies which would more easily fit its able young men and women to assume positions of responsibility in the vast, seething, war economy of North America. There had been a lack in this respect, deeply and honestly regretted by English Canadians of goodwill.

There were now obvious signs that this defect was being repaired by native French-Canadian effort. Every graduate from the Quebec schools of science, engineering, mining, and economics was an obvious token to the English-Canadian industrialist (and to many others besides) that Quebec had embarked on a North American march which would bring it closer in step with the deep industrial trends of the continent of which Quebec itself was so important a part. The knowledge that this was taking place modified the traditional instincts of a class of men who had been, before then, somewhat contemptuous of French-Canadian capacities in this regard. The old notion that there was something inherently inferior about persons who did not speak English began quite quickly to die out. There was in addition the hard-boiled fact that English-speaking managers found they got higher and more continuous production out of men whose immediate leaders were of their own race and spoke their own tongue.

Besides this, there was the fact that many young men from Quebec had joined the armed forces or had been drafted to them. Their English-speaking companions found them likable and made friends with them. They brought them to their own homes on leave, or they wrote home about them. They moved about the country to different camps and air bases. In each one they found the same response and made more friends. Perhaps for the first time there were social and professional contacts between the two major races, and all of them worked out easily and well. These facts too were reported to scores of thousands of English-speaking homes which, for the first time, learned that Quebec boys were in all essential respects like their own boys, and that the divisions caused by race, religion, and language were by no means insurmountable.

On the intellectual level (all-important in the long run) a similar process was taking place. In Quebec a handful of scholars was reaching out to make contacts with their English-speaking counterparts. In English Canada the degree of goodwill and the readiness to co-operate was stronger by far than it had ever been before. This was particularly true in the academic world. In the professions generally the same movement was taking place. Where, before the war, it was a rarity to find a French-speaking scholar or professional man attending a professional gathering—the law always excepted—it became the practice for each racial community to make sure it was at least represented at any so-called national gathering.

What was, of course, most encouraging was that most of these movements, tentatively begun under wartime pressures, persisted and strengthened themselves in the post-war period. The universities and certain schools began exchange programmes which continue year by year. The learned societies now take for granted that certain papers will be delivered in French. There are even stumbling efforts by English-speaking scholars to overcome the inherent British shyness about foreign tongues, to speak at least partly in French. Even so distinctive a body as the Canadian Chamber of Commerce, at its 1955 convention, insisted that some delegates should be present from the Chambres de Commerce de Québec. With traditional courtesy and goodwill, the French-speaking business organizations invite English-speaking delegations.

It would be pleasant to record that the English-speaking provincial departments of education are taking steps to ensure that French is an unconditional prerequisite to further studies. This has not yet become the rule. It is not, however, too risky a prediction that the tide of opinion in favour of a wider racial and cultural understanding will eventually persuade nine English-dominated legislatures that the study of French is a "must" in any Canadian educational curriculum, to an extent greater than anything now in the educational regulations. This will not make English-speaking Canadians bilingual. Continental pressures dictate that English will remain the chief North American language, a fact which Quebec has long recognized, if not formally, then in fact. But it is not too much to hope that the future product of the English-speaking schools of Canada will not open his mouth in bemused amazement when he hears the French tongue spoken. Nor is it too much to hope—in fact the day is already here—that he will not resent hearing the French tongue spoken at any gathering which calls itself national in character.

1956

Les Canadiens français et leur idéologie

JEAN-C. FALARDEAU

Directeur, Département de Sociologie, Université Laval

L'HISTOIRE du Canada contemporain est l'histoire des tensions, du rapprochement graduel et de l'accommodement politique entre les Canadiens de langue française et les Canadiens de langue anglaise. La symbiose de ces deux peuples qui n'ont pas choisi de vivre ensemble a été souvent appelée un « mariage de raison ». *Deux Solitudes* dit le titre, emprunté à Rilke, du célèbre roman de Hugh MacLennan qui raconte un épisode crucial du jeu et du contre-jeu dramatique de cette pacifique coexistence. « We are inescapably, écrit Malcolm Ross, and almost from the first, the bifocal people[1]. » L'équilibre entre les deux grands groupes ethniques et culturels constituant le Canada a tenu historiquement à des compromis qui ont dû être revisés à chaque génération. Il tient surtout à une connaissance plus objective que chaque groupe a acquise de l'autre et à une compréhension plus juste de la perception que chacun a de l'autre.

Un observateur canadien de langue anglaise écrivait l'an dernier dans une lettre adressée au journal *Le Devoir* : « Malgré l'intérêt manifesté à travers le Canada pour le fait français, le public de langue anglaise manque encore de guide capable de le conduire à l'intelligence de cet aspect si fascinant et si important de la vie canadienne[2]. » George Ferguson, pour sa part, affirme dans le présent volume : « Because of differences of race and language, culture and tradition, and, to some extent, religion, Quebec [has] remained a *terra incognita* to almost all English Canadians[3]. »

Cet essai a l'ambition d'éclairer une fois de plus cette *terra incognita* et d'aider à une intelligence plus vive du Canada français. Il ne

[1]Malcolm Ross, *Our Sense of Identity* (Toronto : Ryerson, 1954), p. ix.
[2]Alan Baker (pseudonyme), « Un Mur invisible », *Le Devoir*, 30 avril 1957.
[3]Voir p. 9.

révèlera aucun fait historique nouveau. Il suppose que l'on connaît les études déjà anciennes sur la mentalité canadienne-française de Vattier[4] et de Siegfried[5], certaines analyses plus récentes des chercheurs ou des observateurs canadiens-français, les travaux d'histoire, comme aussi les créations de la littérature canadienne-française contemporaine, de *Bonheur d'occasion* et de *Tit-Coq* à *Poussière sur la ville* et *Zone*. Les plongées des écrivains et les essais des chercheurs ont élargi notre connaissance de la conscience collective et des structures sociales de divers milieux canadiens-français. Mais plusieurs interprétations de nous-mêmes demeurent sujettes à conjectures. Il reste de larges secteurs du paysage psychologique canadien-français à explorer. L'un des buts de cet essai est de stimuler de telles recherches en posant quelques questions anciennes ou nouvelles dans une perspective sociologique.

Le postulat sur lequel sont fondées les réflexions qui suivent est familier aux historiens et aux sociologues. On peut le formuler comme suit : les relations entre les Canadiens de langue française et ceux de langue anglaise tiennent à une certaine conception que ceux-là se font de ceux-ci; cette conception est elle-même un résultat historique et s'insère dans une conception sous-jacente et plus générale que les Canadiens français se font du Canada dans son ensemble, du rôle que les « Anglais » y ont joué et du rôle qu'eux-mêmes estiment y avoir joué. En définitive, c'est à travers une certaine image qu'il a de lui-même dans le contexte canadien que le Canadien français perçoit les autres et qu'il définit ses attitudes et ses comportements envers eux.

I. Ce qu'est le Canadien français

Il importe d'abord d'établir une certaine définition du Canadien français. Et pour cela, il faut rappeler ce que signifie, pour le Canadien de langue française, l'expression « Canada français ».

Le Canada français signifie deux ordres de réalités. En premier lieu, il désigne formellement toutes les régions du Canada où vivent des populations suffisamment nombreuses et socialement visibles de personnes d'ascendance et de langue françaises. Au recensement de 1951, ces populations constituaient plus de 31 pour cent de la population totale du Canada réparties dans les provinces maritimes; dans l'est, le sud-ouest et le nord de l'Ontario; dans les régions septentrionales des

[4]Georges Vattier, *Essai sur la mentalité canadienne-française* (Paris : Honoré Champion, 1928).

[5]André Siegfried, *Le Canada : Les deux races* (Paris : Librairie Armand Colin, 1906).

provinces des prairies et dans le grand Vancouver[6]. Elles accusent des particularismes régionaux qui tiennent soit à leurs traditions locales, soit à leur degré d'ancienneté, soit aux modalités de leurs contacts respectifs avec les divers groupes ethniques, généralement anglophones, auxquels elles ont été mêlées ou par lesquels elles sont entourées. Mais il existe entre toutes de profonds liens. Le Canada français est une réalité à la fois culturelle et géographique, laquelle, bien que discontinue, s'étend à la dimension du pays tout entier. Elle n'est pas donnée ni circonscrite définitivement mais se dilate et se diversifie constamment. C'est à l'ensemble de cette réalité que le Canadien français se réfère lorsqu'il affirme que le Canada est un pays à dualité ethnique et culturelle.

Néanmoins, l'usage a restreint l'appellation de Canada français à la seule province de Québec. Lorsque les Canadiens de langue anglaise ou les Canadiens français eux-mêmes disent « Canada français », ils sous-entendent la plupart du temps le Québec où habitent plus des trois-quarts de la population française totale du pays et dont la population est aux quatre-cinquièmes française. Cette province est avant tout et par-dessus tout le lieu où habitent ceux qui furent les premiers occupants du pays. Les Canadiens français estiment que ce lieu leur appartient en propre. *Leur* Canada, c'est d'abord la province de Québec. Cette province est, en quelque sorte, tout ce qui leur reste de leur ancien domaine. C'est à la fois le cadre historique et l'évidence politique tangible de leur survivance comme groupe culturel. Dans cette province seulement, le Canadien français se sent complètement et parfaitement « chez lui ». A son point de vue, toutes les autres provinces « anglaises » du Canada, malgré leur diversité géographique et les différences régionales dont il n'est d'ailleurs que très peu conscient, sont interchangeables au point de vue du style de vie, des modes de pensée, des attitudes. Elles sont comme découpées dans une même étoffe. Les groupes qui les constituent sont vite devenus politiquement semblables les uns aux autres dans le Canada d'après 1867. Ils sont tous absorbés par la civilisation anglo-saxonne. Le Canadien de langue anglaise peut passer d'une province à une autre sans sortir de « chez lui ». Il n'est étranger nulle part où l'on parle anglais et où l'on vit anglais. Le Canadien français, au contraire, s'il sort du Québec pour voyager ou demeurer, si brièvement soit-il, dans une autre province canadienne, éprouve le sentiment de passer « à l'étranger ». Il a conscience de pénétrer dans un milieu qu'il perçoit comme globale-

[6]Jacques Henripin, « Les Canadiens français et leurs institutions », *Chronique sociale de France*, Cahier 5 (15 septembre 1957), pp. 413–23.

ment inquiétant. De façon peut-être confuse mais très vive, il croit que sa langue, sa culture, peut-être sa religion, y seront en danger. La province de Québec est donc plus que l'une des dix provinces du Canada. Elle n'est pas, non plus, interchangeable. Elle a été et elle demeure la province française du Canada. C'est avec la province de Québec que, spontanément, le Canadien français s'identifie d'abord, parce qu'il s'identifie avec l'histoire de son groupe au Canada, avec *son* histoire du Canada.

II. Le Canadien français et son histoire

L'histoire canadienne à travers laquelle se voit le Canadien français et qui lui est proposée à l'école primaire est, comme l'histoire de chaque peuple, et particulièrement des peuples minoritaires, une histoire ethnocentrique. Tout peuple ou groupe ethnique se fait de lui-même une idée excellente. Chacun des membres du groupe porte en lui une image idéalisée qui lui fait voir le groupe non seulement comme privilégié par rapport à tous les autres mais comme meilleur que tout autre. Un des principaux instruments par lesquels cette image se communique, de génération en génération, est l'enseignement de l'histoire. Le manuel d'histoire est un des principaux véhicules de la transmission de la culture d'une société. Il a comme fonction de provoquer chez les jeunes l'admiration pour les ancêtres qui les ont précédés et, par là, de les entraîner à se solidariser avec le groupe ethnique ou culturel d'où ils sont issus et par rapport auquel ils apprennent à dire « nous ».

Ainsi, du Canadien français. L'histoire du Canada qu'il apprend à l'école primaire pourra subir, au fur et à mesure de l'expérience, des contacts et des lectures de son âge adulte, des transformations d'optique et de contenu. Elle n'en demeure pas moins le point de départ décisif qui constitue pour tous, consciemment ou inconsciemment, un dénominateur commun de perception et d'enterprétation.

« Au Canada français, a écrit Fernand Dumont, l'adolescent découvre son présent en se mettant au passé[7]. » Ce avec quoi le jeune Canadien français apprend à s'identifier en étudiant l'histoire, c'est d'abord et principalement la période du régime français en Amérique. Bien que les manuels récents fassent la part plus grande que jadis aux événements canadiens d'après 1760 et même d'après 1867, le Canada avec lequel le jeune Canadien français est surtout familier est celui d'avant 1760. D'après une recherche actuellement en cours à l'Université Laval[8] sur

[7]Fernand Dumont, « De quelques obstacles à la prise de conscience chez les Canadiens français », *Cité libre*, no 19 (janvier 1958), p. 22.

[8]A l'Ecole de Pédagogie.

le contenu des manuels d'histoire du Canada de langue française et de langue anglaise utilisés dans les écoles primaires de la province de Québec, alors que les manuels anglais consacrent un nombre égal de pages aux régimes français et anglais, les manuels français consacrent les trois-quarts de leurs pages au régime français et un quart seulement au régime anglais[9].

Cette histoire d'un passé français est présentée comme une marveilleuse épopée. Elle provoque une fierté nostalgique de la France de l'Ancien Régime. Le blason de la province de Québec évoque toujours les fleurs de lys et sa devise est « Je me souviens ». Les héros qui dominent le souvenir du Canadien français sont davantage les découvreurs, les fondateurs, les évangélisateurs missionnaires, les pionniers et les hommes de guerre, que les coureurs de bois, les marchands et les administrateurs. L'histoire du Canadien français est une histoire de l'action de Dieu, par l'intermédiaire de l'Eglise, en terre canadienne. Les principaux fondateurs de la Nouvelle-France furent des prêtres, des religieux et des religieuses dont le souci primordial était la conversion des sauvages et le salut spirituel de la colonie. Les grands découvreurs et colonisateurs furent des hommes et des femmes préoccupés avant tout d'étendre le royaume de Dieu. Le Canada français, fondé par des missionnaires, est aussi un peuple élu de Dieu, un peuple missionnaire. Cette « mission » du Canada français est manifestée par toutes sortes d'évidences, en particulier par le fait que le peuple canadien-français fut providentiellement préservé des méfaits de la Révolution française. La France, en 1789, s'aliéna de Dieu. En devenant « athée et séculière », elle abdiqua son rôle historique de fille aînée de l'Eglise. C'est au Canada français qu'échoua alors la responsabilité de perpétuer, en Amérique, le rôle de témoin et d'exemple que la France prévaricatrice avait refusé. Le destin du Canada français est d'être fidèle à cette mission. Bien plus, son salut est associé à cette fidélité.

Mais les Canadiens français se souviennent surtout d'avoir été un jour, en 1760, conquis par les armées anglaises. Ils ont le sentiment d'avoir été, depuis ce jour, dépossédés. La suite de leur histoire de peuple devenu minoritaire par la conquête est une longue série de vexations, de frustrations, de luttes politiques en vue de la reconnaissance de leurs droits élémentaires, de leur langue, de leur religion. Ils se souviennent avec admiration de leurs orateurs et des chefs politiques qui ont obtenu du vainqueur hostile de 1760 leur droit à la

[9]Robert Sévigny, « Analyse de contenu des manuels d'histoire du Canada », thèse présentée pour la maîtrise au Département de Sociologie, Faculté des Sciences sociales, Université Laval, mars 1956, texte dactylographié.

vie. Le nom de Papineau est auréolé d'un prestige égal à celui de Dollard des Ormeaux et la rébellion des « Patriotes » de 1837–8 réitère contre les Anglais un exploit aussi émouvant que celui du Long-Sault contre les Iroquois.

La monotone série de combats parlementaires en quoi se résume, pour le Canadien français, l'histoire du « régime anglais », atteint un point tournant en 1867. Si cette histoire lui apparaît, jusqu'à ce moment-là, comme une litanie des tentatives sans cesse compromises pour empêcher la minorité française du pays d'être assimilée par la majorité numérique et politique anglaise, la Confédération de 1867 marque à ses yeux la mise au point d'un *modus vivendi* relativement satisfaisant entre les deux groupes. A la différence de ses compatriotes de langue anglaise qui ont vu dans la Confédération canadienne principalement sinon exclusivement une entreprise de caractère économique destinée à assurer au pays une plus forte cohésion[10], le Canadien français interprète la loi de 1867 comme un bienfait à un double point de vue : elle associa le Canada français, à titre de partenaire égal et de participant, au gouvernement de l'ensemble de la nation; elle lui accorda son propre gouvernement, celui de Québec. Il la considère surtout comme un « pacte » entre chacune des provinces canadiennes. Plus particulièrement, comme un pacte entre les « Anglais » et les « Français » du Canada. Plus encore, comme un pacte entre Protestants et Catholiques, aux termes duquel tous les droits politiques accordés aux Canadiens français et catholiques du Québec seraient automatiquement garantis à tous les Catholiques dans l'ensemble du pays.

Cette interprétation de la Confédération en tant que pacte étonne encore le Canadien de langue anglaise pour qui la Loi de 1867 ne peut être qu'une loi du Parlement impérial dont l'exégèse doit s'en tenir strictement à la lettre des textes juridiques, lesquels, à nulle part, ne font spécifiquement allusion à aucun pacte. Quoi qu'il en soit, le fait sociologiquement significatif et important est que les Canadiens français, depuis environ la fin du XIXe siècle, ont donné à la constitution canadienne cette signification. Celle-ci s'est incrustée dans leur attitude. Elle est devenue un thème persistant, orchestré avec diverses variations par les chefs religieux et politiques du Canada français jusqu'à l'époque contemporaine. Que les publicistes et les juristes canadiens-anglais la trouvent acceptable ou non, elle persistera comme l'un des éléments les plus tenaces de la définition que le Canadien français donne de l'histoire de son Canada.

[10]Maurice Lamontagne, *Le Fédéralisme canadien* (Québec : Presses Universitaires Laval, 1954).

Cette histoire en est donc une qui a ses propres héros et son propre symbolisme patriotique. Elle est l'histoire d'un peuple qui se sait le premier occupant du pays, qui idéalise son passé français dont il fait un paradis perdu et qui, du fait qu'il est devenu culturellement et politiquement minoritaire par la conquête des armes anglaises, voit la suite de son destin comme une douloureuse dialectique d'oppositions et de compromis avec ses compatriotes dominateurs en vue de faire reconnaître par ceux-ci son droit à l'auto-détermination.

Partant de ces remarques, on sera peut-être plus en mesure de répondre à la question posée au début et que posait récemment, sans trop y répondre, M. Philip Garigue : « Qu'est-ce qu'un Canadien français[11] ? » Etre Canadien français ne signifie pas seulement habiter la province de Québec ou une région française du Canada, se réclamer d'une ascendance française, parler le français, être catholique et partager certaines traditions. Aucune liste de ces caractéristiques, si importantes soient-elles, n'épuise la réalité psychologique et sociologique. Etre Canadien français signifie essentiellement que l'on s'identifie avec la collectivité canadienne-française; avec le peuple auquel spontanément on se réfère quand on dit ou quand on pense « nous »; avec le peuple que l'on perçoit, comme on se perçoit soi-même, dans la perspective d'une histoire.

III. Idéologies et attitudes dominantes

Cette interprétation de l'histoire qui caractérise le Canadien français est un résultat. Elle est une cristallisation qui s'est progressivement formée sous l'action de divers facteurs dont quelques uns sont facilement identifiables. Elle fut surtout l'œuvre de ceux que les sociologues appellent les « définisseurs de la situation ». Dans toute société se retrouvent, de façon épisodique ou continue, des individus auréolés de prestige qui assument la responsabilité de définir, pour l'ensemble de la collectivité ou pour des groupements particuliers, les normes et les modèles de comportement. Ils sont ceux qui proposent aux autres une définition de ce qu'ils sont, des conditions de leur existence, de ce qu'ils ont à faire. Au Canada français, ceux qui ont ainsi défini de façon durable la situation de la société, ont été, d'une part, les chefs ou les porte-parole de l'Eglise, d'autre part, les chefs politiques qui formulèrent les postulats de l'idéologie nationaliste. La prédication et la

[11]Philip Garigue, *A Bibliographical Introduction to the Study of French Canada* (Montréal : McGill University, Dept. of Sociology and Anthropology, distributed by Librairie Dominicaine), Introduction, pp. 5–6.

« pensée sociale » de l'Eglise, l'idéologie nationaliste, ont été les deux courants parallèles, quelquefois concordants, quelquefois divergents, qui ont polarisé les valeurs dominantes de la culture canadienne-française. C'est à ces deux sources qu'il faut remonter pour rendre compte du « caractère national » des Canadiens français[12].

Importance et influence de l'Eglise

Les liens qui unissent l'Eglise catholique et le Canada français ne sont guère différents de ceux que l'on observe en des pays qui furent historiquement catholiques et qui le sont demeurés jusqu'à une époque relativement récente : l'Irlande, l'Espagne, la Pologne ou certains pays d'Amérique du Sud. Dans ces pays, comme dans la Chrétienté du moyen âge, l'Eglise, par son clergé et sa prédication, a en quelque sorte enveloppé la société temporelle. Ses institutions, sa doctrine et son éthique ont informé les groupements et structuré les comportements. Ainsi en fut-il dans l'histoire canadienne-française, au point qu'il est impossible de dissocier, dans cette histoire, ce qui est de caractère purement ethnique et culturel de ce qui est de caractère spécifiquement ecclésiastique ou religieux. L'histoire du Canada français est, dans une très large mesure, l'histoire de l'Eglise catholique au Canada. Un élément déterminant de la mentalité du Canadien français est sa religion. La perception qu'il a des « autres » et la notion qu'il a de ses relations avec les autres dérivent d'une conception de son histoire et de lui-même qu'il tient, au point de départ, de l'Eglise. C'est par l'Eglise qu'il est socialisé. Sa psychologie, sous plus d'un rapport, est d'inspiration théologique. Il n'a pas une condition humaine à comprendre et à assumer. Il a une condition sacrale à défendre et à conserver.

Dès les débuts de la colonisation française en Amérique, l'influence de l'Eglise s'est manifestée dans l'organisation sociale et les attitudes collectives[13]. Le Canadien français a vécu, durant toute la période française de son histoire, sous un régime civil de caractère quasi-

[12]Voir : Maurice Tremblay, « Orientations de la pensée sociale » dans Jean-C. Falardeau, éd., *Essais sur le Québec contemporain* (Québec : Presses Universitaires Laval, 1953), ch. IX; Maurice Tremblay et Albert Faucher, « L'Enseignement des sciences sociales au Canada français », étude spéciale préparée à l'intention de la Commission royale d'enquête sur l'avancement des arts, des lettres et des sciences au Canada, ronéotypée, juin 1950; Marcel Rioux, « Idéologie et crise de conscience du Canada français », *Cité libre*, no 14 (décembre 1955); Pierre-E. Trudeau, « La Province de Québec au moment de la grève » dans *La Grève de l'amiante* (Montréal : Editions Cité Libre, 1956), ch. I.

[13]Jean-C. Falardeau, « Rôle et importance de l'Eglise au Canada français », *Esprit* (Paris), no 193–4 (août-septembre 1952), pp. 214–29.

théocratique et de structure monarchique. L'Eglise a inspiré et modelé les institutions politiques et sociales de la colonie. Les institutions ecclésiastiques, tels le diocèse et la paroisse, furent des éléments vitaux de l'armature sociale. Les normes et les principes religieux ont eu raison de valeurs suprêmes à tous les niveaux de la vie collective, particulièrement dans la vie familiale et l'enseignement.

Le sens d'une mission qu'ont les Canadiens français est principalement d'inspiration religieuse. Il a donné lieu à une attitude de prosélytisme qui s'est perpétuée en s'intensifiant jusqu'à nos jours. C'est lui qui a inspiré, au Canada français, la fondation d'un nombre impressionnant de congrégations et d'ordres religieux comme il a inspiré, au XIXe siècle, de spectaculaires campagnes de prédication populaire. Il a suscité le zèle de centaines et de milliers de prêtres, de religieux et de religieuses qui, au service des congrégations missionnaires, ont essaimé, depuis la fin du XIXe siècle, dans l'Ouest et dans l'Arctique canadiens, dans l'Est et l'Ouest américains, aux Antilles, en Chine, au Japon, en Afrique. Encore maintenant, le Canadien français sait et on lui répète que ses missionnaires, hommes et femmes, sont répartis dans les pays des cinq continents. Il sait que ces contingents canadiens sont parmi les plus nombreux de l'Eglise et il en est fier. Il est en étroit et constant contact avec eux, ses parents ou ses amis, et il les aide financièrement avec une persévérante générosité. On peut affirmer que c'est principalement à travers eux que le Canadien français prend conscience du reste du monde, des autres civilisations, de la vie internationale. Il est présent au reste du monde en tant que Catholique. La Chine, l'Inde, l'Amérique du Sud et l'Afrique du Canadien français sont la Chine, l'Inde, l'Amérique et l'Afrique de ses missionnaires.

Pour autant, il divise l'univers en deux catégories d'hommes : les Catholiques, et ceux qui ne le sont pas. Plus exactement : les Catholiques, et les « païens ». C'est d'après ce clivage élémentaire que non seulement il départage mais qu'il juge et évalue les hommes et les civilisations, y compris les peuples « protestants » dont font partie ses compatriotes de langue anglaise. Il est lui-même dans la catégorie des privilégiés, déjà sauvés. Entre lui et tous les autres, protestants et païens, il y a une distance infranchissable. Nous touchons ici, on le devine, le rempart souvent le moins visible mais le plus résistant dans les relations entre les Canadiens français, catholiques, et les Canadiens anglais, protestants. Le Canadien français oppose confusément mais obstinément à tout ce qui n'est pas catholique une fin de non-recevoir. Son attitude n'est pas nécessairement hostile. Elle se reflète souvent en des manières calmes et pacifiques. Le Canadien français voit dans son compatriote anglophone protestant un être avec qui il ne peut entrer en contact sans risque, peut-être pas sans contamination.

Le prosélytisme religieux canadien-français est donc à sens unique. Il est conquérant à l'extérieur, au loin, très loin. Il est un exemple de ce que les sociologues ont probablement observé très souvent et que mon ami Cyrias Ouellet appelle « le complexe du deuxième voisin » : on est préoccupé et intéressé par ceux qui habitent au delà de sa propre demeure; le voisin immédiat, celui qui habite tout près de chez soi ou chez soi-même, n'a aucun intérêt. Ainsi agit le Canadien français, qui, même du point de vue de sa religion, devrait non seulement s'intéresser à ses compatriotes anglophones protestants, mais chercher à les convertir. Il les craint au contraire et les évite. Ce curieux paradoxe de la religion des Canadiens français a été noté par un des plus lucides observateurs qui se soient récemment préoccupés du problème religieux au Canada : « La religion des Canadiens français, écrit Claude Ryan, n'a pratiquement eu, jusqu'à présent, aucune influence sur la vie religieuse des milliers d'Anglo-Saxons qui entourent les Canadiens français... Réduits à une position de défense contre un conquérant étranger... ils furent tellement occupés à se protéger contre ce conquérant qu'ils n'ont pu que récemment prendre conscience de leur responsabilité spirituelle envers lui[14]. »

Le catholicisme du Canadien français l'éloigne non seulement des non-Catholiques qui l'entourent dans son propre pays et sur son continent mais aussi des Catholiques qui ne sont pas de sa nationalité. Son catholicisme est canadien-français. Sa religion-trésor est aussi une religion-rempart. Depuis toujours, il a identifié religion et langue française. « La langue, gardienne de la foi » est une des convictions les plus profondément gravées dans l'âme canadienne-française : des textes innombrables le rappellent[15], depuis le célèbre discours de Henri Bourassa dans l'église Notre-Dame en 1910. Le catholicisme du Canadien français est de langue française, comme en ont fait l'expérience tous les Catholiques « étrangers » qui ont été en contact ou qui ont vécu avec des Canadiens français, qu'ils fussent Irlandais établis au Canada depuis plusieurs générations, Italiens ou Belges de plus fraîche date, ou même « Français de France ». Il n'y a pas encore si longtemps, à Québec, on disait de quelqu'un qui, le dimanche, assistait à la messe

[14]Claude Ryan, « L'Eglise catholique et l'évolution spirituelle du Canada français », *Chronique sociale de France*, Cahier 5, 65e année (15 septembre 1957), pp. 448–9.

[15]Voir, en particulier : Cardinal Villeneuve, *Le Fait français en Amérique*, conférence donnée à Boston le 4 mai 1938 devant la Société historique franco-américaine (Québec : La Librairie de l'Action catholique, 1938).

dans l'église catholique de St. Patrick, qu'il allait « à la messe chez les Protestants ». Le Catholique non-Canadien français est aussi étranger, parmi les Canadiens français, que le Canadien non-catholique.

Pas plus en milieu canadien-français qu'en d'autres pays traditionnellement catholiques, l'Eglise et son clergé ne furent un bloc monolithique. Divers ont été, selon les tempéraments et les époques, ses représentants. Inégal fut aussi le degré de son contact et de son influence réelle sur la société. Néanmoins, les relations entre le clergé et la société ont toujours eu un caractère personnel. Le clergé canadien-français n'a jamais été extérieur ni supérieur à la société. Il est de la société avec laquelle il se confond à tous les échelons. Pour ces raisons, il serait aussi erroné de considérer l'enseignement social de l'Eglise canadienne-française comme un ensemble de principes superposés à la société que d'y voir un système homogène et absolu de directives morales. La « philosophie de la vie » de l'Eglise canadienne-française est évidemment une explicitation, à divers moments de l'histoire, des principes généraux de l'Eglise de Rome[16]. Mais cette philosophie a été élaborée par un clergé de Canadiens français — bien qu'il ne faille pas méconnaître l'importance des idées et des attitudes apportées ici par un clergé français immigré au Canada, en particulier à deux reprises, au début du XIXe et au début du XXe siècles. Elle n'aurait pas mordu avec tant de facilité sur la mentalité canadienne-française si elle n'eût été l'expression d'un vœu de la collectivité.

Nous avons déjà noté que l'un des thèmes essentiels de la prédication officielle du clergé fut celui d'une mission propre au Canada français. Transposant cette notion de vocation spirituelle à tous les plans de la pensée et de l'action, on en a fait, en particulier, l'équivalent d'une mission rurale du peuple canadien-français. On connaît le célèbre discours de Mgr L. A. Paquet, le 23 juin 1902, qui constitue le « bréviaire du patriote canadien-français[17] ». Le Canadien français a, par dessein providentiel, une vocation agricole; il doit laisser à d'autres les soucis de la vie économique et industrielle, « matérialiste ». Son génie propre doit le river ou le faire retourner à la terre. Les instruments de son destin sont la croix et la charrue.

Etant donné de tels postulats, rien d'étonnant que la pensée sociale et politique de l'Eglise canadienne-française ait traditionnellement privilégié les préceptes d'ordre et de soumission : primauté du pouvoir

[16]Voir : Sister Marie Agnes of Rome Gaudreau, *The Social Thought of French Canada as Reflected in the Semaines Sociales* (Washington, D.C. : Catholic University of America Press, 1946); Pierre-E. Trudeau, *La Grève de l'amiante.*

[17]Mgr L. A. Paquet, *Discours et allocutions* (Québec, 1915); Chanoine Emile Chartier, *Bréviaire du patriote canadien-français* (Montréal, 1925).

établi, quel qu'il fût; nécessité de la soumission à l' « ordre » social représenté par ce pouvoir. Le Canadien français, paroissien souvent récalcitrant mais traditionnellement passif, ayant vécu encadré par des structures sociales de type hiérarchique, a rarement eu l'occasion de s'initier au *self-government* ni de pratiquer l'initiative démocratique. Dans les moments de son histoire où les circonstances se seraient prêtées à une telle expérience, ou bien l'exemple que lui donnaient de la démocratie ses compatriotes-dominateurs anglophones était de nature à le décourager, ou bien l'attitude officielle ou officieuse de l'Eglise le faisait s'en détourner comme d'un péril[18]. Il n'a pas eu de peine à accepter les préceptes paternalistes de soumission, non plus qu'à se désintéresser de son destin temporel. De la démocratie, il n'a pas et ne pourra jamais acquérir la conception que s'en fait l'Anglo-Saxon, à savoir, celle d'une philosophie politique et d'un style de vie. Pour lui, elle désigne exclusivement le régime parlementaire de type britannique auquel il s'est habitué et que ses chefs politiques ont utilisé avec aisance et succès tout au long de son histoire politique.

L'Idéologie nationaliste comme tradition intellectuelle

Le second pôle d'intégration des attitudes collectives au Canada français a été la pensée nationaliste. Mais précisons aussitôt que rien n'est plus ambigu que ce terme. Très souvent, on lui fait inconsidérément désigner seulement l'expression d'un patriotisme authentique, c'est-à-dire l'attachement à sa patrie, à ceux que l'on considère comme les siens, aux souvenirs historiques de son peuple. Nous venons d'évoquer quelques uns des souvenirs et des thèmes qui sont sous-jacents au patriotisme canadien-français. Ceux-ci ont été explicités, formulés, souvent dramatisés, par l'une ou l'autre des écoles de pensée dites « nationalistes ».

L'histoire du nationalisme canadien-français n'est pas facile à résumer. Elle n'est même encore écrite qu'en partie[19]. Néanmoins, si sa genèse exacte et ses avatars contemporains semblent difficiles à dis-

[18]Pierre-E. Trudeau, « Some Obstacles to Democracy in Quebec », *Canadian Journal of Economics and Political Science*, vol. XXIV, no. 3 (August 1958), pp. 299–301.

[19]Voir : Mason Wade, *The French Canadians, 1760–1945* (Toronto : Macmillan, 1955); Jean-C. Bonenfant et Jean-C. Falardeau, « Cultural and Political Implications of French-Canadian Nationalism » in Canadian Historical Association, *Report* (May 23–4, 1946), pp. 56–73; Michael Oliver, « Quebec and Canadian Democracy », *Canadian Journal of Economics and Political Science*, vol. XXIII, no. 4 (Nov. 1957), pp. 506–7; Jean-M. Léger, « Aspects of French-Canadian Nationalism », *University of Toronto Quarterly*, vol. XXVII, no. 3 (April 1958), pp. 310–29.

cerner, il a eu ses chefs de file reconnus. Il a eu ses écoles de pensée caractéristiques, quelquefois opposées les unes aux autres. Sous sa forme extrême, il emprisonne le passé canadien-français dans une interprétation à sens unique, dans un système de pensée qui accentue chez le Canadien français les ressentiments qu'a créés en lui son statut minoritaire. Tout jeune Canadien français traverse, au moment de l'adolescence, une phase nationaliste. Tous ne surmontent pas cet émoi à la fois psychologique et idéologique. Plusieurs demeurent, à l'âge adulte, plus ou moins prisonniers de ce système de pensée qui les empêche de vivre dans le présent, tout au moins d'affronter celui-ci avec une complète lucidité[20].

Il était inévitable que le patriotisme canadien-français, après la conquête anglaise, prît des formes combattives. Comme le rappelait récemment Jean-Marc Léger[21], les principales des « quatre-vingt-douze résolutions » adoptées en 1834 par les représentants des Six-Comtés, ne signifiaient rien d'autre qu'une affirmation collective de conscience culturelle et un désir d'auto-détermination politique. La philosophie sociale du Parti des Patriotes était d'inspiration libérale et proclamait un idéal de réforme, de progrès social, de liberté et de vouloir-vivre démocratique. Papineau, grand parlementaire libéral et fougueusement patriote, fut le porte-parole de cette génération canadienne-française qui fut la plus dynamique de l'histoire canadienne de la première moitié du XIXe siècle et dont il faut regretter qu'elle n'ait été le point de départ d'une tradition continue au Canada français.

Bourassa faillit être l'agent de cette tradition canadienne-française mais ce fut son privilège d'être l'inspirateur d'un plus vaste mouvement de pensée qui s'est étendu, à une époque récente, à la dimension de l'ensemble du Canada de langue anglaise. Un grand nombre de Canadiens anglophones seraient peut-être étonnés d'apprendre que le canadianisme dont ils ont aujourd'hui l'orgueil, que le « nationalisme canadien » qui s'affiche dans les attitudes et les déclarations officielles de notre pays, ont été en grande partie mis au point par le Canadien français Henri Bourassa. Ce fut lui en effet qui, au début de ce siècle, au moment de la guerre sud-africaine, exprima en termes amples et dynamiques les postulats d'une nécessaire autonomie du Canada dans sa vie nationale et internationale. Une telle autonomie exigeait, en particulier, que le Canada coupât enfin le cordon ombilical qui le retenait de façon suffocante à la Grande-Bretagne. Ce fut le grand

[20]Ernest Gagnon, s.j., « Visage de l'intelligence », *Esprit* (Paris), 20e année, no 193–4 (août-septembre 1952), p. 252; Fernand Dumont, « De quelques obstacles à la prise de conscience chez les Canadiens français ».

[21]« Aspects of French-Canadian Nationalism », p. 315.

thème de Bourassa. Il donna naissance, environ trente ans plus tard, à la philosophie politique dont vit le Canada actuel. Il donna cependant naissance, de façon plus immédiate, à un credo nationaliste exclusivement canadien-français qui en réduisit les données à des affirmations d'aigreur et d'exaspération.

L'élaboration de ce credo nationaliste fut l'œuvre des disciples de Bourassa. Il fut l'œuvre, vers les années 1920, de l'historien aigu, combattif et inspirateur, que fut le chanoine Groulx. L'œuvre du chanoine Groulx[22] est trop connue pour la résumer ici. Monumentale, systématiquement poursuivie, élégante de forme, elle a été la doctrine des récentes générations de Canadiens français à qui elle a offert une vision tranchante de la « grande aventure » française en Amérique. Elle les a aussi exaspérés contre « les Anglais ». Elle a surtout débouché sur la notion d'un « Etat français » en Amérique, d'une « Laurentie » dont les jeunes enthousiastes se sont envoûtés dans le rêve d'une utopique réserve québécoise qui serait séparée du reste du Canada, et conséquemment du reste du monde, par un mur de Chine politique, religieux et linguistique.

Comme l'a remarqué en particulier Mason Wade[23], l'idéologie nationaliste québécoise, autour des années 1930, prit une allure et un contenu économiques. L'évidence d'une invasion des industries et des capitaux étrangers dans la province de Québec détermina de nombreux réflexes de frustration et de défense. A des craintes culturelles et politiques se substituèrent des craintes économiques. Aux pénibles souvenirs que laissèrent chez les Canadiens français, comme partout ailleurs, les années de crise et de chômage, s'ajouta le sentiment d'une aliénation devant les phénomènes d'industrialisation et d'urbanisation que ni leur système d'enseignement ni leur philosophie traditionnelle ne les avaient adéquatement préparés à affronter. L'idéologie nationaliste n'en continua pas moins à s'exprimer avec tenacité, de plus en plus distante des phénomènes économiques à l'échelle continentale, de plus en plus retranchée des réalités industrielles et politiques d'un Canada en pleine croissance. Elle inspire, de façon latente ou explicite, l'œuvre de M. Esdras Minville[24], le rapport de la Commission royale nommée en 1953 par le gouvernement de la province de Québec pour

[22]Voir, en particulier : *Histoire du Canada français depuis la découverte* (4 vols., Montréal : L'Action Nationale, 1950–2); *Notre Grande Aventure : L'Empire français en Amérique du Nord (1535–1760)* (Montréal : Fides, 1958).

[23]Mason Wade, « Political Trends » dans Falardeau, éd., *Essais sur le Québec contemporain*, chap. VII, pp. 162 ss.

[24]Esdras Minville, *Invitation à l'étude* (Montréal : Fides, 1943); *Le Citoyen canadien-français* (Montréal : Fides, 1946).

enquêter sur les problèmes constitutionnels[25], ainsi que les travaux de la jeune école d'historiens montréalais dont le pessimisme et le défaitisme font paraître, à distance, l'œuvre du chanoine Groulx comme une symphonie de sérénité.

Réduit à ses positions essentielles, le nationalisme canadien-français n'accepte pas ou, tout au mains, tolère mal le fait du Canada. Orchestrant jusqu'au mythe le thème d'un âge d'or et et d'un paradis perdu, il restreint impérieusement l'intérêt des Canadiens français au Québec et établit une muraille de défense entre eux et les « Anglais » considérés comme une espèce humaine *a priori* hostile et dangereuse. M. Michel Brunet, par exemple[26], maintient que la nation-état qui s'est élaborée au Canada depuis 1760, particulièrement depuis 1867, est «un royaume anglais créé par les *British Americans*... cette nation-état est monarchique, britannique, protestante... le gouvernement d'Ottawa est devenu et demeurera le gouvernement national du Canada anglais... » et il ne peut avoir comme responsabilité que « de veiller à la protection et à l'épanouissement de la culture et de la civilisation *Canadian* ». Le rapport de la Commission royale québécoise sur les problèmes constitutionnels est étayé sur certains postulats qui, sans aller jusqu'à une telle outrance verbale, réflètent une philosophie politique étroitement ethnocentrique : « national » signifie exclusivement « canadien-français »; la culture canadienne-française ne peut s'affirmer qu'en se protégeant, qu'en se refusant à tout contact allogène, qu'en se repliant à la dimension de la vie provinciale québécoise.

L'état actuel des recherches historiques ne permet pas d'établir avec assurance quels secteurs de la société canadienne-française ont adhéré, de façon profonde et durable, à quelque époque donnée, à l'une ou l'autre des principales variations de l'idéologie nationaliste. Il semble que celle-ci a surtout marqué les classes professionnelles, c'est-à-dire une portion très restreinte, mais par contre très influente de la société : celle des « élites » dont les attitudes ou les mots d'ordre ont souvent mobilisé les énergies collectives. Il n'appartient pas à la présente étude de rappeler de quelles façons la pensée nationaliste s'est mêlée aux programmes des partis politiques dans le Québec ni quel usage ceux-ci ont pu en faire[27]. D'autres études de ce volume rappellent pour quelles

[25] *Rapport de la Commission royale d'enquête sur les problèmes constitutionnels* (Québec : Province de Québec, 1956); voir, en particulier, le volume II : *La Province de Québec et le cas canadien-français : Le Fédéralisme.*

[26] Michel Brunet, « *Canadians* » *et Canadiens : Etude sur l'histoire et la pensée des deux Canadas* (Montréal : Fides, 1954).

[27] André Laurendeau, « Y a-t-il une Crise du nationalisme ? », *Action nationale,* vol. XL, no 3 (décembre 1952); vol. XLI, no 1 (janvier 1953).

raisons aucun parti nationaliste n'a jamais réussi à faire long feu dans la province. L'ensemble de la population canadienne-française n'a prêté au nationalisme un intérêt politique réel que de façon sporadique, à des moments de crise[28]. Mais les *leitmotive* du nationalisme sont constamment disponibles pour usage électoral et, à cause de leur association profonde avec les attitudes religieuses, trouvent une résonance facile dans la conscience populaire.

Il est impossible de prévoir ce que sera dans l'avenir, l'évolution de ces sentiments collectifs. Leur forme d'expression dépendra, dans une large mesure, de l'envergure du réveil d'une authentique conscience politique dans le Québec. Il n'est pas impossible qu'une forme atténuée du nationalisme québécois parvienne à se conjuguer avec le nationalisme canadien qui cherche actuellement à s'exprimer sur le plan économique et sur le plan culturel. Car il semble que les Canadiens de langue anglaise seront de plus en plus en mesure de comprendre pourquoi leurs compatriotes de langue française ont été nationalistes. C'est lorsqu'un peuple sent sa culture menacée que celle-ci lui devient chère et qu'il décide de la défendre. Pour les Canadiens français, cette menace a été britannique et c'est contre les Anglais qu'ils ont voulu défendre leur culture. Les Canadiens de langue anglaise ont, depuis quelques années, le sentiment que leur propre culture est compromise par une menace « américaine ». Ils commencent à vivre, sur le plan culturel, une expérience qui depuis cent cinquante ans a été celle des Canadiens français à tous les niveaux de leur existence. De cette conscience d'une expérience commune pourra peut-être surgir, entre les deux groupes, un nouveau type de compréhension.

IV. Valeurs et attitudes nouvelles

Les traits psychologiques que l'on vient d'esquisser s'appliquent à un nombre de moins en moins considérable de Canadiens français. Un des phénomènes les plus marquants de la société canadienne-française actuelle, en effet, est celui d'un décalage entre, d'une part, les idéologies et les valeurs stéréotypées et, d'autre part, la réalité dynamique d'une société qui, sous la poussée de l'industrialisation et de l'urbanisation, est en voie de transformation accélérée dans toutes ses structures.

C'est le mérite de quelques chercheurs et observateurs attentifs d'avoir tenté, depuis dix ou quinze ans, de percevoir et d'analyser ces

[28]Jean-C. Falardeau, « Dualité de cultures et gouvernement d'opinion au Canada » dans *L'Opinion publique* (Paris : Presses Universitaires de France, 1957).

transformations fondamentales de la société canadienne-française[29]. Ils ont commencé à décrire quelques-unes des conséquences immédiatement visibles de l'industrialisation du milieu québécois, quelques-uns des processus de dé-structuration de sa vie traditionnelle, et quelques-unes des innovations qui déjà s'élaborent à un rythme accéléré. Une constatation sur laquelle tous se rencontrent unanimement est justement ce fait que les deux grandes idéologies du Canada français, la « pensée sociale » traditionnelle de l'Eglise et le nationalisme, ont depuis longtemps cessé de mordre sur la mentalité canadienne-française. Plus exactement, par suite de la façon abstraite, routinière, purement verbale, dont elles étaient formulées et répétées, elles sont devenues vides de sens. Ce qu'elles proposaient à la collectivité et aux individus avait perdu toute signification existentielle. En conséquence, la vie du Canadien français s'est déroulée, à l'époque récente, dans une sorte de vacuum moral, au niveau de l'immédiat. « Le Canadien français, écrit Marcel Rioux, a dû s'arranger pour vivre sa vie d'homme à peu près sans modèles idéaux sur lesquels régler sa conduite[30]. » « Un prolétaire spirituel », a-t-on écrit de lui[31].

L'une des conséquences les plus manifestes de l'évolution sociale contemporaine dans le Québec a été l'apparition de classes socio-économiques nouvelles et, en particulier, d'une classe ouvrière de plus en plus distante sinon dissociée du reste de la société. Les valeurs sociales et les modèles d'action que l'on peut discerner dans ces groupes nouveaux ne sont guère différents, dans l'ensemble, de ceux de la société nord-américaine. Leur mode de vivre, de se loger, de se récréer, diffère peu du style de vie américain. On peut affirmer, en empruntant la terminologie de David Riesman, qu'une proportion de plus en plus marquante de Canadiens français se sont soustraits à l'attraction de la tradition (*tradition-directed*) pour adopter des comportements de conformisme à des contrôles sociaux en voie d'élaboration à divers paliers de la société (*other-directed*). Nous connaissons encore mal ce qu'a été pour des milliers et des milliers de Canadiens français le choc graduel ou brutal engendré par leur immigration vers les villes et tout

[29]Les essais de caractère très divers où sont contenues ces analyses sont déjà nombreux et assez connus pour ne mentionner que les principaux : *Essais sur le Québec contemporain*; *La Grève de l'amiante*; les numéros spéciaux des revues *Esprit*, *La Chronique sociale de France* et *University of Toronto Quarterly*, sur le Canada français; un grand nombre d'articles de la revue *Cité libre*, en particulier Marcel Rioux, « Idéologie et crise de conscience du Canada français » dans le numéro 14 (décembre 1955).

[30]« Idéologie et crise de conscience du Canada français », p. 15.

[31]Gérard Pelletier, « D'un prolétariat spirituel », *Esprit* (Paris), no 193–4 (août-septembre 1952), p. 194.

spécialement vers l'agglomération montréalaise qui contient à elle seule plus de la moitié de la population urbaine québécoise. Ceux qui nous éclairent le mieux sur leurs émois et leurs drames sont les jeunes romanciers et dramaturges, de Gabrielle Roy à André Langevin et Marcel Dubé, dont les personnages vivent une existence pirandellienne, à la recherche d'eux-mêmes[32].

« Crise de conscience » du Canada français, écrit-on de plus en plus en ce moment pour caractériser à la fois cette situation collective, et de façon plus particulière, les interrogations que se posent les « intellectuels » et tous ceux qui ont une responsabilité en éducation populaire ou en organisation professionnelle. C'est grâce à ces entraîneurs, qui sont de nouveaux « définisseurs de la situation » que, dans de larges secteurs du milieu canadien-français, depuis une vingtaine d'années, des attitudes nouvelles ont été cristallisées et que des institutions nouvelles ont été élaborées. Les progrès et les réalisations du mouvement ouvrier sont bien connus, de même que les travaux des universitaires, les entreprises des militants sociaux de toute catégorie, y compris une fraction intéressante du clergé qui, avec une vision rajeunie et réaliste, cherche à accorder son effort à celui d'une génération de Canadiens français préoccupée de donner une polarisation nouvelle aux besoins collectifs. Cette œuvre est encore trop récente pour en prédire les résultats. Tout ce que l'on peut affirmer est qu'elle a comme ambition de redéfinir la culture canadienne-française, de rénover les valeurs spirituelles et temporelles qui en sont la clef de voûte, de créer les institutions éducatives, politiques et économiques, dans lesquelles elle doit s'incarner.

Cette ambition comporte aussi l'obligation de redéfinir le champ de perception du Canadien français en tant que Canadien français et en tant que Canadien. Plus exactement, de faire passer au plan de l'acceptation consciente et positive ce qui fait déjà partie de son expérience humaine. Tous les Canadiens français ont vécu et vivront dorénavant davantage, dans les circonstances aussi variées que les événements de la vie quotidienne, en contact avec leurs compatriotes de langue anglaise. L'ouvrier à l'usine, l'acheteuse au magasin à rayons, l'agent d'assurance, le fonctionnaire, l'avocat, l'ingénieur, le militaire, et des centaines d'autres catégories professionnelles, sont en relation avec des Canadiens anglophones. D'autres études de ce volume décrivent les formes qu'ont prises, à l'époque contemporaine, la coexistence, les compromis et la coopération entre les deux partenaires

[32] Jeanne Lapointe, « Quelques Apports positifs de notre littérature d'imagination », *Cité libre*, no 10 (octobre 1954), pp. 17–36.

du « mariage de raison » canadien. Toutes ces études, ainsi que l'observation même superficielle, manifestent que l'équilibre de la vie canadienne, s'il demeure subtil, est maintenant consolidé. Elles manifestent aussi jusqu'à quel point les exigences même de cette vie canadienne contredisent la fiction qui voudrait restreindre la vie canadienne-française aux frontières du Québec. Si la province de Québec demeure le lieu principal de la vie française au Canada, elle n'en circonscrit pas toute la présence ou le dynamisme. Il est de l'intérêt du Canadien français, au point de vue même de sa culture, de ne pas définir ses droits en termes juridiques strictement provincialistes mais en termes culturels qui aient un sens pour l'ensemble du Canada. Ce sont d'ailleurs des voix canadiennes-françaises qui, les premières, ont fait reconnaître et accepter le fait de la dualité ethnique et culturelle au Canada. La définition que le Canada donne maintenant de lui-même proclame ce jumellage de deux grands groupes dominants. Pour que cet équilibre se stabilise, il requiert la présence franche de chacun des deux protagonistes qui ont maintenant prouvé qu'ils « se sont reconnus, qu'ils s'acceptent, et qu'ils s'entr'aident l'un l'autre ».

1958

I. ABSTRACT FACTORS

B. Religion and Philosophy

I. PERSPECTIVES GÉNÉRALES

B. Religion et philosophie

Religion and Philosophy: An English-Canadian Point of View

WATSON KIRKCONNELL
President, Acadia University

WITH THE PROBLEM OF RELIGION, we come to one of the basic issues in a bicultural country such as Canada. At least the distinction between the two main cultural groups is most commonly thought of in religious terms.

At the outset, however, one must avoid over-simplifying a very complex situation. Roman Catholicism in Canada is not synonymous with the Canadian French. Of the 6,260,327 Roman Catholics (including Uniates) listed in the 1951 census, only some 4,200,000, or only about two-thirds, were French. There are also substantial Catholic communities among the Irish, the Highland Scots, the Ukrainians, the Poles, the Italians, and some smaller groups. The sharp line of cleavage between Roman Catholic and Protestant does not, therefore, coincide with the ancient line of demarcation at the conquest of 1760 between the French who lost and the British who won. As we shall note later, there is a measure of association between the two million Catholics who are not French Canadian and the four million who are. In organizations such as the Canadian Catholic Historical Association they meet together, although because of language difficulties some of their sessions are held in separate rooms.

The fact remains, however, that the English Canadians are predominantly Protestant and the French Canadians are overwhelmingly Roman Catholic. Hence it comes about that the Protestant English Canadian tends to think of the French Canadian as the Canadian Roman Catholic *par excellence.* In 12th of July oratory, it is the French rather than the Irish Catholic who now tends to become the target for theological thunderbolts; while to the French Catholic, *les Anglais* are characteristically English-speaking Protestants.

The hostility that is expressed in religious terms is due in part to differentials in growth of population and to the pressure of numbers by which one group consequently displaces the other. Lines of intense friction of this sort are to be found, for example, in eastern Ontario and in northern New Brunswick, where the displacement has been most spectacular. In other areas the stresses have been less marked. In Newfoundland, Prince Edward Island, Cape Breton, and western Nova Scotia there are enclaves of Acadian French who escaped, or returned from, the great expulsion of 1755, but their recent expansion has not been great enough to alarm the English Canadians. The Acadians have, indeed, trebled in the Annapolis Valley during the past two decades, but the increase there has been accompanied by losses on the French Shore in Yarmouth and Digby counties, and so on balance they are losing ground.

In the case of New Brunswick, the advance of Catholicism, largely French, has been spectacular. A clear majority of the province's population now belongs to the Roman Catholic Church (260,742 out of 515,697). The northern and eastern counties are strongholds of Catholicism: Madawaska, 97.3 per cent; Restigouche, 79.2 per cent; Northumberland, 59 per cent; Gloucester, 92.5 per cent; Kent, 88 per cent; Westmorland, 51 per cent.

In the period 1871–1951 the French in New Brunswick increased by 340 per cent, or over eleven times more than the English, who increased by only 30 per cent. This is not, however, the ratio of the birth rates, for although many of the English have migrated elsewhere, few of the French have done so. The French showed an increase in every county in the province in 1951, and they constitute 38.3 per cent of its total population. Of the population of the province under five years of age the French constitute 48 per cent and Roman Catholics 57 per cent.

A good example of a French victory by sheer force of numbers is in the Eastern Townships of Quebec, once predominantly English in population but now just as decidedly French. Figures for six of these municipal areas are as follows:

County	*Pop. 1871*	*French 1871*	%	*Pop. 1951*	*French 1951*	%
Compton	13,665	3,785	27.5	23,856	18,293	77
Brome	13,757	3,471	26	13,393	6,758	51
Huntingdon	16,304	4,924	30	13,457	7,501	56
Richmond	11,213	3,718	34	34,102	28,645	84
Sherbrooke	8,516	3,544	41	62,166	50,356	80
Stanstead	13,138	3,212	24	34,642	26,305	75

In Ontario, Roman Catholics make up 1,181,740 (or 26 per cent) of the total population of 4,597,542. In a band of counties adjacent to Quebec, however, they are markedly in the majority: Glengarry, 77 per cent; Prescott, 88; Stormont, 63; Russell, 85; Nipissing, 63; Sudbury, 62.5; Cochrane, 63. The French in Ontario are largely concentrated in this area and total 477,677. In the old Highland Scottish settlement of Glengarry, the French now constitute 57 per cent of the population and the Scottish Catholics less than 20 per cent. It is a striking example of demographic dynamics.

A clue to relative birth rates is to be found in the census report on age groups. Thus, in New Brunswick, 74,869 (or 14.4 per cent) of the total population of 515,697 are under five years of age; in the province of Quebec, 541,524 (or 13.4 per cent) out of 4,055,681; and in Ontario, 514,722 (or 11.4 per cent) out of 4,597,542. It is clear that so far as natural increase is concerned, Ontario is growing more slowly than either Quebec or New Brunswick. Rural life is a major factor in the birth rate: so far as the under-five group is concerned, French-Catholic Montreal actually has a slightly lower rate (10.4 per cent) than English-Protestant Toronto (10.7 per cent); and both are dwarfed by the rural Catholic counties of Madawaska, New Brunswick (17.4 per cent) and Matapedia, Quebec (18.2 per cent).

The total Canadian population in 1951 is given as 14,009,429, of whom 44.5 per cent are Roman Catholic. However, of the national under-twenty total of 5,308,689, Roman Catholics constitute 2,677,267 (or 50.5 per cent)—a slight majority. Similarly, 50.5 per cent of Canada's children under ten years of age are Roman Catholic. There was a marked upsurge of births in the years immediately after the close of the Second World War. This desire for larger families on the part of many young Protestant couples resulted in a drop in the Roman Catholic percentage in the case of children under five (that is, those conceived and born after the end of the war) from 50.5 to 49 per cent, although this latter figure is still much better than a survival rate. Another way of recording this change is to take the potential parent group (ages fifteen to forty-four) in each denomination as a percentage of that age group in the whole population and compare it with the numbers (in percentages) of post-war children (under five in 1951) that are actually in each denomination:

	Percentage in parent group 15–44	*Percentage in children under 5*
Roman Catholic	44	49
United Church	21	20
Church of England	14.4	13.7
Baptist	3.6	3.3

It will be noted that of all these participants in the post-war baby harvest, only the Roman Catholics are actually increasing.

These facts have given rise to tension and uneasiness. The animus on the Protestant side is partly motivated by a fear of ultimate displacement by the more fertile Catholic stock, chiefly French in origin. In the Protestant communal remembrance, moreover, are the murky horrors of the Inquisition, and the anxieties of the struggle by which English Protestantism narrowly escaped extinction in the days of the Spanish Armada. Transplanted also to Canada was the enmity between Irish Protestant and Irish Catholic, kept warm by long centuries of violence and cruelty on both sides. Racial memories are tenacious things and can linger on undiminished through many generations.

The fears and criticisms in the heart of English-Canadian Protestantism find expression through many organizations. There are groups such as the Protestant Association of Nova Scotia and publications such as *Protestant Action* of Toronto which will propagate uncritically almost any accusation regardless of its source. On the other hand there are groups such as the Inter-Church Committee on Protestant–Roman Catholic Relations, composed of representatives of all of the major Protestant denominations, whose purpose is to study the threat to the welfare of the nation which they anticipate as coming from Catholicism. This latter committee has been made up of sober and estimable men, but they have sometimes been the uncritical victims of anti-Catholic enthusiasts.

The religious issues that burn in the minds of English-Canadian Protestants are of various sorts. Some are false rumours that need to be killed for the sake of good relations among Canadians of both camps. Some are fundamental differences of conviction that need to be understood on both sides for the same reason. And some are contentious issues for which there is no easy solution but regarding which an objective analysis of the facts can do nothing but good.

False Rumours

The following are typical rumours, often believed innocently but, for all that, wholly or partially false.

1. "You have already heard, of course, that far more Roman Catholics are admitted as immigrants into Canada than Protestants. The proportion seems to be about eight to one or ten to one."

Statistics on immigration, secured in connection with the 1951 census, show positively that in no period have immigrating Catholics been more than 41 per cent of the total, a proportion that is slightly less than their percentage (44.5) of the total Canadian population. That maximum percentage of Roman Catholic immigrants was in the period 1949–51. The record in earlier years was as follows (including in all cases the Ukrainian Uniate Church):

Period	%
Before 1911	19
1911–1920	17
1921–1930	27
1931–1940	36
1941–1945	26
1946	23
1947–1948	33
Total R.C. immigrants still living in 1951	25

The facts, therefore, are that until twenty-five years ago Protestant immigrants outnumbered Catholic immigrants by four to one or three to one, and from 1931 to 1948 by two to one. Even in the brief upsurge of 1949–51, the Protestants were still preponderant by three to two.

2. A group calling itself the Protestant Association of Nova Scotia is circulating a printed "Bloody Oath of the Knights of Columbus." It purports to be a solemn vow taken by these Roman Catholics to "make and wage relentless war, secretly and openly, against all heretics, Protestants and Masons," and to "burn, hang, waste, boil, flay, strangle and bury alive these infamous heretics." It is vouched for "as printed from the *Congressional Record*, Sixty-second Congress, Third Session, Vol. 29, Part 4, pp. 3216–17, February 15, 1913."

The facts are that the "Oath" was indeed printed in the *Congressional Record* of that date, but only because it had been produced in an election contest and denounced before Congress as an abominable forgery by the candidate against whom it was circulated. The United States government officially denounced its circulators as traitors to the United States; the forgery was also publicly denounced by the Secretary of State, the Secretary of War, and the Secretary of the Navy; and an agent caught circulating it in New Jersey was arrested and imprisoned. Of the Knights of Columbus, the *Encyclopædia Britannica* (1943 ed., vol. XIII, p. 441) states: "There are four degrees of membership, none having any secret or oath-bound stipulation."

3. A false rumour on the other side of the fence is the frequent Catholic charge that Freemasonry is atheistic, conspiratorial, and aggressively anti-Catholic. Fantastic stories are current, for instance the one about the Freemasons who secured a bit of the Host by

stealth and skewered it with a knife on an altar in their lodge, only to have blood flow from it all over the room. Freemasonry in France at the time of the Revolution was indeed atheistic and revolutionary, and it has tended to preserve that character in some parts of Europe. In English-speaking countries, on the contrary, it is profoundly religious; the open Bible is central to its ritual; and atheism is the first and most deadly offence for which a man can be expelled from membership. Catholics are eligible for membership and some have joined, but their duty to the confessional presents them with a problem, because it conflicts with their duty of maintaining secrecy with regard to their obligations as Freemasons. In thirty-five years as a Freemason, I have never heard an un-Christian word or an anti-Catholic sentiment expressed in any lodge.

4. A Protestant claim is that illegitimacy is more prevalent among Roman Catholics than among Protestants. Statistics show this to be false in Canada. The rate of illegitimacy in the predominantly Catholic province of Quebec is today, and regularly has been, the *lowest* in all Canada. For the period 1932–43, the average annual percentage of illegitimate to live births, by provinces, was as follows: Nova Scotia 6.4, Ontario 4.5, Prince Edward Island 4.1, Alberta 3.95, British Columbia 3.9, New Brunswick 3.75, Manitoba 3.7, Saskatchewan 3.4, and Quebec 3.2.

In the province with the highest rate of illegitimacy—Nova Scotia—provincial statistics prove, moreover, that it is the Protestants and not the Catholics who are responsible. The five counties with the highest rates—Guysborough (11.9 per cent), Queens (7.6), Hants (7.5), Cumberland (6.9), and Shelburne (6.9)—are all predominantly Protestant. The two counties with the lowest rates—Antigonish (3.7) and Richmond (3.5)—are both more than four-fifths Roman Catholic.

Fundamental Differences

Pope Pius XI may have said that "pieces broken from gold-bearing rock themselves bear gold"; and there may be many basic truths—from the Incarnation to the Atonement—that are accepted by all Christians everywhere. It remains true, however, that in some respects the Protestant and the Roman Catholic positions are at present irreconcilable though some misunderstandings of the two positions might helpfully be removed. No amount of sweet reasonableness can merge the two streams without major changes in their channels. Among the aspects of Roman Catholicism that are completely unacceptable to Protestants are the following.

1. The primacy and *ex cathedra* infallibility of the Pope of Rome are rejected alike by all Protestants and all members of the Orthodox Church and even by members of the "Old Catholic Church." A hierarchical system is not unacceptable to Protestant episcopal bodies like the Church of England, but the Roman hierarchy is repudiated. That such a structure falls short of absolutism is sometimes not understood either by Protestants or by Roman Catholics and one sometimes finds even some of the latter interpreting *Extra Ecclesiam non salus est* to mean "there is no salvation outside the Catholic Church." As recently as April, 1949, however, a Jesuit priest in Boston was stripped of his duties for insisting on that very interpretation. The official position of the Roman catechism runs rather as follows: "He who knows the Church to be the true Church and remains out of it cannot be saved. This applies to men of bad faith who sin against the truth; it does not apply to men of good faith who belong to the soul of the Church." In other words, in the official Catholic view, a sincere Protestant, in his invincible ignorance of the Catholic Church's alleged role, can be saved by his fundamental Christian faith.

2. The power of a priest's prayer to transubstantiate the bread and wine of the Eucharist into the veritable body and blood of Christ is denied by Protestants as having no basis in scripture. Protestants themselves, however, vary widely in their interpretation of this sacrament, chiefly in terms of a sacramental presence for the active believer, as held by Luther (Lutherans and Anglicans), and of a holy symbolism, as held by Zwingli (Presbyterians and Baptists).

3. Protestants can find no scriptural evidence for purgatory, no historical acceptance of it prior to A.D. 593, and no institution of Masses for the souls of the dead earlier than a church council in A.D. 1215. Mass money, to deliver souls from torment in purgatory, is regarded by Protestants as an invention of men.

4. The supernatural power of holy oils, holy water, holy candles, holy relics, medals, and scapulars is expressly denied.

5. While deeply respecting Mary, the mother of Jesus Christ, Protestants can find no evidence for her immaculate conception and her assumption into Heaven. The recent ultramontane promulgation of this latter dogma effectively slams and bars the door to any understanding between the two religious groups.

6. The prying of compulsory auricular confession into the intimacies of the marriage bed strikes a Protestant as ruthless and offensive—a sort of never-ceasing investigation into the private life of all the wives and husbands of the community, and this without even the impersonality of a Kinsey questionnaire.

7. The necessity for the celibacy of the clergy is regarded by non-Catholics as a human decree, and contrary to scripture. Even Peter, the first bishop of Rome, was married.

8. Roman Catholicism places a whole range of intermediate beings, on earth and in heaven, between the humble Christian and his God. Protestant bodies, on the contrary, do not see that the priest is a necessary switch in the current of salvation or that the intercession of the saints is a natural part of prayer.

9. Since the Council of Trent, tradition can have the same authority as scripture for Catholicism. A new dogma, pronounced *ex cathedra* by the Pope, becomes a part of tradition as infallible and as authoritative as scripture. This doctrine is repudiated by Protestantism.

To sum up these points at which the Protestant challenges the Catholic, one may cite a simple statement of Protestant principles, set forth in 1951 by Rev. Dr. R. J. McCracken of Riverside Church, New York:

> They were and are simple convictions: that each man and woman is a child of God, whom God loves and for whom Christ died; that human personality has inherent, indefeasible rights, especially the right of direct approach to God; that every individual has infinite worth and must be regarded as an end in himself, never as a means to an end; that a man's conscience should be in the keeping neither of priest nor of magistrate; that the final arbiter of his actions should be his sense of duty and responsibility to God; that freedom of the soul is the supreme freedom, with which no earthly authority can be permitted to interfere.

Confronting these basic Protestant criticisms of Catholicism may be set a major Catholic misgiving about Protestantism: that freedom without authority can produce theological anarchy and demoralization. Protestantism has set the Bible in the hands of Everyman; yet the verdict of scholars for the past two thousand years is that the Bible is a profound and difficult book. Its text, in Hebrew and Greek, has come down to us full of manuscript imperfections and thousands of variant readings. Its various books reflect the conflicting traditions of different stages of civilization. The vernacular translation in common use (the King James Version) employs many deceptive archaisms going back to Tyndale and Wycliffe. While the central message of the Cross makes its appeal to the humblest and most childlike intelligence, the sacred record bristles with problems that have divided even the most learned and pious men into hostile camps. It is easy, in this connection, for the upholders of authority to point to the fact that there are today on the North American continent over two thousand "Protestant" sects and cults, and that each generation, from pioneer times on, has seen a new mushroom-crop of zealous partisans, from Irvingites, Millerites, and Hornerites down to the Russellites and British Israelites of our own day.

Most Protestants would of course agree that the claims of cults such as the British Israelite can hardly be substantiated. This particular cult claims special divine care for the British because of their alleged descent from the so-called Lost Tribes of Israel; yet on all sorts of grounds—historical and linguistic among others—the verdict of science is absolutely against any such identification. Moreover, many Protestants would feel that the basis of the cult is not in keeping with the spirit of Christianity: the Christian places his hope in Christ; the British Israelite puts his hope in race. When a French Catholic hears the tenets of such groups affirmed over the radio or in great public meetings in Toronto which are reported in his own press, he may easily be persuaded that Protestantism must be a disintegrating and meaningless mess. He needs to be assured that the major Protestant denominations are in an utterly different category, with a theology and a philosophy of religion as intellectually respectable as his own.

One issue on which Ontario's Protestants and Quebec's French Catholics have recently experienced a sharp division of opinion is in the disabilities imposed in Quebec on the Jehovah's Witnesses. In the press of Toronto they have largely appeared as down-trodden Protestants, in the press of Quebec as wild-eyed disturbers of the peace. Both views need correction. It would be salutary if there were greater recognition in Ontario of the actual tenets of the Witnesses: to them religion, commerce, and government together form the Kingdom of Satan; all existing churches are condemned and the Witnesses themselves expressly declare that they are not a religious sect or cult; their social doctrines are largely devoted to fomenting class hatred; their political ideal is the destruction of all human governments and societies and their subjection to a dictatorship of Jehovah working through a Witness prophet. On the other hand, the Witnesses raise in an acute form the question of the attitude of a democratic government towards such anarchic groups. It is felt by many that forcible repression cannot be condoned, and it may properly be represented to people in Quebec that, since the Witnesses do not seem to have any conspiratorial general staff to bring about our annihilation, the best way to treat them is to expose the nature of the doctrines their leaders have propagated.

With regard to the question of authority, French-Catholic theologians and English-Protestant theologians might live on better terms if each side realized the amount of basic scholarship incorporated in the training of the others' leaders.

Thus the French prerequisites for theological training call for the classical college B.A., with its six years of Latin, five of Greek, and two of scholastic philosophy. Laval University then intercalates a special pre-theological year devoted to a study of Aristotle in the original Greek and of St. Thomas Aquinas and his commentators in the original Latin. Two, four, and five further years of courses lead to the successive degrees in theology (bachelor's, licentiate, and doctorate), with probably several extra years of work on the thesis before the doctor's degree is conferred. Hebrew is compulsory in the first theological year but is not carried further. Latin is a spoken language and is used for lectures in such courses as dogmatic theology, moral theology, and canon law. A theologian with a doctorate in theology from Laval is a deeply erudite man, but his training is heavily weighted on the side of dogma.

Since Protestantism lays stress on the original languages of the Old and the New Testament rather than on Jerome's Latin (Vulgate) translation, the scholarship of Protestant professors has pushed linguistic studies to great lengths. Thus there is nothing in French-Catholic universities to compare with the advanced work in Hellenistic Greek and in Hebrew, Aramaic, Syriac, Arabic, Sumerian, Babylonian, Egyptian, and Coptic by such Toronto scholars as Meek, Taylor, Winnett, McCullough, and Williams. This scholarship does not permeate the rank and file of theological students, most of whom struggle painfully with small Greek and less Hebrew; but it constitutes a highly learned climate for the mature consideration of biblical theology. Systematic theology is also an integral part of every theological course. One occasionally encounters such Catholic opinions as the rash statement that "Most Protestant ministers have no belief in the Divinity of Christ." No serious examination of the Protestant curriculum would support that contention for a moment. The overwhelming bulk of Canadian Protestantism now co-operating in the Canadian Council of Churches is firmly based on essential dogma and with greater unity than at any time in two earlier centuries.

The points on which that dogma parts company with the Church of Rome are precisely those points already mentioned which have to do with the rites, sacraments, practices, and authority of ecclesiastical bodies. After five centuries of theological controversy, there is little inclination left today to fight the old battles over again and to restate positions that have been stated ten thousand times already. There is more theological controversy in Canada today between Protestant and Protestant and between Catholic and Catholic than there is between serious thinkers on the two major sides.

The same is true of philosophy. Neither tradition is monolithic. On the Catholic side, the Dominicans hold to the theology of Saint Thomas, the Franciscans to the theology of Duns Scotus, the Jesuits to the theology of Suarez, and so on for others; and each article in Quebec's theological textbooks may be preceded by long lists of Catholic theologians who differ in opinion from Saint Thomas. In a learned journal such as *Le Laval théologique et philosophique*, Roman Catholic philosophers occasionally belabour one another's doctrines with great zeal.

Nevertheless, in the education of French-Catholic Canada, the *Summa theologica* of Saint Thomas seems to provide answers to almost all of a pupil's questions and to indoctrinate him with the all-comprehensive dogmas of a single system. The massive scholarship of the great mediaeval institutes in Montreal and Toronto may help to reproduce the vast ramifications of patristic thought out of which Albertus Magnus and his disciple Thomas Aquinas built their synthesis of Aristotle and Christianity; but the average Catholic student in Quebec absorbs no more of this than the Protestant student in Ontario absorbs from the linguistic glories of his professors.

As for English-Protestant philosophy, it is as variable as the spectrum. The approach may be analytical, in the examination of basic problems and concepts; or historical, in a survey of philosophies from Plato down to Wittgenstein; or weighted in terms of logic or ethics or epistemology. The aim is not so much to supply the student with a carefully co-ordinated master plan of thought as to teach him to approach all philosophers with a keenly analytical mind and ultimately to achieve his own personal metaphysic according to his own temperament—whether realistic, idealistic, or pragmatic. In other words, the English-Canadian philosopher is usually a layman and does not necessarily seek to relate his philosophy to Christian dogma. He may even be an experimental psychologist and be more interested in white rats than in entelechies and enthymemes. Plato has exercised a powerful influence in Canada, with men like Lodge and Vlastos; and the late John Watson, of Glasgow and Queen's, was the last of the great Scottish idealists. Typically enough the English-Canadian Protestant will study "formal logic" and sharpen the tools of his dialectic, while the French-Canadian Catholic will add the "material logic" of John of St. Thomas, which seeks not only correctness in reasoning but truth in knowing.

Between the two camps there is no effective communication. Neither side reads the other's current publications.

One might have expected the Royal Society of Canada to be a forum in which the intellectual leaders of French and English Canada would confront each other in an exchange of philosophic doctrine. For better or worse, however, French philosophers are members of Section I and English philosophers of Section II. From 1882 down to 1952, the Jews had no dealings with the Samaritans. Two years ago, however, the precedent was set of holding one joint session of the two sections every year, with a symposium at which either language might be freely used. So far the programme has been discreetly limited to matters of history. Perhaps the time will come when basic differences of philosophy will be amicably discussed.

It is not that the French Canadian is unwilling or unready to enter into basic argument. In 1946 I taught the poetry of John Milton to a postgraduate class in the Summer School at Laval University. Most of my students were priests and nuns from teaching orders. I set them tracking down Milton's patristic erudition in *Paradise Lost* with helpful references to a score of the Fathers, from Augustine to Aquinas, in the Laval Library, and found them very ready to give the Protestant poet his due tribute for profound learning and deep theological thought. He might be unsound at certain points but they readily admitted that he had fundamental truth to communicate.

There have been other contacts, occasional rather than continuing. One of these was a Canadian Hazen Conference held at Duchesnay, Quebec, in June, 1952, which was attended by both French- and English-speaking Canadians of various disciplines, including philosophy and theology. Monseigneur Parent, now Rector of Laval, was the conference chairman, and the "lead" papers, by Dr. Jean Bruchési and others, were published by Laval. Still at the stage of organization is L'Alliance canadienne, with units in Toronto and Quebec City, whose greatest present purpose is a bilingualism that will "promote a better understanding among Canadians." No discussion of religion and philosophy "at the summit," or even on the foot-hills, has yet been contemplated.

Contentious Issues

The basic differences between Catholic and Protestant in theology and philosophy have been taken for granted for at least three centuries. Three hundred years ago, in the Thirty Years' War (1618–48), over twenty million European Christians were slaughtered in one of the bloodiest of all human wars in an effort to settle matters of ecclesiastical authority and spiritual truth. It is inevitable that the bloodshed of that awful period should still coagulate in the hearts of twentieth-century Christians and render difficult any frank discussion of fundamentals. Argumentation is thought of as useless and hence is not even attempted.

There are, however, certain current issues in Canadian life that cry out for more careful examination. Such are the problems of education, of mixed marriages, and of representation at the Vatican.

Education is not an issue in the province of Quebec, where a *modus operandi* has long since been worked out and where Dr. W. P. Percival, the present Director of Protestant Education, has nothing but praise for the relations between the two faiths in the educational field. Friction arises rather in provinces such as Ontario, New Brunswick, and Nova Scotia, where certain overwhelmingly Catholic areas possess separate schools and where the principle of a non-sectarian public school available to Protestants becomes jeopardized.

In the province of Ontario, the Protestant Inter-Church Committee on Protestant–Roman Catholic Relations has given special study to the status of separate schools and has declared itself as "opposed to the principle of state-supported separate or denominational schools." So far as first principles are concerned, I would agree with the Committee, and I am grateful for having had my secondary-school education in a community where children of all creeds were taught together and learned goodwill towards one another as young fellow citizens of the same town. The crux of the matter is religious instruction, however, and no acceptable solution other than separate schools at the elementary level has yet been found. The Committee's frontal attack is on the attempt of *French* Catholics in Ontario to develop a system of *French* separate schools, sought in part on the allegedly equal status of the two languages in Canada. Here one must distinguish between strict legality and the thrust of demographic forces. According to the letter of the law, the French language enjoys equality with English only in the province of Quebec and in the government of Canada. The French of Canada, however, have increased in the past 195 years, without the help of immigration, from 60,000 to about 4,500,000. The English Canadians, in spite of millions of British immigrants, have since 1871 dropped back from over 60 per cent to less than one-half of the total Canadian population.

The famous brief of the Inter-Church Committee starts from the assumptions: (1) that the Separate Schools Act of 1863 was built for eternity; (2) that "there has been no new condition in Ontario to make necessary such a fundamental change in basic policy" (p. 28, re section 21); and (3) that English should by compulsion be "the only language of instruction in all schools" (p. 12), in other words, an essential instrument of racial assimilation. It should be noted, however, that the French population of Ontario has increased from almost nil in 1863 to half a million today (or the equivalent of almost the entire population of the province of New Brunswick), thereby certainly creating "a new condition in Ontario" and a group not lightly to be denationalized by the stroke of a Protestant pen.

In New Brunswick, where, as has already been stated, more than half the total population is now Catholic, the process of taking over the public schools as a separate-school system has inevitably gone a stage further, and the plight of the tiny Protestant minority in some of the northern and eastern counties is sometimes unfortunate. In fact some of the Protestants are now prepared to relinquish the old pattern and envisage Catholic "public schools" and Protestant "separate schools." This would lead almost inevitably to the Quebec solution of two separate and co-equal provincial systems of education, one Catholic and the other Protestant.

The attitude of the Roman Church to mixed marriages is, to Protestants, a scandal. If the marriage is not performed by a Roman priest, the Church declares it void and invalid; the parties are living in sin and their children are illegitimate. The civil law says otherwise; but in marriage the Church claims a higher authority than the state. The mental anguish of the Catholic partner may be imagined. When, however, the Protestant partner agrees to have the marriage solemnized by a Catholic priest, he must make a number of serious concessions: a dispensation must be bought; the wedding cannot take place in church and there can be no music or any other sign of rejoicing; the Protestant partner must sign a witnessed document that all children of the marriage must be brought up as Catholics, even if the Catholic partner dies; the Catholic partner must sign a promise to try to win the Protestant partner to Catholicism; and the Protestant partner must agree to take religious instruction from the priest. It does not help greatly to add that the attitude of the Orthodox Church to mixed marriages is almost identical with that of the Church of Rome.

Another vexatious issue is the question of nominating a Canadian ambassador to the Vatican. The reason why Protestants object to this idea is not that they must automatically be opposed to something that Catholics desire. They object to it because it would give political status and preferential official recognition to a church—to a church, I say, because it is impossible to differentiate between the political and the spiritual significance of an area of one-sixth of a square mile with a population of one thousand persons. The dominant political conviction of Protestantism is the separation of church and state. Protestants consider the true nature of the Church of Christ to be spiritual and not political. They are also nervous about rumours that with the defeat of Catholicism in Marxist Europe the Papacy may consider a transfer to Canada or the United States and may seek an ever-fuller control over the political life of this continent—a control in which special political recognition of Catholicism would play a strategic part. Such rumours may be unfounded, but they influence Protestant thought.

From all this analysis of differences in dogma and organization one might be tempted to forget how much the faith of Catholicism and the faith of Protestantism have in common, and how utterly both differ from Communism, with its atheism, its dialectical materialism, and its utter ruthlessness towards man as an individual. That Catholic and Protestant should stand side by side in a struggle to survive the Red world's conspiracy of destruction is a consummation devoutly to be wished. Yet before that co-operation can be freely given there needs to be a clear understanding by both Protestants and Catholics—and, moreover, by the various "Protestant" sects and cults—of the true nature and spiritual nobility of genuine Protestantism and of its reasons for disliking a form of church government that is the negation of democracy.

For over a decade now, some seven major Protestant denominations in Canada have met together in the Canadian Council of Churches, which represents perhaps eight million Protestants. It imposes no uniformity in dogma or in church government but finds in fellowship and common study a steadily increasing spirit of unity. Both to that Council and to the Roman Church of French Canada one may commend a sober consideration of the issues raised in this essay. It is my hope that my friendly frankness, instead of merely infuriating both sides in the ancient quarrel, may rather have helped to clear away some of the fears and suspicions that have hidden both the real nature of their differences and the great truths which are their common heritage.

1955

La Religion et la philosophie au Canada français

T.R.P. LOUIS-M. RÉGIS, o.p.
Doyen de la Faculté de Philosophie, Université de Montréal

LA PHYSIONOMIE RELIGIEUSE ET PHILOSOPHIQUE du Canada français est toujours une énigme pour l'étranger, c'est-à-dire tant pour nos compatriotes de langue anglaise que pour les voyageurs et les immigrants qui essaient d'entrer en contact avec notre mode de penser et d'en avoir une conception précise. Elle est d'ailleurs, très souvent, un casse-tête chinois pour les Canadiens français eux-mêmes qui, au contact constant d'individus possédant d'autres habitudes de pensée et un autre idéal de vie, deviennent hésitants et perplexes au sujet des valeurs traditionnelles qui ont inspiré et guidé leur jeunesse et qui semblent avoir perdu leur signification et conséquemment leur efficacité au sein de la société qu'ils fréquentent[1].

C'est qu'il y a, dans ce double élément de notre culture, un aspect de stabilité et d'immobilité qui font facilement figure de contradiction dans un univers physique et humain dont toutes les structures semblent vouées à l'évolution et au progrès. A ceux qui nous regardent de l'extérieur nous apparaissons, en effet, comme un étrange phénomène de momification ou de fossilisation, parce que notre religion et notre philosophie ont échappé aux deux grandes sources de l'évolution et du progrès de l'idéologie moderne, je veux dire, la Réforme protestante et l'avènement de la science, ces deux facteurs qui ont changé de fond en comble la pensée religieuse et philosophique des peuples occidentaux. La Réforme a introduit, en effet, le relativisme subjectif ou le dogme du libre examen dans ce qui constituait autrefois ce royaume de l'absolu qu'est la vérité révélée, alors que l'avènement de la science contemporaine a substitué le régime de la probabilité à celui de la certitude. Comment expliquer que dans ce monde où le seul absolu

[1]Voir *Esprit* (Paris), no 193–4 (août-septembre 1952), numéro spécial consacré au Canada français. Voir aussi *Cité libre* (Montréal), 1952–5.

scientifique est celui de la relativité et le seul absolu religieux est celui du libre examen, notre philosophie traditionnelle et notre religion seraient les seules à avoir conservé des critères inchangés et inchangeables de vérité ? Pourquoi aurions-nous le monopole de la certitude dans un siècle où la certitude a été bannie de l'esprit humain comme un mythe inventé par nos désirs de stabilité et notre ignorance du réel ?

Notre dogmatisme religieux et l'intransigeance des principes de notre philosophie sont interprétés par des sociologues contemporains comme des phénomènes de régression individuelle et sociale. Nos attitudes psychologiques ont été pétrifiées lors de la conquête de notre peuple par une nation d'une autre mentalité religieuse et philosophique; pour sauvegarder notre héritage ethnique et religieux, nous nous sommes repliés sur nous-mêmes, nous nous sommes imposés un arrêt de croissance qui va à l'encontre de toutes les lois écologiques qui gouvernent l'évolution et le progrès des individus et des groupes mais qui nous a permis de mettre effectivement en échec les valeurs de transformation radicales que le conquérant trainait à sa suite. Les conséquences de cet arrêt de croissance sont multiples : nous avons conservé le charme des primitifs mais nous sommes des arriérés sociaux et des demicivilisés :

Tout se passe comme si le protestantisme poussait au développement de la civilisation moderne, tandis que le catholicisme exerçait à l'égard de celle-ci une action inhibitrice... L'exemple le plus frappant est certainement celui du Canada... En vérité ces populations fascinent le voyageur par la simplicité de leurs mœurs et ce charme inné qui contraste avec la froideur puritaine de leurs voisins anglo-saxons. Il n'en est pas moins vrai que le Canada français est terriblement en arrière des contrées protestantes environnantes et que ses charmantes et pieuses familles restent généralement au bas de l'échelle sociale, comme d'ailleurs l'ensemble des Franco-canadiens qui font figure de petites gens auprès des Anglais et des Américains qui les entourent[2].

Cette conclusion sans nuance et sans preuves que l'on trouve dans une étude sociologique dont la méthode tient davantage du pamphlet que de l'expérimentation scientifique, exprime assez bien, malgré son manque d'objectivité, l'opinion qu'un grand nombre de nos compatriotes de langue anglaise se font de notre peuple et des valeurs culturelles, philosophiques et religieuses qui l'ont fait ce qu'il est. Nous n'avons pas l'intention d'en manifester la fausseté ni de faire l'apologie de nos idéologies au détriment de celles de nos compatriotes anglosaxons. Si « toute comparaison est odieuse », celle que l'on établit entre

[2]Frédéric Hoffet, *L'Impérialisme protestant* (Paris : Flammarion, 1948), pp. 67–9.

les peuples, pour porter des jugements de valeurs sur les fondements spirituels de leur civilisation, est particulièrement odieuse et pharisaïque. Nos deux groupes ethniques ne vivent pas côte à côte pour se mesurer comme deux pugilistes ni pour s'intenter un perpétuel procès pour libelle, mais pour essayer de mettre en commun leurs qualités respectives qu'un destin historique a voulu unifier dans des cadres géographiques précis et au sein d'une unique nationalité.

Voilà pourquoi, la présente étude ne prétend être rien d'autre qu'un bref essai de clarification de l'énigme que nous sommes dans le but de faciliter, à nos compatriotes de langue anglaise et aux étrangers, la compréhension des attitudes psychologiques fondamentales qui nous caractérisent sur le terrain spécifique de la religion et de la philosophie. Il ne s'agit pas d'une étude sociologique ni d'une description des tendances nouvelles qui se sont manifestées récemment dans l'ordre religieux et philosophique chez une élite intellectuelle, mais des attitudes spirituelles plus ou moins explicites qui ont constitué l'âme de notre peuple et se sont manifestées, à l'extérieur, par un comportement et des structures d'ordre sociologique qui n'en sont que les conséquences visibles. Ce n'est donc pas un travail d'information historique et livresque que nous livrons à nos lecteurs, mais un témoignage portant sur les structures religieuses et philosophiques de notre âme dans l'espoir de rendre cette âme moins obscure à ceux qui nous fréquentent et d'en faciliter la compréhension. Le succès de notre effort dépendra de la bonne volonté qu'ils mettront à accepter ces structures comme un fait humain, qui leur déplaît peut-être, mais dont la réalité historique est aussi inévitable qu'est pour nous le fait de leur présence et de la mentalité qui les caractérise.

I) La Religion du Canada français

L'une des plus grandes sources de l'énigme que nous présentons à nos compatriotes protestants, c'est le caractère catholique et romain de notre christianisme, ce qui fait de nous des papistes selon le vocable séculaire dont ils se servent pour nous désigner. Dans leur bouche cette appellation est injurieuse parce qu'elle désigne des hommes libres qui ont mésusé de leur liberté pour choisir l'esclavage doctrinal alors qu'ils pouvaient opter pour l'affranchissement de leur intelligence et de leur conscience. Etre papistes, c'est pour eux accepter délibérément une tutelle intellectuelle qui va à l'encontre du développement normal de l'esprit dont la maturité consiste précisément dans l'autonomie du jugement personnel dont l'unique guide est l'évidence intérieure et non une autorité qui impose la vérité de l'extérieur. Etre papistes, c'est encore se soumettre ou au moins s'exposer à des ingérences politiques dictatoriales alors qu'on est citoyen d'une démocratie, donc d'une forme de gouvernement qui tire son autorité et son mandat du peuple. Il faut admettre qu'il est difficile pour nos compatriotes protestants de comprendre le caractère des relations religieuses qui nous unissent à l'Evêque de Rome parce que la Réforme qui les a séparés de nous s'est faite précisément contre Rome, à un moment de l'histoire où le Vicaire du Christ sur terre était en même temps un souverain temporel, un roi au sens ancien de ce mot, avec tous les soucis temporels et aussi tous les dangers que la possession d'un tel pouvoir impliquait à cette époque. Et si la Réforme a été, à ses origines et dans l'esprit de Luther, une protestation véhémente contre une ingérence trop fréquente des intérêts temporels dans le domaine des choses de Dieu, il n'en demeure pas moins historiquement vrai qu'elle s'est rapidement transformée en révolution politique et nationaliste et que son succès est dû bien davantage aux intérêts temporels que la noblesse laïque en récoltait (on peut en dire autant de la Réforme en Angleterre) qu'aux libérations spirituelles et doctrinales qu'elle offrait au peuple.

Or, cette situation est complètement changée, et la souveraineté temporelle du Vicaire du Christ n'est plus maintenant que pur symbole. Il n'a pas d'intérêts temporels à défendre ni d'ambition territoriale à sauvegarder; il n'a d'autre fonction, au XXe siècle, que celle que le Christ lui a confiée : garder intégralement toutes les vérités qu'Il est venu nous annoncer de la part du Père et être responsable de la transmission de son message dont le salut des hommes dépend. Il a la puissance d'ouvrir les portes du ciel, de fermer les portes de l'enfer, selon la métaphore traditionnelle, mais il n'a pas celle de construire un royaume temporel ni de nuire aux puissants de ce monde. S'il était possible à l'ennemi le plus acharné du Pape de vivre pendant quelques semaines la vie du Vicaire du Christ il serait bien vite amené à constater que ce n'est pas un mystère de puissance temporelle que cet homme représente mais celui de la cruxifixion, car, comme le Christ, il est un continuel signe de contradiction, aimé, haï, vénéré, méprisé, trahi et renié par certains des siens, craint et traqué par tous ceux qui ont peur que le règne de Dieu ne fasse tort à leur propre règne. Le Christ n'est pas venu instaurer la domination sur terre mais le service (Jn 13, 12–18), et son Vicaire n'occupe pas le trône pour être servi mais pour servir comme l'indique la magnifique formule qui termine les lettres papales : « Serviteur des serviteurs de Dieu ».

Le nom par lequel il se désigne et que nous lui donnons, ne signifie ni un roi, ni un empereur, ni un tyran mais un père; non pas le père qui se tient loin de ses enfants mais le *papa*, celui qui est tout près de ses petits et qui ne se connaît d'autre fonction que de les nourrir et de les éduquer, car en doctrine catholique les enfants ne sont pas pour le père mais lui pour ses enfants[3]. Voilà pourquoi, être papistes, pour nous, cela veut dire tout d'abord que nous avons un père, un *daddy*, dont nous ne sommes ni les serfs, ni les esclaves mais les enfants chéris qui sont l'unique objet de ses préoccupations alors que ceux qui ne sont pas papistes sont des orphelins dont personne ne se préoccupe dans l'ordre spirituel. Etre Catholiques romains, pour nous cela ne représente pas une servitude spirituelle, une tutelle intellectuelle, mais la certitude que le pain de la vérité révélée qui nous sera servi sera pur de tout élément étranger, de tout germe d'erreur et de corruption; c'est avoir reçu la grâce extraordinaire de jouir de la totalité du message que le Christ nous a apporté du ciel; et n'être pas papiste, c'est n'avoir aucune de ces certitudes, c'est être constamment dans la crainte que nos pauvres intelligences humaines déjà si frêles et si portées vers l'erreur dans le strict domaine des vérités naturelles, ne soient constamment déroutées par le caractère énigmatique des textes sacrés, par les hasards imprévisibles et incontrôlables qui accompagnent la transmission écrite et orale des vérités chrétiennes vécues par les générations qui nous ont précédés dans le chemin du salut.

Etre Catholiques romains, pour nous, c'est non seulement avoir reçu la totalité du message du Fils de Dieu mais c'est aussi posséder, pour vivre ce message et le faire fructifier, tous ces moyens, toutes ces ruses de la grâce qui s'appellent les sacrements et dont nos frères séparés sont cruellement privés. Pourquoi désirerions-nous que notre christianisme cesse d'être catholique et romain, puisque c'est précisément ces attaches qui nous garantissent tout ce qu'il y a d'essentiel en christianisme : la réalité de notre foi, la force de notre espérance et la stabilité de notre charité ? Tout cet héritage est assuré parce que nous ne sommes pas orphelins mais que nous avons un père, parce que nous sommes papistes. Telle est la nature réelle mais toujours invisible de notre romanisme religieux. Il est tout cela et il n'est que cela; il est pur de toute immixtion politique et de tout désir de suprématie temporelle, car bien que le Christ soit le roi de ce monde, son royaume n'est pas et ne sera jamais de ce monde.

Il est un deuxième aspect de notre croyance religieuse, qui intrigue également nos compatriotes protestants et nous rend doublement incompréhensibles, et c'est l'aspect visible et social de notre catholicisme.

[3]Cf. Saint Paul, II Cor 12, 14–15.

Nous sommes, en effet, sur un continent totalement laïcisé et voué au libéralisme religieux, l'un des derniers vestiges d'une société dont les structures extérieures demeurent imbriquées dans des cadres ecclésiastiques et fortement influencées par eux. Point n'est besoin d'une longue enquête sociologique pour découvrir l'importance sociale du religieux dans le Québec, car toute l'organisation de l'éducation, l'évolution du problème ouvrier ainsi que les œuvres d'assistance publique, dépendent pratiquement du pouvoir ecclésiastique[4].

Ainsi, il n'y a pas dans notre province de Ministère de l'Education, mais un Comité de l'Instruction publique dont les évêques sont d'office les membres. Les chanceliers de nos universités sont les archevêques de nos villes universitaires, tous les recteurs, plusieurs doyens et un bon nombre des professeurs sont des membres du clergé. Pratiquement tout le secondaire, c'est-à-dire tout ce qui correspond au « college » dans le système anglo-canadien, est aux mains du clergé, ou des communautés religieuses d'hommes ou de femmes. Dans le domaine du primaire et du primaire supérieur, on retrouve, à un degré moindre, le même état de choses. Ce fait s'explique sociologiquement par des causes historiques qui ont forcé les autorités religieuses à prendre en mains tout le domaine de l'éducation et à confier l'enseignement aux seuls individus qui possédaient à la fois un minimum de compétence et assez d'indépendance économique pour vivre sans salaire ou d'un salaire de misère. Seuls les clercs, les religieux et les religieuses réunissaient ces deux conditions, pendant près de deux siècles, et c'est ce qui explique le rôle de suppléance rempli par les clercs et les congrégations religieuses, ainsi que l'absence totale de participation laïque jusqu'à ces dernières années. Mais une étude sociologique des causes historiques ne rend compte que des faits et de leur conjonction dans le temps et l'espace; elle ne nous dit pas pourquoi l'Eglise canadienne, par sa hiérarchie, s'est ainsi chargée d'une besogne très lourde à porter quand on considère la rareté du personnel et la pauvreté des moyens financiers dont elle disposait.

L'explication de ce qui pourrait paraître de l'ingérence cléricale dans la politique terrienne et anti-commerciale de l'Eglise pendant 150 ans de notre histoire présente des difficultés identiques. Pourquoi la hiérarchie religieuse a-t-elle été contre l'exode des Canadiens dans les centres urbains et a-t-elle exalté la fidélité à la vocation paysanne

[4]Cf. J.-C. Falardeau, A. Tremblay, M. Tremblay et Esdras Minville dans Falardeau, éd., *Essais sur le Québec contemporain* (Québec : Presses Universitaires Laval, 1953), pp. 101–22, 169–92, 193–208 et 231–8. Cf. aussi *L'Organisation et les besoins de l'enseignement classique dans le Québec* (Montréal : Fides, 1954).

et minimisé les activités économiques, surtout celles de grande envergure ? Dans le même ordre d'idée, comment expliquer que notre mouvement ouvrier et le syndicalisme qui l'exprime doive son existence à des tractations clérico-patronales ? Quelle relation peut-il exister entre un clergé qui n'a d'autre but que de conduire les hommes au ciel et cet intérêt constant et séculaire qu'il manifeste pour des problèmes aussi temporels et matériels que la colonisation et le syndicalisme ?

De même que le caractère romain de notre christianisme présente des ambiguïtés, des équivoques, à ceux qui n'en aperçoivent que l'extérieur, ainsi l'aspect socialement clérical de notre catholicisme québécois les plonge dans l'étonnement et provoque une réaction de mépris envers la population laïque et de méfiance envers le clergé. Le Canada français leur apparaît comme une « priest-ridden province » où une dictature cléricale s'exerce impitoyablement sur un prolétariat laïque, situation scandaleuse à une époque et sur un continent dont la charte des libertés repose sur une idéologie démocratique et la doctrine du libre examen, c'est-à-dire la non-existence d'une autorité ecclésiastique. Si le christianisme québécois, dans ses manifestations extérieures et l'influence qu'il exerce sur les structures mêmes de la société, devient incompréhensibles pour nos compatriotes anglo-canadiens, comme d'ailleurs il l'est très souvent pour les Catholiques d'Europe et d'Amérique, c'est qu'ils ont tous perdu la mémoire de ce que fut autrefois et de ce que devrait être encore la condition existentielle normale de la doctrine du Christ : celle d'être vécue non seulement par les individus comme tels mais par les peuples comme peuples.

Dieu aurait très bien pu organiser l'œuvre personnelle du salut en éliminant toute influence sociale à la manière de Rousseau; mais sa sagesse, qui a créé la nature humaine et la vie surnaturelle de cette même nature humaine, possède une vision plus profonde des exigences de cette nature que celle qu'en avait Rousseau, et voilà pourquoi sa première manifestation aux hommes, la révélation hébraïque, s'est faite au père d'un peuple et s'est continuée à l'intérieur de la vie publique de ce peuple. La seconde révélation qui nous est venue par le Christ n'est que le couronnement de la première, et elle a conservé le caractère visible et social que son fondateur avait voulu lui imprimer en se faisant homme; car à quoi bon l'Incarnation du Fils de Dieu si la religion qu'Il vient nous révéler n'a besoin d'aucune apparence humaine, n'est conditionnée par aucune exigence sociale ?

Notre christianisme québécois, s'il présente une anomalie dans notre monde contemporain, continue donc d'illustrer l'un des vrais visages de la religion du Christ. Voici une page dont la brièveté ne met que plus en valeur la pénétrante analyse de cet aspect de la religion du Canada français :

On dirait que notre vie religieuse constitue pour les Européens une énigme indéchiffrable, et que même les plus sympathiques d'entre eux se montrent inaptes à découvrir la force obscure qui, lentement, l'a moulée, l'a modelée... Nous estimons que cette incompréhension des Européens est, par suite de la grande différence des milieux et des circonstances, facilement explicable; nous estimons surtout qu'elle est significative. Elle nous révèle que la forme que revêt notre catholicisme fait pour eux figure de phénomène nouveau, déconcertant; elle nous révèle qu'ils n'ont, chez eux, rien qui leur servant de terme de comparaison, puisse les éclairer. S'ils ont, en effet, l'expérience d'un athéisme et d'un matérialisme de masse, ils n'ont pas celle d'un *catholicisme de masse*. Et c'est, selon nous, ce qui caractérise fondamentalement le nôtre que d'en être un de cette nature... Nous n'entendons pas signifier par là qu'il représente une sorte de prolétariat spirituel, ni qu'il a peu à peu conduit à la dépersonnalisation, à l'appauvrissement et à l'aliénation des individus; nous voulons plutôt marquer que notre foi et notre sentiment religieux s'expriment moins par la réflexion, la méditation et la mysticité que par l'action droite et la pratique persévérante... Notre conception de la vie religieuse ne s'est pas projetée dans des constructions doctrinales, mais dans des réalisations collectives de tout genre. L'Eglise est chez-nous particulièrement *charnelle et visible*... Nous concédons que les exigences de notre religion veulent qu'elle soit vécue « en esprit et en vérité », nous concédons que Dieu tire plus de gloire du don de nos esprits que de l'offrande de nos gestes extérieurs... pourtant, nous ne sommes pas sans nous sentir attendris et ébranlés dans nos positions par le *misereor super turbam* du Christ. Car après tout le ciel n'est pas une chasse gardée. Les pauvres, les petits, les ignorants et les gueux ont droit au salut tout comme les riches et les intellectuels. La sagesse surnaturelle à l'encontre de la sagesse philosophique, n'est pas confinée à un cénacle : « elle crie sur les places publiques[5] ».

Ce catholicisme de masse n'est pas le résultat d'une régression infantile, comme le voudraient les psychologues modernes, ni une survivance des valeurs de décadence, comme dirait Nietzsche, mais une fidélité à l'Evangile lui-même et à l'esprit de Celui qui est venu nous l'annoncer. Le message du Christ n'a pas été proclamé dans le secret de l'âme individuelle mais sur les routes et les places publiques; son contenu n'est pas ésotérique ou réservé à des initiés, mais il est destiné à l'humanité toute entière, à laquelle il vient apprendre qu'il existe une hiérarchie de valeurs, et que dans cette hiérarchie les biens surnaturels et éternels priment les valeurs économiques, politiques, temporelles, et qu'elles doivent commander toutes nos actions, tant individuelles que sociales. Et parce que le clergé a comme unique

[5]Louis Lachance, *La Lumière de l'âme* (Montréal : Lévrier, 1955), pp. 9, 10, 12, 13.

mandat de faire connaître et pratiquer ce message du Christ, cela explique que le clergé québécois se soit donné tant de soucis pour organiser le domaine de l'éducation, qu'il ait prôné une politique terrienne et anti-commerciale, pendant 150 ans, qu'il se soit mis à la tête des mouvements syndicalistes, non par crainte de l'émancipation des laïques d'où sortirait une diminution de son pouvoir temporel, mais pour protéger leurs croyances religieuses des dangers qu'offraient les centres urbains et les idéologies matérialistes des fédérations neutres du travail.

Que cet idéal apostolique des clercs se soit concrètement incarné selon toutes les lois de la prudence, qu'il ait toujours été accompagné d'une clairvoyance géniale et d'un désintéressement absolu de la part de tous et de chacun de ses membres, il serait absurde non seulement de l'affirmer mais même de le rêver puisque les clercs sont humains et faillibles. Mais que cet idéal soit juste et conforme à la vocation qu'ils ont reçu du Christ qui en s'incarnant a voulu mettre la loi de l'incarnation dans toutes les œuvres de son Eglise, cela ne fait aucun doute à celui qui accepte le message du Christ dans sa totalité.

Nous comprenons qu'il soit difficile à nos compatriotes anglo-protestants de juger le catholicisme québécois sous l'angle que nous venons d'esquisser et que ses apparences peuvent facilement être interprétées en termes d'ingérence cléricale et de dictature religieuse dans des domaines qui sont de soi purement économiques, parce que pour eux la religion est purement individuelle, chacun recevant de l'Esprit les directives dont il a besoin pour faire son salut; elle est affaire de libre examen, et les structures économiques et sociales du milieu dans lequel elle s'exerce n'ont, en principe, aucune influence sur son évolution. Mais telle n'est pas la situation du Catholique en général, ni celle du Catholique canadien-français, car

> ... à la différence du protestantisme ascétique qui semble historiquement lié à l'expansion du capitalisme, le catholicisme n'a jamais tenté de ramener le royaume de Dieu sur la place du marché. Pour l'Eglise, les valeurs de contemplation sont demeurées supérieures aux valeurs d'action; la grâce et les vertus chrétiennes sont demeurées dissociées du succès des entreprises terrestres. La réussite dans les affaires et dans les occupations séculières n'a jamais représenté, à ses yeux, la valeur symbolique d'une confirmation de la grâce et d'un signe de prédestination. Au contraire, en morale individuelle, on a continué d'y voir une source d'orgueil et un danger de détournement des voies de la vertu et du salut éternel. En pays catholique, le *God's gold* de l'austère et implacable Rockefeller aurait été un sujet de réprobation et de scandale[6].

[6]Maurice Tremblay, « Orientations de la pensée sociale » dans Falardeau, éd., *Essais sur le Québec contemporain*, pp. 204–5.

Il n'est donc pas étonnant que le caractère clérical de nos cadres sociaux soit une énigme pour nos compatriotes, étant donné l'opposition des principes de base qui relient chez eux la vie religieuse et la vie économique. Mais nous croyons que s'ils réussissaient à percevoir l'esprit qui se cache sous ces apparences extérieures qui les scandalisent, leur étonnement diminuerait et leur acceptation de ce que nous sommes serait plus facile. Or, cet esprit, cette mentalité qui se cache sous les aspects cléricaux du catholicisme québécois, est facile à comprendre car il constitue la substance même de notre interprétation de la doctrine du Christ. Tout ce que nous avons dit, plus haut, du rôle du Pape à l'égard de l'Eglise universelle, est également vrai de la hiérarchie et du clergé canadiens : tous ces hommes sont les pères spirituels de leurs ouailles; ils sont par ministère leurs serviteurs, chargés de les nourrir, de les guider, de les éduquer spirituellement de façon qu'ils atteignent le but unique de leur existence temporelle, c'est-à-dire qu'ils fassent leur salut.

Qu'on me permette, au terme de cette trop courte esquisse sur la nature et les modes du catholicisme québécois, de souligner un fait dont l'existence devrait éclairer l'opinion que nos compatriotes se font de la dictature cléricale dans le Québec, et rendre plus critique leur jugement. Comment expliquer que cette « priest-ridden province » soit la seule des dix provinces du Canada à consentir concrètement à ses minorités protestantes la liberté totale de l'enseignement ? Si le papisme était ce qu'on croit qu'il est et si la dictature cléricale n'est qu'un prolongement du papisme, comment se fait-il qu'au lieu de l'Inquisition règne dans notre province la liberté absolue des cultes et de l'enseignement ? La raison en est simple, et elle n'est pas question d'opportunité mais de doctrine, et c'est la doctrine même que le protestantisme réclame comme l'une de ses victoires sur Rome, celle de la liberté de conscience. Près de trois siècles avant la Réforme, voici ce qu'enseignait l'un des plus illustres représentants de la doctrine catholique sur la liberté de conscience dans le domaine religieux :

> Il arrive que la raison estime bon ce qui est mal et mal ce qui est bon... Ainsi, croire au Christ est une chose bonne et nécessaire au salut; mais la volonté n'y consent que sous l'aspect que la raison lui propose. En sorte que *si celle-ci le lui propose comme un mal la volonté agira mal en y adhérant*; non pas qu'il s'agisse là d'une chose mauvaise en soi mais d'un acte accidentellement mauvais à cause de la raison qui se le représente ainsi[7].

Ce respect des libertés religieuses, et de l'éducation qui en fait partie, dont les minorités protestantes ou autres jouissent dans le

[7]Saint Thomas d'Aquin, *Somme de théologie*, Ia, IIae, q. 19, a. V, c.

Québec alors qu'il semble aller à l'encontre des structures sociales de son catholicisme, n'est au fond qu'une conséquence sociale de la doctrine. La foi est un don de Dieu qui l'accorde à qui Il veut; la conscience de chacun est immédiatement responsable de chacun de ses actes libres, et la foi est une acceptation libre de la vérité révélée; et si une conscience est dans l'erreur, on peut essayer de l'éclairer mais on ne peut la forcer, sans aller contre le vouloir même de Dieu, son créateur, à admettre comme bien ce qu'elle voit comme mal. Voilà jusqu'où notre religion pousse le respect de la conscience personnelle, et c'est à cette lumière qu'il faut essayer de comprendre les divers phénomènes contradictoires que présente le catholicisme québécois à ceux qui ne le voient que de l'extérieur; il devient alors une réalité originale parce qu'introuvable nulle part ailleurs mais il cesse d'être une sorte de monstruosité, une gargouille qui se serait détachée d'une cathédrale médiévale pour venir s'insérer dans ce temple protestant qu'est la civilisation capitaliste et matérialiste de notre époque et scandaliser tous ceux qui en admirent la beauté et la nouveauté.

II) La Philosophie au Canada français

Il n'y a pas que la mentalité religieuse du Canada français qui rende ce dernier incompréhensible à ses compatriotes anglo-saxons, sa pensée philosophique est tout aussi féconde en équivoques et en malentendus. Nous allons donc essayer de décrire les paradoxes que présente notre position philosophique à ceux qui les voient de l'extérieur, dans leurs modalités historiques, afin de justifier les jugements qu'ils portent à leur endroit et de montrer, par le fait même, le caractère superficiel de ces paradoxes et le peu d'importance qu'ils ont pour quelqu'un qui vit cette philosophie de l'intérieur. Ainsi envisagée dans ses aspects extérieurs ou historiques, notre philosophie est caractérisée par trois notes ou traits distinctifs qui la dévalorisent aux yeux de nos contemporains et lui enlèvent tout sérieux comme système de pensée rationnelle chargé d'expliquer l'homme et l'univers dans lequel il se trouve. Ces trois traits distinctifs sont les suivants : *a*) elle est chrétienne; *b*) elle est scolastique; *c*) elle est démodée, périmée.

a) *Notre Philosophie est chrétienne*

Ce qui frappe tout d'abord l'esprit de nos compatriotes, ce sont les relations très intimes qui semblent exister entre la religion et la philosophie au Canada français. Cette philosophie est, en effet, officiellement reconnue par l'Eglise romaine, canoniquement imposée dans les programmes de toutes les institutions supérieures d'enseignement, et désignée par les historiens comme une philosophie chrétienne. Il semble donc évident que le mariage entre notre philosophie et notre religion soit indissoluble et que le magistère ecclésiastique exerce la même autorité sur l'une que sur l'autre. La conséquence immédiate de cet état de choses est que le philosophe canadien-français apparaît à ses collègues protestants comme un penseur dont la liberté d'esprit est tellement encadrée par la doctrine de saint Thomas et les directives pontificales qu'elle n'est plus qu'une caricature de liberté, dissimulant un réel asservissement de la raison humaine et de la spontanéité de sa recherche. Or, cette identification juridique et historique de notre philosophie et de notre religion masque concrètement une série d'équivoques qu'il faut dissiper si on veut en percevoir la nature intime. L'épithète *chrétien* peut être appliqué à une philosophie à trois titres différents.

1) Ou bien parce que le Christ est l'inventeur de cette doctrine, et alors le mot chrétien aurait la même signification d'origine que les vocables cartésien, kantien, etc... Mais si le Christ est l'inventeur de notre philosophie, elle cesse d'être une philosophie pour devenir une théologie. La doctrine du Christ dépasse, en effet, la raison humaine; elle est objet de foi et non évidence rationnelle. Et si l'expression philosophie chrétienne désigne un ensemble doctrinal dont la foi serait la source et la lumière qui le guide, elle est en vérité une théologie au sens strict du mot mais une pseudo-philosophie. Or, un examen, même superficiel des structures et des thèmes essentiels de la philosophie du Canada français manifeste à l'évidence que ce n'est pas l'Evangile mais les œuvres de Platon et d'Aristote qui en sont les sources authentiques. Ses principes et sa lumière ne lui sont pas fournis par la foi, mais par les mêmes lois rigoureuses de l'esprit humain et du réel dont, quatre siècles avant Jésus-Christ, ces deux païens de génie qu'étaient Platon et Aristote se sont servi pour découvrir et expliquer à leurs contemporains jusqu'à quelle profondeur l'intelligence humaine devait s'enfoncer pour acquérir une vision intégrale de l'homme et de son univers. Notre philosophie ne peut donc tirer son caractère chrétien du Christ puisque cela va à l'encontre des faits historiques et doctrinaux.

2) Ou bien notre philosophie est dite chrétienne parce que ceux qui l'ont systématisée de façon définitive et ont fait rendre aux intuitions platoniciennes et aristotéliciennes qui lui servent de base tout le potentiel dont elles étaient chargées, étaient des chrétiens. Dans ce sens, il n'y a aucun doute que notre philosophie mérite son nom car ce sont les grands penseurs du moyen âge qui ont travaillé à cette

synthèse et l'ont perfectionnée à l'aide de leur esprit métaphysique; mais le vocable chrétien ne désigne alors qu'une incidence historique qui ne préjuge ni du contenu de la pensée philosophique ni de l'éclairage intellectuel nécessaire à son élaboration. Ici encore, on ne peut donc identifier religion et philosophie chrétienne.

3) Ou bien, et c'est la troisième acception possible de l'expression philosophie chrétienne, ce complexe désigne une doctrine philosophique acceptée, vécue et professée par des hommes dont la religion est le christianisme. Et alors le mot chrétien, ainsi utilisé, devient équivoque car il y a une multiplicité de christianismes depuis le Schisme d'Orient en 1054, et surtout depuis les Réformes de Luther et d'Henri VIII, et aucun groupe de chrétiens, comme tels, à l'exception des Catholiques, n'accepte, ne vit et ne professe le contenu de cette philosophie dite chrétienne. D'ailleurs, à l'intérieur même du groupe des Catholiques romains, l'unanimité est loin d'exister à l'égard de la pensée philosophique dite thomiste alors qu'il y a unanimité pour tout ce qui concerne la substance même de la religion, c'est-à-dire les dogmes chrétiens qui portent sur Dieu, l'homme et sa destinée éternelle. Ici donc, comme dans les deux cas antérieurs, il y a impossibilité d'identification entre philosophie chrétienne et catholicisme.

b) Notre Philosophie est scolastique

Si ce ne sont pas ses attaches à la doctrine du Christ qui caractérisent notre philosophie, par quels traits doit-elle se définir en elle-même et par opposition aux philosophies qui s'y opposent ? Le premier de ses traits, celui sous lequel elle est le plus habituellement classifiée, c'est son caractère scolastique. Depuis Descartes, ce vocable est péjoratif puisqu'il désigne un amas d'opinions discutées et discutables dont le dogmatisme absolu ne cache le plus souvent qu'une ignorance savante dissimulée par un vocabulaire dont la souplesse permet toutes les acrobaties intellectuelles, en particulier celles qui miment le véritable savoir sans jamais l'atteindre[8]. Avec les historiens du XIXe siècle, la scolastique est devenue synonyme de ces âges sombres, *Dark Ages*, où l'intelligence lâchant la proie pour l'ombre se nourrissait de mythes et dédaignait la luminosité du réel.

Pour nous, le mot scolastique signifie tout autre chose; il exprime tout simplement la compétence de ceux qui ont inventé notre philosophie : ils étaient des *scholars*, des hommes dont toute la vie n'avait d'autres préoccupations que celles de chercher la vérité et, l'ayant

[8]Cf. *Discours de la méthode*, édité par E. Gilson (Paris : Vrin, 1925), pp. 135, 165, 167.

découverte, de la transmettre à leurs contemporains non dans le but de s'enrichir ou de se créer une situation enviable, mais parce que la vérité est l'aliment de l'esprit humain et qu'elle vaut la peine qu'on lui consacre tous ses efforts. Les plus grands parmi ces *scholars* auxquels notre philosophie doit son caractère scolastique ce sont Platon, Aristote, Augustin, Abélard, Albert le Grand et Thomas d'Aquin.

Etre scolastique pour une philosophie cela veut donc dire avoir reçu en héritage toute la richesse de la pensée grecque, toute l'évolution que cette pensée a subie en passant par le génie des Latins, ainsi que les purifications successives que les penseurs qui se sont succédé au cours de deux millénaires lui ont fait subir en faisant passer au creuset de leur génie critique et de leurs expériences personnelles les vérités fondamentales plus ou moins explicites qu'ils découvraient dans ce legs des anciens. Etre scolastique pour une philosophie c'est réaliser à la lettre cette pensée de Pascal, si profondément vraie et si conforme aux faits, que « Toute la suite des hommes, pendant le cours de tant de siècles, doit être considérée comme un même homme qui subsiste toujours et apprend continuellement[9]. » Notre philosophie a la stature de l'homme occidental, *parce qu'elle est scolastique*, parce qu'elle n'est pas née du cerveau d'un homme comme Minerve est sortie toute armée du cerveau de Jupiter (ce qui est toujours dangereux puisque c'est au prix d'une tête fendue d'un coup de hache par Vulcain que Jupiter a payé cette génération spontanée), mais qu'elle est le fruit d'une lente et séculaire gestation de la part des esprits les plus puissants qu'ait connu l'humanité dans ce domaine.

c) *Notre Philosophie est démodée*

Or, ce qui devrait faire la gloire et la valeur de la philosophie du Canada français est précisément ce qui la dévalorise aux yeux de nos compatriotes anglo-saxons et des penseurs modernes, car pour eux le caractère scolastique d'une philosophie la rend par le fait même démodée, vieillie; elle a oublié de se mettre à la page, elle n'est pas parvenue à l'état scientifique, elle ne s'est pas mise à la remorque des découvertes et des révolutions que la pensée contemporaine a introduites dans les méthodes d'approche et de saisie de la réalité. Voilà pourquoi le troisième trait, péjoratif lui aussi, qui oppose notre philosophie aux autres et l'en distingue, c'est son aspect démodé.

Ce vocable exprime exactement le jugement de valeur que nos contemporains portent sur la philosophie scolastique, car la mode est devenue aussi importante pour les penseurs contemporains que pour

[9]*Opuscules*, Ière partie (Editions Brunschvicg), L, pp. 79–80.

les femmes de tous les temps. Et pour être à la mode il faut se laisser guider par les grands couturiers, modeler ses goûts sur leurs goûts et s'abandonner passivement aux caprices de leur imagination créatrice dans le but de voiler et de dévoiler les formes humaines pour qu'elles exposent tous leurs attraits et retiennent tout leur mystère. Or, la philosophie, comme la gent féminine, possède aussi depuis plus de trois siècles ses grands couturiers, tous des savants ou des penseurs à mentalité scientifique, qui se sont donnés la vocation de confectionner pour l'intelligence humaine des modes ou des méthodes de pensée qui permettraient à cette dernière de se revêtir de la vérité dernier cri et de mettre au rancart tous les vieux mythes démodés du passé qui l'empêchaient de faire montre de ses véritables attraits et de son mystère intime. Les principaux grands couturiers qui ont créé les modes philosophiques depuis trois cents ans sont, dans l'ordre chronologique : Descartes, Kant, Hegel, Comte, ainsi que les chefs d'écoles phénomé-logistes.

Le résultat net de cette faveur dont jouissent les modes philosophiques nouvelles est enregistré par l'histoire de la philosophie occidentale, histoire qui nous fait penser au récit d'un cauchemar dont serait hanté le sommeil du philosophe qui se voit soudainement dépouillé du vêtement de la vérité et de la certitude par les méthodes scientifiques, et, dans cet état de nudité, exposé au ridicule des penseurs. Il se sent immodeste, indécent et ne peut supporter la honte de se voir déambuler *in naturalibus* sur la place publique. Pour couvrir sa nudité, il tente, d'abord furtivement puis avec une audace que la honte rend astucieuse, de se revêtir des seuls habits décents que la mode expose sur le marché philosophique, l'uniforme scientifique. Il éprouve une certaine gêne à l'intérieur de cet habit dont les lignes rigidement mathématisées ne possèdent rien de la souplesse de l'ancien, dont le caractère analogique permettait une liberté de mouvement dans toutes les directions; mais hanté par l'idée qu'il faut encore mieux s'habiller de la vérité scientifique que de pratiquer le nudisme philosophique, et l'habitude aidant, il finit par décréter que toute philosophie qui ne porte pas l'uniforme scientifique sera désormais considérée comme naïve et populaire, et indigne par conséquent du nom dont elle se réclame. Et comme le Thomisme, philosophie officielle du Canada français, n'a pas voulu passer chez les couturiers scientifiques pour endosser une livrée qui non seulement la déguiserait mais l'emprisonnerait dans une tunique de Nessus et la détruirait comme philosophie, elle a perdu toute valeur aux yeux de nos contemporains et est devenue un objet de ridicule, tout comme les costumes de nos aieules; elle est démodée et dénote une mentalité d'arriéré mental puisqu'elle correspond, paraît-il, à la mentalité d'un enfant de neuf ans !

Mais le problème demeure de savoir qui a raison, des philosophies qui suivent les modes scientifiques et périssent avec elles, ou d'une philosophie qui fait fi, non de la science ni de ses méthodes, mais d'une tutelle scientifique dans le domaine philosophique parce que cette tutelle est une absurdité ? Il n'est pas facile de résoudre de façon satisfaisante un tel problème en quelques lignes, car il a été l'objet de milliers de volumes et demeure le grand point en litige parmi les penseurs contemporains. Essayons d'aborder la difficulté de l'extérieur et de justifier notre adhésion à la philosophie traditionnelle par les fruits qu'elle a produits et qu'elle continue de produire là où cette pensée dite démodée et archaïque n'est pas remplacée par des philosophies dites scientifiques.

Pendant quinze siècles, la pensée de Platon et d'Aristote, reprise et complétée par les penseurs chrétiens, a incarné pour le monde occidental l'idée même de sagesse naturelle, c'est-à-dire l'idée d'un savoir qui n'avait pas la prétention de raconter l'histoire de la genèse de l'univers, de son évolution, mais qui avait pour but de faire pénétrer l'homme dans le secret même de sa substance, de découvrir les origines de sa vie ainsi que la destinée à laquelle elle était appelée. Ni l'expérimentation contrôlée, ni la statistique, ne fournissaient à ce savoir ses données et ses méthodes pour la raison très simple que la substance des êtres, leur origine et leur destinée ne sont pas objet d'expérimentation instrumentale ni ne tombent sous les lois de la statistique, mais relèvent d'une réflexion métaphysique. Or, cette réflexion métaphysique a réussi à donner à l'humanité le sens de sa royauté vis-à-vis de toutes les choses matérielles et temporelles par l'affirmation de l'existence d'un élément spirituel chez l'homme, en même temps qu'elle lui infusait le sens de sa dépendance d'un absolu béatifiant par l'idéal qu'elle lui proposait d'une destinée qui n'est ni de ce monde ni de ce temps. Et par ce joint, la philosophie rencontrait le message du Christ et unifiait l'homme dans sa vision de lui-même, de l'univers dont il est partie et de sa destinée personnelle qui est d'un autre ordre que celui de l'univers physique.

Que constate-t-on maintenant après trois siècles de prédominance des systèmes de pensée à la remorque des méthodes scientifiques ? L'univers physique s'est agrandi, les diverses pièces dont il est fait se sont unifiées, la domination de l'homme sur les forces matérielles s'est décuplée, mais la véritable royauté de l'homme est disparue; il est devenu l'esclave de ses propres engins qui tendent de plus en plus à diminuer son importance pour le remplacer par des robots. La sociologie a remplacé la sagesse dans la conduite des hommes, et les statistiques économiques qui ne travaillent que sur les ensembles ont été substituées à ce sens de l'homme individuel, de son importance personnelle qui le faisait autrefois le centre et la fin de tout l'ordre temporel qu'il avait vocation de reconduire à Dieu, sa source et sa fin. On parle beaucoup de psychologie, on ne s'est jamais tant préoccupé de l'éducation, de la rééducation, et jamais peut-être l'humanité n'a tellement manqué de connaissance sur l'âme humaine et son caractère spirituel. Tout est jaugé en fonction du social, donc d'une organisation qui est le fruit d'une convention humaine, et l'idée de nature humaine, de ses exigences intellectuelles et morales n'ont jamais été aussi absentes des critères de valeur que l'on utilise pour essayer d'orienter l'être humain vers le bonheur.

Or, cette perte du sens de la nature humaine, elle a commencé avec la première philosophie scientifique, celle de Descartes, qui a mis au rancart toute la sensibilité humaine comme moyen de connaître la vérité, c'est-à-dire de connaître l'homme et l'univers qui l'entoure. Elle a continué avec Kant qui a coupé les ponts entre l'intelligence et le réel dans sa *Critique de la raison pure* qui est l'éloge funèbre de toute pensée métaphysique. Elle a fait un autre bond avec Hegel qui a supprimé toute contingence dans la réalité historique pour chanter la naissance de l'esprit dans la conscience collective. Et l'existentialisme athée contemporain n'est que l'aboutissement normal de toutes ces philosophies contre nature dans la revendication fondamentale que l'homme est absurde, que sa vie est essentiellement sans but et que l'univers dans lequel il se trouve participe également à cette absurdité. Il en est de même du Marxisme, qui veut établir un paradis terrestre parce qu'on a tronqué l'homme de cette partie de lui-même qui l'appelle à un paradis éternel qui dépasse l'économique et le politique, de toutes les dimensions de l'esprit.

Si les philosophies, à la mode scientifique, conduisent progressivement l'humanité au chaos, c'est qu'il leur manque peut-être ce qui a toujours été proclamé comme le fruit normal de toute sagesse, c'est-à-dire la puissance d'engendrer la stabilité. Aristote proclamait cette vérité dans une phrase assez humoristique : « Il est impossible d'imaginer le sage comme un caméléon[10] », et les médiévaux, en affirmant que « c'est en devenant stable qu'on devient sage[11] ». Or, la

[10] *I Eth. Nic.*, chap. x, 1100b, 5–7.

[11] Cf. Saint Thomas d'Aquin, *I Eth. ad Nic.*, lect. xv, n. 186; *In I De An.*, lect. vii, n. 125; *III Cont. Gentes*, chap. 48.

science est toujours en mouvement, et ses procédés vont toujours dans le sens d'une désintégration de plus en plus radicale des moyens naturels que l'homme possède pour se connaître et connaître l'ensemble des êtres. Voici un texte qui rend magnifiquement cette idée, et heureusement pour moi, il provient de la plume d'un grand savant qui ne risque pas d'être soupçonné de partialité :

When we have eliminated all superfluous, what have we left ? We can do without taste, smell, hearing, and even touch. We must keep our eyes or rather one eye, for there is no need to use our faculty of stereoscopic vision... With this reduced equipment we can still recognize geometrical form and size... But it was found that the observers were still quarreling even when they had only form and size to quarrel över. So, in 1915, Einstein made another raid on their sensory equipment. He removed all the retina of the eye except one small patch. The observer could no longer recognize form or extension in the external world but he could tell whether two things were in apparent coincidence or not... Since we have so mutilated him (the observer), he cannot make the experiment himself. We perform the experiments and let him keep watch. The point is that all our knowledge of the external world as it is conceived to-day in physics can be demonstrated to him. If we cannot convince him, we have no right to assert it[12].

Il est difficile d'inventer une méthode plus draconienne de réduire les querelles entre les hommes de science par l'élimination des sources mêmes dont la nature l'a doté pour prendre contact avec la réalité. La méthode est efficace, sans aucun doute, et la science, telle que conçue, se devait de l'appliquer. Mais le résultat net de tout ce processus d'élimination est que ce n'est plus l'homme mais l'instrument qui juge, et ce n'est plus la nature mais une fiction de nature qui est objet de connaissance : « La vie sensible, la chaleur, la couleur, l'odeur et le son, la nature, privée de tout cela, n'est plus qu'une fiction intellectuelle[13]. »

Ce qu'il y a de plus intéressant pour le sujet que nous traitons, c'est-à-dire pour porter un jugement sur la valeur réaliste des philosophies à procédés scientifiques, c'est que la brutalité nécessaire des procédés scientifiques qui appauvrissent simultanément et l'homme et la nature sont les symptômes d'une mentalité antinaturelle et antiphilosophique. La nature, en effet, n'est pas isomorphiste; elle ne tend pas vers l'homogénéisation des réalités mais se manifeste comme une source inépuisable de différenciations qui s'opposent entre elles et cependant s'entr'aident continuellement. Dans la nature, rien ne se perd, rien ne se crée : son pragmatisme est inimaginable. La nature n'a pas de dépotoirs; elle ne jette rien à la voierie; il n'y a ni décombres,

[12]Sir Arthur Eddington, *New Pathways in Science* (Cambridge, 1935), chap. I, pp. 12–13.

[13]F. H. Bradley, *Appearance and Reality* (London : Macmillan, 1893), p. 493.

ni détritus, ni restes, ni ordures. Ce qui est laissé-pour-compte par un être devient un principe de fécondité et d'alimentation pour un autre. Son sens de l'utile et de l'utilisable est extraordinaire comparé au nôtre, comme le prouvent les immenses cimetières de ferrailles, de débris, d'ordures de toutes sortes qui entourent nos villes industrielles.

Or, c'est cette nature que la philosophie veut comprendre, non pour la mesurer et s'en servir, mais pour se laisser mesurer par elle, ce qui implique qu'elle accepte la nature dans toute son intégralité, en commençant par la nature humaine elle-même. Voilà pourquoi la véritable philosophie ne laissera rien perdre des instruments variés dont l'homme est armé pour entreprendre ce labeur difficile d'une vision sûre et intégrale de la complexité de sa nature et de la nature. Contrairement à la science et aux pseudo-philosophies qui empruntent à celle-ci leurs méthodes, la philosophie scolastique, qui est nôtre, ne considérera pas comme inutilisable et nuisible le monde de la sensation; elle ne fera pas de ce monde un cimetière d'illusions, mais elle l'acceptera avec la même humilité et la même gratitude que celles dont faisait montre le pauvre de l'Evangile en présence des miettes tombées de la table du riche, car elle sait que les moindres parcelles de réalité qui lui sont communiquées par le canal des sens sont un reflet fragmentaire mais vrai de l'infinie perfection qui est source de toute réalité.

L'attachement du Canada français à la philosophie traditionnelle qui est sienne ne s'explique adéquatement ni par le caractère chrétien, ni par le caractère scolastique de cette synthèse doctrinale, mais d'abord et avant tout par la pureté philosophique de la connaissance qu'elle donne et de la méthode qu'elle utilise. Le monde occidental a oublié, en effet, depuis trois siècles, que la véritable philosophie est une sagesse parce que Descartes et Kant l'ont recouverte d'un masque scientifique qui nous en cache le vrai visage. Or, une sagesse ne reçoit que d'elle-même les clefs de son royaume et la structure des vérités dont elle est la reine, et aller quémander à la science, au sens moderne du mot, des consignes qu'elle mettrait ensuite à exécution serait pour une sagesse non seulement un non-sens mais un acte de démagogie. Or, c'est ce régime absurde que Descartes et Kant, ces pères putatifs de la méthode philosophique, ont imposé à l'intelligence lorsqu'au nom de la clarté et de la certitude des sciences mathématique ou physique, ils ont conçu une méthode *rationnelle* de connaissance à laquelle la sagesse devait se soumettre sous peine de renoncer à l'existence. Ils n'avaient pas pris conscience que cette soumission forcée de la méthode et de la pensée philosophiques à des procédés scientifiques était une abdication pure et simple, et qu'elle néantisait non seulement les philosophies antérieures mais encore toute possibilité d'existence. Cette conclusion à laquelle Kant est arrivé, au terme de son œuvre, ne justifie pas sa *Critique* mais manifeste à l'évidence que lorsque la science essaie de fonder la sagesse, cette dernière est inévitablement vouée au néant.

Pour retrouver le vrai visage de la philosophie et la débarrasser à tout jamais de ce masque scientifique sous lequel elle mascarade depuis des siècles, il faut pasticher la maxime évangélique, c'est-à-dire « rendre à la science ce qui appartient à la science et à la sagesse ce qui est sien ». A partir du XIVe siècle on a cessé de pratiquer cette justice. Pendant trois siècles, la science s'est vu refuser, par une prétendue sagesse, sa liberté de méthode dans le champ de l'expérimentation et de la mathématisation des faits expérimentés. Depuis le XVIIe siècle c'est la philosophie qui a été ligotée par la science, qui a décrété son arrêt de mort par des injections répétées et à dose massive du prétendu vaccin scientifique contre l'erreur. Notre philosophie a refusé ce vaccin parce qu'elle a voulu demeurer fidèle à sa nature de connaître sapientiel; elle ne prétend exercer aucun despotisme à l'égard de la science et de ses méthodes propres; mais elle compte bien demeurer maîtresse dans le royaume des vérités qui lui sont propres, vérités qui nous mettent en contact avec le mystère de l'existence et de la vie parce qu'elles relient toute existence et toute vie à Celui qui est l'Exister et la Vie.

Telles sont la véritable nature de notre pensée philosophique et les raisons qui nous la font préférer à tous ces systèmes pseudo-philosophiques qui se sont succédé à un rythme accéléré depuis que la science s'est introduite au sein de la sagesse : car nous connaissons les trésors de stabilité et de sécurité intellectuelles et morales qu'elle renferme dans un monde où la pensée devient de plus en plus fuyante et instable, de plus en plus semblable à un caméléon. Nous soutenons, avec Aristote, « qu'il est impossible d'imaginer le sage comme un caméléon ». Et voilà pourquoi, en dépit de ses apparences démodées, nous estimons que notre philosophie possède encore au XXe siècle la capacité d'introduire l'esprit humain au cœur même du réel et de le lui faire voir en profondeur ce qui est, en définitive, la définition même d'une véritable philosophie.

III) Conclusion

On a l'impression très vive, en lisant l'histoire du Canada, de revivre le récit d'une guerre de deux cents ans entre des frères ennemis que des circonstances géographiques et politiques obligent à la cohabitation au sein d'une atmosphère de méfiance et d'antipathie réciproques. On pourrait trouver un paradigme analogique de cette situation dans l'histoire biblique d'Esaü et de Jacob, deux frères qu'un ensemble de circonstances rendirent ennemis. Cet ensemble de circonstances est résumé par deux faits : la vente, par Esaü, de son droit d'aînesse, et le vol, par le cadet, de la bénédiction paternelle à laquelle se rattachaient des biens présents et futurs de toutes sortes. Or, historiquement parlant, il semble que les Canadiens français fassent revivre le personnage d'Esaü alors que les Canadiens anglais personnifient Jacob. Venus près de deux siècles avant les Anglais sur la terre canadienne, professant un christianisme qui est de seize siècles antérieur à la Réforme, nous possédons incontestablement le droit d'aînesse religieux et politique, et nos compatriotes anglo-saxons sont nos cadets à ces deux points de vue. Et pourtant depuis deux siècles nous avons l'impression d'avoir été dépouillés de ce double droit d'aînesse, et c'est notre cadet qui a hérité de la bénédiction paternelle, c'est-à-dire de la supériorité économique et de la liberté politique avec tout ce que cela comporte de facilité et d'avantages dans le domaine de l'éducation et de l'avancement social; d'où le complexe de frustration et d'antipathie qui nous caractérise, et auquel s'oppose un complexe de supériorité et de mépris de la part de nos compatriotes anglophones.

Or, nous oublions un fait de première importance, c'est que ce n'est pas nous qui avons vendu notre droit d'aînesse politique et ce ne sont pas nos compatriotes qui nous ont volé la bénédiction paternelle, mais une tierce personne. C'est la France qui en 1763 a échangé notre droit d'aînesse pour un plat de lentille, et c'est l'Angleterre qui a hérité des nombreux avantages de cet échange. Puisque la source de ce changement de situation n'est imputable à aucun de nos deux groupes ethniques, puisque notre nationalité canadienne est une réalité que nous avons conquise ensemble dans un pays qui n'est ni la France ni l'Angleterre mais en terre d'Amérique, rien, sinon des préjugés, ne nous force à nous considérer comme des frères ennemis; tout nous invite, au contraire, à devenir des partenaires engagés dans un immense labeur d'édification des destinées de notre peuple.

Ce n'est pas la multiplication de nos échecs respectifs, provoqués par les traquenards multipliés que réciproquement nous nous tendons, qui construira cet avenir, mais le travail d'équipe entre nos deux races, dont l'une n'est pas conquise et l'autre conquérante, mais deux races dont l'homogénéité des origines culturelles et religieuses est une invitation continuelle à la coopération dans les divers domaines qui font la force et la richesse d'une nation. N'oublions pas, en effet, que nos deux cultures sont dans leur sub-structures, scolastiques et chrétiennes, et que sous les oppositions idéologiques qui nous divisent se dissimulent des traits communs dont la mise en évidence serait beaucoup plus efficace pour la construction de l'unité canadienne que des moyens d'ordre économique ou politique. Si, pour utiliser une expression chestertonienne, le monde occidental « ne vit que sur un capital d'idées chrétiennes devenues folles », et si d'autre part, ces idées chrétiennes ont absorbé, au cours des âges, tout l'apport philosophique inventé par les Grecs et les Latins, nos deux races dont la grandeur et la valeur reposent en définitive sur ce capital culturel antique et chrétien sont reliés entre eux par des liens spirituels qui ni les nationalismes racistes ni la Réforme ne devraient avoir la puissance de couper.

Dans la mesure où nous demeurerons fidèles aux plus stables traditions de la culture et de la religion occidentales, dans la même mesure nous découvrirons des terrains d'entente qui dépasseront les intérêts politiques et économiques et nous permettront de travailler dans la paix à l'évolution et à l'épanouissement de la patrie canadienne. Mais pour ce faire, il faut méditer l'avertissement que donne saint Paul aux premiers chrétiens, avertissement dont l'opportunité n'a jamais été aussi réelle que de nos jours : « Un temps viendra où l'on ne supportera plus la saine doctrine. Au gré des passions, l'on se donnera des maîtres à la douzaine dans la démangeaison d'apprendre. On détournera l'oreille de la vérité pour la tourner vers les mythes[14]. »

Or, ce temps est venu; on a délaissé la vérité chrétienne et philosophique pour les mythes historiques et scientifiques dont le changement, la probabilité, sont les seuls attributs. Demandons à l'Evangile et à la sagesse humaine de nous fournir les cadres sprituels stables et indéfectibles dans lesquels la destinée humaine doit se dérouler et servons-nous de la science pour améliorer les conditions temporelles qui doivent faciliter à l'homme la réalisation de son bonheur mais non l'en détourner ignominieusement. C'est dans le respect de cette hiérarchie des valeurs que notre pays se donnera simultanément la paix et la prospérité, au sein d'une unité politique jalousement fidèle à préserver et à favoriser les deux traditions culturelles qui constituent notre originalité au milieu d'un monde voué à la monotonie de la standardisation.

1955

[14]II Tim 4, 3–4.

I. ABSTRACT FACTORS

C. Law

I. PERSPECTIVES GÉNÉRALES

C. Normes légales

Areas of Conflict in the Field of Public Law and Policy*

F. R. SCOTT

Macdonald Professor of Law, McGill University

THE PUBLIC LAW of Quebec, unlike the private law, derives its principles and general content from the public law of England. By the Treaty of Paris in 1763 the sovereignty over New France passed from the King of France to the King of England; and automatically the law relating to the Crown, the government, and the political rights of citizens became those of an English colony. The legislative, executive, and judicial organs, which were established and developed after the cession, copied the patterns of the new mother country, as formerly they had those of the old: in this sense New France became New England. But the underlying social institutions, such as the Church, the seigneurial system, and the family, with the French language, private law, and traditions, did not change:[1] in this sense New France became Old France. Thus Quebec offers an early example of British institutions of government being first imposed upon, and then accepted by, a non-British people, who in other respects guarded jealously their own laws and customs.

Through the successive constitutional changes in Canada after 1763, such as in 1792, 1841, and 1867, the public law of Quebec remained English in character, though new institutions of government were introduced. These new institutions, with few exceptions, were not peculiar to Quebec but followed the model set up also in other Canadian jurisdictions. Quebec was integrated into a developing imperial system. Though French-Canadian nationalism steadily increased during the nineteenth century, the law of the constitution takes little note of

*This paper appeared as an article in 3 *McGill Law Journal* (1956–7), pp. 29–50.

[1]I leave aside the question of whether the French private law was temporarily displaced by the royal proclamation of 1763.

it. The British North America Act of 1867 contains few special provisions for Quebec. Outside sections 71–80, establishing the Quebec legislature, most of which concern the Legislative Council, there are few references to the province by name. Some of the clauses applicable to Quebec were for the protection of the Protestant minority only, or were equally beneficial to Catholic and Protestant; an example of the former is the special vote required for changes in the representation from the Eastern Townships (s. 80), predominantly English in 1867; of the latter, the extending to Quebec of the rights to separate schools guaranteed to Ontario (ss. 93–2) and the protection for the two official languages (s. 133). These rules, far from enlarging autonomy in the province, all impose restrictions on it in the interest of minority rights which are not exclusively French or Catholic.

The most noticeable singling out of Quebec, as a province, in the constitution is to be found in the uniformity provisions of section 94,[2] where Quebec is omitted, and section 98, which provides that judges in Quebec courts must always be drawn from the bar of Quebec. Section 94 does not permit the legislature of Quebec to delegate to Ottawa jurisdiction over "property and civil rights" by the easy process which other provinces may employ, and shows that the preservation of the French law was one of the purposes of the Union of 1867 as it had been of all previous constitutions since the Quebec Act of 1774. This is also the reason for the requirement that judicial appointments in Quebec must be made from among the members of the provincial bar (s. 98). Like the guarantee for the use of the English and French languages, these provisions recognize the bicultural nature of Canada. They do not add to provincial autonomy, however, but rather restrict it. Nor do they prevent a transfer of jurisdiction by the amendment of the constitution, as for unemployment insurance and old age pensions. Cultural differences in 1867 were not expressed in greater legislative autonomy for the provinces; indeed, the dangers to unity which they entailed were one of the reasons for establishing a strong government at Ottawa with the residue of power in the hands of the central authorities.

In the basic distribution of legislative powers under sections 91–2 of the constitution, there is no mention of Quebec: the original legislatures are all given the same powers. Preservation of the two cultures was a principle on which the Canadian nation was built, but the constitution did not create in Quebec a special kind of "state" to which

[2]This section, which has never been used, enabled provinces to abandon jurisdiction to the federal Parliament by consent.

was entrusted an exclusive guardianship over French culture. On the contrary, minority rights and provincial autonomy are kept quite distinct, and autonomy is frequently subordinated to the higher value of minority rights. This is shown by the fact that Ottawa is specifically given power to legislate on education in certain circumstances, in Quebec as elsewhere, for the protection of minorities (ss. 93–4), and to veto provincial laws (s. 90), a provision which was intended to operate as a control over any legislature abusing its power. As Cartier himself said during the Confederation debates, "I would recommend it (disallowance) myself in case of injustice."[3]

The superstructure of the constitution, however, is one thing; the living forces within peoples are another. The states of the American Union, under its constitution, are treated with even more equality among themselves than are Canadian provinces, yet the deep-seated differences between North and South are still patent, though not based on language and religion, and have produced a doctrine of nullification and claims to secession which could not be resolved by judicial process. From 1867 Quebec became an autonomous community in the sense in which any state in a federation is autonomous: it could exercise its legislative powers as it chose in any way that did not conflict with the law of the constitution. In particular, its jurisdiction over "property and civil rights" which it shares with other provinces gave it a wide field for self-expression, particularly as the extent of its jurisdiction was greatly expanded through judicial interpretations. Over the course of the years it has, by provincial legislation, changed certain parts of the public law in ways that differ from the direction taken in other parts of Canada, though a basic similarity remains. More important even than the differences which such local legislation produces—and Quebec is not unique in this form of regionalism—are the attitudes and feelings about "provincial autonomy"; here the opinions expressed with increasing conviction in Quebec often stand in strong contrast to those prevalent elsewhere. While opinions are not law, they tend to produce interpretations of law and certainly produce conflict in the judicial as well as in the political sphere.

Some of these contrasting views will now be analysed. But while the emphasis is on differences of outlook, it must be remembered that not all French Canadians think alike and still less do all other Canadians. Quebec is by no means the only defender of provincial autonomy,

[3]*Confederation Debates*, pp. 407–8. See also F. R. Scott, "Dominion Jurisdiction over Human Rights and Fundamental Freedoms," 27 *Canadian Bar Review* (1949), at p. 530.

though under Premier Maurice Duplessis, as often in the past, this has been a leading characteristic of its policy. Hence cross-currents soften opinions which, if too rigid, might make impossible that degree of ethnic co-operation without which Canadian federalism could not survive. The areas of conflict here outlined must be seen against a much wider background of day-to-day collaboration in almost every phase of Canadian activity.

Statute or Compact?

A primary question, still unresolved by Canadian publicists, is this: What is the nature of the British North America Act of 1867? Is it simply a statute of the British Parliament, distributing powers afresh among Canadian governments through the exercise of an ancient imperial sovereignty? Or is it a solemn compact or treaty not only between provinces but between the French and English races in Canada? On the answer given this question many others will inevitably depend.

The view that the constitution is a statute, a view which commands wide though not universal support in English Canada, sees all the present provinces as deriving their governmental powers from a superior legislative grant which is equally binding on federal Parliament and provincial legislatures. The authority of the Parliament at Westminster, which established the present system of government, is still used to change its fundamental provisions, and for the amendments this Parliament alone can make, no provincial consent is legally necessary, however politically wise it may be to secure it. The law of the constitution does not give any province, or any number of them, a veto on changes requested by the federal Parliament. Moreover, "provincial autonomy" is no more a chief purpose of Confederation than federal autonomy, or decentralization than centralization; the B.N.A. Act was an act for the union of provinces, not for disunion, and while a federal form of government was adopted, the provinces, in the words of the Act, "shall form and be one Dominion under the name of Canada" (s. 3).

On this understanding of the B.N.A. Act, the struggle of the French-Canadian minority for its due share of status and power in Canada and for the recognition of its fundamental rights must express itself through the Parliament of Canada, as well as through the Quebec and other provincial governments. Federal institutions, as well as provincial ones, are its proper outlet. Quebec is and doubtless will remain a "homeland" to all French Canadians, except perhaps the Acadians, but this is an historic fact rather than a constitutional rule. All Canada is the homeland for all Canadians. Canada is thus two cultures but not two states; a federal system and not a diarchy. The ten provinces are equal in status, and French culture, while geographically centred in Quebec, radiates outward through various social and political channels but not through any special governmental institutions. The government of Quebec, though controlled by French Canadians, is neither French nor Catholic, being designed for all its inhabitants, 20 per cent of whom are not of French origin. "Dans notre pays il n'existe pas de religion de l'Etat," says Mr. Justice Taschereau.[4] Indeed, since all government in Canada is carried on in the name of the Crown, and the Queen must by law be in communion with the Church of England, Quebec has a Protestant as formal head of the government, whatever may be the religion of the premier and cabinet.

If the B.N.A. Act is viewed as a compact or treaty rather than a statute—an opinion almost official in Quebec[5]—at once different aspects of the federal relation are stressed. Ottawa becomes, in a very real sense, the "creature" of the provinces,[6] which agreed in 1867 to set up a new form of government. The creators, being equal in rights, would seem to have an equal voice in proposing and approving changes in the constitution. On this argument every province has, or should have, the power of veto over amendments. Though it is true that some provinces were established or admitted after Confederation, and cannot strictly be considered as parties to the compact, and though Quebec and Ontario were united in a single Province of Canada when the compact was formed, the basic fact of provincial pre-existence remains in so far as Quebec opinion is concerned. French Canada had its separate existence as New France until 1763, as Lower Canada from 1792 to 1841, and was recognized as a distinct entity by the tacit federalism that was practised under the Union government of the Province of Canada from 1841 to 1867. Its sense of identity survives and pervades every form of constitution. Lower Canada also had its own delegation, separate from that of Ontario and composed of both French and English members, at the Quebec and London conferences preceding Confederation. These facts lend special strength to the compact theory in Quebec.

Some recent thinking in Quebec goes far beyond the compact theory and defines Confederation as a fundamental agreement, not merely

[4]In *Chaput* v. *Romain*, [1955] S.C.R. 834 at p. 840.

[5]It has been written in to the preamble of the Quebec statute 2–3 Eliz. 11, c. 17.

[6]This view has also English-Canadian support: see, e.g., S. J. Watson, *The Powers of Canadian Parliaments* (1880), p. 51; D. A. O'Sullivan, *A Manual of Government in Canada* (1879), p. 21.

between provinces, but between the two races, French and English. This notion, like the compact theory, opens up new lines of constitutional analysis but leads to quite different conclusions. Not unnaturally, among all the influences that shaped the constitution, the French-English relation stands out most vividly in the Quebec mind. There seems no straining of history in calling the eventual agreement a treaty between races, even though the text of the B.N.A. Act mentions no race at all except the Indian. In this approach there exists a dualism in the constitution that reflects a predominant fact of Canadian life, and the government of Quebec at once appears as a "French" and "Catholic" government, a champion of the race, set over against the English and Protestant government of Ottawa. Symbolization of the racial and religious struggle takes place on the constitutional level, though the language of the law is neutral. The treaty-between-races theory explains the importance for Quebec of having its own flag, as a sign of nationhood, and its own anthem—"O Canada!"—whose French version hymns the traditions of Old France rather than the aspirations of the new federal state stretching from sea to sea.

If the races in Canada are equal, so the theory goes, then the governments representing the races should be equal. Therefore Quebec is the equal of Ottawa and not just one part of a larger whole. Such is the easy transition from the aspirations of the people to the supposed law of the constitution. This concentration on the provincial government as defender and sole representative of Quebec's rights, as distinct from merely regarding the province as a focus of culture, is something relatively new in Quebec though the ideas being defended are as old as the cession of 1763. The degree to which these ideas have penetrated into the realms of constitutional theory can be seen in the following typical statements. One is from a speech of Hon. Antonio Barrette, Minister of Labour in Quebec, who said in May, 1955:

> There is now such a thing as a French-Canadian nation. Not only have we accomplished the miracle of survival but we have reached the point where we have our own government, our own religion, our own language, our own culture, our own universities, and our own literature.
>
> The acts of heroism of Quebec's early settlers are beginning to pay off in a tangible manner.
>
> We have reconquered our autonomy and we are now well on the way to retake possession of our taxation rights which are at the very basis of our existence. Without our power to tax, our freedom of legislation would be a sheer illusion.[7]

[7]Quoted by J. Harvey Perry, "What Price Provincial Autonomy?" 21 *Canadian Journal of Economics and Political Science* (1955), at p. 445.

Another is from the recommendations of the Tremblay Commission on Constitutional Problems, the second of which states: "2. With regard to French-Canadian culture, the Province of Quebec assumes alone the responsibilities which the other provinces jointly assume with regard to Anglo-Canadian culture."[8] A third is from an article by a member of the bar of Quebec, M. Philippe Ferland, Q.C., published in *Thémis*, the law journal of the Université de Montréal.[9] Writing of the meeting of Prime Minister St. Laurent and Premier Duplessis in "neutral" Montreal on October 5, 1954, to discuss a new taxation agreement, M. Ferland said:

> Nous sommes ramenés au point de départ, à l'origine de la Confédération. Deux parties sont en présence: l'Etat canadien-français et l'Etat canadien. Pour la première fois depuis 1867, ces deux Etats se rencontrent seul à seul. Le dialogue doit s'engager entre les deux seules parties qui n'ont ni négocié ni signé: Québec et Ottawa. La discussion doit s'engager entre les véritables délégués qui se font face: l'Etat fédéral, représentant de l'union législative, l'Etat provincial du Québec, représentant le peuple qui veut refaire ses chances de survie, celui des Canadiens-français. Deux Etats, deux conceptions, deux peuples.

What would surprise a Canadian from Nova Scotia or Alberta who read this last statement (assuming he understood French), is the notion that Ottawa speaks for all the other "English" provinces as well as for itself, and that because the population of Quebec is predominantly French and Catholic, all provinces except Quebec disappear, leaving only two "states" on the Canadian scene. Yet this has become a deeply felt reality in Quebec, where the idea that federalism in Canada exists solely to guarantee the survival of French culture, and that without it Canada would be a unitary state, finds ready acceptance. The regional loyalty of the Maritimes, for example, or the separatism, inherent in geography, which imposed federalism on Canada quite regardless of feeling in Quebec, are factors to which no attention is paid.

The "dual state" theory is quite inconsistent with the compact theory, since the latter claims only that all provinces are equal sovereign entities whose rights cannot be changed without their consent, whereas the former denies the existence or importance of all provinces save Quebec. The attractiveness of the theory for Quebec lies in its attribution of equal status to the smaller of the two Canadian communities: it thus plays the same role as "Dominion status" within the Commonwealth and "sovereignty of states" in the international order. That it

[8]Summary of the *Report*, 1956, p. 18.
[9]No. 14 (Dec. 1954), p. 105 at p. 109.

is revolutionary in its implications is obvious. It could not be worked out to its logical conclusions without totally destroying the present constitution of Canada. Already certain extremists in Quebec have no hesitation in dismissing all French-speaking federal members of Parliament from Quebec (though duly elected) as *vendus*, as indeed by definition they must be for associating with "the other side." Even though *Le Devoir*, traditional defender of Quebec nationalism, may protest at the injustice to Quebec of having too few French Canadians in the federal civil service, any Quebecer who takes an Ottawa post is likely to suffer the accusation of having lost his essential French character.

Unless Quebec is to become an independent state outside Confederation, an eventuality which virtually no one in Quebec seems to desire, the limitation of legislative and executive powers imposed by the present constitution on the Quebec government would seem to make it wholly inadequate as the *exclusive* defender of French culture, even if all French minorities in other provinces are disregarded. The elevation of this government as the sole champion of the race has therefore grave dangers for that race: it might have the unexpected effect of imprisoning the vital energies of the French-Canadian people. A "state" such as a Canadian province, deprived by the constitution of control of money and banking, foreign and interprovincial trade, transportation and telecommunications (including radio and television), the armed forces, and the criminal law, whose taxing powers are limited and whose laws can be vetoed, is not in a position to control all the important areas in which a culture flourishes, still less to provide a secure economic base for that culture. Besides these legislative limitations, the constitution gives to the government at Ottawa the appointment of all the senators from Quebec, all the judges of the Superior Court and Court of Appeal in Quebec, and the Lieutenant-Governor of Quebec, while the Parliament of Canada can declare any public work in Quebec to be for the "general advantage of Canada" and thus gain control over it.

These provisions were not aimed at Quebec, but apply to all provinces equally; they are part of the traditional fabric of Canadian federalism. The Fathers of Confederation, witnessing the American Civil War, drew the lesson that an exaggerated provincial autonomy could spell disaster, and took steps to avoid any such danger in the Canadian constitution. There is little in Canadian history to suggest that they were mistaken in this view. The Quebec nationalist is far from being alone in his dislike of federal authority. Before Confederation was a year old, Nova Scotia (not Quebec) was endeavouring to secede; secessionist movements were developing on the Prairies during the 1930's; the Social Credit party's attempts to secure financial autonomy for Alberta under Premier Aberhart fully match the similar efforts of Mr. Duplessis in Quebec. The Canadian nation, in demographic shape still a long ribbon of population broken at several points, has difficulty at all times in holding itself together against strong centrifugal forces. That is the reason why Canadian federalism contains the unitary features, already referred to, which mark it off from other systems, more typically federal.

Behind the rather outspoken claims of supporters of the compact and racial theories of Confederation lies a natural desire for survival and expansion that is constantly seeking new symbols to express its aspirations. The French Canadian is at home in Quebec; so is the English Canadian, though some other minorities are perhaps not so secure. The French Canadian wants to feel as much at home when he lives in Ontario; that is, he wants his own language, his own school, his church and parish, and his French-Canadian way of life. To some extent he has achieved this in districts adjacent to Quebec. But his minorities farther from the homeland have not achieved it, and the English-speaking inhabitants of the other provinces are surprised, if not startled, to discover that they are expected to adapt their local laws (for example on separate schools) so as to make possible the steady development of a French-speaking cultural minority as an island colony in the midst of their already heterogeneous populations. Meeting this resistance, the French minorities look to Quebec for help, which in turn reacts with stronger claims. The fact that an exaggerated provincial autonomy may actually weaken the outside minorities by subjecting them still further to local majorities and depriving them of the protection of Ottawa does not deter the nationalists in Quebec. An "autonomous" Quebec is a fortress in a dangerous land, without which the struggle for survival seems hopeless. Thus a strong Quebec government seems necessary to pry loose more freedom for its minorities outside as well as inside, using at the same time provincial autonomy, influence at Ottawa, and pressures of every kind to achieve the single purpose. The conflicting interpretations of the constitution as between statute and compact, or as racial treaty, are phases of this wider engagement. For this reason legal argument is of little avail in changing opinions, and proofs that the B.N.A. Act is or is not founded on a compact or treaty do not go to the real issue, which is one of power rather than of law.

New Functions of Government

While debates about the nature of the Canadian constitution continue, new functions of government arise to alter the basic foundations of federal-provincial relations. These new functions create new conflicts of opinion. The provision of social services, and the maintenance of economic equilibrium, make demands upon Canadian governments which the original constitution was ill equipped to fulfil. Economic equilibrium and high employment are inevitably federal responsibilities, for no province has sufficient control over taxation or finance to be capable of maintaining them. The Social Credit Government's record in Alberta between 1935 and 1940 exposed this provincial weakness, both in fact and in law. Social legislation, about which Quebec is deeply concerned, is more easily conceived of in provincial terms in so far as administration goes, and even the financing of minor services can be borne by provinces, but the larger social insurances affecting unemployment, health, and old age are too costly for most provincial budgets without federal participation. Already unemployment insurance and old age pensions have been attributed to Ottawa by constitutional amendment. Other provincial services are developing so fast that they too are demanding federal aid. University education is a case in point. National economic policies and demands for social services tend toward centralization, no matter what interpretations the courts place upon the constitution or what arguments are brought forward for provincial autonomy. Hence Quebec's fears for the future of her distinctive way of life are increased, and the conflicts of opinion which are always present in the federal system are exacerbated.

The most powerful centripetal forces are created by the fundamental dynamic in Canadian society—industrialization. This is the real enemy to provincial autonomy as conceived in racial or any other terms, and the most serious challenge which French Canada must face—more dangerous than the English majority in Canada, also carried along by the forces of change, or than "Ottawa" or any other external symbolization of the "threat to Quebec." Industrialization and technical change are sweeping Quebec as never before in her history, for the rugged Laurentian country which for so long maintained the near-subsistence agriculture on which Old France could survive in North America is now found to be rich with minerals and resources which an expanding economy requires for its voracious mills and factories. The remotest regions of the province are being brought under exploration and development. Great amounts of capital are needed which few French

Canadians can provide, and the large private corporations which, in a capitalist society, are the chief instruments used in development, relentlessly transform the ancient pattern of Quebec life, introduce new centres of authority, and tie the province to world markets. The movement from farm to factory is accentuated, despite Quebec's belief in the "colonization" of marginal lands; immigrant labour can for the first time be absorbed in French communities; international trade unions reach out to protect workers who feel themselves to be unsympathetically treated even by their own government. Even the Catholic trade unions, originally designed to protect Quebec, have discussed affiliation with the single Canadian Labour Congress. The cultural curtain which history and institutional policy have placed around Quebec is being brushed aside at every point.

It is ironic that the man who most invokes the political appeal of provincial autonomy, Premier Maurice Duplessis, is the one who has most encouraged the very process which is undermining his own philosophy. Being conservative in background and political outlook, he promotes private enterprise in its purest forms, so that while it is true, as *Le Devoir* said,[10] that "the only government over which the people of Quebec exercise absolute control is the Quebec Government," the Quebec population has very little control over the policies of the financiers and entrepreneurs who are shaping the future relations of Quebec to Canada and to the outside world. Corporate undertakings of the modern type are themselves a form of government, and to use the words of an American constitutional authority, "corporations, in the process of conducting their operations in a number of states, render control by any state extremely difficult, leaving the federal government the only potentially effective master."[11] Even Ottawa seems powerless in face of the general trend. The forces threatening Quebec are international in scope, and battles over provincial status seem peculiarly beside the point.

It is not only economic forces, however, which play this formative role in the federal system. Canada's international obligations, and her essential part in the defence system of the Western world, also change the basis of federalism. During the Second World War, Canada became virtually a unitary state. The emergency necessitated a high degree of centralization. That this did not permanently destroy the autonomy of provinces is evidenced by their present strength. But some after-effects

[10]Quoted and translated in *Montreal Gazette*, March 31, 1955.

[11]C. B. Swisher, *The Growth of Constitutional Power in the United States* (Chicago: University of Chicago Press, 1956), p. 208.

of war show no signs of disappearing. One is the continuing need to spend large sums on defence, which necessitates a high level of federal taxation. Both in law and in policy the demands of defence have priority over provincial claims. Money for this programme must be obtained from taxation spread over the whole country, including Quebec. In addition, Canadian industry must be available as needed for defence supplies; this has necessitated federal legislation under which very stringent controls can be imposed by Ottawa upon sources of production. Each individual industry in a province forms part of the national defence potential. No industry falls exclusively within the jurisdiction of the province in which it is situated, though "property and civil rights" are provincial matters under the constitution. Given nothing worse than a cold war, Ottawa's use of the defence power leaves room for provincial freedom, but no concession which threatens defence planning for the security of Canada and her Western allies can be made to provincial governments. The conflicts that occur in the field of public law in Canada, and the constant attempt to find new solutions to the financial problems facing provincial governments, are carried on under the overriding necessity of facing the realities of the international situation.

Fiscal Policy and Provincial Autonomy

It may be admitted that provincial autonomy must have a sound financial base or it is an empty formula. In insisting on this point, Quebec voices a widespread belief. With federal taxes geared to the double requirement of equilibrium economics and defence spending, the field of taxation is so largely occupied by the federal government that provincial legislatures are hard pressed to find the additional funds needed for their expanding social services. Under the constitution they are denied the right to levy any but direct taxes. All provinces other than Quebec—and, for a time, Ontario—accepted Ottawa's solution to this problem up to 1957, in the form of five-year tax rental agreements by which, in return for their withdrawal from the income and corporation tax fields, they received additional grants from the federal treasury on formulae equally available to all. Quebec refused to enter these arrangements after 1945, though she was a party to the wartime tax agreements, 1941–5. Mr. Duplessis has consistently interpreted his refusal as a defence of the fundamental rights of Quebec, and Ottawa's taxation policies as an attack upon those rights. The following extracts from a speech he delivered at Rouyn on August 21, 1955, state his position clearly enough:

The Premier said the efforts of the Government were limited by the amount of taxes collected. . . . "To do what is required to meet the growing needs of our province and our people, additional funds will be required. . . ."

"As far as I am concerned," the Premier asserted, "I don't know how many more years Providence will allow me to continue as the head of the Government. I know it would be simple for me to take the easy way out and sell the rights of Quebec for a few million dollars. It would be easy but it would not be honourable.

"I have said before and I say it again," declared the Premier, "that I will never betray the province of Quebec whether the price is a few pieces of silver or millions of dollars. . . ."

"We must have additional funds to provide our schools with the educational facilities to which they are entitled; we must have financial independence to build our own hospitals and to provide the people of this province with the social services which they have come to expect from their government."[12]

Stated in these general terms, these propositions have evoked almost universal support in Quebec and a good deal outside. The problem is to know whether in fact the rejected taxation agreements, or others which may replace them, are the real danger to autonomy which they are painted to be. Sharp conflicts of opinion between Quebec and the rest of Canada have arisen on this point. Other provinces find it difficult to believe that a French-Canadian Prime Minister of Canada, or the Quebec members of the Senate and House of Commons, would have approved the tax arrangements had they contained a betrayal of Quebec's rights. The general view outside Quebec seems to be that some such form of financial co-operation among all the Canadian governments is essential for the economic well-being of the whole country, and that any province that attempts to "go it alone" will not only injure its own people but others as well. The smaller and poorer provinces in particular want a federal policy which redistributes national income through federal support of social insurances and direct subsidies to provincial governments. The opposition of so powerful a province as Quebec could mean the collapse of national plans and a general free-for-all in which the existing inequalities of regions and classes would be greatly accentuated.

From the Quebec point of view, however, the problem is not at bottom economic. Or rather, its economic aspects are not as important as its cultural implications. To be subsidized is to be in some degree

[12]As reported in *Montreal Gazette*, Aug. 23, 1955.

dependent. The donor is psychologically and politically stronger than the recipient of the gift; hence if Quebec accepts money from Ottawa, the dual-state theory of Canadian government is difficult to maintain. In receiving subsidies the people of Quebec learn to look outside their borders for assistance; their local loyalty is weakened; they become less defensive of their special position. If it is pointed out that subsidies have always existed in the constitution, and that they were an integral part of the agreement of 1867, obviously not destructive of provincial autonomy, the reply is that the original provinces were weak and undeveloped, not obliged to assume the wide functions of their present governments, and not faced with the challenge to autonomy which now threatens them. The very strength of the present centripetal forces justifies further measures for safeguarding local self-government. Even though some "efficiency," from the purely economic point of view, be lost, the value of autonomy, particularly for Quebec, far outweighs this cost.[13]

Even deeper motives can be sensed in Quebec's hesitancy to commit herself to certain forms of tax centralization. Long-range fears, as much as present dangers, compel caution. A particular scheme, such as the tax rental agreements, on its surface may appear fair and reasonable. It avoids dual taxation, supports national fiscal policy, and redistributes wealth to the poorer provinces. What can be said against it? The answer often given in Quebec is that it is the beginning of a road, the end of which no one can foresee. Today there may be nothing but benefit in the scheme, tomorrow the strength of Quebec may be undermined beyond repair. Such is the line of thought which has produced a refusal to co-operate in national fiscal plans even when this refusal has cost Quebec millions of dollars of revenue. And since fiscal needs constantly increase, the government of Quebec chooses to impose dual income taxation and to demand that the federal government withdraw from direct taxation fields which the province wishes to enter. Unless Ottawa moves out there is little room for Quebec to move in, since under the law a province has no priority in the exercise of the direct taxation to which it is restricted.[14] But if the federal government is obliged to withdraw from a given field of taxation at provincial request, then not only does national fiscal policy go by the board but a doctrine of nullification or veto by provinces over Parlia-

[13]This danger is not felt exclusively in Quebec: see, e.g., H. F. Angus, "Two Restrictions on Provincial Autonomy," 21 *Canadian Journal of Economics and Political Science* (1955), at pp. 445–6.

[14]See discussion in F. R. Scott, "The Constitutional Background of Taxation Agreements," 2 *McGill Law Journal* (1955–6), at p. 1.

ment becomes part of Canadian constitutional practice, regardless of what the law may be. It was on this point that Mr. St. Laurent stood firm when Mr. Duplessis first imposed his provincial income tax in 1954, and on which the Quebec government eventually gave way by removing the claim to priority from the statute.[15]

In every federal state the division of taxing powers and public revenues presents grave difficulties. In the United States, Australia, and Switzerland, as well as in Canada where they are part of the original law of the constitution, subsidies to the states and cantons have had to be instituted.[16] Yet these countries have remained federal in form, though the central authority has grown stronger. Quebec's claim for fiscal autonomy is by no means peculiar to herself; it is echoed by other Canadian provinces and in other federations. But in her case it takes on added strength and colour because it becomes part of the general defence of a minority culture.

Conflicts over Education

Some of the most acute conflicts in the field of public law have occurred over the educational provisions of the Canadian constitution. The story is a long one, reaching back to the vain attempts of the English not long after the cession to establish the Royal Institution for the Advancement of Learning as a general educational system for the province. Against this unifying tendency Quebec stood firm, claiming the right to separate French parochial schools. In the course of the constitutional evolution since those days Canada has achieved a peculiar school system which varies from province to province and which ranges in theory from the complete separation of Protestant and Catholic schools, as in Quebec, to the notion of the single, undenominational, state-supported public school, as in British Columbia. In between are several variations on these two themes, with varying types of separate schools in Ontario, Saskatchewan, Alberta, and the North-west Territories. Newfoundland has added a new note with five kinds of religious schools receiving state support: Catholic, Anglican, United Church, Seventh Day Adventists, and Salvation Army. Needless to say, the Canadian constitution does not contain a fundamental rule barring "an establishment of religion," as in the opening clause of the First Amendment to the United States Constitution.

The conflicts that arise in this area are numerous and stem from

[15]See amendment in Statutes of Quebec, 1954–5, c. 15.
[16]K. C. Wheare, *Federal Government* (3rd. ed.), pp. 115–16.

different motives. They are by no means exclusively disagreements between French Catholics and English Protestants. Sometimes English-speaking Catholics are ranged against French-speaking co-religionists, as in the lawsuit which tested the validity of Ontario's attempt to restrict the use of French as the language of instruction.[17] Sometimes two different churches are allied in their opposition to a school law, as in the attack upon the Manitoba School Act of 1890 when Anglicans and Catholics joined forces.[18] The Jewish communities in Quebec have difficulty in fitting themselves into a system divided into two Christian groups, and some Doukhobors refuse to send their children to any school, a refusal that results (in British Columbia) in the forceful separation of children from parents. Ontario law still has provision for separate schools for "coloured people," though the last of such schools ceased to exist in 1891.[19] The heterogeneity of the Canadian population, which steadily increases as new immigrants arrive, produces many claims on provincial governments for educational privileges.

From the point of view of Quebec, however, there is one claim which has priority over all others, and that is the right of the French-Canadian minority in all the other provinces to possess as fair a system of separate schools as exists for both Catholics and Protestants in Quebec. Spokesmen for Quebec take justifiable pride in pointing out the favourable situation of the Protestant minority in the province, and claim that no other provincial government treats the minority so well. They contend that the principle of separate schools, written into section 93 of the constitution, while not universally extended in the early days to all Canada, should be admitted in every province as the French-speaking population grows. They have been bitterly disappointed in certain leading court decisions which have denied their claims, notably with regard to separate schools in New Brunswick and Manitoba, to the use of the French language in Ontario, and to the distribution of school funds in Ontario. They feel aggrieved that British Columbia does not accept their views. Gérard Filion, Editor of *Le Devoir*, lists the inequalities in the school system as one of the great causes of friction between the two races, and he adds somewhat optimistically: "On the day when every French-Canadian, wherever he may be in the country, enjoys the same advantages and the same privileges as his English-speaking compatriot, the last obstacle to the unity of the country will have disappeared."[20]

[17]*Ottawa Separate Schools* v. *Mackell*, [1917] A.C. 62.
[18]*Winnipeg* v. *Barret*, *Winnipeg* v. *Logan*: [1892] A.C. 445.
[19]Information supplied by the Ontario Dept. of Education.
[20]In *Saturday Night*, Nov. 24, 1954.

The opponents of this view employ much the same argument as can be heard in the United States against the claims of parochial schools to a share of tax revenues, though in Canada there is no constitutional barrier to such payments. The need to develop a common sense of citizenship, and to overcome the racial and religious hatreds that too often follow segregation, exists in Canada as well as in the United States. Groups that feel unable to use state schools on conscientious grounds are at liberty to set up and pay for private schools. A belief in the advisability of the complete separation of church and state is firmly held in many parts of Canada, though not written into the fundamental law. The conflict of ideas here is one of principle, not easy to resolve since there is no common point of departure. In the result, Canada remains partly committed to separate schools, and partly not.

The differences of view over schools reach out to other fields of education. Universities in Canada have traditionally been established or regulated by provincial legislation. Some, like McGill, have a royal charter antedating Confederation; others, like the Université de Montréal, have both a civil and a pontifical charter. All are having difficulty in securing the necessary finances. In 1951 the federal Government, which had long been making special grants for particular forms of university research, adopted a recommendation of the Massey Commission and embarked upon a scheme of subsidization for all universities based on a formula equally applied in all the provinces. In Quebec, a special committee appointed by the Quebec Government supervised the distribution of the funds. All Quebec universities at first accepted the plan, but after one year the Quebec Government refused to participate further and declared that Ottawa's subsidies were an invasion of the province's exclusive jurisdiction over education. As no other province took this view, the result has been that all universities save those in Quebec have continued to receive federal funds. Meanwhile the Quebec Government has instituted payments on a year-to-year basis to replace those lost by its own institutions. This additional drain on its resources is urged as a further argument for exclusive use of the direct tax fields allotted to it under the constitution.

The same dispute goes beyond school and university into the realm of culture generally. Is "culture" a provincial matter? The very idea seems to denude the word of any meaningful content, yet many defenders of provincial autonomy claim that it is included by analogy in the term "education," over which provinces have the main jurisdiction. It would follow that Ottawa should not assist at all in the development of the arts and sciences, or in adult education. Yet radio and television broadcasting have been ascribed to federal jurisdiction by legal interpretation of the constitution, and federal responsibility for the whole Northwest Territories and for Canada's 160 thousand Indians as well as its need for trained personnel in every branch of government are patent facts. Legally there is no invasion of any legislative field in a province if the federal Crown, legal proprietor of public funds, offers a subsidy to any institution or group engaged in educational or cultural work, since the making of gifts is not the same as the enacting of laws.[21] Moreover, as the Massey Report said: "If the Federal Government is to renounce its right to associate itself with other social groups, public and private, in the general education of Canadian citizens, it denies its intellectual and moral purpose, the complete conception of the common good is lost, and Canada, as such, becomes a materialistic society."

Despite these facts and this argument, opposition from Quebec is credited with the prevention of the establishment of the Canada Council, as recommended by the Massey Report, thus leaving Canada without any arts council or any national commission for UNESCO.[22] Meanwhile Canadian artists and writers must rely on the generous assistance of American foundations and such help as may come from provincial institutions (among which the Quebec Government is most generous) supplemented by federal aid in the form of radio and television contracts or fellowships paid out of blocked European currencies. This *Kulturkampf* has its casualties in fewer creative artists and lost cultural opportunities.

Disputes over Language

The law of the Canadian constitution recognizes English and French as the two official languages of the country, within certain limits. They are on an equal footing as regards their use in the Parliament of Canada, in federal statutes, and in federal courts. Since these statutes and courts may operate anywhere in the country, every province is in this sense bilingual. But in provincial legislatures, statutes, and courts outside Quebec, English is the sole official language. This results from the wording of section 133 of the B.N.A. Act, which reads as follows:

> 133. Either the English or the French Language may be used by any Person in the Debates of the Houses of the Parliament of Canada and of the

[21]Cf. n. 14.

[22]On November 12, 1956, Mr. St. Laurent announced that his Government intended to establish the Council.

Houses of the Legislature of Quebec; and both these Languages shall be used in the respective Records and Journals of those Houses; and either of those Languages may be used by any Person or in any Pleading or Process in or issuing from any Court of Canada established under this Act, and in or from all or any of the Courts of Quebec.

The Acts of the Parliament of Canada and of the Legislature of Quebec shall be printed and published in both those Languages.

Thus the simple description of Canada as a "bilingual country" is misleading, unless understood in the special Canadian sense.

The incompleteness in Canadian bilingualism is a source of irritation in Quebec, just as any extension of French annoys certain elements in the English-speaking provinces. Attacks upon the whole notion of bilingualism have come from several parts of the country. These two languages, which happen today to be the two working languages of the United Nations, are frequently felt to be a handicap to be overcome, rather than a source of cultural richness. Thus in 1890 Manitoba repealed that section of its original constitution which had made French an official language for the province. In 1877 Ottawa introduced French into the Northwest Territories, but in 1891 permitted the Legislative Assembly of the Territories to decide the question itself; and in 1892 the latter abolished the use of French for debates—a further example of how local autonomy may be used to restrict minority rights.[23] Ontario's decision in 1912 to limit the use of French as a language of instruction in her schools raised a storm of protest, not alleviated by court rulings that the law was constitutional. In 1937, Mr. Duplessis put through an amendment to make the French text of the Civil Code and statutes of Quebec prevail over the English in case of conflict, but as this was clearly contrary to section 133 of the B.N.A. Act he was induced to repeal the law, so that the two languages remain on an equal footing in Quebec.

French has thus lost some of the status it once held in the law of western Canada. On the other hand the federal control over broadcasting has brought French programmes into areas which, had radio been a provincial matter, would not have permitted it. Strong pressure from Quebec, and a somewhat more rational attitude to bilingualism, have resulted in the establishment by the Canadian Broadcasting Corporation of French-language stations on the Prairies. A French network has been set up, bringing programmes to French minorities far from their homeland. Radio and television are important influences in the extension of the French language in Canada and of English in Quebec. Since, however, the French are concentrated in the Quebec

[23]French continues, however, as an official language in the courts of the Territories.

region and represent less than 30 per cent of the total Canadian population, a widespread familiarity with the second official language is hardly to be anticipated, however desirable it may be.

Civil Liberties

The Canadian constitution does not contain a bill of rights such as is found in the American and other written constitutions. Some constitutional guarantees, such as those for separate schools, the two languages, and annual sessions of Parliament, are in the text of the B.N.A. Act, but freedom of religion, speech, assembly, and the press are not mentioned in the written law. As in England, they remain sacred by tradition but at the mercy of legislation. The only question for Canada is which legislature has jurisdiction—the federal or the provincial; the rights themselves are seemingly not beyond parliamentary modification.

Perhaps nowhere in the public law of Canada is the difference of outlook between French and English more marked than in respect to civil liberties. The order of values is not the same in the two peoples; the tradition and situation of Quebec make its people emphasize their own minority rights at all times, while in other provinces the stress is much more on individual rights. The "village Hampden" that Wolfe was reputedly hearing about as he was rowed under the cliffs of Quebec in September 1759 was unknown to New France, where representative institutions, even on the municipal level, had never existed. The Declaration of the Rights of Man, France's great contribution to modern liberal thought, came after the cession, and was then so closely associated with anti-clericalism as to render it ever afterwards suspect by the Catholic Church in Canada. On the other hand, English public law had not worked out any theory of minority rights guaranteed by law.

The British conquest was the first revolutionary experience French Canada had ever had, and though the new sovereign soon introduced an elected Legislative Assembly, and replaced the *lettre de cachet* by Habeas Corpus, the cession created racial tensions not favourable to the growth of an indigenous sense of personal freedom. Individual liberties thenceforth had an English face, and the democracy thus begun was discovered by the French to possess unexpected limitations when it seemed likely to transfer power to their hands. Lower Canada's fight for responsible government, as Durham rightly perceived, was a struggle not of principles but of races, though democratic slogans were used. The prime purpose was to assert minority rights against the English, rather than, as in Upper Canada, to secure personal freedom from arbitrary power of any kind. Since those days the concept of the "état de siège" has persisted in Quebec and in French minorities in other provinces, making them subordinate individual liberty to the common racial goal, and to ostracize those of their own group who deviate from the official line of action.

In the matter of religious toleration, similar differences of outlook appear. No Protestant was ever allowed into New France after 1627; Protestantism was the religion of the conquerors which the French were forced to tolerate. The British, intolerant of Catholicism at home, were obliged to give legal status to Catholics in Quebec by the sheer necessities of Canadian life as well as by the need for allies against the growing threat of revolt in America. Toleration in these circumstances did not carry much conviction. The strong Catholic tradition in Quebec has remained ultramontane rather than Gallican, and authoritarian rather than liberal. Quebec has seen in parliamentary institutions a valuable instrument for asserting cultural differences, while the English have accepted toleration and minority rights in inverse proportion to their distance from Quebec.

These various strands have shaped and are still shaping the evolution of the laws relating to civil liberties. Examples can be found on both sides of a disregard for the types of fundamental rights proclaimed in the Universal Declaration of Human Rights of the United Nations. Only since the Second World War, for instance, have the federal election laws removed several forms of racial discrimination, and Ottawa's attempt to deport some 4,000 Canadian Japanese in 1945–6 will stand as a solemn reminder that racial prejudice can spring up anywhere in Canada. Quebec did not grant votes to women until 1941, and her Civil Code still subjects married women to serious incapacities. But while Ottawa and various provincial governments have been removing discrimination from their laws, Quebec has been moving in the opposite direction. Recently, certain Quebec statutes have curtailed the traditional freedom of religion, of speech, and of the press in a manner which has marked off its legislation sharply from that of other provinces, and has created conflicts both in public opinion and in the courts.

These statutes were all introduced by Premier Duplessis and backed by his Union Nationale party. The most notorious of them, adopted in 1937, and popularly known as the Padlock Act, makes it an offence to propagate "communism or bolshevism" by any means in a "house" in the province, or to publish or distribute any literature propagating or even "tending to propagate" these undefined doctrines. Any house may be padlocked, and the occupant evicted, by the Attorney General "on satisfactory proof" that the Act is being violated, without any notice or trial in a court of law; to remove the padlock the owner must institute an action in court and prove either that the house was not in fact being so used or that he was ignorant of it. Thus there is punishment without trial, and the burden of proof is cast upon persons presumably innocent. Since the federal Government refused to disallow the Act, it remained in force and has been applied on numerous occasions to activities of suspected communist groups. Its constitutionality was upheld by the Quebec courts, but a final appeal to the Supreme Court of Canada is pending. While Canadian opinion, both in Quebec and outside, is overwhelmingly opposed to the spread of communism, this type of legislation is in direct conflict with traditional concepts of freedom and nothing similar to it has existed in Canadian law in peacetime.

Other examples may be given of recent Quebec legislation restricting ancient civil liberties. A provincial statute enacted in 1947 enables municipalities to prohibit the distribution on their streets of any literature or pamphlets without the permission of a municipal chief of police. Thus a local policeman becomes a press censor. Many municipalities have adopted such by-laws, and even candidates in federal elections have found themselves obliged to submit their election literature to the police for approval.[24] The prohibition appears to be aimed at the activities of Jehovah's Witnesses and communists; like all such laws, in striking at minorities it deprives everyone of rights. In 1950 the Quebec legislature adopted the Act Respecting Publications and Public Morals, by which the Board of Cinema Censors may issue a censure order against magazines and certain other publications which are found to contain "immoral illustrations," whereupon all copies may be seized by the police with or without warrant. Another Quebec statute enabled municipalities to close commercial establishments on certain Catholic feast days, whether or not they were owned by Catholics. Montreal's attempt to apply the law was, however, held unconstitutional by the Supreme Court of Canada, which overruled the Quebec Court of Appeal, and the statute itself was held to be criminal law, a subject outside provincial powers under the B.N.A. Act.[25] Still other Quebec statutes have seriously restricted the rights of trade unions. One bars all strikes and lock-outs, and imposes compulsory arbitration, in all "public services" in the province, including

[24]See F. R. Scott, "Correspondence," 31 *Canadian Bar Review* (1953), at p. 591; also *Dame Dionne* v. *The Municipal Court*, [1956] S.C. 289.

[25]See *Henry Birks & Sons* (Montreal) Ltd. *et al.* v. *City of Montreal*, [1955] S.C.R. 799.

municipal and school corporations, public transportation systems, and public utilities. No other province in Canada feels such drastic curbs to be necessary. Another Quebec law requires that the certificate of recognition of all trade unions must be refused or revoked if they tolerate so much as one organizer or officer who adheres "to a communist party or movement," thus limiting the unions' freedom to choose its own leaders. And in 1954, the Freedom of Worship Act, dating from before Confederation, was amended so as to narrow considerably the toleration hitherto allowed.[26]

While these Quebec laws are in conflict with traditional freedoms in Canada, provisions not so dissimilar have been found in other parts of the country at various times. Certainly the Quebec community is not alone in reacting against communists, Jehovah's Witnesses, and trade unions. British Columbia prevented a qualified student from practising law because he was a communist;[27] the Labour Relations Board of Nova Scotia refused to certify a union whose Secretary-Treasurer was a communist;[28] Prince Edward Island in 1948 adopted a law amounting almost to the total prohibition of trade unions;[29] Alberta has passed a statute limiting the right of Hutterite colonies to purchase land.[30] The Quebec laws, particularly the Padlock Act, are severe, but may well represent a temporary reaction to a new situation. There are some signs that within Quebec society itself, particularly among trade unionists, there is a growing awareness of the need for protecting individual rights against Quebec authorities. Industrial disputes place the French-Canadian worker in opposition to French-Canadian employers and provincial police. Racial categories break down before economic facts. Catholic teachers once went on strike in Montreal against the Catholic School Commission, and their union fought valiantly, though unsuccessfully, for its rights to collective bargaining.[31]

[26]Statutes of Quebec, 1953–4, c. 15. The amendment forbids "abusive or insulting attacks against the practice of a religious profession."

[27]E. Meredith, "Communism and the B.C. Bar," 28 *Canadian Bar Review* (1950), at p. 893.

[28]*Smith & Rhuland Ltd.* v. *The Queen,* [1953] 2 S.C.R. 95; 32 *Canadian Bar Review* (1954), at pp. 85, 353.

[29]E. A. Forsey, "The P.E.I. Trade Union Act," 26 *Canadian Bar Review* (1948), at p. 1159.

[30]See Communal Property Act, Statutes of Alberta, 1947, c. 16.

[31]The union, having been illegally decertified by the Quebec Labour Relations Board, won back in the Supreme Court of Canada (overruling the Quebec Court of Appeal) its right to recognition as the bargaining unit, only to have the right taken away by retroactive legislation put through the Quebec legislature. See *Alliance des Professeurs catholiques* v. *Labour Relations Board,* [1953] 2 S.C.R. 140: 2–3 Eliz. 11, c. 11 (Quebec).

Surveying the recent battles over civil liberties which have for the first time been presented to the Quebec courts, it seems fair to say that the judges in Quebec are far more inclined than are the common law judges to uphold the authority of the state as against the individual, though generalizations here must be used with caution. In five recent leading cases, dealing with the definition of sedition,[32] with arbitrary decertification of a trade union,[33] with the control by cities of the distribution of pamphlets,[34] with the liability of police officers for unlawfully disturbing a meeting of Jehovah's Witnesses,[35] and with compulsory observance of Catholic feast days,[36] the Supreme Court of Canada took a more liberal view of private rights than did the Quebec Court of Appeal, which was overruled every time. Two further cases, involving the validity of the Padlock Act[37] and the legality of the cancellation of a liquor licence held by Witnesses of Jehovah[38] seem to show the same support of authority by Quebec judges. It is only to be expected that Quebec courts, like any others, will reflect in large part the prevailing attitudes of the community from which they are drawn; and that community is still highly authoritarian.

Conclusion

It is necessary to repeat what was said earlier about the relation between areas of conflict and areas of co-operation. Conflict in any acute sense between Quebec and the rest of Canada is the exception, not the rule, but it is often vivid and sometimes profound, and its existence throws light upon the root differences between the two cultures. Within the legal order, cultural conflicts present no different problem from class conflicts or international conflicts; they are one among the many types which it is the purpose of the law to resolve by peaceful means with the minimum of effort. If contained within the bounds of constitutionalism, they are a creative force moulding the law and adapting it to the satisfaction of larger numbers of people.

[32]The *Boucher* case: [1951] S.C.R. 265; 29 *Canadian Bar Review* (1951), at p. 193.

[33]The *Alliance* case: [1953] 2 S.C.R. 140; 31 *Canadian Bar Review* (1953), at p. 821.

[34]The *Saumur* case: [1953] 2 S.C.R. 299.

[35]The *Chaput* case: [1955] S.C.R. 834.

[36]The *Birks* case: see n. 25.

[37]The *Switzman* case: Padlock Act upheld by Quebec Court of Appeal, [1954] Q.B. 421. Appeal pending in Supreme Court.

[38]The *Roncarelli* case: cancellation upheld by Quebec Court of Appeal, [1956] Q.B. 447. Appeal pending in Supreme Court.

Canadian public law, with its mixture of English and Canadian rules, has shown itself to be sufficiently humane in principle and adaptable in practice to suit the needs of most Canadians, as is evidenced by the small number of substantive changes made in the constitution since 1867. That the French minorities however, still feel dissatisfied on certain issues has already been indicated, and conflicts of opinion about the nature of Canadian federalism are as acute today as they have ever been.

What immediately lies ahead of Canadians is the problem of completing the "nationalization" of the constitution. The B.N.A. Act remains a British statute; its very name belongs to an age that is past. Fundamental changes in its provisions cannot be made wholly within Canada, for the quaint procedure known as the "Joint Address" of the Senate and House of Commons to the United Kingdom Parliament for proposed amendments has survived Canada's achievement of nationhood. Until a new procedure is agreed upon for these amendments, capable of being carried out inside the country, legal sovereignty cannot be finally transferred from England to Canada. The Constitutional Conference of 1950 failed to achieve this solution because Quebec insisted on the right of veto over every amendment affecting "property and civil rights," though the other provinces were quite willing to entrench the minority rights clauses.[39] Hence the English-French complex is responsible for the continuing element of colonialism in Canada's relations with Great Britain. The fear of Ottawa is seemingly greater in Quebec than the fear of London, though since London by constitutional convention must always act at Ottawa's request, the retention of the sovereignty of Westminster does not remove the danger of overriding by the majority.[40] By tacit agreement the political parties now leave in abeyance a question fraught with so much danger of racial conflict. Perhaps the drafting of a Canadian bill of rights, placing fundamental freedoms as well as minority rights beyond the risk of diminution without the unanimous consent of all the provinces, might provide a basis on which a reasonably flexible amending process for other parts of the constitution might be established, and the legislative independence of the country finally secured.

1957

[39]See the two volumes of *Proceedings of the Constitutional Conference of Federal and Provincial Governments* (Ottawa, 1950).

[40]Despite the contrary argument in Gérin-Lajoie, *Constitutional Amendment in Canada*, and in the same author's "Du Pouvoir d'amendement constitutionnel," 29 *Canadian Bar Review* (1951), p. 1136 at p. 1149.

Conflits nés de la coexistence juridique au Canada

LOUIS BAUDOUIN

Faculté de Droit, Université McGill

LES DONNÉES DU PROBLÈME

NÉ DANS UNE ATMOSPHÈRE CANADIENNE-FRANÇAISE, reflétant à l'époque où il fut promulgué les mœurs des habitants de cette province, le Code civil de la province de Québec (1866) porte en soi les germes d'une pensée dont on a trop souvent tendance à méconnaître hors de ses frontières géographiques, voire même parfois à l'intérieur de celles-ci, la richesse et la fécondité.

La codification du droit privé dans la province de Québec, fait français par excellence, ne s'est jamais entièrement alignée, dans sa vie réelle, dans le sillage du pur droit français. Historiquement parlant et tout naturellement, droit de cité devait être accordé dans ce Code au droit anglais, quoique dans une mesure plus restreinte. L'empreinte anglaise, fruit de la Cession, s'est en effet marquée dans certains secteurs de la vie juridique de cette province désormais coupée de la Mère-patrie. Ayant reçu mission en 1865 de codifier le droit encore en vigueur, les codificateurs restèrent fidèles à ce devoir. Ils inclurent dans des articles du Code des textes d'origine sinon d'inspiration anglaises. L'apport anglais s'est manifesté notamment dans les textes sur le droit de la preuve, dans certains secteurs du droit commercial civilisé, notamment dans celui de la fiducie du droit testamentaire par la double adoption du testament dérivé du droit anglais, et du principe de la pleine liberté testamentaire, dans le domaine de l'exécution des contrats par le principe de la *specific performance.* La jurisprudence depuis la Cession a servi de canal naturel à l'infiltration de certaines formes de pensée anglaise dans le domaine de la responsabilité civile.

Le Code de la province de Québec est donc par essence même et historiquement, le produit de deux expressions de formes de pensées juridiques dont la dominante certes est canadienne-française, mais dont la mineure, canadienne-anglaise, a sa part d'influence qu'on ne saurait méconnaître sous peine de commettre de graves erreurs sur l'intelligence de ce pays.

Un étranger – j'entends un non-Canadien ou même un néo-Canadien de trop fraîche date – ne saurait saisir les subtilités de la pensée juridique canadienne-française dans cette province sans tenir compte tout d'abord de sa traduction vivante : le Code. L'existence même de celui-ci est sans doute la manifestation la plus éclatante de la personnalité canadienne-française au sein d'une majorité canadienne de langue, de pensée et de mœurs canadiennes-anglaises. Mais, tout l'arrière-plan de ce Code est éclairé par la vie politique et judiciaire dont cette province a été le théâtre depuis qu'elle existe géographiquement et qu'elle s'est intégrée politiquement dans la communauté canadienne, sans perdre pour cela certaines de ses caractéristiques fondamentales. On a écrit : « Il y a deux miracles dans l'histoire du Canada. Le premier, c'est la survivance du Canada français, et le second, la survivance du Canada[1]. » On peut ajouter sur le plan plus précis du droit privé : il y a le miracle de la survivance du droit privé de la province de Québec, qui a su résister parfois à certaines lames de fond du droit anglais, soit en absorbant certains de leurs remous, soit en brisant la hauteur de certaines vagues sur le récif du Code.

Ce miracle s'est opéré dans des conditions d'autant plus remarquables que tout l'appareil judiciaire canadien est un fait de création anglaise. Le magistrat canadien est nommé suivant le système anglais, parmi les avocats les plus réputés. Ce n'est pas un magistrat de carrière, comme en France par exemple. Les décisions judiciaires de ce pays sont rendues suivant le mode anglais, le juge parle à la première personne, il découvre sa pensée, il donne une véritable consultation judiciaire. On peut étendre ici la maxime anglaise. « Our judges are our jurists ». En outre, le Comité judiciaire du Conseil privé, jusqu'en 1949, avait le dernier mot dans les affaires judiciaires canadiennes. Les juges de la province de Québec, comme leurs collègues canadiens-anglais, attachaient aux avis du Conseil privé une sorte d'autorité de fait issue d'une tradition ancienne, que d'aucuns auraient souhaité voir élevée à la hauteur d'un principe véritable aussi strict que celui du droit judiciaire anglais.

Dès lors, sous le manteau du précédent et du *stare decisis*, le droit privé de la province de Québec s'est parfois trouvé indirectement

[1]F. R. Scott, « Canada et Canada français », *Esprit* (Paris) (août-septembre 1952), p. 178.

soumis à un travail d'érosion dont on ne semblait guère prendre ombrage au lendemain de la Codification.

La pensée juridique au Québec semble donc s'aligner, en partie au moins, sur la pensée anglaise dont elle épouse, dans le domaine judiciaire, certaines formes expresses de raisonnement qui vont jusqu'à l'adoption de l'*obiter dictum*, sorte de doute émis par le magistrat sur un point de droit. On a pu écrire que cet usage dans les affaires judiciaires de la province de Québec « n'ajoute rien à la force de l'exposé des motifs, dont il embrume l'éclat; il n'y a là qu'une faiblesse qu'il peut accentuer ».

Ainsi donc, le Code civil de Québec, héritier de l'ancien droit français, modelé sur le Code Napoléon, parsemé de notions de droit anglais, devait-il engendrer à son tour dans sa vie judiciaire, des conflits aigus de pensée juridique. Le fait qu'un texte soit d'origine française n'implique pas en effet nécessairement que seule l'interprétation française doive prévaloir. Un texte d'origine ou d'inspiration anglaise n'emporte pas forcément de son côté une interprétation d'obédience anglaise.

Avant que d'entrer dans le détail de ces conflits qui sont particulièrement significatifs, notamment dans le domaine du droit de la famille, des contrats en général, de la responsabilité civile ou dans certains actes juridiques spéciaux tels que le mandat, le trust ou le testament, une note prédomine dont il faut souligner l'importance majeure. Son règne sans doute a-t-il duré jusqu'au jour où le Conseil privé est demeuré le dernier échelon semi-judiciaire des affaires canadiennes. Pourtant l'état d'âme qu'elle a pu créer, même après la rupture du nœud gordien avec Londres, au sein des juridictions québécoises, n'est pas près de s'éteindre. Celui qui vit dans cette province peut mesurer en effet combien le facteur temps, si précieux pour la lente évolution voire même la stagnation du droit anglais, prend un sens identique au Québec dans le domaine juridique.

Jusqu'en 1949, date de l'abolition des appels au Conseil privé, une tendance générale prévalait au sujet de l'interprétation à donner aux textes du Code civil. Les Lords en Conseil privé étaient naturellement enclins à interpréter comme un statut le Code civil de la province de Québec; ils lui réservaient les principes d'interprétation que les cours anglaises réservent à tout statut purement britannique.

C'est ainsi, notamment que Lord Summer dans l'affaire *Vandry*[2], espèce relevant du droit de la responsabilité civile des articles 1053 et suivants du Code civil de Québec, n'a pas craint d'affirmer que : « the

[2]*Vandry* v. *Quebec Railway Light Heat and Power*, [1920] A.C. 622.

statutory character of the civil Code of Lower Canada must always be borne in mind ». Lord Moulton dans l'affaire *Despatie Tremblay*[3] (droit du mariage) affirmait ce qui suit : « The Codifiers have no doubt the task of examining the various authorities on each point... but when they have done this, and the Code has become a Statute the question whether they were right or wrong in their conclusion becomes immaterial. From then forth, the Law is determined by what is found in the Code and not by a consideration of the conclusions which have been framed. » On peut lire également dans l'affaire *Symes* v. *Cuvellier*[4] : « The only authority which the learned Counsel could invoke is that of the Commissioners charged with the preparation of the Civil Code... this authority is no doubt entitled to respect, but the opinion of the Commissioners has not the weight of a judicial opinion pronounced after discussion and argument. »

La plupart des juridictions anglaises de Grande-Bretagne, placées devant un statut anglais, éprouvent par tradition historique une méfiance certaine à l'égard des travaux préparatoires des lois. Elles font alors prévaloir le plus souvent la lettre du statut sur son esprit. L'interprétation judiciaire anglaise se situe donc aux antipodes de l'interprétation française, et même de l'interprétation canadienne-française, lorsque c'est le Code civil de la province de Québec qui en est l'objet.

Il a fallu un long et patient travail de mise au point entrepris par certains hauts magistrats et juristes canadiens-français, dont l'Hon. Juge Mignault a été l'incarnation même, pour détruire cette tendance interprétative réservée au Code civil de Québec :

> Le Code civil ne doit pas être interprété comme un simple statut; il est beaucoup plus que cela, et j'aime encore moins qu'on lui applique le système de l'interprétation purement littérale comme le voudrait Lord Summer... L'interprétation littérale du Code aboutirait à le tuer... elle empêcherait le développement de notre droit civil et l'immobiliserait dans des formules rigides interdisant tout espoir de progrès, à moins que ces formules ne soient sans cesse élargies par l'intermédiaire du législateur[5].

En orientant l'interprétation du Code civil de Québec en ce sens, les Lords ont cru en toute bonne foi se conformer à l'esprit même du droit civil. Le Code, en effet, se présente en livres, chapitres, titres ou sections, formellement au moins, comme un statut. Son titre préliminaire qui contient des définitions d'ordre juridique, n'est-il pas dans sa présentation même le frère du *glossary* propre à tout statut anglais ?

[3][1921] 1 A.C. 702. [4][1880] 5 A.C. 138.

[5]« L'Avenir de notre droit civil », *Revue du droit* (1923), p. 56 à p. 65 et p. 104 à p. 116 *passim*.

Sans doute cette attitude des Lords se justifie-t-elle au point de vue formel. Mais les juristes canadiens-français leur ont démontré que les cloisonnements du Code ne sont pas des cloisons étanches: ils ne sont que les parties d'un tout. Le plus souvent, l'absence d'une règle précise à l'intérieur d'une des cloisons peut et doit être suppléée par analogie avec d'autres règles d'un caractère ou d'un esprit semblable qui se trouvent dans d'autres secteurs. Il existe dans ce Code une sorte de plasma qui circule à travers tous ses tissus organiques. Les déficiences du Code se comblent à l'aide du Code lui-même.

L'attitude du Conseil privé a pesé de tout son poids sur la vie juridique du droit civil de Québec dès sa naissance officielle. Celui-ci a parfois été sauvé grâce à certaines interprétations de la Cour suprême du Canada dont les réactions ont été d'autant plus dignes de remarque qu'une autorité considérable était attachée par toutes les juridictions canadiennes aux avis du Conseil privé. Un usage judiciaire, par la lenteur même avec laquelle il pénètre, répond une fois établi de façon si intense aux besoins ressentis qu'il est difficile sinon impossible de le mettre en échec. Depuis la suppression des appels au Conseil privé, les décisions de la Cour suprême du Canada vont sans doute se revêtir à leur tour d'une importance capitale. L'autorité qui s'y attache est d'autant plus considérable pour l'avenir que la Cour se prononce sur des problèmes juridiques qui sont nés de la Common Law ou du droit civil de la province de Québec. Cette situation de fait permet de comprendre que tout juge de la Cour suprême, comme ses collègues de Québec, est en quelque sorte un comparativiste forcé et né. Il se fait dans l'esprit de ces magistrats une interpénétration profonde des deux manières de pensée, la pensée propre au droit civil et celle propre à la Common Law. Si le dualisme de systèmes juridiques dont le Code civil de Québec est gros engendre des crises, il ne faut pas le regretter. Celles-ci sont des plus instructives et riches de conséquences. Ce sont elles que nous voudrions mettre en vedette, car elles seules permettent de saisir sur le vif toutes les subtilités de la pensée juridique découvrant d'immenses perspectives d'enrichissement intellectuel et d'ordre pratique à la solution de problèmes qui participent des deux grands systèmes juridiques. Le problème québécois devient un problème qui se pose à l'échelon international.

Les conflits de pensée dans le domaine du droit de la famille et des contrats sont assez significatifs.

Tout récemment une décision de la Cour suprême[6] mettant en jeu le principe de la puissance paternelle au Québec révélait l'existence

[6]*Donaldson* v. *Taillon,* [1953] 1 S.C.R. 257.

d'un conflit latent de pensée juridique entre juges canadiens de langue anglaise et leurs collègues de langue française au sein de cette juridiction. Un père avait, quelques années auparavant, délégué l'exercice de sa puissance paternelle sur l'un de ses enfants à un membre de sa famille. Il demandait à recouvrer définitivement l'exercice de sa puissance paternelle. A la majorité des voix des juges canadiens-anglais, la Cour devait décider que : « The natural right of parents to the custody of their children as sanctioned by article 243 C.c. is displaced where it is shown that they are unfit or incapable ».

Le droit positif de la province de Québec s'accomode en matière de puissance paternelle de la notion d'Habeas Corpus. La pratique judiciaire dans la province de Québec donne droit de cité à l'Habeas Corpus qui devient l'instrument propre à régler les conflits de ce genre. Mais la scission qui s'est opérée en l'espèce entre les magistrats canadiens-anglais et les magistrats canadiens-français vient de ce que les premiers ont méconnu, en toute bonne foi, les caractères fondamentaux de la puissance paternelle du droit québécois, trop imbus qu'ils sont de la pure liberté individuelle. Dans l'esprit d'un juge canadien-anglais, un père qui ne s'est pas préoccupé pendant sept ans du sort de son enfant est moralement coupable. Un juge canadien-français pensera certainement la même chose; mais la physionomie juridique de la puissance paternelle en droit civil ne se dégage pas de cette simple constatation d'ordre purement moral. La puissance paternelle est, dans cette province, une véritable institution. Le père de son vivant l'exerce seul, il ne peut être déchu de son exercice qu'à titre exceptionnel et pour des motifs graves. Il faut qu'il en soit véritablement indigne. Le terme d'indignité s'attache à des faits d'une gravité exceptionnelle qui conduisent, s'ils sont prouvés, à la déchéance des droits de puissance paternelle. La déchéance a des accents de droit pénal. La stabilité et la cohésion de la famille canadienne-française ne peuvent être ébranlées que pour des motifs extrêmement graves. La décision de la Cour suprême met en évidence ce fait que l'Habeas Corpus, instrument de fabrication anglaise, ne devrait pas aux yeux des magistrats québécois, faire échec aux droits fondamentaux de la puissance paternelle du Code civil de la province de Québec. Le simple instrument de procédure ne devrait pas réagir à ce point sur le fond même du droit.

Il y aurait beaucoup à écrire au sujet des conflits nés dans le domaine des contrats ou des obligations. Il suffit pour s'en convaincre de rappeler ici le conflit, non encore complètement résolu, créé par l'admission, sur pied d'égalité, de la notion de cause et de *consideration* dans les textes du Code civil. L'article 984 du Code civil de Québec donne effectivement droit de cité dans ses deux versions française et anglaise à la notion française de « cause » et à la notion anglaise de « *consideration* ». L'une et l'autre, ou l'une ou l'autre, sont des éléments fondamentaux de la validité des contrats. Sont-elles des notions complémentaires l'une de l'autre, en ce sens que s'il n' y a pas de cause dans un contrat la *consideration* peut y suppléer ou inversement ? Il est curieux de noter qu'il existe au sein même de ce conflit, malgré parfois des divergences de détail dans l'esprit des juristes canadiens, une tendance générale à admettre de fait, en droit québécois, que les deux notions malgré des caractéristiques fondamentales divergentes de pur droit français et de pur droit anglais, paraissent des notions équivalentes en droit québécois[7]. L'esprit juridique d'un Canadien anglais et celui d'un Canadien français s'accommodent parfaitement de l'emploi des deux notions, alors que ni le juriste anglais d'Angleterre ni le juriste français de France ne le peuvent.

Le domaine de l'exécution des obligations est aussi la source d'un conflit qui reste encore mal défini et dans lequel on peut distinguer des tendances soit vers l'alignement au droit anglais, soit vers certaines solutions adoptées par le droit français. Le conflit vient de ce que l'article 1065 du Code civil a traduit l'expression française « l'exécution de l'obligation même » par l'expression anglaise « *specific performance* ». Or, cette notion de *specific performance* est pour le juriste anglais extrêmement spéciale. Elle correspond à une conception contractuelle qui se situe, en principe, à l'opposé des conceptions québécoises et françaises. Le droit anglais prend moins en considération l'exécution des obligations contractuelles envisagées séparément, qu'il n'attache d'importance à l'exécution du contrat pris dans son ensemble. La *specific performance* s'est développée, dans le droit de l'équité, à contre-pied de la Common Law qui n'accorde en principe, en cas d'inexécution, que des dommages-intérêts. Le droit français et le droit québécois semblent apparemment, le premier surtout, considérer que l'inexécution ne se résoud en fait dans la vie pratique que par des dommages-intérêts. Alors que la *specific performance* est devenue le principe général, le droit à l'exécution de l'obligation même, en droit français, semble être resté l'exception. Par un processus fort curieux, mais assez fréquent ici, la confrontation du droit anglais et du droit français a donné naissance à une position originale dans la province de Québec. La pensée du juriste québécois reste en principe fidèle à

[7] *Ross* v. *The Royal Institution for the Advancement of Learning*, [1932] S.C.R. 57.

la pensée du juriste français en ce sens que le problème de la non-exécution est envisagé avant tout sous l'angle obligation plutôt que sous l'angle contrat. Mais la tendance à l'alignement de la pensée québécoise vers le concept anglais de *specific performance* s'est trouvée favorisée par l'adoption en procédure civile québécoise du *contempt of court* et de l'*injunction.* Ce sont là des procédés techniques directement importés d'Angleterre. Tous deux sont l'affirmation indirecte d'un droit, pour tout créancier, d'obtenir l'exécution même de l'obligation avant qu'il ne lui soit accordé en dernier lieu des dommages-intérêts. Alors que le droit français semble faire dépendre davantage le droit à l'exécution même de l'obligation du seul pouvoir discrétionnaire des juges, ce même droit dépend avant tout, ici, de la volonté première du créancier[8]. Parachevant cette évolution, l'esprit juridique québécois a poussé jusqu'à l'extrême les conséquences du système qu'il adopte. En effet, tandis qu'il voit dans la force majeure un obstacle à l'exécution qui libère le débiteur, il proclame cependant que cette exécution s'impose si l'événement, cause de cette force majeure, n'a qu'un caractère momentané. La volonté du magistrat se tend pour essayer de faire aboutir, bon gré mal gré, l'exécution du contrat[9].

Enfin, il faut signaler le conflit qui s'est élevé à propos de la notion d'« *estoppel* », sorte de « fin de non-recevoir » en matière contractuelle. Le fait d'admettre, ici, dans le langage judiciaire, la « fin de non-recevoir » sous le nom d'« *estoppel* », a fini par créer chez certains juristes des deux langues une tendance, instinctive mais fausse, à l'assimilation des deux notions. Il a fallu une décision de la Cour suprême rendue par l'Hon. Juge Mignault pour mettre en garde contre cette erreur.

This does not mean that in many cases, when a person is held to be estopped in England, he would not be held liable in the Province of Quebec. Art. 1730 CC is an example of what in England is referable to the principle of estoppel, and where a person has, by his representation, induced another to alter his position to his prejudice, liability in Quebec could be predicated under art. 1053 and following of the civil code; whether such liability could be relied on as a defence to an action in order to avoid what has been called a circuit d'action, is a proposition which, were it necessary to discuss it here, could, no doubt, be supported on the authority of Pothier. May I merely add, with all deference, that the use of such word as estoppel, coming as it does, from another system of law, should be avoided in Quebec cases, as possibly involving the recognition of a doctrine which, as it exists to-day is no part of the law administered in the Province of Quebec[10].

[8] *Canada Paper* v. *Brown*, [1922] 63 S.C.R. 243.
[9] *Boudreau* v. *Cie Hydraulique de St. Félicien*, [1924] 36 B.R. 455.
[10] *Grace and Cy* v. *C. E. Perras*, [1921] 62 S.C.R. 166, 172.

*
* *

La fréquence même des conflits dans le domaine de la responsabilité civile délictuelle trouve sa justification directe dans le laconisme extrême des quatre seuls articles du Code qui englobent cette matière. Le conflit s'est manifesté tant au sein des juridictions de la province de Québec qu'au sein du Conseil privé jusqu'en 1949.

Ces quatre articles du Code ont reçu leur souffle et leur vie réelle directement de la jurisprudence des cours et tribunaux. C'est pendant cette période de crises que se sont manifestées les tendances contraires de la pensée.

Pour saisir toute l'ampleur du problème, il faut remarquer que l'esprit juridique d'un Canadien anglais s'accommode plus volontiers de tendances sociales ou socialisantes que l'esprit juridique d'un Canadien français. Le juriste canadien-anglais vivant dans la province de Québec éprouve un sentiment naturel de solidarité sociale auquel le fait qu'il y soit minoritaire n'est peut-être pas étranger. C'est en pensant social d'abord que l'unité et la cohésion canadiennes-anglaises peuvent subsister dans cette province.

Par contre, sur le juriste canadien-français qui vit dans la province de Québec, un système juridique qui est le sien propre réagit tout autrement. Attaché par tradition et par une ligne de pensée constante à un système de droit privé autonome, il cherche avant tout la valeur sociale à travers l'individu. C'est dans la personne de l'individu qu'il mesure le sens et la valeur de la responsabilité. Cet état d'esprit se marque d'ailleurs dans les textes mêmes du Code civil. Les articles 1053 et suivants du Code ont fait de la faute l'impératif catégorique de toute la responsabilité civile. Il ne saurait être question de responsabilité sans faute. Le droit à la réparation du préjudice causé n'est pas rivé à la seule survenance du dommage pris comme un simple fait matériel qui s'est manifesté socialement, mais avant tout à la liaison entre ce simple fait et la faute de celui qui en est l'auteur.

On conçoit aisément, dans ces conditions, que la jurisprudence de cette province s'attache à trouver la justification de la solution des problèmes de responsabilité civile en puisant directement dans les racines profondes de ce Code, et non pas en allant chercher à l'étranger, que ce soit en Angleterre ou en France, des solutions qui sont inadaptables ici parce qu'elles correspondent à d'autres mœurs à d'autres réactions sociales, en un mot à une autre conception philosophique de la vie.

Trois exemples typiques de pensée et de méthode illustrent cette double tendance.

La divergence de pensée et de méthode est saisissante, tout d'abord, à propos de l'interprétation de l'article 1054, alinéa 7, du Code civil. Ce texte, on le sait, rend responsables les maîtres et commettants du dommage causé par leurs domestiques et préposés ou ouvriers « dans l'exécution des fonctions » auxquelles ces derniers sont employés. C'est en recherchant le sens exact de l'expression « dans l'exécution des fonctions », que les deux tendances se sont fait jour. L'Hon. Juge Anglin, près la Cour suprême, éprouve le besoin de rechercher tout naturellement les précédents anglais sur ce point. Il s'offre même le luxe de les analyser tout au long de son rapport. La « manie » de citer des précédents, dénoncée par le grand juriste canadien Mignault, est la réaction instinctive du magistrat de formation canadienne-anglaise. Il semble qu'il veuille se donner à lui-même, et bien qu'il s'agisse de textes du Code civil, les raisons de la justification de la solution qu'il préconise, alors même qu'il doit, comme dans cette espèce, écarter expressément tous les précédents cités parce qu'ils ne font pas autorité, à son avis, dans l'affaire qu'il a à juger.

L'attitude du magistrat canadien-français est légèrement différente. Il n'échappe pas, lui non plus, à la manie de citer des précédents français et même anglais, mais c'est semble-t-il pour affirmer presque aussitôt, en s'appuyant sur l'esprit du Code, l'inadaptabilité des uns et des autres.

Il est quelquefois dangereux de sortir d'un système juridique pour chercher des précédents dans un autre système, pour le motif que les deux systèmes contiennent des règles semblables, sauf, bien entendu, au cas où un système emprunte à l'autre une règle qui lui était auparavant étrangère. Alors même que la règle est semblable, il est possible qu'elle n'ait pas été entendue ou interprétée de la même manière dans chacun d'eux. Il peut très bien arriver que, malgré une apparente similitude, elles ne soient pas du tout identiques[11].

Cette phrase est très caractéristique de la mentalité québécoise. Elle dénonçe l'esprit de similitude entre le Québécois et le Français. Tous deux, s'élevant au dessus de la simple espèce, aiment à énonçer un principe général.

Il semble en définitive que pour un juge canadien de formation anglaise, la question se solde comme par une sorte de regret de devoir abandonner les précédents anglais, alors que pour le magistrat de formation canadienne-française c'est presque un bulletin de victoire à l'actif du seul droit de Québec, au sein de la communauté canadienne.

La responsabilité du fait de la garde des choses (article 1054, alinéa 1, du Code civil) permet également de vérifier le dualisme de pensée.

[11]J. Mignault dans *Curley* v. *Latreille*, [1920] 60 S.C.R. 131 à p. 176.

La jurisprudence a recherché si l'individu doit être tenu pour responsable du seul fait qu'il a la garde d'une chose (responsabilité sans faute) ou si l'on doit faire la preuve contre lui d'une faute. En 1909, devant la Cour supérieure de Montréal, l'Hon. Juge Cannon s'était prononcé pour une responsabilité stricte du seul fait de la garde des choses. Devant la Cour du Banc du Roi, et parlant au nom de la majorité, l'Hon. Juge Archambault renversait la décision : il faut prouver la faute. En Cour suprême enfin les Hon. Fitzpatrick et Anglin notamment se prononcèrent dans le même sens que le juge de la Cour supérieure[12].

En 1920 le Conseil privé, saisi d'une affaire québécoise,[13] avait admis que la responsabilité était indépendante de la preuve de la faute, « Upon the true construction of art. 1053 CC, a person capable of discerning right from wrong, is responsible without proof of negligence for damage caused by things which he has under his care, unless he establishes that he was unable to prevent the event which caused the damage ». Il s'agissait ainsi dans l'esprit des Lords d'une « strict liability ». En 1922, le même Conseil privé dans une autre affaire québécoise[14] revint quelque peu sur sa première interprétation, dans une sorte de sursaut de pudeur. Il devait essayer de corriger sa décision antérieure en ajoutant que, « in their Lordships' opinion, unable to prevent the damage complained of, means unable by reasonable means. It does not denote an absolute liability. » Cette décision rétablissait ainsi indirectement la nécessité de la preuve d'une faute, mais elle devait garder à cette preuve son sens anglais résultant de l'emploi du qualificatif « *reasonable* ». Ce terme emprunté au vocabulaire juridique anglais paraît plus difficilement acceptable dans un système juridique d'esprit français. On aurait pu croire alors qu'après l'emploi du qualificatif *reasonable* qui, apparemment tout au moins, paraît énoncer un principe, le sens de la responsabilité de l'article 1054 du Code civil était définitivement fixé. Il n'en a rien été. Tout est devenu question de fait. Comme l'écrivait un magistrat de la Cour du Banc du Roi, « les jugements sont et seront désormais des questions d'espèce[15] ». Dans ce conflit, on le voit, l'esprit juridique anglais domine.

La rupture de pensée est également très nette à l'occasion de la question des dommages-intérêts en matière délictuelle. L'article 1056 du Code de Québec, qui donne à certaines personnes limitativement

[12]*Doucet* v. *Shawinigan Carbide Cy.*, [1909] 35 S.C. 385; [1909] B.R. 271; [1910] 42 S.C.R. 281.

[13]*Vandry* v. *Quebec Railway Light Heat and Power*, [1920] A.C. 622.

[14]*City of Montreal* v. *Watt and Scott*, [1922] A.C. 558.

[15]*Liverpool London and Golden Insurance Cy* v. *Cie Giguère Ltd.*, [1921] 31 B.R. 305.

énumérées le droit de réclamer des dommages-intérêts en cas de décès de la victime à l'auteur de l'accident, a fait naître une querelle précise entre la Cour suprême du Canada et les cours de la province de Québec. Dans une décision que l'on a voulu qualifier de décision de principe, la Cour suprême, faisant état des origines anglaises de l'article 1056 du Code de Québec, aurait posé le principe que l'on ne saurait accorder de dommages-intérêts du chef de *solatium doloris*. Le chagrin, la douleur morale que l'on éprouve à la perte d'un être cher ne sont pas appréciables en argent. Sans doute les juridictions québécoises sont-elles obligées de se soumettre à cette décision, mais bien des juristes n'en expriment pas moins leur dissidence. Certains le font ouvertement. On peut lire sous la plume de l'Hon. Juge Jetté[16] que « le sens moral d'un juge français se révolte contre une pareille doctrine et que c'est là un principe barbare qui n'est pas admissible. Si vous avez un grand-père à votre charge et qu'il vient à mourir des suites d'un accident, non seulement vous ne pouvez pas demander de dommages-intérêts à l'auteur du délit, mais vous devriez le rémunérer pour vous avoir déchargé d'un fardeau pécuniaire par cet accident mortel.»

D'autres magistrats commencent par proclamer qu'ils se soumettent à la décision de la Cour suprême, mais ils cherchent à déguiser en même temps sous un *item* matériel la douleur morale et le chagrin, de façon à pouvoir les comprendre indirectement dans des dommages-intérêts, sans heurter de front le respect dû au précédent. On parlera volontiers alors de la « privation des sourires candides d'un enfant »; de la perte de soutien « moral »; de « dislocation du foyer ».

Ces attitudes contraires proviennent d'une divergence plus profonde qui tient à la différence de conception que réserve le droit anglais à la notion de dommages-intérêts. Dans l'esprit de ce droit, il semble que le terme *to repair* soit synonyme de *to replace*. Pour le juriste canadien-français, les dommages-intérêts ne sont qu'un mode de compensation par équivalent et non pas une valeur véritable de remplacement. Or, fait curieux, le juriste anglais comme le juriste canadien-français invoque l'éthique à l'appui de sa thèse. Le juriste anglais considère comme moralement choquant le fait d'apprécier en argent la douleur morale et le chagrin. Le juriste canadien-français estime que le fait important n'est pas dans l'attribution d'une somme d'argent de ce chef. La condamnation même à un symbolique dollar à titre de dommages-intérêts est la sanction morale supplémentaire que l'on doit infliger à l'auteur du délit qui, par sa faute, a causé la mort de la victime.

[16]*Dame Jeannotte* v. *Couillard*, [1894] 3 B.R. 461.

*

* *

Certaines institutions du droit civil, telles le testament ou le mandat, par exemple, ont également donné lieu à des divergences d'interprétation ou de justification des solutions proposées.

On sait que le Code civil de Québec a adopté le principe de la pleine liberté de disposer de ses biens par testament. La province de Québec a donc officiellement répudié la « Légitime » de l'ancien droit français, qui a été conservée dans le Code Napoléon sous le titre de « Réserve ». Sans doute la chose ne s'est pas faite sans réaction de la part de juristes canadiens-français. Certains sont allés jusqu'à traiter l'adoption de ce principe de « barbare ». Ils y ont dénoncé un principe « immoral que n'ont connu que la civilisation anglo-saxonne et la barbarie des Romains de la Loi des Douze Tables[17] ».

Là n'est pas la question. Ce n'est pas là que se trouve le conflit. Celui-ci s'est révélé à l'occasion de décisions de la Cour suprême et du Conseil privé. Les unes et les autres ont cherché à faire prévaloir, sous le couvert de l'adoption du principe anglais de liberté testamentaire, les principes de la jurisprudence anglaise sur les conditions incluses dans les testaments ou sur les questions de capacité du testateur.

En 1902 la Cour suprême[18] décidait que « in the Province of Quebec the English law rules on the subject of testamentary dispositions, and therefore in that Province a testator may validly impose as a condition of a legacy to his children and grand children, that marriage of the children should be celebrated according to the rites of the Church recognised by the laws of the Province... » Un juge canadien-français près la Cour suprême affirmait que « si notre code décrète un principe du droit anglais, n'est-il pas raisonnable de recourir à la jurisprudence anglaise pour l'interpréter ? Or — et ce n'est pas contesté — , la liberté pleine et entière de tester nous vient de l'Angleterre. La France ne l'a jamais connu. Peut-on alors mieux faire que de suivre les principes consacrés par le Conseil Privé ? »

Cette décision a eu l'heur de soulever quelque réaction tant en doctrine qu'en jurisprudence.

La première s'insurge contre la conclusion hâtive que l'on voudrait tirer du principe de la liberté testamentaire. On ne doit pas confondre le droit de tester avec ce que l'on est convenu d'appeler la liberté illimitée de tester. Le premier laisse subsister les règles de la loi de

[17] J. E. Billette, « Traité théorique et pratique de droit civil canadien », 1 *Donations et testaments* (1933), à p. 94.

[18] *Renaud* v. *Lamothe*, [1903] 32 S.C.R. 357.

fond du lieu où le testament à été rédigé. La liberté testamentaire n'a rien à voir avec ce principe.

La seconde, de son côté, affirme que l'on ne saurait prendre prétexte du principe de liberté testamentaire pour introduire indirectement les principes anglais de la preuve relatifs, par exemple, à la capacité du testateur. Comme conséquence absolument erronée de l'introduction de la liberté testamentaire, l'on a fait constamment sanctionner la jurisprudence anglaise lorsqu'il s'agit de la preuve de l'insanité du testateur. Il faut revenir sur cette matière à la seule et vraie doctrine juridique, celle de notre code. Comme l'ajoute un juriste canadien-français : « ce n'est pas la common law anglaise qu'on introduit au pays par l'Acte de Québec, sauf la forme dérivée de la loi d'Angleterre, mais uniquement le droit de tester selon les termes de cet acte ».

• • •

Dans le domaine du mandat du Code civil, une scission de pensée s'est également opérée à propos de l'interprétation à donner à l'article 1716. Cet article spécifie que « a mandatary who acts in his own name is liable to the third party with whom he contracts without prejudice to the rights of the latter against the mandator also ».

Les juristes de formation canadienne-française et ceux de formation canadienne-anglaise se sont trouvés en désaccord sur la justification à donner au recours du tiers contre le mandant ou le mandataire s'il n'a pas reçu satisfaction contre le premier qu'il a assigné.

A l'échelon de la Cour suprême, l'Hon. Juge Idington fit une déclaration reposant sur deux arguments distincts. Partant du point de vue que « in this case there is no settled jurisprudence of Quebec », il développait cette idée que,

> instead of adopting for the first time a novel rule to be peculiar to Quebec, we should so far as we can, when applying relevant law in which the substance is identical with that of the other provinces wherein the law is founded on, and is English law, aim at a degree of uniformity in its administration, instead of deciding in a way that will tend to produce confusion and unjustifiable expense. So far as the principles applicable thereto are concerned, the rule adopted in English decisions is in accord with reason and justice, as well as that practical business sense which always tends to minimizing the operation of the purely religious spirit[19].

Les deux magistrats canadiens de langue française, et l'un des magistrats de langue anglaise à la Cour suprême, s'employèrent à démontrer que le droit anglais préconise la doctrine de l'élection :

> In English law, both agent and principal cannot be liable as principals simultaneously and jointly... the merger implied in the maxim « transit in

[19] *Desrosiers* v. *The King*, [1920] S.C.R. 105 à p. 106.

rem judicatam » as understood in English law has no application in the legal system of this Province... this case affords an excellent illustration of the danger of treating English decisions in Quebec cases which do not depend upon doctrines derived from the English law[20].

Fidèles à la méthode de raisonnement propre à la discipline du droit civil, c'est-à-dire, au principe de référence aux travaux préparatoires des Codificateurs, les deux magistrats canadiens de langue française près la même Cour se sont employés à démontrer que le droit au recours est basé en droit civil sur une conception de fond totalement différente de celle du droit anglais. « Le mandat québécois crée à l'égard des tiers deux débiteurs, le mandant et le mandataire. Le mandant, parce qu'il est d'ordinaire responsable des actions de son mandataire, et le mandataire, parce qu'il n'a pas jugé à propos de dénoncer sa qualité d'agent. » Ce fut l'occasion pour l'un des juges de rappeler que « sur tous ces points et surtout en matière de mandat, le code civil et la Common Law contiennent des règles semblables. Cependant le droit civil constitue un système complet par lui-même et doit s'interpréter d'après ses propres règles[21]. »

L'exemple tiré du mandat montre donc, comme nous le signalions, que la similitude apparente de conception n'emporte pas toujours similitude de solution. Si la finalité à laquelle répond le mandat en droit québécois ne diffère guère de celle du droit anglais, leurs structures respectives ne sont cependant pas complètement similaires.

Conclusion générale

Ce tableau, quoique bref et forcément incomplet, met au moins en vedette l'existence d'une différence marquée de tempérament entre le juriste de formation et de langue anglaises et celui de formation et de langue françaises.

Le juriste canadien-anglais est tout naturellement enclin, en présence des lacunes du droit positif, à les combler suivant son propre tempérament et la discipline de son esprit. Le juriste canadien-anglais comme celui d'Angleterre se fait du rôle du magistrat une conception à peu près identique. Pour eux, le magistrat est avant tout un homme sage. On doit alors, à ce seul titre, lui donner le maximum de liberté pour juger le différend. La philosophie platonicienne le veut ainsi.

Le juriste canadien-français, né dans cette province, élevé dans la discipline d'Aristote, conçoit au contraire le juge comme n'étant pas

[20] *Ibid.*, J. Anglin, à p. 119.
[21] *Ibid.*, J. Mignault, à p. 126.

aussi sage que le voudrait Platon. Les lacunes du droit civil doivent sans doute être comblées par interprétation judiciaire, mais celle-ci est, peut-être, considérée comme d'ordre mineur, parce que n'étant pas totalement créatrice du droit civil. Il y a une sorte de dirigisme judiciaire en fonction de la tradition qui est, par excellence, l'élément formateur du droit civil et présente un caractère de pérennité que le temps n'altère pas.

C'est dans la tradition que le juriste canadien-français va tout d'abord puiser. Il le fera d'autant plus volontiers qu'il professe une défiance naturelle à l'égard des lois fédérales ou même provinciales qui, pour lui, s'inspirent encore trop souvent, semble-t-il, de concepts sociaux qui ne sont pas les siens propres.

Par contre, le juriste canadien-anglais appartient par esprit et par culture au monde canadien-anglais qui est l'élément dominant et dirigeant du Canada. Il pense plus naturellement d'emblée à l'échelon fédéral et ne professe nullement cette défiance à l'égard d'une législation en marge du Code civil. Ce juriste canadien-anglais, tout au moins celui qui ne vit pas dans cette province, semble manifester une tendance naturelle à aborder les problèmes de droit privé, spécialement le Code civil, comme le juriste anglais aborde la Common Law. Dans son comportement intellectuel, il est enclin à donner au pouvoir judiciaire, à l'égard du droit civil, un rôle presque aussi créateur que celui reservé par les cours anglaises au pur droit anglais. Pour ce juriste, il semble que les textes du droit civil ne sont qu'un simple point de départ et qu'ils ne prennent leur valeur réelle que par la seule décision judiciaire comme s'il s'agissait de droit anglais. C'est la jurisprudence, et elle seule, qui constituerait la structure même du droit civil. Aussi son esprit le pousse-t-il du même coup à contenir le processus de cette interprétation judiciaire dans les limites propres à celles du droit de la Common Law. Ceci explique son goût inné pour l'adoption du « précédent » et du *stare decisis*, procédés de formation par excellence du droit anglais. Ainsi donc, l'interprétation judiciaire plus largement ouverte pour lui, à son point de départ, se trouve-t-elle bridée dans son propre fonctionnement par une technique qui épouse les rigueurs du droit judiciaire purement anglais.

Il faut d'ailleurs signaler à cet égard la situation plus nuancée du juriste canadien-anglais vivant dans cette province. Il réagit différemment de son collègue canadien de l'extérieur. Il sait pertinemment que le « précédent » et le *stare decisis* ne sont pas, selon les conceptions québécoises, le précédent et le *stare decisis* du pur droit anglais. Il sait, pour avoir été élevé dans l'atmosphère du droit civil de cette province et en avoir mesuré les subtilités, que, selon la démonstration magistrale de Mignault, le grand juriste canadien, « l'insistance ou la persistance » d'une cour québécoise à maintenir une décision contraire à celle de la Cour suprême, ou tout au moins à exprimer des dissidences, peut amener celle-ci à reviser plus tard ses positions sur des problèmes du pur droit civil. Il sait que le précédent n'est pas, ici, une institution constitutionnelle judiciaire canadienne, mais une simple coutume judiciaire qu'un certain engoûment pour les avis du Conseil privé antérieurement à 1949 avait contribué à renforcer, sans avoir jamais, cependant, réussi à la transformer en un principe aussi rigoureusement technique que son ancêtre d'Angleterre.

Ainsi donc, le juriste canadien-anglais de l'extérieur de cette province tend à ne voir le droit civil qu'à travers une succession de décisions judiciaires qui deviennent pour lui des règles impératives et pour ainsi dire définitives. Le droit civil se fige à l'image de la Common Law, dans le moule préparé du précédent. Il devient aussi rigide que le droit judiciaire anglais. La jurisprudence est, pour ce juriste, sa Bible.

Le juriste canadien-français, auquel il faut assimiler son collègue de langue anglaise vivant ici, part des textes qui sont pour lui son Evangile. Ces textes, apparemment du moins, semblent si brefs, si succints, si tranchants dans leur énoncé, que toute vie réelle paraît s'en être retirée. Les textes n'énoncent que des résultats et ne donnent pas leurs raisons. Mais tout juriste, ici, sait pertinemment que ces textes d'apparence squelettique sont le fruit d'une longue expérience. Ils sont la traduction concise d'un état jurisprudentiel coutumier antérieur qui a été codifié à un moment donné, parce que la Codification en soi correspond au besoin naturel de synthèse ressenti par tout esprit latin ou de formation latine. Ces juristes canadiens, vivant au Québec, savent que ces textes contiennent en germe toute la vie juridique qui les a faits ce qu'ils sont encore aujourd'hui.

On conçoit, dans ces conditions, que le juriste canadien de Québec professe d'emblée une sorte de méfiance à l'égard de tout ce qui, directement ou indirectement, tendrait à interpréter les textes du Code civil selon un esprit qui ignorerait d'abord leur sens historique. C'est pourquoi il opère ce repli constant vers la tradition, afin que celle-ci demeure une réalité vivante et que l'interprétation trop littérale des textes n'en tue pas l'esprit. Guiyot n'écrivait-il pas que le progrès consiste quelquefois à revenir en arrière ?

Cette première attitude, qui intéresse directement et en profondeur la substance interne du droit privé, se double d'une autre.

Redoutant, étant minoritaire au Canada, que le sens du droit civil ne soit par trop axé sur une ligne fédérale qui peut lui être étrangère, le juriste de cette province favorise la souplesse dans l'interprétation même des textes. Cette attitude permet d'écarter parfois la technique du droit anglais et de faire ressortir du même coup, et par contraste, l'esprit général du pur droit civil. Celui-ci a été conçu comme un élément séparé au sein de la communauté canadienne et est doté de qualités intellectuelles qui lui sont propres.

Ce libéralisme permet ainsi à ce juriste de redonner au droit civil ses caractéristiques propres et fondamentales. Si l'on a constamment à l'esprit que le code est, tout au moins en apparence, pour un juriste anglais, une sorte de « statut », on mesure toute l'importance fonctionnelle de ce libéralisme pour la sauvegarde de l'esprit du droit privé québécois.

On assiste ainsi à ce paradoxe que, tandis que le droit de la Common Law dans son processus de formation judiciaire se fige par étapes et va jusqu'à prendre une certaine immobilité, le droit privé de cette province, apparemment figé au départ, reprend une mobilité extrême au cours de sa vie judiciaire. Il atteint une mobilité et une souplesse enviables, dont les résultats positifs ne heurtent pas les caractères spécifiques de ce droit, puisque c'est en lui, et en lui seul, qu'ils trouvent la substance nourricière de sa constante régénération.

Tandis que le juriste canadien-anglais hors du Québec conçoit le code civil comme s'intégrant dans la communauté canadienne, ce qui se traduit pour lui, dans la communauté juridique canadienne d'origine majoritaire anglaise, le juriste canadien du Québec estime que l'intégration de la communauté québécoise dans la nation canadienne ne comporte pas forcément l'intégration aux fins d'absorption de son système juridique de droit privé. Il pense au contraire au maintien de ce droit, à la nécessité de sa survivance comme système autonome, parce que, tant au point de vue juridique qu'au point de vue social, il reflète la vie même de cette province et ses éléments de culture propres.

Cette tendance générale en sens contraire se marque, au fond, par une idée plus générale encore, semble-t-il, qu'il faut dégager.

Le juriste hors de cette province, pense naturellement « uniformisation » ou « unification » du droit. Il flirte facilement avec cette idée. Elle lui paraît nécessaire ou, à tout le moins, souhaitable pour un grand pays comme celui-ci. Sa ligne générale de pensée est constamment tendue vers cet objectif. Elle a parfois conquis certains juristes canadiens-français, tant est grande, on le sait, l'influence du milieu fédéral et la force attractive propre au droit anglais lorsque celui-ci pénètre dans toutes les veines de la vie des pays où il s'installe avec le temps.

Le système juridique du droit de Québec développe, par contre, chez tout juriste qui vit dans cette province, une dualité de pensée, une sorte de bipartisme juridique. La constitution même de ce Code civil qui renferme des éléments du droit français de France et des éléments de droit anglais invite l'esprit à ce bipartisme. A la tendance centralisatrice juridique canadienne-anglaise se substitue, ici, une tendance décentralisatrice québécoise commandée par la nature même des choses.

Le droit de la Common Law reste le droit majoritaire au Canada. Il correspond à des conceptions sociales, économiques, qui sont pour le juriste canadien-anglais l'expression de la nation canadienne. Il va de soi que ce juriste ait tendance à le considérer un peu comme le droit commun de tout le pays, dans la mesure, bien entendu, où ses conceptions ne heurtent pas de front ou pas trop visiblement des concepts juridiques québécois fondamentaux et solidement assis. S'il en est ainsi, il ne faut pas croire cependant que ce même juriste renonce pour cela à toute tentative d'uniformisation. La pénétration de l'esprit « Common Law » s'opère alors dans les interstices des textes du Code, dans les lacunes que certains d'entre eux n'ont pas voulu ou n'ont pu combler. Les obstacles sont alors contournés. D'esprit plus franchement socialisant, le juge canadien-anglais, notamment hors de cette province, trouve naturel d'enrober certains concepts mal définis du droit privé dans la masse majoritaire des concepts dérivés du droit anglais. La jurisprudence devient l'instrument naturel de cette réalisation.

De son côté le juriste du Québec n'entend abandonner les idéaux juridiques du droit privé que s'il ne trouve pas, même par analogie forcée, dans les solutions jurisprudentielles ou doctrinales françaises de France, un point d'appui satisfaisant. La conscience qu'il a du sens de l'héritage juridique français, même lointain, ne va cependant pas jusqu'à lui faire adopter aveuglément les solutions du pur droit français, comme il semblait le faire au lendemain de la Codification. Il sait parfaitement que les mœurs et la civilisation françaises de France ne sont pas les siennes.

Y a-t-il rien de plus significatif en ce sens, que ce propos rapporté par un avocat canadien il y a quelques années déjà ? « Tout récemment un publiciste français nous conseillait de nous rapprocher du droit anglais et il ajoutait : Ce n'est pas en se recroquevillant, et en s'en tenant aux traditions anciennes que le Canada se maintiendra en liaison avec nous, car nous marchons de l'avant, tandis qu'il court le risque de rester en arrière et de se trouver moins bien adapté que le droit anglais aux nécessités de la vie moderne[22]. » Cet avocat ajoutait : « Nous voulons apporter notre contribution à ce progrès et nous voulons rester nous-mêmes et nous guider sur l'esprit de nos institutions. Il y va de notre survivance et de la conservation de notre génie propre. » Ce langage français couvre parfaitement la pensée canadienne-française.

Le juriste canadien-français, par suite du repli sur des positions françaises de base, dresse en quelque sorte un premier rempart contre l'envahissement peu souhaitable à ses yeux de toute pensée issue d'un système juridique qui paraît étranger à sa propre façon de vivre et de réagir. C'est à ce moment et sur ce point précis que la ligne séparative se creuse entre le juriste canadien-français et son compatriote canadien-anglais. Cette manie de citer qui existe à l'état latent chez les juristes des deux langues a fini par engendrer dans la personne de tout juriste vivant dans la province de Québec une prise de conscience des plus significatives.

Sans rien perdre de cette mobilité et de cette souplesse qui parfois déroutent et qui lui ont permis d'éviter les écueils du pur droit français ou du pur droit anglais, le juriste québécois a franchi maintenant le stade de la simple tentative d'adaptation, pour celui de la prise de conscience. La comparaison constante qu'il faisait naguère entre les solutions préconisées en France et celles préconisées en Grande-Bretagne à l'occasion de nouveaux problèmes de droit propres à la discipline du droit québécois prend maintenant un autre sens. Ce juriste cherche moins désormais à savoir quelle est la solution française ou anglaise qu'à découvrir dans cette recherche même les raisons profondes et surtout d'ordre juridique d'une solution purement québécoise. La méthode comparative, instrument quotidien nécessaire à tout juriste vivant ici et qui servait alors de simple procédé d'alignement vers le droit français ou même le droit anglais, a maintenant une fonction propre. Elle a pour mission de dégager la philosophie du droit québécois et de découvrir les assises réelles du monde juridique de cette province en leur redonnant leur pureté.

Tout ce travail d'affinement juridique ne se fait pas sans heurts. Des crises sont encore à redouter. Elles sont même à souhaiter, car elles sont le signe évident que l'indifférence ou le laisser-aller des premiers jours est désormais lettre morte. Certains de ceux qui, ici même, préconisaient naguère une unification du droit privé au Canada, soit par l'absorption par voie législative de certaines institutions du droit privé québécois, soit par l'influence plus voilée de la jurisprudence, sem-

[22]C. E. Dorion, « La Philosophie du droit civil », *Revue du droit* (1925–6), p. 134 à p. 211.

blent maintenant hésiter à persister en ce sens. La personnalité juridique québécoise qui a déjà rayonné au delà des limites géographiques de la province est la preuve manifeste que non seulement le droit privé du Québec n'est pas un élément mort ou isolé au Canada, mais qu'il commence à devenir une source d'enrichissement pour le Canada tout entier.

Le juriste d'ici croit maintenant à la possibilité de la coexistence juridique des deux systèmes de droit qui se partagent le monde. Sans doute cette coexistence ne se réalise-t-elle pas toujours sans heurts. Il s'y mêle parfois des facteurs d'ordre politique ou économique qui mettent à vif les réactions sentimentales. Certaines décisions judiciaires rendues dans cette province dépassent parfois de beaucoup le seul cadre étroit des intérêts privés et locaux qui les ont fait naître. Les répercussions d'ordre social ou économique qu'elles peuvent avoir les portent d'emblée, souvent même malgré elles, à l'échelon national. La politique pure s'en empare et leur enlève leur seule objectivité juridique.

Faut-il conclure que cette coexistence juridique, qui développe à l'état latent dans le domaine du droit privé une sorte d'esprit d'opposition au sein de la communauté canadienne, soit nuisible à la culture canadienne ? Il n'en est rien à notre avis. Existe-t-il, dans un pays comme les Etats-Unis, un régime de droit privé unitaire ? Sans doute le droit de base est-il la Common Law anglaise. Celle-ci est devenue par la suite une Common Law américaine. Mais à l'intérieur de ce droit privé il existe un grand nombre de secteurs particuliers qui font de ces Etats un véritable damier juridique. Les *Restatements* américains s'efforcent d'établir des dénominateurs communs à des institutions identiques de droit privé, mais en l'état actuel des choses ils ne sont le plus souvent que des vœux et ne constituent pas même un système juridique organique. L'unification du droit privé au Canada est-elle plus souhaitable que le maintien d'une coexistence au sein d'une même communauté politique ? Cette coexistence porte déjà ses fruits. Malgré les heurts qu'elle engendre elle est, par elle-même, une source d'équilibre. Elle élargit les horizons dans un esprit de mutuelle compréhension nécessaire. Le dualisme d'esprit juridique favorisé, et heureusement épaulé par un bilinguisme réel dans cette province, est une source d'enrichissement intellectuel inégalé.

La disparition de l'une ou de l'autre des pensées juridiques de ce pays serait pour lui et même pour le monde entier une perte irréparable.

1956

II. MATERIAL FACTORS

A. Demographic Considerations

II. POPULATION ET ÉCONOMIE

A. Facteurs démographiques

Some Demographic Aspects of French-English Relations in Canada

NATHAN KEYFITZ
Department of Political Economy, University of Toronto

THE FIRST CENTURY AND A HALF of Canada's population history, from 1605 to the war that ended with the cession of the colonies, was almost exclusively French-Canadian history. Fortunately the keeping of records both civil and ecclesiastical was an early habit of the colonists. The records include baptisms and a series of complete censuses at dates starting from 1666; more is known of what was happening demographically in Canada prior to 1760 than in some periods since.

The first significant event in the history of European settlement in Canada was the founding of Port Royal in 1605, and the survival of forty-four settlers out of seventy-nine who had undertaken to spend the winter on Ile Sainte-Croix.[1] In 1608 Champlain with twenty-seven French settlers spent the winter at Quebec, and in 1613 sixty-two English wintered at St. John's, Newfoundland. French settlement moved up the river from the base now established in Quebec, and Montreal was founded in 1642. But population grew slowly in those days; between disease and wars with the Iroquois and the English, births in the small colony did not exceed deaths until 1638.[2]

Growth of Canadian Population

By 1666 the population of New France was 3,215.[3] This number is known as the result of a census taken in modern style, showing the name, age, sex, and other facts concerning each person. The census of 1666 is one of which Canadians are proud, for in basic method it is

[1]Samuel de Champlain, *Œuvres*, Edition Laverdière, Tome III, pp. 41, 42, 78.

[2]Paul Veyret, *Population du Canada* (Paris: Presses Universitaires de France, 1953).

[3]Public Archives of Canada, Series G 1, vols. 460–1, Archives des Colonies, Series B, vol. 1, pp. 136–7, vol. IV, Census 1871, pp. 2–4.

the earliest expression of the census-taking tradition which spread through the countries of western Europe and North America in the nineteenth century.

Canada, unlike the British colonies to the south, did not receive a flood of dissenters who sought an opportunity to practise their religion; in fact it was by royal intention closed to French Huguenots. Immigration was slow, but some 2,500 colonists arrived between 1660 and 1672 in the favourable atmosphere created by Louis XIV and fostered within the colony by Intendant Talon. Henceforth the population grew rapidly and by the end of the seventeenth century New France contained a white population of 14,000.[4] At the same time Acadia showed 800 persons; Newfoundland had 2,400 British residents in 1702 and 600 French in 1706. The eighteenth century showed a continuance of the rapid rate of increase so that by 1736 New France had reached 40,000 persons, thus almost trebling in thirty-eight years, an increase of 3 per cent per year. The largest part of this high increase was due to the excess of births over deaths. Thus it is stated that: "With the end of the work of Talon little interest in colonization was taken and emigration from France practically ceased at the end of the century—apart from some Acadians who moved to the St. Lawrence and some discharged soldiers."[5]

It is not certain how many immigrants there were in the whole period of the French colony; A. R. M. Lower refers to estimates varying from 4,000 to 10,000.[6] There was a good deal of travel in both directions; while new settlers were coming some of the old were returning. The population of New France by 1758 was estimated[7] at 72,000, an increase of 80 per cent in 22 years, or 2¾ per cent per annum. This number somewhat exceeded the count made in 1765 of 69,810 for Canada, which included substantially the territory of New France; there was some return to France after the conquest and Louisiana was no longer included.

That fewer than 10,000 immigrants could be the ancestors of the 70,000 or so who were present in 1763 implies fairly settled conditions and a rate of fertility among the highest ever reached, even among small populations occupying practically limitless areas. That the 70,000 of 1763 could be the recognized ancestors of over 4½ million Canadians and perhaps 1½ million Americans implies a continued high fertility,

[4]Census of Population and Agriculture, 1698.
[5]"Immigration" in *Encyclopedia of Canada*, vol. III, p. 241.
[6]*Colony to Nation* (Toronto: Longmans, Green, 1946), p. 44.
[7]E. Rameau, *La France aux colonies* (Paris, 1859), deuxième partie, p. 127.

as well as a degree of cultural continuity in the face of majority pressures of many kinds that has few parallels in world history.

Since immigration from France was negligible subsequent to the Peace of Paris it is of special interest to calculate the annual rate of growth that is implied by the fact that in the eighty-six years preceding 1851 the population of Lower Canada multiplied by thirteen to 890,000. Population (or money) which multiplies by thirteen in eighty-six years is growing at the rate of 2.7 per cent compounded annually. If the deaths were at least 25 per thousand the births would have to be at least 52 per thousand. All the differentials which later, more detailed statistics have revealed favoured this population; it was rural, farming, Roman Catholic, and not wealthy.

The British had taken Nova Scotia in 1713, and in 1749 Halifax, the first British settlement, was founded. It seemed to the leaders of the time that the best way out of their difficulties was to expel the Acadians, and this expulsion altered the demographic balance. After 1763 when the British took over the administration of the St. Lawrence Valley, the growth of the British population was slow, for the richer colonies to the south exerted a strong attraction. With the revolt of the Thirteen Colonies the United Empire Loyalists, estimated at 35,000,[8] came north, and helped found what became the provinces of New Brunswick and Ontario. At the same time the current of emigration from the Mother Country was deflected towards a more northerly destination; after the Napoleonic Wars, Upper Canada, established as a separate entity in 1791, began to receive British immigrants in considerable numbers.

The French Canadians continued to farm, and each generation sought new lands for its sons. When the lands that were available within the boundaries constituted by the English holdings in the south and the infertility of the north were fully occupied there was a migration, most of it to the United States. Montreal became a largely English city during the first half of the nineteenth century, and only about the time of Confederation did some of the overflow from Quebec farms enter it in the search for jobs, and restore the French majority.

Confederation had important consequences for Canadian population through the integration of vast new territories. One of the tasks of the new federation was the development of the west.[9] In 1870 the province of Manitoba was established and British Columbia joined the Con-

[8]Lower, *Colony to Nation*, p. 118. Veyret, *Population du Canada*, p. 14.

[9]Maurice A. Lamontagne, *Le Fédéralisme canadien: évolution et problèmes* (Québec: Presses Universitaires Laval, 1954).

federation in 1871. However, the growth of the prairies seemed to have to await the filling of the United States west, and it was only towards the end of the nineteenth century that population figures start to rise rapidly. Manitoba was the first of the three prairie provinces to be occupied, and it counted 62,000 inhabitants in the 1881 census, 153,000 in 1891, 255,000 in 1901, and 461,000 in 1911. The cycle of expansion of the other two was only slightly behind that of Manitoba; the largest growth of any of these in any intercensal period was that of Saskatchewan between 1901 and 1911, when an increase of over 400,000 was shown.

Partly to guide federal activities aimed at settling the country, a ten-year census had been made one of the articles of Confederation in 1867. When the prairies attained a growth early in the century of nearly a million persons per decade, it was plain that more frequent censuses would be necessary to keep track of it. Accordingly a special five-year census of the present prairie provinces was arranged, and this continued from 1886 to 1946. In 1956 the scope of the prairie census will be somewhat reduced, and it will be extended to the whole of Canada. The purpose is to take account of a new phase of population growth, not primarily agricultural but rather urban, suburban, and oriented to the development of resources.

The number of French in 1881 was 1,299,000 and by 1951 these had increased to 4,319,000. This multiplication by three and one-third or an increase of 1¾ per cent per annum in the period of seventy years is rapid but somewhat lower than the phenomenal rates previously shown: it would imply an average birth rate of 40 to 45 per thousand and a death rate of 20 to 25 per thousand if there had been no emigration, but we shall see below that emigration was important and that the birth rate must have averaged over 45.

It is convenient to arrange population data in the form of a table which shows how the changes from one census to the next have occurred (see Table I). The four possible ways in which people can enter or leave a population are by birth, death, immigration, and emigration. But when we seek to analyse changes from one census to the next in terms of these four items we find that the official vital statistics series for Canada only go back about thirty years. We are compelled to make estimates of the births and deaths; for deaths we can only assume the applicability to Canada of rates tabulated for other countries at the dates concerned. The assumption that mortality in Canada was similar to that in England and Wales a hundred years ago fortunately has rather little effect on the calculation as compared with mortality 10 per cent higher or lower. The number of children under ten years recorded at the successive censuses gives adequate information on births once we assume infant mortality rates.

Among others Coats, Hurd and MacLean, Marshall, and the writer have made estimates for the period prior to that covered by the national registration system.[10] Reconstructions of the past are difficult to verify, but something can be done by comparing the outgo of Canadian-born, estimated census by census, with the increase in the Canadian-born population of the United States. This method serves (among other things) as a check on the assumed mortality rates, because too low an estimate of deaths would exaggerate the number of immigrants from Canada, but diminish the apparent immigration into the United States, and so reveal itself. The general conclusion from the checks used is that most of the figures in Table I are within 100,000 of the truth.

To sum up the sources of data: official figures on immigration are at hand for at least a hundred years; the number of births is inferred from the count of those less than ten years old at the successive censuses; and the rate of mortality is taken to be the same as in other countries whose registration systems antedate that of Canada.

Given this information emigration may be calculated as a residual. The writer followed a well-beaten path in making this calculation[11] and there is no point here in taking the reader over all the statistical hurdles again; it should be explained, however, that the data from 1941 to 1951 are corrected on the basis of the 1951 census, that official vital statistics are used for 1921 to 1951 in place of the previous life table methods, and that an attempt is made to make the reconstruction throw light on the relative growth of the French and the English.

The purpose of the construction in Table I is to show the roles played by natural increase and migration in the building of Canada. It appears that the difference between the numbers of immigrants and of emigrants during the hundred years is only about 700,000, whereas the difference between births and deaths is over 10 million. The 700,000 net does not mean that of the 7 million immigrants only

[10]R. H. Coats, "Canada" in Imre Ferenczi, ed., *International Migrations* (2 vols., New York: National Bureau of Economic Research, 1929). W. B. Hurd and M. C. MacLean, "Projection of Canada's Population on the Basis of Current Birth and Death Rates, 1931–1971" in Canadian Institute of International Affairs, *Canadian Papers*, vol. IV (1936). For Herbert Marshall, see Proceedings of the Standing Committee of the Senate on Immigration and Labour, July 30, 1946, and May 14, 1947. N. Keyfitz, "The Growth of Canadian Population," *Population Studies*, vol. IV, no. 1 (June 1950).

[11]"The Growth of Canadian Population."

TABLE I

A RECONSTRUCTION OF CANADA'S POPULATION RECORD, 1851–1951
(000's omitted)

	Births	Deaths*	Immigration	Emigration (residual)	Population at end of decade
–1851	—	—	—	—	2,436
1851–1861	1,281	611	209	86	3,230
1861–1871	1,369	718	187	377	3,689
1871–1881	1,477	754	353	439	4,325
1881–1891	1,538	824	903	1,110	4,833
1891–1901	1,546	828	326	505	5,371
1901–1911	1,931	811	1,782	1,067	7,207
1911–1921	2,338	1,018	1,592	1,330	8,788
1921–1931	2,414	1,053	1,195	967	10,377
1931–1941	2,291	1,070	150	241	11,507
1941–1951†	3,205	1,216	548	380	14,009
1851–1951	19,390	8,903	7,245	6,502	

*Includes 36,000 overseas casualties of the Second World War, and 150,000 extra deaths due to the First World War and the influenza epidemic.

†Including Newfoundland from 1949; estimated population at that date 345,000.

10 per cent stayed, but rather that if the doors of both immigration and emigration had been closed the total population at the present time would have been less by the descendants of 700,000 persons. This statement does not fully clarify the role of immigration in attaining our present population, for we have the "loan" of population if the immigration comes before the emigration, and we receive some "interest" if the people in question are more than reproducing themselves. Thus, through immigration, we had a net gain of 700,000 in the first decade of the century; if we were to lose 700,000 at the present time—a highly unlikely contingency presented only as an example of the arithmetical point—we would still be ahead of where we would have been if the doors both ways had been closed in 1901–11. In so far as the immigrants have high birth rates and the emigrants lower ones, the process gives Canada an additional demographic gain—though, some writers insist, a cultural loss.

The extent to which the immigrants are themselves the emigrants of the same period has been much discussed. Successive censuses provide data on this point when set alongside statistics on immigration. It turns out that from January 1926, to May 1931, the number of immigrants who were recorded as entering Canada was 742,000, but that only 468,000 people reported to the 1931 census enumerators that they had come to Canada in that period. The latter figure is only 63 per cent of the former—our rate of retention to the end of a five-year period was not high. The next census that was preceded by a major amount of immigration was that of 1951, and this time we find that the number of immigrants in the preceding five-year period was 491,000, and that the census counted 386,000 of these, or 70 per cent. It looks as though Canada's ability to hold immigrants was much higher then than in former times, perhaps partly owing to some closing of the United States immigration doors, but mostly to our solid growth and the opportunities it offers for satisfying and remunerative work.

Birth and death rates for the period of Canadian history covered by Table I, and indeed for a longer period, are discussed in the chapter of this volume written by Mr. Henripin. In Table II we shall attempt to split the totals from Table I into French- and English-speaking persons.

TABLE II

PERSONS OF FRENCH ORIGIN AND TOTAL POPULATION
1851–1951
(000's)

Year	Total population	French	French % of total
1851*	1,842	696	37.8
1861*	2,508	881	35.1
1871†	3,486	1,083	31.1
1881	4,325	1,299	30.0
1891	4,833	1,405	29.1
1901	5,371	1,649	30.7
1911	7,207	2,062	28.6
1921	8,788	2,453	27.9
1931	10,377	2,928	28.2
1941	11,507	3,483	30.3
1951‡	13,648	4,309	30.8

*Upper and Lower Canada only.
†Nova Scotia, New Brunswick, Quebec, and Ontario only.
‡Exclusive of Newfoundland.

The periods of immigration (for example 1901–11) tend to show a decline in the percentage of French, whereas the negligible immigration of the 1930's brought the French to a higher proportion than had been seen during the present century. One may summarize by saying that after some decline, the proportion of French by 1951 was not appreciably different from that shown by the first census after Confederation.

Birth and death rates are shown in Table III, and from them it seems a reasonable guess to take the French births as 39 per cent of all births, and French deaths as 32 per cent of all deaths for the period prior to the time for which complete statistics are to be had. For our rough purpose we can take it that there was no French immigration, and we will infer the amount of French emigration.

TABLE III

FRENCH AS PERCENTAGE OF ALL ORIGINS*

Years	Births %	Deaths %
1921–30	39.2	34.2
1931–40	38.9	31.7
1941–50	38.8	29.6

*Exclusive of Newfoundland, Yukon, and Northwest Territories.

The result of all this for the French is 7.6 million births, 2.9 million deaths, and 1.2 million emigrants. For the non-French the corresponding figures are 11.8 million births, 6 million deaths, 7.2 million immigrants, and 5.3 million emigrants. The most important of these figures is the 1.2 million French emigrants, presumably largely to the United States; this figure is too low by any immigration from France into Canada, too high by any understatement of deaths or overstatement of births. Esdras Minville speaks of a million departures in the century that ended in 1932.[12] Such figures may be compared with the United States census, which shows the number of Canadian-born divided into French and other. The absolute number of French who were born in Canada reaches a peak of 395,000 in 1900, and is 238,000 in 1950. The proportion of French Canadians in the population of Canadian birth residing in the United States is declining, being almost one-third in 1890, and less than one-quarter in 1950.

The United States census does not ascertain origin, but it does ask the birth-place of parents; and the number of persons described as being of French-Canadian parentage was 908,000 in 1940 and 758,000 in 1950. We do not know how many of the people of French-Canadian ancestry who now reside in the United States are the grandchildren of emigrants; there seems no basis for proceeding from our 1.2 million emigrants to an estimate of their descendants now living. The literature abounds in figures, however. Senator Belcourt gives 1¾ million as the

[12]Quoted by Veyret, *Population du Canada*, p. 50.

number of French Canadians living in the United States.[13] In the same issue of the *Annals* (pp. 10, 12) G. E. Marquis, Statistician for the province of Quebec, gives their number as one million. Other estimates run a great deal higher—O. A. Lemieux has drawn my attention to a recent one of 2½ million. The wide range of figures quoted on a simple fact is an example of the difficulty of providing a clear picture of an aspect of our social world for which the necessary statistics are not present.

The Division of Labour

Census figures throw light on the division of labour—how the French and English associate with one another in earning their individual livelihoods and in turning out the product of their joint industry. The way in which French- and English-speaking Canadians are related to one another in the world of work is no new topic. It has been studied by Jamieson, Roy, and above all by Hughes.[14] In an earlier essay this writer introduced the issue with some thoughts, largely due to Hughes, which constitute an extension of the notion of qualification for a job beyond that ordinarily understood.[15]

The process of qualifying for a job begins of course with the technical knowledge which is gained in schools; it includes experience gained on the job as well as such qualities as initiative and reliability and the ability to fit into a social organization. For some posts, as Professor Hughes points out, an appointee's background must be such that he can be safely and comfortably entertained at dinner. For other posts this is not a requirement at all. Where the confidence of management is primary to the job, the appointee is likely to resemble management, both ethnically and in other ways, but when the confidence of staff is primary to the job, he will resemble staff. The suitability of a person is not established once and for all, but in a series of separate gestures, in the form for example of promotions, each of which constitutes, in Hughes's words, a "vote of confidence."

In the sorts of occupations in which the French and English work,

[13]"The French Canadians outside of Quebec," *Annals of the American Academy of Political and Economic Science*, vol. CVII, no. 196 (May 1923), p. 13.

[14]S. Jamieson, "French and English in the Institutional Structure in the Province of Quebec," M.A. thesis, McGill University, Montreal, 1935. W. J. Roy, "French and English Division of Labour in the Province of Quebec," M.A. thesis, McGill University, Montreal, 1935. E. C. Hughes, *French Canada in Transition* (Chicago: University of Chicago Press, 1943).

[15]N. Keyfitz, "The Demographic Development of Quebec" in J. C. Falardeau, éd., *Essais sur le Québec contemporain* (Québec: Presses Universitaires Laval, 1953).

no great change was revealed between the 1931 and 1941 censuses. The situation is described by a French-Canadian writer after a review of the literature:[16]

The English owner establishing himself in Quebec saw the advantage of labour which was cheap, docile, demanding little because it did not know what to demand. He did not entrust responsibilities to these people. . . . The situation has probably greatly changed since the war, particularly now that the people who had rushed from the countryside to the city could send their children to the primary schools for a longer period and then on to the technical schools. . . . In brief a majority of French language and culture is invaded by an English-speaking minority which gives it work, but at the same time keeps it in subordinate positions. Only a small number of French Canadians can rival the English, and it seems that these are French Canadians who are anglicized, that is to say who have adopted this impersonal attitude in business.

To quote an English-Canadian writer[17] on the division of labour:

"The French education system of Quebec has, until very recent years, been slow in adapting itself to the needs of an industrial society. It has turned out an excellent supply of practitioners of the older professions, but few experts in engineering, chemical industry, commerce, and finance. This is being remedied, but the remedy comes somewhat late."

M. Lortie goes on to discuss the resentment which French Canadians feel because so few of their group are in high-salaried positions. The problem is of course only partly that the educational system does not provide the background needed in modern industry, but partly also that "the control of capital is largely in English-language hands."

The French were under-represented in high-salaried positions in proportion to their numbers in 1941 as in 1931, especially where the activities of modern industry were involved. Among professional groups, for instance, there were three in which the French were found in greater proportion than in the working population—lawyers, clergymen, and professors and college principals; but among chemists, architects, and especially engineers they were a much smaller proportion. It is plainly not education that was lacking, but certain kinds of technical education.

We said then that though there did not seem to be a change between 1931 and 1941 the figures were not entirely unambiguous, and besides the 1930's were a time of regression for everybody.[18] It was therefore with keen anticipation that the 1951 census data were awaited. The

[16]Monique Lortie, "Les Relations biculturelles au Canada," *Contributions à l'étude des sciences de l'homme* (1952), pp. 32–4.

[17]B. K. Sandwell, "The French Canadians," *Annals of the American Academy of Political and Social Science* (Sept. 1947), pp. 171, 172.

[18]Keyfitz, "The Demographic Development of Quebec."

war had brought many changes to Canada—a change in the division of labour between French and English might be one of the most fortunate.

Occupations of course do not tell the whole story, for an occupation as recognized by the census is something of a mixed bag. Thus carpentry includes many grades of skill and experience; when we say that the proportion of carpenters who are French is the same as the proportion of the whole working population who are French we have said nothing about how the French carpenters stand in skill and in pay in relation to other carpenters—they may be higher or lower. However, the classification of occupations used by the census contains the most homogeneous classes that can be devised if the number of these classes is to be kept small enough for the results to be easily reviewed.

Extensive results for men are given in Table IV; a few figures may be extracted and presented here with simplified occupational titles. The construction trades group is a good place to start. For the whole of Canada, this group of occupations was 34 per cent French in 1951. But among foremen and inspectors, whom we may expect to be better paid and regarded, only 28 per cent were French, while among carpenters 37 per cent were French, painters and decorators 34 per cent, and plumbers 36 per cent.

Logging is another activity in which the French are represented in greater numbers than they are in industry as a whole; 48 per cent of persons in all the logging occupations are French. But only 40 per cent of foremen are French against 49 per cent of lumbermen, and these figures, like those for construction, had not changed greatly since 1941.

To turn to transport, we find that 42 per cent of taxi drivers are French, but only 20 per cent of locomotive engineers. Since driving a locomotive is more highly regarded than driving a taxi the question arises (this writer does not have the data to answer it) why the French should have a higher proportion in the one than in the other. Such a question, like similar issues elsewhere in Table IV, can be answered on many levels and the answers in general will turn on historical considerations. We only note here that this is one situation in which there has been an improvement between 1941 and 1951, in the sense of an increase in the proportion of locomotive engineers who are French and a decline in the proportion of taxi drivers.

About 35 per cent of labourers both in agriculture and elsewhere are French, as against 28 per cent in all occupations. At the other end of the scale are the proprietary and managerial ranks in mining (10 per

TABLE IV

Percentage of French to Total for Selected Occupations, Canada and Quebec, 1931–51

Occupation	Canada*									Quebec								
	1931†			1941			1951			1931†			1941			1951		
	Total	French	%	Total	French	%	Total	French	%	Total	French	%	Total	French	%	Total	French	%
ALL OCCUPATIONS‡	3,260,014	808,490	24.8	3,353,416	939,769	28	4,070,384	1,151,704	28.3	822,946	621,764	75.6	924,713	731,852	79.1	1,108,700	883,606	79.7
Proprietary and managerial	209,101	43,237	20.7	209,256	45,278	21.6	357,893	76,581	21.4	55,029	35,834	65.1	55,893	37,015	66.2	94,827	62,073	65.5
(*Owners, managers, officials*) *in:*																		
Forestry, logging	1,879	649	34.5	1,414	524	37.1	4,516	1,652	36.6	660	590	89.4	419	384	91.6	1,388	1,222	88
Mining, quarrying, oil wells	1,249	131	10.5	1,360	93	6.8	2,654	252	9.5	169	91	53.8	173	54	31.2	363	161	44.4
Manufacturing§	28,611	5,983	20.9	26,398	4,771	18.1	65,870	11,877	18	8,860	5,064	58.3	7,982	4,022	50.4	20.295	9,761	48.1
Construction	9,411	2,122	22.5	6,739	1,440	21.4	22,415	4,793	21.4	2,445	1,775	72.6	1,786	1,202	67.3	5,192	3,736	72
Transportation, storage, communication	9,431	1,490	15.8	10,323	1,657	16.1	19,363	3,299	17	1,751	1,110	63.4	2,176	1,186	54.5	4,358	2,497	57.3
Retail trade	94,644	20,699	21.9	100,756	23,486	23.3	127,034	29,988	23.6	23,866	16,853	70.6	25,701	19,014	74	30,902	24,093	78
Wholesale trade	12,848	1,444	11.2	20,188	2,871	14.2	39,308	6,013	15.3	2,837	1,235	43.5	5,226	2,381	45.6	10,625	5,083	47.8
Government service	9,970	2,039	20.5	12,502	3,190	25.5	23,158	5,713	24.7	2,296	1,694	73.8	3,339	2,650	79.4	5,965	4,669	78.3
Recreation service	3,077	449	14.6	3,348	478	14.3	6,304	1,157	18.4	545	309	56.7	596	320	53.7	1,262	843	66.8
Personal service, n.e.s.‖	17,005	4,246	25	17,977	5,430	30.2	31,853	9,214	28.9	5,537	3,652	66	6,314	4,627	73.3	10,319	7,695	74.6
Professional	120,293	25,414	21.1	152,166	37,585	24.7	217,902	46,739	21.4	34,105	21,512	63.1	48,956	32,385	66.2	61,924	39,254	63.4
Architects	1,296	234	18.1	1,186	271	22.8	1,697	313	18.4	431	206	47.8	447	247	55.3	572	280	49
Artists, art teachers	1,909	296	15.5	2,328	404	17.4	3,671	685	18.7	551	256	46.5	708	345	48.7	1,087	594	54.6
Authors, editors, journalists	2,880	432	15	3,434	731	21.3	5,596	1,115	19.9	725	370	51	1,076	652	60.6	1,642	981	59.7
Chemists, and metallurgists	3,200	488	15.3	7,233	1,112	15.4	7,698	1,279	16.6	915	427	46.7	1,881	907	48.2	2,060	1,045	50.7
Clergymen, priests	12,662	3,695	29.2	14,077	4,514	32.1	15,825	5,245	33.1	3,599	2,881	80.1	4,106	3,396	82.7	4,862	4,059	83.5
Dentists	4,007	674	16.8	3,695	727	19.7	4,540	855	18.8	824	577	70	856	640	74.8	1,016	734	72.2
Draughtsmen, designers	4,596	526	11.4	5,596	855	15.3	12,379	2,229	18	1,368	435	31.8	1,810	731	40.4	3,765	1,930	51.3
Engineers	15,818	1,938	12.3	18,547	2,378	12.8	31,417	3,563	11.3	4,507	1,629	36.1	5,548	2,000	36	8,164	2,899	35.5
Lawyers, notaries	8,004	2,081	26	7,791	2,249	28.9	8,841	2,217	25.1	2,347	1,869	79.6	2,582	2,034	78.8	2,639	1,999	75.7
Physicians, surgeons	9,817	2,204	22.5	10,339	2,470	23.9	13,665	3,163	23.1	2,723	1,909	70.1	3,103	2,159	69.6	3,979	2,772	69.7
Professors, college principals	2,941	1,570	53.4	3,858	2,208	57.2	4,610	2,221	48.2	1,710	1,478	86.4	2,157	1,920	89	2,205	1,874	85
Teachers—school	18,274	4,649	25.4	21,988	5,519	25.1	29,322	8,086	27.6	4,687	3,901	83.2	5,780	4,753	82.2	8,250	6,911	83.8
Clerical	143,041	26,930	18.8	151,439	30·443	20.1	243,900	59,149	24.3	42,519	226,65	53.3	42,838	24,585	57.4	71,936	48,136	66.9
Office appliance operators	239	28	11.7	365	111	30.4	1,237	253	20.5	55	24	43.6	133	94	70.7	297	161	54.2
Stenographers, Typists	3,531	667	18.9	3,331	820	24.6	5,038	1,479	29.4	1,088	518	47.6	1,129	664	58.8	1,890	1,215	64.3
Other clerical occupations	139,271	26,235	18.8	147,743	29,512	20	237,625	57,417	24.2	41,376	22,123	53.5	41,576	23,827	57.3	69,749	46,760	67
Agricultural	1,107,766	275,738	24.9	1,064,847	302,004	28.4	797,874	223,455	28	225,914	200,252	88.6	251,539	228,740	90.9	187,846	171,984	91.6
Farmers, stock raisers	625,628	141,052	22.5	630,709	158,155	25.1	539,112	131,599	24.4	113,904	100,283	88	131,406	118,376	90.1	108,145	98,556	91.1
Farm labourers	479,116	134,258	28	431,102	143,490	33.3	254,946	91,235	35.8	111,606	99,680	89.3	119,788	110,144	91.9	79,187	73,040	92.2
Fishing, hunting, trapping	47,408	10,067	21.2	51,126	11,047	21.6	52,742	9,602	18.2	6,418	3,704	57.7	8,081	4,855	60.1	5,538	3,320	59.9
Fishermen**	33,620	9,017	26.8	33,273	9,904	29.8	46,184	8,500	18.4	4,063	3,282	80.8	5,237	4,347	83	3,515	2,843	80.9
Hunters, trappers, guides**	13,788	1,050	7.6	17,853	1,143	6.4	6,558	1,102	16.8	2,355	422	17.9	2,844	508	17.9	2,023	477	23.6

*Not including Yukon and Northwest Territories. Including Newfoundland in 1951.
†Ten years of age and over in 1931.
‡Not including males in "not stated" classification.
§Including owners, managers, officials in "Electricity, gas and water."
‖N.e.s. = Not elsewhere specified.
**The 1951 figures do not include Indians living on reserves.

NOTE: The "Gainfully occupied" rather than the "Labour force" concept was used prior to 1951 for determining the labour force status.
The labour force figures exclude a few persons seeking work who have never been employed.
Occupations for 1931 and 1941 were rearranged on the basis of the 1951 classification, though some adjustment of the 1951 occupations was necessary.
The 1941 figures in this Table do not include persons on active service on June 2, 1941.

TABLE IV (*cont.*)

Occupation	Canada*									Quebec								
	1931†			1941			1951			1931†			1941			1951		
	Total	French	%	Total	French	%	Total	French	%	Total	French	%	Total	French	%	Total	French	%
Logging	42,116	17,965	42.7	78,834	39,871	50.6	101,331	49,118	48.5	14,897	13,608	91.3	30,038	27,998	93.2	34,563	32,811	94.9
Foremen	912	384	42.1	1,321	663	50.2	3,726	1,492	40	339	295	87	613	541	88.3	1,185	1,099	92.7
Forest rangers, timber cruisers	3,182	1,190	37.4	2,923	1,292	44.2	5,030	2,049	40.7	1,114	937	84.1	1,136	986	86.8	1,646	1,486	90.3
Lumbermen	38,022	16,391	43.1	74,590	37,916	50.8	92,575	45,577	49.2	13,444	12,376	92.1	28,289	26,471	93.6	31,732	30,226	95.3
Mining and quarrying	57,336	7,779	13.6	70,501	12,984	18.4	65,273	16,638	25.5	5,959	3,930	66	9,804	6,206	63.3	11,883	8,757	73.7
Manufacturing and mechanical	367,532	89,062	24.2	544,810	152,716	28	737,238	219,293	29.7	103,333	72,702	70.4	167,992	124,153	73.9	220,367	174,022	79
Bakers	10,539	3,256	30.9	11,310	3,896	34.4	10,070	4,016	39.9	3,333	2,782	83.5	3,906	3,314	84.8	3,950	3,456	87.5
Foremen	13,658	3,685	27	19,671	5,284	26.9	46,342	12,130	26.2	4,813	3,110	64.6	6,933	4,455	64.3	14,514	10,167	70
Stationary engineers, power station operators	23,069	4,092	13.4	32,120	7,910	22.4	53,167	11,892	22.4	3,496	2,009	57.5	7,925	5,538	69.9	10,566	8,111	76.8
Construction	183,506	54,767	29.8	195,770	66.928	34.2	290,486	99,800	34.4	57,540	45,130	78.4	65,489	54,118	82.6	90,068	77,985	86.6
Foremen, inspectors	5,381	1,360	25.3	4,481	1,293	28.9	13,186	3,675	27.9	1,589	1,099	69.2	1,355	1,046	77.2	3,467	2,787	80.4
Carpenters	81,778	26,528	32.4	90,470	32,897	36.4	129,045	47,293	36.6	24,852	21,075	84.8	29,218	25,647	87.8	39,881	36,150	90.6
Painters, decorators, glaziers	35,227	10,129	28.8	39,058	13,374	34.2	46,273	15,661	33.8	11,025	8,576	77.8	13,261	11,028	83.2	14,304	12,331	86.2
Plumbers, pipe fitters	17,471	5,365	30.7	19,484	6,633	34	29,531	10,681	36.2	6,090	4,680	76.8	6,884	5,632	81.8	10,049	8,691	86.5
Transportation and communication	229,980	56 016	24.4	252,607	72,231	28.6	379,617	112,454	29.6	57,575	44,690	77.6	68.775	56,820	82.6	101,655	85,561	84.2
Chauffeurs, taxi and bus drivers	15,388	6,398	41.6	15,242	6,639	43.6	32,458	13,523	41.7	7,107	5,614	79	6,702	5,664	84.5	13,187	11,308	85.8
Locomotive engineers	7,920	1,021	12.9	7,088	907	12.8	9,366	1,832	19.6	1,460	766	52.5	1,184	623	52.6	1,934	1,341	69.3
Locomotive firemen	5,948	919	15.5	5,235	909	17.4	7,254	1,246	17.2	952	664	69.7	931	636	68.3	1,199	795	66.3
Longshoremen, stevedores	7,358	2,881	39.2	10,922	4,804	44	10,634	4,419	41.6	2,938	2,569	87.4	4,437	4,073	91.8	4,042	3,810	94.3
Messengers	12,880	3,041	23.6	11,711	4,418	37.7	10,668	3,878	36.4	4,230	2,523	59.6	4,931	3,724	75.5	4,028	3,203	79.5
Postmen, mail carriers	6,700	1,640	24.5	7,310	2,044	28	8,786	2,554	29.1	1,561	1,350	86.5	1,848	1,667	90.2	2,302	2,101	91.3
Sectionmen trackmen	23,587	3,871	16.4	24,422	4,928	20.2	30,353	6,780	22.3	2,873	2,539	88.4	3,689	3,226	87.4	4,337	3,728	86
Teamsters, draymen	22,286	6,879	30.9	18,844	6,559	34.8	12,845	4,621	36	6,403	680	10.6	6,279	5,437	86.6	4,218	3,795	90
Truck drivers	49,942	13,100	26.2	85,172	26,745	31.4	152,728	50,579	33.1	12,757	10,522	82.5	23,909	20,895	87.4	42,636	38,358	90
Commercial	156,592	34,156	21.8	152,115	38,462	25.3	195,426	49,622	25.4	43,365	29,007	66.9	44,608	32,340	72.5	55,518	40,836	73.6
Sales clerks (incl. service station attendants)	100,537	22,680	22.6	81,270	24,282	29.9	85,264	26,747	31.4	27,591	19,092	69.2	25,683	20,384	79.4	26,602	22,040	82.9
Financial	27,695	4,965	17.9	22,335	4,445	19.9	30,755	6,018	19.6	7,028	4,204	59.8	5,993	3,888	64.9	7,519	5,078	67.5
Insurance agents	17,049	3,795	22.3	14,571	3,596	24.7	18,032	4,604	25.5	4,867	3,271	67.2	4,506	3,199	71	5,435	3,975	73.1
Service	137,438	28,775	20.9	153,555	38,969	25.4	269,680	66,893	24.8	35,332	22,736	64.3	43,354	30,793	71	64,814	47,600	73.4
Barbers, hairdressers, manicurists	16,368	5,406	33	14,889	5,137	34.5	13,561	4,688	34.6	4.657	4,088	87.8	4,420	3,901	88.3	4,028	3,530	87.6
Cooks	17,832	3.300	18.5	17,847	4,263	23.9	19,513	5,801	29.7	3,929	2,288	58.2	4,637	3,099	66.8	5,902	4,335	73.4
Guards, watchmen, n.e.s.‖	13,411	3,663	27.3	20,815	5,821	28	25,298	8,040	31.8	4,177	3,125	74.8	6,477	4,843	74.8	8,235	6,730	81.7
Janitors, sextons	14,691	1,878	12.8	19,221	3,628	18.9	31,120	6,105	19.6	2,612	1,379	52.8	4,054	2,707	66.8	5,715	4,304	75.3
Launderers, cleaners, dyers	9,789	1,040	10.6	8,898	1,560	17.5	9.928	2,984	30.1	2.326	896	38.5	2,609	1,271	48.7	3,456	2.496	72.2
Policemen, detectives	10,900	2,799	25.7	15.9[illegible]0	4,711	29.5	19,874	5,943	29.9	3,099	2,453	79.2	5,241	4,158	79.3	6,261	5,216	83.3
Waiters	11,203	2,149	19.2	13,735	3,728	27.1	20,341	6,781	33.3	3,578	1,804	50.4	4,075	2,782	68.3	7,171	5,369	74.9
Labourers (not agricultural, fishing, logging, or mining)	430,210	133,619	31.1	254,065	86,806	34.2	330,267	116,342	35.2	133,932	101,790	76	81,353	67,956	83.5	100,242	86,189	86

cent French) manufacturing (18 per cent French), and wholesale trade (15 per cent French). These have not shown any important change since 1941. On the other hand clerical occupations have changed. The proportion of French among clerks has gone up from 20 per cent in 1941 to 24 per cent in 1951.

We suggest that the reader glance over the occupations listed in Table IV and make interpretations from his own knowledge. What the table does not show is that almost everybody has gone up in income between 1941 and 1951, and this applies both to French- and English-speaking Canadians. Also shared as far as we know are mechanization and its consequent substitution of lighter work, shorter hours, and similar changes. What the table reports on is only the relative position of the French, and it seems to this reader of the table that the relative position of the French has not improved.

A regional qualification may be mentioned. The first column of the table is concerned with the situation in the whole country; if there was a shift of some activity into the province of Quebec, there would probably also be an increase in the proportion of French in the occupations concerned. The last set of columns of the table shows the figures for the province of Quebec, and is presumably free of this effect.

One explanation of the figures which has been suggested may be quickly dismissed. If the French who rise in the world were in a certain proportion of cases to forget that they were French when asked their origin by the census enumerator, then the French would be under-represented in the upper-income occupations. However, the French whose conception of their origin has changed would most likely answer "Canadian" and the number of persons who so answered the question of origin in 1951 was small enough (about 75,000 in all occupations and both sexes), that this possibility must be dismissed.

Although the qualifications ought not to be overlooked, the news from the 1951 census shows little change in the relative standing of French and English in Canadian industry. But educational measures have been taken—the provision of courses for construction workers in the province of Quebec is one example—and the effect of these may be expected to appear in later censuses.

Population and Public Opinion

Students of politics from Plato to Gallup have always seen opinion as associated with a date. During the past twenty years there have been times when almost everybody in Canada thought there ought to be immigration, and there have been times when almost nobody wanted it. The birth of this question as an issue in Canadian thinking and politics occurred about the time of the peace settlement of 1763 when the English victors looked out over a vast territory taken from France after a costly struggle, occupied largely by French settlers who had little wish to return to France.

The colony had few people compared with the other portions of British North America, and many felt that it was only a question of time before the French would be swamped. This notion even then overlooked some important facts, and it has become increasingly untenable during the years since the Thirteen Colonies separated in 1783. The thought that the French might in some way be assimilated has turned up from time to time, and as eminent an observer as Lord Durham thought they might be drowned in a flood of immigration. It is an aspect of the subsequent fine adaptation of Canadians to biculturalism that the suggestion that either group simply disappear no longer enters public discussion. Everybody desires Canadian unity first of all and a fine etiquette has developed by which it is not proper to make public remarks on whether our neighbour's religion is right or wrong, and whether he has too many or too few children. Published observations on population are strictly non-normative, confined to the presentation of facts in a tone set by the restrained publications of the census. There is one exception—immigration is an aspect of population that is fair ground for controversial discussion. So extensive in fact is this discussion that it appears to channel the sentiment on the forbidden topics; whether it actually does so would furnish an interesting theme for investigation.

The excerpts from this discussion which we shall present make it clear that the differences between French and English have their place in a spectrum of opinion that includes differences between farm and city people, between employers and labour, between growing provinces and those that are stable.

One might speculate on how immigration would be regarded in an economy in which limited natural resources were the economic base, and how in one centred on manufacturing, which offered productive work for a more expandable labour supply. We need not formulate this issue here, still less try to resolve it. Whether Canadian wealth is a cake of fixed size so that we should keep down the number of people for whom slices are cut, or whether newcomers expand the cake, would seem to be a matter of fact, though one on which agreement has not been reached; our being divided on this issue may account for some of the ambivalence with which Canadians face the immigration issue.

The Canadian Chamber of Commerce considers that immigration will make the cake bigger. It says that Canada should aim at 30 million people by 1975, and that immigration "creates more jobs, creates more homes and raises the standard of living. . . . Immigration has increased employment rather than unemployment. . . . Of every 100 immigrants 50 are dependents or self-employed. . . . Each year in the past five years immigration has added to Canadian life a consumer population larger than many of our fair-size cities. There is no doubt that these new consumers have helped to maintain the momentum of Canadian prosperity."[19]

Moderate opinion has tended to insist that it is not a question of immigration versus no immigration, but rather one of finding the right kind of immigrants, and in the right numbers. Thus Herbert Marshall, testifying before the Immigration Committee of the Senate as far back as 1947, gave the statistics on past immigration, and then was asked about the future; he developed his viewpoint in terms of Canada's "absorptive capacity." More recently Walter Harris, Minister of Immigration, said that "Canada cannot absorb more than from 150,000 to 200,000 each year . . . [the labour unions] don't want immigrants admitted beyond the country's absorptive capacity."[20]

This limitation of numbers is to be taken both in reference to the economy as a whole and to particular occupations. After the war it was assumed by nearly everybody that Canada needed forestry workers, miners, farm help, and domestic servants. The need for farm help was especially stressed, in continuance of a tradition going back long before the Second World War that immigration ought to be primarily a handmaid to our agricultural development. Even during the 1930's when the stream of immigration had dwindled to its lowest point in a century, farmers and persons with capital were still wanted. H. F. Angus comments that "Canada's economic vicissitudes should not be interpreted as a settled belief that in nation-building capitalists and peasants are more important than the petite bourgeoisie or the proletariat. It does however indicate the political strength of the two latter classes in Canada, who have been able to exclude those most likely to compete with them."[21] It perhaps also reflects the view, especially prominent during the 1930's, that at the worst the farmer could eat his produce but that the unemployed industrial worker would be a burden on others.

[19]*Montreal Gazette*, Nov. 26, 1954, reporting on brief presented to the Canadian Government.

[20]*Ottawa Citizen*, April 28, 1954.

[21]"The Need for an Immigration Policy," *Annals of the American Academy of Political and Social Science* (Sept. 1947), p. 17.

The Gallup Poll of May 31, 1952, turned up an interesting result on this topic. It asked, "Would you say that Canada needs immigrants, or does not need immigrants at the present time?" Thirty-six per cent thought that Canada needed immigrants. People were asked to name those occupations in which immigrants were particularly needed, and the most common answer was "farm help." But it turned out that the proportion of farmers who thought that Canada needed immigrants was no greater than the proportion of the general public. This result surprised some of those who had thought of the farmers as so desperate that their need for help would determine their opinion on the subject of immigration. However, spokesmen for the farm community, notably James G. Gardiner, Minister of Agriculture, have been consistent in urging measures for a larger population.

Labour has in all periods looked on immigration in the light of the unemployment position. Says one newspaper writer, "Labour, of course, favours immigration in principle—but only if there are already more than enough jobs to go round."[22] Many well-reasoned expressions through the post-war years by organized labour and by organizations speaking for labour impress the need for caution on the part of the government. A Canadian press dispatch of October 7, 1954, reports a convention of the army, navy, and air force veterans of Canada, in which one resolution urged the federal Government to control the number and types of immigrants. It was explained that the resolution was directed against new Canadians working for too low wages while veterans were idle. Gallup polls, at various dates, in particular in August 1947 and May 1952, showed that a majority of business men wanted more immigrants, while a majority of white collar and manual workers wanted fewer.

We might perhaps identify attitudes on immigration with economic strength and weakness, real or imagined. The people who see newcomers to the country as providing a labour force for them to command will take a different attitude from those who see them as potential competitors for jobs. And the census indicates a larger proportion of English among employers and of French among employees.

But thought on immigration is not entirely determined by economic issues. One cultural concern is the ethnic composition of the country. Rather little has been heard since the 1930's to the effect that immigrants drive out native Canadians. Mabel Timlin shows some of the weaknesses of the "displacement theory."[23] It was never easy to show that the native Canadians who left did so in greater numbers than they

[22]Arthur Blakely in *Montreal Gazette*, April 16, 1955.
[23]*Does Canada Need More People?* (Toronto: Oxford University Press, 1951).

would have if there had been no immigration. The decline of this view happens to coincide with the decline of emigration from Canada; the number of immigrants coming in was greater earlier in this century than it is now, but there has never been a time in our history when the number of immigrants retained has been greater.

Underlying some declarations on immigration appears to be the view that the number of unemployed in the country has been equal to the "excess" of our population—in other words, if the population had been less by the number of unemployed and their families through more restraint in our past admittance of immigrants there would be no unemployed. The over-simplified economics which this implies is no longer current. Immigration and unemployment have been linked in a much more reasonable argument that immigrants should not be admitted during the winter months when unemployment reaches its seasonal peak.

There are clear regional differences in opinion on the need for immigration. The Gallup Poll of May 1952 showed that in Ontario 37 per cent of the respondents thought the country needed immigrants, in Quebec only 20 per cent, and in British Columbia 47 per cent. This and other polls indicate that the regions that are growing the fastest are the ones that want immigrants—British Columbians, for instance, see a greater need than Maritimers.

In this inventory of the directions in which Canadian opinion is split on the need for immigrants we come at last to the cultural dimension. The generalization that the English want immigrants as a weapon to counter French children does not cover today's expression of opinion. All groups would like to see more Canadians born—to all this is the ideal way of filling the empty spaces. But more Canadians are being born than ever before, and it is especially the former low fertility groups that have shown the increase—the better off, the urban, the English-speaking. That the differential has diminished is often mentioned by French-Canadian writers. The tendency of birth rates to approach one another may have helped bring about a convergence of opinion on immigration between French- and English-speaking Canadians.

Father Mailhiot asked a series of questions of a sample of French and English residents of Montreal, and used the answers to divide his subjects into six classes of attitude to immigration.[24] The class that was most adverse favoured the immediate abolition of all immigration. It turned out that in his sample 43 per cent of the French were in this class, and 23 per cent of the English. Within the two culture groups

[24]*Contributions à l'étude des sciences de l'homme* (1952).

there were differences according to income. Of the French who were well off only 12 per cent favoured abolition of all immigration, against 32 per cent of the French who were middle class and 58 per cent of the poor. The three corresponding percentages for the English were 5, 21, and 29. It looks as though income is more decisive than being French or English in determining opinion on migration. Father Mailhiot's careful study went much further and attempted to find the kind of thinking that lay behind these opinions. He found prominent among the reasons for the opposition the housing shortage, unemployment, and inflation. Father Mailhiot's students have extended this research in various directions.

The debate on immigration on the cultural side has recently tended to focus on where the immigrants ought to come from. A *mémoire* presented by the Société d'Assistance aux Immigrants to the Royal Commission on Constitutional Problems lays a good deal of stress on the fact that even among the immigrants who settle in the province of Quebec some three-fifths become assimilated into the English-speaking community. Quebec, says the brief (p. 38), ought to attack this matter in a positive way, for example by doing something about the selection and recruitment of the immigrants who will settle in Quebec, as the constitution permits it to do, and as some other provinces are actually doing.

A Canadian Press dispatch of September 27, 1954, quotes Antoine Rivard, Solicitor General for the province of Quebec, as saying that "The right to immigrate is a natural right," but that if "the apostolic role of French Canada is to be continued effectively with regard to the immigrants of tomorrow those immigrants must come to us only after being judged able to integrate themselves into the Quebec family." *Le Droit*[25] then complained that there were too few "Franco-Latin" immigrants. Shortly after this the *Globe and Mail* made the suggestion that Canada should seek more French immigrants, who could bring new blood to Quebec. *Le Devoir*[26] does not agree. In the first place it points out that Quebec has been a source from which immigrants have gone forth to the other provinces. However, it considers that some immigrants would be valuable, preferably solidly educated technicians rather than intellectuals, fewer than Ontario needs, but more perhaps than in the past.

One element that lies in the background of all Canadian thinking is an awareness that American ways of doing things are making inroads on local cultures everywhere in the world. This fact is variously evaluated; but both those speaking English and those speaking French

[25]Sept. 28, 1954. [26]Nov. 17, 1954.

consider that as Canadians they have something distinctive to defend and to create. It has been suggested that the French are perhaps more sensitive on this matter; Hughes observes that the intellectuals of Cantonville "decry the banality of the American newspaper and magazine, as of most things American."[27] Says Edgar McInnis, "To the French, clinging to their distinctive culture, American influences have seemed not only alien but dangerous in a way that has little real parallel for English-speaking Canada."[28]

It has not been easy for the Government to find a consistent immigration policy that would meet these varied viewpoints and their changes from year to year. The matter has been much discussed outside as well as inside official circles. Dr. Timlin's book *Does Canada Need More People?* is a useful attempt to indicate needs and the policies that might meet them. The *Annals of the American Society of Political and Economic Science* has had two volumes on Canada; the earlier, dated May 1923, contained a chapter entitled "Canada's Immigration Policy," while in the latter the corresponding chapter was "Need for an Immigration Policy." The more critical spirit of the present generation of scholars is exemplified in a book by William Petersen on the immigration into Canada from Holland, in which he says in effect that there never has been a Canadian immigration policy.[29] The difficulty is that in a democracy government must be sensitive to opinion and to changes of opinion.

But there are some constants in Canadian thinking on immigration. Thus most Canadians want to see a larger population for this would increase the labour force and the market.[30] Most want to see the immigrants who are admitted come at such times and be selected in such a way that they match the country's absorptive capacity. Professor Angus mentions two points which come increasingly to the fore as Canada orients itself to the outside world. One is security; the other is national prestige—"A larger population might give greater influence in world affairs."[31] This writer agrees whole-heartedly even though he has no clear idea of how population fits into measures designed for national security in an atomic age.

1955

[27]*French Canada in Transition*, p. 92.

[28]"The People" in G. W. Brown, ed., *Canada* (Berkeley: University of California Press, 1950), p. 24.

[29]*Some Factors Influencing Postwar Emigration from the Netherlands* (The Hague: Nijhoff, 1952).

[30]Gallup polls, Feb. 1945, Oct. 1946, Jan. 1948.

[31]"The Need for an Immigration Policy," p. 20.

Aspects démographiques

JACQUES HENRIPIN
Faculté des Sciences sociales, Université de Montréal

IL Y A LONGTEMPS que le problème des relations entre « Canadiens » et « Canadians » se pose en termes démographiques. Au reste, on peut dire qu'il s'est posé en ces termes même avant qu'il y eût des Canadians au Canada. En effet la conquête militaire de 1760 ne pose plus beaucoup de problèmes quant à ses causes profondes, si l'on veut bien se rappeler que les 65,000 Canadiens d'alors faisaient face à des voisins dont le nombre était d'environ un million et demi. Cette situation a été éloquemment rappelée par M. Alfred Sauvy :

> Il a suffi que, dans un des deux pays en lutte pour un immense continent, l'un envoie, chaque année, quelques milliers de colons, l'autre quelques centaines, pour que le cours de l'histoire reçoive une formidable impulsion. Et, symbole tragique, au moment même où la langue française s'assurait en Europe la prédominance internationale, grâce à sa forte démographie, elle était en train de la perdre à terme dans le monde, parce que quelques bateaux de plus... quittaient tous les ans la petite Angleterre[1].

Cette évocation se situe à l'échelle du monde, mais les conséquences de ces « quelques bateaux de plus » ont été singulièrement analogues, plus « tragiques » peut-être, à l'échelle du Canada. De 1780 à 1930, on a assisté à une lutte entre les deux groupes ethniques, qui s'est livrée surtout sur deux plans : politique et démographique. Quant à la vie économique, il semble bien que les Canadiens français n'ont jamais pu opposer une concurrence bien sérieuse à leurs co-nationaux. Sur le plan démographique, les armes sont bien connues : l'immigration britannique, prolongée par son accroissement naturel, était en concurrence avec l'accroissement naturel des Canadiens français; ceux-ci, loin de recevoir des renforts de l'extérieur, virent des centaines de milliers des leurs émigrer aux Etats-Unis, de 1830 à 1930. Résultat : depuis 1871, les Canadians – auxquels se rallient plus ou moins en

[1]Préface à Marcel Reinhard, *Histoire de la population mondiale de 1700 à 1948* (Paris : Domat-Montchrestien, 1949).

définitive la plupart des Canadiens dont l'origine ethnique n'est ni française ni britannique – comptent 70 pour cent environ de la population et les Canadiens 30 pour cent.

Depuis 1930, la situation est plus compliquée : d'une part, les facteurs démographiques traditionnels de la concurrence ethnique semblent se stabiliser autour des proportions que nous venons de signaler; d'autre part – et c'est ici que le phénomène se complique – d'autres facteurs, de nature économico-sociologique, interviennent et ils ne sont pas étrangers aux préoccupations des démographes : une partie importante des Canadiens d'origine française vivant hors de ce qu'on a appelé le glacier québécois, adoptent la culture ou en tout cas la langue anglaise. Ce phénomène n'est lui-même qu'un aspect plus apparent d'une réalité qui prend de plus en plus d'ampleur : c'est l'importance des facteurs socio-économiques dans le problème des relations entre les deux groupes culturels majeurs du Canada. La répartition professionnelle de la population active est, à ce point de vue, très significative.

Laissant à monsieur Nathan Keyfitz l'étude de la croissance et de la distribution géographique de la population, des migrations et de la répartition professionnelle, nous nous attacherons à décrire le comportement de chacun des groupes culturels[2], en ce qui concerne : 1) les mariages; 2) les naissances; 3) l'assimilation ou le passage d'un groupe culturel à l'autre; 4) la mortalité infantile.

I. Nuptialité

L'étude de la nuptialité comporte un double intérêt : d'abord parce qu'elle conditionne le volume des naissances; ensuite parce qu'elle est l'expression d'une réalité socio-économique. La première proposition va de soi, étant donné que plus de 95 pour cent des enfants naissent de mères mariées. Quant à la seconde, mentionnons seulement à titre d'exemple que le mouvement des mariages est étroitement dépendant de la situation économique. Nous allons le voir un peu plus loin.

Un certain nombre de particularités existent concernant le comportement comparé des Anglais et des Français à l'égard de la nuptialité. La principale est peut-être l'espèce de renversement qui s'est produit, au cours des cinquante dernières années, et surtout depuis 1920, dans

[2]Les statistiques disponibles lèvent, à toute fin pratique, l'imprécision de la notion de culture; les comparaisons seront établies d'après l'origine ethnique, bien que l'« origine » ne corresponde pas toujours, tant s'en faut, à la culture ou même à la langue.

les positions respectives des représentants des deux cultures. En 1891, le Québec avait la plus forte nuptialité du Canada; en 1941, il occupait le dernier rang, parmi les provinces[3]. Le Québec était également, en 1941, la seule province ayant subi une diminution de la proportion des mariés, par rapport à 1891. On peut élaborer un indice montrant l'évolution, pour chaque province, de la proportion des personnes mariées. Si l'on choisit l'année 1891 comme base (=100), on trouve les indices suivants pour 1941 : Canada, 103; Ontario, 107; Québec, 92. C'est surtout depuis la première guerre mondiale que le Québec s'est dissocié, dans son évolution, des autres provinces[4].

Il semble donc que les Canadiens français, après avoir été sujets à une propension au mariage relativement forte, ont vu ce caractère perdre de sa vigueur ou rester stagnant alors que les autres Canadiens évoluaient en sens contraire. Le pivot de ce mouvement de bascule se situe vers les années 1910–20. Depuis ce temps, la nuptialité française s'est restaurée, mais elle garde toujours – et plus encore, semble-t-il, depuis quelques années – son infériorité par rapport à la nuptialité anglaise.

Ainsi, depuis 1921, sauf pour les années 1943, 1944 et 1945, les taux de nuptialité (nombre de mariages pour mille habitants) de la province de Québec sont légèrement inférieurs à ceux de l'ensemble du Canada et le sont passablement à ceux de l'Ontario[5]. Mais cet indice mesure mal le comportement à l'égard du mariage car il est légèrement affecté par la composition par âge de la population. Cependant, comme justement la structure par âge du Québec favorise un taux de nuptialité élevé, l'infériorité constatée pour Québec doit avoir une signification. Nous reviendrons d'ailleurs sur ce fait, avec un indice plus précis.

Sensibilité différente à la conjoncture

Ce qu'il est intéressant d'observer, à l'aide de ce taux, c'est l'évolution comparée de la nuptialité, au cours des trente dernières années. Le Tableau I donne les taux de nuptialité des provinces de Québec et d'Ontario, de 1921 à 1953, par période de cinq ans.

En plus de l'infériorité des taux québécois, on constate que dans la mesure où les différences entre les deux provinces représentent à peu près les différences entre les deux ethnies, les Canadiens français ont réagi davantage à la crise économique des années 1930–4 : le taux de

[3]Recensement du Canada, 1941, vol. I, p. 139.

[4]*Ibid.*, p. 137, Tableau I.

[5]Les statistiques officielles ne donnent pas la répartition des nouveaux mariés par origine ethnique.

TABLEAU I

NOMBRE DE MARIAGES POUR MILLE PERSONNES (TAUX DE NUPTIALITÉ), 1921–53, ONTARIO ET QUÉBEC

Années	Ontario	Québec
1921–25	8.0	7.2
1926–30	7.8	6.9
1931–35	6.9	5.7
1936–40	8.9	8.5
1941–45	9.7	9.6
1946–50	10.3	9.2
1951–53	9.6	8.6

la période 1931–5 n'est qu'à 82.6 pour cent du niveau de la période 1926–30, pour le Québec, à comparer avec 88.5 pour cent pour l'Ontario. La chute a donc été plus forte pour le Québec : 11.5 pour cent contre 17.4 pour cent. Cela n'est pas étonnant lorsqu'on sait que dans l'ensemble, les Québécois comptaient beaucoup moins sur la restriction volontaire des naissances que les Ontariens pour atténuer les difficultés de la crise économique; ils devaient donc se rabattre davantage sur l'abstention ou tout au moins le retard du mariage. Les difficultés économiques sont toujours un facteur de diminution des mariages[6]. Mais elles le sont d'une manière beaucoup plus efficace lorsque le mariage est suivi de naissances sur lesquelles presque aucun contrôle n'est exercé. Or nous verrons plus loin que la société canadienne-française compte beaucoup plus de couples se conformant à cette attitude que n'en comptent les autres Canadiens.

Par contre c'est la population de la province de Québec qui est la moins affectée, au point de vue de la nuptialité, par la guerre. Dans l'ensemble du Canada et pour les autres provinces, on observe, entre 1942 et 1944–5, une chute du taux de nuptialité variant de 16 à 30 pour cent par rapport au niveau de 1942. Pour le Québec, la baisse n'est que de 9 pour cent. Si l'on se rappelle l'ampleur prise par l'opposition à la conscription, chez les Canadiens français, on ne sera pas étonné de ces résultats.

Comportement actuel

Nous serons parfois forcé d'examiner les différences interethniques par l'intermédiaire de comparaisons interprovinciales. Des recoupements parfois possibles ont montré que les provinces de Québec et d'Ontario représentaient assez bien les Français et les Anglais.

[6]La corrélation entre l'évolution de l'emploi et celle des mariages le montre de façon frappante. Voir : Recensement de 1941, vol. I, p. 141, Graphique 1.

La nuptialité est beaucoup plus précoce et aussi plus répandue chez les Ontariennes que chez les Québécoises. Il en va de même d'ailleurs pour le sexe masculin. On peut le constater de deux façons : 1) en calculant des taux de nuptialité par âge, c'est-à-dire en rapportant, pour des âges ou groupes d'âges déterminés, le nombre des nouveaux mariés auparavant célibataires aux célibataires du même âge, ce qui exclut le phénomène des remariages; 2) en calculant la proportion des personnes mariées pour différents âges ou groupes d'âges.

Taux de nuptialité

Le Tableau II et le Graphique 1 montrent que pour les deux sexes et presque à tous les âges (à tous les âges pour le sexe féminin), les taux de la province d'Ontario sont supérieurs à ceux de la province de Québec.

TABLEAU II

TAUX DE NUPTIALITÉ (POUR MILLE) PAR GROUPES D'ÂGES, ONTARIO ET QUÉBEC, 1951*

	Sexe féminin			Sexe masculin		
Age	(1) Ontario ‰	(2) Québec ‰	(3) Rapport (1)/(2)	(4) Ontario ‰	(5) Québec ‰	(6) Rapport (4)/(5)
15–19	85.6	42.8	2.00	20.2	7.1	2.86
20–24	243.7	163.2	1.49	160.0	116.3	1.38
25–34	158.5	96.4	1.64	161.0	157.1	1.03
35–44	43.7	29.9	1.46	61.0	57.1	1.07
45–54	16.0	12.2	1.31	23.7	21.5	1.10
55–64	5.9	3.3	1.88	9.5	7.8	1.22

*On trouve des différences un peu moins fortes mais de même sens lorsqu'on compare la province de Québec au reste du Canada.

Les différences entre les deux provinces sont beaucoup plus marquées pour le sexe féminin, sauf pour le groupe 15–19 ans (voir colonnes 3 et 6). Un ajustement graphique de ces taux donne les courbes du Graphique 1. La différence de nuptialité, pour le sexe féminin, a une ampleur inattendue et le maintien de cette différence jusqu'à un âge avancé laisse entendre que les jeunes Québécoises qui ne se marient pas (et qui le feraient si la nuptialité était aussi forte qu'en Ontario) ne se « rattrapent » pas à un âge plus avancé : il n'y a pas de récupération. Pour les célibataires masculins, la différence entre les provinces est forte, de 15 à 25 ans environ.

Le fait que l'écart est plus fort pour le sexe féminin s'explique, au

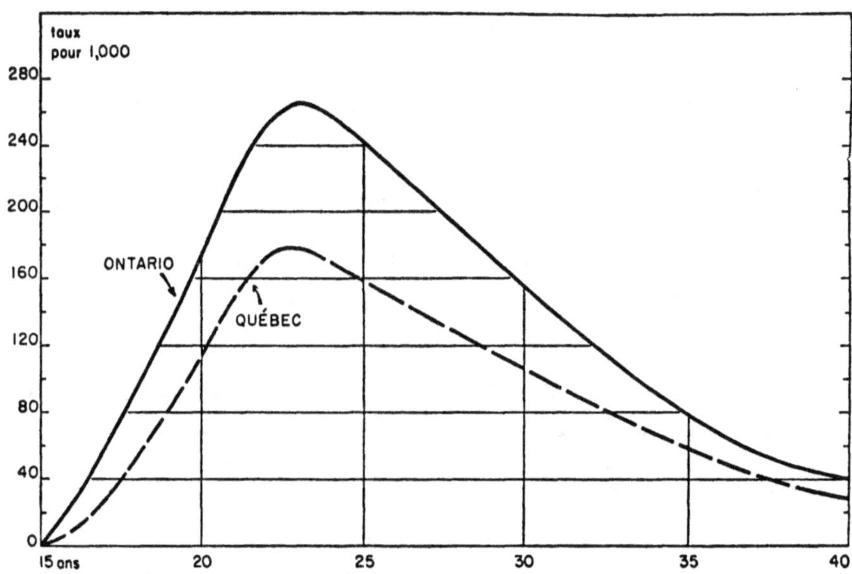

GRAPHIQUE 1a. Taux de nuptialité des célibataires (sexe féminin), par âge, 1951

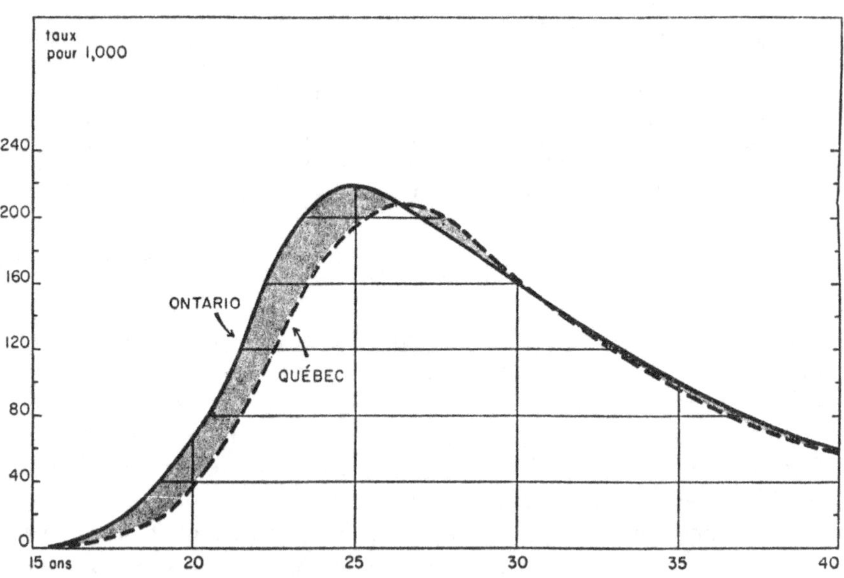

GRAPHIQUE 1b. Taux de nuptialité des célibataires (sexe masculin), par âge, 1951

moins en partie, par le fait que la proportion des sexes, aux âges où l'on se marie le plus, est défavorable aux femmes célibataires du Québec, probablement à cause de l'émigration des jeunes hommes. Telle est la situation en 1951. Il semble qu'elle soit exceptionnelle, c'est-à-dire que l'écart entre les provinces est probablement plus grand en 1951 qu'il ne l'est d'ordinaire. Les chiffres du Tableau III, par exemple, expriment le résultat d'une nuptialité moins inégale. Il s'agit de la proportion des individus restés célibataires, vers l'âge de 50 ans pour les femmes et 60 ans pour les hommes.

TABLEAU III

PROPORTION DE CÉLIBATAIRES À 45–54 ANS (SEXE FÉMININ) ET À 55–64 ANS (SEXE MASCULIN), 1951

Ethnie et région	Sexe féminin 45–54 ans %	Sexe masculin 55–64 ans %
Canadiens britanniques	11.6	11.7
Canadiens non-français	9.8	11.9
Canadiens français	15.4	10.7
Canadiens français, Québec	16.7	10.6
Canadiens britanniques, Ontario	12.3	10.3

L'ensemble des Canadiennes non-françaises semblent jouir d'une forte nuptialité qui doit s'expliquer par les excédents de population masculine. Cette hypothèse est confirmée par la proportion des Canadiens (masculins) non-français qui restent célibataires vers l'âge de 60 ans; celle-ci est la plus forte de tous les groupes mentionnés. Il est plus significatif de comparer les Britanniques de l'Ontario avec les Français du Québec[7]. Notons cependant que ceux-ci sont un peu moins urbanisés que ceux-là. La proportion des femmes restées célibataires à 45–54 ans est de 16.7 pour cent pour les Françaises du Québec et de 12.3 pour cent pour les Britanniques de l'Ontario.

Cette différence entre Britanniques ontariennes et Françaises québécoises n'est pas due uniquement au fait que les premières ont relativement plus de partenaires masculins possibles que les secondes. Elle tient probablement à une attitude différente à l'égard du mariage, attitude qui dépend d'ailleurs des deux sexes. Elle pourrait s'expliquer en partie par le fait que la charge des enfants que suppose le mariage n'est pas envisagée de la même façon par les Britanniques, qui la contrôlent, que par les Françaises, qui la contrôlent moins.

[7]La distribution de chacun de ces groupes suivant l'habitat n'est pas très différente et cette ressemblance est intéressante car elle élimine à peu près l'influence importante que pourrait avoir ce facteur.

Facteurs influant sur la nuptialité

On peut se demander si c'est à cause de leur culture (langue, religion, éducation, etc.) ou encore à cause de leur situation économique que l'un et l'autre groupes diffèrent dans leur comportement à l'égard du mariage. Dans son excellente étude basée sur le recensement de 1941, Mme Enid Charles a dégagé les principaux facteurs qui influencent la nuptialité[8]. Il appert que pour les femmes alors âgées de 45 à 54 ans, la religion catholique avait constitué un important facteur de persistance dans le célibat, aussi bien pour les Canadiennes de langue anglaise que de langue française[9]. Mais le facteur instruction avait joué un rôle encore plus important : pour les femmes étudiées, l'instruction supérieure semble avoir été la cause d'une réduction de la proportion des femmes ayant déjà été mariées. Cette réduction est d'environ 23 pour cent par rapport aux femmes moins instruites. Il est également intéressant de constater qu'elle a été beaucoup plus forte pour les Catholiques françaises (30 pour cent) que pour les Protestantes de langue anglaise (16 pour cent). Il semble donc que la contribution des femmes instruites au renouvellement de leur génération est plutôt désastreuse, au moins quantitativement. Signalons aussi qu'en plus d'exclure complètement un certain nombre de femmes de la vie conjugale, l'instruction repousse l'âge du mariage de celles qui se marient : on a noté une différence de 4.5 ans (pour l'âge médian au premier mariage), entre les femmes ayant fréquenté l'école de 0 à 4 ans et celles qui avaient reçu plus de 13 ans d'instruction.

Contrairement peut-être à ce qu'on pouvait attendre, le facteur langue française pris isolément, – c'est-à-dire une fois éliminée l'influence de la religion, de la durée de la scolarité et de l'habitat, – avait favorisé le mariage par rapport à la langue anglaise. Ici, la « langue » recouvre en fait une réalité sociologique qui dépasse l'aspect purement linguistique et inclut les traditions, le complexe professionnel et économique et tous les facteurs sociologiques qui entourent le mariage.

Nous ne savons pas si l'action des facteurs mis en relief par l'étude de Mme Charles a persisté jusqu'à maintenant. Peut-être le rôle joué par les différences de niveau de vie est-il maintenant prépondérant et explique-t-il l'infériorité actuelle marquée de la nuptialité française ? Peut-être aussi le travail féminin n'exerce-t-il pas une influence égale sur la nuptialité, dans les deux provinces ?

[8]*The Changing Size of the Family in Canada* (Ottawa : Imprimeur du Roi, 1948).

[9]Il faut cependant noter que la différence de religion n'est pas simple : elle inclut, par exemple, des différences de niveau de vie, ce qui doit aussi exercer une influence.

Cette infériorité se manifeste aussi bien dans les régions rurales que dans les villes. C'est du moins ce que laisse voir la comparaison des provinces de Québec et d'Ontario : pour la population agricole comme pour la population rurale non-agricole et la population urbaine, on trouve relativement plus de personnes mariées en Ontario que dans le Québec. Il y a cependant une exception : les fermes de l'Ontario ont plus de célibataires masculins que celles du Québec, ce qui doit s'expliquer par une différence dans la structure des fermes de chaque province, celles de l'Ontario employant plus de travailleurs salariés. Ici aussi on retrouve quelque chose du type d'exploitation souvent exclusivement familial du Québec; la « terre » du Québec ne fait pas beaucoup de place aux célibataires de l'un comme de l'autre sexes.

Veuvage et divortialité[10]

Malgré le petit nombre des personnes engagées dans ces situations matrimoniales, les problèmes posés ont leur importance et il nous paraît utile d'indiquer ici les principales différences observées entre les Anglais et les Français.

L'une des principales différences est bien connue : le divorce est beaucoup plus répandu chez les Britanniques que chez les Français et la cause principale de cette différence est religieuse. En 1953 par exemple, le taux de divortialité de l'Ontario était près de neuf fois plus élevé que celui du Québec : 55.6 et 6.4 pour cent mille habitants. Cependant, dans l'Ile-du-Prince-Edouard, très britannique, le taux n'était que de 14.2. Il était de 120.2 dans la Colombie-Britannique, province elle aussi britannique mais beaucoup moins catholique. On voit qu'il n'y a pas là qu'un facteur ethnique.

Le Tableau IV montre, pour les Britanniques de l'Ontario et pour les Français du Québec, la proportion des veufs et divorcés, par sexe et par groupe d'âges. La supériorité des pourcentages britanniques, pour le sexe féminin, s'explique par la fréquence des divorces et aussi par le fait que la surmortalité masculine – phénomène universellement répandu et qui accroît le nombre des veuves – est remplacée dans le Québec par une surmortalité féminine[11], ce qui tend à diminuer pour cette province le nombre des veuves. Malgré que les différences inter-

[10]Le mot «divortialité» est un néologisme qui est en voie d'être accepté, sinon par les littérateurs, du moins par les démographes. Voir : Nations-Unies, *Dictionnaire démographique multilingue* (édition provisoire, volume français, New York, 1954).

[11]Celle-ci coïncidant avec la période où la fécondité est la plus forte, il se peut que la surmortalité féminine québécoise s'explique, du moins en partie, par les accidents provoqués par les accouchements. C'est dans le Québec que la proportion des accouchements ayant lieu dans une clinique ou un hôpital est la plus faible.

TABLEAU IV

PROPORTION DES VEUFS ET DIVORCÉS, PAR SEXE ET GROUPES D'ÂGES —BRITANNIQUES DE L'ONTARIO ET FRANÇAIS DU QUÉBEC— 1951

Age	Sexe féminin		Sexe masculin	
	Britanniques %	Françaises %	Britanniques %	Français %
25–34	1.40	0.79	0.45	0.30
35–44	3.64	2.80	1.09	1.08
45–54	9.50	8.40	2.65	3.20
55–64	20.88	19.40	6.32	8.55
65 et plus	48.30	46.25	22.60	27.80

provinciales qu'on trouve pour le sexe masculin soient assez différentes de celles qui s'appliquent aux veuves et divorcées, ce sont les mêmes facteurs qui les expliquent. Cependant le rôle joué par ces deux facteurs (divorces surtout et surmortalité) est beaucoup plus important que ne le laissent voir les résultats du Tableau IV, au moins jusqu'à 40 ans. Ces résultats en effet masquent un phénomène important : les taux de remariages sont deux fois plus élevés en Ontario qu'au Québec, jusqu'à l'âge de 40 ans environ. C'est-à-dire qu'un veuf, une veuve, un divorcé ou une divorcée a en moyenne, jusqu'à l'âge de 40 ans environ, deux fois plus de chances de se remarier en Ontario que dans le Québec. C'est du moins la situation de l'année 1951.

Résumé

De nombreux indices montrent une infériorité marquée de la nuptialité française, par rapport à celle des Britanniques, qui est beaucoup plus précoce et répandue. Cette situation correspond à un renversement des positions respectives des deux ethnies, depuis une cinquantaine d'années. Comment expliquer ces phénomènes ? Il est probable qu'à l'époque où la restriction des naissances était encore assez peu pratiquée chez les Anglo-Protestants, ceux-ci envisageaient le mariage avec plus de pondération – nous allions dire avec plus de froideur – que les Franco-Catholiques, probablement moins soucieux de tenir compte des conditions qui modèlent leur vie et de les contrôler.

Pour la période actuelle, la limitation des naissances très largement pratiquée par les Britanniques, appuyée par la supériorité de leur niveau économique et aussi par la perspective du divorce possible, leur permet sans doute de se marier plus allègrement que les Français.

C'est probablement aussi la diffusion, très différente pour chaque ethnie, du contrôle des naissances qui explique que les Français ont été plus sensibles à la crise économique de 1930–5, au point de vue de la nuptialité. Le rôle que nous imputons au facteur contraception (ou limitation des naissances) semble confirmé par l'étude de Mme E. Charles dont nous avons fait mention. Cette étude a en effet montré que la religion catholique avait constitué un facteur d'éloignement de la vie conjugale.

Nous avons enfin vu que la fréquence des dissolutions de mariages était beaucoup plus grande en Ontario qu'au Québec, surtout à cause des divorces. Cette différence est plus que compensée pour le sexe féminin, et à peu près compensée pour le sexe masculin, par des taux de remariages deux fois plus élevés en Ontario.

En plus d'être chargée de signification socio-économique, l'extension prise par le mariage a une répercussion directe sur le niveau de la natalité. Nous aurons l'occasion de constater, dans la section suivante, que la poussée récente de la nuptialité, surtout chez les Britanniques, n'a pas été sans influence sur le mouvement des naissances vers la hausse qu'on a enregistré au cours des dernières années.

II. Natalité et fécondité

L'expression « la revanche des berceaux » n'est ni un fruit de l'imagination, ni un pur slogan qui aurait servi à promouvoir ou maintenir une forte natalité chez les Français; elle évoque une réalité : la natalité des Canadiens est depuis longtemps plus forte que celle des Canadians. L'a-t-elle toujours été ? Le sera-t-elle encore longtemps ? Peut-on du moins dégager une tendance à une amplification ou à un rétrécissement de cette différence ? A quoi est due la forte natalité des Canadiens ? Est-elle imputable à une nuptialité précoce ou plus fréquente ou bien au comportement des couples à l'intérieur du mariage ? Et quel est l'effet de cette différence sur les taux de croissance ? Ces phénomènes sont à la base de la vie économique et sociologique d'un peuple. Ils la conditionnent et sont en même temps un reflet d'un certain ordre de valeurs.

Natalité et fécondité générale

Les statistiques concernant le mouvement naturel de la population[12] non-française, au Canada, n'existent pas depuis longtemps : à peine trente-cinq ans. Pour les Français, on est mieux renseigné grâce au

[12]Les phénomènes relatifs à la natalité et à la mortalité sont désignés en français par l'expression « mouvement naturel de la population » ou, par abréviation, « mouvement de la population ».

dépouillement des registres paroissiaux effectué par Mgr Tanguay et à la publication qu'en a faite le gouvernement fédéral, à l'occasion du recensement de 1871. Cependant, certains indices permettent de croire que la natalité était à peu près la même pour les deux ethnies, vers 1850. M. Nathan Keyfitz[13] a calculé le taux brut de natalité pour le Canada, de 1851 à 1941, à l'aide des données des recensements. Dès le début de cette période, le taux de natalité de l'ensemble du Canada est un peu plus faible (d'environ 8 pour cent) que celui des Canadiens français. Cette différence s'accentue dans la suite jusqu'à la première guerre mondiale; plus exactement, la baisse de l'ensemble du Canada est plus rapide que celle des Français : de 1851 à 1951, la première est d'environ 40 pour cent et la seconde de 20 à 25 pour cent seulement.

Reportons-nous à l'année 1921, alors que débutent la collection et la publication des statistiques du mouvement de la population pour tout le Canada. A ce moment, la natalité des provinces britanniques est nettement inférieure à celle de la province de Québec : pour la période 1921–5, on observe un taux annuel moyen de natalité[14] de 35.5 pour mille au Québec, de 23.7 en Ontario et de 27.4 pour l'ensemble du Canada. Mesurons maintenant la natalité des deux groupes culturels principaux : en 1926, le taux était de 19.7 pour mille pour les Britanniques et de 34 pour mille pour les Français.

A l'heure actuelle, même si cette différence persiste entre les deux ethnies, elle n'apparaît plus aussi clairement dans les chiffres relatifs aux provinces : pour les années 1951–3, le Québec ne vient qu'en troisième place avec un taux de 30.1 pour mille, après Terre-Neuve (33.2) et le Nouveau-Brunswick (31.2); l'Ontario avait une natalité beaucoup plus faible : 25.8. Où en est la natalité de chaque groupe ethnique ? Le Tableau V donne, pour l'année 1951 et pour les personnes d'origine britannique et française, d'abord le taux de natalité (colonne 3) puis le nombre de naissances pour mille femmes de 15 à 44 ans (colonne 5). Ce dernier indice est encore plus précis que le taux de natalité car il ne fait intervenir que des personnes dont l'âge ne les exclut pas de la possibilité de procréer.

Sous une forme ou sous l'autre, la différence interethnique est encore très appréciable; moins cependant qu'en 1926. Comparons par exemple les taux de natalité de chaque groupe culturel : en 1926 et 1927, la différence était de 42 pour cent par rapport au niveau du groupe français; elle est en 1951, de 24 pour cent; en 1939, on trouvait 39 pour

[13] « The Growth of Canadian Population », *Population Studies*, vol. IV, no 1 (juin 1950).

[14] Le taux de natalité est le nombre annuel des naissances pour mille habitants.

TABLEAU V

TAUX DE NATALITÉ ET NOMBRE ANNUEL DE NAISSANCES POUR MILLE FEMMES DE 15 À 44 ANS, EN 1951—ORIGINE BRITANNIQUE ET FRANÇAISE—CANADA MOINS TERRE-NEUVE

Origine	(1) Nombre de naissances*	(2) Population	(3) Taux brut de natalité %	(4) Femmes 15–44 ans	(5) Nombre de naissances pour mille femmes, 15–44 ans
Britannique	153,693	6,364,081	24.1	1,380,844	111
Française	137,298	4,307,727	31.9	980,144	140

*Naissances issues de pères ayant l'origine indiquée auxquelles nous avons ajouté les naissances issues de mères non-mariées de cette origine.

cent et en 1942, 36 pour cent. Il y a donc depuis trente ans une tendance à la diminution de l'écart entre la natalité des Britanniques et celle des Français. Le Graphique 2 montre l'évolution du taux de fécondité totale[15], au cours des trente dernières années, pour chacune des deux provinces. Il est facile de constater que la reprise de la fécondité qui a suivi la crise des années 1930–4 a été beaucoup plus accentuée en Ontario que dans le Québec. On peut noter, sur le même graphique, la différence encore importante entre les deux provinces malgré la tendance à la diminution de cette différence.

Fécondité légitime

Pour une population où presque toutes les naissances proviennent de mères mariées (au Canada : 96 pour cent), la fécondité générale peut se décomposer en deux facteurs isolables : la proportion des personnes mariées, aux différents âges de la procréation, et la fécondité des couples mariés, appelée fécondité légitime.

Dans la première partie de ce chapitre, nous avons comparé la nuptialité des Britanniques et des Français : les Britanniques qui, jusqu'à 1920 environ, se mariaient à un âge plus avancé en moyenne que le Français, ont fini par rattraper et dépasser ces derniers; de sorte que leur nuptialité est maintenant plus précoce et plus généralisée que celle de la population française. Ce premier facteur favorise donc la fécondité non-française.

Mais le deuxième facteur, la fécondité légitime, fait beaucoup plus que compenser l'influence du premier, puisque la fécondité de l'en-

[15]Le « taux de fécondité totale » est le nombre d'enfants qu'auraient, *en moyenne*, au cours de leur vie, les femmes qui vivent jusqu'à l'âge de 50 ans, étant donné les conditions de nuptialité et de fécondité du moment.

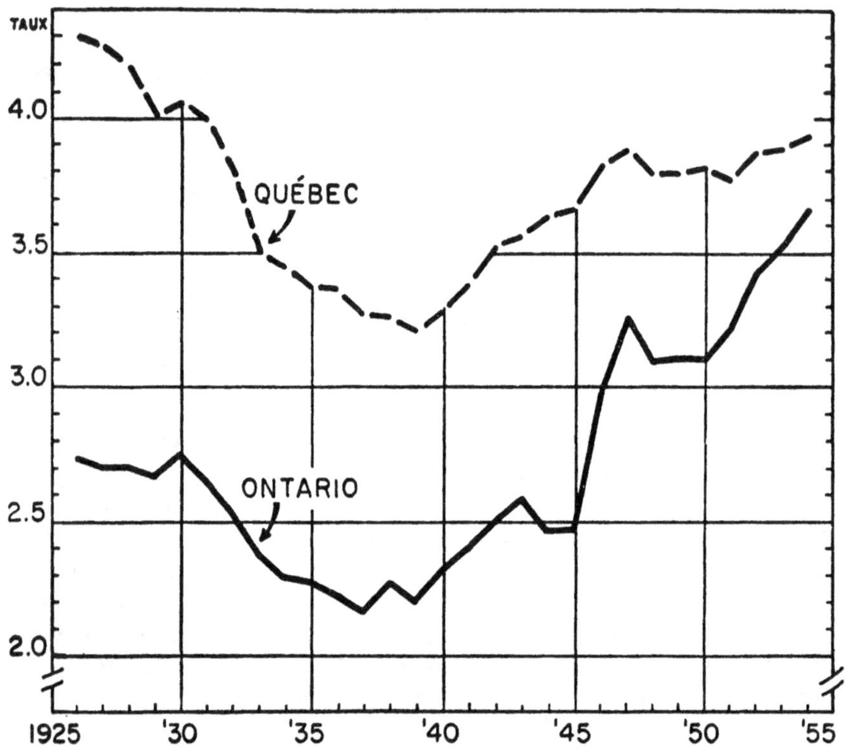

GRAPHIQUE 2. Taux de fécondité total, 1926–53. Sources:

	Qué.	Ont.		Qué.	Ont.		Qué.	Ont.
1926	4.31	2.73	1935	3.37	2.28	1945	3.67	2.47
1927	4.27	2.7	1936	3.36	2.22	1946	3.83	2.97
1928	4.2	2.7	1937	3.27	2.16	1947	3.9	3.28
1929	4.01	2.67	1938	3.26	2.27	1948	3.81	3.1
1930	4.06	2.75	1939	3.21	2.2	1949	3.8	3.11
1931	4	2.65	1940	3.29	2.32	1950	3.81	3.11
1932	3.8	2.53	1941	3.39	2.4	1951	3.78	3.22
1933	3.5	2.37	1942	3.53	2.51	1952	3.86	3.41
1934	3.44	2.29	1943	3.57	2.59	1953	3.88	3.54
			1944	3.64	2.47			

semble des femmes (mariées et non-mariées) est beaucoup moins forte pour les Britanniques. Comparons donc la fécondité des deux groupes ethniques, à l'intérieur du mariage. Nous donnerons d'abord un aperçu historique, puis nous analyserons de façon un peu plus détaillée la situation récente et présente.

Malgré l'insuffisance des matériaux statistiques avant 1921, on peut, grâce aux recensements, élaborer un taux assez significatif : il consiste à rapporter au nombre des femmes mariées de 15 à 44 ans, le nombre des enfants de 0–4 ans. Cet indice est criticable, mais nous croyons que son imperfection n'affecte pas beaucoup la comparaison interethnique. Les résultats du calcul sont donnés dans le Tableau VI et dans le Graphique 3. Ils s'appliquent aux années 1851, 1861, 1871, 1931, 1941 et 1951, pour les provinces d'Ontario et de Québec. Pour les trois dernières années, nous avons ajouté les taux correspondant aux Britanniques de l'Ontario et aux Français du Québec : on voit que la comparaison des deux provinces atténue la différence qui existe entre les Britanniques et les Français. Il nous a paru intéressant d'indiquer sur le graphique les taux enregistrés par les Canadiens en 1681 et en 1734.

TABLEAU VI

FÉCONDITÉ COMPARÉE: QUÉBEC ET ONTARIO—RAPPORT DU NOMBRE DES ENFANTS DE 0–4 ANS AUX FEMMES MARIÉES DE 15–44 ANS, POUR CERTAINES ANNÉES, 1851–1951

Années	Ontario	Québec	Ontario Britanniques	Québec Françaises
1681	—	—	—	1.71
1734	—	—	—	1.45
1851	1.50	1.67		
1861	1.58	1.59		
1871	1.33	1.41		
1881	1.19	1.38		
1891	1.02	1.33		
1931	0.71	1.14	0.66	1.27
1941	0.60	0.90	0.57	1.05
1951	0.77	1.02	0.72	1.10

Les faits les plus importants qui ressortent de ces chiffres sont les suivants : 1) au milieu du XIXe siècle, la fécondité des couples ontariens était à peu près aussi forte que celle des couples québécois (on doit pouvoir transposer cette égalité sur le plan ethnique); 2) le niveau de cette fécondité ne semble guère éloigné de celui des Canadiens de la fin du XVIIe siècle; 3) dès le début de la deuxième moitié du XIXe siècle, s'inaugure le mouvement de baisse constante de la fécondité; cette baisse est beaucoup plus marquée en Ontario que dans le Québec; 4) ici encore on observe, depuis 1931 et davantage depuis 1941, une tendance à la diminution de l'écart entre la fécondité de chacun des deux groupes. En 1931, la fécondité des Ontariennes britanniques n'atteignait qu'un peu plus de la moitié du niveau atteint par les Québécoises françaises; en 1951, la fécondité des premières était aux deux tiers de celle des dernières.

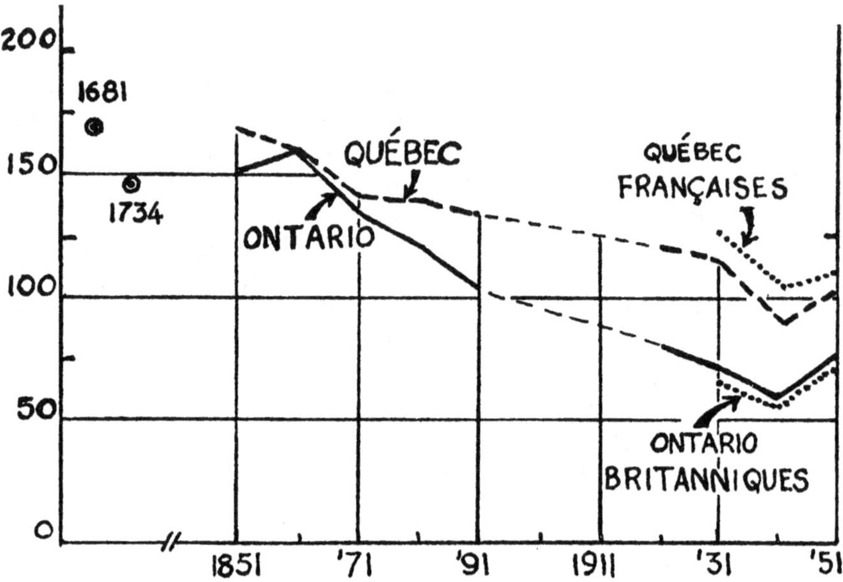

GRAPHIQUE. 3. Fécondité légitime : nombre d'enfants de 0–4 ans pour cent femmes mariées de 15–44 ans

Faut-il supposer que dès le milieu du XIXe siècle, les pratiques anticonceptionnelles ont commencé à s'introduire au Canada, alors que dans les pays européens autres que la France, ce n'est que vers 1880 que ces procédés se sont répandus ? Nous le croirions difficilement. Pour les Françaises en particulier, cette hypothèse semble assez invraisemblable. Nous savons que même à l'heure actuelle, les familles agricoles françaises du Québec ont une fécondité à peu près aussi forte que celle qu'avaient leurs ancêtres du XVIIIe siècle. Nous croyons donc que la diminution de la fécondité enregistrée à partir de 1850 tient à d'autres causes et il n'y a pas de raison de penser que la même explication ne peut pas être appliquée aux Britanniques du XIXe siècle. Il est probable que l'émigration nette importante qui a caractérisé la période 1861–1901 et qu'ont bien montrée les travaux de M. Keyfitz (voir son chapitre dans cet ouvrage) explique une bonne partie de la baisse de fécondité des couples. En effet, parmi les personnes mariées, ce sont les jeunes couples qui émigrent le plus facilement, c'est-à-dire les plus féconds. De plus – et ceci a probablement joué surtout pour les Français – on croit que de nombreux couples ont été séparés, le mari laissant ici sa famille pour aller travailler en Nouvelle-Angleterre. Ces deux catégories d'émigration peuvent très bien ne pas être étrangères à la baisse de fécondité illustrée par le Graphique 3, surtout au cours de la deuxième moitié du XIXe siècle.

On peut montrer de façon simple et frappante l'évolution qui s'est produite dans la vie des couples canadiens, depuis le XVIIIe siècle, à l'aide du Tableau VII illustré par le Graphique 4. On y trouve des taux de fécondité par groupe d'âges, pour les femmes mariées. Ces taux correspondent au nombre annuel de naissances pour mille femmes mariées de l'âge indiqué. Les chiffres ou les courbes permettent de comparer les différents niveaux de la fécondité, suivant l'âge, pour les populations suivantes : *a*) Canadiens du début du XVIIIe siècle; *b*) Canadiens britanniques en 1951; *c*) Canadiens français en 1951.

TABLEAU VII

TAUX DE FÉCONDITÉ LÉGITIME PAR GROUPES D'ÂGES: NOMBRE DE NAISSANCES POUR MILLE FEMMES MARIÉES DE CERTAINS ÂGES, 1951 ET DÉBUT DU XVIIIE SIÈCLE

<table>
<tr><th rowspan="2">Age</th><th colspan="3">Taux de fécondité légitime</th></tr>
<tr><th>Canadiens du début du XVIIIe siècle*</th><th>Canadiens britanniques 1951†</th><th>Canadiens français 1951†</th></tr>
<tr><td>15–19</td><td>493</td><td>476</td><td>538</td></tr>
<tr><td>20–24</td><td>509</td><td>303</td><td>423</td></tr>
<tr><td>25–29</td><td>496</td><td rowspan="2">177</td><td rowspan="2">266</td></tr>
<tr><td>30–34</td><td>484</td></tr>
<tr><td>35–39</td><td>410</td><td rowspan="2">53</td><td rowspan="2">112</td></tr>
<tr><td>40–44</td><td>231</td></tr>
<tr><td>45–49</td><td>30</td><td></td><td></td></tr>
</table>

*Voir J. Henripin, *La Population canadienne au début du XVIIIe siècle* (Paris: P.U.F., 1954), pp. 60 et 124.

†SOURCES: Recensement du Canada, 1951 et Statistique de l'état civil, 1951.

Il importe avant tout de noter que les différences observées ne concernent que les femmes mariées, donc que les variations de la nuptialité n'interviennent pas pour expliquer la diminution très forte de la fécondité. Ainsi isolée, l'évolution de la fécondité légitime est chargée de signification sociologique. Mais examinons d'abord les courbes du Graphique 4.

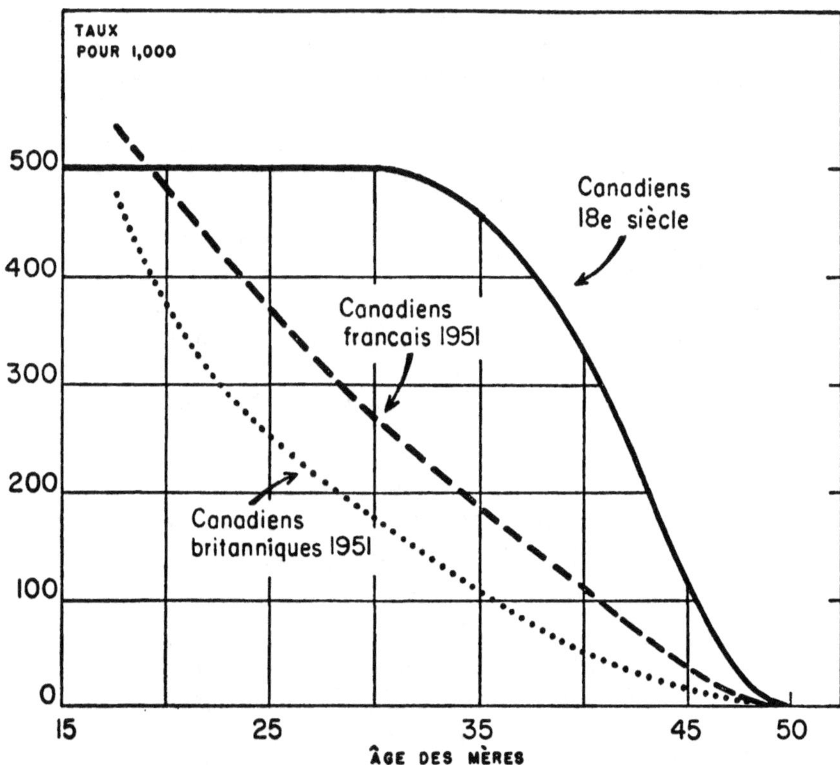

GRAPHIQUE 4. Fécondité légitime suivant l'âge des femmes : nombre de naissances pour mille femmes mariées de chaque âge

Ce qui frappe le plus, c'est la différence entre la courbe correspondant au XVIIIe siècle et les courbes actuelles. Elle est plus prononcée dans le cas de Britanniques. Mais il est quand même surprenant de constater jusqu'à quel point les couples canadiens-français ont évolué dans un domaine qui touche de si près la racine même de la vie de ce peuple pour qui, espérait-on encore naguère, « rien ne doit changer ». Vers l'âge de 20 ans, la fécondité est restée à peu près la même. Mais tandis qu'autrefois la fécondité des couples restait constante jusqu'à ce que la femme atteigne 30 ou 35 ans, aujourd'hui il n'y a plus de palier et le taux baisse régulièrement dès l'âge de 20 ans. Voici, en pourcentage, la baisse enregistrée au cours des deux derniers siècles pour certains âges compris entre 20 et 50 ans : 25 ans : 28 pour cent; 30 ans : 48 pour cent; 40 ans : 66 pour cent.

Dans l'ensemble, baisse de près de la moitié. Dira-t-on que la baisse de la fécondité physiologique ou de l'aptitude physiologique à la procréation explique cette évolution ? Rien ne permet de le penser et au contraire plusieurs raisons peuvent être invoquées pour montrer qu'il s'agit là surtout du résultat d'une intervention volontaire : en effet l'évolution qui a modifié à bien des points de vue l'attitude des hommes devant la vie a conduit à ce qu'on a appelé les pratiques anticonceptionnelles. Empressons-nous d'ajouter qu'un autre facteur est peut-être en cause, mais sûrement beaucoup moins : la vie urbaine, avec ses nombreuses distractions, favorise sans doute moins que la vie rurale d'autrefois les rapprochements conjugaux pouvant donner lieu à une fécondation.

Il y a un phénomène classique qu'on peut constater sur le Graphique 4 : ce n'est pas au début de la vie conjugale que la limitation volontaire des naissances se fait le plus sentir. Les couples qui planifient leur descendance préfèrent en général avoir les enfants souhaités à un âge assez jeune, tout en respectant cependant un certain espacement des naissances. Quand le nombre souhaité est atteint, la restriction devient plus rigoureuse. On observe ce phénomène par rapport à la fecondité du XVIIIe siècle; on l'observe également dans la différence entre les courbes de 1951.

La courbe du XVIIIe siècle correspond à peu près à la « fécondité physiologique » des Français. Celle des Britanniques ne doit pas en être très éloignée; de sorte que l'écart entre la courbe du haut et celle des Britanniques de 1951 doit mesurer l'évolution de ces derniers. Elle semble plus poussée que celle des couples français. Ce qui est certain, c'est que la fécondité des couples britanniques est nettement plus faible. Voici les différences constatées en 1951 entre les taux de fécondité des deux ethnies, suivant l'âge (en pourcentage par rapport au niveau français) : 20 ans : 11 pour cent; 25 ans : 30 pour cent; 30 ans : 33 pour cent; 40 ans : 54 pour cent.

Dans quelle mesure ces différences, constatées en 1951, sont-elles permanentes et non accidentelles ? Nous croyons que, étant donné que la conjoncture favorable de 1951 semble avoir influé davantage sur les couples britanniques, la différence interethnique constatée en 1951 est plutôt sous-évaluée que surévaluée. En 1941, les différences, à chaque âge, étaient passablement plus fortes qu'elles ne l'étaient en 1951 : 20 ans : 24 pour cent; 25 ans : 40 pour cent; 30 ans : 45 pour cent; 40 ans : 65 pour cent.

Il serait intéressant de savoir quels moyens sont utilisés pour limiter la dimension des familles. De toute façon, la limitation volontaire — quel que soit le procédé employé — a une signification sociologique et culturelle importante : entre la soumission aveugle et spontanée aux lois de la nature et le désir de connaître ces lois et de contrôler leurs effets possibles, il existe une notable différence au point de vue de la conception de la vie. Mais en plus, – au moins pour les fidèles catholiques, – l'emploi d'un moyen dit naturel (continence) et permis par les moralistes de l'Eglise catholique ou de moyens dits artificiels et condamnés, n'a pas du tout la même signification : l'un et l'autre supposent des attitudes intérieures tout à fait différentes à l'égard de l'observance religieuse et de la tradition. Malheureusement, nous ne disposons pas de renseignements sur ce point.

Facteurs affectant la fécondité

On peut se demander quels sont les facteurs de cette évolution ou de ces différences interethniques; quelles sont les couches sociales ou culturelles qui sont le plus soumises au désir de limiter le nombre des enfants et de prendre les moyens pour y arriver. L'étude remarquable que Mme E. Charles a faite à l'aide du recensement de 1941 apporte sur ce sujet des renseignements aussi nombreux que précieux. Malheureusement il est impossible, la plupart du temps, de faire le partage entre l'effet de l'âge au mariage et celui de la fécondité après le mariage.

L'étude a confirmé la faible fécondité des femmes de langue anglaise, comme on peut le voir dans le Tableau VIII. Les différences sont fortes : dans toutes les catégories, le nombre d'enfants qu'avaient eus les Françaises catholiques est à peu près le double de ceux qu'avaient eus les Anglaises protestantes. Même si l'on tient compte du fait que beaucoup de femmes de langue anglaise sont catholiques, l'inégalité persiste. On peut aussi remarquer qu'à l'intérieur de chaque groupe culturel, on observe des différences de même sens et de valeur com-

TABLEAU VIII

NOMBRE D'ENFANTS QU'AVAIENT EUS LES FEMMES MARIÉES ÂGÉES EN 1941 DE 45 À 54 ANS

Durée de l'instruction et habitat	Femmes anglo-protestantes	Femmes franco-catholiques	Femmes anglo-catholiques
0–8 ans			
Rurales nées sur une ferme	3.97	8.33	5.68
Urbaines nées hors d'une ferme	2.85	5.46	3.92
Plus de 13 ans			
Rurales nées sur une ferme	2.70	6.25	4.21
Urbaines nées hors d'une ferme	1.85	3.62	2.57

parable quand on passe des femmes moins instruites aux plus instruites et des rurales aux urbaines. L'instruction semble cependant influencer surtout les Anglaises protestantes et l'urbanisation les Françaises catholiques; ce fait a d'ailleurs été noté par Mme Charles[16]. Les Canadiennes françaises rurales catholiques, par exemple, sont plus influencées par une transplantation à la ville que par l'accès à un niveau supérieur d'éducation, ce qui est contraire à ce qui se passe pour les Canadiennes non-françaises.

Les inégalités interculturelles constatées font appel à plusieurs facteurs pour les expliquer : langue, religion, instruction, habitat, niveau économique, etc. Mme Charles a tenté de mesurer l'influence propre de chacun de ces facteurs. Nous ne pouvons ici donner les résultats de cette analyse et nous renvoyons le lecteur à l'étude originale. Signalons cependant que c'est l'instruction qui semble avoir contribué le plus efficacement à limiter la dimension des familles; on peut d'ailleurs s'en rendre compte en examinant les chiffres du Tableau VIII : les femmes ayant reçu plus de 13 ans d'instruction avaient des familles de 40 pour cent inférieures à celles des femmes qui n'avaient été à l'école que pendant 0 à 8 ans. Mais attention : les familles restreintes des femmes instruites sont dues à peu près autant, sinon plus, à leur mariage tardif qu'à leur comportement après le mariage. L'adhésion au protestantisme, le fait d'habiter à la ville, la langue anglaise (qui synthétise l'apport de la tradition, des habitudes, etc.), un haut niveau de vie, chacun de ces facteurs avait eu sur la dimension des familles des femmes étudiées un effet comparable : diminution de 30 pour cent environ. Le niveau de vie semble avoir eu autant d'influence sur les Françaises que sur les Anglaises.

Situation en 1951

Les femmes étudiées par Mme Charles avaient eu leurs enfants surtout entre 1910 et 1930. Beaucoup de choses ont pu changer depuis ce temps mais, faute des renseignements nécessaires, on ne peut refaire ce travail pour la période actuelle. Le Tableau IX donne quelques chiffres significatifs qu'on peut tirer des données du recensement de 1951, sur la fécondité actuelle des couples.

On remarque une différence d'environ 25 pour cent entre Britanniques et Français, entre l'Ontario et le Québec et entre Toronto et Montréal. L'écart est beaucoup plus accentué entre les Britanniques de l'Ontario et les Français du Québec (35 pour cent) ainsi qu'entre les deux provinces au niveau des régions agricoles (40 pour cent). De

[16]*The Changing Size of the Family in Canada*, p. 68.

TABLEAU IX

RAPPORT DU NOMBRE D'ENFANTS DE MOINS DE 5 ANS AU NOMBRE DES FEMMES MARIÉES DE 15 À 44 ANS (TAUX POUR CENT FEMMES)

Habitat et ethnie	Régions							
	Canada	T.-N.	I.-P.-E.	N.-B.	Qué.	Ont.	Montréal	Toronto
Ensemble	86	—	—	—	102	74	69	53
Régions urbaines	—	—	—	—	87	67		
Régions rurales, non-agricoles	—	—	—	—	127	92		
Régions rurales, agricoles	—	146	116	—	154	90		
Britanniques	79	129	108	—	—	72		
Français	108	—	—	142	110	92		

plus la différence entre villes et campagnes est plus grande pour le Québec (43 pour cent) que pour l'Ontario (26 pour cent). Nous laissons au lecteur le soin de faire les autres comparaisons possibles à l'aide du Tableau IX.

Fécondité illégitime

Les naissances illégitimes sont relativement peu nombreuses au Canada : en 1953, 15,980 sur 416,825, soit 38.3 sur mille. Il y en avait 26.3 sur mille en 1926. Comparons les Britanniques et les Français à l'aide d'un taux plus précis : la différence est plus faible que ce qu'on est porté à présumer, en général, lorsqu'on pense à l'intensité – surtout sous son aspect moral – de la fidélité et du sentiment religieux des Canadiens français. En 1951, le rapport des naissances illégitimes aux femmes non-mariées de 15–44 ans était de 12.98 pour mille pour l'ensemble du Canada, 9.72 pour les Canadiennes françaises et 12.78 pour les Britanniques. Les statistiques ne sont cependant pas comparables pour les différentes provinces; celles de l'Ontario tendent à sous-évaluer la fécondité illégitime. Une évaluation grossière de l'erreur ainsi entraînée nous amène à adopter un taux de 14 pour mille environ pour les Britanniques et de 10 pour les Françaises.

Résumé

Comment résumer tout ce que nous venons de dire ? Retenons surtout que, tout en étant soumises l'une et l'autre aux effets des mêmes facteurs et tout en étant affectées pas ceux-ci dans une mesure relativement comparable, la fécondité des couples britanniques et celle des couples français sont très différentes. La première reste très inférieure à celle des couples français et cette différence est assez faiblement compensée par la nuptialité plus précoce et plus forte des Britanniques. Le résultat global du jeu combiné de la nuptialité et de la fécondité des couples peut s'exprimer de la façon suivante : une Canadienne britannique qui vivrait jusqu'à l'âge de 50 ans et qui se conformerait au comportement moyen de son groupe ethnique, en 1951, au point de vue de la nuptialité et de la fécondité, aurait au cours de sa vie 3.12 enfants; tandis qu'une Canadienne française se conformant au comportement des femmes de son groupe, aurait 4.11 enfants, ce qui représente une différence de 30 pour cent[17].

Si l'on tient compte du fait que la mortalité est plus forte pour les Français que pour les Anglais, on obtient ceci : les Canadiens français ont un taux net de reproduction qui dépasse de 25 pour cent celui des Canadiens britanniques : si chaque groupe est représenté à un moment donné par un million d'individus, les Français seront environ 1,750,000, trente ans plus tard et les Anglais 1,400,000.

Si nous connaissions l'évolution future du taux de reproduction de chaque groupe culturel, – cela suppose que nous connaissions l'évolution future de la nuptialité et de la fécondité légitime et nous en sommes loin, – nous pourrions prévoir quelle sera la proportion des individus représentant l'une et l'autre cultures au Canada. Mais il faudrait encore tenir compte de deux choses : les migrations (surtout l'immigration, qui joue en faveur du groupe anglais) et l'assimilation des Canadiens français à la langue anglaise, ce que nous allons étudier dans la troisième section de ce chapitre. Négligeons ces deux derniers phénomènes pour le moment et appliquons aux Canadiens français de 1951 leur taux de reproduction et aux autres Canadiens le taux des Britanniques (ce qui n'est pas très correct mais nous pouvons nous contenter d'un calcul grossier). Vers 1980, on compterait au Canada environ 7,550,000 Canadiens français sur une population totale de 21 millions, soit 40 pour cent. Ceci n'est pas une prévision mais une *perspective hypothétique* basée sur le maintien des taux de reproduction et l'absence de migrations. Une immigration exclusivement de langue anglaise d'environ trois millions de personnes serait nécessaire pour empêcher la proportion des Canadiens d'origine française de passer de 30 à 40 pour cent. Répétons que ces chiffres n'ont rien à voir avec ce qui va se passer; ils ne servent qu'à indiquer l'ordre de grandeur des effets que peuvent avoir certains phénomènes.

Il est probable que la fécondité des couples baissera et il est possible que ce phénomène soit encore plus sensible pour les Français que

[17]Pour l'ensemble des Canadiennes, on trouve 3.43 enfants.

pour les autres Canadiens, ce qui modifierait passablement les chiffres que nous venons de lire. Le mouvement d'urbanisation, l'accès de plus en plus répandu à l'éducation moyenne ou supérieure, l'influence de notre milieu où triomphe la publicité en faveur du bien-être matériel et intellectuel et du confort, l'émancipation à l'égard des prescriptions morales de la religion et aussi le désir de contrôler les facteurs essentiels de sa vie et de mieux équiper ses enfants pour la leur, tous ces facteurs jouent en faveur de la limitation des naissances.

Les allocations familiales ou les autres moyens qui peuvent être mis en œuvre pour atténuer l'espèce de pénalisation économique qui frappe les familles moyennes et nombreuses pourraient ralentir cette baisse de la fécondité. Il faudrait au moins que les allocations familiales et les privilèges concernant l'impôt sur le revenu soient un peu plus substantiels qu'ils ne le sont présentement et orientés davantage dans le sens d'un soutien des familles moyennes et nombreuses. Il ne s'agit pas de préconiser la généralisation des familles de huit ou dix enfants, mais il faut rappeler ceci : si une forte natalité coûte cher en allocations pour enfants, une faible natalité ne coûte pas moins cher : le déclin de la natalité est en effet la cause principale du vieillissement des populations occidentales et du coût relativement élevé entraîné par les pensions de vieillesse, sans compter les autres conséquences pénibles de ce phénomène.

III. Assimilation

Dans l'étude de la croissance d'une population, on doit tenir compte, en général, de deux facteurs : le mouvement naturel (naissances, décès) et les mouvements migratoires. Dans la mesure où l'on se préoccupe du caractère culturel d'une population, il faut ajouter à ces facteurs biologiques et physiques, celui de l'assimilation, c'est-à-dire de l'adoption, au cours ou dès le début de la vie, d'une autre culture que celle qui correspond à l'origine ethnique[18]. Ce phénomène se produit de façon générale pour les immigrants et surtout pour leurs enfants. Au Canada, la plupart de ceux-ci adoptent la culture ou tout au moins la langue anglaise. Mais une proportion importante des Canadiens français vivant hors de ce qu'on a appelé le « glacier québécois », se convertissent aussi à la culture anglaise et souvent, concurremment, à d'autres religions que celle de leurs pères. On verra que le phénomène est assez important pour qu'on ne puisse pas

[18]L'origine ethnique d'un individu peut être très complexe. Elle l'est toujours quand on remonte indéfiniment les différentes lignées de l'ascendance. Pour les fins du recensement, l'origine d'un individu est déterminée par celle de la lignée paternelle et en pratique, elle correspond à celle de son père.

considérer les Canadiens d'origine française comme étant de culture ou au moins de langue française, sans risquer de faire des erreurs d'interprétation importantes. Un exemple : entre 1941 et 1951, la population d'*origine* française a vu croître l'importance relative de ses effectifs dans toutes les provinces; cependant la population de *langue maternelle* française a vu son importance relative décroître dans six provinces et ses effectifs absolus le faire dans trois. S'il est certain que le milieu ambiant joue un rôle important dans l'assimilation (v.g. la plus ou moins forte « densité » de certains éléments culturels et linguistiques au sein de la population locale), il semble bien que le phénomène se produise surtout à l'occasion du mariage.

Exogamie

L'exogamie (mariages mixtes) joue de deux façons : 1) elle favorise l'assimilation des deux conjoints ou de l'un d'eux surtout; 2) pour l'éducation des enfants, elle peut annuler en pratique les effets possibles de l'« instinct de persévérance culturelle » du conjoint dont la culture est minoritaire. Ainsi un Français de Halifax épousant une Britannique verra probablement ses enfants (d'origine française) adopter la langue anglaise. Voyons donc d'abord jusqu'à quel point l'exogamie est répandue parmi la population des deux ethnies principales. Nous verrons ensuite le résultat le plus tangible de l'assimilation : l'abandon de la langue maternelle originelle.

Lorsqu'on veut se rendre compte du degré d'assimilation de certains immigrants, on mesure la fréquence d'un certain nombre d'indices correspondant à divers degrés d'assimilation ou d'intégration à la vie du pays d'adoption. Or l'un des indices (sinon l'indice) qui signifient la plus complète assimilation est précisément le choix d'un indigène comme conjoint. Cela étant, il y a lieu de faire une remarque : le problème de l'unité nationale n'en est pas un d'assimilation. Comme pour la Suisse – mais dans des conditions, semble-t-il, plus difficiles ou peut-être moins mûries – l'unité canadienne doit reposer sur la coexistence, la participation, l'acceptation volontaire mutuelle de cultures différentes. Il ne s'agit donc pas d'assimilation. Cependant on ne peut s'empêcher de faire un lien entre le nombre des mariages interethniques et la facilité relative des rapports, la compréhension mutuelle, entre Canadiens et Canadians. Voyons donc quelle est la proportion des conjoints susceptibles de devenir des « assimilés » – certains diront : « en danger » de le devenir !

Les statistiques ne donnent ni l'origine ethnique ni la langue maternelle des nouveaux mariés. Nous devons donc nous rabattre sur la statistique des familles. En 1951, 87.6 pour cent des Françaises mariées et 89.7 pour cent des Français mariés avaient un conjoint de même origine ethnique. Dans la province de Québec, les pourcentages correspondants étaient 95.4 et 96.5. Les trois quarts des mariages exogames (ou mixtes) restants faisaient intervenir un conjoint britannique. Dans l'ensemble donc, du côté français, les chances d'assimilation par le mariage ne paraissent pas très nombreuses. Mais elles le sont beaucoup plus hors du Québec. Ainsi, dans l'Ontario, 37.6 pour cent des Françaises mariées et 33.8 pour cent des Français mariés ont un conjoint « étranger »; les cinq sixièmes de ces conjoints étrangers sont britanniques et il est probable qu'il s'agit d'individus de culture anglaise, puisqu'au Canada – surtout hors du Québec – les Canadiens d'origine française sont à peu près les seuls qui se rattachent à la culture française, encore qu'ils soient loin de le faire tous.

Que se passe-t-il du côté des Britanniques ? Dans le Québec, – où ils occupent, au point de vue du nombre, une place relativement équivalente à celle qu'occupent les Français en Ontario, – les Britanniques se marient beaucoup plus entre eux que les Français de l'Ontario[19]. En 1951, 20 pour cent des Québécoises britanniques étaient mariées à des non-Britanniques et 15 pour cent seulement à des Français. Les Britanniques masculins du Québec étaient un peu plus exogames : 18 pour cent avaient une épouse française. Dans l'ensemble du Canada, 4.1 pour cent des femmes et 4.8 pour cent des hommes britanniques avaient épousé des personnes d'origine française, dont on n'est d'ailleurs pas sûr qu'ils fussent francophones.

Nous avons supposé que les mariages mixtes sont l'occasion d'une certaine assimilation, mais rien ne nous dit dans quel sens joue cette assimilation ni quelle est son importance. Pour le cas qui nous occupe, nous ne savons pas si c'est le conjoint de culture française ou l'autre qui abandonne plus ou moins sa langue ou encore si les enfants issus de parents de langues différentes adopteront l'anglais ou le français comme langue maternelle. Les indications qui suivent répondent à ces questions.

Abandon de la langue originelle[20]

En 1931, 4.78 pour cent des Canadiens d'origine française avaient l'anglais comme langue maternelle. En 1941, le pourcentage était de

[19]Cependant les calculs à l'échelle provinciale sont faiblement significatifs. En ce qui concerne les Britanniques du Québec, il faut remarquer que leurs effectifs sont plus concentrés (à Montréal surtout) que ceux des Franco-Ontariens, ce qui explique l'endogamie relativement forte des premiers.

[20]Les chiffres qui ont servi de base à cette étude sont tirés des recensements. Les constatations que nous faisons ne sont donc justes que dans la mesure où l'origine ethnique et la langue maternelle sont déclarées correctement.

5.89 et en 1951 de 7.77[21]. Pour les Britanniques, ceux dont la langue maternelle était le français formaient pour les mêmes années les proportions suivantes : 0.59, 0.87 et 0.96 pour cent. Il semble donc que l'assimilation croît autant pour les Britanniques que pour les Français. Mais elle est beaucoup plus importante pour les derniers que pour les premiers.

Il est préférable, pour mieux cerner le phénomène, de découper le territoire canadien en régions. Cela permet de voir dans quelle mesure l'assimilation varie, lorsqu'on passe d'une région à l'autre. On peut même se faire ainsi une idée des facteurs en cause.

On se doute bien que l'assimilation est d'autant plus intensive que l'ethnie des assimilés est plus faiblement representée dans le milieu où ils vivent. Ainsi, dans le Québec, où ils sont relativement peu nombreux, 8.4 pour cent des Britanniques ont le français comme langue maternelle. Le pourcentage est de 6.1 pour Montréal, où les Britanniques forment 17.7 pour cent de la population. Prenons maintenant les Français vivant hors de leur « glacier » : 29 pour cent ont abandonné leur langue originelle.

C'est au niveau des divisions de recensement ou même des municipalités locales qu'il faudrait analyser le phénomène de l'assimilation, ce que nous ne pouvons faire ici. Voici cependant les principaux résultats d'une étude plus poussée :

1) Il y a une forte corrélation négative entre la proportion des assimilés et celle de leur ethnie dans l'ensemble de la population locale. Le Père O.-J. Ferguson a calculé, pour différentes régions du Canada, des indices de corrélation montrant, au niveau des divisions de recensement, la relation qui existe entre la « densité française » et la proportion des Français ayant abandonné leur langue maternelle originelle[22]. Pour la région des Maritimes[23], l'indice trouvé est —0.82 en 1941 et —0.87 en 1951. Pour l'Ontario[24], l'indice est —0.8.

2) On trouve des résultats analogues, si au lieu de considérer la langue maternelle, on tient compte de la simple connaissance (ou ignorance) de la langue française.

3) Pour une même « densité ethnique » les Canadiens français semblent s'assimiler plus facilement que les Canadiens anglais. Cela peut tenir aux plus grandes difficultés que rencontrent les Français, là où ils sont minoritaires, dans l'établissement d'un équipement culturel minimum (écoles, radio).

[21]On a exclu Terre-Neuve de ces calculs.

[22]Oneil-Joseph Ferguson c.s.c., « Le Comportement linguistique de la population d'origine française », thèse présentée à l'Ecole des hautes études commerciales, Montréal, 1953.

[23]Moins certains comtés français. [24]Moins certains comtés français.

4) L'assimilation varie aussi avec la proportion des mariages mixtes.

5) Pour les Canadiens français, la perte de la langue maternelle est systématiquement moins fréquente pour les agriculteurs que pour les ruraux non-agricoles et elle est moins fréquente pour ceux-ci que pour les citadins. Il y a exception pour la Colombie-Britannique.

6) Toutes choses étant égales, l'assimilation présente un état plus avancé là où elle peut s'exercer depuis plus longtemps (dans les Maritimes par exemple).

Il existe un phénomène assez inattendu sur lequel le Père Richard Arès[25] a attiré l'attention et qui a une importance capitale au point de vue du rapport qui existe entre l'accroissement de la population d'*origine* française et l'accroissement de la population de *langue* française. D'après les chiffres des recensements de 1941 et de 1951, l'accroissement des Canadiens d'origine française vivant hors du Québec a été compensé dans une large mesure par ceux d'entre eux qui adoptent la langue anglaise. Voici, pour les provinces où le phénomène est le moins grave, le pourcentage que représentent les transferts linguistiques par rapport à l'accroissement des Français d'origine : Québec, 3.2; Nouveau-Brunswick, 21.4; Ontario, 53.7; Manitoba, 57.8; Colombie-Britannique, 62.3; Alberta, 77.5. Il y a mieux : dans trois provinces (Ile-du-Prince Edouard, Nouvelle-Ecosse et Saskatchewan), le contingent des Canadiens français qui passent à l'anglais est plus fort que l'accroissement des Canadiens d'origine française ! Dans le Québec et le Nouveau-Brunswick seulement, les Français d'origine fournissent plus de francophones que d'anglophones.

On ne peut donc pas, du moins en général, confondre « origine française » et « culture française », du moins pas dans les milieux où les Français sont minoritaires. A Terre-Neuve, 26.3 pour cent seulement des Français d'origine savaient le français en 1951; en Colombie-Britannique, 45.4 pour cent; les autres provinces (sauf le Québec et le Nouveau-Brunswick) ont des proportions variant entre 50 et 80 pour cent.

Il y a là matière à s'interroger sur les chances de la survivance de la culture française dans l'ensemble du Canada.

IV. Mortalité infantile

Les statistiques sur la mortalité générale ne sont publiées que par province et non par ethnie. Aux différents âges de la vie, les taux du

[25]Voir Richard Arès s.j., « Position du français au Canada », *Relations*, avril à septembre 1954.

Québec sont supérieurs à ceux de l'ensemble du Canada. Il y a sûrement là une différence qu'on peut transposer sur le plan ethnique. La province de Québec se signale aussi par une surmortalité féminine entre les âges 24 et 38 ans, c'est-à-dire que pour cette période de la vie, les taux de mortalité du sexe féminin sont supérieurs à ceux du sexe masculin.

Mais c'est la mortalité de la première année de la vie qui a toujours retenu le plus l'attention des démographes et de tous ceux qui s'intéressent aux problèmes sociaux. D'une part, la mortalité infantile (décès de moins d'un an) se situe à un niveau très élevé[26]; d'autre part une grande partie de ces décès sont dus à des facteurs sociaux ou culturels. Des enquêtes faites en France et en Grande-Bretagne ont montré en effet que la mortalité varie beaucoup lorsqu'on passe d'un milieu socio-culturel à l'autre. Ainsi en France, en 1950–1, le taux de mortalité variait du simple au triple lorsqu'on passait de la classe la plus favorisée (professions libérales) à la classe la moins favorisée (manœuvres).

Or, on trouve au Canada de grandes différences entre les ethnies, en ce qui concerne la mortalité infantile. En 1951, le taux de mortalité infantile[27] du Canada était de 37.8 pour mille. Après les Indiens (115 pour mille) venaient les Canadiens français, avec un taux de 49.4. Le groupe ethnique qui suit est constitué par les Anglais (à l'exclusion des Irlandais et des Ecossais, qui ont des taux plus faibles) : 33.1 pour mille. Tous les autres groupes ethniques ont des taux inférieurs à 30 pour mille. Une analyse plus poussée montre que cette différence de mortalité est imputable surtout à des maladies apportées à l'enfant par le milieu où il vit : il s'agit en particulier de maladies infectieuses et de mauvaise alimentation. Les enquêtes citées ont montré que la lutte contre ces maladies dépend avant tout de deux facteurs : l'éducation sanitaire ou l'éducation tout court de la mère; un niveau minimum de bien-être économique qui permet à la mère de s'occuper efficacement de ses enfants. Il serait extrêmement utile de savoir quels sont les facteurs socio-culturels qui affectent la mortalité infantile, au Canada.

Ajoutons cependant que les progrès enregistrés dans ce domaine depuis une trentaine d'années semblent avoit été aussi rapides pour la province de Québec que pour le reste du Canada. L'écart absolu entre les taux s'est même partiellement résorbé.

[26]Au Canada, malgré une réduction de cette mortalité des deux tiers de ce qu'elle était en 1920, le taux des décès d'enfants de moins d'un an est aussi élevé que celui des vieillards de 70 ans.

[27]Nombre de décès au cours de la première année de la vie pour mille enfants nés vivants.

V. Conclusion

Toutes les valeurs culturelles ne sont pas reflétées – du moins pas directement – par les phénomènes démographiques analysés. Ainsi la préoccupation d'insérer dans l'activité des hommes des formules humaines, non entièrement mécaniques, n'est pas facilement perceptible. Cependant certains aspects démographiques soulignés par l'étude de M. Keyfitz ou la nôtre sont liés assez directement à la culture; nous entendons par là qu'ils ont un rapport avec les objectifs que se fixent (ou ne se fixent pas) les individus et les institutions, avec l'ordre de valeurs auquel ils se conforment et avec la façon dont ils se « proportionnent » à leur milieu et aux buts poursuivis. Nous nous intéressons ici aux Canadiens français.

La répartition professionnelle montre qu'ils sont moins adaptés à la structure économique de leur milieu; en tout cas, ils ont moins « réussi ». Peut-être cela reflète-t-il une conscience bien tardive du besoin d'un équipement intellectuel et éducatif d'ailleurs encore très insuffisant.

Quant à leur résistance à l'immigration, elle peut s'expliquer d'abord par les forts accroissements naturels que le milieu économique arrive avec peine à accueillir. Un accroissement de population de plus de 2 pour cent par an requiert des investissements qui peuvent être doubles de ceux que nécessite une population à peine croissante. Il y a aussi des facteurs psycho-sociologiques : les individus qui n'ont pas la compétence ou la richesse suffisantes pour concurrencer efficacement les arrivants se réfugient facilement derrière leurs « droits » de premiers occupants. De plus, on trouve des traces encore marquées de la crainte traditionnelle d'être noyés par la quantité des « étrangers » et le désir facilement justifiable de maintenir ou d'accroître la proportion des Canadiens français au Canada. Cette crainte et ce désir s'appuient sur le fait qu'une proportion importante des Canadiens d'origine française adoptent la langue anglaise.

La forte mortalité infantile des Canadiens français a une signification socio-culturelle dont il est difficile de préciser les aspects principaux. Un niveau de vie inférieur, une déficience de l'éducation sanitaire ou de l'éducation tout court, la surcharge de plusieurs mères, peuvent être en cause.

La faveur relativement restreinte dont semble jouir la vie conjugale, chez les Canadiens, est peut-être la conséquence de difficultés économiques ou peut-être d'un sentiment plus prononcé de la gravité du mariage auquel s'ajoute une certaine modération devant les charges familiales qu'impose l'observance de la morale catholique. On observe également des indices de stabilité et de fidélité à une tradition socio-religieuse : abstention du divorce, fécondité illégitime plus faible et forte fécondité légitime, sur laquelle nous allons insister un peu.

Cette force des Canadiens français est probablement l'élément de leur vie qui est évoqué avec le plus de satisfaction. Dans plusieurs milieux, on souhaite un retour à la fécondité du XVIIIe siècle ! On a une conscience très vive du rôle qu'a joué cette forte natalité dans la survivance des Canadiens français; et il ne s'agit pas uniquement de l'existence de quatre millions d'individus d'origine française mais du maintien d'une société — si imparfaite soit-elle — ayant réussi à conserver une vie propre avec ses institutions, son droit, sa pensée, sa religion, ses romans, bientôt son théâtre, ses arts, etc. On croit fermement que ce qui a permis cette survivance dans le passé saura bien le faire dans l'avenir. Mais peu de penseurs, de dirigeants, s'interrogent sur les problèmes économiques que pose la forte croissance de la population du Québec. On a accepté fort mal ou pas du tout le fait que la « terre » ne semble pas pouvoir absorber une partie même minime de l'accroissement démographique; on ne s'est donc pas soucié davantage de la quantité d'investissements industriels nécessaires pour encadrer, faire travailler les jeunes générations qui se présentent chaque année sur le marché du travail, surtout dans un milieu qui a peut-être peu d'épargne et peut-être aussi, bien peu de sens de l'épargne pour faire face à la nécessité de ces investissements.

Pour notre part, nous n'avons jamais vu posée directement ou indirectement cette question qui nous paraît essentielle : si la forte natalité des Canadiens français les a servis dans le passé — et cela du moins semble un fait certain puisque sans elle ils auraient été engloutis — si cette forte natalité les a servis, parce qu'alors il s'agissait surtout d'un objectif quantitatif, ne peut-on pas se demander si un retour à la fécondité « naturelle » (celle d'avant 1850), ne va pas les desservir ? Les objectifs à poursuivre désormais ne sont-ils pas surtout d'ordre qualitatif ? Et la quantité ne jouerait-elle pas dans certains cas contre la qualité ? La faible scolarité du Québec après la limite de la scolarité obligatoire et certaines enquêtes de la Jeunesse ouvrière catholique le laissent entendre[28].

Quelle est la fécondité souhaitable, compte tenu de la capacité d'absorption de l'économie d'une part et, d'autre part, des possibilités pour les familles d'éduquer et d'instruire convenablement leurs enfants

[28]Voir en particulier dans *L'Action catholique ouvrière*, octobre 1952, le rapport de l'« Enquête sur la vie professionnelle des jeunes travailleurs du Québec ».

et pour l'état de faciliter cette éducation ? Certains penseurs se sont inquiétés de cette question, Bourassa entre autres : « Ce n'est pas tout d'avoir beaucoup d'enfants; le principal, c'est de les élever au triple sens du mot : physique, intellectuel et moral[29]. »

Mais le plus souvent, pour expliquer les défections à l'égard de la tradition des familles nombreuses, on évoque surtout des « péchés ». Certes c'est l'égoïsme qui est en cause la plupart du temps. Mais il y a peut-être parfois un souci « d'éduquer les enfants au triple sens du mot ». On a parfois « excusé » la baisse de la natalité par l'insuffisance des salaires des chefs de famille. Comme remède, on a souvent préconisé le « salaire familial »; mais on s'est assez peu inquiété du niveau du revenu national capable d'étayer ces salaires familiaux et des investissements nécessaires pour atteindre ce revenu.

Bref, les Canadiens français sont restés jusqu'à maintenant moins sensibles que leurs co-nationaux à la civilisation occidentale moderne. Mais l'évolution rapide de la pensée sociale, souhaitée et amorcée énergiquement ou impétueusement par les jeunes intellectuels, rend impossible un jugement d'ensemble sur l'interprétation de la vie démographique des Canadiens.

1955

[29]Henri Bourassa, « La Famille canadienne, ses périls, son salut » dans « Semaines sociales du Canada », IVe session, sur *La Famille*, tenue à Montréal en 1923 (Ottawa, 1924).

The French-Canadian Family*

PHILIPPE GARIGUE

Dean, Faculty of Social Sciences, University of Montreal

THERE IS NO LACK OF THEORIES about the French-Canadian family. Practically all writers on the French Canadians have said something about their family organization. Most have seen it as the institution through which the survival of the French Canadians was achieved. The "battle of the cradles," as their high birth rate has been called, has either been applauded or vilified. To explain it has taxed the ingenuity of all who have written about it. Some have seen it as the survival of an older society, some as the expression of a manifest destiny, and others as the result of environmental conditioning. In this paper we shall deal only with those hypotheses which are thought to be sociologically relevant. As a rough and ready classification of these hypotheses at least two extreme types can be separated: first, those which stress origin, and second, those which stress environment. Most of the sociological explanations are of the second type. However, the few authors who have used the first have had so much influence that it is thought worth while to begin with them.

Among these authors it has been the practice to identify the French-Canadian family with the French family of the seventeenth century. Sometimes it is also generally classified as the equivalent of the French peasant family. These can also be called the oldest theories about the French-Canadian family, for one of the first courses of lectures on the family ever taught in Montreal, in 1880, and given to the students of the Jacques Cartier School of Teachers, identified the French with the French-Canadian family.[1] Half a century later, Miner, in his study of

*The author wishes to acknowledge the award of a grant from the Faculty of Graduate Studies and Research of McGill University, which enabled him to collect the data upon which this paper is based. He also wishes to acknowledge his debt to Prof. Father Norbert Lacoste, who in discussions with him helped him to clarify a number of points.

[1]L. A. Brunet, *La Famille et ses traditions* (Montréal, 1881).

St. Denis, made the statement that the French-Canadian family system is one which was brought over from France in the seventeenth century, and has remained unchanged.[2] This identification of French Canadian and French is at the core of a number of propositions about the traditional nature of French-Canadian society and family organization. Its acceptance can be seen in all the theories which have a tendency to overstress what are thought to be the French characteristics of the French Canadians.

However, an examination of the traditional French family and of the early French-Canadian family will show that although certain traits show close similarities, the total organization is different. The first French settlers who arrived in Canada left a rural France in which life was still mainly regulated according to custom.[3] The enclosure of land, which was to revolutionize rural life, had not yet had any influence on family organization.[4] What existed was a customary mode of life in which land tenure, ties of kinship, and other social relationships maintained a highly specific form of family organization to which the name of *communauté taisible* has been given. This type of family unit has been traced back to the tribal structure of early France, and recent research has shown that it was in existence, in some rural areas, as late as the beginning of the twentieth century. These *communautés taisibles* were based on the practice, among commoners, of a father keeping with him his married sons, and of married brothers often remaining together after the death of their father as a joint family living under the same roof.[5] Property, and especially land, was held for the benefit of all the members of the household, who pooled their resources. More than two generations thus lived together, and the household could be composed of anything up to seventy persons.[6] At marriage, a woman came to live with her husband's family, and so came under the authority of her father-in-law, who appropriated the product of the couple's labour as well as the marriage dowry.[7]

The *communauté taisible* was never introduced as an institution into New France. There were a number of reasons. First of all, the migration from France was very slow and relatively limited. Altogether,

[2]H. Miner, *St. Denis: A French Canadian Parish* (Chicago, 1939), p. 72.

[3]A. Esmein, *Cours élémentaire d'histoire du droit français* (14th ed., Paris: Recueil Sirey, 1921), p. 114.

[4]M. Bloch, *Les Caractères originaux de l'histoire rurale française* (Oslo: Inst. for Samm. Kulturforskning, 1931), p. 210.

[5]Esmein, *Cours élémentaire*, p. 223.

[6]Bloch, *Les Caractères originaux*, p. 170.

[7]G. Fagnez, *La Femme et la société française dans la première moitié du XVIIe siècle* (Paris, 1929), pp. 144–5.

about 10,000 persons, most of them single, are said to have made the crossing in the 150 years of New France. At the time of the conquest, in 1760, the population of 60,000 persons was overwhelmingly Canadian-born. Rather than migration it was the high birth rate which had peopled New France, since in that period over 25,000 weddings, and 138,000 births, had taken place,[8] or an average of about nine births for every mother who lived through her normal child-bearing life.[9] Furthermore, the migrants did not come as organized communities, but as small groups from practically all the regions of France, many of them from the growing urban centres.[10] It is not surprising, therefore, if the special family structure of rural France was never transplanted. Instead, the family organization which came to be had features which had not existed in France.

The organization of the French-Canadian family of that period can be described as that of a conjugal household with strong ties of kinship with other households, but with a high degree of autonomy. For instance, married brothers would take adjoining lots, and not work together on the same property. The economic difficulties, the dangers, the scarcity of women in the early days, resulted in a different type of family relationship. It was very early remarked that women had a higher status there than in France.[11] Peter Kalm, who visited New France in 1749, reported that they had a tendency to assume an equal, if not a superior, status to that of their husbands.[12] Much of the law of France was set aside in the new situation.[13] For instance, in France, both law and custom had discouraged remarriage, but in New France the law was ignored and the custom changed, so that even the usual year of mourning was not observed. Most widows remarried within three months, and one instance is recorded of a widow who remarried before her husband was in his grave.[14] Many women and men married twice, or three times, thus making for an extreme complexity of kinship, as well as extending the child-bearing life of the women. Because of the high frequency of death among the men, as well as their frequent

[8]G. Langlois, *Histoire de la population canadienne-française* (Montréal, 1935), p. 258.

[9]G. Sabagh, "The Fertility of French Canadian Women during the 17th Century," *American Journal of Sociology*, vol. XLVII, no. 5, pp. 680–9.

[10]A. Godbout, *Origine des familles canadiennes-françaises* (Lille, 1925).

[11]I. Foulché-Delbosc, "Women of New France (Three-Rivers: 1651–63)," *Canadian Historical Review*, vol. XXI, no. 2 (June 1940), pp. 132–49.

[12]*Travels into North America* (London, 1771), vol. III, p. 82.

[13]L. Baudouin, *Le Droit civil dans la province de Québec* (Montréal, 1953), pp. 67–79.

[14]Foulché-Delbosc, "Women of New France," p. 141.

and long absences in either the fur trade or the wars, the women were often left in complete control of family affairs, and they thus built for themselves a tradition of independence, better education than their menfolk, and self-reliance. It was they who looked after the family property, and assumed custodial rights in their husband's absence. The only type of discrimination which seems to have been practised against them only underlines their new status. In France the practice has developed, according to the Law Code of the Kings of France, which also became the Law Code of New France, of redistributing property equally among all the children of a commoner, irrespective of sex. In New France the law was often set aside, and property was often inherited by the sons only, to the detriment of the daughters.[15] The reason was that sons needed the inheritance to set up a new household, whereas the poorest girl was certain of a husband. But women could, and often did, inherit property, many of them acquiring real wealth with the corresponding high social status.[16]

The relationship between parents and children was also different from that in France. The inhabitants of New France were in a situation in which great advantages were to be had from having many children. This was different from the situation in France for the same period.[17] In New France there was a close relation between social security, wealth, status, government policy, and large families.[18] Children were regarded as a most welcome addition and this attitude was reflected in the way they were treated. Writing in 1709 a Jesuit missionary remarked that "it was here different than in France, they love their children too well to make them do anything against their will, and the children have so little respect for their parents that they leave them when they want."[19] The economic opportunity of being able to live independent of their parents, as well as the frontier mentality, gave French-Canadian youth a status unknown in the France of that period.

While the lack of data about the period prevents a more thorough analysis, there is no doubt that by the middle of the eighteenth century the French-Canadian family had become a special form of family, different from that of the French. As a type it had many similarities with the description given by Cahoun of the families of New England in the same period.[20] The French-Canadian family is more North

[15] *Ibid.*, p. 143.

[16] A. Tessier, *Canadiennes* (Montréal, 1946), pp. 88–91.

[17] Langlois, *Histoire*, pp. 5–14.

[18] G. Frégault, *La Civilisation de la Nouvelle France* (Montréal, 1944).

[19] A. Silvie, *Relations par lettres de l'Amérique septentrionale (années 1709 et 1710)* (Paris, 1904), p. 4.

[20] A. W. Cahoun, *A Social History of the American Family* (Cleveland, 1918), vol. II, pp. 11–26.

American than European. Furthermore, it is not a variation of another national family form, but a specific form by itself. The characteristics which the French-Canadian family had acquired by the end of the eighteenth century were not to remain static, but to change further. The conquest of 1760, the end of the fur trade, the agricultural, commercial, and early industrial developments, and the gradual change from a predominantly rural to a predominantly urban society created situations which were peculiar to French Canada and which further heightened its characteristics as a special type. It is beyond the scope of this paper to trace in detail the historical changes which took place, and how these influenced the structure of the French-Canadian family. It is enough if it is stressed that these historical changes were correlated with a demographic and geographic expansion, as well as with an intensification of social differentiation. While it has been repeated before and after Lord Durham that French-Canadian society was remarkable for its equality of status and wealth,[21] there are indications that important social differentiations came to exist among its various communities, as well as within each community.

It is this background of extensive social differentiation which clashes with a number of "situational" theories which have been advanced about the French-Canadian family. Practically all these theories analyse the French-Canadian family according to a simple logical model. A number of indices are selected and said to be the elements of a homogeneous, traditional, French-Canadian rural culture and society. In opposition to these, other elements are also selected and said to be caused by the development of an Anglo-Saxon industrial and urban culture. As far as the family is concerned, these assumptions are based on the belief that what is traditional French-Canadian is rural. This rural culture is held to have remained unchanged for some two centuries, and it is only now, under the pressure of an industrial urbanization brought about by English-speaking persons, that a new type of family structure is emerging. What is interesting about these theories is that they are found among such different authors as the French-Canadian Catholic reformers of the Semaines sociales du Canada,[22] and the anthropologists and sociologists trained at the University of Chicago. Not only do these authors stress the supposed traditional rural characteristics of the French-Canadian family, but they also present the change from rural to urban as implying the development of "instabilities" unknown in the rural areas.

[21]Lord Durham, *Report on the Affairs of North America* (London, 1839), p. 13.

[22]Semaines sociales du Canada, *La Famille* (Montréal, 1923); *Le Chrétien dans la famille* (Montréal, 1940); *La Jeunesse* (Montréal, 1946); *Le Foyer* (Montréal, 1950).

The theories which have been used to explain these traditional characteristics do, however, differ widely in their stress. A classification of them would place at one end those which use the folk society frame of reference as a method of analysis, and those which stress that the urban-rural continuum in the province of Quebec rests on an important social difference. The folk society concept is now so well known that there is little need here to do more than outline its premises. According to Redfield's latest formulation, it is a small community, isolated, illiterate, and with strong solidarity, in which the sacred prevails over the secular. Behaviour is traditional, spontaneous, acritical, and personal. Kinship, its relationships and institutions, are the typical categories of experience, and the family group is the unit of action.[23] In its totality the folk society concept obviously does not apply to French Canada at the present day, or at any moment of its history. However, even Redfield's statement, in his Introduction to Miner's book on St. Denis, that rural French Canada was half way along the continuum between the fold and the urban type of societies, is not a valid generalization.

Redfield's argument rests on Miner's presentation of the data he collected at St. Denis. According to Miner this community had remained untouched, since its foundation, by industrialization and urbanization, and the traditional customs of the French Canadians had remained unchanged. The information which he reports does not, however, support this "survival" theory. By 1936, when Miner did his field research, St. Denis had known fifty years of decline in population. The birth rate for that year was given by Miner as 25 per thousand, which is below the average of 27.1 per thousand for the whole of Kamouraska County.[24] Furthermore, two demographic trends have been observed for this county: a high birth rate and an increase in population for a number of rural parishes situated in the interior; and a low birth rate and a decrease in population for a number of rural parishes situated on the shore of the St. Lawrence. According to this report St. Denis had the second-lowest birth rate among the parishes of this county.[25] The decrease in population is noticeable in St. Denis in the abandonment of farms: not only do sons not follow their fathers as farmers, but whole families migrate from the parish.[26] Miner's study was of a community which was withdrawing into itself, with all the social and

[23]R. Redfield, "The Folk Society," *American Journal of Sociology*, vol. XLII (1947), pp. 292–308.

[24]*Quebec Statistical Year Book*, 1937, p. 94.

[25]R. Blanchard, *L'Est du Canada français*, vol. I (Montréal, 1935), p. 190.

[26]Miner, *St. Denis*, p. 27.

psychological effects of such a trend. It cannot, therefore, be a suitable example on which to base generalizations about rural French Canada.

There are a number of other reasons why the folk society concept cannot be used in analysing the French-Canadian family. Social institutions of the sort which exist in rural French Canada are the product of complex social change, whose complexity demands a different analysis from the one carried out in the logical model which has been described. There are a large number of institutions within each community whose nature is contrary to the basic assumptions of the folk society. Among these are the *rang* and the parish organization. The *rang* is the peculiar long-lot system of land tenure developed by the early settlers along the shores of the St. Lawrence, a system which is specific to French Canada. All the farms are at one end of the long lot and they are connected by a road, the length of the road being called the *rang*. Its use throughout Quebec has given to that province its peculiar appearance of rural urbanism, reminiscent of ribbon development. Each *rang* is to a point a social unit, and the ties between immediate neighbours become very important through the daily exchange of services. These ties are of greater importance than certain ties of kinship. Gérin, in his study of St. Justin in the 1890's, reported a farmer as saying to him that his daughter was having a quiet wedding as he had only invited his brothers and his two neighbours in the *rang*. The *rang* is thus a secular institution, whose size varies with the number of farms on the road, and whose social cohesion is due to propinquity. While ties of kinship may develop between members of the same *rang* through marriage, or through the settlement of kin in farms along the same road, its social function does not arise from familistic conceptions, but from an administrative and general preference for this form of land tenure.[27]

The other social institution whose presence prevents the development of anything like a folk society is the parish organization. Miner's presentation of the function of the Catholic religion in St. Denis stressed its integrative and traditionalistic role within the parish.[28] However, the parish organization must also be seen as part of the organization of the Catholic Church in Quebec, and, for that matter, of the Catholic Church everywhere. The parish organization is not an autonomous unit, resulting from the functional operations of the communal life of the members of the parish. This organization is imposed

[27]P. Deffontaines, *Le Rang: type de peuplement rural du Canada français* (Québec: Presses Universitaires Laval, 1953), pp. 23–5.
[28]*St. Denis*, pp. 91–105.

upon the community, and its structure is based on the acceptance, by the members of that community, of directives formulated elsewhere. The implication of this for an understanding of French Canada is that the parish, a religious unit found in rural and urban areas, is not only, or mainly, determined by the social characteristics of a community, but by an ideology involving the whole history of the Catholic Church.[29] The life cycle of the people of St. Denis as described by Miner, or the yearly cycle of ceremonies in Cantonville listed by Hughes, could be used, with only slight modifications, for describing the life cycle, or the yearly ceremonials, of all the communities that use the Roman ritual. These are not the product of the special social life of a community, but the result of pronouncements and discussions which have taken place in the intellectual life of the Catholic Church, and which must be accepted by anyone who wants to be a Catholic. The French Canadians do not have a religion which is derived from the communal life of their rural communities, or directed at maintaining a rural society in the province of Quebec, or at perpetuating the type of behaviour described by Miner. While it can be shown that, for a long time, there was a tendency among some of the Catholic hierarchy of Quebec to present the rural way of life and the rural family as superior to urban life and the urban family, the development of a new Catholic "spirituality" in urban centres, and recent pronouncements of the Catholic hierarchy, show that they are convinced that there is nothing incompatible between urban life and the Catholic family.[30]

The folk society concept sees the integrative and traditionalistic character of religion, but it ignores religion as the cause of change or minimizes its ability to reformulate some of its teachings. This concept also ignores religion as a factor breaking down the isolation of separate communities, seemingly because it has no criteria within itself for differentiating between a tribal cult and a universal church. There can be no doubt that even a watered version of the folk society concept cannot be used in the formulation of a research hypothesis about the French-Canadian family. There are rural communities in Quebec, but they are not folk societies.

There are equally good reasons why the theory advanced by a number of authors that the French-Canadian family is essentially rural is not a satisfactory explanation. The weakness of this generalization is that it reduces itself to one major proposition, and that is that French

[29]Semaines sociales du Canada, *La Paroisse* (Montréal, 1953).
[30]Lettre Pastorale Collective, *Le Problème ouvrier* (Montréal, 1950).

Canada was formed as a peasant community and can only retain its characteristics by remaining a peasant community. The historical evidence does not support this. New France was for long a "frontier" society, whose main activity was the fur trade. As late as the eighteenth century agriculture was still a secondary occupation. Furthermore, the dominant activities of the period were located in the towns. In the middle of the eighteenth century, one-quarter of the population lived in three towns, while the other three-quarters lived in a continuous settlement along the shores of the St. Lawrence.[31] The economic life of the period was diversified, and commercial as well as industrial enterprises were active. After the conquest of 1760 many of these fields of activity were no longer open to the French Canadians, and it was then that agriculture became the dominant activity. But a considerable proportion of the French Canadians continued to live in the towns, and many had non-agricultural occupations. One author remarked on the existence of a proletariat in the Province of Quebec in the first decade of the nineteenth century,[32] and urbanization spread rapidly during that century.

While the classification of what is rural and urban in Quebec was long far from clear, one author has commented that by 1941 only a very small number of communities in Quebec could be called rural. The overwhelming majority of communities, if the criterion of density is taken, were semi-urban.[33] Since 1951 the Canadian census has classified any community larger than 1,000 inhabitants as urban. According to this there were 212 rural communities in Quebec in 1951, of which 75 had come into existence since 1921 and had remained below the 1,000 inhabitant mark.[34] However, density alone is not a safe criterion for assessing rural life. The greatest majority of these rural communities are within the belt of territory, 200 miles by 50, through which the St. Lawrence passes, and which forms the centre of French Canada. There is a complex system of communication which links rural and urban, and an easy diffusion of ideas among all these communities.

A clearer idea of the relation between rural and urban can be had by following the fluctuation in farms. In the period between 1841 and 1951, there was a total decrease of about 10,000 farms in the province of Quebec. There were, however, many periods of rapid fluctuation.

[31]Frégault, *La Civilisation de la Nouvelle France*, pp. 100, 217.
[32]E. Rameau, *La France aux colonies* (Paris, 1859).
[33]E. Charles, *The Changing Size of the Family in Canada* (Ottawa: King's Printer, 1948), p. 141.
[34]*Ibid.*

Between 1844 and 1861, for instance, nearly 40,000 farms were abandoned, or over a third of the 1861 figure. Similarly, since 1891, about 40,000 farms have also been abandoned, or under a third of the 1951 figure. By 1931, when the first count of persons living on farms was taken, the proportion was 27 per cent. By 1951 it had decreased to 18.9 per cent of the population of Quebec, irrespective of their occupation.[35] The impression which remains from a study of the statistics of farming in Quebec is of recurring cycles of migration and colonization, not of an over-all stable agricultural population. It seems, therefore, that many qualifications must be made about what is called the traditional rural character of French Canada.

Criticism can, in fact, be directed against a very high number of generalizations about the supposed traditional characteristics of the French-Canadian society. For instance, one of Miner's statements, which has been repeated by a large number of other social scientists, was that one of the characteristics of rural French Canada is that the farm is handed over to one son, and that the other children leave home to make their living elsewhere. This statement does not take into account the fact that there were periods in the history of Quebec when a large proportion of farmers did not hand over their farms, but migrated with their whole families. Furthermore, it is to be recalled that since 1865, with the coming into force of the Civil Code of Quebec, a person can leave his property to whom he chooses, and cut off his relatives from inheritance.[36] If Miner's report is taken to be purely a description of a rural custom, it is found that it does not describe the historically oldest, or the only way of rural inheritance. Writing in 1832, Bouchette remarked that a very minute subdivision of land had taken place because of the equal division of property by inheritance.[37] Another author has pointed out that in certain areas, by 1820, the size of farms differed according to the subdivision practised at inheritance, and also according to the number the land could support.[38] Another author has remarked that in the parish of St. Justin, in the last decade of the nineteenth century, there were two systems of inheritance, varying according to the size of the farms and the wealth

[35] *Quebec Statistical Year Book*, 1953, pp. 309, 311; and F. A. Angers, "Documentation statistique" in A. Minville, éd., *L'Agriculture* (Montréal, 1943), pp. 486, 483.

[36] Baudouin, *Le Droit civil dans la province de Québec*, pp. 1129–31.

[37] J. Bouchette, *The British Dominion of North America* (London, 1832), p. 379.

[38] W. S. Reid, "The Habitant's Standard of Living on the Seigneurie des Mille Isles, 1820–50," *Canadian Historical Review*, XXVIII, no. 3 (Sept. 1947), pp. 266–78.

of the families concerned: the farm was either equally divided between a number of sons, or handed over to one son. At St. Dominique, at the turn of the century, the same author found that inheritance was equally divided between all siblings, irrespective of sex.[39]

There are indications that other variations in inheritance procedure can be found in rural Quebec, and that they are not limited to a single item. For instance, Miner reported that, at St. Denis, it was the father who decided which one of the sons was best suited for taking over the farm. However, Gérin has also reported that there was a period, at St. Justin, when the position was reversed, and the father had to convince one of his sons to stay and take over the farm, and that a son would impose his own conditions regarding his obligations to his parents and other relatives, if he agreed to stay.[40] Furthermore, a farm is not always handed down from father to son. Gérin described an instance at St. Dominique, at the beginning of the century, in which a wife inherited the farm and administered it with complete rights of disposal.[41] It can be seen that far from having become traditional behaviour, the handing over of a farm shows many variations. Hughes's remark that around Cantonville the practice of handing over a farm to a son had fallen into desuetude is, therefore, not to be taken as an indication of critical changes, but simply of the application of a mode of behaviour which existed in French Canada before the development of industrialization. Another instance of generalization on the basis of limited evidence is Hughes's hypothesis that there is friction among siblings as the result of competition over the farm.[42] There is no doubt that instances of competition for a farm can be found, but there are also indications that conditions in Quebec have always tended to minimize friction between siblings over a farm.

Far from showing homogeneity, the French-Canadian family has many variations within the same general form. This diversity is not simply a question of a difference in the stress given to certain items, but of important variations in the relationship of family members. For instance, Gérin, in his study in 1898 of an area on the north shore of the St. Lawrence, was able to point to the differences which existed in the modes of relationship of family members in the three communities of Maskinongé, St. Justin, and St. Didace, all within a few

[39]L. Gérin, "L'Habitant de St. Justin" in *Proceedings and Transactions of the Royal Society of Canada*, 2nd series, vol. V, pp. 139–216; and *Le Type économique et social des Canadiens* (Montréal, 1937), p. 119.
[40]"L'Habitant de St. Justin," p. 195.
[41]*Le Type économique et social des Canadiens*, p. 121.
[42]E. C. Hughes, *French Canada in Transition* (Chicago, 1943), pp. 184–8.

miles of each other.[43] At Maskinongé and St. Didace, he found family relationships which he labelled "instable" for two different sets of reasons: at Maskinongé, the extensive social differentiation which existed in the community was said by him to have weakened family cohesion; and at St. Didace, economic hardships had caused friction between family members. Only the families of St. Justin were classified by him as having a "stable" relationship.

This high degree of variation in family relationships in a small geographical area was shown by Gérin to exist also in the various regional subdivisions of Quebec. In a later analysis of four more rural families, spread between 1900 and 1930, he was able to show quite clearly the differences to be found between the families of: (1) the farmer of the lower St. Lawrence, who also colonized the Saguenay; (2) the stay-at-home farmer of the middle reaches of the St. Lawrence; (3) the progressive farmer situated at the junction of the main roads of the St. Lawrence Valley; (4) the uprooted farmer on the sandy soils of southern Quebec; (5) the emancipated farmer of the St. François Valley.[44]

From Gérin's evidence it seems that, cutting across similarities, there are extensive variations in family behaviour in rural French Canada. Neither the word "traditional" nor the word "rural" means "homogeneous" in the province of Quebec. In fact, considering that the urban way of life has always been a part of French-Canadian society, the theories which have been advanced about the "essentially" rural nature of the French-Canadian family, or its uniformity, could be considered as the "myths of origin" of the French-Canadian family, with no more empirical foundation in them than most myths.

According to Gérin all these variations in family behaviour were caused by geographical, economic, and historical differences, which influenced the various communities of Quebec.[45] It would seem possible, simply by extending his classification, to cover all the communities to be found in Quebec. Each of these community types could then be duplicated by a family type, whose range would form a classification of the French-Canadian family types. The present situation, for instance, could be analysed, if this suggestion is taken over, according to the classification of communities suggested by Hughes. According to him the following types of communities could be distinguished in Quebec: (1) the old settled agricultural parishes; (2) the

[43] "L'Habitant de St. Justin," p. 215.
[44] *Le Type économique et social des Canadiens*, p. 9.
[45] *Ibid.*

new agricultural fishing communities; (3) the old French-Canadian towns which have recently become industrialized; (4) the frontier towns where industry came first; (5) the former English towns where French Canadians have moved in; (6) the cities of Montreal and Quebec as special instances.[46]

Falardeau has offered a revised version of this classification, according to an economic continuum of at least ten subdivisions, which even more clearly points out the variety of communities in Quebec.[47] It can readily be expected that variations in family behaviour are to be found in such a wide-ranging typology. The problem, however, is whether these classifications cover all the important differences in family behaviour, and whether there is a constant relationship between community organization and family organization. The problem here is whether the major determinant of Hughes's and Falardeau's classification—the economic organization of the community—is the major determinant of family organization in Quebec. This stress on the economic determinant is hinged on the proposition that industrialization is the criterion of differentiation, not only between rural and urban, but also between all communities. Underlining this are the personal criteria of the authors of these classifications who see in industrialization the disintegrating cause of a previously integrated society. The industrialization of Quebec is blamed for having "abruptly disturbed a pastoral symphony," as Falardeau states it. The theoretical implication of this attitude has been the drawing of too sharp a distinction between rural and urban, so that at least one author was led to make the puzzling remark that "the transitional character of the family behaviour is seen in the wide and rather inexplicable variations in urban fertility of French Catholic towns."[48]

While it is apparent that urbanization and industrialization have exercised a powerful influence on the fertility rate of the French Canadians, this influence has been modified by other, more complex, social and cultural conditions, which are as valid in urban as in rural areas. The argument which is here presented is based on three main generalizations: (1) the French Canadians have always had an urban life; (2) the social and cultural differences in Quebec have never been as wide apart as the use of an extreme rural-urban dichotomy tends to present them; (3) the French Canadians have always possessed

[46]J.-C. Falardeau, "The Changing Social Structures" in Falardeau, éd., *Essais sur le Québec contemporain* (Québec: Presses Universitaires Laval, 1953), p. 104.
[47]*Ibid.*, p. 120.
[48]Charles, *The Changing Size of the Family in Canada*, p. 98.

numerous institutions which have tended to maintain their cohesion as a separate ethnic group.

French Canada has neither a completely homogeneous family type nor variations in family behaviour so extensive as to necessitate their being classified as separate autonomous forms. For instance, Lamontagne and Falardeau have reported that the urban working-class families they studied in Quebec City were similar in size to those of rural communities. This similarity in size has, they explain, been caused by the retention of a "rural" culture in urban surroundings.[49] The authors also imply that French-Canadian culture is paradoxical in as far as it does not seem to be aware of the industrial revolution which has taken place in Quebec. This theoretical conclusion seems to be caused by their expectancy that major differences should exist between rural and urban families.

That such a differentiation is not as sharp as an extreme urban-rural dichotomy would present it was seen in a recent study of families in Montreal. In comparing the range of kinship knowledge of informants born in Montreal with that of informants recently migrated from other ports of Quebec, it was found that there was only a limited adjustment in the second generation. Furthermore, informants reported few or no difficulties in the adaptation of their family members to city life. One of the characteristics of kinship organization in Quebec is that all the informants so far interviewed have been able to name relatives in both rural and urban areas. This is not to say that persons cannot be found in Quebec whose relatives are all in a rural or all in an urban area, but simply that a type of family organization exists in Quebec which maintains a high degree of contact among relatives who reside in different communities. This high degree of contact is kept, even though each sibling group of each generation scatters itself in all directions. The fact that the sibling group is large means that through this scattering a person has relatives in practically every major centre of French Canada.[50] One of the peculiarities of the French-Canadian family is the great strength of sibling and lineal recognition, which is correlated to a high degree of family identity and reciprocity of services. Links among persons who recognize ties of kinship are maintained even though migration may separate them for the rest of their lives.

[49]M. Lamontagne and J.-C. Falardeau, "The Life Cycle of French-Canadian Urban Families," *Canadian Journal of Economics and Political Science*, vol. XIII, no. 2 (May 1947), pp. 233–470.

[50]P. Garigue, "Kinship and Urban Life," unpublished MS, 1955.

The cultural background of French-Canadian family life can be shown to have two major characteristics: a strong sense of grouping and integration, superimposed on an extensive pattern of migration. Furthermore, this problem of migration cannot be reduced to a simple, one-dimensional proposition, like Miner's statement, repeated by others, that it is caused by population pressure which in turn is caused by the large birth rate. This, of course, does not explain the tradition of the *coureur de bois*, which constantly drained the population of New France. Neither does it face the problem, mentioned by Blanchard, that the agricultural land of Quebec could support a much greater density of population.[51] Furthermore, it does not account for the cycle in migration, for the frequent moves of families from one parish into the next.[52] This migratory practice of the French Canadian can, in fact, become pathological, as in the instance of one household that moved twenty times in fifty years across the Quebec–United States frontier,[53] or in the instance of the family of *Maria Chapdelaine*, whose head was only happy when he was opening up new land. The migration of the French Canadians seems to be as much a cultural trait as the geographical mobility of the population of the United States. To refer to this migration as land hunger, or land pressure, is to forget that the French Canadians were forced, at one stage of their history—after the conquest—to turn to the land to survive.[54] It seems that as soon as they could they left their farms for other places and other occupations: witness the fact that by the 1930's it is reported that there were two million French Canadians in the United States, and three million in Canada.[55]

But this migration took place without the complete loss of the cultural characteristics of family unity and obligation. One instance of this can be seen in the practice of the family reunion, which rural and urban French Canadians have maintained. It is also found in the development of anniversary meetings attended by those having the same family name. Notices can be found in French-Canadian newspapers asking persons having the same family name to come together at certain dates. These gatherings vary in size from a few hundred to thousands of persons. In 1939, for instance, the descendants of nine Frenchmen named Poulin, who had come over in the seventeenth century but who

[51]R. Blanchard, *L'Ouest du Canada français*, vol. I (Montréal, 1953), p. 86.
[52]Gérin, *Le Type économique et social des Canadiens*, pp. 17–18.
[53]*Ibid.*, p. 174.
[54]Minville, éd., *L'Agriculture*, p. 285.
[55]G. Lanctôt, *Les Canadiens français et leurs voisins du sud* (Montréal, 1941), p. 294.

were not related, gathered together for the third centenary of the arrival of the first Poulin. It is estimated that about 7,000 Poulins attended Mass at Ste-Anne-de-Beaupré on that day. In 1940, a smaller reunion brought together 836 Gagnons in an anniversary ceremony in Quebec City. One hundred and eighty-six of these Gagnons were from Quebec City, 81 from Montreal, 509 from other communities in the province of Quebec, 29 from other provinces in Canada, and 37 from the United States.[56] Some of these had travelled over a week to come to this family gathering. The range of status among them varied, from a member of Parliament, priests, university professors, farmers, working men, shopkeepers, and so on, through practically every possible occupation. The fact that one of the organizers of this reunion was born and brought up in the United States, and that a number came from there, shows that this practice is no rural "survival" limited to the province of Quebec.

The mechanism of social change in the French-Canadian family is then more complex than it has usually been presented as being in the theoretical model which assumes a transition from a rural to an urban type of family. The functions of the French-Canadian family cannot, furthermore, be limited to a direct correlation with the community in which the members of the household are living. In order to understand the family, the analysis must be transferred to the totality of French-Canadian society, and the role of the family as an institution peculiar to French Canada. Furthermore, any theories which assume that it is the English-speaking persons who are the dynamic cause of change only present a limited side of the problem. To say, as Keyfitz does, that the influence of the English-speaking world is transmitted to French Canada through the towns[57] is to assume that the social changes within French-Canadian society are the after-effects of changes in the English-speaking groups. This is to ignore the vitality of French Canada's institutions. Besides schools and universities, its own press, and the radio and television stations, all of which provide for the diffusion of French-Canadian ideas about the family, the church organization is one of the most important means of spreading new ideas about the family.

A recent study of Catholic literature on the family has shown that it has changed from interpreting the family as a hierarchical structure

[56] *Compte-rendu des fêtes du troisième centenaire de la famille Poulin* (Québec, 1939); *Livre-souvenir des fêtes du troisième centenaire des Gagnon* (n.d.).

[57] N. Keyfitz, "Population Problems" in Falardeau, éd., *Essais sur le Québec contemporain*, p. 95.

involving a scale of duties for its members to presenting it as reciprocal love among persons who have different, but not subordinated roles.[58] The spreading of these ideas is helping to change family relationships in Quebec. A recent study of French-Canadian rural youth has shown that they are conscious that their own level of expectation with regard to the family relationship is changing as the result of their coming into contact with this new interpretation.[59] Although the total influence of this change for the whole of the province cannot be assessed for lack of data, it has been estimated that 30 per cent of all Catholic weddings in Montreal in 1954 were between persons who had followed the ten weeks' course of lectures on preparation for marriage given by the Jeunesse ouvrière catholique.[60] In 1947, another Catholic association had over 200 groups throughout the province of Quebec making a study of problems facing the French-Canadian family.[61] In 1954, 5,925 persons attended the course of lectures on the family given by another association in Montreal. The number of these associations interested in the family includes practically every major Catholic association in Quebec. Other associations, directly interested in family affairs, have also been started, such as the Ecole des parents, the Ecoles ménagères, and so on.

In this examination, the following basic facts seem to have been established about the French-Canadian family. (1) It is North American, rather than European. (2) It has gone through a number of changes since the first settlement of New France, but these changes have not been uniform, and they have created variations in types of family behaviour. (3) These variations do not, however, result in different kinds of family organization, but in degrees of variation within the same general family form. (4) At the same time, a number of factors are operating to maintain similarities. (5) Changes in family organization have a complex origin, in which the influence of the English-speaking world is only one element. (6) The main characteristics of the French-Canadian family can be said to be an extensive kinship recognition only partially weakened by geographical scattering, an extensive exchange of services among recognized kin, a strong sense of household unity, and a large sibling group.

These characteristics have been reported as existing to a greater or

[58]S. de Lestapis, "Evolution de la pensée exprimée de l'Eglise catholique" in *Renouveau des idées sur la famille* (Paris, 1954), pp. 254–8.

[59]G. Lemieux, *Vu et vécu : La Vie familiale des jeunes ruraux* (Montréal, 1955).

[60]Rapport de l'Action catholique ouvrière (1954), "Service de préparation au mariage."

[61]*Le Mouvement ouvrier* (Montréal, 1955), p. 117.

smaller degree in all French-Canadian communities, even outside the province of Quebec. A hypothesis which explains these characteristics as peculiar to French Canadians cannot, moreover, be correlated with the origin of the French Canadians in France, or with the supposed folk character of rural French Canada, or with the "survival" of an inherent rural culture and family form. Neither can present-day French-Canadian society be compared to that of underdeveloped countries, for the history and scale of industrialization in the province of Quebec is closely similar to that of other areas of Canada.

Arising out of these findings are a number of postulates which can be isolated, and from which a hypothesis can be built. In the historical dimension it can be offered, as one of the postulates, that although there have been important social changes in a number of social institutions, such as the political and economic organizations, as well as a shift from a predominantly rural to a predominantly urban society, no particular period can be pointed out as the breaking-up of a traditional family structure. In the functional dimension it can also be stated, as another postulate, that important supports have always been provided by other institutions, such as religion, law, education, and so on, to the maintenance of the characteristics of the French-Canadian family.

Presented as statements, these postulates can be correlated in the following manner, which as a totality could provide the main structure of a hypothesis for further empirical research. The characteristics of the French-Canadian family are the results of: (1) an early history within a society whose survival demanded a rapid growth of population as well as a strongly integrated society; (2) the acceptance, when New France was founded, of a family ideal based on extensive reciprocal rights and duties which merged into religious obligations, and the need for the survival of French-Canadian society as its members fought the climate, the forest, the Indians, and the British; (3) the development, after the conquest of 1760, of a society in which the religion, the language, and the family were the main social institutions left over from the period of New France, and in which these institutions were highly valued because they were the links with the previous society, as well as because they became the accepted characteristics of the French Canadians as a separate ethnic group; (4) the maintenance, to the present, of a strong ethnic consciousness, with its accompanying refusal of social and cultural assimilation.

A sociological analysis of the French-Canadian family must, therefore, emphasize the fact that, besides its normal functions of fitting its members into the various communities composing French Canada, it has been the instrument of survival of the French Canadians as a special group. This need to survive, both in the period of New France and after, has been so important that the other social determinants, which normally have important bearings on family behaviour, have taken second place. Survival needed both numbers and a well-integrated society. The most efficient sociological instrument for achieving those aims is the family. For that reason it can be stated that, as long as a feeling of ethnic difference exists among the French Canadians, then the special characteristics of the French-Canadian family will continue to exist.

The research hypothesis presented here as a conclusion is that the family has been and is even now the major instrument of cultural continuity of the French Canadians. Because, after 1760, the political and economic as well as other institutions became English in character, and because gradually the Catholic Church, with an ever increasing proportion of non–French Canadians among its members, ceased to identify the survival of Catholicism with the survival of French Canada, the family has been the means of cultural continuity.

Even today, family life does not, for French Canadians, mean only the socialization of children, and the providing of economic and psychological security. It is for the overwhelming majority of them the centre of their cultural and social activities, the centre of what they hold to be French-Canadian values. It is therefore possible to suggest that the maintenance of over-all cultural similarities between the various rural and urban communities, the strength of kinship ties, the central position of the family in the behaviour of French Canadians, are the results of a compensatory attitude resulting from loss of control over the other institutions. Because the conquest decreased their participation, as well as their identification, with the political, legal, and economic, as well as other institutions developed by the English, French Canadians withdraw into their families, creating for themselves the only social and cultural world over which they were masters. Against a mainly Anglo-Saxon continent they found in their family the needed social and cultural security.

This hypothesis would also explain another cultural characteristic of French Canada: the identification between the general cultural values and the family values of French Canadians. Without under-estimating the role and importance of other values in the history of French Canada, it can be said that the general cultural world view of French Canadians has been familistic. The reason why urbanism has not had the same disintegrating consequences on the French-Canadian family as it has on other societies is that, on the one hand, French Canada was not a folk society or a peasant society, and, on the other hand, there was an over-all familistic culture which minimized the impact of the urban way of life. These familistic values are not the result of a rural way of life, or of a folk survival, but seem to have resulted from, first, an adaptation to certain conditions, and, second, a compensatory reaction against a minority status in a dominant Anglo-Saxon world.

The importance of familistic values in the cultural world view of French Canadians can be seen in the dominant role played by these values in the development of nationalistic values. A number of the most famous slogans used by the nationalists, such as "la langue, la paroisse, la famille," "la terre de nos ancêtres," "la revanche des berceaux," and so on, are to be seen as an identification of familistic and nationalistic values. The French-Canadian national anthem, *O Canada*, carries two verses which epitomize this identification: "O Canada, terre de nos aïeux," and "protégera nos foyers et nos droits." Poets like Fréchette speak of the respect French Canadians have for those who started New France: "Ces hommes qui furent nos pères." Henri Bourassa, speaking in 1920, identified the society and the family: "Toute loi civile, toute mesure administrative qui porte atteinte directe ou indirecte à la famille, est anti-sociale." The thread which links all the various aspects of French-Canadian culture and social life seems to be, in all instances, the family.

1955

II. MATERIAL FACTORS

B. Economic Considerations

II. POPULATION ET ÉCONOMIE

B. Facteurs économiques

A Comparison of Manufacturing Industry in Quebec and Ontario, 1952

J. H. DALES

Department of Political Economy, University of Toronto

MANUFACTURING INDUSTRY in Canada is largely a growth of this century and to an amazing extent a growth of the last fifteen years. It is not surprising then, given the usual "academic lag," that scholarly work in this field of Canadian development is just beginning.[1] What is surprising is that when one starts thinking about manufacturing industry one can find so few guides to its analysis—and this in spite of the fact that for the better part of a century manufacturing has been the very core of economic life. Historians and statisticians have written of the relative importance of manufacturing to the economy as a whole and theorists have analysed the workings of the individual and firm, but only rarely have students taken the manufacturing *sector* of the economy as a unit of study and sought to lay bare its anatomy and physiology.[2] Perhaps the main reason for this neglect is the in-

[1]Two recent essays in the field are: A. Maddison, "Productivity in an Expanding Economy," *Economic Journal* (Sept. 1952), and G. D. Sutton, "Productivity in Canada," *Canadian Journal of Economics and Political Science* (May 1953).

[2]The field is not entirely unmapped, of course. Location theorists have sought to throw light on the spatial patterning of manufacturing; empirical workers, usually interested in filling empty theoretical boxes, have dealt with such things as size of firm and plant, productivity, type of market organization, and, more recently, the structure of industry in terms of input-output tables; the National Bureau of Economic Research has devoted much study to such things as production indexes and the cyclical behaviour of different industries. Professor P. S. Florence's notable work, a combined statistical, empirical, and theoretical approach to manufacturing industry which stems from an interest in the subject itself rather than from theory, illustrates an unfortunately much rarer treatment of the material. But the very diversity of approach is eloquent of the absence of any accepted framework for the analysis of that economic conglomerate we call manufacturing industry.

credible variety of manufacturing activities in a highly industrialized economy. As contrasted with the relatively few primary activities, and thus their tractability to Marshallian analysis, manufacturing presents the student with a dismaying array and variety of data whose very classification presents formidable difficulties. It may be, as E. M. Forster once wrote of the poor, that manufacturing should be approached only by statisticians or poets—but economists are bound to have their say!

This paper presents a simple quantitative comparison between manufacturing industry in Quebec and Ontario. Its purpose is to describe, and in some measure to suggest explanations for, the differences in the size and composition of manufacturing industry between Quebec and Ontario. In particular an attempt is made to test the relative strength of two hypotheses about these differences, namely, a congeries of suggestions that the differences are due to differences in skills, wages, and general cultural factors on the one hand, and on the other hand, the perfectly definite thesis of MM. Faucher and Lamontagne "that Quebec's industrialization had nothing specific to do with, and was not fundamentally influenced by its cultural environment," but was on the contrary simply a manifestation of "economic and geographic factors" and trends in the location of industry in the North American continent as a whole.[3]

"Comparative analysis" is at best an inexact technique, as much a matter of art as of science, but, carefully used, it seems to offer some hope of illuminating economic jungles such as "manufacturing industry" where the precision tools of deductive economics are apt to be blunted by tangled masses of facts. Unfortunately, the term itself has been subjected to much abuse: it is often used in a very loose sense to refer to any general discussion of similarities and differences between two entities. Even when used with greater scientific pretension, the "comparative method" can take a number of forms, so that it can scarcely be said to enjoy the status of a standard intellectual strategy. It is necessary, therefore, to make clear the use made of "comparative analysis" in this paper, and this can most easily be done by giving an outline of the procedure and argument.

The purpose of the comparison is to improve our understanding of manufacturing development in Quebec and Ontario. We can classify the *possible* determinants of manufacturing activity in the two provinces into three categories: A, factors which are *known* to differ

[3]A. Faucher and M. Lamontagne, "History of Industrial Development" in J.-C. Falardeau, éd., *Essais sur le Québec contemporain* (Québec, 1953), pp. 24, 34.

between the provinces, the best example of which in our case is the different resource endowment and geographical position of the two provinces; B, factors which are considered to be roughly similar in the two provinces, for example, climate, the political setting, and economic institutions; and C, all other factors which differ between the provinces, but whose significance to manufacturing development is *not* known or *imperfectly* known, for example, a wide range of cultural factors. We then set up the hypothesis that the differences between industry in Quebec and Ontario are due to differences in natural resources. In comparing manufacturing in the two provinces we therefore classify in one category all resource-oriented industries. In the event, the difference between employment in resource-oriented industries in Quebec and Ontario proves to be a minor part of the total difference in all manufacturing employment. This suggests that the "resource hypothesis" is inadequate, and that the major explanation of the differences in industrial development between Quebec and Ontario—since group B factors are considered to be common to the two provinces—are to be found in group C, or "cultural" differences.

So much for logic. But as we have already commented, comparative analysis involves judgment as well as logic, and before any comparison is undertaken it should pass two tests: Is the comparison intelligible, that is, are the two terms of the comparison comparable, and, Is the comparison likely to be a useful one? The latter test requires that the B factors be numerous and the C factors few, for if it turns out that the initial hypothesis (that the A factors are of major importance) is wrong, one would like the field of search for the important factors, that is, the C factors, to be as circumscribed as possible. We must now subject our proposed comparison to these tests.

The first question, put in terms of the present problem, can be rephrased as follows: Is there reason to expect that the manufacturing structures of the two industrial regions should be predominantly similar in composition and intensity? If there is no reason to expect this, if manufacturing structures are growths *sui generis*, or if manufacturing structures are predominantly *specialized* economic phenomena, then manufacturing developments in different regions are simply non-comparable phenomena: a "comparison" between them would in fact become a contrast, a mere enumeration of differences. What, then, is the situation? Is the manufacturing sector of an economy a formless growth with no regularities or rationale of its own—no more, in brief, than the sum of its component firms? Or, is the manufacturing sector of each region unique and therefore not comparable with manufacturing in other regions? Certainly, academic emphasis on the

Law of Comparative Advantage, Alfred Weber's work on the location of industry, and lay impressions of the special character of industrial areas—textiles in New England and steel in Ohio, for examples—tend to make us think of manufacturing developments as being rather highly specialized and individual economic structures. Despite these suggestions, two considerations lead us to believe that we should expect similarities rather than differences to characterize manufacturing developments in different regions.

First, we have the testimony of Professor Florence who, at the end of a detailed analysis of British and American manufacturing industry, wrote as follows:

> The main dissimilarities [between manufacturing in Great Britain and in the United States] are in the degree of mechanization and in the strength of the incentives to labour and . . . management, together accounting largely for the higher physical output per head in America. In spite of these fundamental industrial differences and others such as area, climate, [economic] structure (notably the greater scope of agriculture in America) and law (notably the British nationalization of coal, transport and utilities) striking similarities were found. . . . Corresponding manufacturing industries [in the two countries] had roughly the same selling costs, patterns of location, integration, and prevailing sizes of plant measured in men; and manufactures generally much the same average size of plant and firm and average staff ratio (and trends in these averages), and much the same unequal distribution of size.[4]

Even in mechanization, measured by the number of horsepower per worker, it was found that "though the general level of mechanization is higher in America, any one industry will tend to have the same relative position in degree of mechanization among British and among American industries."[5] Professor Florence's work thus provides strong support for the view that manufacturing industry, far from being a haphazard development, displays enough "character," enough stability in its structure and functioning, to be a fit object of scientific inquiry.[6]

[4]P. S. Florence, *The Logic of British and American Industry* (London, 1953), p. 348.

[5]*Ibid.*, p. 335. Some of the difference in mechanization is illusory because British and American statistics of horsepower are compiled in different ways. See P. S. Florence, *Investment, Location and Size of Plant* (Cambridge, 1948), p. 184. To the present writer the differences in compilation seem to be major ones, sufficiently important, perhaps, to account for a large part of the apparent discrepancy in the horsepower-per-worker ratios between the United States and Great Britain.

[6]For the observed trend in the United States toward a more equal regional distribution of industry, and to a greater similarity of industry between regions, see E. M. Hoover, *The Location of Economic Activity* (New York, 1948), pp. 154–65.

Second, we can approach the problem analytically. The bias of international trade theory and of location theory has been to emphasize differences rather than similarities in industrial developments. The reason is not far to seek: both theories base their arguments on assumptions of various immobilities, trade theorists on the interregional immobility of all factors of production, and location theorists on the fixed spatial patterning of natural resources and of "the market." These assumptions are partly true of course, and the shorter the period under consideration the more realistic they become. But for a period relevant to the study of industrial development—a minimum of a decade, or even a quarter-century perhaps—they are not obviously reasonable assumptions to make. Labour and capital have always displayed a considerable degree of international mobility, and domestically, as economies develop, labour and capital, and thus markets, tend to become increasingly mobile. Not even natural resources are quite immobile in the long run, for old resources can be depleted, new resources discovered—not only by chance but also by search—and new technologies or tastes can change the very catalogue of resources.

Most important, however, is the other general category of the factors of production, namely, partly finished materials, and it must be stressed that these materials are usually very mobile indeed. Thus while a relatively few "first stage" or "early stage" industries like metal smelting, cotton ginning, fruit preserving, pulp and paper production, and sawmilling, are usually tethered closely to the natural resources they process, the metals, cotton, paper, and lumber they produce, being valuable in relation to their bulk, are very mobile and the thousand and one industries for which these products are "raw materials" therefore normally have a wide choice of location. Professor Florence comments that:

> The twenty industries which are most highly localized . . . in Britain and in America . . . are in localizations that have existed for some time, but nearly all of them not particularly near their market or their material. . . . Weber's law that the location of industry will be such as to make the total ton miles of transport to and from the industry a minimum, applies to localized heavy material industries. . . . But these industries employ today relatively few workers either in Britain or America. . . .[7]

In brief, the assumptions of immobilities that underlie trade theory and location theory seem the lesser part of the truth for most manufacturing industries, at least in the long run, and when we make the opposite assumptions, theory no longer creates any presumption of

[7] *Logic of British and American Industry*, pp. 83–5.

major dissimilarities (other than in those industries based directly on natural resources) in the manufacturing developments of different regions. Indeed in two regions with populations of similar tastes we should expect to find the development of similar industrial structures.

As to our second question—Is the comparison likely to be useful?—we can simply note the assumption on which we proceed and let the reader judge its reasonableness for himself. Our argument presupposes that Quebec, Ontario, and the northeastern United States are sufficiently similar in important economic respects to permit useful comparison between them, and yet sufficiently dissimilar in geographical and cultural respects to be distinguished as different regions. Two procedural points may be noted here. First, we compare industries only on the basis of the numbers of people employed in them: although an important, and in many ways a fundamental criterion, "number of employees" is of course only one of several possible measures of industrial importance. Second, although comparison logically tolerates only relative, not absolute statements, and although there is no logical reason for taking one area, or industry, as a yardstick for another—so that to say, for example, that the clothing industry is overdeveloped in Quebec in relation to Ontario is logically the same thing as saying that the clothing industry is underdeveloped in Ontario in relation to Quebec—everyone uses yardsticks in practice, logic or no logic, and we do not hesitate to do so here. We first use the manufacturing structure of the northeastern United States as a yardstick against which to measure manufacturing in Ontario and Quebec, and we do so simply because the northeastern part of the United States provides the outstanding example in the modern world of what we mean by an industrialized area. Later in the paper we measure Quebec against Ontario; we take Ontario as a yardstick for Quebec, rather than vice versa, because the preliminary analysis shows that Ontario's industrial pattern conforms much more closely to the American "standard" than does Quebec's. There can surely be no harm in speaking thus in terms of absolutes, provided we realize that the "absolutes" are arbitrary, especially since the reader can easily translate statements from an absolute into a relative form if he so wishes.

II

Table I provides a summary statement of the size and composition of manufacturing in Quebec, Ontario, and the northeastern United States (that is, the East North Central, Middle Atlantic, and New

TABLE I

EMPLOYMENT IN MANUFACTURING INDUSTRY IN THE NORTHEASTERN UNITED STATES,* ONTARIO, AND QUEBEC, 1952

A. Canadian designation† B. American designation	Percentage distribution‡			Numbers employed per 10,000 population‡		
	U.S.	Ont.	Que.	U.S.	Ont.	Que.
1. A. Foods and beverages B. Food and kindred products	6.9	11.6	10.2	99	149	105
2. A. Tobacco and tobacco products B. Tobacco manufacturers	.2	.3	1.7	3	4	18
3. A. Rubber products B. Rubber products	1.9	2.5	1.4	27	32	14
4. A. Leather products B. Leather and leather products	2.7	2.1	4.1	39	27	42
5. A. Textile products (exc. clothing) B. Textile mill products	5	4.6	9.4	72	59	97
6. A. Clothing (textile and fur) B. Apparel and related products	7.6	6.3	16	109	81	165
7. A. Wood products (exc. furniture) B. Lumber and products (exc. furniture)§	1.5	3.8	5.4	21	49	56
8. A. Furniture B. Furniture and fixtures	2	2.2	2.1	29	28	22
9. A. Paper products B. Paper and allied products	3.1	5.3	7.5	44	68	77
10. A. Printing, publishing, and allied industries B. Printing and publishing industries	5	5.3	4.1	72	68	42
11. A. Primary iron and steel *and* non-ferrous metal products B. Primary metal industries	9.4	9.8	6.1	134	126	63
12. A. Iron and steel products (exc. primary products) B. Fabricated metal products *and* machinery (exc. electrical)	21.3	14.2	8.3	305	182	85
13. A. Transportation equipment B. Transportation equipment	10.5	13.1	9.8	150	168	101

*The American figures are the totals for the New England, East North Central, and Middle Atlantic census divisions. These statistics result from a sampling procedure, the last enumeration of manufacturing establishments in the United States having been made in 1947. We omit from our figures the category "Administrative and auxiliary" personnel.

†The Canadian categories have been rearranged in a few cases to make them approximately comparable to the American statistics.

‡All percentages and ratios have been calculated on a slide rule.

§Includes logging whereas the Canadian figures do not.

SOURCES: D.B.S., *The Manufacturing Industry of Canada*, Section C, *Province of Quebec* and Section D, *Province of Ontario* (1952); *The Canada Year Book, 1954;* U.S. Bureau of the Census, *Statistical Abstract of the United States* (1952).

TABLE I (*cont.*)

A. Canadian designation† B. American designation	Percentage distribution‡			Numbers employed per 10,000 population‡		
	U.S.	Ont.	Que.	U.S.	Ont.	Que.
14. A. Electrical apparatus and supplies B. Electrical machinery	8	8	4.4	114	102	45
15. A. Non-metallic mineral products B. Stone, clay, and glass products	3	2.6	2.2	43	33	23
16. A. Products of petroleum and coal B. Petroleum and coal products	1.1	1.4	.9	16	18	9
17. A. Chemicals and allied products B. Chemicals and allied products	3.7	3.9	4.6	53	50	47
18. A. Miscellaneous industries B. Miscellaneous manufacturers *and* instruments and related products	7.3	3	2.1	104	38	22
ALL INDUSTRIES	100.2	100	100.3	1,430	1,280	1,030
"Coefficient of specialization"‖	0	.138	.282			

‖See text, n. 8.

England census regions). It gives a measure of quantitative expression to common impressions of the similarities and differences in the manufacturing developments of these three regions. Measuring the extent, or intensity, of manufacturing by the proportion of the total population employed in manufacturing, the relative positions of the northeastern United States, Ontario, and Quebec are roughly as 14:13:10. Quebec makes a somewhat better showing when we use a measure of intensity which makes allowance for the proportionately larger number of children in Quebec than in the other areas. Thus the number of employees in manufacturing per thousand of the labour force is 354 in the American area (based on the 1950 labour force), 324 in Ontario, and 292 in Quebec (based on 1951 labour force figures). With respect to the composition of manufacturing the table suggests two main points: first, the general—I should say the quite striking—similarity between Ontario and the United States; and, second, the imbalance of Quebec's manufacturing structure. Measured against the American standard, the food industries bulk unusually large in Ontario; more understandably, the wood and paper industries are over-represented; and the transport equipment industries are slightly over-represented. The clothing industries are under-represented in Ontario, while the leather, electrical apparatus and non-metallics groups, though about the same proportion of all manufactures in Ontario as in the United

States, are slightly under-represented in Ontario when related to total population. The really striking features of the Ontario–United States comparison, however, are Ontario's deficiencies in the other iron and steel and miscellaneous categories (items 12 and 18): the former is largely a deficiency in the manufacture of machinery, and both are probably to be explained by the relative smallness of the Canadian markets. Despite these differences, Ontario's manufacturing industry is clearly recognizable as a small-scale version of the great industrial economy of the northeastern United States.

The same can hardly be said of Quebec's manufacturing industry. Here we have an industrial structure which, by comparison with that of the United States, is heavily, but understandably, biased toward the wood and paper industries and even more heavily, and much less appropriately, biased toward the tariff-fostered textile and clothing industries. The gaps in Quebec's manufacturing are even more apparent, with serious deficiencies in the primary metals, other iron and steel, electrical apparatus, and miscellaneous groups (items 11, 12, 14, and 18) and significant under-representation in the rubber goods, printing, transportation equipment, and non-metallic categories (items 3, 10, 13, and 15). Only in the chemical and furniture industries (items 17 and 8) does Quebec have a relatively "normal" number of employees.[8]

[8]Some quantitative expression can be given to these comparisons by calculating the "coefficients of specialization" for Ontario and Quebec in relation to the United States. This coefficient is calculated by summing the plus (or minus) percentage point deviations of one area's percentage distribution of employees in the various categories as distinguished from the percentage distribution in the "standard" area, and then dividing the result by 100. The coefficient can vary from 0, complete identity of an area's manufacturing distribution with that of the standard, to nearly one, complete specialization of manufacturing in one grouping. See the United States National Resources Planning Board, *Industrial Location and National Resources* (Washington, D.C., 1943), pp. 120–4. The coefficients for Ontario and Quebec measured against the standard of the northeastern United States are respectively, as shown in Table I, .138 and .282. No significance should be given to the absolute size of the coefficient—it will vary depending on the classification of industry which is used, and it does not of course distinguish between variations in "important" and "less important" groups of industries—but the difference in the coefficient for Quebec and Ontario does support the generalizations made in the text.

It will be urged that while it is reasonable to compare Ontario with the northeastern United States, it is unreasonable to stretch Quebec on this particular rack, and that for a number of reasons, among them historical reasons, Quebec is to be more appropriately compared with New England. What is reasonable is of course always a matter of judgment. Those who urge that Quebec is the Canadian counterpart of New England sometimes forget that the manufacturing structures of the two regions display major differences as well as major similarities. Thus the leather goods, textile, and clothing industries comprise 29.5 per

III

Table II employs a finer classification of industries (derived from the still finer classification given in the Canadian census of manufacturing) and therefore provides for a more detailed comparison between manufacturing in Ontario and Quebec. The classification is not based on any one criterion: the first three groupings are, for different reasons, considered to be in the nature of special cases; the other groupings are distinguished roughly on the basis of the markets which their component industries mainly serve.

In section A of the table we list those industries whose location is likely to be largely determined by geographical factors and especially by the location of natural resources. The first six items need little comment: they are all "early stage" industries closely tied to the natural resources they process. Shipbuilding (item 9) must take place on navigable water, and sugar refining (item 8)—the figures for which cannot be separated from the wines and animal fats industries, though the former is also resource-oriented—is most economically carried on at import points.

In the introductory section of this paper it was noted that the products of resource-oriented industries are usually quite mobile and that therefore the industries which use these products as raw materials are normally quite foot-loose. Modifying this generalization is the well-recognized fact that for a variety of technical and economic reasons later stage industries are sometimes "linked" to earlier stage industries and tend to locate near them. How important this "linkage" effect is in different industries we do not know, for we have no reliable measure of it. It is often argued, however, that the location of the *primary* iron and steel industry in Ontario, because of that province's proximity to American resources of iron ore and coal, gives Ontario an overweening advantage in *all* iron and steel industries. This overstates the point in my opinion, for while Quebec has no blast furnaces and very little rolling mill capacity, it competes on fairly even terms with Ontario in some later stage iron and steel industries, such as bridge building and structural steel (section G), certain types of machinery,

cent of industry in Quebec and 27.8 per cent of industry in New England—though the relative importance of textiles and clothing is almost reversed in the two areas, New England employing 15 per cent of her manufacturing employees in textiles and 5 per cent in clothing while Quebec has 16 per cent of her employees in clothing and 9.4 per cent in textiles—but in New England the metallic and electrical industries account for 36 per cent of the employees in manufacturing while in Quebec these industries account for only 18.7 per cent of all employees in manufacturing.

miscellaneous iron and steel products, and machine shops (section F). Why then, with a proportionate, or better than proportionate share of these industries, should Quebec make such a poor showing in such industries as machine tools (section F), heating and cooking apparatus (section E), and hardware, tools, and cutlery (section F)? The answer, we suggest, is not obvious, but is obviously not that these industries are ineluctably tied to primary iron and steel centres. Nevertheless, the "linkage" argument has some force and to make

TABLE II

EMPLOYMENT IN MANUFACTURING INDUSTRIES IN QUEBEC AND ONTARIO, 1952

Industries	Quebec	Ontario	Ratio, Que. to Ont.	Ontario–Quebec Surplus	Ontario–Quebec Deficit
A. *"Resource-located" industries*					
1. Pulp and paper	23,928	18,883	127	—	5,045
2. Saw and planing mills	18,992	16,870	112	—	2,052
3. Non-ferrous metal smelting and refining	9,768	10,018	98	250	
4. Canning and processing	3,653	10,004	37	6,351	
5. Tobacco processing and packing	401	1,289	31	888	
6. Asbestos products	1,344	423	137	—	921
7. Primary iron and steel	4,503	23,479	19	18,976	
8. Sugar refineries, wines, animal oils and fats	1,206	696	173	—	510
9. Shipbuilding	8,458	4,088	207	—	4,370
10. Castings, iron	3,793	10,256	37	6,463	
11. Boilers, tanks, and platework	1,482	6,087	24	4,605	
TOTAL: Section A	77,528	102,093	76	24,635	
B. *"Special" industries*					
1. Railway rolling stock	17,127	7,220	237	—	9,907
2. Aircraft and parts	14,705	16,174	91	1,469	
3. Miscellaneous electrical apparatus	12,020	9,033	133	—	2,987
4. Motor vehicles, motor vehicles parts and supplies	1,319	50,332	3	49,013	
TOTAL: Section B	45,171	82,759	55	37,588	
C. *"Cheap labour" industries*					
1. Clothing (textile and fur)	68,578	38,453	179	—	30,125
2. Woollen goods	4,462	9,774	46	5,312	
3. Textile products (exc. clothing), other than woollen goods	35,755	18,277	196	—	17,478
4. Leather products other than tanning	16,942	9,645	176	—	7,297
5. Leather tanning	497	3,281	15	2,784	
6. Tobacco, cigars, and cigarettes	6,935	518	1,340	—	6,417
TOTAL: Section C	133,169	79,948	167		53,221

TABLE II (*cont.*)

Industries	Quebec	Ontario	Ratio, Que. to Ont.	Ontario–Quebec Surplus	Deficit
D. *Other "ordinary consumption goods" industries*					
1. Bread and other bakery products	9,668	14,548	67	4,880	
2. Butter and cheese	5,431	7,627	71	2,196	
3. Slaughtering and meat packing	4,568	8,724	52	4,156	
4. Carbonated beverages	2,709	2,864	95	155	
5. Confectionery	2,552	4,792	53	2,240	
6. Miscellaneous food preparations	2,594	4,856	53	2,262	
7. Biscuits	2,411	2,247	103	—	164
8. Breweries	2,448	3,036	81	588	
9. Distilled liquors	2,140	1,852	116	—	288
10. Feeds, stock and poultry, prepared	1,524	2,731	56	1,207	
11. Other foods	2,978	6,700	44	3,722	
12. Rubber products	6,139	15,403	40	9,264	
13. Furniture	9,212	13,536	68	4,324	
14. Wood industries (other than furniture and saw and planing mills)	4,073	5,914	68	1,841	
15. Paper products (other than pulp and paper)	8,445	13,631	62	5,186	
16. Chemicals and allied products (other than primary plastics and acids, alkalis, and salts)	14,878	18,947	78	4,069	
TOTAL: Section D	81,770	127,408	64	45,638	
E. *"Standard of living goods" industries*					
1. Heating and cooking apparatus	1,656	5,752	29	4,096	
2. Non-ferrous metal products (exc. metal smelting and refining)	8,125	16,844	48	8,719	
3. Radios and radio parts	3,886	7,524	52	3,638	
4. Refrigerators, vacuum cleaners, and appliances	1,877	6,103	31	4,226	
5. Clay products	1,618	3,078	52	1,460	
6. Miscellaneous industries (exc. scientific and professional equipment)	7,585	14,316	55	6,731	
7. Bicycles and parts, boat-building, carriages, wagons, and sleighs	402	2,134	19	1,732	
TOTAL: Section E	25,149	55,751	45	30,602	

TABLE II (*cont.*)

Industries	Quebec	Ontario	Ratio, Que. to Ont.	Ontario–Quebec Surplus	Ontario–Quebec Deficit
F. *Other producers goods industries*					
1. Agricultural implements	266	16,743	2	16,477	
2. Hardware, tools, and cutlery	3,579	10,286	35	6,707	
3. Machinery, household, office, and store	4,233	5,379	79	1,146	
4. Machinery, industrial	7,442	12,204	60	4,762	
5. Machine tools	—	2,299	0	2,299	
6. Sheet metal products	4,999	9,943	50	4,944	
7. Wire and wire goods	2,289	5,453	42	3,164	
8. Miscellaneous iron and steel products	3,853	5,125	75	1,272	
9. Batteries	132	1,655	8	1,523	
10. Machinery, heavy electrical	1,189	24,218	5	23,029	
11. Primary plastics	1,412	414	342	—	998
12. Acids, alkalis, and salts	3,314	4,142	80	828	
13. Scientific and professional equipment	1,278	4,002	32	2,724	
14. Machine shops	1,897	2,248	84	351	
15. Abrasives, artificial	403	2,204	18	1,801	
TOTAL: Section F	36,286	106,315	34	70,029	
G. *Construction goods industries*					
1. Bridge building and structural steel	3,464	4,878	71	1,414	
2. Cement	746	610	123	—	136
3. Glass and glass products	2,419	3,543	68	1,124	
4. Lime, salt, brick, stone, and miscellaneous non-metallic mineral products	2,900	5,898	49	2,998	
TOTAL: Section G	9,529	14,929	64	5,400	
H. *Ancillary and service goods industries*					
1. Commercial printing	6,961	12,352	56	5,391	
2. Engraving, stereotyping, and allied industries	1,553	5,785	27	4,232	
3. Printing and publishing	6,772	12,463	54	5,691	
4. Publishing (only) of periodicals	2,215	1,590	139	—	625
5. Products of petroleum and coal	3,665	8,303	44	4,638	
TOTAL: Section H	21,166	40,493	52	19,327	
TOTALS, all industries	429,768	609,696	70.5	179,998	

some allowance for it (whether adequate or not, there is no way of telling) we have included in section A two iron and steel industries —iron castings, and boilers, tanks, and platework—which because they use very large tonnages of iron and steel might be expected to be located near primary iron and steel mills.[9] This is the only allowance we make for the advantage in manufacturing generally which Ontario allegedly enjoys over Quebec as a result of her favoured position in the primary iron and steel industry: our procedure thus amounts to assuming that there is no reason, from the point of view of natural resources or geographical position, why iron and steel industries other than those listed in section A should be more heavily concentrated in one province than in the other.

Ontario had some 180,000 more people employed in manufacturing in 1952 than Quebec had, of whom about 24,000, or 13 per cent of the total, were accounted for by the industries listed in section A.

Section B of Table II lists four important "special" industries, "special" in the sense that each of them is composed of only a few major firms, and that "historical accident" may therefore have played an important part in their location. The net balance of employment in these industries in 1952 was about 38,000 in favour of Ontario, or some 20 per cent of Ontario's over-all superiority in manufacturing employment.

In section C of the table we list four industries in which Quebec clearly leads Ontario. The usual explanation of Quebec's disproportionately large share of these industries is that they are attracted by Quebec's "cheap labour." We shall not here call that explanation into serious question, but two points are worth noting: the "cheap labour" explanation requires us to believe that Quebec's "advantage" in this respect disappears when it has about 64 per cent of the combined clothing industry of the two provinces, 59 per cent of the textile industry, and 58 per cent of the leather goods group; it also applies, apparently, to cotton and synthetic fibres, but not to wool, for Quebec

[9]For a rough measure of linkage, the "coefficient of geographic association," see U.S. National Resources Planning Board, *Industrial Location and National Resources*, pp. 107–20. I have worked out from the American data for 1939 there listed the coefficients between various iron and steel industries and the "steel works and rolling mills" industry. They are as follows (the higher the coefficient, the more closely associated are the industries): steel castings, 55; fabricated structural steel, 61; power boilers, 61; stoves, ranges, and water heaters, 50; wire, drawn from purchased rods, 49; hardware, not elsewhere classified, 36. Other coefficients are listed in *ibid.*, p. 119, among them coefficients between steel works and rolling mills and electric generating equipment, 55; and motor vehicles and bodies, 35. Significance should be attached only to the relative magnitudes of the coefficients; even then, in my opinion, not much weight should be given them. See *ibid.*, p. 120, for some of the shortcomings of the coefficient.

is under-represented in all branches of the woollen industry. Quebec has an excess over Ontario of more than 52,000 employees in these industries. If one wanted to "pair off" the three categories we have discussed so far, one could say that Quebec's "advantage" of cheap labour has roughly offset its resource disabilities and its deficiencies in the "special" industries listed in section B.

Section D of the table comprises industries which may be considered to produce goods for ordinary, or routine, consumption purposes. With some 64 per cent of Ontario's employment in this group Quebec is under-represented in these industries whether we measure under-representation by reference to total manufacturing employees, where Quebec's proportion to Ontario is 70.5, by reference to total population, where the Quebec–Ontario ratio is 87.5, or by reference to the labour force, where the ratio is 78. In terms of individual industries Quebec has an above-normal employment in distilled liquors, carbonated beverages (Montreal is said to have the largest per capita Coca-Cola consumption of any city in North America), and biscuits. Serious deficiencies are evident in rubber products, slaughtering and meat packing (low meat consumption? much local butchering?), confectionery (where one would have expected cheap labour to be important), and miscellaneous food preparations. On balance Quebec has nearly 46,000 fewer employees in these industries than Ontario.

Goods produced by the industries listed in section E of the table may be considered as semi-luxuries, mainly consumer durables, or, in general, as "standard of living" items. Quebec is very deficient in all these industries, and especially in the heating and cooking apparatus and the refrigerators, vacuum cleaners, and appliances categories, where employment in Quebec is less than a third of that in Ontario. How can we explain Quebec's shortcomings in the consumer goods industries of sections D and E? They are of course a reflection of lower incomes in Quebec, but to say this is merely to rephrase the question, for precisely what we should like to know is why industrialization, or income, or standard of living, or economic development, *is* at a lower level in Quebec than in Ontario.

The industries of Section F manufacture producers goods. It is here that Quebec's industrial deficiencies are most manifest, employment in this group in Quebec being only about a third of what it is in Ontario. When one looks at individual industries, however, the picture is rather spotty. Quebec almost monopolizes the primary plastics industry, and has an above-average share of the acids, alkalis, and salts industry, machine shops, certain types of machinery production, and miscellaneous iron and steel products. On the other hand Quebec has no machine tool industry, and only a token representation in two very important industries, agricultural implements and heavy electrical machinery. Quebec's weakness in the agricultural implements industry no doubt reflects the small market for these products in that province, which in turn reflects a low level of agricultural technique, but a similar argument could not be applied to electrical machinery since Quebec accounts for over a half of the hydraulic turbine capacity for all Canada and has an installed capacity which is more than twice as large as Ontario's. Some observers might suggest that this group of industries—and also, perhaps, the industries in section E—demands highly skilled labour, and be inclined to attribute Quebec's deficiency in this group (some 70,000 fewer employees in Quebec than in Ontario) to a low average degree of skill in Quebec's labour force. But an employment of over 15,000 in the machinery (except electrical) and hardware, tools, and cutlery industries suggests that skilled labour is available in considerable quantities in Quebec. Doubt is also cast on the "low skill" thesis by the fact that Quebec's employment in the two census classifications of iron and steel and electrical apparatus in 1952 was about the same as Ontario's employment in these industries in 1939, and by the fact that between 1939 and 1952 these industries, along with others such as chemicals, transportation equipment, and non-ferrous products expanded somewhat more rapidly in Quebec than in Ontario. In a modern economy deficiencies in skill can quickly be remedied—as wartime experience suggested—and can scarcely be considered as a satisfactory explanation of persistent weakness in manufacturing.

The last two sections of Table II require little comment. Quebec has an over-all deficiency of employment in manufacturing industries closely related to construction, but has a roughly normal representation in the bridge building and structural steel and glass and glass products industries. Quebec's deficiency in the printing industries is somewhat surprising—one might have expected "cheap labour" to be important in these trades—but perhaps the deficiency mainly reflects the generally lower degree of commercialization of Quebec's economy as compared with Ontario's.

Table III summarizes the results of our comparison in three ways. The first column lists the actual differences between the provinces in employment in the different groupings. This is the appropriate basis of comparison if one holds that on purely economic grounds Quebec should be expected to have as large a population and labour force as Ontario and should also be as highly industrialized as Ontario. The figures of columns 2 and 3 are computed numbers. Column 2 states

TABLE III

SUMMARY STATEMENTS OF QUEBEC'S DEFICIENCIES IN MANUFACTURING EMPLOYMENT AS COMPARED WITH ONTARIO, 1952

(Italicized figures represent an excess of employment in Quebec)

Category	Actual deficiency	Deficiency related to labour force*	Deficiency related to total employment in manufacturing†
"Resource-located" industries	24,565	2,175	*6,482*
"Special" industries	37,588	19,381	13,174
"Cheap labour" industries	*53,221*	*70,810*	*76,806*
"Ordinary consumption goods" industries	45,638	17,608	8,053
"Standard of living goods" industries	30,602	18,337	14,155
"Producers goods" industries	70,029	46,640	38,666
"Construction goods" industries	5,400	2,116	996
"Ancillary and service goods" industries	19,327	10,419	7,381
TOTALS: all industries	179,928	45,867	

*The Quebec-Ontario ratio for the labour force in 1951 was 1,471,840 to 1,884,941 or 78.

†The sum of this column should be zero but is actually 137: the discrepancy results from our taking the Quebec-Ontario ratio of total employees in manufacturing to be 70.5 instead of the actual ratio of 70.477.

what the differences in employment in the two provinces would be if Quebec, with its present labour force, had as many employees per thousand of the total labour force in the different groupings of manufacturing industry as Ontario has. The assumption underlying this comparison is that the size of Quebec's labour force is appropriate to its economic base, but that the degree and composition of manufacturing in the province should be expected to be the same as in Ontario. Column 3 is based on the assumption that both Quebec's present population and its present degree of industrialization are appropriate to its resources, and the figures in this column merely compare, therefore, the composition of industry—employees in each grouping per thousand employees in all manufacturing—in the two provinces. There will be general agreement, I think, that Quebec has not yet reached its saturation point in manufacturing industry, and even, perhaps, that given greater industrialization it could support a larger labour force at the present, or a higher, standard of living. If we are interested in a quantitative measure of Quebec's "backwardness," the figures of column 2, or some average of columns 1 and 2, appear to be the appropriate ones.

IV

Our comparison suggests that deficiencies in resources account for only a minor part of Quebec's industrial backwardness as compared with Ontario. Quebec's deficiency in the "resource-located" industries is only some 14 per cent of the total deficiency in column 1 and about 4 per cent of the total deficiency in column 2. Even if we add to resource-oriented industries the "special" industries listed in section B of Table II and assume that Quebec has simply had bad luck in not getting her share of these industries, the deficiency in these two groups together amounts to less than 35 per cent of the total deficiency in the figures of column 1, and slightly less than half of the deficiency in column 2. Column 3 shows that Quebec employs a larger proportion of all her manufacturing employees in resource-oriented industries than Ontario does.

If the assumptions underlying our comparison be accepted, we must conclude that the major part of Quebec's backwardness in manufacturing is to be explained on the basis of differences in factors other than resources. We can reasonably refer to these "other" factors as cultural differences, for even the terms which economists might use to describe them—differences in tastes, skills, entrepreneurship, propensity to consume, mobility, and so on—are themselves to be explained largely in sociological terms.

* * *

It is not the purpose of this essay to attempt to explain the differences between the industrial structures of Quebec and Ontario that our comparison has disclosed, but we should like, in lieu of conclusion, to make three general comments on this subject. First, a negative point. Economists, if pressed for an explanation of why Ontario is more highly industrialized than Quebec, may be tempted to answer in terms of the size of the market, external economies, and agglomerative factors. May we point out that this is merely a rephrasing of the question and that the question is precisely why the market is larger, and external economies more in evidence, in Ontario than in Quebec? And if external economies, agglomerative forces, and so on, are presented as cumulative factors that lead to a snowballing of economic development, why has Ontario's lead in manufacturing not tended to increase? At the turn of the century the Ontario–Quebec ratio of employees in manufacturing was 146; during the 1920's it averaged about 155; in the 1930's it fell to an average of around 146; and since the last war (during which the ratio fell to a low point of 130 in 1943) it has averaged about 143. The division of manufacturing between Quebec and Ontario has been relatively stable on the average during the last fifty or sixty years, but the rate of growth in manufacturing employment in Quebec has been slightly higher than that in Ontario during the last twenty-five years.[10]

Second, one suspects that the traditional bias of Quebec's culture against engineering education has been an important inhibiting influence on Quebec's manufacturing growth, and it has certainly been an important factor leading to the paucity of French-Canadian managers and executives in the province's industry. For while engineers do not necessarily become entrepreneurs, they often supply the ideas for promoters, or at least translate promoters' ideas into practicable plans; and in a going concern, particularly in an environment of rapidly changing technology, close liaison between the entrepreneur and his engineers is crucial to business survival. In a country which in fact is *not* bilingual it is not practicable to have executives and engineers who speak different languages.[11]

Third, in searching for an explanation of the differences between Quebec and Ontario in industrial development we would urge the importance of agricultural technique. In 1951 land under crops in Quebec was 67 per cent of that in Ontario, but the male agricultural labour force in Quebec was 96.5 per cent of Ontario's. With these figures in mind it not surprising to learn that cash farm income in Quebec was only 54 per cent of that in Ontario—a figure which suggests a negative marginal product for farm labour in Quebec. Another significant statistic showed that Quebec farmers were summer-fallowing only 14 per cent as much land as Ontario farmers were in 1951. Although economists have devoted surprisingly little attention to the interrelations of agriculture and industry, an economic historian, with the comparative history of agricultural reform in England and on the Continent in mind, may advance the hypothesis that an inefficient agriculture creates major distortions in the allocation of a region's resources and acts as a serious drag on its economic development.

1955

[10]Inspection of the Ontario–Quebec ratios from 1890 on suggests that the First World War led to a greater expansion of industry in Ontario than in Quebec, and in the twenties the ratios tend to fall back to the 1910 value; in the Second World War it was apparently Quebec that expanded more rapidly, for the ratios fall during the war years and rise in the post-war period.

[11]See the very interesting article by Huet Massue, "Contribution de polytechnique au génie canadien" in a special number of the *Revue trimestrielle canadienne* (novembre 1949).

La Dualité canadienne et l'économique: tendances divergentes et tendances convergentes

ALBERT FAUCHER

Professeur d'Histoire économique, Université Laval

L'ACTIVITÉ ÉCONOMIQUE a-t-elle rapproché ou éloigné les deux groupes ethniques ou culturels qui dominent le paysage démographique du pays ? Telle est la question à discuter. Du point de vue économique, on peut dire que les groupes culturels se caractérisent par l'intensité de leurs besoins, de leurs propensions vers des objectifs de consommation et de production, et par leur génie d'adaptation dynamique. Pour mieux cerner ces spécificités, nous userons tout au long de ce travail d'une typologie qu'on retrouve, sous des formulations diverses, chez Tawney, Delaisi et Handman[1]. Selon ce dernier, deux types sociaux ont caractérisé le monde occidental : le type bureaucratique et le type pécuniaire.

L'organisation de type bureaucratique ou fonctionnelle caractérise une société hiérarchique, primitivement établie sur la richesse foncière et dont le gouvernement peut être, tour à tour, ou simultanément, aristocratique, théocratique, militaire. L'adhésion à ce type d'organisation sociale entraîne donc l'exercice d'une « fonction » communautaire. C'est l'instinct de conservation et l'idée de promotion hiérarchique, et non l'instinct d'acquisition, qui dominent ce type de société. La base est rurale, l'inspiration féodale. Le pouvoir d'acquisition que chacun y exerce n'est pas basé sur le procédé mercantile d'achat et de vente, mais sur le statut social.

L'organisation de type pécuniaire implique l'esprit d'entreprise au

[1]R. H. Tawney, *The Acquisitive Society* (New York : Harcourt, 1946); F. Delaisi, *Les Deux Europes : Europe industrielle et Europe agricole* (Paris : Payot, 1929); Max Handman, « The Bureaucratic Culture Pattern and Political Revolution », *American Journal of Sociology*, XXXIX, 1933. L'élément fondamental de cette typologie, l'accumulation du capital, se trouve dans John Stuart Mill, *Principles*, Book I, chap. XI.

sens économique du terme, c'est-à-dire un goût du risque doublé d'une aptitude aux investissements productifs. Dans cette société, le prestige social dépend de l'aptitude à manipuler les biens et services en vue d'un gain, à *investir* pour acquérir la richesse. Le prestige attaché au pouvoir politique n'est, dans la société de type pécuniaire, qu'accidentel ou dérivé.

Ces types représentent deux pôles d'intégration; ils peuvent, à certaines phases historiques, s'imposer tous les deux à l'intérieur d'un même groupe ethnique et créer une situation de duopole social. Mais on ne peut pas dire que cette dualité d'objectif détruit le caractère du *we-group*, car les facteurs de cohésion culturelle sont plus nombreux que n'en peut révéler l'organisation sociale, surtout au niveau de l'économique dont il est ici question. Par contre, l'intégration culturelle en fonction d'un type unique, soit bureaucratique soit pécuniaire, intégration qui finit par s'imposer sur le plan architectonique de la politique, peut marquer profondément l'économie d'un groupe ethnique.

Heckscher a démontré que la formation des états nationaux, français et anglais entre autres, s'est opérée sous le signe du duopole social[2]. En d'autres termes, la politique de ces états apparut, disons au XVIIe siècle, comme la résultante de deux forces sociales tendant vers des objectifs différents. En France, les tendances bureaucratiques l'auraient emporté, cependant que les tendances pécuniaires auraient dominé la politique anglaise.

On retrouve une semblable dichotomie dans les entreprises colonisatrices des états européens. Le mercantilisme continental (hispano-français) s'appuie sur les terres; le contrôle territorial est son instrument. Et dans la mesure où il est tendu vers la conquête du territoire ou l'occupation des terres, il emprunte à la féodalité certaines normes d'organisation. Le mercantilisme anglo-hollandais, de type maritime, s'appuie sur la mer et le littoral; son objectif est commercial ou, s'il est aussi territorial, c'est qu'il considère les terres comme un point d'appui. Mais le mercantilisme maritime respecte son élément féodal représenté par la Couronne : il laisse à l'exécutif (la Couronne) son contrôle des terres.

Dans les deux types mercantilistes, anglais et français, les éléments bureaucratiques (de caractère féodal) et les éléments pécuniaires (de type commercial) coexistent. Ce qui donnera à l'un ou à l'autre son caractère final, ce sera la prédominance des éléments de première espèce sur les autres, ou vice versa.

* * *

[2]Eli F. Heckscher, *Mercantilism* (London : Allen & Unwin, 1935).

La première phase du développement économique de la colonie française en Amérique du Nord se réduit presque uniquement à l'histoire du commerce des fourrures dont l'organisation avait été de structure compétitive d'abord (annexe des pêcheries), de structure monopolistique ensuite, avec les compagnies de Rouen et des Cent-Associés, et enfin, de structure semi-monopolistique, marquant, avec la Compagnie des Habitants, un mouvement en faveur d'une certaine décentralisation. Ces compagnies de l'époque pré-Colbertienne inaugurèrent une politique de gratification de pouvoirs à un groupe délégué de la Couronne, sorte de féodalité marchande, instrument d'une société bureaucratique[3].

Par suite de l'expansion territoriale de la traite et de la multiplication des coureurs de bois – rendue nécessaire d'ailleurs après la destruction de la Huronie – il devint très difficile de contenir l'activité commerciale dans les limites du contrôle administratif. Le système de licence établi par Lauzon en 1654, et maintenu par D'Argenson, pour soumettre l'initiative privée à l'administration, ne réussit pas à enrayer l'individualisme de Chouart des Groseilliers et de Radisson. Des recommandations faites par Colbert à Talon, en 1665, au moins les cinq premières se rapportent au prestige de l'autorité royale; les autres révèlent des soucis d'ordre social ou économique, mais aucune d'elles ne souligne l'importance d'une classe économique soustraite au paternalisme d'état[4].

La règle générale des relations entre métropole et colonie fut celle du pacte colonial : monopole du commerce et de l'industrie réservé à la métropole, prohibition d'entreprises susceptibles de heurter les intérêts métropolitains imposée aux colonies. Mais il y eut des dérogations; et c'est précisément dans le mécanisme de celles-ci et dans leur résultat final qu'on peut saisir la portée générale de la règle. Les recommandations de Colbert à Talon semblent contenir quelques-unes de ces dérogations : encouragement aux manufactures, aux chantiers maritimes, aux mines... La chapellerie, petite industrie coloniale qui remontait à 1660, fut supprimée en 1736 par ordre du ministre[5]. L'industrie des textiles lancée par Talon subsiste à force de gratifications : ce fut le cas de l'industrie des frères Charron, par exemple[6]. La

[3]La charte de la compagnie des Cents-Associés (27 avril 1627) reflète l'esprit de cette politique.

[4]Pierre Clément, éd., *Lettres, instructions et mémoires de Colbert*, vol. III (Paris, 1865).

[5]H. A. Innis, ed., *Select Documents in Canadian Economic History, 1497–1783* (Toronto : University of Toronto Press, 1929), p. 392.

[6]P. E. Renaud, *Les Origines économiques du Canada* (Paris : Mamers, G. Enault, 1928), p. 384.

malversation règne dans l'entreprise de la tannerie, avec l'intervention d'une intendance qui distribue des quotas de production[7]. La construction navale, industrie gratifiée de subsides aux constructeurs, et aux armateurs qui y feraient leurs premières commandes de navires, n'a pas réussi à produire une bonne qualité de vaisseaux[8]. Quant aux mines, les Forges de Saint-Maurice en illustrent assez bien l'histoire : les forges ont subsisté grâce à l'intervention du roi. En somme, les tentatives pour introduire l'industrialisme en Nouvelle-France ont échoué. On a réussi à introduire un réseau de moulins assez imposant dans l'économie du Canada du XVIIIe siècle; mais ces entreprises ne justifient pas de parler d'industrialisme, dans le sens métropolitain du terme.

La réglementation (protection aux étrangers ou forains de France, contrôle et surveillance des marchés) a favorisé le petit commerce des autochtones, petit commerce inféodé à l'administration. Le grand commerce s'y opère par infiltration des étrangers, avec l'appui plus ou moins avoué des administrateurs. Nous retrouvons les éléments d'une société bureaucratique : une masse populaire à faible pouvoir d'achat, des *petits bourgeois* en mal de s'ennoblir et de s'enrichir, des administrateurs collaborant clandestinement avec les gros riches venant de l'extérieur[9].

On peut, semble-t-il, dégager deux aspects fondamentaux de l'empire français en Amérique : un aspect géographique, un aspect social.

L'empire comprenait deux types d'économie, maritime et continental, géographiquement disloqués, mais que la tradition impériale aurait voulu intégrer dans un même réseau commercial. Or l'on sait que, pour des raisons géographiques, techniques ou autres, on n'a jamais réussi à intégrer ces deux types d'économie. Pour autant que le progrès de cet empire dépendait d'un avant-poste maritime, la perte de l'Acadie en 1713 y introduit une brèche que les efforts péniblement tentés à Louisbourg n'ont pas réussi à réparer.

Du point de vue social, l'empire était divisé en lui-même. Cette dichotomie trouvait son expression la plus frappante dans l'opposition entre petits marchands, boutiquiers, détaillants d'une part, qui s'appelaient « habitans » et auxquels s'associaient les paysans (après la conquête le terme n'eut plus qu'une connotation rurale), et les marchands-entrepreneurs, capitaines de navire ou autres. Dans l'organi-

[7]*Ibid.*, pp. 398–9.

[8]*Ibid.*, p. 438.

[9]G. Frégault, *François Bigot, administrateur français* (2 vols., Montréal : Les Etudes de l'Institut d'Histoire de l'Amérique française, 1948). Voir en particulier, vol. I, troisième partie, et vol. II, quatrième partie.

sation militaire, division semblable, qui engendra « un vif antagonisme entre les officiers canadiens et ceux qu'on envoyait de France pour conduire la guerre. Les frictions, les rivalités et l'amertume qui en résulta, contribuèrent beaucoup à amoindrir les premiers succès du côté français, succès qui étaient dus à une meilleure préparation, obtenue aux dépens des intérêts normaux du Canada et de sa population[10]. »

En résumé, on retrouve dans l'organisation économique de la Nouvelle-France les caractères originaux de l'organisation économique de la France métropolitaine. Dès l'origine de la Nouvelle-France apparaît une féodalité marchande; à sa phase finale, on retrouve une dualité de structure dans laquelle l'habitant, au sens commercial du terme, qu'il fût boutiquier, artisan ou autre, prend figure de vassal. Transposé dans le nouveau monde, cet héritage métropolitain a quand même subi l'influence constante des conditions du milieu. Et ces conditions expliquent, dans une grande mesure, le manque d'intégration de l'empire français en Amérique; elles ont servi de prétexte au zèle de l'administration locale, par exemple, dans la lutte de l'administration contre l'expansionisme commercial. Mais les efforts d'adaptation aux conditions géographiques font ressortir d'autant les tendances du type bureaucratique. L'organisation administrative d'une telle société, inspirée d'un mercantilisme de tradition hispano-française, nous permet-elle de parler d'un état en Nouvelle-France ? Et l'organisation économique elle-même justifierait-elle de conjecturer l'existence de bourgeois-entrepreneurs répondant aux exigences des milieux où prédomine le type pécuniaire ?

* * *

La conquête a provoqué l'exode de tous ces Français qui étaient venus en Nouvelle-France soit pour l'administrer ou la défendre, soit pour l'approvisionner en temps de guerre; elle a provoqué aussi l'exode d'une catégorie de seigneurs habitués à un certain niveau de dépenses somptuaires. Les habitants sont restés et ils ont gardé les deux institutions essentielles à leur survivance : la seigneurie et l'Eglise.

A l'administration française, depuis longtemps militarisée, on a substitué une administration anglaise de type militaire. On l'a confiée à des généraux d'armée, qui ont reconstitué la société bureaucratique, à l'aide d'un « tiers état » que leur avait légué la bureaucratie française.

[10]Adam Shortt, éd., *Documents relatifs à la monnaie, au change et aux finances du Canada sous le régime français* (Ottawa : Archives du Canada (F. A. Acland), 1925), pp. lxxx–lxxxii.

It was on the whole a friendly period of laissez-faire; every effort was made to preserve the French way of life in matters of seigneurial law or habitants' custom. Although most of the administrative officials had left the Colony, the old hierarchy of seignior, priest and peasant remained, and their good will was secured by a policy which leading French-Canadian historians have accepted as being just and merciful[11].

Ce mode de vie – ce *French way of life*, a pu se perpétuer après la conquête, et malgré la conquête, grâce à l'indifférence économique de l'Angleterre envers le Canada, indifférence de l'époque et commune à la France et à l'Angleterre. La remarque d'Adam Shortt sur l'attitude de la France envers le Canada s'applique aussi bien à l'Angleterre conquérante; le Canada, économiquement inutile, doit jouer un rôle stratégique; il faut le confier à une bureaucratie militaire.

Les détails du programme de l'action française en Amérique n'étaient que le corollaire de visées plus importantes, tendant à enrayer le développement de l'empire britannique, dont l'agrandissement menaçait gravement les ambitions impérialistes de la cour de France. De ce moment, le Canada ne fut donc plus considéré au point de vue de ses propres intérêts, mais seulement de l'appui qu'il pourrait donner aux ambitions de la France. On y voyait une base d'attaque contre la puissance grandissante de la Grande-Bretagne en Amérique. Aussi, sa population et ses ressources furent-elles complètement utilisées dans ce but. Durant la dernière lutte coloniale, les dépenses faites pour le Canada et pour les opérations militaires poursuivies sur son territoire, ou au delà de ses frontières, furent toutes décidées et effectuées d'après la méthode européenne, et sur une échelle non moins européenne[12].

Ce point de vue explique que l'Angleterre ait hésité dans son choix entre la Guadeloupe et le Canada jusqu'aux négociations de 1762. Un groupe d'intérêts fit pencher la balance en faveur du Canada : celui des planteurs anglais qui ne voulaient pas une Guadeloupe anglaise susceptible d'être résorbée dans le réseau yankee. Terre-Neuve, avec ses pêcheries, était, dans l'opinion du Board of Trade, réputée supérieure au Canada et à la Louisiane réunis. C'était le point de vue économique. Mais à la crainte des planteurs des îles d'Amérique allait se conjuguer le point de vue militaire et impérialiste, qui voyait dans le Canada une région-tampon, une base pour enrayer le courant autonomiste des Yankees. Le Canada fut confié à des militaires. Solution impérialiste qui favorisait la survivance des Français en Amérique : « a fortunate thing for Canada that a precedent should have been set

[11]G. S. Graham, *Britain and Canada* (London : Longmans Green, 1943), p. 6.
[12]Shortt, éd., *Documents relatifs à la monnaie*, p. lxxx.

during the military regime for an administration which was sympathetically adjusted to the needs and feelings of the new subjects[13] ».

Les Anglais y sont donc venus sans rompre la continuité; ils y ont restauré un régime bureaucratique auquel les Canadiens étaient habitués depuis longtemps. Certes, l'administration devenait anglophone, mais elle ne dérangeait rien à la base. Il est vrai que l'élément pécuniaire, relativement faible à cette époque, devait créer un certain déséquilibre en contestant le droit que s'arrogeaient les militaires de diriger la colonie de façon non conforme aux exigences du progrès commercial. Mais leur récrimination ne portait pas à conséquence aussi longtemps qu'il s'agissait du commerce traditionnel[14].

Les entrepreneurs du commerce des fourrures avaient besoin, pour régner économiquement, d'une main d'œuvre rompue au dur métier du trappeur, du canotier, et du *winterer*, comme les militaires, à qui l'on confiait l'administration de la colonie, avaient besoin d'une petite noblesse, et d'un clergé uniquement préoccupé de survivance, pour régner politiquement. Ainsi s'effectuait un rapprochement qu'on pourrait qualifier d'équivoque. L'Ancien Régime, soit l'organisation sociale perpétuée par les paysans, les curés et les seigneurs, fournissait la base d'une société bureaucratique dont la nouvelle administration anglaise, représentée par l'élément le plus conservateur de la culture anglo-saxonne, constituait maintenant la superstructure. Mais la nouvelle administration n'eut pas la vertu de rallier tous les éléments de la culture anglo-saxonne. « By all I can find, écrivait Maseres, the English and the French agree together tolerably well and speak well of each other : but there are great animosities between the English themselves one with another[15]. » Les Canadiens, par contre, que l'ancienne administration avait entraînés à la docilité, surtout au cours de circonstances de guerre, n'affichaient aucune ambition politique.

Il n'en fut pas ainsi des commerçants, sitôt qu'ils eurent à réclamer auprès de l'administration des réformes politiques conformes à leurs besoins. Ils s'attaquèrent à ce système,

> but in this period their attack was directed only at the apex and not at the base of the social and political system of Quebec. Their quarrel, in the first few decades of British rule, was not against the great mass of the French Canadians; it was against the British governors, the British military, the

[13]Graham, *Britain and Canada*, p. 6.

[14]D. G. Creighton, *The Commercial Empire of the St. Lawrence, 1760–1850* (Toronto : Ryerson, 1937), chap. II.

[15]W. S. Wallace, ed., *The Maseres Letters, 1766–1768*, cité en Creighton, *Commercial Empire of the St. Lawrence*, p. 34.

British and French bureaucracy, and the French-Canadian *noblesse*. The merchants accepted the bulk of French-Canadian institutions and customs because they were the superstructure of which the fur trade was the base[16]. »

L'organisation sociale de type bureaucratique avait obtenu, après la conquête, une politique conforme à ses aspirations, soit une intégration à partir du principe ou du type bureaucratique. Au début du XIXe siècle, elle devait perdre ce type d'intégration et subir, dans la défensive, le gouvernement des autres, et chercher ailleurs un nouveau principe d'intégration. Cette désorientation avait un fondement économique.

Au début du XIXe siècle, le pays avait déjà subi de grandes transformations, la plupart attribuables à l'introduction de nouveaux types d'activité commerciale et, fondamentalement, à l'immigration de milliers de Loyalistes. Ces types nouveaux, beaucoup plus complexes que le commerce traditionnel des fourrures, requéraient une armature financière. De plus, au cours des guerres napoléoniennes, le gouvernement britannique avait découvert une valeur économique au Canada et jetait son dévolu sur ses ressources forestières.

Enrichie de nouveaux apports et fortifiée dans son commerce par une politique mercantiliste tout à fait appropriée, la « société acquisitive » afficha une attitude d'intolérance envers l'autre société (comprenant aussi le groupe de paysans et boutiquiers anglophones du Haut-Canada) qui refusait de l'appuyer dans ses desseins; et ses desseins, elle les associa à la cause britannique. Elle s'attaqua, non plus à la superstructure administrative, mais à l'infrastructure. Dans l'impossibilité de gouverner par voie majoritaire dans une assemblée qu'elle avait pourtant réclamée, conformément à la tradition britannique, elle va se retrancher dans l'exécutif qu'elle associe à la famille financière (« Family Compact » et « Clique du Château »).

C'était, dans la tradition britannique, prendre une attitude réactionnaire et, pour ainsi dire, renverser le cours de l'évolution historique. Mais un tel renversement n'était pas sans fondement pragmatique, car une économie continentale appuyée sur la richesse foncière fournissait au plus fort, s'il s'associait à l'exécutif (dans la tradition britannique, celui-ci s'attribuait le revenu des terres), l'occasion de gouverner sans majorité populaire. Une administration de mentalité militaire avait jadis retardé la concession d'une assemblée populaire; maintenant une classe mercantile devenue réactionnaire et réfractaire aux enseignements de la tradition britannique va retarder la concession du gouvernement responsable.

[16]Creighton, *Commercial Empire of the St. Lawrence*, pp. 32–3.

De la sorte, le gouvernement britannique heurtait un groupe de descendance bureaucratique qui, en dépit de son inexpérience démocratique, avait résolu de se prévaloir de la nouvelle constitution de 1791. Ainsi s'amorçait pour les Canadiens français, une période de luttes, qui devait durer une trentaine d'années, au moins. Cette période s'est déroulée en deux phases; l'une de défensive inaugurée sous le régime de la Terreur et qui dura jusqu'en 1820 environ : Britanniques et Canadiens s'insultent réciproquement; l'autre d'offensive, menée à la lumière du principe constitutionnel (la question des subsides soulevée par nécessité en 1817) : ce point de vue attira la sympathie de divers groupes anglophones au sein de l'empire britannique. Par un étrange renversement des rôles, les Canadiens français devenaient les défenseurs de la cause libérale et, comme tels, s'assimilaient à l'aile réformiste du Haut-Canada.

Mais la politique, envisagée dans cette perspective, n'est qu'une mise en scène; et l'alignement des forces sociales qui la provoque dépend des circonstances de milieu et de la position de ces forces les unes vis-à-vis des autres et par rapport à leurs aspirations respectives. De même le nationalisme n'est qu'une affirmation d'un groupe particulier à partir du principe de nationalité; il n'épuise pas, tant s'en faut, la signification historique de la culture qu'il veut affirmer.

Dans la querelle des subsides au XIXe siècle, deux types d'aspiration se heurtent, deux mondes s'affrontent. Le choc les replie sur elles-mêmes, et l'on peut dire que, durant tout le XIXe siècle, les deux groupes vont leurs cours économiques, de façon parallèle, divergente même, un peu comme deux étrangers, que la politesse ou la diplomatie rapprochent fortuitement ou accidentellement. Bien plus, l'économie les divise ou les éloigne même; car l'action économique procède de l'intime même des cultures, pour autant qu'elle implique un choix. Or, ce choix se traduit tangiblement par des investissements qui, une fois réalisés, commandent des attitudes, sociales ou politiques, ou exigent une protection d'état. Mais un tel choix qui engendre des investissements n'est pas, pour autant, un geste matérialiste. Au contraire, c'est plutôt, sur le plan de la culture, un geste de première valeur, puisqu'il manifeste les modes de réaction d'une société à son milieu. Les investissements sont la manifestation d'aspirations culturelles; ils expriment, avec les institutions et les groupes dominants qui les suscitent, les stimulent ou les protègent, un système de valorisation sous-jacent à la société même qu'ils tendent à promouvoir et à protéger. Ils expriment un ensemble de propensions qui, précisément, s'élaborent au sein même d'une culture.

On peut donc distinguer trois phases dans l'élaboration des caractères originaux du groupe culturel canadien-français.

a) La première génération est composée d'un groupe d'immigrants; elle est, selon Parkman, systématiquement soustraite à l'influence calviniste[17]. Il serait difficile de prouver que cette espèce d'immigrants accusât une *intensité sociale* supérieure à celle de la société française de l'Ancien Régime, telle que définie par Hauser[18].

b) Les générations suivantes n'eurent pas la chance d'*intensifier* le groupe. L'esprit de thésaurisation, selon Shortt, domine le milieu rural[19]. Les exigences militaires de la traite des fourrures assujettie à la concurrence anglo-hollandaise d'abord, et à la double concurrence anglaise ensuite (nord-sud), imprimèrent à l'administration un caractère fortement bureaucratique. La tradition mercantiliste française, inefficace en région maritime, et incapable d'y maintenir ses positions, affaiblissait la région continentale, en la privant d'un avant-poste maritime jugé essentiel à son développement économique. A cette faiblesse, s'ajoutait la faillite de l'industrialisme en Nouvelle-France.

c) La société rurale, édifiée sur une agriculture de subsistance en majeure partie, a vécu en marge du grand commerce. Elle ne s'est guère aperçue de la transition au régime britannique jusqu'au jour où, affirmant la supériorité britannique, on mit en cause la question raciale. Ce fut, pour les Canadiens français, le début d'une période de repli, l'occasion d'une prise de conscience. Ils sont devenus une *race* retranchée dans le terroir et dans l'Eglise; et tels ils sont demeurés durant tout le XIXe siècle.

• • •

Si l'évolution économique et politique influe sur l'organisation sociale, celle-ci, à son tour, conditionne le développement économique. Mais comment relier cette notion à un schéma d'étude économique; en d'autres termes, en quel sens établir que les attitudes sociales ont pu conditionner, disons, un volume ou un taux de production ? En ce sens que tel groupement culturel exprime des propensions susceptibles d'orienter la courbe de développement économique. Telles sont, par exemple, les propensions à s'accroître et à se multiplier, les propensions

[17]Francis Parkman, *The Old Regime in Canada* (Boston : Little, Brown & Co., 1874), chap. XVII.

[18]Voir H. Hauser, « The Characteristic Features of French Economic History from the Middle of the Sixteenth to the Middle of the Eighteenth Century », *Economic History Review*, vol. IV, no. 3, pp. 257–72.

[19]Shortt, éd., *Documents relatifs à la monnaie*, p. lxxxiv.

à s'instruire et à rechercher les innovations scientifiques, ou à les accepter, à accroître le capital productif, ou encore à accepter des immigrants, à bâtir des églises, des presbytères, des couvents, à importer des communautés religieuses (ce qui est une espèce de propension à accepter des immigrants)[20].

Il est remarquable qu'à l'époque où débute l'immigration massive destinée à s'associer à la société de type pécuniaire, les Canadiens français, se multipliant à un rythme supérieur à celui de l'augmentation de leur richesse matérielle, commençent à émigrer. Quant à leurs propensions à investir, elles expriment une tendance au capital improductif de l'espèce la plus propre à soutenir le terroir et l'Eglise. L'espèce d'immigration admise dans cette société reflète les mêmes caractères, ou répond aux mêmes aspirations.

Durant la période de l'Union, la société de type bureaucratique, qu'on identifiait alors au groupe francophone et catholique romain, a fondé 234 paroisses nouvelles, établi vingt communautés religieuses, dont cinq d'hommes et quinze de femmes; elle a confié à des communautés religieuses la direction de quatre-vingt-douze écoles nouvelles ou maisons d'enseignement, de neuf hospices et hôpitaux, de douze institutions diverses, fondé sept collèges classiques et une université[21]. La liste est impressionnante et, transposée en termes financiers, elle pourrait révéler un volume d'investissements comparable à celui des investissements effectués, durant la même période, sous le signe de Mercure, du moins dans le secteur privé.

Cependant que la nouvelle constitution laisse place à un gouvernement d'inspiration pécuniaire, comme en témoignent les grands travaux publics effectués sous le régime d'Union, et, plus tard, sous le régime de Confédération, cette même constitution assure liberté d'action à la société de type bureaucratique. Celle-ci s'exprime par des investissements qui lui sont propres. A l'intérieur de son univers, elle fait preuve d'un dynamisme proportionnel à celui de l'autre société.

Les investissements publics d'inspiration pécuniaire destinés à l'aménagement de l'espace national et à l'extension du marché eurent pour parallèles les investissements d'inspiration bureaucratique centrés sur la terre et sur l'Eglise. Deux sociétés coexistent sous un même régime constitutionnel. Dans le rajustement constitutionnel de 1840, les deux sociétés ont trouvé un *modus vivendi.* Un nationalisme de terroir, doublé de cléricalisme, depuis longtemps stimulé par les attaques

[20]Voir W. W. Rostow, *The Process of Economic Growth* (Oxford : Clarendon, 1953), Part I, chap. III.

[21]Données compilées d'après *Le Canada ecclésiastique*.

passionnées d'un britannisme qui prenait des attitudes de *jingo*, trouve un élément de sécurité dans le duumvirat ministériel du régime d'Union. Mais cela ne pouvait durer. Pour des raisons politiques, et pour des raisons économiques, dont les principales furent indiquées par George Brown dans son discours sur la Confédération, on dut reviser les conditions de cette coexistence. Au cours de l'Union, on avait déjà remarqué que les dépenses émargeant au budget pour le compte du Bas-Canada ne répondaient pas à la conception qu'on se faisait alors d'un budget national. Ces dépenses étaient de nature plutôt locale, disait-on alors. Il était normal que les revenus d'état, pour la plupart provenant des douanes, fussent appropriés à des dépenses d'intérêt national; et il était inadmissible qu'on les affectât au service d'une société étrangère au grand commerce (une agriculture de subsistance ne contribue pas au revenu des douanes) et absolument réfractaire à la taxation directe.

Aussi fut-il conclu en 1867 que les affaires locales seraient dévolues aux législatures provinciales, ainsi que toutes prérogatives locales associées au contrôle des terres, source de revenus. Ainsi, les prérogatives traditionnelles de la Couronne, c'est-à-dire, ce qu'il y avait de féodal dans l'héritage canadien fut défini comme relevant normalement des législatures provinciales.

La définition des pouvoirs du gouvernement général et des pouvoirs des législatures provinciales accuse, à cette époque, la supériorité de la société pécuniaire sur la société bureaucratique refoulée par la constitution de 1867 au secteur local. L'expansion vers l'ouest, la grande politique nationale inaugurée par Macdonald, mais virtuellement contenue dans la constitution de 1867, manifestent un comportement politique d'inspiration pécuniaire. La politique provinciale du Québec, au contraire, du moins considérée dans ses grands gestes du XIXe siècle, affirme des prérogatives féodales exploitées par une bureaucratie bipartite : les politiciens et les curés. Même le rôle de la province de Québec en matière de chemins de fer, disons à la fin du siècle dernier, assume au regard des grands objectifs de l'époque (la colonisation en particulier, c'est-à-dire la route et la chapelle, selon une définition du XIXe siècle) une signification bureaucratique. Seul l'élément militariste, caractère important d'une société bureaucratique, paraît manquer; mais on le retrouve dans les luttes électorales, dans les querelles d'Eglise, et dans les procès entre voisins.

Durant tout le XIXe siècle, et même au delà, les deux types d'organisation sociale ont évolué parallèlement, chacun à sa façon et dans sa sphère économique propre. L'organisation de type bureaucratique, représentée en majeure partie par le groupe francophone, a développé son terroir, elle a amplifié son contrôle clérical. L'association du Curé Labelle avec Mercier est caractéristique : donne-moi la terre et la route, je te donnerai la chapelle et la paroisse. Mais il ne faudrait pas croire que tout le groupe francophone et catholique romain s'est conformé aux normes de cette organisation. Ce qu'on a appelé exode rural fut, dans une grande mesure, la manifestation d'une tendance à s'associer au mode de vie pécuniaire. On quitte la paroisse, on émigre vers des contrées lointaines, ou vers la ville, pour gagner de l'argent et pour y relever son niveau de vie matérielle. Pour quelques-uns, sans doute, c'était une façon de prendre congé de certaines institutions.

Au niveau des classes dirigeantes (les gens instruits ayant place dans la hiérarchie de l'univers bureaucratique), la plupart prêchaient *l'attachement au sol*, la poursuite d'un mode de vie rural à tout prix : on peut, dans la perspective contemporaine, les appeler « agriculturalistes ». Mais d'autres, timidement d'ailleurs, et tout en protestant de leur attachement à la hiérarchie, proposaient une autre solution au problème de la désertion du terroir. Pour eux, il eut été possible, sans risque de contamination, d'évoluer vers un mode de vie pécuniaire : on les appelle « industrialistes ». Leur point de vue implique que même les institutions évoluent et qu'elles n'ont pas été établies dans le dessein de tyranniser la société qu'elles avaient la tâche de servir.

La technologie contemporaine a mis un terme aux divergences économiques entre les deux types d'organisation sociale que nous avons décrits. Aujourd'hui, leurs opérations économiques sont convergentes, elles se confondent même dans certains secteurs d'activité. Le charbon et la vapeur avaient inauguré cette tendance; il fallait l'électricité pour la confirmer. L'électricité a placé sur la carte économique du pays certaines régions que la technologie du XIXe siècle avait ignorées. La province de Québec, bastion d'une société de type bureaucratique, est devenue la base géographique d'un développement industriel; elle a été projetée dans l'univers anglo-américain.

Cet aspect soulève une question fondamentale. Quelle influence exercent les techniques sur un type d'organisation sociale donnée; ou quelles sortes de transformation peut-on leur attribuer ? Notons que les techniques, comme les investissements, procèdent de l'intime d'une culture : elles manifestent des aspirations qui, fondamentalement, sont loin d'être matérialistes. Elles s'élaborent au sein même des sociétés qui affirment des propensions à la recherche scientifique. Le terme « technologie » évoque la dignité de leur origine.

Normalement, les techniques ne se plaquent pas sur une organisation sociale, mais elles en procèdent. Et cependant, il peut arriver qu'elles s'imposent du dehors à certaines organisations sociales traditionnellement réfractaires au type de culture qui les engendre. Alors l'aptitude à les assimiler dépend de l'aptitude ou de la propension à substituer un enseignement scientifique, commercial, technique, universitaire, à l'enseignement traditionnel d'un collège classique destiné à servir une société de type bureaucratique.

Il n'est pas question ici de discuter les influences de la technologie « étrangère » sur un type d'organisation fermée[22]. On peut toutefois choisir d'en indiquer quelques-unes en prenant pour *critères* certains problèmes qui ont orienté le cours de la « dualité canadienne » ou qui ont, en tous cas, marqué l'histoire de la province de Québec. Tels sont les problèmes suivants : les terres, l'hydro-électricité, les coûts de production industrielle.

• • •

A l'origine du déplacement des lignes de forces des deux cultures vers un foyer commun de convergence, on peut situer cette transformation discrète, mais profonde, du rôle traditionnellement assigné à la terre, dont le contrôle avait constitué une prérogative féodale. La terre est devenue, au XIXe siècle, fonction du capitalisme financier. Lorsque s'opéra cette transformation, l'organisation pécuniaire, formée dans l'atmosphère du début du XIXe siècle, a cessé de se retrancher dans l'exécutif pour devenir parlementaire, car c'était au niveau parlementaire que devaient se discuter les problèmes de l'entreprise ferroviaire. Le chemin de fer a donné à la terre une valeur rentable et bien plus, elle en a fait un objet de spéculation.

La province de Québec, en tant qu'elle représentait un type d'organisation bureaucratique, n'a jamais connu cette connotation capitaliste conférée à la terre. Quelques individus ont pu s'y enrichir, au moyen des terres, mais à la façon bureaucratique, ou de la façon qu'avait pu s'enrichir Bigot par d'autres moyens. La terre est restée territoire, c'est-à-dire, une surface pour étendre ou propager le terroir et l'Eglise.

Cette fonction nouvelle de la terre, issue du capitalisme financier, fut saisie par les artisans de la Confédération, qui ont soustrait aux

[22]Voir : Herbert Frankel, *The Economic Impact on Under-developed Countries* (Oxford : Basil Blackwell, 1953), Essay II; Ragnar Nurkse, *Problems of Capital Formation in Underdeveloped Countries* (Oxford : Basil Blackwell, 1953), Introduction.

provinces de l'ouest le contrôle des terres pour en faire un instrument d'expansionisme d'inspiration pécuniaire. Cette politique a laissé indifférente la province de Québec, car celle-ci, grâce à la Confédération, prenait possession entière d'une législature locale à laquelle fut dévolu le contrôle des terres. Vis-à-vis l'ouest canadien, le gouvernement fédéral, refuge des éléments pécuniaires, se justifiait d'agir ainsi. Il avait ses propres objectifs, les provinces de l'ouest, sans tradition féodale, étaient ses propres créatures. La tradition aborigène a toutefois pris ombrage. L'affaire Riel l'a en quelque sorte associée à la tradition bureaucratique du Québec.

La situation se révéla plus complexe lorsque la terre, à cause de la technique hydro-électrique, devint fonction du capitalisme industriel. A ce stade technologique, sa mise en valeur exigeait des investissements massifs. Pour attirer de tels investissements, il fallait une politique des terres favorable à l'entreprise capitaliste. Aussi bien les hommes politiques, ceux du premier quart du siècle en particulier, se firent-ils les propagandistes de leur province en proclamant l'abondance des ressources hydrauliques et forestières qui s'offraient aux capitalistes désireux d'investir dans la province de Québec. Et pour bien marquer que l'abondance des ressources n'épuisait pas le potentiel capitaliste de cette province, on proclamait également la frugalité de sa population, qu'un régime d'éducation avait prédisposée de longue date à rejeter toute forme de socialisme et à accepter des conditions de travail favorables à l'entrepreneur.

Cette politique d'inspiration pécuniaire n'était-elle pas de nature à alerter une population demeurée fidèle à la tradition bureaucratique ? Tout naturellement, le parti de l'opposition devenait le défenseur de cette tradition, mettant la population en garde contre les idées et les mœurs qui s'insinuent avec le capital étranger. Que vaut la mise en valeur de nos terres lorsqu'elle n'est pas dirigée par « les nôtres » ? Ne vaut-il pas mieux rester pauvres et maîtres chez soi que de devenir riches malgré soi en aliénant ses biens aux étrangers ?

Ce thème de propagande politique à l'endroit des capitalistes *étrangers*, de même que l'avertissement exprimé par l'opposition, avaient fourni des sujets de discours aux rhétoriciens de notre génération. Mais ces discours, comme les graves et courageuses dissertations sur le rapport entre l'*économique* et le *national* dont ils s'inspiraient, ne devaient pas modifier le cours des événements. La terre du Québec était devenue fonction du capitalisme industriel.

Pour cette province, c'était subir, à sa base même, la plus grande transformation de son histoire. La terre, maintenant synonyme de ressources naturelles, fournit de l'électricité, du papier, des métaux non-ferreux, et des métaux ferreux. Cette transformation s'était préparée lentement, en laboratoire, et en dehors du Québec. Elle était le produit du génie scientifique que la société traditionnelle de type bureaucratique, plutôt tournée vers les belles-lettres, ne s'était guère souciée de produire. Mais ce qu'on n'avait pu produire, on dut l'accepter du dehors et ré-adapter l'enseignement à l'avenant des nouvelles exigences avec la collaboration de scientistes naturellement entraînés à l'étranger. C'était, du jour au lendemain, passer de la féodalité au capitalisme et tourner le dos au vieux quartier latin.

L'évolution technologique des derniers trente ans n'a fait qu'amplifier la fonction nouvelle assignée à la terre; et les événements saillants de cette dernière période, tels que la dépression des années 1930 et la prospérité des années 1940, n'ont pu que ralentir ou accélérer le processus de rapprochement entre les deux types d'organisation sociale, qu'une espèce nouvelle d'activité économique tend à confondre dans une communauté d'intérêts.

Le dernier aspect de la question implique le problème des coûts de production. Une organisation sociale qui, traditionnellement, se montre réfractaire aux innovations, se trouve dépourvue lorsqu'elle est projetée dans un univers de concurrence; car les concurrents, grâce à leurs mises au point techniques, opèrent sur une base de coûts décroissants. L'organisation sociale de type bureaucratique, dans sa phase d'imperméabilité, n'a pas été alerte à cette forme d'adaptation qui caractérise le capitalisme industriel. Elle a bien pu se donner des extensions commerciales ou industrielles, à divers degrés, depuis la fabrication de chandelles jusqu'à l'entreprise de transport maritime; mais elle n'a pas été capable de s'ajuster aux exigences du capitalisme contemporain.

Comment expliquer en effet que ses entreprises aient disparu ou aient perdu leurs raisons sociales ? C'est que, à une phase particulière de leur histoire, elles ont subi le choc de la concurrence. Elles n'étaient pas conçues à l'avenant d'un univers capitaliste; elles ont été résorbées dans ce grand univers. On a essayé d'enrayer cette tendance, on a fondé des ligues d'achat chez nous et on a désigné des boucs émissaires. On a mesuré les tailles économiques.

S'il faut parler en termes d'adaptation dynamique, on peut dire toutefois que la grande corporation a inauguré une ère d'espérance pour tous ceux qui ont à cœur de conserver certains caractères originaux de l'organisation sociale de type bureaucratique; car la technologie, elle-même un produit de l'histoire, ne détruit pas ce que l'histoire édifie.

Or, la grande corporation d'aujourd'hui comprend trois fonctions distinctes[23], qui représentent trois paliers de collaboration. C'est d'abord la fonction de ceux qui y investissent : cette fonction est devenue universelle, et l'épargne recueillie par la plus pure des compagnies d'assurance d'aujourd'hui est résorbée dans une fonction universelle, qui est capitaliste. Il y a ensuite la fonction de ceux qui participent à la marche de l'entreprise. Elle est accessible à tous les groupes ethniques. C'est celle des ingénieurs et scientistes formés à l'université, mais c'est surtout celle des dirigeants qui détiennent la clef des ressources naturelles, et la clef de l'usine contemporaine. Et enfin, la fonction de ceux qui dépendent de l'entreprise assume une signification nouvelle depuis l'avènement des grands syndicats. On peut dire que les problèmes de travail ont eu, sur les deux types de sociétés, l'influence d'un dissolvant. Les syndicats ouvriers sont un signe de rapprochement des deux groupes, le symbole le plus caractéristique de la convergence économique que nous avons tenté de définir.

* * *

Les deux groupes ethniques, anglophone et francophone, appartiennent historiquement à des types d'organisation sociale différents. Ces types eux-mêmes portent la marque des cultures européennes auxquelles ils se rattachent. Transposés en Amérique, ils affirment leurs caractères originaux, que l'influence d'un milieu nouveau modifie, atténue ou amplifie, mais ne détruit pas. Les classes sociales dominantes et les institutions qu'elles dirigent canalisent ces propensions vers des objectifs économiques. La politique est le moyen, direct ou indirect, grâce auquel les propensions engendrent des conséquences économiques. Mais la politique est fortement conditionnée par la technologie. Elle peut, par conséquent, varier en fonction de facteurs exogènes au groupe social qu'elle a mission de servir, surtout dans un monde dominé par des investissements internationaux au service de techniques productives. C'est ce qui arrive lorsqu'une société de tradition bureaucratique doit accepter une technologie qu'elle n'a pas engendrée. Une société ainsi exposée aux pressions de la technologie contemporaine doit reviser son système éthique en fonction du temps qui passe et modifie tout, même les structures sociales.

1955

[23]Voir Adolf A. Berle, Jr., and G. C. Means, *The Modern Corporation and Private Property* (New York : Macmillan, 1947), Book I, chaps. V–VI.

III. FORMS OF ASSOCIATION

A. Politics

III. ORGANISATION SOCIALE

A. Vie politique

Some Obstacles to Democracy in Quebec*

PIERRE ELLIOTT TRUDEAU

Associate Editor, Cité libre, *Montreal*

HISTORICALLY, French Canadians have not really believed in democracy for themselves; and English Canadians have not really wanted it for others. Such are the foundations upon which our two ethnic groups have absurdly pretended to be building democratic forms of government. No wonder the ensuing structure has turned out to be rather flimsy.

The purpose of the present essay is to re-examine some of the unstated premises from which much of our political thinking and behaviour is derived, and to suggest that there exists an urgent need for a critical appraisal of democracy in Canada. No amount of inter-group back-slapping or political *bonne-ententisme* will change the fact that democracy will continue to be thwarted in Canada so long as one-third of the people hardly believe in it—and that because to no small extent the remaining two-thirds provide them with ample grounds for distrusting it.

I

French Canadians are perhaps the only people in the world who "enjoy" democracy without having had to fight for it. Before 1763 they had known only an authoritarian rule, implicitly founded on a belief in the divine right of kingship. The people were subjects of an autocratic monarch and were governed by administrators responsible only to him. Their church was also authoritarian, their seigneurial system was quasi-feudal, and even on a strictly local plane the farmers and townsfolk had never been active participants in public affairs. As Gustave Lanctôt demonstrated: "Les habitants de la Nouvelle-

*First published, with slight variations, in the *Canadian Journal of Economics and Political Science,* vol. XXIV, no. 3 (Aug. 1958), pp. 297–311.

France n'avaient aucune idée d'une action commune dans le domaine politique. Sans organisation quelconque qui pût les grouper et les diriger, ils avaient pris l'habitude de se soumettre passivement aux ordonnances des intendants, aux ordres du gouverneur et aux édits de Versailles."[1]

That whole political structure was challenged in 1760 *by an outside force*. And its gradual replacement by forms of sovereignty which were to give an ever widening place to the principles of self-government was first brought about not by the Canadiens but by the English colonists. It was the latter who protested against the Act of 1774 and demanded an elective assembly; it was the former who circulated petition after petition in opposition to such an assembly. In 1788, Lord Dorchester advised the Colonial Office that only one-fifth of the total population wanted a "change of laws and form of government";[2] and fully three-quarters of the French Canadians were actively opposed to such a change.[3]

Consequently, when the Constitutional Act of 1791 ushered in—after a fashion—representative government, the Canadiens were neither psychologically nor politically prepared for it. As Durham later remarked, they were being initiated to responsible government at the wrong end; a people who had not been entrusted with the governing of a parish were suddenly enabled through their votes to influence the destinies of the state. And as was natural with a vanquished people, they valued their new form of government less for its intrinsic value than as a means to their racial and religious survival. Thus, though the elections of 1792 failed to evoke much enthusiasm in the Canadiens, they were quick to realize that, though their ethnic group composed 94 per cent of the population, it had elected only 68 per cent of the Assembly; and that furthermore they were in a minority in both the non-elective bodies—the Legislative and Executive Councils, where the seat of power truly rested.

Such a situation, soon to be aggravated by Governor Craig's despotic disposition, stifled what otherwise might have been a nascent belief in democracy. French Canadians felt that they had been deceived by

[1]*L'Administration de la Nouvelle-France* (Paris, 1929), p. 140. See also F. Ouellet, "M. Michel Brunet et le problème de la conquête," *Bulletin des recherches historiques* (juin 1956), p. 99: "La société canadienne à l'époque de la Nouvelle-France avait vécu sous l'absolutisme le plus complet."

[2]Quoted by Mason Wade, *The French Canadians, 1760–1945* (Toronto, 1955), p. 96.

[3]M. Trudel, "L'Essai du régime parlementaire," *Notre Temps* (Montréal), 2 avril 1955.

the pre-1791 propaganda extolling the virtues and powers of representative assemblies; and they would forevermore look with distrust at majority rule, so called. True, they soon took to the electoral process like ducks to water; and 1837–8 even found many of them fighting and dying to uphold its logic. But such conduct cannot be ascribed to a sudden miraculous conversion to parliamentarianism. They had but one desire—to survive as a nation; and it had become apparent that parliamentary government might turn out to be a useful tool for that purpose. Consequently, in adopting piece by piece the British political system, their secret design was not merely to use it, but to abuse it if need be.[4]

Such abuse was apparent in the extremism of the assemblies which opposed first Aylmer's and then Gosford's conciliatory attitudes, and brought the racial issue to a head. Though the *Quatre-vingt-douze Résolutions* reflected the republicanism of the leaders of the revolt, there is little doubt that the effectiveness of the document among the people stemmed mainly from the anti-British violence which it contained. And whereas the Mackenzie rebellion in Upper Canada was a clear struggle for democratic self-government, most of Papineau's followers took up their pitchforks to fight for national self-determination. It was because of that issue that Durham observed: "I expected to find a contest between a government and a people: I found two nations warring in the bosom of a single state: I found a struggle not of principles but of races."[5]

The Canadiens fought at Saint-Denis and Saint-Eustache as they would eventually rally for electoral battles or parliamentary debates whenever their ethnic survival seemed to be imperilled, as men in an army whose sole purpose is to drive the *Anglais* back. And, as everyone knows, the army is a poor training corps for democracy, no matter how inspiring its cause.

That is not to deny the existence of radical currents in French-Canadian political thought. For instance, one cannot ignore the fact that during part of the nineteenth century a significant section of the bourgeoisie was notoriously *rouge*. But if historical events are any guide at all to the discovery of underlying ideologies, it seems fair to assert that the dominant ideologies in French Canada turned out to be more nationalistic than democratic. A lengthy study would be necessary to

[4]See F. R. Scott, "Canada et Canada français," *Esprit* (Paris) (août 1952); and also P. E. Trudeau, "Réflexions sur la politique au Canada français," *Cité libre* (décembre 1952). I have drawn heavily from this earlier article of mine in a few of the following paragraphs.

[5]*Durham Report* (Coupland ed., Oxford, 1945), p. 15.

show how French-Canadian radicalism was crushed, mainly by agreement between the English-Canadian governing class and the French-Canadian higher clergy. Quite typical of such a pincers operation was the seizure of *Le Canadien* by Governor Craig, and the approval of that seizure by the Bishop of Quebec. The end result was that, for the mass of the people, the passage from French to British rule was remembered—not unnaturally—more as an enslaving defeat than as a liberation from Bourbon absolutism; regardless of how liberal were the conqueror's political institutions, they had no intrinsic value in the minds of a people who had not desired them, never learned to use them, and who finally only accepted them as a means of loosening the conqueror's grip.

How then were the French Canadians to use the arsenal of democratic "fire-arms" put at their disposal? There were two possibilities: sabotage of the parliamentary works from within by systematic obstruction which, like the Irish strategy at Westminster, might lead to Laurentian Home Rule; or outward acceptance of the parliamentary game, but without any inward allegiance to its underlying moral principles. The latter choice prevailed, no doubt because the years 1830 to 1840 demonstrated that sabotage would lead to suppression by force. Moreover, a show of co-operation would have the added advantage of permitting French Canada to participate in the governing councils of the country as a whole. Such a decision guided most French-Canadian politicians after the union of Upper and Lower Canada, and continued to do so after Confederation.

Fundamentally, all French-Canadian political thinking stems from these historical beginnings. In the opinion of the French in Canada, government of the people by the people could not be *for* the people, but mainly for the English-speaking part of that people; such were the spoils of conquest. Whether such a belief was well founded (an issue I shall discuss in the following section) is entirely irrelevant to the present argument. So the Canadiens believed; and so they could only make believe in democracy. They adhered to the "social contract" with mental reservations; they refused to be inwardly bound by a "general will" which overlooked the racial problem. Feeling unable to share as equals in the Canadian common weal, they secretly resolved to pursue only the French-Canadian weal, and to safeguard the latter they cheated against the former.

In all important aspects of national politics, guile, compromise, and a subtle kind of blackmail decided their course and determined their alliances. They appeared to discount all political or social ideologies, save nationalism. For the mass of the people the words Tory and Grit, Conservative and Liberal, referred neither to political ideals nor to administrative techniques. They were regarded only as meaningless labels, affixed to alternatives which permitted the auctioneering of one's support; they had no more meaning than *bleu* and *rouge* which eventually replaced them in popular speech. French Canadians on the whole never voted for political or economic ideologies, but only for the man or group which stood for their *ethnic* rights: even condemnation of liberalism by the Church did not prevent Mercier and Laurier from being elected in 1886 and 1896; and the advantages to Quebec's economy of Laurier's reciprocity did not prevent Bourassa from being returned as an anti-imperialist in 1911.

In such a mental climate, sound democratic politics could hardly be expected to prevail, even in strictly provincial or local affairs where racial issues were not involved. For cheating becomes a habit. Through historical necessity, and as a means of survival, French Canadians had felt justified in finessing at the parliamentary game; and as a result the whole game of politics was swept outside the pale of morality. They had succeeded so well in subordinating the pursuit of the common weal to the pursuit of their particular ethnic needs that they never achieved any sense of obligation towards the general welfare, including the welfare of the French Canadians on non-racial issues. Consequently, apart from times of racial strife such as the Riel Rebellion, the schools question, conscription, the plebiscite, and the like—when the Canadiens banded together avowedly to fight for survival within the national whole—they came to regard politics as a game of every man for himself. In other words, their civic sense was corrupted and they became political immoralists.

The foregoing explanation of the lack of civic-mindedness must not be taken to exclude religious factors. French Canadians are Catholics; and Catholic nations have not always been ardent supporters of democracy. They are authoritarian in spiritual matters; and since the dividing line between the spiritual and the temporal may be very fine or even confused, they are often disinclined to seek solutions in temporal affairs through the mere counting of heads. If this be true in general, it is particularly so in the case of the clergy and laity of Quebec, influenced as they were by the Catholicism of nineteenth-century France, which largely rejected democracy as the daughter of the Revolution.

But there was quite a separate reason why the Church in Quebec was suspicious of popular sovereignty. When Canada passed into

British hands, the Church naturally concerned herself with safeguarding the faith by protecting her authority. And, as it turned out, she discovered that her position had in a sense improved. For after the débâcle of 1760 she remained alone as a social beacon to give strength and guidance to a vanquished people, and to the victor she had the potentialities of a formidable opponent. So, after difficult beginnings, both powers found it advantageous to work out a *modus vivendi*. Loyalty was bartered for religious freedom, and the Church was as good as her word. During the wars of 1775, 1812, 1914, and 1939, the Catholic hierarchy preached submission to His Majesty's government; they even launched an appeal against the Fenian raiders in 1870. And at the time of the 1837 rebellion, they used their powers to check the *patriotes*.

When the faith lay safe, no distant call to democratic liberty held much appeal to the churchmen. The reason may have been partly that the torch of freedom so often appeared to be borne by enemies of the faith, as in the case of nineteenth-century revolutionaries whose staple stock-in-trade was anti-clericalism. But more profane rivalries are not to be discounted. Until the rise of democratic politics, a French Canadian's only access to positions of command lay through holy orders; but with the coming of the politicians, a career was opened to the Canadiens whereby they might compete with ecclesiastical authority. It is no coincidence that leaders such as Papineau, Mercier, Laurier, and even Bourassa, to say nothing of a host of lesser men, all incurred varying degrees of ecclesiastical censure.[6]

A conquered people therefore not only faced a state which they feared as the creature of a foreign nation, but also belonged to a church which distrusted that state as a rival power and as a child of the Revolution, liable to be dominated by anti-clericals, Protestants, or even socialists. The resulting popular attitude was a combination of political superstition and social conservatism, wherein the state—any state—was regarded as an ominous being whose uncontrollable caprices were just as likely to lead it to crush families and devour crucifixes as to help the needy and maintain order.[7] Electoral processes for the mass of the people remained mysterious rituals of foreign origin, of

[6]P. E. Trudeau in *La Grève de l'amiante* (Montréal, 1956), p. 59. See also the author's "Obstacles à la démocratie" in *Rapport de la Conférence de l'institut canadien des affaires publiques*, 1954.

[7]That and that alone can explain why nationalist Quebec has never dared to translate into public ownership and a demand for the welfare state its unending clamour for economic emancipation; and why a people—so moral in other areas—has no sense of moral obligation in its relation to the state.

little value beyond that for which the individual can barter his vote: a receipted grocery bill, a bottle of whiskey, a workman's compensation, a contract to build a bridge, a school grant, a community hospital. For it is noteworthy that in Quebec, a school or a hospital is not expected by the citizens as of right, being their due from an obedient government and for which they pay, but as a reward for having returned a member to the Government benches.[8] And many a respectable citizen or prelate who would deem it dishonourable to sell his vote for a keg of beer thinks nothing of advising his *gens* to barter theirs for a load of bricks.

I see little use in illustrating these latter points, not only because that task was excellently done after the last Quebec general election[9] but also because such illustrations would not, *per se*, prove my point that French Canadians as a people do not believe in democracy, for other people who do profess to believe in democracy have none the less succumbed to corrupt electoral practices, the system of spoils, and so on. I prefer to quote some recent[10] and typical instances which exemplify not corruption, but the complete lack of a democratic frame of reference for French-Canadian political thinking.[11]

On the morning of the last provincial general election (June 20, 1956), the following was read over radio station CBF during the programme called "Prières du matin: Elévations matutinales":

L'autorité souveraine, par quelque gouvernement qu'elle soit exercée, découle uniquement de Dieu, principe suprême et éternel de toute puissance.

[8]This doctrine was given its classic expression and official sanction in Mr. Duplessis' speeches to the electors of Verchères during the 1952 elections, and to those of Shawinigan during the 1956 elections.

[9]See André Laurendeau's series, "La Politique provinciale," *Le Devoir*, juillet et août 1956, during the course of which appeared the devastating denunciation written by the abbés Dion and O'Neil. See also Pierre Laporte's lengthy investigation "Les Elections ne se font pas avec des prières," *Le Devoir*, octobre et novembre 1956. For material on the 1952 provincial elections see *Cité libre* (décembre 1952), *passim*.

[10]The present paper was first drafted in August, 1956. As time went by I began to add references to current events, but soon discontinued this practice as it added more to the length than to the strength of my demonstration. Consequently my *recent* and *typical* instances are more typical than recent.

My original draft was written when the national Liberal party was at the height of its glory. The accusations I shall level at it later on in this paper remain historically valid; but I must recognize that I felt less cruel in writing them a few years ago than I do in publishing them now. If it be a sop to anybody, I sadly add that the campaign waged by the Conservative henchmen in Quebec for the election of March, 1958, has hardly given me reason to hope that by the sole grace of the new régime will there be a rebirth of democracy in "la belle province."

[11]For less recent examples of that authoritarian frame of mind, see the author's chapter in Trudeau, comp., *La Grève de l'amiante*, pp. 22–7.

. . . C'est donc une erreur absolue de croire que l'autorité vient de la multitude, du nombre et du peuple, de prétendre que l'autorité n'appartient pas en propre à ceux qui l'exercent, mais qu'ils n'ont qu'un simple mandat toujours révocable par le peuple. Cette erreur, qui date de la Réforme, repose sur le faux principe que l'homme n'a d'autre maître que sa raison individuelle. . . . Toute cette explication sur l'origine, la base et la constitution de cette prétendue [!] souveraineté du peuple est purement arbitraire. Elle aurait, en outre, comme conséquence, si elle était admise, d'énerver l'autorité, d'en faire un mythe, de l'établir sur une base instable et changeante, de stimuler les passions populaires et de favoriser les séditions.[12]

Think *that* over before you cast your vote!

French-Canadian lack of concern for the liberties and traditions of Parliament was admirably brought out during the pipeline debate of 1956. The Toronto *Star*, the *Telegram*, the *Globe and Mail*, the Ottawa *Journal*, the *Citizen*, the *Montreal Gazette*, and many other English-language papers were all pressing for Mr. Speaker's resignation, but *L'Action catholique*, *Le Droit*, and *Le Devoir* looked with disdain on such childishness. Mr. Lorenzo Paré, a parliamentary correspondent of some repute in French-Canadian circles, wrote: "Il n'y a pas raison de soulever, pour une pareille bagatelle, toute une crise parlementaire. . . . Le plus surprenant est qu'elle se soit prolongée si longtemps, et

[12]This programme apparently is under the guidance of the Comité interdiocésain d'Action radiophonique. To sociologists, it is no doubt an interesting example of the intermeshing of two institutions as different as the Church and the Canadian Broadcasting Corporation. I need hardly add that Catholicism is not *per se* incompatible with democracy; as a matter of fact, many a Catholic would claim that democracy follows naturally from the Christian belief that all men are brothers and fundamentally equal. But the historical fact remains that the clergy in Quebec made no such deductions. On the contrary, the foregoing quotation shows a remarkable continuity of thought with the anti-democratic theories which Mgr Plessis imparted to Quebec Catholics 150 years earlier. F. Ouellet has written with considerable insight on "Mgr Plessis et la naissance d'une bourgeoisie canadienne" in a paper presented to the Congrès de la Société canadienne de l'Histoire de l'Eglise catholique at Chicoutimi in August 1956. The following opinions of Mgr Plessis are quoted from that paper. In 1799 the Bishop warned the faithful that if they were not protected against the influences of revolutionary France, "le funeste arbre de la liberté sera planté au milieu de vos villes; les droits de l'homme seront proclamés; . . . vous serez libres, mais d'une liberté oppressive, qui vous donnera pour maîtres la lie des citoyens, et abîmera dans la poussière les respectables chefs qui possèdent maintenant votre amour et votre confiance." In 1810 he denounced "le système de souveraineté du peuple" as "le plus faux et le plus absurde" of sophisms, and told his flock that "J.C. en vous donnant une religion toute propre à vous conduire en Ciel, ne vous a pas chargés de contrôler et de surveiller les souverains sous lesquels vous vivriez." In 1815 and 1823 he was still writing against the constitution of 1791, "constitution mal calculée pour le génie des Canadiens et qui n'a eu d'autre effet réel que de rendre les administrés insolens envers les administrans. L'esprit de démocratie et d'indépendance a gagné le peuple, et passé de là au clergé, et vous en voyez les fruits."

que les Communes aient donné, durant toutes ces semaines, le spectacle d'un surprenant enfantillage." *Le Devoir*'s two parliamentary *courriéristes* had the same reaction. Mr. P. Laporte wrote: "A force d'envenimer les choses la presse anglaise et l'opposition avaient réussi à faire perdre à trop de monde les véritables données du problème. . . . M. Saint-Laurent a mis les choses au point. Il a presque dit qu'on a fait une tempête dans un verre d'eau." And Mr. P. Vigeant:

> C'est une situation qui s'explique assez mal à des Canadiens français. Il faut avoir été formé depuis l'enfance dans le culte des institutions parlementaires pour réagir vigoureusement devant des incidents qui nous paraissent, à nous, plutôt secondaires. Le respect de la présidence de la Chambre . . . a de quoi nous surprendre. . . . Ces incidents illustrent bien les difficultés qu'éprouvent nos représentants à Ottawa à s'adapter aux institutions parlementaires anglaises dont le fonctionnement . . . répond si peu à notre génie français.[13]

Indeed, had the crisis over the Speaker's office aroused any considerable excitement at all in Quebec, it most surely would have been interpreted as a racial attack on Mr. Louis-René Beaudoin!

An unusual approach to civil liberties might also be considered as typical of French Canada. At the time of the decision on the Jehovah Witness case, enforcing freedom of religion, public opinion in Quebec was quick to point out that the judges of the Supreme Court had been somewhat divided along racial and religious lines. The judgment of the Supreme Court on the Padlock Law drew the same kind of reaction. For instance, *Montréal-Matin* emphasized Judge Taschereau's dissent, and spoke of a Communist victory, good news for all revolutionaries in Quebec; Mr. P. Sauriol of *Le Devoir* (March 19, 1957) questioned whether "la Cour Suprême aurait inversement le même souci s'il s'agissait de protéger les juridictions provinciales contre une intrusion fédérale," and underlined "l'une des différences profondes qui existent entre les Canadiens anglais et nous. . . . Il s'agit de savoir si la défense de la liberté doit aller jusqu'à la défense et au respect d'un prétendu droit à propager l'erreur."

Writing about the debate on the subservience of the C.B.C. to the party in power, and the whole issue of freedom of opinion, Mr. Gérard Filion of *Le Devoir* (April 10, 1957) remarked that if opposition parties were looking for an electoral issue,

> on a probablement fait fausse route pour ce qui concerne le Canada français. L'opinion publique n'a pas l'habitude chez nous de se pâmer pour ces sortes de débat. C'est probablement un tort, mais c'est comme ça.

[13]These quotations are from *Le Devoir*, 3, 4, 10, 12 juillet 1956.

D'autre part, le sentiment général du Canada français, c'est que M. Saint-Laurent a eu raison de [protester auprès de M. Dunton pour] mettre à sa place ce jeune blanc-bec qui, à peine débarqué chez nous, vient nous faire la leçon sur nos devoirs vis-à-vis de l'Empire.

If I have quoted heavily from *Le Devoir*, the reason is that it is generally recognized even in English Canada as a truly independent daily of exceptionally high intellectual standards. But it should go without saying that in the lesser French-Canadian press, democracy, if it is known at all, is known as an evil. Mr. Duplessis' paper, *Le Temps* (Quebec, Sept. 24, 1956) in condemning the Rassemblement, accused it of the greatest of all sins: leading the people "vers la laïcisation et la démocratisation." Another weekly refers to citizens as "subjects" and preaches realism:

Les véritables maîtres d'une province ou d'un pays sont et demeureront les puissances d'argent. . . . Il ne faut pas non plus se scandaliser à outrance au sujet du favoritisme qui naît avec la partisannerie politique. Que ce soit en démocratie ou en monarchie . . . normalement, il s'établit entre lui [le chef du gouvernement] et ses seconds une camaraderie, parfois une amitié sincère qui fait naître les compromis et le favoritisme aux dépens des autres, aux dépens du peuple en définitive. Ce n'est pas l'idéal mais c'est humain et c'est une chimère que de rêver d'un gouvernement qui pourrait se maintenir longtemps au pouvoir sans aucune sorte de favoritisme.[14]

Mr. Léopold Richer, long-time parliamentary reporter, and now director of *Notre Temps*, a self-styled "hebdomadaire social et culturel" with (until recently) a wide support among the clergy, is prone to mock "the new religion of democracy," and uphold authority everywhere. The following case is interesting because Mr. Richer was indignant at the "libertarianism" of what many a democrat might feel to be a rather authoritarian conception of civil government. Mr. G. Filion had written in *Le Devoir*: "La liberté n'est pas un don gratuit, mais une conquête. Il n'est de liberté que celle qu'on arrache à l'autorité." At which Mr. Richer fumes: "Vous avez bien lu? Vous avez bien compris? . . . C'est de l'insoumission à l'autorité établie, qu'elle soit religieuse ou civile. C'est de la sédition. C'est de la révolte. Gérard Filion en est réduit à prêcher ouvertement la révolution. Ou il ne comprend pas le sens des mots . . . ou on doit le tenir pour un journaliste extrêmement dangereux." And so on.[15]

If I were to quote all the material proving that French Canadians fundamentally do not believe in democracy, and that on the whole

[14]Quoted by André Laurendeau in a scathing editorial, *Le Devoir*, 20 juillet 1956.

[15]*Notre Temps* (Montréal), 27 octobre 1956.

neither the pulpit, nor the Legislative Assembly, nor the radio, nor the press is doing much to instil such a belief, I would "exhaust time and encroach upon eternity." In 1958, French Canadians must begin to learn democracy from scratch. For such is the legacy of a history during which—as a minority—they hammered the process of parliamentary government into a defensive weapon of racial warfare, and—as Catholics—they believed that authority might well be left to descend from God in God's good time and in God's good way.

II

Parliamentary democracy I take to be a method of governing free men which operates roughly as follows: organized parties that wish to pursue—by different means—a common end, agree to be bound by certain rules according to which the party with the most support governs on condition that leadership will revert to some other party whenever the latter's means become acceptable to the greater part of the electorate. The common end—the general welfare—which is the aim of all parties may be more or less inclusive, and may be defined in different ways by different men. Yet it must in some way include equality of opportunity for everyone in all important fields of endeavour; otherwise "agreement on fundamentals" would never obtain. For instance, democracy cannot be made to work in a country where a large part of the citizens are by status condemned to a perpetual state of domination, economic or otherwise.[16] Essentially, a true democracy must permit the periodic transformation of political minorities into majorities.

In Canada the above conditions have never obtained. As to ends, the French Canadians would never settle for anything less than absolute equality of political rights with the English Canadians, a demand which, as I shall show below, was never seriously considered by the Colonial Office before the advent of responsible government, nor by the English-speaking majority since then. In brief, one-third of the nation disagreed with the common good as defined by the other two-thirds. Consequently parliamentary government was unworkable, for, given this situation, there arose a fundamental cleavage between a majority and a minority which could therefore not alternate in power.

16With others, Elton Mayo, *The Social Problems of an Industrial Civilization* (London, 1949), p. xiii, has observed that "representative government does not work satisfactorily for the general good in a society that exhibits extreme differences in the material standards of living of its various social groups. . . . [Nor can] representative government be effectively exercised by a society internally divided by group hostilities and hatreds."

It may be that after 1760 the French were just as unrealistic in their demands as the English were uncompromising in their attitude; the point remains that the English-speaking Canadians, rightly considering that self-government is the noblest way of regulating social relations among free men, proceeded to claim its benefits for Canada, but only after serving standing notice on the French that such benefits were not for members of a subject race.

It is a matter of record that the purpose of the Royal Proclamation of 1763 was complete assimilation of the French Canadians; yet it was through that instrument that the French Canadians first became acquainted with representative government. "The proclamation tacitly assumed such an influx [of English settlers] by providing for the establishment of English law and by promising an assembly."[17] And when Governor Murray tried to protect the *habitant* against the voracious English merchants, the latter "demanded the immediate calling of an assembly for whose candidates the French might be allowed to vote, but of which only Protestants were to be members."[18] Of such an assembly, Maseres, the incumbent Attorney General, was to write in 1766: "An assembly so constituted, [because of the laws against popery] might pretend to be a representative of the people there, but it would be a representative of only the 600 new English settlers, and an instrument in their hands of dominating over the 90,000 French."[19] Instead of an assembly the Quebec Act of 1774 was brought down, welcomed by the Canadiens, but attacked by the English colonists for being undemocratic and establishing popery. Such attacks could only impart a peculiar understanding of democracy to a people who through the act had only received what they considered their birth-right: freedom of faith and of language.

When at last French Canadians were initiated into the sanctuary of representative government, by the Constitutional Act of 1791, they discovered that it did not mean majority rule through an elected assembly, but rule by the representatives of the conquering minority, nominated to the Executive and Legislative Councils. Moreover, at its very first meeting, the elected Assembly itself split along ethnic lines over the language qualifications of the Speaker. The history of democracy in Lower Canada from 1793 to 1840 was that of one long process of warping. As Mason Wade puts it, the English colonists "were badly scared men." In 1793, Richardson, the able leader of the Opposition, was to explain: "Nothing can be so irksome as the situation

[17]E. McInnis, *Canada: A Political and Social History* (New York, 1947), p. 130.
[18]*Ibid.*, p. 138.
[19]Quoted by Wade, *The French Canadians*, p. 60.

of the English members—without numbers to do any good—doomed to the necessity of combating the absurdities of the majority, without a hope of success." In 1806, the English merchants raised the cry of "French domination" because of a tax they disliked, and during the fray the *Montreal Gazette* and the Quebec *Mercury* were summoned to the bar of the Assembly for contempt of that body. In 1810, Chief Justice Sewell proposed the establishment of high property restrictions upon the franchise, to prevent French dominance in the Assembly; the union of Upper and Lower Canada for more prompt and certain anglicization. Governor Craig also regretted the presence of a French majority in the Assembly, proposed various schemes for reducing it, and advocated the playing of one ethnic group against the other.[20]

As is well known, the situation deteriorated steadily until it led to the rebellion of 1837–8. When the smoke of battle had cleared, Lord Durham observed that

> the most just and sensible of the English . . . seem to have joined in the determination never again to submit to a French majority. . . . The English complained that they, a minority, suffered under the oppressive use to which power was turned by the French majority. . . . They assert that Lower Canada must be *English*, at the expense, if necessary, of not being *British*. . . . Nor have the English inhabitants forgotten in their triumph the terror with which they suddenly saw themselves surrounded by an insurgent majority. . . . Their only hope of safety is supposed to rest on systematically terrifying and disabling the French, and in preventing a majority of that race from ever again being predominant in any portion of the legislature of the Province.[21]

That latter design was finally[22] realized through the Act of Union in 1840. A single Legislative Council was appointed and a single Assembly was elected, with equal representation for Upper and Lower Canada, in spite of the fact that the latter province had 650,000 inhabitants against the former's 450,000. Moreover, English was to be the sole official language.

The final irrational upsurge of the frightened minority occurred in 1849, when the passing of the Rebellion Losses Bill unleashed the English-Canadian riots which led to the pelting of Governor Elgin, the burning of the Parliament buildings, and the Annexation Manifesto. But a year or so later, demographic change had at last made English-speaking Canadians the more numerous ethnic group; and forever

[20]*Ibid.*, pp. 93, 97, 102, 108, 110, 112, 202.

[21]*Durham Report*, pp. 18, 35, 43.

[22]It had been advocated many times before: by Sewell and by Craig (1810), by the Duke of Richmond (1819), by Lord Dalhousie (1820). And it had almost succeeded in 1822, when a petition was signed by some fourteen hundred English-speaking Montrealers.

after they were able to preach the grandeur of true democracy and to back up their preachings by their own virtuous submission to majority rule. Unfortunately, it was then too late for French Canadians to unlearn their first seventy-five years of schooling, during which time the notion of representative government had been identified with domination by an English-speaking minority. And they could hardly be expected to greet as the millennium the advent of representation by population in 1867, which could only mean continued domination, but this time by an English-speaking majority.

Future events confirmed French-Canadian scepticism with reasonable regularity: the wanton use of majorities to do away with a bilingual legislature in Manitoba, and with *droits acquis* over separate schools in various provinces; the formation of a Union Government in 1917 to ride roughshod over the whole of French Canada; the use of the plebiscite in 1942, by which English Canada pretended to absolve the Liberals from their twenty years of solemn (if unwise) pledges to the French Canadians; the long-standing practice of favouring immigration from the British Isles as opposed to that from France.[23] Such examples of the use of majorities as a bludgeon to "convince" minorities should remind us that if French Canadians made the mistake of using democracy as a tool of ethnic warfare, the English Canadians offered them the wherewithal to learn. In all cases where fundamental oppositions arose on racial lines, the French felt that a stronger force (first an army and later a majority of citizens) could always be mustered against them. Of course it would be wrong to conclude that cultural relations between the two groups in political matters were a complete failure. The converse is happily the case. But sadly enough, even in cases where complete co-operation has seemed to exist between the French minority and the English-speaking majority, within the framework of the national parties for instance,[24] democracy appears to have been thwarted.

[23]As early as 1763 the implicit assumption of British policy was that the French group was to be swamped by immigration (see McInnis, *Canada*, p. 130). Durham recommended that policy in his famous report (p. 180). And the laws of Canada favoured it until after the Second World War, when P.C. 4849 was amended by P.C. 4186 (Sept. 16, 1948) and by P.C. 5593 (Dec. 10, 1948). In fairness, it must be added that the French on either side of the Atlantic were not militant advocates of migration to Canada; but the fact of inequality under the law is not changed for all that.

[24]The following remarks apply mainly to the Liberal party, since for nearly seventy years French-Canadian representation in the others was not numerically significant. At the present time, it is too soon to generalize about the Conservative party.

Towards the end of the nineteenth century a well-known combination of factors brought French Canadians *en masse* into the fold of the Liberal party. The choice of Laurier as leader, and the way the Conservatives handled the Riel Rebellion and the Manitoba schools question convinced the French-Canadian voters that their ethnic survival could be better guaranteed by the Liberals than by the Conservatives. And so, in every federal election from 1891 to 1958 Quebec returned a majority of Liberals to Ottawa, nearly always an overwhelming majority.[25]

I shall not belittle the amazing astuteness, foresight, and (in the very early days) courage that made such a performance possible. No doubt the Liberals received great help at various times from their bungling Conservative and socialist opponents; but they still deserve credit for preventing the growth in Quebec of a federal nationalist party, even at the height of Mercier's and later of Bourassa's influence, and even when the Bloc populaire was in full sway. For they learned to cater to French Canada's intuition that its destinies would be better protected at Ottawa by a more or less independent bloc within the party in power rather than by a nationalist party, bound, because of its ethnic basis, to remain forever seated on opposition benches.

But power entails responsibilities; and there is no doubt that the Liberals tragically failed to shoulder theirs. A party cannot have the approval of a majority of the electorate for well over half a century without accepting much of the blame for that electorate's political immaturity. If French Canadians even today have learnt so little about democracy, if they twist its rules so shockingly, if they are constantly tempted by authoritarianism, it is to a large degree because the Liberal party has been miserably remiss in its simple political duty. Instead of educating the French-speaking electorate to believe in democracy, the Liberals seemed content to cultivate the ignorance and prejudice of that electorate.[26]

I should not like to apportion blame between French- and English-speaking Liberals in this regard. The gravest faults no doubt fall squarely on the former. It is they who have failed to inject valid

[25]Provincially the Liberal grip on power was only broken in 1936, when an even more "nationalist" party was born.

[26]There were some rare exceptions. For instance, a short but meritorious effort was made during the Second World War by groups that founded the Institut démocratique, but it was soon to perish. Today, a minority within a splinter group is trying to build a democratic Fédération Libérale provinciale with the help of a weekly, *La Réforme*; both are still very far from the electorate. Whether the Liberal débâcle at Ottawa will strengthen the provincial reformers remains an open question.

democratic concepts into the innumerable campaigns waged during the present century. On the contrary, forgetful of the common weal, they have always encouraged Quebecers to continue using their voting bloc as an instrument of racial defence, or of personal gain. Their only slogans have been racial slogans. Until 1917 their cry was: Vote for a party led by a French Canadian. After 1917 it was: Vote against Borden's party. This cry was still used in recent years, though between 1947 and 1957 more sophisticated politicians were able to revert to the French-Canadian leadership slogan, as well as to attack the Conservatives for being "anti-French Canadian Protestants and imperialists" and the C.C.F. for being "anti-French Canadian atheists and centralizers." And it was largely on the strength of such slogans that they were elected.

But the fact remains that throughout most of its existence the federal Liberal party was overwhelmingly an English-speaking party. And that majority in my view should bear the blame for serious faults of omission with respect to the backwardness of democracy in Quebec. They might, *à la rigueur*, be excused for not having liked to poke into the hornet's nest of their French-Canadian bloc. But the pity is that they seemed to encourage such a state of affairs. The shameful incompetence of the average Liberal M.P. from Quebec was a welcome asset to a Government that needed little more than a herd of *ânes savants* to file in when the division bell rang. The party strategists had but to find an acceptable stable master—Laurier, Lapointe, Saint-Laurent—and the trained donkeys sitting in the back benches could be trusted to behave. Even the choice of front-benchers very often smacked of shysterism. Excepting the French-Canadian leader, who was usually a man of quality, many ministers of that ethnic group were chosen not so much for their ability to serve democracy as for their ability to make democracy serve the party; their main qualification was familiarity with machine politicians and schemers, and until lately they were traditionally put at the head of patronage departments such as the Post Office and Public Works. To sum up, English-speaking Canadians have long behaved in national politics as though they believed that democracy was not for French Canadians.

That this is so is forcefully confirmed by English-Canadian behaviour in local politics in Quebec. In precisely that province where the people had been historically conditioned to believe that government is a function of wealth and power, rather than of the will of the majority, it so happened that the English-speaking Canadians had wealth and power but not numbers. In such circumstances, it was perhaps inevitable that the English-speaking element should choose to govern with what means they had, rather than be thankless apostles of democracy, preaching in the wilderness that they had partly created. None the less, the net result is that incredible amounts are spent in Quebec at every election, many times more per capita than in other provinces.[27] Now it is all very well to denounce the dishonesty of voters who accept refrigerators and television sets in exchange for their votes, but it must be recognized that the offering of bribes is just as detrimental to democracy as the taking of them. So the question remains: Who makes those bribes possible?

As the President of Quebec Beauharnois stated, after his Company had contributed three-quarters of a million dollars to various campaign funds: "Gratefulness was always regarded as an important factor in dealing with democratic governments."[28] Of course, to some extent party funds come from French-Canadian business men and seekers after petty favours. But the *real* money comes from huge corporations and wealthy enterprises that give willingly to parties which, apart from being an insurance against socialism, promise (and deliver) favourable labour laws, exemptions from property taxes, special franchises, valuable contracts without tender, mining or hydro rights of inestimable value in exchange for a row of pins—to say nothing of openly tolerating profitable infringements of the law (as in the case of timber-cutting regulations). Those powerful financial interests are not to any extent directed or owned by French Canadians. Thus it is somewhat paradoxical to observe that wealthy, upper-class, English-speaking Quebecers may sometimes return an Opposition member in their riding, thereby rejecting as individuals the undemocratic practices of the Duplessis Government; but as directors and managers of wealthy concerns what a part they must play in making his elections a success!

Perhaps the prize example of such political schizophrenia is found in the *Montreal Star* and the *Montreal Gazette*. Unparliamentary procedure at Ottawa or undemocratic practices by national politicians are denounced with the vigilance which befits truly democratic organs. But these papers never have editorials on, indeed often neglect to report, the innumerable cases of violation of parliamentary and

[27]This is common knowledge among professional politicians. Attempted estimates for the 1952 provincial elections can be found in G. Pelletier and P. E. Trudeau, *Cité libre* (décembre 1952), at pages 35 and 61. Guesses at amounts spent in the 1956 elections have ranged from $15 million to $25 million, though this seems hard to believe. (See *Le Devoir*'s articles referred to in n. 9.)

[28]Quoted by R. MacGregor Dawson, *The Government of Canada* (Toronto, 1949), p. 573.

democratic rights which are standard procedure for the Government they support in Quebec. It is safe to assume that a person whose reading of politics was limited to the *Star* and *Gazette* would never realize that the Premier constantly shouts orders to the Speaker of the Lower House, and has even participated in a loud voice in the conduct of the Upper House; that he vociferously commands the Speaker to expel members from the House on the flimsiest of pretexts; that several times during debate he has accused an honourable member of ingratitude for sitting on the Opposition benches after having, as a student, received assistance from the Government side; that he has introduced retroactive and vindictive legislation, sometimes bearing on individual adversaries (for example the Guindon bill, and the Picard bill in 1954; and since then the concerted legislative warfare against elected municipal representatives belonging to the Civic Action League); that he frankly tells the electorate that they will not get roads or bridges in their riding if they return a member of the Opposition; or that during the last provincial campaign his party repeatedly branded the Liberals as Communists because "their friends in Ottawa" had given money to the Colombo Plan instead of to the farmers of Nicolet.[29]

Indeed it is hard to escape the conclusion that if in the past English Canadians went far to instil a distrust of representative government in French-Canadian minds, in the present they are doing precious little to eradicate that distrust and to spread the gospel of honest parliamentarianism in Quebec.

III

In the two foregoing sections I will perhaps have managed to displease all Canadians. Both French and English may claim that I put too much blame on their particular ethnic group. But that would be silly, for under the democratic form of government all citizens are jointly and severally responsible for the procedures by which they choose their leaders; all men are to blame who fail in their duty of denouncing undemocratic practices and shady politicians.

[29]These are miscellaneous examples of fairly recent occurrences. Concerning the "discretion" of the English press in relation to more distant instances, see a pamphlet by F. R. Scott, *The Montreal Star and the C.C.F.* (Montreal, 1944). See also G. Pelletier, "La Grève et la presse" in Trudeau, comp., *La Grève de l'amiante*. As of late, this topic has drawn more and more attention. For instance, see the indignant editorials by P. Vigeant and G. Filion, *Le Devoir*, 21 février, 7 décembre 1957; and André Laurendeau's editorials on "La Théorie du roi nègre." Also, probably for the first time in English, the subject was dealt with in a very remarkable editorial, "The Shame of English Canada," which appeared in the *McGill Daily*, Feb. 26, 1958.

Democracy is not easy, even under the best of circumstances. But it is no consolation to know that under other climes other pitfalls beset democratic ways. It is important for Canadians to realize what particular pitfalls beset *them*. And there is no doubt that the unpleasant facts I have evoked play an important part in conditioning Canadian political behaviour on both sides of the ethnic barrier. I have tried to pry those facts away from the back of the collective minds of French and English Canada, and fit them into an explanatory hypothesis, for I believe that such exercises are necessary if Canadians are to know how to provide the whole of Canada with a common and enduring democratic faith.

If my hypothesis is right, the current vogue for preaching political morality in Quebec will by itself be of little avail. For so long as people do not believe in democracy there is no reason why they should accept its ethics. Political behaviour in Quebec can be described as immoral, objectively speaking; but subjectively the people are not conscious of wrongdoing, and consequently they see no reason to change that behaviour.

But this essay has run its course; further thoughts would lead me towards ground where men of action take over. And this book is no place to publish a tract for the times.

1958

The National Political Scene*

NORMAN WARD

Department of Economics and Political Science, University of Saskatchewan

THIS CHAPTER IS AN ATTEMPT TO APPRAISE some of the important contemporary elements in relations between English- and French-speaking Canadians in national politics, so as to show the kind of understandings and misunderstandings that can develop when two different peoples, one of them a minority consciously seeking equality with the other, must work together within a framework of liberal democratic institutions in which majority rule is presumed to prevail. The emphasis is on the means of communication, or their absence, between the two, and on some of the causes of friction between them that are less well known outside Ottawa than the more traditional and sometimes spectacular disagreements over conscription and the British connection.

The study is admittedly subjective, for at least two reasons. Abstracting from the whole complex of French-English relations in Canada the specific situation in politics in Ottawa inevitably involves distor-

*This chapter was written when the Liberal party had enjoyed twenty-one years of uninterrupted power, and appeared, in terms of both public confidence and internal organization, to be in an impregnable position. The general election of 1953 had given the party, as part of a large majority, sixty-six of Quebec's seventy-five federal seats, and fifty of Ontario's eighty-five. The Progressive Conservatives, by contrast, held four seats in Quebec and thirty-three in Ontario. In the general election of 1957 the Liberals retained sixty-three Quebec seats, but the Progressive Conservatives made enormous gains in Ontario, capturing sixty-one seats. In 1958, the national Progressive Conservative sweep saw that party make gains in Quebec which made its victories in Ontario in 1957 seem of minor significance: it took fifty seats in Quebec and sixty-seven in Ontario. The Liberals retained only twenty-five seats in Quebec and fourteen in Ontario.

So cataclysmic a change in the fortune of the two parties would at first sight seem to invalidate many of the findings of this chapter. In fact, if the chapter were to be rewritten in 1960, I would change little of it beyond altering a few sentences to read "Conservative" instead of "Liberal," and deleting a few references which now have about them a quaint antiquarian air. The electoral turnovers have not only produced almost no evidence to justify the alteration of the basic conclusions presented here, but seem to me to confirm their validity, in so far as one can assess them so soon after the events of 1957 and 1958.

tion, perhaps sufficiently serious to result in an artificial picture that is unrepresentative of the whole. In addition, the study deals largely with attitudes, and with one individual's assessment of attitudes. The material is drawn partly from interviews and correspondence, and partly from official documents. A depressing number of impressive details have been supplied either off the record, or with the injunction that if used they be so disguised as to be unrecognizable even to their donors. The weaknesses in the approach need no comment; but the approach has at least a partial validity, for it will demonstrate in itself some of the problems in French-English relations in Canada. The term "French-English" is one of the minor problems, for at the national level in politics its two components cannot be taken at equal value, but as: "On the one hand, Canadians whose mother tongue is French and who are usually bilingual; and on the other, Canadians whose mother tongue is English and who are not usually bilingual."

Political relations between English and French Canadians, because they are in some aspects so controversial, are rarely discussed fully in public by the journalists and politicians who have reason to know most about them. Our politicians, in particular, have not often been bookish men interested in doctrinaire analyses, and there are few books either by or about Canadian statesmen which offer much information about contacts between the two groups. Nor, since relations between Canadians form the context within which they do their daily work, are politicians necessarily self-conscious in regard to all they accept or reject. They may, and generally do, talk freely in private about their attitudes to the language and mores of their own and other groups, and these attitudes affect their public utterances as well as the day-to-day routine of Parliament. Yet in public many things are left unsaid, sometimes because it is difficult to say them without sounding more intolerant than shrewdness would allow; sometimes because of a genuine desire to avoid irritating members of a group different from one's own. We have in politics been successful in establishing an elaborate system of *ad hoc* compromises, one of which is that while battle lines may be clearly drawn on individual issues, French-English relations as such are rarely considered a fit topic for public debate.

It is true that as spokesmen from the minority, French Canadians are listened to politely when they complain of the disabilities which their compatriots must suffer, and French Canada and allied topics can still be found, although not as frequently as in the past, as separate categories in the index to the *House of Commons Debates*. There are few parallel entries for English Canada. One of the annoyances that some English-Canadian parliamentarians feel they must endure is that the desire to woo or placate French Canada often prevents them from expressing themselves as forthrightly as French-speaking representatives, the more nationalistic of whom speak with some *bravura* on matters about which English Canadians are sensitive. The possible significance of the statistical evidence that Canadians of British origin are now themselves a minority has not as yet been realized by either English or French in national politics; but it is highly improbable that the French Canadians will yield their specialized monopoly as the country's leading minority without a struggle.

Some of the main compromises between the two peoples have been institutionalized with a classical symmetry. With occasional exceptions the Speaker of the House of Commons has been for decades alternately a French and an English Canadian, with his deputy drawn from the group to which he does not himself belong; a prime minister whose majority includes a shortage of representatives from one side can encounter extraordinary embarrassments in equipping the Speakership with its two-member team, as Sir Robert Borden did in 1917. The Library of Parliament has had, in effect, two heads, one French and one English.[1] The parliamentary staff, like the cabinet, always includes a judicious mixture of French and English Canadians. In some instances the practical necessity of recognizing the claims of both groups has undoubtedly militated against the establishment of useful traditions. A Speaker of the House of Commons, for example, who may be chosen in the first place because there was not room for another representative from his province in the cabinet, usually serves for only one Parliament, so that few Speakers have had an opportunity to build up the prestige of the Speakership, and thus of Parliament.

Within the private affairs of the political parties, full caucuses are conducted in English, while provincial caucuses are conducted in the language best suited to the majority of the members. An English-Canadian prime minister does not attempt to take personal leadership of his party in Quebec, but relies on French-speaking lieutenants, whereas a French-Canadian leader must exert himself considerably in English Canada. The parties naturally strive to have ample representation from both groups on their executives and at their conventions, and to choose leaders acceptable to both groups. For parties

[1]A bill to reorganize the Library under one head is before Parliament as this is written, and has stirred up the usual controversy. See *Debates of the Senate of Canada*, Feb. 22 and 23 and March 2, 1955.

other than the Liberal, French-speaking supporters may exert an influence in party affairs that, in the opinion of their English-speaking colleagues, is not matched by the delivery of a proportionate number of seats in general elections. The Liberal hold on Quebec has as one of its by-products a capacity to contribute to internal strains in other parties, a phenomenon which most members of the House of Commons view with some detachment.

While the requirements of Parliament and the parties necessitate a continuing series of attempts to establish a rapport between French and English Canadians, another essential element in Canadian democracy—the Press Gallery in Parliament—presents a different picture. Personal relations between French- and English-speaking newsmen are excellent, and both groups are invariably represented in the organization of the Gallery. But English reporters write almost exclusively for journals published in English, and French write for French. The efficient news-gathering services of the Canadian Press collect and distribute news of national interest and translate from one language to the other. No need exists, especially for English-Canadian writers, to be bilingual, and, what is probably more important, the division of the Press Gallery into two sections, reporting independently to newspapers in the two languages, inevitably means that attempts by English-speaking journalists to understand and interpret French-Canadian points of view, and vice versa, are more uncommon than not. In addition, as one veteran Canadian journalist has noted, the national press service has the peculiar bias of an individual paper's news room, "which reduces its value in spreading understanding and promoting national feeling. . . . This means that Canadians tend to be very fully informed about fatal highway accidents of Nova Scotia but know little or nothing about that province's amateur drama. We hear much of the Dionne quintuplets but little of revolutionary changes in the social attitude of the working man in Quebec. . . ."[2] Many important aspects of French-English relations in fact are not news, and those which are discussed in interpretative articles tend to be found on editorial pages, which are not read by large numbers of citizens. The mechanical transmission of news in the two languages in any event places a heavy emphasis on literal translation, and political bilingualism involves not merely the use of two languages, but the comprehension of two sets of attitudes to national affairs, including Parliament itself.

[2]W. Eggleston, "The Press of Canada" in *Royal Commission Studies: A Selection of Essays Prepared for the Royal Commission on National Development in the Arts, Letters and Sciences* (Ottawa, 1951), pp. 49–50.

Until 1952 the excellent wire services of the Canadian Press were available only in English, and that French-language newspapers need no longer provide their own translations is one significant indication of the changing status of the French language in national affairs. Section 133 of the British North America Act ensures the use of English and French only in Parliament, the legislature of Quebec, and certain courts. These minimal constitutional guarantees of bilingualism have been profoundly modified in recent years by the development of radio and television, by the needs of modern administration in government, by the needs of political parties to gain or keep support in Quebec, and not least by the growth of the idea that a Canadian who speaks either French or English has a right to be entertained, instructed, and appealed to for support, in his own language.

Since so high a proportion of French-Canadian parliamentarians, newsmen, and civil servants are bilingual, language as a barrier to communication has never been insurmountable. But surmounting the barrier of language has come to include a steady expansion of the use of both languages far beyond the limits defined in 1867. Limiting the use of French to the areas mentioned in the British North America Act is indeed not a practical possibility within a liberal democratic framework, and only a few die-hard conservatives, who can be found in all parties, still think that it is. The French Canadians are no slower now than they were during the nineteenth-century struggle for responsible government to turn political (and now technical) devices to their advantage, and few of them would agree wholly with a statement on bilingualism once made by Sir Wilfrid Laurier. In opposing a motion that would have put French "on a footing of equality with the English language in all public matters," the French-Canadian Prime Minister said: "Instead of affirming pedantically on every occasion our right to speak the French language . . . it is sufficient for all French Canadians, I am sure, that we have obtained the right to speak French and to use our mother tongue on the floor of this Parliament. . . . But to affirm, as he does, that the French language should be used upon every occasion . . . is, I think, going a little too far."[3]

Bilingual postage stamps, paper money, and sundry other public documents have long been a reality in Canada, but French is not now on a footing of equality with English. English is the language of Parliament, and the working language of the public service. A French member of Parliament who wants a hearing must speak English or he may empty the House; even many of his compatriots will leave, for

[3]*House of Commons Debates*, Feb. 25, 1907, p. 3655.

they believe that when a French-speaking member speaks in French he is usually addressing not Parliament but his constituents. French is the language of translation, and the French edition of committee reports and other documents, to the occasional irritation of French Canadians, is often not available until well after the English original. Briefs to parliamentary committees are not often in French, and many official documents tabled for the use of committees are in English only. The rules of the House of Commons affirm that a bill must be available in both languages before proceeding to second reading, but supporting documents (according to an opinion held by Mr. Speaker Fauteux, Mr. St. Laurent, and an overwhelming majority of the House, including French Canadians) may be only in English.[4]

A growing number of English-Canadian elected representatives (about thirty-five in 1955) are finding bilingualism useful, whereas it is within the memory of sitting members that a bilingual English Canadian from outside Quebec was something unusual. Yet an awareness of the continuing inferiority of the status of the French language cannot be avoided by either French or English Canadians, and is one element in the differing attitudes to Parliament and politics taken by the two groups. Most French members have a mission no other member need consider: the defence and extension of their language and everything remotely connected with it. Areas of governmental activity that especially concern language (such as the Canadian Broadcasting Corporation, in which French Canadians have a double interest, for they believe it is protecting the quality of spoken French as well as extending its use through French stations and networks) provide institutions in which French members take a proprietary interest that distinguishes them from most English-Canadian M.P.'s. The French-speaking member gets an additional sense of mission from the frequency with which his constituents enlist his support, as a compatriot, in approaching some branch of a federal government believed to be predominantly English Canadian. French- and English-Canadian M.P.'s agree that the French representatives must concern themselves with much routine detail which the English Canadian is spared because so many of his electors, as a matter of course, deal direct with departments and agencies.

The French-Canadian voter, in the view of some of his own representatives, is less likely than the English to have formed or joined a lay organization that would channel his interests. He is accustomed, especially outside the urban areas, to organizations authorized by his

[4]See *ibid.*, April 1, 1947, pp. 1918–21.

church which are not necessarily established through the initiative of individual private citizens, and French Canadians in national politics are sometimes astonished by the array of sectarian and non-sectarian clubs and interest groups that they find in Protestant English Canada. What Mason Wade has called the French Canadians' lack of civic consciousness is a related element in their attitude to Parliament and politics; and Pierre Trudeau has observed that to the French-Canadian mind, electoral goings-on "sont des divertissements protestants et anglo-saxons dont la signification profonde reste obscure."[5] Such attitudes constitute one factor which helps the French-speaking parliamentarian to believe that he is a diplomatic representative in at least a semi-foreign capital, of each individual in his constituency. One result of this is that the French member, possibly rationalizing something he would do anyway, asserts that he must spend a good deal of time at home with his electors. The week-end delinquency from Ottawa of French-Canadian M.P.'s, which exceeds even that of members from Ontario,[6] has a peculiarly aggravating effect on many English-Canadian politicians, and notably on those who live too far from their districts to go home regularly themselves.

Many points of difference between French and English Canadians are sharpened in Ottawa by the traditional grouping of the vast majority of the French-speaking members on one side of the House, in both Commons and Senate. The adherence of French Canadians to the Liberals, and of the southern United States to the Democrats, suggests the hypothesis that it may not be possible within the structure of representative government for a large compact minority either to divide its allegiance between two or more political parties, or to alternate freely between parties. The single-member constituency system, by throwing whole blocks of seats to one party, sustains and encourages it in its special role as protector of the minority; at the same time, members of other parties are continually divided and confused over the apparent hopelessness of obtaining the minority's support. Symptoms of the last-named phenomenon are not hard to find in Canada, but some of the other relevant by-products are less obvious.

Just as the great majority of the French-Canadian members, through having sat so long on Government benches, have little parliamentary experience in criticism, attack, and questioning (or even, as several

[5]See Pierre Trudeau, "Réflexions sur la politique au Canada français," *Cité libre* (Dec. 1952), pp. 53 ff.

[6]Confirmed by a check of recent division lists for well-attended sittings of the House of Commons.

have pointed out, in speaking, for government back-benchers are not encouraged to clog the parliamentary time-table, and days and weeks may pass with no French private member saying a word) the Opposition parties have for many years had little experience in dealing with French Canadians as trusted colleagues in caucus. Lasting traditions based on an absence of personal contact can develop, for the turnover of members in the House of Commons is high, and each new parliamentarian is introduced to the mysteries of representative government chiefly through caucus colleagues. Personal friendships that cut through party lines are of course not uncommon, and non-parliamentary contacts between the two groups, within each party, are systematically fostered; but space and the federal nature of Canadian parties seriously limit the number of contacts that can be made within parties. It is possible, and not unusual, for the veteran politicians on one side of the House of Commons to spend years in national politics in virtual isolation from those who speak a different language on the other.

Inevitably, French and English Canadians thus separated develop their own notions and stereotypes about honourable members across the floor. On the one side, bilingualism can readily become regarded as "a necessary nuisance," "an expensive waste of time," and even "childish." All these terms have been used in good faith in my hearing, and I was once asked a singular question: "Suppose we did have a substantial number of French Canadians in our caucus, what would we do with them?" (One of the obvious answers—count them every time the division bells ring—under the circumstances seemed rude.) Attempts by French Canadians to secure their language a little more, to expand the French operations of the Canadian Broadcasting Corporation, or to increase the number of French Canadians in the civil service (in all of which the French Canadians insist they want no concessions, but only their rights) sometimes come under suspicion almost as if they were linked with some dark plot to reverse the decision of 1760. English Canadians in the civil service, faced with French-Canadian attempts to increase the proportion of their compatriots on the public payroll, can naturally argue that a citizen's training should be the prime requisite for an appointment, and can refer to the apparent inability of the French-Canadian educational system to produce large numbers of technically qualified people, a point returned to below. It is understandably difficult for a technically qualified English Canadian to accept as his equal a less qualified French Canadian, or to tolerate as his superior a French Canadian whose chief qualification is not his training but his language—especially when, as many argue, English is demonstrably more flexible than French in the development of technical terminology.

French-Canadian parliamentarians who have few contacts with the Opposition side can, and do, produce views of their own about Parliament and the English-speaking members whom they know only by sight. Criticism from the Opposition benches of the Senate, the Canadian Broadcasting Corporation, the parliamentary handling of divorce bills, or any one of many diverse subjects in which French Canadians feel they have a special stake, can sound like an underhanded attack on French Canada and its rights; it is the misfortune of all the parties in Opposition that some of the things they criticize most effectively can arouse members on the government side not only because they are Liberals, but because they are French Canadians.

Permanent residence on Mr. Speaker's right does not facilitate the growth of an impassioned devotion to free speech. The French-Canadian political tradition, reinforced in Ottawa by the dependence of the French on executive rather than parliamentary action for the securing of many of their rights, does not lead French-speaking members to share Opposition distrust of growing executive power. The C.C.F. party's attitude to executive power is conditioned by its socialistic theories, and is not as far removed from the French Canadians' as one might suppose; but the C.C.F.'s interest in British political traditions, when added to the British origin of many of its spokesmen, paradoxically gives to the C.C.F. a taint of "imperialism" not unlike that enjoyed by the Conservatives. In a different way, the English origins of Social Credit and the championing by some Social Credit spokesmen of a sort of pan-Anglo-Saxonism allow French-Canadian members to assert that Social Credit is "imperialistic to the core."[7] Few French Canadians seem to understand, or to wish to understand, how a patriotic English Canadian can have an honest admiration for Great Britain which interferes in no way with his putting Canada first in all things. English Canadians who are willing to admit that French Canada is one of the fundamental factors that distinguishes Canada from the United States are puzzled and annoyed by French-Canadian reluctance to find a similar utility in the Commonwealth connection.

The isolation on the Opposition side of many western representatives who are accustomed to constituencies containing far more citizens of continental European than of French-Canadian extraction tends to a serious under-estimation on their part of the problem of bilingualism,

[7] *H. of C. Debates*, March 6, 1947, p. 1084 (Mr. Bertrand).

which they see often as a series of private issues between Ontario and Quebec. Members from each of the two central provinces, who naturally think of bilingualism as particularly related to the central province they do not belong to themselves, are by the same token led to under-estimate the importance to the Canadian nation of the other eight provinces. An outstanding bilingual member of the House of Commons only slightly over-stated a common sentiment when he observed that "After all, Canada is here, in Ontario and Quebec." The same viewpoint has permeated parts of the civil service, for the Department of External Affairs, seeking potential employees in 1955, listed as a qualification "a Canadian outlook derived from knowledge of the people and life of our two races." (How one could possibly obtain a Canadian outlook without also knowing something of the other "races" in Canada was not indicated.) Indeed, a well-travelled member of Parliament today, because of the war and delegations to such bodies as the United Nations, the Commonwealth Parliamentary Association, and the NATO Parliamentary Association, can easily have more first-hand knowledge of foreign countries than of his own. Some French Canadians appear to have a rather special interest in the U.N. and NATO partly because these are not connected direct with the Commonwealth, and partly because foreign centres have an attraction which the provincial Ontario city of Ottawa lacks; it is therefore sometimes easier to recruit French Canadians for civil service posts abroad than for work in Ottawa.

While language and regionalism create serious barriers to unity, the Liberal party has been demonstrating for decades a number of ways of negotiating the obstacle course. So far as the rank and file members are concerned, the negotiating is not always of a sort to necessitate or even encourage a wide knowledge on the part of Liberals from one province of the affairs of Liberals in another; mutual concessions can be made, each side knowing only what the other wants conceded, without asking why. Liberals can disagree on important specific issues (such as parliamentary divorces, the word "Dominion," or a Canadian flag[8]) but relations between French and English Canadians within Liberal ranks are regarded by both as good; they get along, as one well-informed French Canadian put it, with "joviale indifférence." French Canadians attribute the relative comfort they find within the Liberal party to the attitude taken by the English-

[8]See, e.g., *Joint Committee of the Senate and House of Commons, Appointed to Consider and Report upon a Suitable Design for a Distinctive Flag for Canada, Minutes of Proceedings and Evidence, 1945 and 1946*; *H. of C. Debates*, April 25 and June 2, 1950.

Canadian majority to the French Canadian and his language: both have a status so secure that it can be taken for granted. But even within the Liberal party the *Canadian Liberal*, a quarterly magazine which is probably the most ambitious political publishing venture in Canada, circulates only in English.

Status in the national government is what the French Canadian really seeks, not only for his language in Parliament, public affairs, and national broadcasting, but also for himself as a citizen. Apart from Parliament and the parties, this means that he has a special claim on the civil service of which the following, although the figures are now out of date, is a typical expression: ". . . in 1918, before the creation of the Civil Service Commission under the federal administration, the proportion of French Canadian civil servants amounted to 21.58 per cent while in 1946 the proportion was down to 12.5 per cent. What is worse, with respect to salaries of $6000 or more a year, the proportion of French Canadians fell from 25 per cent in 1918 to 9.52 per cent in 1946."[9]

The interesting variant on the spoils system in modern administration that is implied in the quotation is no doubt an inevitable product of a bilingual situation such as ours. It is no accident that the French-Canadian complainant correlated the decline of the French with the reform of the civil service beginning in 1918, for the expansion of the Dominion government in the last few decades was at first characterized, as was the entire civil service after Confederation, by exclusively English-Canadian thinking. Applicants for civil service posts have for years been able to elect to write examinations in French or English anywhere in Canada, and French Canadians have always held a share of posts, usually among the minor ranks, and especially in departments staffed by the patronage method. But as the technical requirements of the service have grown, and as English Canadians staff most of the higher ranks, the senior departmental officers have not unnaturally sought more English Canadians to work with, and until after the Second World War the proportion of French Canadians in the total service was dropping steadily. As recently as the war a French-Canadian cabinet minister could find himself marooned at the head of a predominantly English-Canadian organization in which English was the only departmental language and only English-Canadian ideas influenced the formation of policy and the organization of the department itself.

[9] *H. of C. Debates*, July 16, 1946, p. 3520 (Mr. Dorion). Complaints of this type can be traced back well beyond Confederation.

An enormous change in the status of French-speaking citizens in the public service has occurred since the war (even though the preference given to war veterans in public employment has inevitably benefited more English Canadians than French) and with it have come new attitudes to the national government among both French and English. The war itself is responsible for much, for the great bureaucracy which developed across Canada encountered problems of establishing contacts with citizens, and of getting their active co-operation, on a scale which threw into sharp relief some of the major needs of national administration in a bilingual country. The Wartime Prices and Trade Board, for instance, which used voluntary co-operation wherever it could, found that approaches that were efficient in English Canada were not necessarily so in Quebec, where the pattern of voluntary organization is so different. Legal concepts necessary to the enforcing of price regulations fell on barren ground in French civil law, and publicity that appealed to English Canada often did not translate at all into French. The wartime bureaucracy as a whole left a legacy of great importance: a national policy that closely concerns the welfare of citizens can be "sold" to French Canada only by French Canadians; and French Canadians interested in undertaking such a task are not readily found.

The proliferation of federal services since the war has been influenced by wartime experience, and during the past few years more serious attempts (which have sometimes involved the creation of sinecures) have been made to strengthen French-Canadian representation in the public service than in the whole period from 1867 to the Second World War. A contributory factor has been pressure from interested French Canadians, including an active group of members of Parliament, as a result of which a Solicitor General, Hon. Joseph Jean, made a study of French Canadians in the civil service.[10] But while improving the status of French Canadians in the civil service has become a Dominion policy, with the specialized agencies usually showing the most stubborn resistance to French-Canadian infiltration, progress has not always been made without difficulty. The moderate successes of the policy have produced a reaction, for the fairly obvious appearance of an increasing number of French Canadians in the higher ranks of the public service has led some English Canadians to feel that the French are "overplaying their hand" (the phrase is

[10]*Ibid.*, March 18, 1948, p. 2335. The Jean report was not published, but appears to have been read by some French-Canadian M.P.'s. See *ibid.*, Feb. 24, 1949, p. 885 (Mr. Langlois).

quoted from an interview). In political circles some impetus has been given to the theory that Opposition parties should perhaps abandon their time-consuming and expensive attempts to win Quebec, in order to seek a parliamentary majority in the rest of Canada. The prospect of confronting French-Canadian electors with a choice between becoming a permanent Opposition minority in Parliament, and being obliged to cast themselves loose from the Liberal party if they wish to influence governmental policy, makes an increasing and understandable appeal to some politicians the longer the Liberal monopoly of Quebec's seats goes on. They feel, as Mr. Speaker Edgar observed to Laurier as long ago as 1897, "your weakness is your great appearance of strength in Quebec."[11]

It is one thing to decide to have more French-Canadian civil servants, and another to get them. Ottawa is in Ontario, and to a well-educated French Canadian living in Montreal or Quebec it is more distant from the social milieu of those cities than a glance at a map might suggest. French-speaking members of Parliament and civil servants alike have vividly described how Ottawa is a "foreign" city, and predominantly English Canadian in its foreignness; and as if that were not enough, a French Canadian who settles down in Ottawa must sometimes also run the risk of being suspected of having deserted his own people. Furthermore, a large number of private corporations operating in Quebec have until recently been almost exclusively English Canadian in their executive ranks, partly because the French educational system has not produced large proportions of people trained for technical or administrative posts. French Canadians qualified for executive posts in either private or public enterprises are thus sufficiently scarce that they can probably earn higher salaries, and avoid Ottawa, by staying in Quebec. Lower ranks in the administrative machinery are more readily staffed with French Canadians (almost all of whom for practical purposes must be bilingual, a qualification not often required of English Canadians), but even there many problems are found. As this is written, for instance, the chief personnel officers in all departments are English Canadian, most of them with a French-speaking assistant or associate; French Canadians who have problems connected with their employment (and in a basically English-Canadian system they are likely to have problems which others are spared) find themselves encountering theories of organization and personnel administration derived mainly from the English-speaking world. It will be seen that for many particular kinds of positions,

[11]Public Archives of Canada, Laurier Papers, nos. 17443–4.

French-Canadian civil servants, despite conscientious efforts by various branches of the Dominion public service, are not easy to find and keep. Some departments have less trouble than others, because their work is more attractive to French Canadians, or less oriented towards an English-Canadian educational system. In some departments there are important posts which have not since 1867 been held by French Canadians. Even of the Canadian Broadcasting Corporation, whose services daily demand the use of the French language and French-speaking employees, and are probably better known to more French Canadians than those of any other part of the government of Canada, the highest-ranking French Canadian in the Corporation once said: ". . . whereas it is difficult to find proper help for English programs, at times it is impossible to obtain what we want for the French network."[12]

The Canadian Broadcasting Corporation, because its operations must be in both French and English, is an interesting focal point for many of the political and administrative problems that accompany bilingualism, and is worth more serious study on this score than it has yet received. Although not our largest or most expensive governmental enterprise, it is one of the most conspicuous, and is examined more often by a parliamentary committee than most public activities. The committee brings French- and English-speaking parliamentarians together in a study of the national broadcasting system, and since the same members tend to be appointed to the committee each time it is created, they have ample opportunity to learn of the attitudes taken by French and English Canadians to the two languages. The corporation illustrates, too, some of the added costs and complexities that go with bilingualism. Giving evidence to a committee on June 4, 1946, the Chairman of the Board of Governors deposed: "Another heavy cost factor is that the CBC operates in two languages. This necessitates a large amount of dual programming and also some duplication of broadcasting facilities." In other branches of the Dominion government, it should be added, some of the added costs of bilingualism arise not so much from French-Canadian insistence on the use of French as from the persistent refusal of so many English Canadians to speak anything but English.

The broadcasting system also offers ample proof of a proposition that is of great importance to relations between French and English Canadians, but which in Ottawa seems to be better understood by the

[12]House of Commons, Special Committee on Radio Broadcasting, *Minutes of Proceedings and Evidence*, June 2, 1942, p. 271 (Dr. Frigon).

former: more is involved in bilingualism than the translation of words from one language to another. Words translate more readily than ideas, and the C.B.C., in endeavouring to give French and English Canada services which are as similar as possible, has been obliged to set up in effect two broadcasting systems. The Chairman of the Board told a committee in 1951: "A lot of different broadcasting is put on the two networks. We often wish that they were closer together, but there is a difference of atmosphere and wants and needs." No greater proof of that last statement is needed than the following evidence once given by the Corporation's General Manager: "there is a much more avid appetite for political speeches in the province of Quebec than elsewhere. In fact, I think in the province of Quebec it is regarded not only as information but also as entertainment."[13]

One result of the bilingual broadcasting system is that the C.B.C. services divide citizens, and in some ways more than they unite them. It is a rather ironic fact that the services of the national system are now so comprehensive that the great bulk of Canadians, whether English- or French-speaking, need never listen to broadcasts or telecasts in a language other than their own. This is no doubt satisfactory to large numbers of people in both groups, and a particular gratification is afforded to the French Canadians who like to point out, and rightly, that while English Canadians are daily exposed to large gobbets of American propaganda of all kinds, the French system remains comparatively impenetrable. But the dichotomy of C.B.C. services, considered as an aspect of the government of Canada, raises important questions about what biculturalism means in national politics, and what it is going to mean in the future.

In the past, biculturalism in national politics has meant that the French Canadians in Quebec remained French (on "some sort of reservation," as one of their representatives remarked sardonically in Parliament) and the English Canadians spoke English; and whenever the two groups made contact, the French spoke English too. We have entered a phase in which the public use of French has been extended widely, thanks to modern techniques of communication, and in which the status of the French Canadian in the Dominion government has improved rapidly, thanks to the needs both of political parties and the Dominion bureaucracy. A significant and growing number of English-Canadian politicians and civil servants appear to be working at becoming bilingual. If it is true that biculturalism is one of the fundamental elements that differentiate us from our southern neighbours,

[13]*Ibid.*, Nov. 20, 1951, p. 43; and May 29, 1942, p. 234.

and thus in the long run one of our great bulwarks against absorption, the bulwark appears to be in the process of being strengthened at the national political level.

The very strengthening brings with it a danger that the group of politicians and civil servants who dominate the national political scene may become increasingly isolated from the rest of Canada. Rightly or wrongly, both French and English Canadians agree that the fluently bilingual French Canadian who gets along well in Ottawa is unlike the "real" French Canadian of Quebec. The bilingual English Canadian, or even the unilingual English Canadian who works familiarly with French Canadians, is marked off from most English Canadians who have survived only their provincial educational systems. The Dominion government can do little to encourage bilingual education within the provinces, and nobody would resist federal attempts to influence provincial educational policies more fiercely than the leading proponents of bilingualism, the French Canadians. Apart from the language, the eight provinces outside central Canada already accustomed to acting the role of claimants for favours within a political and economic environment dominated by Ontario and Quebec, may find the role increasingly complex and difficult.

Since communications are fundamental to the practice of politics, the changing status of the French Canadian and his language would appear to have limits beyond the control of participants in the affairs of the Dominion government. Thoughtful French Canadians may regret this, for they believe that all Canada is enriched by biculturalism, and wish to persuade increasing numbers of English Canadians to accept the obvious truth that they too have a direct stake in the French language and in French Canada. But whether Canadians, and especially French Canadians, will be better off in the long run if more Canadians from both groups become bilingual, or better off if the two groups maintain their traditional separation with the addition of important lines to French-Canadian roles in national politics, is a question to which few have yet given attention. If increasing numbers of citizens become bilingual, will the gain in national feeling be offset by the increased exposure of French Canada to propaganda and sales talks in English and American? How great would become the danger that French Canada would be assimilated at last not by English-speaking Canada, but by English-speaking North America? The French Canadian, concerned with the immediate means for the defence of his language and his people, has no fears about the long-run implications of what he regards today as the continuing improvement in the condition of his compatriots. Even the most sympathetic English Canadian, also concerned with the immediate, is of two minds: he cannot but approve in principle (at least in public) anything that gratifies his fellow citizens who speak French; but it is impossible not to feel impatient on occasion with people who seem so preoccupied with their status, and in general hold so high an opinion of their opinions. Changes in relations between the two groups inevitably rub many edges raw, and a wide tolerance, shown daily by large numbers of individuals on both sides, is still needed to keep as many as possible of the ragged edges from showing. Nobody is yet thinking of the days when the main sources of difference may have disappeared.

1956

III. FORMS OF ASSOCIATION

B. Labour

III. ORGANISATION SOCIALE

B. Monde ouvrier

Le Syndicalisme canadien-français

GÉRARD PELLETIER

Directeur, Cité libre, *Montréal*

L'ÉVOLUTION OUVRIÈRE au Canada français, c'est d'abord l'histoire d'une double désillusion, puis celle d'un courage remarquable. Pour en comprendre la marche, il faut partir de ce que les anthropologues appellent notre « idéologie nationale » et des rêves qui nous permirent de vivre à travers tout le XIXe siècle. Il faut, qu'on aime ou non les souvenirs historiques, remonter à la « conquête ». Elle seule, en effet, explique de façon valable notre repliement sur nous-mêmes. Nous avions vécu jusque là au niveau d'une haute destinée. Le continent nord-américain n'était pas trop grand pour nous. Solidement ancré à la terre par sa majorité paysanne, notre peuple produisait de surcroît sa quote-part d'aventuriers, de risque-tout, de voyageurs et de conquérants. L'Amérique nous appartenait. Tandis que les uns grattaient la terre, d'autres couraient les grands espaces; le commun dénominateur des deux groupes était fait d'un sentiment très fort de possession, de courage conquérant, de course à l'avenir.

Mais à compter de 1760, nous nous absentons du continent pour devenir des provinciaux. L'Amérique appartient aux autres, à ceux qui sont venus et qui nous ont « vaincus ». Nous abandonnons le sud aux Américains, l'ouest aux Anglais. Nous serons désormais sur la défensive. Notre vocabulaire s'enrichit du mot « survivance ». L'accent est mis tout entier sur la terre. Les Canadiens français se resserrent autour de leurs clochers. Ils aborderont encore les terres neuves mais seulement de proche en proche, ne quittant plus leurs villages que pour en bâtir de nouveaux. Ils se sentent isolés, menacés. Ils ne quittent plus guère leurs foyers, ne se coupent jamais de leurs bases de ravitaillement spirituel. Ils ne luttent plus pour la conquête d'un continent; ils aménagent une forteresse, communauté humaine disciplinée, resserrée sur elle-même, unanime, inexpugnable. Les voyageurs sont rentrés à la maison; ils labourent, engrangent, s'inquiètent et défendent « leur foi, leur langue, et leurs institutions ».

Notre idéologie prend naissance. Désormais, nous nous donnons pour mission d'édifier une civilisation agricole dont l'unité est la consigne. Toute l'insistance est portée sur les liens très forts qui nous unissent : une seule foi religieuse, une seule langue que du reste nous sommes seuls à parler et qui fait de nous un groupe culturel unique en Amérique; une profession quasi unique : la terre; une organisation sociale qui est la paroise. Et, comme il arrive sous la pression du danger, ces éléments divers de notre vitalité finissent par se confondre un peu.

Fin et moyen prennent une importance égale. La langue est-elle gardienne de la foi ou la foi de la langue ? La vocation paysanne est-elle fonction de la chrétienne, ou celle-ci de celle-là ? En pratique, ces questions ne se posent guère et l'on finit par faire du tout un seul bloc où le temporel, par contagion, devient sacré lui aussi. Nous en viendrons à croire que notre âme est menacée si nous abandonnons l'agriculture et c'est ici que je retrouve mon sujet.

Car les Canadiens français du XIXe siècle avaient beaucoup d'enfants. Ils avaient surtout un nombre prodigieux de fils. Eussent-ils été capables de les établir tous sur des terres (hors une minorité de prêtres, d'avocats et de médecins) ils l'auraient fait sans hésiter. Mais ce ne fut pas toujours possible. Dans un pays immense, la politique les privait de terres.

L'industrie ? Elle ne faisait pas partie de notre paysage intérieur. Dans notre idéologie, l'industrie ne jouait aucun rôle. Il faut bien dire aussi que nous n'en possédions pas les leviers : le capital n'était pas de la famille et nous avions renoncé à l'aventure. Il fallait donc nous acharner à réclamer des terres. Et quand nous n'arrivions pas à en arracher aux pouvoirs publics l'étendue nécessaire, nous n'avions pour nos fils aucune solution de rechange. Ils devaient, bon gré, mal gré, adopter celle que le hasard offrait.

Elle prit la forme, cette solution, d'un service de diligence, établi vers 1840, pour relier Montréal à la Nouvelle-Angleterre. Et dès lors, la saignée commença. Chaque omnibus amena outre-frontière son contingent de jeunes Canadiens français en quête de travail. Notre révolution industrielle était dès lors amorcée. Mais comme elle s'accompagnait d'un exil, d'un éloignement, pour l'époque, considérable, l'expérience ne nous profita guère. Ces départs ne nous familiarisaient pas avec la réalité industrielle; il nous enfonçaient dans notre entêtement agricole, dans notre acharnement à réclamer des terres. L'usine devint l'ennemi à qui nous devions, de toute force, soustraire le plus grand nombre possible de jeunes. Quand ils quittaient la terre, n'étaient-ils pas en effet perdus pour notre groupe ?

« Perdus » c'est le jugement que prononçait sur eux la majorité paysanne, rivée à la sécurité de la terre. De ce jugement devait naître bientôt, et fatalement, chez les « perdus », le sentiment qu'on les abandonnait.

L'histoire en effet continuait d'avancer. L'industrie n'était plus confinée outre-frontière; elle envahissait le Canada à pas de géant. Bientôt la diligence perdit son utilité. Les usines poussaient à nos portes. Montréal et Québec attiraient plus de jeunes que « la terre ». Toute une partie de notre peuple et bientôt la majorité de ses fils aménageaient dans la misère les quartiers ouvriers de nos villes.

Tous ceux qui étudient aujourd'hui cette période de notre évolution, avec le recul que nous donne le temps, s'étonnent de la lenteur que nous avons mise à prendre conscience du fait industriel.

Sur le plan pratique, l'industrialisation s'opérait implacablement, avec une rapidité rarement observée en Occident. Cette révolution, toutefois, la pensée officielle de notre groupe humain se contentait de la refuser, de la décrier, d'en peindre les conséquences néfastes, sans jamais s'aviser, semble-t-il, qu'elle était irréversible. Bloqués sur le thème traditionnel de « la terre », nos maîtres à penser produisaient une étonnante quantité de littérature à la gloire de l'agriculture et à la honte de la vie malsaine des villes, comme s'ils avaient cru possible d'empêcher ainsi l'exode de la population vers l'industrie en pleine expansion.

Est-il seulement besoin de noter que cela préparait fort mal les Canadiens français à la nécessaire transition qui leur était imposée ? Ils arrivaient dans les villes sans aucune tradition urbaine à laquelle se raccrocher. Ils devenaient ouvriers comme on prend la typhoïde, par une sorte de fatalité aveugle dont ils s'accommodaient le mieux possible. Pour une génération au moins et parfois davantage, ils restaient des paysans déplacés, conservant de leur mieux, dans les semi-taudis des rues ouvrières, les mœurs inadaptées, les habitudes en lambeaux de leurs traditions campagnardes. Très souvent, eux-mêmes restaient convaincus en théorie que la ville n'était qu'un pis-aller temporaire, qu'il fallait s'accrocher quand même au grand rêve de « la terre »...

Le patronat, du reste, ne faisait rien pour les dissuader. Toutes les révolutions industrielles ont connu leurs périodes initiales d'exploitation intense; ce cauchemar ne fut pas épargné aux travailleurs canadiens-français. Il suffit, pour s'en convaincre, de relire quelques documents comme l'Enquête fédérale sur les établissements industriels (1889) ou celle, plus récente, sur l'industrie textile (1937). Les salaires de famine, l'infâme régime des amendes, des conditions de travail effroyables, une criminelle carence d'hygiène industrielle, des heures de travail parfois meurtrières, sans oublier le travail des enfants, tel fut le lot de notre population ouvrière pendant le dernier quart du XIXe et le premier quart du XXe siècle.

Après les quelques notations qu'on vient de lire, qui pourra s'étonner du fait que les Canadiens français, engagés dans l'industrie comme travailleurs, furent lents à trouver leur voie vers le syndicalisme ?

Rien ne les disposait à comprendre le sort qui leur était fait. Au premier abord, ils voulurent se convaincre que rien n'était changé, que l'idéologie expliquait tout. Formés au respect le plus scrupuleux de l'autorité, imbus du sens de l'ordre, il ne leur venait même pas à l'idée de revendiquer, de tenir tête, d'entrer en lutte avec le patronat. Leurs traditions paysannes en faisaient d'ailleurs des individualistes peu ouverts aux idées de collaboration. Des solutions de groupe leur eussent-elles été présentées, à la toute première phase de notre urbanisation, il y avait bien peu de chances qu'elles fussent reçues.

Dans le jeu de valeurs héritées de leurs familles et de leur communauté paysanne, ils auraient cherché en vain la trace d'une solidarité autre que celles du sang, de la paroisse et de la nationalité. L'idée d'une solidarité basée sur leur condition économique n'effleurait même pas leur esprit.

Et pour corser encore l'équivoque, pour augmenter la confusion, l'incidence culturelle venait de surcroît brouiller les cartes davantage. Car si le fait de l'oppression s'imposait avec l'aveuglante autorité d'une évidence, l'origine de cette oppression et les intérêts qui la soutenaient n'apparaissaient pas aussi clairement. Face à un patronat en presque totalité anglophone, les travailleurs canadiens-français avaient toutes les raisons de croire que rien n'avait changé. Ce qui s'éveillait en eux, sous les brimades d'un contremaître, d'un gérant ou d'un super-intendant « anglais », n'était-ce pas le vieux réflexe de méfiance et d'agressivité hérité de la « conquête » ? Dans la personne même de l'oppresseur, l'Anglais cachait complètement le patron.

C'était donc la « défaite » qui continuait sous une forme renouvelée. Et personne ne songeait à chercher au delà de cette explication, tant elle paraissait naturelle. On constatait seulement que dans l'industrie, les Canadiens français étaient moins aptes à se défendre des Anglais que sur la terre. Mais puisqu'on n'avait pas le choix, puisqu'en dépit de tous les rêves agrestes, les usines offraient désormais le seul gagne-pain accessible, il fallait bien y rester. Ainsi intégrée au contexte historique, la révolution industrielle se trouva pour plusieurs années travestie en lutte ethnique. Au pays de Québec, rien n'avait changé.

Dans l'industrie comme sur la ferme, on travaillait à survivre en dépit des « maîtres anglais ». Comme les paysans, les travailleurs industriels restaient attachés à l'idéologie, vivaient des mêmes slogans (y compris ceux qui chantaient la terre comme planche unique du salut national).

On ne peut toutefois rester longtemps fidèle à des principes ni à des rêves qui ne correspondent plus à la réalité concrète. L'élan initial met du temps à s'épuiser tout à fait mais assez tôt le doute commence de s'insinuer, à travers les fissures d'un système ébranlé par la progression massive et inéluctable des faits. L'oreille est conditionnée à certains discours. On continue de les écouter, d'abord par routine, ensuite par conformisme (des ouvriers ignorants auraient eu mauvaise grâce à protester quand le consensus des notables était unanime) enfin par distraction. Mais à mesure que la conscience ouvrière évacuait les schèmes de pensée traditionnels, d'autres préoccupations et d'autres inquiétudes venaient combler les vides.

C'est ici que s'amorce la double désillusion dont j'ai parlé au début du présent chapitre.

Désillusion d'abord devant une idéologie en pleine déroute. Inquiétude profonde (longtemps inconsciente) de sentir que les « mots d'ordre nationaux » s'ajustaient mal aux problèmes de la nouvelle condition ouvrière, si mal en vérité que « l'élite » renonçait à les propager en milieu ouvrier, prenant pour acquis qu'ils n'y seraient pas entendus. L'Association catholique de la Jeunesse canadienne-française donne un probant exemple de cette démission. Pendant vingt-cinq ans, cette association occupe le territoire presque entier des préoccupations de jeunesse, étant le seul mouvement d'éducation nationale. Elle allie typiquement, fidèle incarnation de notre idéologie, action religieuse et action temporelle, c'est-à-dire nationale. Elle a l'ambition d'assumer tous les problèmes de la jeunesse citadine. Or, elle n'a jamais compté dans ses rangs qu'une infime minorité d'ouvriers d'usine. Tous ses efforts étaient misés sur les collégiens et les étudiants universitaires.

Et ce n'est là qu'une manifestation, du reste assez bénigne, d'un esprit très général. Le milieu ouvrier, en quittant les campagnes, avait comme glissé subitement hors des préoccupations de la communauté. On songeait à lui pour le plaindre assez platoniquement, pour citer l'exemple de sa déchéance et faire valoir par contraste la dignité du cultivateur « roi de son domaine et maître de lui-même ». Mais on ne songeait guère à l'aider, à prendre en charge ses problèmes, à connaître sa condition. La politique restait agricole. Plus près des humbles, l'Eglise suivait à la ville ses fidèles, mais sans que le clergé comprît très clairement ce qui se passait. Personne n'imaginait possible la formation d'une élite ouvrière, hors quelques songe-creux dont il sera bientôt question.

Cette démission de la communauté se manifeste clairement dès les premières tentatives d'organisation syndicale. Celles-ci, comme on le devine sans peine, ne furent pas d'origine autochtone. Circonstance inévitable, mais qui aggravait encore l'équivoque dont nous avons parlé, les premiers organisateurs ouvriers nous vinrent d'outre-frontière. Quand il arriva au Canada français, le syndicalisme, lui aussi, parlait anglais.

Ce n'est pas là, pourtant, qu'il faut rechercher la raison principale de ses maigres succès. Sans doute les Canadiens français se trouvèrent-ils dépaysés, au premier abord, dans ces organisations américaines. Sans doute, le caractère « étranger » de la Fédération américaine (F.A.T.) ou des Chevaliers du Travail devait-il rebuter beaucoup de travailleurs. Il faut peut-être attribuer à ce dépaysement la pauvreté du *leadership* ouvrier canadien-français des débuts du siècle.

Mais quand on trouve par ailleurs au Québec, 16,000 membres chez les Chevaliers et des douzaines de locaux de la F.A.T. vers l'année 1900, c'est l'afflux des travailleurs dans des cadres aussi mal adaptés qui nous étonne. Le divorce du milieu ouvrier d'avec la communauté canadienne-française dans son ensemble se manifestait déjà.

Il faut souligner en effet que notre « élite » et notre paysannerie se trouvaient en accord profond pour répudier toute forme de syndicalisme. Entre 1875 et 1925, il se développe chez nous toute une littérature anti-syndicale d'un rare conservatisme. On croirait, à lire les dénonciations dirigées contre les unions ouvrières, que le pays se trouvait au bord de l'anarchie. En milieu canadien-français, cette réaction devait se nourrir d'abord de tous les arguments nationalistes imaginables. On dénonçait les « agitateurs étrangers », les « idées subversives importées d'ailleurs »; on adjurait les « braves ouvriers canadiens-français » de ne pas suivre ces mauvais bergers « qui ne partagent pas notre foi et ne parlent pas notre langue ». Mais le conservatisme ne tarda pas à montrer l'oreille : quand naquirent, à compter de 1902, les premiers syndicats confessionnels, seule une minorité de clairvoyants en acceptèrent le principe. Pour les cultivateurs et la majorité de l'élite (en dépit des positions fort modérées de ces nouveaux groupes) les syndicats chrétiens constituaient un scandale à peine moins irritant que les unions « anglaises ».

Comment expliquer un refus aussi net dans une communauté aussi pauvre, aussi inapte au capitalisme que l'était alors le groupe canadien-français ?

Plusieurs facteurs poussaient dans le sens de la réaction. Au premier rang, l'autoritarisme et l'individualisme traditionnels. On n'admettait pas qu'un employeur, même anglais, dût accepter de discuter d'égal à égal avec ses employés (ses inférieurs) alors qu'il était propriétaire de son usine. Le sens de l'ordre prenait le pas sur le sens national.

Sans doute aussi trouverions-nous chez les « notables » du temps la crainte de voir leur autorité compromise par l'émergence de l'organisation ouvrière. Ces notables (médecins, notaires, avocats et marchands), seule minorité instruite en dehors du clergé, formaient alors une petite oligarchie imbue de ses privilèges et persuadée de sa qualité d'élite. L'époque était celle des notables et de leur règne indiscuté. C'est sur eux que l'on comptait alors pour assurer notre salut et notre survivance; l'intrusion de la force ouvrière les dérangeait trop pour qu'ils n'en sentissent pas la menace à longue portée, pour qu'elle n'éveillât pas en eux l'instinct de conservation.

Il faut souligner aussi le rôle du patronat canadien-français. Si restreint que fût celui-ci et en dépit du rôle insignifiant qu'il jouait dans l'expansion industrielle, il n'en avait pas moins l'oreille des notables, voire celle des clercs. Beaucoup plus efficacement que les travailleurs, il influençait l'opinion publique et la pensée officielle canadiennes-françaises. Cette influence joua à bloc dans le sens de la réaction, du conservatisme le plus aveugle. Engagés pour la plupart dans des entreprises marginales, les employeurs canadiens-français, pour défendre leur existence même, devaient se montrer plus mesquins et plus durs encore que les puissants exploiteurs d'origine anglaise ou américaine. Plus d'une fois, ce sont eux qui, craignant de voir s'élever le niveau des salaires, exhortèrent les grandes compagnies à ne pas dépasser les taux établis dans telle ou telle région, conseil que les employeurs richissimes devaient suivre avec une rare ferveur...

Quant au clergé, en dépit de lenteurs irritantes et souvent lourdes de conséquences désastreuses, il devait évoluer pourtant à meilleure allure que les notables. D'abord braqués contre les syndicats américains, à la fois neutres (c'est-à-dire non-confessionnels) et étrangers, les clercs et l'épiscopat firent longtemps figure d'anti-syndicaux convaincus. Pour eux aussi, la plupart des organisateurs syndicaux prenaient figure de dangereux agitateurs. Et quand des tendances radicales se firent jour dans certains secteurs du syndicalisme américain et dans l'ouest canadien, quand surtout les affiliés montréalais de la F.A.T. se prononcèrent, vers 1900, en faveur d'une réforme de l'enseignement au Québec, l'hostilité cléricale s'intensifia dangereusement.

Mais dans l'Eglise, un autre courant prenait forme. En 1891, le Pape

Léon XIII dans sa lettre encyclique *Rerum novarum*, avait endossé clairement le principe du syndicalisme et fait à tous les chrétiens un devoir de hâter la constitution d'une force ouvrière. A travers la broussaille des intérêts et des préjugés, cette impulsion ne pouvait cheminer qu'avec lenteur. Quand elle finirait pourtant par atteindre ici la majorité des Catholiques et de leurs pasteurs, beaucoup d'attitudes en seraient profondément modifiées.

Mais nous n'en étions pas encore là quand, à côté des succursales du syndicalisme américain, le syndicalisme chrétien prit naissance au Québec. Seuls quelques évêques et quelques prêtres plus éclairés en comprenaient l'importance. Encore devaient-ils soumettre ces syndicats naissants à de telles tutelles ecclésiastiques et leur imposer une modération si timorée qu'on se demande aujourd'hui comment ils ont pu survivre. Mais à l'époque, ni cette tutelle abusive ni cette modération exagérée n'étaient suffisantes pour rendre acceptable à la majorité des clercs un syndicalisme pourtant catholique et canadien-français...

A quelle date doit-on situer le second aspect de la désillusion ouvrière canadienne-française ? Si je risquais d'en citer une, je la choisirais quelque part entre 1910 et 1920, probablement au début de la première guerre mondiale. A ce moment-là, une conscience ouvrière a déjà pris naissance. Un peu partout, des militants se sont mis à réfléchir. Ils se rendent compte que la communauté canadienne-française ne comprend pas grand'chose aux problèmes des travailleurs, qu'elle refuse la plupart des solutions que les ouvriers eux-mêmes tentent d'y apporter et soutient des gouvernements pour qui, dans le domaine industriel, seuls comptent les grandes corporations et leurs chefs anglophones ou les patrons de langue française.

A ces militants, deux chemins sont ouverts, deux outils sont offerts, mais tous deux inadéquats.

L'histoire du syndicalisme américain au Québec, si un jour on peut l'écrire en détail, étalera un bien curieux mélange du luttes et de compromis, de clairvoyance et de confusion, de résolution et d'incohérence. Reconnaissons tout de suite à la F.A.T. comme aux Chevaliers du Travail l'indiscutable mérite d'être venus chez nous au secours des travailleurs et d'avoir hâté de vingt, peut-être même de trente ans, l'accession au syndicalisme de notre population ouvrière.

Que cela ne nous aveugle pas toutefois sur l'inadaptation grave de ces organisations à nos particularités culturelles ni sur l'impérialisme latent qui caractérisait leur action. Le syndicalisme américain (comme d'ailleurs plusieurs syndicats « nationaux » d'origine ontarienne) a toujours considéré la culture française des ouvriers québécois comme un problème, un obstacle à la communication efficace de l'esprit syndical et pour tout dire un embarras. Jamais il ne leur est venu à l'esprit que le caractère français des travailleurs québécois pût être mis à contribution comme un enrichessement pour l'ensemble du mouvement ouvrier. La branche québécoise des « internationales » américaines devait *suivre* de son mieux le reste de la F.A.T., qui ne chercha jamais à s'adapter, si peu que ce soit. Aujourd'hui encore on trouve à Montréal, à la tête de syndicats ouvriers presque exclusivement canadien-français, des représentants qui n'ont jamais appris notre langue ni même adopté la nationalité canadienne après vingt ans de séjour ! Le plus grave de cette histoire c'est l'incapacité où se trouvent ces dirigeants de comprendre en profondeur les aspirations, les besoins et les ressources des ouvriers qu'ils représentent. Mal à l'aise dans un milieu où ils séjournent sans le connaître, leur confiance dans l'esprit militant de leurs membres reste limitée. On les voit souvent paralyser par leur ignorance les syndicats mêmes qu'ils jugent « peu évolués » mais dont l'évolution est précisément bloquée par leur présence encombrante. Ce sont les gens qui vous diront par exemple : « Au Québec, l'action politique du syndicalisme est impossible». Mais grattez un peu et vous découvrirez qu'ils sont les premiers à l'empêcher, effrayés des risques qu'elle présente pour eux, à cause de leur ignorance du milieu. Il en résulte trop souvent des attitudes timorées qu'ils font d'ailleurs partager à leurs associés canadiens-français, ces derniers étant soigneusement choisis pour leurs qualités de soumission et de prudent conformisme.

Qu'en tel milieu le militant de langue française ne se soit pas toujours senti à l'aise, personne ne s'en étonnera. Avant la traduction simultanée, initiative toute récente au Congrès du Travail du Canada, la connaissance de l'anglais primait toute autre considération quand il s'agissait de déléguer des représentants, ce qui n'amenait pas toujours aux congrès annuels les meilleurs militants. De même, la F.A.T. fut de loin le groupe le plus retardataire en matière d'éducation ce qui explique la pauvreté de son *leadership* québécois.

D'où une certaine incohérence dans l'action : campagnes d'organisation aussi brusquement interrompues qu'entreprises : promesses non tenues : capitulations subites et inexplicables, toutes misères bien connues de tous les syndicalismes mais qu'on ne prenait pas toujours la peine d'expliquer aux intéressés, avec comme résultats la conviction chez ces derniers qu'on les « manipulait ».

Or, pour des raisons différentes, l'autre route ouverte aux ouvriers, celle des syndicats chrétiens, ne conduisait pas plus directement aux objectifs désirés. Car si la C.T.C.C. connaissait davantage le milieu, si l'atmosphère y était plus accueillante et plus familière, on y souffrait par ailleurs, à l'époque dont nous parlons, d'inhibitions tout aussi paralysantes quand elles ne l'étaient pas davantage.

Je ne voudrais pas attribuer au seul moralisme clérical l'impuissance des premiers syndicats chrétiens au plan de l'action. Il faut concéder à leur décharge qu'ils démarrèrent avec trente ans de retard sur la F.A.T., qu'ils ne pouvaient compter que sur les seules ressources humaines du milieu local et qu'ils n'avaient pas à l'origine le prestige du nombre ni l'appui financier d'un groupe comme la F.A.T. Il reste pourtant que beaucoup de prêtres mêlés au mouvement avaient tendance à en faire d'inoffensifs cercles d'études et que les aumôniers y exercèrent à l'origine une autorité gauche et abusive. Un seul exemple : l'unanimité des clercs à empêcher la constitution d'un fonds de grève lors de la fondation de la C.T.C.C., sous prétexte qu'un tel fonds « inciterait au désordre social ». Privé de moyens, modéré par une timidité déguisée en morale, le syndicalisme chrétien constitua longtemps une illusion sur le plan de l'action concrète.

Le travailleur de l'époque se trouvait donc alors, en milieu canadien français, acculé à un choix pénible : ou bien donner son allégeance à un syndicalisme où sa part était celle du parent pauvre; ou bien jeter son dévolu sur un syndicalisme mieux adapté à sa mentalité mais peu capable d'améliorer sa condition économique.

On se souviendra aussi des luttes violentes où se trouvèrent engagés ces deux groupements dès la naissance du second; division profonde, hostilité rageuse, rivalités qui, dans certains secteurs, n'ont jamais désarmé depuis.

• • •

Ce n'est pourtant pas sur cette note pessimiste qu'il faut terminer notre article. Au contraire, ce sont les chances nouvelles de l'unité ouvrière, au Québec comme au Canada, qui caractérisent notre temps. Les quinze dernières années ont en effet marqué un rapprochement sensible des principaux groupes syndicaux à l'intérieur du Québec et de meilleures relations entre la masse ouvrière canadienne-française et l'ensemble des travailleurs canadiens.

Au Canada français, le choc de la dernière guerre a ouvert tous les yeux. Tandis que la C.T.C.C. manifestait subitement une combativité et une maturité nouvelles, désormais pourvue de dirigeants laïcs compétents et de services adéquats dans les domaines de la recherche et de l'organisation, les autres groupes syndicaux « découvraient » de leur côté la réalité ouvrière canadienne-française. Longtemps convaincus qu'il n'existait pas au Québec d'interlocuteurs valables en matière syndicale, ils revisaient désormais leurs positions à la lumière de quelques luttes où les syndiqués canadiens-français avaient montré un esprit militant rarement égalé au Canada.

C'est à ce point que nous en sommes aujourd'hui. Des animosités subsistent : des incompréhensions et des ignorances font encore obstacle à l'unité. Mais le courant semble porter dans la bonne direction...

Les travailleurs canadiens-français ont imposé à la communauté canadienne-française, au syndicalisme majoritaire et à l'ensemble de la nation canadienne, la reconnaissance de leur importance. Le dialogue est engagé, chaque groupe tendant l'oreille. Il n'est pas vain d'espérer qu'ils se comprendront bientôt !

1959

Labour Unity in Quebec

STUART JAMIESON

Department of Economics and Political Science, University of British Columbia

IT IS AN ACCEPTED AXIOM of social scientists that among the most fruitful situations for studying human behaviour, particularly in its collective aspects, are those in which the people of two distinct cultures come into close and continuous contact. The province of Quebec is one of the most interesting laboratories of this kind, for in it a French-speaking and Catholic culture, protected by constitutional guarantees and various legal and political arrangements, has survived and grown in the midst of an overwhelmingly English-speaking and Protestant continent.

Forces from outside that appear to threaten the unity and survival of French Canada evoke defensive attitudes and collective action of a kind that has been loosely termed "nationalistic." The Roman Catholic Church, by far the most important or influential single institution in Quebec, has played a key role in this regard. For it has been a basic tenet of Catholic social doctrine in that province that the maintenance of the French language, the Catholic faith, and the distinct culture of French Canada are mutually dependent. The Church has been the main source of inspiration and leadership in a wide variety of more or less exclusively French-speaking and Catholic organizations, both sacred and secular, that have been formed at one time or another to combat "alien" influences. Its doctrines and policies in Quebec are not fixed and immutable, however. They have undergone substantial change in recent years.

Organizations from English-speaking Canada or the United States that seek to extend into Quebec face special problems, and in trying to solve them they acquire unique characters and structures. For, in attempting to compete, co-operate, or amalgamate with exclusively French-speaking and Catholic organizations, they have to make special concessions, devise special means of communication, and develop special systems of administration in which both major ethnic groups are represented at strategic levels.

Trade unionism presents an outstanding example of this kind. For in Quebec during the past half-century or more there have been not only branches of the main trade unions of the United States and English-speaking Canada, most of which now belong to the Canadian Labour Congress (C.L.C.), but also indigenous French-speaking Catholic unions belonging to the Confédération des Travailleurs catholiques du Canada, or Canadian and Catholic Confederation of Labour (C.T.C.C.). Affiliates of the two groups were in almost continual conflict until fairly recently. During 1956–7, however, delegates of both groups at their respective conventions voted overwhelmingly in favour of affiliation, and representative committees from each have been seeking means of bringing this about. There are numerous difficulties to be faced, however. As these arise primarily from the special background and character of the Catholic Confederation of Labour, most of the analysis that follows will be concerned with that organization.

The C.T.C.C. is unique in the annals of organized labour on this continent, for it is only in Quebec that the Church actively sponsored and organized exclusively Catholic trade unions, while vigorously opposing the so-called international unions of the American Federation of Labor (A.F.L.) and the Congress of Industrial Organizations (C.I.O.) and their respective affiliates in Canada—the Trades and Labor Congress (T.L.C.) and the Canadian Congress of Labour (C.C.L.), which in 1956 merged into the Canadian Labour Congress (C.L.C.). The main authority that the Quebec hierarchy offered as justification for this policy was Pope Leo XIII's encyclical, *Rerum novarum*, of 1891. That statement, however, did not lay down detailed and specific directives. It enunciated broad principles, such as labour's "natural" right to organize into unions, and the "natural" harmony of interests between workers and employers—principles that were open to widely varying interpretations in different countries. The Church's policy in Quebec was to be explained primarily on ethnic or nationalistic rather than religious grounds, to the degree that these could be distinguished realistically in that province.

The major factors underlying the special viewpoint and policy of the Church in Quebec have been analysed in a number of studies by Everett C. Hughes, Mason Wade, and others.[1] Rapid and large-scale industrialization during the twentieth century wrought major transformations in the economic and social structure of French Canada.

[1]Everett C. Hughes, *French Canada in Transition* (Chicago: University of Chicago Press, 1943); Mason Wade, *The French Canadians, 1760–1945* (Toronto: Macmillan, 1955).

Quebec changed from a predominantly rural into one of the most highly urbanized provinces in Canada within hardly more than a generation. Industrialization represented, in a sense, a process of *invasion* of predominantly French-speaking and Catholic Quebec by a culturally alien English-speaking and mainly Protestant minority—American and British as well as Canadian—armed with large amounts of capital, modern techniques, and specially trained personnel. Members of this group became dominant in the higher-paid managerial or executive, professional, and technical positions in the new industrial system, while French Canadians were brought into the structure largely as unskilled, semi-skilled, and, to a lesser extent, skilled and minor supervisory workers.

Trade unionism as one important by-product of industrialization also represented a process of invasion of French Canada, in a sense. The main centres of control and decision-making of most unions in Quebec, as of most corporations, have been outside that province, in the hands of predominantly English-speaking executives and members. The Church and many prominent laymen in Quebec, therefore, tended to look upon industrialization, urbanization, and unionization alike as alien forces that threatened the unity and survival of French Canada. For, in an economic system dominated by outside capital and English-speaking personnel, the main avenues for seeking material advancement, whether as "career men" rising in the main business or professional hierarchies, or as wage earners joining trade unions, seemed in danger of inducing French Canadians to forsake their traditional language and faith.

The Church had a more specific reason, perhaps, for opposing the so-called international unions in Quebec. Historically, its special status in that province had rested to a large degree on the fact that the clergy, along with political leaders drawn mainly from a small professional élite, had been the main intermediaries, not only between social classes in French Canada, but also between French-speaking and English-speaking Canadians. Up to the twentieth century the two language groups had been spatially and socially separated for the most part, and relations between them had been essentially formal and diplomatic. In the new industrial system, however, their relations became direct and symbiotic. Trade unions constituted a potentially new source of power, inspired and controlled from outside, that threatened to take over both intermediary functions simultaneously. The Church's answer to this threat was to encourage, and sometimes coerce, French-Canadian workers to join exclusively French-speaking and Catholic unions controlled largely by the clergy.

The history of the Catholic labour movement in Quebec, from the first local *syndicats* and study clubs in the early 1900's to the formation and growth of the C.T.C.C. in the 1920's and after, has been documented in some detail by A. B. Latham, H. A. Logan, and others.[2] No attempt will be made here to summarize their findings, other than to comment on some of the more controversial aspects of Catholic trade unionism.

The Church's labour policy in Quebec up to and including the Second World War has been criticized on a number of grounds. Catholic syndicates have been pictured as essentially artificial organizations that were imposed on French-Canadian workers to exploit nationalistic sentiments, rather than as bona fide unions that were organized to meet the real and pressing needs of industrial workers. The results achieved by the syndicates, after several decades of intensive effort, seemed mostly negative; they prevented international unions from organizing effectively in Quebec, but they apparently had little to show on their own account prior to the Second World War. Their total membership did not exceed 45,000 until the later 1930's, and the proportion they claimed of all organized workers in the province was only 30–40 per cent at the most.[3] This small minority was poorly distributed in terms of bargaining power. Catholic unionism owed what limited success it did have in previous decades largely to the special status and close personal contacts that the clergy had with their parishioners in the smaller, predominantly French-Canadian towns. It was not suited to the large-scale, impersonal, and heterogeneous environment of a metropolis such as Montreal. The ineffectiveness of the clergy in this regard is reminiscent of Gertrude Stein's classic observation about Ezra Pound: "He was a village explainer, excellent if you were a village, but if you were not, not." Thus throughout its history less than one-quarter of the Catholic Confederation's locals and members have been in the key Montreal area. Most of its affiliates were scattered in the more marginal firms or industries in Quebec City and numerous less important industrial centres. The movement's organizational structure, furthermore, was weak and decentralized. Most local syndicates lacked the resources and personnel to be effective bargaining agents. But, as autonomous legal entities under the control of local clergy, they were virtually a law unto themselves. The various trade and industry "federations" that were

[2]A. B. Latham, *The Catholic and National Unions of Canada* (Toronto: Macmillan, 1930); H. A. Logan, *Trade Unions in Canada* (Toronto: Macmillan, 1948).

[3]Canada, Dept. of Labour, annual reports, *Labour Organization in Canada*, 1921–56.

organized later, lacked the strike funds and disciplinary powers to co-ordinate local syndicates effectively.

The organizational and bargaining tactics of the Catholic syndicates furnished special grounds for criticism. Their weakness of organization and their control by members of the clergy, whose traditional role was that of peacemaker in the community, led them for many years to acquiesce in a policy of subservience to employers. This was also a matter of deliberate strategy in many cases. To head off the threat of organized campaigns or strikes by other unions, local priests and employers on many occasions negotiated personal "deals" that enrolled workers in Catholic syndicates regardless of their own wishes. Spokesmen of the international unions continually denounced the syndicates for "scabbing," "strike-breaking," and "selling out to employers."[4] Even some prominent members of the clergy who were actively associated with the Catholic labour movement now concede that in former years many of its affiliates were essentially "company unions."[5]

Although most of these allegations about Catholic unionism are undoubtedly true, some of the more widely accepted conclusions regarding its total impact on organized labour in Quebec should perhaps be modified. In the first place, it is not entirely valid to brand the early Catholic syndicates as "artificial" or "phony" unions merely because they were organized and dominated by the clergy rather than by bona fide wage earners or professional trade unionists. In the early stages of unionism in newly industrialized regions labour often looks to other classes for leadership. History is replete with examples of effective and militant labour movements in Europe and Asia that were first organized by intellectuals, professional men, and others. The *curés* in many Quebec communities were traditionally looked upon as the "natural" leaders who were expected to initiate and direct new organizational ventures. A large part of the Church's strength and influence in Quebec, particularly in small towns and rural communities, has lain in the fact that its clergy have been recruited mainly from farm and lower middle-class families. In many newly industrialized communities the local clergy came from essentially the same backgrounds as the workers and members of the syndicates that they helped organize. And, as exclusively Catholic and French-speaking organizations under the leadership of supervision of local clerics, as Everett Hughes[6] brought out in his study, the syndicates were often an

[4]Logan, *Trade Unions in Canada.*

[5]Le R.P. Cousineau, s.j., "Commentaires" dans Jean-C. Falardeau, éd., *Essais sur le Québec contemporain* (Québec: Presses Universitaires Laval, 1953), p. 212.

[6]*French Canada in Transition.*

integral part of a rich and varied French-Canadian institutional life that could be an important element of support and strength in a crisis.

Again, a second look perhaps needs to be taken at the widely held conclusion that the Church's efforts to organize a separate French-speaking Catholic movement retarded the cause of trade unionism as a whole in Quebec. The clergy did undoubtedly prevent international unions from organizing in many areas in the province. On the other hand, there are also good grounds for arguing that Catholic unions managed to become established in many communities and plants in which international unions could not have won a foothold in any case prior to the Second World War. Until fairly recently, Quebec in many respects resembled the Old South more than it did Ontario or the industrial middle western states. It was a relatively over-populated, low-wage region specializing in the more marginal types of industries, culturally insular or separatist in viewpoint, and intensely hostile to trade unionism or other social movements inspired from outside. There was no legislation protecting labour's right to organize or compelling employers to recognize and bargain with unions. In the face of similar obstacles the American Federation of Labor and its affiliates had failed in several attempts to organize major industries in the southern states prior to the Second World War, and in all likelihood their Canadian counterparts would likewise have failed in Quebec even had there been no separate Catholic labour movement to contend with. The latter had certain special advantages in its favour. Against the prevailing anti-union "open shop" ideology of major business enterprises, the papal encyclicals did proclaim the natural right of labour to organize and bargain collectively. In view of the Church's power and influence in Quebec, the doctrine of natural right enabled the clergy in many cases to exert moral and social pressure on employers, English-speaking and Protestant or Jewish as well as French-speaking and Catholic, to recognize and bargain with Catholic syndicates. Often these were hardly more than company unions, as pointed out. Nevertheless, they did give previously unorganized workers the taste or experience, at least, of being organized, negotiating with employers, and developing some sort of articulate leadership. In the Catholic Confederation, as in the C.I.O. during the later 1930's, a number of affiliates that had begun as company unions subsequently became militant and effective bargaining organizations.

Finally, the relatively small size and apparently weak, decentralized structure of the Catholic labour movement in Quebec were not, and still are not, entirely accurate indices of its real strength or significance, for its main role in earlier decades was primarily defensive rather than offensive. The main objective of the lay and clerical organizers of Catholic unions was to keep French-Canadian workers loyal to their language and faith, rather than to enrol as many dues-paying members as possible. Hence, as compared to other labour movements, the Catholic Confederation devoted far more time, money, and personnel to education or indoctrination than to organization as such—an intensive rather than extensive cultivation of labour, so to speak. This policy did pay dividends in one important respect, and continues to do so. Considering its limited size, organizational weaknesses, and marginal positions in the economy, the Catholic labour movement in Quebec proved to have remarkable staying power and unity of purpose. During and after the Second World War it survived many long and costly strikes, and held its own against several large and well-financed organizing campaigns directed against it by other unions.

The great depression of the 1930's, followed by the Second World War, wrought drastic and permanent changes in the Catholic Confederation. Economic nationalism and ethnic tensions between the English and the French in the province of Quebec were brought into sharp relief. The English-speaking minority, concentrated in the more secure and better-paid executive, professional, and salaried positions, were to a large extent insulated from the depression. Its main burden fell on the masses of French-Canadian wage earners and small proprietors. The dominant role that English-Canadian or American-owned and managed corporations had played in Quebec's rapid industrialization during the 1920's made them a special target of attack by lay and clerical spokesmen of various nationalist organizations.[7]

Intense economic nationalism temporarily imbued the Catholic Confederation with a new strength and militancy. During the recovery of the later 1930's it expanded rapidly in hitherto unorganized industries such as textiles, asbestos mining and smelting, aluminum, iron and steel, and shipbuilding. Several of its affiliates became involved in long and bitter strikes, particularly in the textile and shipbuilding industries. These were accompanied by scattered but highly publicized incidents of property damage and violence.[8]

[7] *Ibid.*, pp. 212–19; Wade, *The French Canadians*, pp. 902–3.

[8] During a series of textile strikes in 1937, for instance, numerous plants were attacked by mobs of strikers, and violent clashes broke out with the police. Stones were thrown through the windows of some English-speaking executives' homes. The American manager of a silk mill in one town was kidnapped while playing golf, driven across the American border, and told to stay in his own country. An

These developments coincided with, and undoubtedly were influenced by, the new and dramatic upsurge of industrial unionism under the leadership of the newly formed C.I.O. Much of the violence and disorder could be attributed to the inexperience of hitherto unorganized workers and the weak and decentralized structure of the Catholic Confederation. Such conditions made it difficult for the leaders to hold the members in line once industrial relations had reached the stage of overt conflict. The violence and disorder, however, also brought out a basic contradiction in Catholic unionism that presented a serious dilemma to its leaders and to the Church itself in Quebec. Catholic unions, in principle, based their policies on *Rerum novarum* and on later encyclicals that counselled harmony and co-operation between workers and employers, and the avoidance of strikes and class conflict. An important force behind the new growth and militancy of Catholic unionism in Quebec, however, was the intense nationalism which members of the clergy, among others, had been instrumental in arousing. It tended to reach violent proportions among low-paid and hitherto docile French-Canadian workers in mass production industries. The hardships of the depression had engendered widespread unrest and smouldering resentment against employers. These feelings were intensified where employers were culturally alien and English-speaking. Adding to the tension and hostility was the stubborn open shop policy of a number of prominent employers, who refused to recognize and bargain with *any* unions, even those as conciliatory as the Catholic syndicates had been.[9]

The Church finally felt compelled to resist the mounting tide of ethnic and class conflict. Several strikes were settled by informal negotiation between representatives of the Church, the employers, and the provincial government, without consulting the workers involved. This policy aroused a good deal of latent anti-clerical sentiment among French-Canadian workers, and greatly weakened the Catholic labour movement for several years.[10]

---

inkpot was thrown in the face of the President of the Dominion Textile Company when he visited a plant that was on strike. (See *Montreal Gazette*, Aug. 20, 21, 22, and 23, 1937; Hughes, *French Canada in Transition*, pp. 212–13.) Again, during a shipyard strike in Sorel, two fires of suspected incendiary origin threatened the home of a prominent employer (*Montreal Gazette*, Aug. 25, 1937, p. 11).

[9]See, for instance, statement by Blair Gordon, President of Dominion Textile Company, as reported in *Montreal Gazette*, Aug. 23, 1937, p. 11.

[10]The turning point came in the bitter and violent four-week strike of the National Syndicate of Textile Workers against the Dominion Textile Company during the summer of 1937. Cardinal Villeneuve intervened to end the strike on

The Second World War brought unprecedented industrial expansion and a new surge of French-Canadian "nationalism" to Quebec. The C.T.C.C. was revived and strengthened by this double stimulus, but came into sharper and more frequent conflict with other groups. Catholic syndicates consolidated their position in a number of rapidly growing industries of major wartime importance, such as aluminum, chemicals, and asbestos. They became involved in intense and at times violent conflict with affiliates of the T.L.C. and the C.C.L. in these and other industries, such as textiles and pulp and paper. Spokesmen of the C.T.C.C. repeatedly charged that the federal government and prominent English-speaking employers connived with international unions and discriminated against the Catholic syndicates because of their lukewarm attitude to Canada's participation in the war.[11] The provincial Government and a number of leading industrial concerns, on the other hand, tended to discriminate against T.L.C. and C.C.L. unions in favour of Catholic syndicates. The Church continued to support the C.T.C.C., and prominent members of the clergy attacked international unionism in the strongest terms.[12]

A number of major developments during and after the war, however, brought about substantial and permanent changes in the Church's labour policy in Quebec, and in the character of the Canadian and Catholic Confederation. These prepared the way for closer co-operation and ultimately, perhaps, affiliation with the other main labour bodies. Industrialization and urbanization proceeded at an accelerated

---

the grounds that, as he put it, it "constitutes an entirely dangerous state of affairs for the public peace" (*Montreal Gazette*, Aug. 28, 1937, p. 1). He prevailed on the strikers to return to work on the promise of the company to negotiate an agreement within three months. The result was disastrous to the National Syndicate. The agreement, signed without the consent of the membership, established minimum rates of only 18 cents an hour, and raised hourly rates by only 4 per cent. The union, which had more than 13,000 members at its peak in 1937, declined to only 642 by 1940. (See Gilles Groulx, "Le Syndicalisme dans l'industrie textile du Québec," M.A. thesis, Université de Montréal, 1954, p. 78.) Similar tactics were used to settle a strike of clothing workers in Montreal. (See Eugene Forsey, "Clerical Fascism in Quebec," *Canadian Forum*, vol. XVII (June 1937), pp. 90–2.)

[11]See, for instance, speeches of F. Charpentier, President of the C.T.C.C., at the 1942 and 1943 conventions, as reported in *Labour Gazette*, Oct., 1942, p. 1228, and Oct., 1943, pp. 1452–3.

[12]The auxiliary bishop of Rimouski, Mgr C. E. Parent, for instance, addressed a meeting of Catholic syndicates in the following words: ". . . Have nothing to do with neutral unions, albeit they have made gains in the great cities. Communism glides in their shadows like a snake. . . . Such unions stir up the workers against the employer, against religion, and against the clergy." (Wade, *The French Canadians*, p. 1019.)

pace in the province.[13] Improved transportation and communications greatly increased the mobility of French Canadians and broke down much of the local isolation that had hitherto characterized many Quebec communities. Large-scale organizing campaigns by international unions in strongholds of the Catholic Confederation forced the syndicates to become more militant and effective bargaining agents for their members, and to open their ranks to other than just French-speaking and Catholic workers. New federal and provincial labour legislation provided further pressure in these directions. Finally, the social doctrine and policy of the Church in Quebec moved away from "clerical nationalism" to advocate co-operation between French-speaking and English-speaking organizations having common interests. The clergy withdrew from positions of direct control in trade unions and other secular bodies. A new group of young, technically or professionally trained and aggressive lay leaders, several of whom were graduates of the new Ecole des Sciences sociales at Université Laval, rose to top positions in the C.T.C.C. and its major affiliates shortly after the war.

The Catholic labour movement rapidly lost its separatist character in the course of these developments. Jurisdictional disputes with international unions declined in frequency and bitterness. The C.T.C.C., supported by the C.C.L. and to a much lesser extent by the T.L.C., took the lead in opposing provincial legislation that was considered dangerous to organized labour in Quebec.[14] In so doing, however, it came into increasing disfavour in official circles. Paradoxically the C.T.C.C., which hitherto had been an outstanding symbol of French-Canadian nationalism, now became one of the most vociferous opponents and a major target of attack of the supposedly nationalistic Duplessis régime.

The critical turning point in the post-war development of the Catholic labour movement—or even of the social history of Quebec itself, in the view of some observers[15]—came in the spectacular strike of asbestos workers in 1949. It signified, in the words of Jean-C. Falardeau, "the significant *rite de passage* of the Catholic syndicates

[13]Employment in manufacturing in Quebec, for instance, almost doubled from 1941 to 1951, while the urban population increased by more than 30 per cent.

[14]Indeed, from 1950 on, the Quebec Federation of Labour (an affiliate of the T.L.C.) increasingly supported the provincial Government, in opposition to the Quebec Federation of Industrial Unions (an affiliate of the C.C.L.) and the C.T.C.C.

[15]Pierre-E. Trudeau, comp., *La Grève de l'amiante* (Montréal: Editions Cité Libre, 1956).

to adulthood and to maturity."[16] This bitter and prolonged struggle brought forth the unusual spectacle of the Church's openly supporting the union against the employers and the provincial Government, after the Minister of Labour had officially declared the strike illegal and the Labour Relations Board had decertified the union. The dispute was finally settled after four months through the mediation of Mgr Maurice Roy, Archbishop of Quebec.[17]

Victory in this long and highly publicized struggle brought the Catholic Confederation new prestige and strength and, for a few years, rapid organizational gains. By 1953 it had reached a new membership peak of more than 100,000. That apparently represented the limits to its growth, however, as it declined in numbers subsequently. Attempts to establish a solid base of membership in manufacturing and heavy industry in the Montreal area brought Catholic syndicates into new and costly conflict, not only with employers but also with other unions, particularly affiliates of the Trades and Labor Congress. In the course of a strike of nine weeks' duration against the Vickers Shipyards in 1952, for instance, a prominent official of an international union that had separate jurisdiction in the plant[18] was seriously injured while attempting to go through a Catholic syndicate picket line. Ironically, Catholic unionism, which had been condemned formerly by spokesmen of A.F.L. unions for its excessive timidity and submissiveness, was now criticized for its excessive militancy and violence. A protest meeting sponsored by the Quebec Federation of Labour passed a resolution that "deplores and denounces the use of gangster methods on the part of the Catholic syndicates," and expressed amazement at "the alliance between Communist elements, professional gangsters, and the leaders of the Catholic syndicates in Montreal."[19] Similar difficulties have attended the C.T.C.C.'s attempts to expand its organizational base in other industries in which the international unions are established.

The main labour groups in Quebec have been at a virtual impasse for several years, and have been unable to carry out effective organizing campaigns among the vast majority of workers in the province who remain outside the unions. The main weaknesses of the Canadian and

[16]Falardeau, éd., *Essais sur le Québec contemporain*, p. 116.

[17]Trudeau, comp., *La Grève de l'amiante*, pp. 240–62.

[18]Spokesmen of the C.T.C.C. claimed that the A.F.L. union had managed to retain jurisdiction of its local in the Vickers plant only because of "illegal" decisions by the Labour Relations Board, favouring A.F.L.–T.L.C. unions as against Catholic syndicates.

[19]*Montreal Gazette*, Sept. 13, 1952, p. 15.

Catholic Confederation have been outlined before, and are made evident, as has already been noted, by the inability of this organization to win a firm foothold in the key metropolitan Montreal area, where they are opposed by the international unions. By the same token, however, certain weaknesses of the international unions are made just as apparent in the fact that, although they have dominated organized labour in the strategic Montreal area for many years, they have been unable to expand effectively into other Quebec communities in which the Catholic syndicates have been dominant.

The main limitation of the international unions in this regard is their inability, or perhaps unwillingness in some cases, to provide the special facilities and personnel that would be needed to bridge successfully the linguistic, religious, and other cultural differences between Quebec and English Canada or the United States. The problem of communication alone, between the national or international headquarters and the French-speaking membership in Quebec, is a formidable one that most international unions have failed to deal with adequately. To take the most elementary example: of some eighty national or international unions that have branches in Quebec, only twenty-two, or about one-quarter, put out special editions or sections of their trade union papers in French.[20] It is especially difficult, therefore, to develop among the French-speaking locals and members any strong sense of identification with their international unions, much less with the labour movement as a whole.

A fear of factionalism and disunity is also an important consideration among a number of international unions that have branches in Quebec. It arises from past difficulties with French-Canadian "nationalism" within their own ranks, and from conflict with the Church-supported Catholic syndicates. Often it leads them to choose their Quebec officials on the basis of their personal or institutional loyalty rather than their organizational abilities or their representativeness. There is a distinct tendency on the part of some unions to avoid having officials who are too French Canadian in character and viewpoint. In a number of organizations that have a predominantly French-speaking membership in Quebec, the higher officials at the district or provincial level speak English only. More often such officials are selected from the more Anglicized and bilingual type of French Canadian who is able to communicate and mix easily with English-speaking confrères at collective bargaining sessions and union council meetings or conventions. Such types, while probably most appropriate and effective in the

[20]*Labour Gazette*, 45th annual report, 1956, pp. 34–83.

predominantly bilingual and heterogeneous Montreal area, often are not representative of, or acceptable to, workers in predominantly French-speaking communities in other parts of Quebec.

Affiliation of the Catholic Confederation with the Canadian Labour Congress appears to offer the only prospect of a solution to the problems that face these organizations in Quebec. Delegates of both groups voted in favour of it, in principle, at their respective conventions in 1956. So did the delegates of the T.L.C.–Quebec Federation of Labour and the C.L.C.–Quebec Federation of Industrial Unions at their merger convention in 1957.[21] Not only would affiliation of the C.T.C.C. with the C.L.C. serve to break the present impasse; it would also combine the considerable assets of the two labour bodies. Affiliates of the Canadian Labour Congress, on the one hand, have vastly greater membership, resources, and bargaining power to put into a concerted organizing campaign. The Catholic Confederation and its affiliates, on the other hand, have a long-established and special status in many Quebec communities, and, perhaps more important, a large corps of unusually able and dynamic French-speaking executive and professional leaders who could make up for various deficiencies in policy and personnel among C.L.C. unions in that province.

A number of difficulties stand in the way of affiliation between the two groups, however. These may be considered, for purposes of analysis, from three broad but necessarily related aspects: the ideological or cultural; the organizational or structural; and the personal.

The ideological and cultural barriers, or their more formal and easily recognizable symbols at least, seem on the face of it to have disappeared. The clergy no longer dominate the Catholic Confederation or its affiliates, nor does the Church in Quebec continue to oppose international unions. The C.L.C. and its affiliates can no longer be looked upon as "alien" organizations that threaten the security of French Canada, for the President of the new Congress and two of its three Quebec vice-presidents are French-Canadian Catholics. So are the highest Canadian officials of more than a dozen international unions, as well as the vast majority of the local and provincial officers of practically all the C.L.C. unions in Quebec. The Canadian and Catholic Confederation of Labour likewise is no longer objectionable to other unions for the reasons that it once was. The stigma of clerical domination and company unionism has been removed, and the

[21]The merger of the Trades and Labor Congress and the Canadian Congress of Labour at the national level was the first move. It took several months for their subsidiary bodies to merge at the provincial and local level.

C.T.C.C. is generally looked upon as a bona fide progressive labour movement. And, in principle at least, it is no longer an exclusively Catholic and French-speaking organization.[22]

The cultural factor, albeit vague and amorphous, is still, however, a barrier to successful affiliation. A majority of the executive of the C.T.C.C. are opposed to affiliating unless their union can come in as an intact, autonomous unit. This is desired not only to preserve the distinct character and identity of the Catholic Confederation, but also to maintain its efficiency as an organization. In fact, if not in principle, the composition of the C.T.C.C. is almost entirely French-speaking and Catholic. A minority of spokesmen among unions in the C.L.C. express the fear that affiliation on this basis would introduce a divisive sentiment of French-Canadian nationalism that would stir up conflict among the unions and factional strife within the Congress.

The main problems involved in affiliation, however, are structural or organizational in character. In this regard the resolutions passed at conventions of both labour bodies are, as yet, hardly more than statements of good intentions. The Catholic Confederation is a much smaller organization than were the Trades and Labor Congress and the Canadian Congress of Labour before they merged into the Canadian Labour Congress in 1956. These federations consisted of hundreds of autonomous international, national, provincial, and local bodies. However, since the formation of the C.L.C., the affiliates of the C.T.C.C. have conflicted with those of the C.L.C. over jurisdiction in Quebec to a far greater degree than the affiliates of the T.L.C. and C.C.L. used to conflict in Canada as a whole. The two latter federations merged on the basis of an agreement that was designed to lead to their eventual disappearance as distinct entities. The negotiations conducted by the C.T.C.C., however, as noted before, have been aimed at *affiliation* rather than merger, in order to preserve its autonomy and separate identity, and this would tend to perpetuate divisions or conflicts in jurisdiction with C.L.C. unions in a number of industries and trades. An agreement for eventual merger that would eliminate these conflicts, which some C.L.C. spokesmen demand, would be exceedingly difficult to achieve.

There are important minorities in both organizations that are at best cool, and in some cases strongly opposed, to the proposed affiliation.

[22]The C.T.C.C.'s "Declaration of Principles," like that of the C.L.C., states that it ". . . does not admit discrimination based on language, nationality, race, sex or religion" (*What We Stand For*, Statement of Principles, Canadian and Catholic Confederation of Labour, Montreal, 1955, p. 4).

The whole issue becomes confused at this point, in a bewildering maze of conflicts between persons, between unions, and within unions, as well as ideological conflicts within and between both labour federations. It becomes exceedingly difficult to distinguish what might be called the institutional interest or consensus of each union from the personal interests and viewpoints of its various officials. Perhaps some sort of orderly classification and analysis of the main viewpoints could be made along the following lines.

First, paradoxical as it may seem, the most articulate opposition to acceptance of the C.T.C.C. in affiliation does not come from the predominantly English-speaking executives of the C.L.C. at the national or international level; they are, in a sense, a step removed from the immediate issues. The main opposition comes from various Quebec executives of certain international unions formerly affiliated with the A.F.L.–T.L.C., in such industries as printing and publishing, construction, textiles, and pulp and paper. These unions have had a long history of conflict with Catholic syndicates in many different communities, because the industries over which they claim jurisdiction are comparatively decentralized or scattered in operation in various centres throughout the province. Opposition to the Catholic Confederation also stems partly from the suspicion with which conservative "business" unionists tend to view younger, more aggressive and radical "industrial" unionists, a situation reminiscent of the original split between the A.F.L. and C.I.O. a generation ago. More specifically, there is the fear that, after affiliation, leaders of the Catholic Confederation would soon dominate the Quebec Federation of Labour, the provincial branch of the C.L.C. merger.

Spokesmen of craft unions, such as those in the building and printing trades, appear to be most strongly opposed to the C.T.C.C.'s affiliation as an autonomous organization. Craft unionists, particularly in the construction industry, tend by nature to be most unwilling to share jurisdiction with other organizations. Building tradesmen and construction workers are a relatively mobile occupational group, many of whom work on a variety of projects of short duration in different communities. The security and bargaining power of their unions rest on having the fullest possible control of the labour supply as well as opportunities for jobs over a wide territory. The C.L.C.'s affiliates in the building trades have been confined for the most part to the Montreal area, in which they control more than 80 per cent of the organized workers in construction. The unprecedented construction boom in Quebec during the past two years—particularly the new industrial plants and projects for the development of resources in hitherto remote and undeveloped areas—gives the building trades in the C.L.C. a new incentive and new opportunities to expand into communities now dominated by Catholic syndicates. This situation has led to several bitter, and sometimes violent, conflicts between the two groups.[23] Spokesmen of the C.L.C. building trades unions in Quebec take the view that the C.T.C.C., if it is to affiliate with the Congress, should agree to disband its organization within a definite time, and turn its local affiliates and members over to the appropriate international unions.

Much the same considerations account for the opposition from spokesmen of international unions in the pulp and paper industry to the proposed affiliation of the C.T.C.C. with the C.L.C. The most sustained and bitter conflict between international unions and the Catholic syndicates in Quebec's history occurred in that industry.[24] Catholic pulp and paper workers' syndicates are now in a highly vulnerable position because the international unions negotiate agreements with the main companies that establish regional patterns for the industry as a whole throughout Ontario and Quebec. The C.T.C.C.'s Federation of Paper Workers is thus left with little or no room to manœuvre independently. It tends to lose prestige where it merely "goes along" with the established patterns or "rides on the back of the internationals" as its critics allege. Attempts to "break out of the pattern" and win special concessions for its own members, on the other hand, tend to involve it in long, costly, and sometimes illegal strikes. Under provincial labour legislation, disputes have to be submitted to conciliation or arbitration boards before strike action can be undertaken. This the syndicates are loath to do, because of the Duplessis Government's well-publicized hostility to the C.T.C.C. The only alternative is illegal strikes, and these bring the risk that the unions involved will be decertified and lose members to the competing international unions. That was what happened, for instance, in a strike of pulp and paper workers' syndicates in Shawinigan and Grand'Mère in 1955.[25]

[23]During February and March of 1957, for instance, spokesmen of the C.T.C.C. on several occasions charged that the teamsters' and carpenters' unions of the C.L.C. were "strike-breaking" and using "strong-arm men," in attempting to break a strike in Baie Comeau, led by the Building and Construction Trades Federation of the C.T.C.C. (See *Montreal Star*, March 2, 1957, p. 2; *Le Devoir*, March 2, 1957, p. 2.)

[24]See W. E. Greening, *Paper Makers in Canada* (Ottawa: International Brotherhood of Paper Makers, 1952), pp. 34–64.

[25]Albert Plante, s.j., "Les Grandes Lignes d'un conflit industriel," *Relations* (Montréal) (Sept. 1955), pp. 227–30.

Whereas spokesmen of C.L.C. unions in the construction and pulp and paper industries oppose affiliation with the C.T.C.C. from positions of strength, prominent spokesmen of the C.L.C. unions in the textile industry appear to oppose it from a position of weakness. The National Catholic Textile Federation is considerably stronger than either of the two internationals in Quebec, and on the whole it seems to have an abler and more dynamic leadership. There tends to be the fear, therefore, that if the C.T.C.C. were to join the C.L.C., its textile union would in effect absorb the international locals, and the executives of the latter would lose in status.

The Quebec branches of former C.I.O.–C.C.L. unions have generally been less hostile to the C.T.C.C. in recent years, and are more favourable to its affiliation with the Canadian Labour Congress. The divergence in viewpoint from that of many former A.F.L.–T.L.C. unions rests on a number of factors. Like the majority of C.T.C.C. affiliates, the former C.I.O.–C.C.L. unions in Quebec are predominantly industrial rather than craft organizations. Most of them were organized during or after the war, and they have generally been more flexible in policy and leadership than the former A.F.L.–T.L.C. unions. Perhaps most important is the fact that they do not, and have not, overlapped or conflicted in jurisdiction with Catholic syndicates to the same degree as a number of former A.F.L.–T.L.C. unions. They are concentrated in a few industries that are largely confined to the Montreal area, such as meat-packing, iron and steel, and street railway and bus transportation—industries that had been left virtually unorganized by the other two main labour groups. Leading spokesmen of former C.C.L. unions in Quebec, officially at least, tend to look upon the C.T.C.C. as a great potential asset to the Canadian labour movement, and are favourable to the principle of accepting it into the Congress as an autonomous unit.

A similar divergence in viewpoints is found within the Catholic Confederation. As is the case in the C.L.C., the strongest opposition to affiliation seems to come from spokesmen of the Building and Construction Workers' Federation. This stems partly from the fact that this organization has experienced frequent and bitter conflict with C.L.C. affiliates in recent months, and partly from the fact that it enjoys lucrative closed shop agreements with employers in many communities, particularly those engaged in the large volume of construction on behalf of the Catholic Church in Quebec. Spokesmen of some smaller C.T.C.C. affiliates have also expressed opposition to joining the Canadian Labour Congress, perhaps for fear they would lose in relative status and be "swallowed up" in the much larger labour body.

Representatives of some other C.T.C.C. unions, by contrast, appear to favour affiliation with the C.L.C. on just about any terms. The leaders of a few individual syndicates, indeed, are reported ready to bolt the Catholic Confederation and join certain C.L.C. unions. They are attracted, perhaps, by the prospect of the greater gains in organization and collective bargaining to be made for their members as well as themselves if they were to link up directly with international unions having greater financial resources and bargaining power.

The executives of the C.T.C.C. are virtually unanimous in agreeing that their organization should affiliate with the C.L.C. only if the whole Confederation is accepted as an autonomous "national union" like, for instance, the Canadian Brotherhood of Railway Employees. They feel that if the C.T.C.C. were to enter into affiliation on the "bits and pieces" terms demanded by the spokesmen of some international unions, its leaders might, in effect, be "frozen out" of the C.L.C. or relegated to positions of minor status. It is almost a sociological law that no institution that is a going concern willingly votes itself out of existence, particularly if it has able and dynamic leaders who have won a considerable, and unique, prestige in the community.

To join the C.L.C. as an autonomous national union, however, the C.T.C.C. would have to drastically reorganize its present loose and decentralized structure. The executive of the Confederation has proposed to do this by raising per capita dues, payable by local syndicates directly to the central "confederal bureau" rather than to their industry or trade federations, and by grouping the fifteen federations into six "departments" directly under the bureau's control. This proposal according to some reports has aroused intense factional conflict within the C.T.C.C., particularly from the leaders of the larger and more prosperous affiliated federations, who see themselves relegated to a distinctly subordinate status in the proposed new structure.

It would appear to this observer that the various difficulties of affiliation discussed above will have to be settled, if they ever are, by numerous compromises and individual "deals," union by union. The Catholic Confederation may have to sacrifice some of its affiliates in such industries as pulp and paper and, possibly, mining and smelting, and perhaps gain new locals in such industries as textiles, in order to be accepted into the C.L.C. as an autonomous unit and preserve anything of its present character.

Regardless of the particular methods by which such fusion or affiliation may come about, it seems likely that organized labour in Quebec will continue to be a distinct and different segment of the trade union movement in Canada, for Quebec itself, even though it has become more closely integrated with the rest of Canada economically and organizationally, remains different culturally and highly autonomous politically. Like most trade union movements, the Canadian Labour Congress and its affiliates are essentially "political" rather than "business-like" in character and structure. And, in common with governments and political parties in Canada, they are likely to find that their organizational objectives can be achieved more effectively if they make special concessions to French Canada and allow more autonomy to their branches in Quebec than is usual in the other provinces.

1957

IV. OUTSIDE QUEBEC

A. The West

B. Ontario

C. The Maritimes

D. New England

IV. EN DEHORS DU QUÉBEC

A. L'Ouest canadien

B. L'Ontario

C. Les Provinces maritimes

D. La Nouvelle-Angleterre

French and English in Western Canada

GEORGE F. G. STANLEY
Head, Department of History, and Chairman, Arts Division
Royal Military College of Canada

THE FIRST EUROPEANS TO OPEN UP WHAT IS NOW WESTERN CANADA were men who spoke the French language, men from Old and New France. For a century and more, adventurers from the valley of the St. Lawrence, explorers, fur traders, and *coureurs de bois* followed the Ottawa and French rivers to Georgian Bay, passed Sault Ste Marie, skirted the rocky shores of Lake Superior, travelled over the height of land and along the waterways leading to Lake Winnipeg, until at last they reached the great plains of the west. Champlain himself started this westward movement. Others, of names known and unknown, followed in his wake. Jean Nicolet discovered Lake Michigan in 1634; the brothers Desfosses reached Lake Superior in 1649, Radisson and Groseilliers traded trinkets for furs at Fond du Lac in 1659; and in 1679 Dulhut is said to have built the first post on Thunder Bay. Then came Jacques de Noyon, Henri de Tonti, and Zacharie Robutel de la Noue; and finally Pierre Gaultier, Sieur de la Vérendrye, explorer in spite of himself and fur trader through necessity, bearer of the greatest name in the history of French expansion in the west.

Impelled by the desire to expand the fur trade of his native land, to save the souls of the pagan Indians, and to discover the Western Sea, La Vérendrye and his sons paddled along the western rivers and journeyed over the prairies, dotting the countryside with trading posts and French names: Fort Saint-Pierre on Rainy Lake (1731); Fort Saint-Charles on Lake of the Woods (1732); Fort Maurepas on Lake Winnipeg (1734); Fort La Reine on the Assiniboine River (1738); Fort Rouge on the site of the present city of Winnipeg (1738); Fort Dauphin at the mouth of the Mossy River (1741); and Fort Paskoyac at the Pas on the Saskatchewan River (1743). Under La Vérendrye's successor, Le Gardeur de Saint-Pierre, the French trader-explorers pressed still farther towards the west. In 1750 Indians told the Hudson's

Bay Company agent at Fort Prince of Wales that no less than thirty Canadians with seven large canoes laden with trade goods were in the interior of the country: and in 1751 twelve Canadians are said to have erected a fort far up the Saskatchewan and called it Fort La Jonquière. Neither La Vérendrye nor those who succeeded to his command of the western posts ever discovered the Western Sea; what they did do was to establish the west-east economic axis along which furs and later wheat were to flow, and to place in French hands an area almost half a continent in size, and rich in the richest furs. Champlain may be regarded as the father of New France; but La Vérendrye is the father of the Canadian west.

Actual settlement or colonization was not a feature of the history of the west during the days of the Ancien Régime. The men who came from Canada came to trade, to make money; not to colonize or cultivate the soil. And even the traders were soon to be forced to direct their energies elsewhere. By the middle of the eighteenth century the hundred years' struggle between England and France for supremacy, economic and political, in North America, was entering its final and decisive phase; and with the outbreak of fighting on the Monongahela in 1754 came the gradual withdrawal of available French manpower from the west. First to go was the Chevalier Saint Luc de la Corne, last of the French commandants of the western posts, who returned to lead his *coureurs de bois* and Indians in battles which could not save his native land from defeat. One by one the posts of the west were abandoned, until by 1760 there were no more in operation. Then came the negotiations for peace. British statesmen balanced the speculative assets of a West Indian sugar island against those of Voltaire's "quelques arpents de neige" and chose to keep the latter. In 1763 Canada and its dependencies were ceded to Great Britain. A new chapter in the history of western Canada began.

The fall of New France did not, however, mean the extinction of the French fact or the French tongue in the western plains and woodlands. The Canadians of earlier days had acquired too strong a position for the memory of their activities and achievements to be lightly forgotten with the closing of a few trading counters. Many of those who had come to the west in happier times chose to remain. Some of them threw in their lot with the Indian nations, with whom they had contracted marital as well as economic alliances. Others simply made the best of an unfortunate situation. To both, Quebec was far away and international politics had little meaning. Said the trader at Fort Bourbon to Joseph Smith in 1757, "What if the King of England and the King of France are at warrs together, that is no reason why we should, so let us be friends." These isolated elements of French civilization, weak and unsure of themselves though they were, carried the flickering torch of French survival during the years of doubt, until the return of peace made possible the revival of trade connections with Montreal and the return of the traders from the St. Lawrence Valley.

One outcome of the British victory at Quebec was the rush of Scottish and English fur traders and fur-trading capitalists to Montreal. These men became the legatees of the old French Indian trade and the entrepreneurs, financiers, and directors of the new. The Indian trade was much too profitable a business to be left long to languish, and within a few months of the signing of the Capitulations, trade canoes were moving once more over the familiar waterways west of Montreal.

There were the inevitable Scots and a few Englishmen and Americans among the new generation of traders; but there were Canadian French too. Better than anyone else they knew the country and they knew the Indian psychology. By 1765–6 they had reoccupied many of their old bases of operations in the west. Maurice or Barthélemy Blondeau took possession of Fort La Reine; François LeBlanc appeared at Fort Dauphin and, later, with a dozen companions, at Paskoyac. William Tomison of the Hudson's Bay Company believed that in 1786 there were no fewer than 400 French Canadians west of the Grand Portage. Their peculiar qualities were thoroughly appreciated by the moneyed Scots in Montreal, and when unrestricted competition compelled individual traders to come together in that remarkable profit-sharing enterprise, the North West Company, it was to Lower Canada that they looked for recruits. Handicapped though it was in the economic struggle with its English rival, the Canadian company always enjoyed one advantage, the French-Canadian *voyageur*. Unambitious yet proud, undisciplined yet accepting the necessity of discipline, liking and liked by the Indians, he was the indispensable instrument of every bold and startling design planned by the fur barons of Beaver Hall. Beyond the prairies, into the rocky stillness of the Shield, into the country of the Lower Albany, over the Methye Portage to the northern rivers, the French-Canadian *voyageur* was ever in the forefront of the continental marathon. François Bériau (Barrieau), Charles Doucette, Joseph Landry, and Pierre Delorme were Alexander Mackenzie's companions on his dash to the Arctic in 1789. Charles Doucette, Joseph Landry, François Beaulieu, François Comtois, Baptiste Bisson, and Jacques Beauchamp accompanied him on his journey to the Pacific Ocean in 1792–3, the first white men to penetrate beyond the Rocky Mountain barrier into what is now British Columbia.

Like their predecessors of the Ancien Régime who had remained in the country during the Seven Years' War, the new group of French *hivernants* (winterers), while retaining the tongue of their fathers, tended to lose touch with Quebec and with the culture of their homeland. Only a few days each year did they renew their contacts with the *mangeurs de lard* from the east, when they exchanged their cargoes of furs for the cargoes of goods brought from Montreal to the Grand Portage. Their life and their living was in the west. Many of them abandoned any lingering ideas of returning to the villages of their boyhood, and, for love or convenience, took unto themselves Indian wives. Marriages *à la mode du pays* were easily contracted and just as easily dissolved; and an Indian woman was a necessity for survival in the wild and primitive country, as well as a useful if not indispensable auxiliary to the Indian trade itself.

When and how rapidly *métissage* developed in the west is a question incapable of accurate answer. It probably began with the appearance of the first white men; it definitely began when the early traders were compelled to spend the winters in the lonely scattered outposts instead of returning to their eastern homes. References on the part of English traders to "French Indians" seem to suggest the existence of a distinct mixed-blood group by the middle of the eighteenth century. This process of racial assimilation, once begun, apparently accelerated with the expansion of the fur trade during the later 1700's; for, by the beginning of the nineteenth century, the emergence of a clearly defined Métis population, with such well known Métis names as Breland, Vandal, Desjarlais, Cardinal, Delorme, Dumont, Beaulieu, Deschamps, and others, is obvious. It is, however, in the absence of suitable statistical data, impossible to establish either the rate of increase of the Métis population or even its total strength over the whole of the northwestern territory during these formative years. Such estimates as have been made (such, for instance, as that of W. J. Snelling, who gives a numerical strength of 4,000 to 5,000 to the Métis during the years 1800 to 1810) are no more than conjectures. Not until the establishment of sedentary colonies do the demographic obscurities begin to disappear.

With the fixation of the Métis groups begins the real history of French colonization in western Canada. Alexander Henry mentions the existence of a small Métis colony at Pembina in 1807; and Miles Macdonnell reported another along the banks of the Assiniboine in

1814. In the vicinity of Edmonton there was a similar group of Canadian "freemen." Out of these and similar groups grew that sense of community and consciousness of identity which later found expression in the name "the New Nation."

II

Although the French Canadians were the first, they were not the only Europeans to make their way into the western wilderness. The establishment of the Hudson's Bay Company in 1670 placed another race, the Anglo-Saxons of the British Isles, in a favourable position to press forward into the interior and to anticipate their French rivals from Montreal. Geography imposed fewer and less formidable obstacles on the northern route than it did upon the south; the rivers were there, the Hayes, the Nelson, and the Churchill, flowing from the west into Hudson Bay. But the servants of the company were, for the most part, content to cling to the shore line. Although York Fort (later called York Factory), the oldest continuous settlement in Manitoba, was built in 1684, it was not until six years later that Henry Kelsey set out on the journey which took him as far west as Saskatchewan; nor was it until 1754 that Kelsey's exploit was duplicated by Anthony Henday, when he travelled along the Hayes River and the Saskatchewan and reached the rolling prairies of southern Alberta. In 1770–2 Samuel Hearne journeyed northwards through the Barren Lands from Fort Prince of Wales to the Coppermine; and in 1772 Matthew Cocking visited the country of the Blackfoot Indians. These journeys, Hearne's excepted, were undertaken with the one object of drawing remote Indian tribes to the company's trading posts on the Bay. There was no determined collective effort, no building of forts, no community of action similar to that put forward by La Vérendrye. The English journeys were isolated, individual, sporadic efforts; and as such, important though they may be in the general history of travel and exploration, they lack the same significance in the history of western Canada as those of the French from Canada.

The increased economic pressure which followed the resumption of the fur trade by the Montreal merchants led to a change of attitude and policy on the part of the Hudson's Bay Company. No longer did the Gentlemen Adventurers wait upon the littoral. They carried aggressive war into the very heart of Rupert's Land. They had the advantages of a shorter route and cheaper goods; and they built a series of forts from James Bay to Lake Superior to cut off entry into the interior, and along the well-travelled route of the Saskatchewan, and even in the remote regions of the Athabasca. Philip Turnor began his surveys in the spring of 1779 and Hudson's Bay Company posts sprang up at Brandon House, Cumberland House, Marlboro House, Manchester House, Chesterfield House, Carlton House, Edmonton House, Fort Chipewyan, nearly all of them offsetting a post erected not far distant by the North West Company. It was with some bitterness that Alexander Mackenzie wrote in 1801: "From this period [the founding of Cumberland House] to the present time, they [the Hudson's Bay Company] have been following the Canadians to their different establishments, while on the contrary, there is not a solitary instance that the Canadians have followed them. . . ." The outcome was a rivalry which drove both companies inexorably across the continent and forced them into competitive methods that debauched the Indians and finally wrecked the Canadian company. Under the pressure of such unrelenting competition the hard facts of geography and economics were bound to triumph; and in 1821 the Nor'Westers gave up the struggle and accepted a union with their rivals which was, in effect, complete absorption.

The factors which had led to *métissage* among Canadian traders and *voyageurs* were not without their impact upon the employees of the Hudson's Bay Company. At first English policy was rigidly exclusive: Indians would not be admitted to the interior of the company's forts and traders would in no way molest the Indians or depart from the generally accepted standards of moral conduct. But theoretical rigours proved weaker than the rigours of reality: loneliness and promiscuity were hard to resist, and regulations made in the board room at London were even harder to enforce on the shores of Hudson Bay. When Kelsey returned to York Fort in 1692 accompanied by an Indian woman he merely set the precedent which others were to follow, first secretly and later openly. These Indian alliances proved an asset to the trade and by 1768 the Scottish or Anglo-Saxon Métis formed an important human group about the posts of the littoral. As the company extended its activities to the interior this group increased in size and significance.

The presence of two half-breed peoples in the west, the one speaking French and the other speaking English did not, however, create difficulties either for the half-breeds themselves or for the companies which they served. Between the two groups there always existed a solidarity born of a common origin and a common way of life. Not infrequently Scottish half-breeds adopted the French tongue for no other reason than that it was spoken by the dominant group in which they moved. For them the transition from English to French had no political or cultural significance. Both were sons of the same mother, and both, when necessary, spoke the tongue of their Indian forbears. Material life was simple and elemental and the Métis were scarcely conscious of the cultural forces which their fathers represented. For the time being their ambitions were limited to the realities of the moment; the prejudices of race and language had not, as yet, arrived on the prairies of the northwest from the provinces of old Canada.

III

It was the attempt to establish a European colony which gave rise to the first racial crisis in western Canada. In 1811 the Hudson's Bay Company granted to Lord Selkirk an area of 116,000 square miles covering much of what is today the most fertile land in Manitoba, Saskatchewan, North Dakota, and Minnesota. The purpose of this munificent grant was to assist the Earl in establishing a colony at Red River. From the outset the men of the North West Company viewed the project with suspicion. Was it not an astute attempt on the part of their rivals to interfere with the Canadian fur trade, if not even to bar them from the country from which they drew their wealth? Accordingly the Nor'Westers opposed the colonization scheme with bitterness and determination. They fought it while it was still in the project stage in London; they fought it on the spot when Miles Macdonnell led the first Highlanders and Orkneymen from York Factory to the Red River Valley in 1812.

A powerful and dangerous weapon was close at hand, the growing national consciousness of the half-breed peoples. Their nationalism was still an inchoate thing, a vague stirring from within, an idea which could, and did, become a faith. By subtly suggesting to the Métis that the newcomers were interlopers, come to rob them of their lands and deprive them of their heritage, the Nor'Westers were able to lead them as they willed; for the new allegiance of their hearts and simplicity of their minds made them obedient servants to a familiar master. Finally, the antagonism of colonist and fur trader, transformed by the insinuations of the North West Company into an antagonism between the old and the new inhabitants and between the Métis and the Europeans, degenerated into violence and bloodshed. Led by Cuthbert Grant, "Captain General of all the half-breeds in the country," the New Nation determined "to clear their native soil of intruders and assassins." "It must end," wrote Laughlin McLean, "in some sickly work at the long run." It ended in June 1816 with a one-sided exchange of shots at Seven Oaks in which the newly appointed Governor of the colony, Robert Semple, and twenty colonists met their death. Grant lost but a single follower.

Seven Oaks did not put an end to the Red River Settlement. With the dogged determination characteristic of their race, the Highlanders stood their ground and Selkirk fought their battles in the courts of Canada. But there was no further European immigration, beyond a few Swiss soldiers and colonists who would not stay to face the grasshoppers and the floods. It had been one of the terms of Selkirk's grant that lands in the settlement should be given to servants of the company who chose to settle down rather than return to their homes across the sea, and Red River became the favourite retreat of company employees with their Indian wives and half-breed progeny. After 1821 this movement towards Red River developed rapidly. The union of the Hudson's Bay and North West companies threw many clerks and *voyageurs* out of work, and it was to Red River that they came. By 1831 the population numbered 2,417, and by 1840, 4,369. For the most part the newcomers were men of mixed blood, Métis both French and English. Evidence of this development is afforded by the fact that between 1849 and 1856, although the total population increased by 1,232 souls, the number of whites decreased by 102. Finally, in 1871, the first federal census in the area revealed the overwhelming Métis composition of the settlement. The official figures showed a total population of 11,400, of whom 1,600 were whites, 5,720 French-speaking Métis, and 4,080 English-speaking Métis.

As the colony grew, so too did the factors which tended to fix the two language groups and emphasize the cultural differences between them. One of these factors was the influence of the Christian missionaries. In 1818 Bishop Plessis of Quebec, yielding to the request of Lord Selkirk and the petition of a group of French Métis, sent two Catholic priests to the Red River Settlement, the abbés Provencher and Dumoulin. Missions were established at St. Boniface and Pembina, and journeys were made to more remote areas of the western vineyard, to the valleys of the Souris and the Qu'Appelle and even to the shores of Hudson Bay. At the end of five years Provencher, who had been consecrated bishop in 1822, was able to report numerous baptisms, marriages, and first communions and, in addition, the establishment of a boys' school (1818), a college (1822), and a school for girls (1829). In 1833 the foundations of a stone cathedral were laid at St. Boniface and a few years later the northwest became a separate diocese independent of that of Quebec. But priests were always hard to get. The secular clergy could not carry the burden of the western mission and Provencher turned to the Orders. In response to his appeals came the Grey Nuns in 1844, and in 1845 the vanguard of that missionary group whose name has long been associated with the history of the west: the Oblates of Mary Immaculate. With them was a young man, scarcely in his twenties, Father Alexandre Tâché, who, as Bishop and later Archbishop of St. Boniface, was to leave a lasting imprint upon the country to which he devoted his life.

The Anglicans were next in the field. In 1820 the Rev. John West arrived in Red River to minister to the spiritual needs of the Selkirk settlers; but they, Scottish Presbyterians almost to a man, were not disposed to welcome an Anglican without the Gaelic who refused to water down his ritual to suit the wishes of his congregation. In 1823 he returned to England, leaving behind him as an enduring monument a school, the Red River Academy, later St. John's College. After West came the Rev. D. T. Jones and others. Finally, in 1849, the erection of the Anglican diocese of Rupert's Land and the consecration of David Anderson as bishop fairly established the Anglican Church as an enduring element in the religious life of the western community.

The Methodists and Presbyterians came later to the western mission field. In 1840 the Rev. James Evans was placed in charge of the Wesleyan missions in the Northwest; and in 1851 the Presbyterian missionary, John Black, was welcomed at Kildonan with tears of joy, by the Scottish Highlanders of Red River.

The immediate result of the coming of the Christian missionaries was the pacification of the settlement, the regularization of many Métis marriages, and the spread of the Christian gospel. The incidental, but none the less important, result was to give vitality and strength to the waning cultures of the two basic language groups which made up the population of Red River. Brought up by their Indian mothers and acquiring the cultural concepts of their fathers only from the post servants of the fur companies, the Métis, French and English, had become, in many instances, more Indian than white in their habits of thought and life. While working to restore Christian *mores* to a people whose religion was more superstition than conviction, the Catholic and Protestant clergy also restored to them the cultural ideas, the historic aspirations, and the prejudices too, of the language groups from which they had originally sprung. Faith and language seemed to go together, and the missionary, as he revived the feeble flame of

Christian faith, revived the flame of an almost forgotten culture. The French fact gained new vigour. But if there was a French fact in the west, there was likewise an English fact; and, as the French Métis in becoming more Catholic became more French, the English-speaking half-breed was drawn by his pastors to identify himself more closely with the culture of the British settlers whom Selkirk had brought into the country.

There were, of course, instances of tension between the two linguistic groups and between the Métis and the whites. These were, however, few in number and were occasioned by the Hudson's Bay Company's rigorous enforcement of its monopoly of trafficking in furs with the Indians, and by the growing political awareness of the Métis as they developed their own native bourgeoisie. Generally speaking, the life of the colony was marked by comparative tranquility and mutual toleration. In 1835 Bishop Provencher and Cuthbert Grant were both invited to attend the meetings of the governing body of the colony, the Council of Assiniboia, thus giving representation to the French and to the half-breeds. In 1849 an armed gathering of French Métis protested against the arrest of Guillaume Sayer for an infraction of the company's monopoly and against his trial before Adam Thom, regarded by all the French-speaking inhabitants of Red River as a confirmed francophobe. In consequence, the Council unanimously recommended that in future the recorder should "in all cases involving either Canadian or Half-breed interests" address the court "in both languages" (that is, French and English), and that there should be an "infusion" into the Council of "Canadian and half-breed members." In 1850 several Métis, both French- and English-speaking, were appointed magistrates. In the same year Father Laflèche, later Bishop of Trois-Rivières, was appointed to the Council, and in 1853 François Bruneau —one of the demonstrators in 1849—became the first French Métis to sit on the Council of Assiniboia. In 1857 Pascal Breland, Solomon Hamlin, and Maximilien Genthon were appointed members; in 1866, Roger Goulet; and in 1868 William Dease, Thomas Bunn, and Magnus Berston, all of whom were of mixed Indian and European origin. In 1856 two surveyors were appointed for the Settlement, "one for the Canadians, and the other for the Europeans," or in other words one who spoke French and one who spoke English; and in 1861 the appointment of collector of customs was shared by four men representing the linguistic and ethnic groups in the colony. At the session of the Council held in May 1851, the Rev. William Cockran moved and Father Laflèche seconded a resolution "that £100 be granted from the public funds to be divided, equally, between the Bishop of Rupert's Land and the Bishop of the North-West, to be applied by them at their discretion for the purpose of education": when, in 1852, £15 was granted the Rev. John Black for educational purposes, a similar grant was made to Bishop Provencher, in order not to disturb the balance between the two religious and linguistic groups. The policy of thus giving official recognition to these several groups did much to relieve such tensions as did exist and to encourage a co-operation which, if not enthusiastic, was at least realistic.

The second great racial crisis in the history of the Red River Settlement came with the arrival in the colony of immigrants from Canada during the 1850's. They were for the most part Ontarians, openly contemptuous of all half-breeds and French Canadians, militantly Protestant and aggressively English. They were not a popular element in Red River, even among the white settlers, and their advocacy of the annexation of the colony to Canada scarcely endeared them either to the Métis or to the Hudson's Bay Company. The government of Canada had for some time contemplated the acquisition of the company's territories—if only to save them from a similar fate at the hands of the Americans pushing rapidly northwards and westwards—and negotiations had been under way with the British authorities and the Hudson's Bay Company in London for the transfer of the company's territorial rights to Ottawa. Unfortunately, neither the local government nor the local inhabitants were consulted or prepared for the change, and the doubt in their minds soon yielded place to fear. To the Canadians the annexation of the northwest was simply and obviously a necessary corollary to their own confederation; to the people of Red River it meant their transfer to a foreign power, whose interests and whose ways were very different from their own, a supposition which hardened into fact when Canadian surveyors arrived in Red River to lay out the land in a new, unfamiliar, symmetrical manner, taking little heed of the irregularities of the original holdings. Was this not another attempt "pour piller notre pays?" Were not the sons of Isaac advancing upon the lands of the sons of Ishmael?

Fundamentally the rising led by Louis Riel in 1869 differed little from that led by Cuthbert Grant fifty years before. It was the clash between a primitive and complex social organization, between a simple and highly competitive economy, between the prairie and the plough. But in the minds of the people of Canada, both French and English, it was something more: it was the revival on the banks of the Red River of the traditional rivalries of French and English on the St.

Lawrence. Beginning by fighting the battle of ethnic survival, Riel ended by fighting the battle for the survival of the French fact in western Canada, and his fate became the shuttlecock of the self-appointed champions of language and religion in Old Canada. The Métis movement resulted in victory; but it was less a victory for the Métis than for their French supporters. When Riel's delegates went to Ottawa they bore with them a list of rights, demanding, in addition to provincial status, provision for separate schools and official equality of the French and English languages. These demands were subsequently embodied in clauses 22 and 23 of the Manitoba Act of 1870. French survival, at least, seemed assured.

As far as the Métis were concerned, they were compelled to fight a second time the battle for their own survival. The defeat on the banks of the Saskatchewan River was final, and with the execution of Louis Riel in 1885 the New Nation disintegrated. Their battle ended not in the death of their bodies but in the death of their minds. Today the remnants of the group (with the exception of those who have been assimilated to the culture of the whites), destitute and discouraged, cling precariously to the outer fringes of European society.

IV

The new province of Manitoba that emerged from the Riel insurrection continued, with official sanction, the duality of language and education which had been the feature of the colonial period. In the first legislature, almost half of the twenty-four members were French-speaking, and it was a French Canadian, Marc Girard, whom the Lieutenant-Governor called upon to form the first provincial ministry. In 1871 a school system was established which took as its model that of the province of Quebec, with its two governing boards, Protestant and Roman Catholic. In its early days Manitoba was a bilingual province; French and English were spoken in its towns and villages, taught in its schools and heard in its legislative chambers. And yet the whole bilingual edifice, so carefully erected and so strongly buttressed with constitutional guarantees, was essentially unstable. It depended, in the long run, upon the unlikely continuation of equality of numbers between the French and English populations, or failing that, upon the equally unlikely goodwill of the majority in power.

The Catholic clergy, upon whom the burden of French survival now securely rested, were under no illusions about the uncertain nature of the victory which Riel had won for them in 1870. "Le nombre va nous faire défaut," wrote Bishop Tâché, "et comme sous notre système constitutionnel les nombres sont la force, nous allons nous trouver à la merci de ceux qui ne nous aiment pas." Even before Riel's delegates had gained their point at Ottawa, Bishop Tâché and others had persuaded several young French Canadians to leave the old province of Quebec and migrate to Manitoba, Joseph Dubuc, Marc Girard, Joseph Royal, and Alphonse LaRivière, all of whom were to play major roles in the political life of western Canada. During twenty-five years of his episcopate, Bishop Tâché never relaxed his efforts to induce French-speaking settlers to come to Manitoba and the northwest. It was his great hope; for the Métis were too weak a reed upon which to rely for security in the rising flood of English immigration. French-Catholic colonists were needed and needed badly to bolster the sagging fact of French existence. In France they were sought, in Quebec, and in the eastern United States. They came. They strengthened the old parishes at St. Boniface and along the Red River. They established new ones at St. Malo, Fannystelle, Notre Dame de Lourdes, St. Claude, and elsewhere. But they did not come in numbers; not in numbers sufficient to match the thousands from other parts of Canada and from Europe. All too soon it became clear that the French element in Manitoba, even with ecclesiastical backing at home and abroad, was getting only the sympathy of its compatriots, not the compatriots themselves.

Within a few years of the passing of the Manitoba Act, the Manitoba French had irretrievably lost the battle of numerical equality. They failed, too, to hold the goodwill of the English-speaking majority. In Ontario D'Alton McCarthy's anti-French, anti-Catholic agitation was in full voice, and its echoes had reached the Protestant parishes of the western province. To a shaky Liberal administration, anxious to divert attention from its political failures, the French Catholics looked like suitable whipping boys. Moreover, assimilation and "national" schools seemed an easy way to deal with the problems arising out of the multitude of nationalities then pouring into the country. Accordingly, despite constitutional guarantees, and despite, too, the fact that few real objections had up to this time been raised to the existing school system, the provincial legislature in 1890 abolished both the official status of the French language in the province and the dual system of separate denominational schools.

This was a challenge which could not be let go by default. There was the law; there were the courts. Between the years 1890 and 1896 the provincial legislation was challenged in the courts of Manitoba, of

Canada, and even of Great Britain. The Catholics based their case on section 22 of the Manitoba Act and section 93 of the British North America Act, both of which seemed to guarantee the rights of the minority. They gained this much, that although the legislation was declared *intra vires* of the province, the Judicial Committee of the Privy Council recognized their legal right, as an injured minority, to appeal to the federal authorities to remedy the injury suffered. Headed by their Archbishop, the Roman Catholics of Manitoba appealed to Ottawa. To the Government the appeal was a source of embarrassment, for Parliament was nearing its allotted span and the Conservative party was on its last legs; but to the credit of Mackenzie Bowell and his successor, Sir Charles Tupper, the Government grasped the nettle and introduced the necessary remedial legislation. Time, however, was running out, and before the bill could be passed in the face of a determined opposition led by a French Canadian—Wilfrid Laurier—the life of Parliament expired and a general election was fought, not over the rights of the French and Catholics in Manitoba, but over the right of the federal authorities to coerce a province in a matter admittedly within its own jurisdiction. The Catholic Church did its best. But the faithful voted for provincial rights rather than for Catholic rights.

The school issue in Manitoba was finally settled by agreement between the Prime Minister, Wilfrid Laurier, and the Premier, Thomas Greenway, in 1896. Under the Laurier-Greenway compromise religious teaching might be permitted in the schools for half an hour at the end of each school day, and where ten or more pupils spoke French (or any other language) elementary teaching might be carried on in that language. As far as Catholic schools were concerned, they were free to continue as private, voluntary institutions, not entitled to any funds from the public purse. If Roman Catholics were determined to have their own schools, then they would have to pay for them, and pay, as well, for the new non-denominational "national" schools.

For all Catholics the Laurier-Greenway agreement was a bitter one; but for the French there were still the dregs to swallow. Their language was now no more than another "foreign" tongue like Ukrainian or Icelandic. It enjoyed no distinction in its own right; and when the linguistic provisions of the compromise began to pose serious problems to a province rapidly being peopled by many races and many tongues, it was probably inevitable that this portion of the compromise should be repealed. In 1916 the Manitoba legislature, dominated by a Liberal majority pledged to furthering Canadian unity, did away with bilingual schools. The French Canadians thus lost even the meagre privileges of 1896. Forgotten was the history of Manitoba; forgotten was the history of Canada; forgotten, too, was the whole understanding which had made Confederation a possibility in British North America. There were some opponents of the measure who tried to argue that the legislation of 1916, by violating the Laurier-Greenway compromise, cleared the way for the federal authorities to resume the powers which they had abdicated in 1896; but the minority was weary of litigation and political guarantees which were no guarantee. Thus French, the original language of the plains, the tongue of the explorers, the *voyageurs,* the traders, and the first settlers, a language which enjoyed "official" status in the Red River Valley for the greater part of the nineteenth century, was proscribed in the schools of twentieth-century Manitoba. And yet the voice which spoke the outlawed tongue would not be silenced. "The French are a distinctive race," cried P. A. Talbot, in the Manitoba legislature in 1916, "and we will not be assimilated, whether you like it or not."

V

The story of the French fact in the Northwest Territories follows much the same plot as that in Manitoba. At first the French sought to fortify their case with immigration, and when this proved illusory, they turned for help to the legislative enactments with which Ottawa had provided them. But these too proved powerless before the will of the majority. Everywhere prejudice seemed to triumph over toleration and politics over justice.

The earliest settlements in the Territories were those of the Métis. They were to be found at Qu'Appelle (now Lebret) and at Wood Mountain in the southeastern regions, and at St. Laurent de Grandin and St. Paul de Métis in the north. Efforts were made to reinforce these colonies with French-Canadian Catholic missions and with French-speaking immigrants. Prospective settlers, ranging from dukes and counts to simple artisans and peasants, came from France, from Belgium, from Quebec, and from the Franco-American regions of the eastern United States. They expanded the old settlements and established new ones at Ponteix, Gravelbourg, Coderre, Laflèche, St. Hubert, Montmartre, Bellegarde, Dumas, Forget, in southern Saskatchewan; at Bellevue, Bonne Madone, Domrémy, St. Brieux, Périgord, Vonda, Prud'homme in northern Saskatchewan; at Trochu, Castor, Tinchebray, Chauvin, Pincher Creek in southern Alberta; at St. Albert,

Lafond, Brosseau, Thérien, Ste Lina, Bonnyville, McLennan, Falher, Grouard, Donnelly, and elsewhere in northern Alberta. These settlements, of course, were not all founded at the same time—they grew up over many years; nor is the list more than a sampling. But, numerous though they may appear, they were outnumbered and outvoted. Frenchmen simply did not emigrate; and Quebecers, while trotting off freely to the mills of Massachusetts, showed small enthusiasm about becoming farmers in the far-distant west of Canada. There were, moreover, many who felt that emigration was a debilitating process for the mother province. Archbishop Tâché might beg and pray and Father Lacombe search far and wide, but French-speaking immigrants never came near equalling in numbers those of other tongues and other races.

Like their confrères in Manitoba, the French-Catholic settlers of the northwest were not lacking in what appeared to be legislative guarantees of great solidity and strength. The federal government itself had promised them separate schools and official status for their language. The Northwest Territories Act passed in 1875 had provided that whenever a school system should be set up in the Territories, the minority ratepayers, Catholic or Protestant, should have the right to establish their own separate schools and be liable "only to assessments of such rates as they may impose upon themselves in respect thereof." Two years later, in 1877, Parliament extended the application of section 133 of the British North America Act to the Territories, thus giving the English and French languages equal status in the legislature and in the courts. The territorial government, too, committed itself to the principle of duality in instruction. The first regular school system in the Territories, set up in 1884, was modelled largely on that of Quebec. There was to be a board of education composed of two sections, one Catholic and the other Protestant. Each section could pass regulations for the conduct of its own schools, select its own textbooks, and train its own teachers. One restriction, and one only, was imposed upon the board; no more than one hour, the last hour of the day, was to be devoted to instruction in religion.

By the 1890's, however, the Territories had undergone considerable change. The frontier days were almost over. The Métis had fought and lost their final battle at Batoche. The transcontinental railway, the colonization companies and the federal government had combined to fill the plains with people. There were new men and new ideas. The settlers were clamouring for responsible government; they were talking in terms of provincial status. The political attitudes and the prejudices of Canada were spreading to the Territories, as they had already spread to Manitoba; and the legislators at Regina were inclined to keep one ear cocked towards Winnipeg, and even beyond, towards Ontario. But the territorial Assembly moved with care and circumspection. Its rights in the matter of school legislation were by no means clearly defined. It did not possess full provincial powers and there were doubts whether it could validly pass ordinances which might be repugnant to the federal Act of 1875. Thus the school ordinances of 1892 and 1901, while radically curtailing the privileges of separate schools within the Territories, did not do away with them entirely. The old board of education was replaced by a new commissioner who was to have sole authority over educational matters, but there was still to be an advisory council comprising both Protestant and Roman Catholic members, albeit without any powers save to advise. Religious instruction was to be retained in the schools, the time devoted to it cut to half an hour. The new ordinances met with opposition; but the resistance encountered was neither as prolonged nor as bitter as that which assailed the School Act in Manitoba. Frederick Haultain had not gone as far as Thomas Greenway. He had, indeed, affirmed the right of the minority to state-supported separate schools, even if he had hedged them around with restrictions which, according to his opponents, had made them "dependent on such conditions that they are virtually suppressed." Said Israël Tarte: "Mr. Haultain has done indirectly what he could not do directly."

The French language, too, lost ground along with the Catholic schools. Although D'Alton McCarthy was formally defeated in his effort in Ottawa in 1890 to deprive the French language of its legislative sanctions in the Northwest Territories, the federal government, in effect, withdrew its support when, in 1891, it gave the local legislature power to settle for itself the status of the two languages then regarded as official. The majority, it knew, was hostile; and the linguistic rights of the French minority would never be safe in the hands of the legislators at Regina. Nor was there even a decent interval before the obsequies were performed. In January 1892 Haultain moved in the territorial Assembly that henceforth English should be the sole language of recording and publishing the proceedings of the House. The motion was carried on a division. He could not move quite so quickly to eliminate French from the schools; that touched upon a matter still under federal jurisdiction. Nevertheless, in 1892 provision was made that English should be the language of instruction in the schools of the Territories, permitting only the use of French, in "a primary course," for those pupils who spoke no other tongue.

Further battles remained to be fought. The Territories were moving towards a change of political status and the French-Catholic minority was fearful and apprehensive of what its own fate might be. Experience in Manitoba had taught only one lesson, that mercy and tolerance were not to be hoped for from a hostile or unfeeling majority. The only hope, weak as it had proven to be, still lay with Ottawa, where French-Catholic representation was not without some influence upon the course of government policy. After all, the Northwest Territories were the political creation of Parliament, and the terms upon which the Territories would enter Confederation as provinces would be for Ottawa to decide. To Ottawa flocked the delegations of various and opposing points of view; and to Ottawa were addressed the many petitions bearing upon the various problems attending the granting of provincial status. The *Toronto News*, suspicious of the Roman Catholic Church and strong in its support of provincial status for the Territories, was inclined to blame every delay attending the consummation of the new political marriage upon "the Hierarchy of the Roman Church" which, it declared, had "served notice that when the [autonomy] Bill . . . is drafted it must contain a provision establishing Separate Schools . . . as a permanent portion of the Western system." It would, indeed, have been very odd had they not! To the Catholic, religion was not something to be taught as a subject thirty minutes a day: it was something which permeated the whole educative process. Schools were either godly or godless. Men like Archbishop Langevin of St. Boniface, and Bishops Pascal of Prince Albert, Légal of St. Albert, and Breynat of Mackenzie, were not to be expected to remain neutral in a controversy of this nature. They wanted no repetition of the events which had taken place in Manitoba in 1890, no more ambiguities "and consequent misunderstandings." And behind them was the full support of French-Canadian opinion in Quebec.

When the autonomy bills were finally introduced in Parliament in February 1905, the educational clauses not only provided for the application to the new provinces of section 93 of the British North America Act, but also that any provincial school acts were bound to make special provision for state-supported separate schools. The new legislation proposed was virtually a reproduction of clause 11 of the Northwest Territories Act of 1875.

The educational terms of the autonomy bills came as something of a surprise to the general public. In the west they excited some dissatisfaction on the part of the English-speaking Protestant population, but in eastern Canada they led to a prolonged protest from Orange lodges, ministerial associations, Protestant clergymen, and others bitterly opposed to the whole principle of denominational education. Sir Wilfrid, who, in drafting these terms, had probably thought to mollify his co-religionists who had never quite forgiven him for his concessions to Greenway, found himself faced with a cabinet crisis. Clifford Sifton of Manitoba, a former member of the Greenway Administration, resigned his portfolio as Minister of the Interior; W. S. Fielding, Minister of Finance, intimated his intention of doing likewise should no change be made in the offending clauses. Laurier attempted to justify his course by appealing to the principles of toleration and forbearance, the twin pillars upon which the structure of Confederation had been labouriously erected. But to no avail. It was the old dilemma of Manitoba all over again—provincial rights or minority rights; and the ghost of the Greenway compromise of 1896 could not be laid in 1905 by conjuring up those of Galt, Blake, Mackenzie, and Macdonald.

Sir Wilfrid had no choice but to make his peace with the proponents of provincial rights and to revise the educational clauses of the autonomy bills. There would be guarantees for a system of separate schools, but separate schools hedged around with the restrictions imposed by the territorial ordinances of 1901. Some French-Canadian newspapers, notably *La Patrie* and *Le Canada*, on the familiar argument of the half a loaf, professed to regard the new clause as a "consecration of the rights of Catholics to their schools." But Archbishop Langevin was probably nearer the truth when he said that the new guarantee guaranteed very little; that it would probably be a "source of great sadness and grave anxiety for the future."

The events which followed seemed to bear out the Archbishop's forebodings. The school acts passed in each of the two new provinces of Alberta and Saskatchewan were based upon the ordinances of 1901. Religious teaching might be allowed, but only during the last half hour of the school day; textbooks, with the exception of the catechism, were to be neutral; and teachers were to qualify for their appointments at non-denominational normal schools. As far as teaching in French was concerned, it was to be limited to the primary grades.

For the present the matter rested there. In Alberta, indeed, it remained there without substantial alteration; but in Saskatchewan it was not long before the old familiar quarrels once more broke out. During the years between 1913 and 1917 there were charges and counter-charges over the proportion of taxes paid by corporations to be allotted to public and to separate schools. These were, however, mild when compared with the bitter criminations and recriminations which arose out of the controversial school legislation introduced into the Legislative Assembly in 1930 by Dr. J. T. M. Anderson.

The tinder was ready for the spark. As early as 1912 provincial Conservatives had declared their intention of using every means, political and legislative, to make English the sole language of instruction. Only through the tactful intervention of Mgr Mathieu of Regina was French retained as a language of instruction in accordance with the terms of the original school act. However, during the late 1920's the Conservatives were able to make political capital out of the refusal of several Protestant parents to allow their children to attend a school in which a crucifix was suspended on the wall. The crisis was temporarily averted by the personal intervention of the Premier, James Gardiner; but the whole unfortunate episode revealed the strength of those latent animosities which underlay the apparent veneer of toleration. Anderson, the Conservative leader, although publicly dissociating himself from the anti–Roman Catholic, anti-foreign agitation of the Ku Klux Klan (an importation from the United States which flourished briefly in the western provinces and then disappeared from the Canadian scene), did not hesitate to disinter the old appeals of prejudice, charging the Government of the province with compelling Protestant children to attend schools taught "by garbed clericals." He waved the Union Jack in one hand and the Orange banner in the other, frightened the people with a non-existent bogey of "French domination," and shouted for uniformity in the name of national unity.

Elevated to power in 1929, following an election in which the Klan played an important part, Anderson proceeded to carry out his campaign promises and introduced into the Assembly an amendment to the school act which provided that English should henceforth be the sole language of instruction. The only concession to the people of French origin was one which permitted the teaching of French reading, grammar, and composition for a period "not exceeding one hour each day"; pupils not wishing to receive this instruction were to be "profitably employed in other school work." Further legislation made certain that school trustees should be able to speak and write English, and that all school meetings should be conducted in that language. Restrictions were also placed upon the separate schools, many of which were taught by members of religious Orders. "No emblem of any religious denomination, order, sect, society, or association" was henceforth to be "displayed in or on any public school," nor should any teacher be permitted, while engaged in teaching, to wear "the garb of any such religious denomination, order, sect, society or association." Should any school board, unsympathetic with the Government's policy, be inclined to turn a deaf ear to the new regulations, it would promptly be deprived of financial assistance from the public purse until the regulations should be obeyed.

VI

It seemed as if French culture in western Canada was a lost cause. It had been a battle almost every year since the first Ontario settlers had made their way into the Red River Valley in the 1850's. Immigration had failed to ensure a numerical victory for the French population, and the cradles were too few to permit talk of *revanche.* French-speaking settlers, Canadian, French, and Belgian, had, indeed, increased their numbers from 64,020 in 1911 to 113,603 in 1921; but during the same years the English-speaking population had grown from 710,123 to 1,103,228, and the foreign group from 538,466 to 739,151. The people of French origin were still very much of a minority and a very small minority at that.

The law, too, had been of small assistance. The walls erected around French culture by section 93 of the British North America Act of 1867, by section 22 of the Manitoba Act of 1870, by section 11 of the Northwest Territories Act of 1875, and by section 17 of the Saskatchewan Act of 1905, had been battered, broken, and breached by the repeated assaults of hostile provincial legislation. All that was left to the western French Canadians of the equal status of former years was a state of uneasy truce in Manitoba (where French was taught on sufferance in defiance of the law), one hour a day of instruction in the French language in the schools of Saskatchewan, and one hour daily in Alberta after the first two primary school grades. In the two last-named provinces separate schools admittedly existed by law; but theirs was an existence threadbare and scanty from the Catholic point of view. And yet the French Canadian and his culture survived; not only survived but grew in strength.

Behind the miracle of French survival in western Canada was the remarkable tenacity of the French fact; the same tenacity and will to live which had made it possible for French Canada to outlive its defeat at arms in 1759 and the cession of the country to Great Britain in 1763. Immigration and acts of Parliament might fail them; they would not fail themselves. And behind them was the strong moral leadership, the unity of purpose, and the organizing genius of the Catholic Church.

A ready instrument was at hand, the parish. The parish organization had contributed much to French survival in eastern Canada after 1763; in western Canada it became the custodian of French traditions and the maternal tongue. From the first days of French settlement the Catholic clergy had sought to group the French-speaking population, Métis and white, in parishes along the Red and Assiniboine rivers and elsewhere where church and school would serve as twin fortresses of faith and language. It was from the pulpit that the faith was taught in the tongue of France; it was at the church door that the faithful gathered to exchange views and impressions as did their cousins in the rural parishes along the St. Lawrence; it was in the churchyards that the crumbling tombstones stood—silent, perpetual reminders of the traditions of endurance and courage of the French fact; and close by was the parish hall, gathering place for parish *fêtes*, church suppers, and political meetings. Faith and language were the essentials of survival.

But something more was necessary, and that something was an active organization in which laymen could play a major part. A Société du Parler français had been founded at St. Boniface in 1912, but the first vital step towards effective organization was taken in 1916 under the impact of the restrictive Norris legislation, with the founding of the Association d'Education des Canadiens français du Manitoba. The Hon. James E. Prendergast became the first President of the new body. Archbishop Béliveau sounded the keynote of the new organization. "Il nous faut cette union pour vivre et faire notre quote-part pour la cause du droit et de la justice en notre pays," said the Archbishop. "Les nôtres seront fiers et forts quand en face des lois scolaires injustes; ils sauront individuellement prendre rang parmi les défenseurs du droit et collectivement s'entendre pour garder à Dieu et à l'Eglise l'âme de leurs enfants, et transmettre à leurs descendants le parler de leurs aïeux." The principal object of the Association was to preserve French culture and ensure French survival in the primary schools. Accordingly it set out to recruit teachers and to prepare programmes of study. A special teachers' society was formed, the Ligue des Instructrices de Langue française, and a monthly bulletin was published. Since no Catholic normal schools existed, special courses were organized in French and religious pedagogy. An educational programme covering the whole twelve years of schooling was also prepared and a series of contests, *concours de français*, were organized in May of each year. Between 1923 and 1936 the numbers participating in these contests increased four times over. In the latter year no fewer than 2,758 students were entered from 109 schools and 47 parishes; of this number, 338 belonged to the high school grades. A system of inspection was also organized, and two inspectors were sent to visit the schools where French was being taught. Many errors were undoubtedly made during the early years; but the Association steadily improved its technique and gradually developed into an unofficial department of French education for the province of Manitoba. It was not without justifiable pride that Camille Fournier, Vice-President of the Association, said in 1937: "Nos positions légales nous ne les avons pas reprises, nos droits nous ne les avons pas reconquis, mais nos efforts constants ont établi un état de fait qui honore les chefs qui nous ont guidés et qui équivaut presque à une reconnaissance juridique."

French Canadians in the other two provinces quickly followed the lead of their Manitoba compatriots. As early as 1912 an Association catholique des Canadiens français had been organized in Saskatchewan, following the first great Congress of the French Language held at Quebec; but it was not until the 1920's that it became aggressively active, drawing up teaching programmes, visiting schools, issuing pedagogical directives, and conducting annual examinations in French. In Alberta the Franco-Albertans organized a national association, the Association des Canadiens français de l'Alberta in December 1925. In this province the same policy was followed as in Saskatchewan and Manitoba, special attention being devoted to the placing of competent teachers in the bilingual schools and assisting them with special courses in pedagogy, religion, and French. The Association did much to popularize singing and reading in French, and was responsible for the founding of the Avant-Gardes in order to stimulate the French and Catholic spirit among the children of the province. One of the major activities of the Association was the preparation of the annual courses in French studies extending over the whole academic year and concluding with an examination.

The various national associations concentrated upon the work in the primary schools. Secondary education was already well organized by the Church. At St. Boniface there was the college which had been founded by Bishop Provencher, with its sister institution conducted by the Sœurs des Saints Noms de Jésus et de Marie. St. Boniface College, administered at various periods of its history by the secular clergy, the

Christian Brothers, the Oblates, and the Jesuits, became in 1871 an affiliated college of the University of Manitoba. In Saskatchewan the Collège Mathieu, founded in 1917 by the Bishop of Regina, was placed under the direction of the Oblates. It was affiliated with the Catholic University of Ottawa. In Alberta the Juniorat des Oblats, founded originally at Pincher Creek in 1908, was moved to Edmonton in 1910, where, in a burst of enthusiasm, a second college was built in 1913 by the Jesuits. Both colleges existed side by side until, in 1940, the Collège d'Edmonton was obliged to close its doors. The Juniorat continued under the name of the Collège Saint-Jean. Other colleges have been founded at Prince Albert and at Falher.

Another factor of importance in bolstering French survival in the west was the French press. In 1871 Joseph Royal established *Le Métis*; and in 1881 Alphonse La Rivière founded *Le Manitoba*, for many years the principal organ of French opinion in the west. But these were frankly party papers, and in 1913 *La Liberté* was founded on a non-party basis. Further west *Le Patriote de l'ouest* was founded at Duck Lake in 1910; subsequently it moved to Prince Albert. This paper, however, fell upon evil days, and in 1941, it merged with *La Liberté*. In 1898 Fred Villeneuve founded *L'Ouest canadien* at Edmonton, the first French newspaper in the Northwest Territories. This paper, like its successors, was comparatively short-lived, although the Hon. P. E. Lessard's *Courrier de l'ouest* lasted ten years (1905–15), and *L'Union*, founded in 1917 by V. E. Feguenne, continued to exist until 1929. In 1928 *La Survivance* was founded by the Association des Canadiens français de l'Alberta. For fifteen years this paper was under the direction of Father P. E. Breton, O.M.I.

The economic depression of the 1930's resulted in a temporary setback to the work of rebuilding French morale. Many franco-westerners found themselves out of work, while those on the farms were discouraged by the low prices and the long years of drought. Some, indeed, packed their few belongings and joined the steady stream of English-speaking prairie people moving towards the warmer climate west of the Rocky Mountains. But the leaders of the French revival never lost their hopes or abandoned their task. Farmers' clubs and schools of handicrafts were started. Co-operatives were organized and *caisses populaires* opened. Scholarships were also made available to students to enable them to attend normal school or to continue their studies at university. At the same time new strength was derived from closer ties with the living centre of French culture in central Canada. In 1937, following the second Congress of the French Language at

Quebec, western representatives were elected to the new Comité permanent de la Survivance française. This committee had as its declared purpose the promotion of French culture and the co-ordination of the efforts of all the national associations. It was thus able to place at the disposal of the western associations the resources and influence of the whole body of French-speaking people in North America.

And the new access of strength was needed. The development of radio broadcasting during the 1920's and 1930's posed new problems from a cultural and religious point of view. Hitherto his home had been for the French Canadian the sanctuary of his language. The men in the mills and factories might be exposed daily to the impact of English language and culture; the children in the schools might be taught in English and play with English-speaking schoolmates; when they crossed the threshold of their homes they returned to the tongue and to the ways of their fathers. But the radio was an insidious thing which penetrated both the walls and the minds of the population, and its language was English and its culture neutralist, materialist, sometimes immoral, pagan, or frankly anti-Catholic. It was a matter of deep concern both to the Church and to the national associations how to counter the new threat to their culture. Several courses were possible; to obtain free time on the English radio stations for broadcasts in French; to buy time; or to construct new stations to broadcast wholly in French. Some free time was made available, notably by CKUA, the University of Alberta station in Edmonton; but it was limited and wholly inadequate. The establishment of the Canadian Radio Commission appeared at first to offer some hopes for a less expensive solution than that of erecting special French-language stations. Radio was a federal responsibility; and it was expected that in accordance with the spirit of Confederation, if not the letter, broadcasts would be bilingual in character. But bilingual radio was limited to the province of Quebec. A French network extending the length and breadth of the country never emerged from the chrysalis of wishful thinking. Representations were sent to the Radio Commission and to its successor, the Canadian Broadcasting Corporation. The response was sometimes sympathetic, occasionally encouraging, even promising, but little more.

In 1939 the national associations, with the assistance of the Comité permanent de la Survivance, took up the question of French-language broadcasts over the federal radio system. The C.B.C. was prepared to recognize the principle of bilingualism, and to authorize a limited number of French broadcasts over the C.B.C. station at Watrous. But demands for broader coverage were set aside with the answer that funds were not available. All that could be obtained was one hour a day out of sixteen hours' broadcasting; and that hour was not always at a suitable time for listening. If there was to be a French-language radio system in the west, it would have to be built by the French Canadians themselves. In 1941, without renouncing any of their rights to bilingual broadcasts over the federal radio network, western French Canadians formed an association known as Radio-ouest-française, made up of representatives from the three prairie provinces, which studied the whole question of French-language broadcasts both from the financial and technical points of view; and in 1943 Dr. L. O. Beauchemin, President of Radio-ouest-française, announced: "Nous avons absolument besoin pour survivre de postes radiophoniques français. Nous les aurons." His words were but an echo of those of the President of the Comité permanent de la Survivance, Adrien Pouliot of Quebec, who after a visit to western Canada returned home convinced that the problem of radio broadcasting in the west was a most acute one from the standpoint of the western French Canadians, and that a French-language radio system was the only solution to the problem of cultural survival in the prairie provinces. In March 1944 a request was made to the C.B.C. for permission to establish private French stations in all three provinces. An appeal was then made for funds. Money poured in from clergy and laymen alike, from men rich in dollars and from men rich only in children. Two years later the C.B.C. granted the necessary authority for the operation of Radio St. Boniface, and on May 27, 1946, CKSB, the first French-language station in western Canada, began its broadcasts. The success of the new station assured, Radio-ouest-française approached the Board of Governors of the C.B.C. in the summer of 1947 with a request for licences for private stations in Alberta and Saskatchewan. These were granted, and in 1949 CHFA was opened in Edmonton. Subsequently two more French-language stations were built in Saskatchewan at Gravelbourg (CFRG) and Saskatoon (CFNS). These two stations began broadcasting in 1952. More recently two hours of programmes on television have been made available in French on Sundays, over CBWT, Winnipeg.

The establishment of the French-language radio system was not achieved without opposition. Few if any were the discordant voices raised in Manitoba, where a number of prominent English Canadians backed the establishment of Radio St. Boniface; but in Alberta militant Protestants, supported, surprisingly enough, by some English-speaking

Roman Catholics, opposed any further extension of broadcasting in the French language. One member of the Alberta Government, the Hon. W. A. Fallow, added his voice to those in opposition. In a memorandum to the C.B.C. he argued that Canada was not a bilingual country and that special concessions to the French language would only make it impossible to refuse similar concessions to a multitude of other tongues. There were, however, English-speaking people who deplored these efforts to revive old ethnic prejudices, and who conceded that, even if French were not, from a narrowly legal standpoint, an official language in the western provinces, it should, nevertheless, for historic reasons, enjoy a special status in all the provinces of Canada. The Massey Commission gave its blessing to the extension of facilities for French broadcasting; and on September 19, 1947 the editor of the *Montreal Gazette* wrote in an editorial ". . . it is a lamentable thing that there exist to this day . . . people who are prepared to stand up in public to deny this fact and to make stupid arguments about the 'Balkanization' of Canada, suggesting that the grant of a licence to a French-language station would lead inevitably to broadcasting in a dozen other tongues as well."

The years which witnessed the successful struggle for the establishment of French radio broadcasting in western Canada also witnessed the emergence of an old controversial issue in a new garb. In all three western provinces the basic unit of the school system was the small, autonomous, school district controlled by a board of trustees elected locally by the ratepayers. The school board was responsible for engaging teachers and for all financial arrangements in the district. Each school thus tended to reflect the personality of the community in which it was located. The system was not the most efficient or the most economical; although it did have the virtue of being essentially democratic. However, during the 1930's an agitation, supported by many teachers and school inspectors, developed in favour of doing away with the small school districts and replacing them with larger units which would not only improve administrative efficiency but make possible improved educational facilities in the schools.

Both Manitoba and Saskatchewan, aware of the sensitivity of the minority in all matters relating to educational policy, trod slowly; but the Alberta Government rushed ahead and in 1936 introduced legislation providing for the amalgamation of local school districts and the adoption of large administrative units. The French and Catholic minorities at once saw the dangers implicit in the proposed legislation. The merging of such districts as they already controlled into larger units in which they would, in many instances, be outvoted, would seriously limit, if not completely nullify, the privileges which they enjoyed and the influence which they possessed under the school legislation of 1905. The Association des Canadiens français de l'Alberta sprang to the defence of French and Catholic privileges, and sufficient pressure was put upon the Government to bring about, not a substantial change in the new legislation, but at least the insertion of safeguards for the rights of French Canadians and Roman Catholics. It was provided that when the board of an ordinary school district, forming a part of a large administrative unit, requested religious instruction in the school in conformity with existing regulations, the board of the large unit would engage a teacher for this purpose, nominated by the smaller. A similar provision was made for bilingual instruction in the primary grades. Moreover, should three or more local school boards ask to be excluded from the larger divisional grouping on the grounds of dissatisfaction with the treatment accorded them in the matter of religious or bilingual instruction, they might withdraw from the divisional grouping, following a majority vote of the ratepayers in a referendum held under the auspices of the Minister of Education. The minority had saved its rights by prompt and effective action on the part of the national association of French Canadians; but there were still many who felt apprehensive of the future. In April 1947 Bishop Routhier of Grouard urged the faithful to resist all further attempts at educational centralization. "Il importe, avant qu'il ne soit trop tard," he wrote, "de rappeler, par une ferme attitude et de légitimes représentations, à nos legislateurs qu'il y a des bornes à leurs droits et que les droits des parents en matière d'éducation priment ceux de l'Etat."

The other two prairie provinces followed the lead of Alberta. In 1944 the Saskatchewan legislature passed a new school act introducing the large unit system, but with safeguards for the teaching of religion and French. In Manitoba, after several years of careful study, the Government submitted to the Assembly in April 1945 legislation designed to reduce the number of school districts in the province from 1,800 to 34. The proposed bill was attacked strongly by the Association d'Education des Canadiens français and by the Société d'Enseignement postscolaire; and in the Legislative Assembly Edmond Préfontaine argued that administrative efficiency and improved teaching conditions could be achieved without reducing the number of school districts and awakening the slumbering animosities of past years, by adjusting the school grants in accordance with the needs of the districts concerned. The bill was not withdrawn as a result of the backing which Préfontaine received from other members of the legislature; but it was modified so that for the time being only two large units would be organized on an experimental basis; the power to nominate members of the board of the large unit was also surrendered in favour of appointment by election; and a clause giving the Government power to abolish small school boards by simple regulation was suppressed. It was a victory, but only a modest one. The legislation still remained on the books, and although the Government encouraged its implementation, it did not attempt to impose the large school units upon the objecting school districts.

VII

One of the interesting developments within recent years has been the substantial increase in the number of people of French origin living in British Columbia. The first French Canadians to reach the Pacific Coast were those who accompanied Mackenzie, Fraser, and Thompson on their early explorations, and the missionaries who followed in the footsteps of Fathers Blanchet and Demers after 1838. From time to time various Catholic institutions, such, for instance, as St. Paul's Hospital, founded in Vancouver by the Sœurs de la Providence in 1894, were established; but the French population remained small and its influence ineffective. Early in the present century (1907) a number of French Canadians were brought from Quebec to work in the lumber mills along the Fraser River. At their head came Father R. Maillard, an Oblate priest, who gave his name to the parish organized near New Westminster in 1909. French Canadians also settled in Vancouver, in the Okanagan Valley, and on Vancouver Island. Nevertheless the growth of the French-speaking population was slow; and as late as 1931 the Franco-Columbians numbered only 15,028. During the economic depression of the thirties they were reinforced by the arrival of French-Canadian immigrants from the distressed prairie provinces, principally from Alberta and Saskatchewan. The big increase, however, came after the Second World War. Large numbers of French Canadians had passed some time in the west with the armed services during the war years. They were attracted by the high salaries and the warmer climate. Some of them married British Columbia girls and chose to take their discharge on the west coast when hostilities came to an end. Thus the population of French origin jumped almost 100 per cent between the years 1941 and 1951.

The same years witnessed a rebirth on the part of the Franco-

Columbians of a consciousness of their French heritage. The Union canadienne-française de Vancouver had been organized as early as 1905; but it had petered out within a few years. From time to time various social and dramatic clubs were formed by French Canadians; not, however, until 1941 was a proposal advanced for the federation of all such groups into a strong provincial organization. Thus was born the Fédération canadienne-française de la Colombie-Britannique in 1945, with headquarters at Victoria. The new Fédération, following the precedent established in the Prairies, set out to organize new parishes, arrange for regular meetings of the branches of the Fédération, hold classes and contests in French, build up French libraries, sponsor special celebrations such as Saint Jean-Baptiste Day, and conduct weekly half-hour radio programmes from New Westminster. They also encouraged the establishment of *caisses populaires* at Maillardville and Vancouver.

The big problem facing the French-speaking Canadians of British Columbia was that of schools. British Columbia had never had a separate school system, and Catholics resident in that province had never enjoyed the privileges of which their co-religionists had, in part at least, been deprived in the other western provinces. They had never lost anything because they had never had anything to lose. Petitions had been sent to the provincial legislature as early as the one prepared by Bishop Durieu in 1881, asking for recognition of the principle of separate schools, but no steps had ever been taken in that direction. It had been necessary for Catholics, both French and English, to erect and to maintain their own schools, while at the same time paying their share of taxes for the support of the regular public schools. The burden was a heavy one. Roman Catholics, and particularly those who spoke French, were not found among the wealthier members of the population. Finally, in 1951, the schools maintained by the French Canadians at Maillardville suddenly were closed. It was a dramatic action designed to bring to the attention of the government and of the people of the province generally the plight in which the Catholic minority found itself. Catholics, French and English, organized the British Columbia Catholic Education Association and undertook a vigorous campaign with a view to obtaining some modification of the educational system which would permit the establishment of state-assisted separate schools. In 1953 the Association presented a formal petition to the legislature. The response, however, was unfavourable, and the issue of separate schools in British Columbia remains unsettled. Meanwhile appeals were made by the French Canadians to their compatriots in other parts of Canada, and funds poured in from Quebec for the construction and support of a new school for French-speaking children in Vancouver. This school was opened in September 1954 with 107 pupils under the direction of the Sisters of the Good Shepherd from Quebec.

As far as the northern territories are concerned, cultural survival on the part of the French-speaking population has never developed into a major problem. In northern British Columbia and the Yukon the French fact is practically non-existent. Contrary to what took place in the Prairies, very few French trappers or fur traders established themselves in the north country. A number of French Canadians took part in the Gold Rush to the Yukon in 1898; but the great majority went back home again after a few years, wiser but poorer, and thoroughly disappointed with what they had found; those who remained stayed single, or married Indian or Métis women and became absorbed into the Indian or English-speaking population.

In more recent years some French Canadians have moved into the north with the construction of the Alaska Highway. These came, for the most part, from the Prairies. They had already been partly anglicized and mixed freely with the workers and settlers of other races and nationalities whose one common bond was the English language. They had few opportunities to group together and to form a French unit which might preserve the language and the traditions of the past. The only French-Canadian families in the Yukon anxious to maintain their cultural individuality are the families of men in the Canadian army or air force, who have but recently arrived from other parts of Canada and who are not permanently settled in the north. Although most of the Catholic missionaries and sisters are French-speaking, they have found it next to impossible to organize distinctive French groups for the sake of preserving the French heritage. The country is not one which lends itself to agriculture and the settlement on the land of a compact group of settlers; so the prospects for a homogeneous French group in the Yukon appear very slim. And while settlers come into the north in ones and twos in search of employment or adventure, they will inevitably be absorbed by the English-speaking population with which they are surrounded.

The situation in the Northwest Territories differs little from that in the Yukon. The French-speaking population is weak, both in numbers and in will to survive. In 1951 only 1,202 people were classified by the census as speaking French, and of these, 1,031 were classified as speaking English as well. Although the total French-speaking population equals more than 17 per cent of the English-speaking population (6,929), and 7.5 per cent of the whole population of the Territories (16,004), in no place does it form a compact community. Scattered groups of French Canadians and French-speaking Métis are to be found throughout the District of Mackenzie, the largest individual groups living within the vicinity of the major centres of settlement at Yellowknife, Hay River, and Forts Smith, Resolution, Providence, and Simpson. Lacking the incentive and the opportunities to remain French, these groups are becoming more and more assimilated to the culture of the majority. The language of the majority is English, and so too is the language of the schools. According to section 98 of the Northwest Territories School Ordinance of 1952, French may be taught in a primary course, but no school in the District of Mackenzie has as yet taken advantage of this provision. Opposition to the use of French as a language of instruction is strong on the part of the majority—witness the debates in the Northwest Territories Council in 1952 when Louis Audette proposed that French should enjoy equal status with English in the territorial schools—and the French-speaking minority has been reluctant to press even for such privileges as have been accorded it by law. Religious instruction in the schools is given in English or in one of the several Indian tongues, for these are the languages understood by all, or almost all, the people concerned. Even in the mission schools French did not survive beyond the 1930's as a medium of instruction. Owing to the fact that French was not taught, and owing too to the mixing of French, English, Indian, and other races in the settlements of the Territories, the French spoken is oftentimes crude and incorrect; this, in itself, adds to the sense of inferiority felt by those who use it. English is not only the language of the majority, it is the mark of social superiority. The Catholic Church, the living force behind French survival in other parts of western Canada, appears to have accepted without resistance the course which history has taken in the Northwest Territories. The fact that no pastoral letters have considered this question for the past twenty-five years is evidence of the reluctance of the Church to lead a cause which is virtually lost or to attempt to revive a culture which possesses no real vitality or strength in this region of Canada. Only by increased immigration of French Canadians to the Territories, by granting the French language complete equality with English in the schools, and by giving more French-speaking Canadians government appointments there, would it be possible to strengthen the French fact and give prestige to a waning culture; and these are developments which are unlikely to emerge from pious hopes on the part of the few into realities for the many.

VIII

In the light of this historical survey of the issues and problems attending French survival in western Canada, the question at once arises whether this survival is now assured. Is the French fact a temporary or a lasting thing in the history of the four western provinces?

On the surface, at least, there is every evidence of durability. Numerically the people of French origin in the west have gained rather than lost ground. During the last decade, from 1941 to 1951, their numbers have improved from 169,023 to 217,653, an increase of 35 per cent. By provinces the figures are: Manitoba from 52,996 to 66,020; Saskatchewan from 50,530 to 51,930; Alberta from 42,979 to 56,185; British Columbia from 21,876 to 41,919; and the Yukon and North-West Territories from 642 to 1,599. More significant, however, is the fact that in every instance there has been an increase in the French population in proportion to the total population of each province. The respective percentages for 1941 and 1951 are: Manitoba, 7.2 and 8.5; Saskatchewan, 5.7 and 6; Alberta, 5.4 and 6; British Columbia, 2.6 and 3.5.

Broadly speaking, the French-speaking population in western Canada is a rural one, with the one exception of the Franco-Columbians. In Manitoba 34,996 people of French origin, or approximately 53 per cent, live in the country. Of the urban population, however, two-thirds, or over 20,000, live in the Winnipeg–St. Boniface urban area, thus concentrating the great bulk of the French-Catholic population within the region of St. Boniface and the Red River Valley. In Saskatchewan over three-quarters of the people of French origin may be classified as rural, but they are scattered and dispersed throughout the whole province. The largest single group is to be found within the general vicinity of Prince Albert. In Alberta 60 per cent of the French-speaking population lives in the country, or 33,807 out of 56,185. As in Manitoba, however, the bulk of this population is concentrated in the north of the province between Edmonton and Peace River. Of the 22,378 French-Canadian city dwellers, 9,047 live in Edmonton, thus adding the strength of their proximity to the rural group. In British Columbia the situation is reversed. Here 66.5 per cent of the people of French origin live in the cities, principally in Vancouver, New Westminster, and the Fraser Valley.

Not only have the people of French origin retained their proportionate strength in numbers, they have also clearly demonstrated the strength of their will to retain and maintain their distinctive culture. Despite the whittling away of privileges conceded in 1870 and 1875, as a result of the legislation of 1890 and 1916 in Manitoba and of 1905 and 1930 in Saskatchewan, the western French Canadians have shown the living force of their heritage through the achievements of their national associations, colleges, convents, schools, newspapers, radio stations, and economic organizations, to say nothing of their 200 parishes and missions. For fifty years they have resisted all attempts at assimilation. To some extent this was the inevitable response to a challenge; much of it, however, was the positive result of the leadership afforded by the clergy, by men like Tâché, Langevin, and Béliveau, like Lacombe, Routhier, and Baudoux. Today in Manitoba the French-speaking clergy control three of the four Roman Catholic dioceses in the province—St. Boniface, Keewatin, and Hudson Bay; in Saskatchewan they control two of five dioceses—Gravelbourg and Prince Albert; and in Alberta two of four—St. Paul and Grouard. There are no French-Canadian bishops in British Columbia, but in the Northwest Territories the vicariates apostolic of Whitehorse and Mackenzie are held by French-speaking clergy.[1] From the heart at the Archdiocese of St. Boniface, through the several dioceses to the individual parishes and homes, the faith has flowed, giving strength to the old traditions and to the new aspirations. Faith and language have been inseparable, Catholicism and the French tongue indivisible. Home, school, church, press, and national society (to which should be added radio) have been the basic factors which have assured French survival; but within, through, and behind all of them, can be detected the guiding hand and encouraging voice of the French-Canadian clergy. As long as the identification of faith and language, one with the other, is an accepted principle within the Catholic hierarchy, so long will the battle for the rights of French Canadians continue; and so long will the French fact remain a real and living part of western Canadian history.

But is the picture of the future wholly without its sombre colours? Complete confidence and goodwill has not always existed among Irish and French Roman Catholics in western Canada. French and Irish rivalries have not been unknown in other parts of Canada, and in the west the great expansion of non–French-speaking immigration during

[1]These include Mgr M. Baudoux, Mgr P. Dumouchel, Mgr M. Lacroix, Mgr A. Décosse, Mgr L. Blais, Mgr L. P. Lussier, Mgr H. Routhier, Mgr J. Coudert, and Mgr J. Trocellier.

the early years of the present century gave strength to the demand on the part of the Irish for a greater share of ecclesiastical control. In 1905 a letter was addressed to Cardinal Merry del Val, the Papal Secretary of State, complaining of the domination of the western Canadian dioceses by French Canadians, and suggesting that the spread of Catholicism among the newcomers was being hindered by the lack of English-speaking clergy. This internal rivalry was brought vividly to the fore in 1910, when Archbishop Bourne of Westminster, in his address to the Eucharistic Congress in Montreal, urged the Canadian clergy to make English, rather than French, the language of the faith in western Canada, and to abandon the struggle for the survival of French culture in a part of country where immigration had already determined that English would be the tongue spoken by the majority. French Canadians, believing that the Holy See would never have sanctioned such a plea unless it had been misinformed about conditions in Canada, brought about the recall of the Papal Legate, Mgr Donato Sbaretti. But to their acute disappointment Sbaretti's return to Rome was followed by the establishment of Winnipeg as a diocese separate from St. Boniface and immediately subject to the Holy See, and by the appointment of Arthur Sinnott, who had been Mgr Sbaretti's secretary, as the first incumbent. Soon afterwards, Henry O'Leary was made Archbishop of the heretofore French diocese of St. Albert, renamed Edmonton. In 1913 Calgary was erected into a diocese under Bishop McNally, and the Oblates and French clergy were withdrawn.[2] To mollify the French Canadians, a French Canadian was appointed to Prince Albert, and Mgr O. E. Mathieu to Regina. Every effort was made by the French clergy to consolidate their position in southern Saskatchewan, but Bishop Mathieu himself accepted what he felt was inevitable. His successor was James McGuigan; and the French Canadians had to be content with the establishment of Gravelbourg as a French diocese.

This rivalry of language, among Roman Catholics themselves, has been a constant source of weakness to the French Canadians whenever and wherever they have tried to press their claims within the provinces dominated by indifferent English-speaking Protestant majorities. Not only did the agitation for the extension of radio facilities for French broadcasting receive little or no assistance from English-speaking Catholics, in some instances it was actually opposed by them. In 1954 both French- and English-speaking Roman Catholics revealed the extent of the split between the two ethnic groups when they aired

[2]A French-speaking parish in Calgary (Ste Famille) was re-established in 1928.

their quarrels over the control of separate schools in the city of Edmonton, in the press of that city. Much has been done by men like Bishop Mathieu, Cardinal Villeneuve, Cardinal McGuigan, and Archbishop O'Neill to achieve harmony and understanding between the two linguistic groups within the Catholic Church; nevertheless racial jealousies and internal quarrels have, in the past, militated against the successful outcome of the French-Canadian struggle for equality of rights.

Nor has there been an unbroken and effective united front on the part of all French Canadians. Within his own province of Quebec, the French Canadian is secure; he is one of the majority; he is therefore inevitably a supporter of the rights of that majority and of the rights of his province. In western Canada, however, the French Canadian is a member of the minority. For him, provincial autonomy has held few virtues. At its hands he has lost what rights he once enjoyed. For the western French Canadian the guarantees of his privileges have, in every instance, come from the central government, not from the province; and to the central government he has been obliged to turn for help in periods of crisis. The British North America Act, the Manitoba Act, the Northwest Territories Act, were all acts of the federal Parliament; it was from the provincial legislatures that emanated all the anti-French and anti-Catholic legislation of the last half century and more.

The point of view of French Canadians of the west and those of the east is therefore different. The westerner argues that bilingualism and biculturalism should be recognized throughout the length and breadth of Canada as a moral if not as a legal right. For him the frontiers of French Canada extend far beyond the Ottawa River and the Bay of Chaleur, to the Pacific and to the Atlantic oceans. His vision of *la patrie* is a broad one, a vision which, he feels, does not always inspire his compatriots in the province of Quebec, and which too seldom elicits their strongest political support. Talk of separatism, not infrequently heard on the banks of the St. Lawrence, brings forth no responsive echo on the banks of the Red and the Saskatchewan. There is no denial that Quebec has given aid to the French cause in the west, that from Quebec have come men, funds, books, encouragement, and advice; but assistance has always been less practical than moral. And what political support has been available has had to be made effective through the federal Parliament. A province such as Quebec, which demands respect for its own autonomy, is restrained by its own convictions from interfering in the affairs of other provinces, even on behalf of the people to whom it has given birth. It was these convictions that defeated the Conservative attempt to coerce Manitoba in 1896 and prevented section 93 of the British North America Act from becoming the real buckler of minority rights. The western French Canadian, while not unappreciative of the attitude of his Quebec brother to the perils of over-centralization, must, as long as he is in the minority, still look to Ottawa, if he is to realize his political aspirations.

During the sittings of the Rowell-Sirois Commission, all three western French-Canadian national associations presented strong briefs demanding redress of grievances suffered at the hands of the several provinces; and in 1949 the Association canadien-français de l'Alberta, testifying before the Royal Commission on the Arts and Sciences, advocated the establishment of a permanent, national, cultural committee comprising two autonomous sections, French and English, which would be responsible for cultural matters in the whole country: "Ce Corps aurait pour fonction de s'occuper de tout ce qui touche au caractère biculturel au Canada." This was followed by a revealing editorial in *La Survivance* written by Father Breton, pointing out that notwithstanding the prerogatives of the provinces in the field of education, cultural problems were a federal matter, for Canada was a bilingual, bicultural state, in which the two cultural groups possessed equal rights if unequal privileges. He wrote:

> On se plaint parfois et à bon droit des agissements de nos adversaires qui veulent faire du Québec une "Réserve" en dehors de laquelle le français n'a pas droit de cité. N'allons pas donner raison à de telles prétensions en voulant délimiter le Canada français aux frontières de Québec. N'oublions pas que 25 pour cent des Canadiens français vivent en dehors de ces frontières et sont répandus à travers tout le Canada. Si nous avons le droit de réclamer du fédéral le respect du bilinguisme et des droits égaux pour les deux grandes races du pays, on ne saurait omettre le plus important de ces droits; le respect de la double culture dans toute l'étendue de la Confédération. Car si la culture relève en bonne partie des provinces, elle n'est pas absente tant s'en faut de l'Etat fédéral.

This was not an argument which would find a full-throated echo from Quebec.

But different points of view, such as these, do not constitute the major problems of survival at the present time. There are still others, even more significant. Every effort possible has admittedly been made to encourage the teaching of French and to utilize to the fullest the meagre opportunities offered by law or by tolerance.[8] But the pro-

[8]French is now taught in the public schools in Manitoba from Grade IV.

visions of the school acts, even the most liberal, such as those in Alberta, are manifestly insufficient to give the pupils a thorough knowledge of their language or an understanding of their cultural heritage. The results are not always encouraging. Too frequently the French spoken by the western Canadian is marked by poverty of vocabulary and by the use of English forms and expressions. Many parents fail to make the effort required to speak correctly, and adolescents sometimes feel that to do so is to expose themselves to the derision of their comrades. Much better are the results achieved in the residential colleges, such as those at St. Boniface, Gravelbourg, and Edmonton. Boys and girls who are privileged to attend these institutions emerge far superior to the general run of those who pass through the ordinary provincial schools. Unfortunately for the survival of a vigorous French culture in the west, the graduates of these schools all too often drift eastwards to central Canada where they find greater opportunities. It is the old story of the drift of educated Canadians to the United States on a smaller scale. The very people who might be expected to provide the leaders of the French community—the doctors, the lawyers, the teachers—have enriched the life of other provinces than those in which they saw their birth and education. In 1937 Mgr Yelle said to the second Congress of the French Language at Quebec: "L'autre danger est d'un autre ordre, c'est l'émigration de nos jeunes laïcs plus instruits vers l'est, où ils semblent pouvoir plus facilement s'orienter et trouver leur chemin. Cela pose le problème chez nous de la classe dirigeante et des chefs de demain." There are, of course, exceptions. Some, like Bishop Routhier, have entered Orders and remained in western Canada; others like Lucien Maynard in Alberta and Sauveur Marcoux in Manitoba, have entered provincial politics and become cabinet ministers; but the general rule holds true. And in consequence, not a few French Canadians, believing that their professional future would be better assured among the majority of the population, prefer to follow their studies at English-speaking colleges, or at the provincial universities at Edmonton, Saskatoon, and Winnipeg. This loss of leaders is something which the French community in the west can ill afford if it is to maintain its own life without loss of vitality.

And has there not been a real loss of vitality? Despite the efforts of the Church and the activities of the national associations, a considerable group of those classified by the census as being of French origin have ceased to speak their mother tongue; some too have lost their faith, thus giving ground for the familiar argument that when the

French Canadian loses his maternal language he all too frequently loses his Catholic faith as well. Broadly speaking, the last two decades reveal a slow but steady decline in the numbers of those who cling to faith and language, the twin safeguards of their French heritage; and the farther west we go, the more obvious the decline. In Manitoba no fewer than 13,799 people of French origin (or 20 per cent of the total French population) were classified in 1951 as no longer speaking or understanding French. In Saskatchewan the corresponding figures were 16,394 and 31 per cent; in Alberta, 21,859 and 38 per cent; and in British Columbia, 22,852 and 54 per cent. From the standpoint of religion, 90.2 per cent of the people of French origin in Manitoba were Catholics; in Saskatchewan 85.5 per cent; in Alberta, 80 per cent; and in British Columbia, 65.6 per cent. In every instance there has been a percentage increase in the number of non-Catholic French in the years between 1931 and 1951. In most instances the French Canadians retained their language where they were grouped together in rural areas where the influence of the Church could most effectively be exercised. It is in communities which were virtually swamped by surrounding English-speaking communities, in cities, where mixed marriages were more easily contracted, and in schools where the children were exposed to teaching solely in English and to an atmosphere wholly English, that the French language tended to disappear in favour of the other tongue.

The outlook for French cultural survival is not, however, one of unrelieved gloom. Both in Manitoba and in Alberta there are militant, compact groups, strongly attached to the soil and sufficiently concentrated to make it possible to put up some effective resistance to the penetration of English language and culture. This concentration has greatly facilitated the work of the Church and enabled the clergy to exercise their cultural as well as religious leadership. St. Boniface, St. Norbert, Ste Agathe, Lorette, Notre Dame de Lourdes, Edmonton, St. Paul, Bonnyville, Falher, Peace River, are all seats of active French and Catholic life. In both provinces too, the radio and the newspapers have a fair circulation and wide influence. Could bilingual instruction but be extended to half each school day, the maintenance of French culture would be assured, beyond all doubt.

In Saskatchewan, however, the situation is less hopeful. The extensive dispersion of the French-speaking population is a source of great weakness. It exposes the scattered French communities to the full impact of the English-speaking population and prevents them from drawing strength from close association with other French groups.

More than ever English becomes a necessity as well as a convenience. In no diocese are the French a majority and in no constituency are they numerous enough to elect one of their own people either to the Legislative Assembly or to Parliament. In the other two prairie provinces the fact of concentration has made it possible for the French-speaking constituencies to elect four French Canadians to the legislature in Manitoba and three in Alberta;[4] moreover, two French Canadians from Manitoba and one from Alberta sit in Parliament.[5] For the present the northern group of French Canadians in Saskatchewan would seem to be in a stronger position than the southern group, despite a heavy financial commitment, including the Collège Mathieu, in the diocese of Gravelbourg. The latter diocese embraces such centres as Swift Current, Maple Creek, and Assiniboia, where, for the most part, French is not spoken; and the bulk of its Catholic constituents resent the presence of a purely French clergy. Unless there is an access of strength by immigration from Quebec, this southern Saskatchewan group, like the small community in the vicinity of Pincher Creek in southern Alberta, may well be absorbed by the larger and more aggressive English-speaking population. In British Columbia, too, the battle would seem to be a losing one against time and assimilation. The future of the French fact in western Canada would appear to rest with the traditional stronghold at the junction of the Red and Assiniboine and with the dioceses of St. Paul and Grouard, to which there has, in recent years, been a fairly steady flow of immigrants from the mother province of Quebec.

And yet one must hesitate before attempting to sound too soon or too loudly the funeral bell of French culture in Saskatchewan or in British Columbia. The tenacity with which the western French Canadian has clung to his language and his culture in the face of hostility, indifference, and defeat, has been a source of admiration to the French Canadian of Quebec, and of amazement to the English Canadian in other parts of Canada. Even at the price of hard sacrifices he has gained his victories in the battle for survival; victories, however, more often moral than legal. Absorption, if it comes, will come slowly and painfully, for even in adversity the French Canadians' will to live has always been a mighty thing: "Nous avons une indéfectible confiance en la victoire finale."

1956

[4]Manitoba, the Hon. H. Préfontaine, E. Brodeur, R. Teillet, F. Jobin; Alberta, the Hon. L. Maynard, L. Joly, J. R. Desfosses.

[5]R. N. Jutras (Provencher), F. Viau (St. Boniface), and J. M. Dechêne (Athabaska).

Ontario: The Two Races

LÉOPOLD LAMONTAGNE

Head, Department of Modern Languages
Royal Military College of Canada

TO A CONTEMPORARY OBSERVER Canada looks like an immense laboratory in which Providence is supervising the various phases of an experiment begun about two centuries ago. Each province is a huge test-tube into which are thrown the most diversified substances. The Ontario one contains elements of at least twenty-five ethnic groups, all with different temperaments and characteristics, living in different regions and climates. The mixture is fermenting; certain forces develop, some components lose their properties, some in accordance with variable laws, undergo a transmutation toward an undetermined status. The nature of the substances involved, their quantities, and the influence of the material conditions in which they are set up necessarily produce combinations which deeply affect the destiny of the province and even of the nation.

An analysis of that experiment, limited to the study of the relations between the two more important organic elements, French and English, will bring out historical, demographic, sociological, educational, and religious phenomena.

I

From a historical point of view the French and English descendants living side by side in Ontario could find many good reasons for either quarrelling or living in good understanding. Those two groups, more than any others, deserve to be called fraternal enemies.

They are brothers by virtue of their common heritage of a European culture which dates back to the Romans. For centuries the English fought on the soil of France, and their soldiers had an influence which can still be felt, to some extent, in the coastal provinces as far as Bordeaux and even the Basque country, where many of them settled permanently. On the other hand, William the Conqueror and his

Normans left in England some names and customs still to be found today among the noble families of the kingdom. A study of vocabulary reveals that the two languages have a common stock of about two thousand words. The English court and nobility have faithfully kept the usage of the French language: "Honi soit qui mal y pense" is the motto of the Order of the Garter, and the tune of the English national anthem was retained from a religious hymn of the former school of St. Cyr. Finally those trends of *entente cordiale* and even of political union —such as was advocated on a memorable occasion by Sir Winston Churchill—are the undeniable results of an undisguised reciprocal esteem.

However, the common heritage of those two great nations carries with its load of assets an equal load of debts. There is many a conflict to be forgotten between them, defeats and victories on both sides. There is Joan of Arc, Henry VI, Richelieu, Napoleon, and Wellington. There is the Hundred Years' War and the Seven Years' War.

This last conflict, partly waged on Canadian territory, was the logical issue of long political and economic strife. For a century and a half the French and the English had been fighting for the possession of Canada and its rich fur trade. Whenever they did not fight among themselves, they kept busy stirring up the Indians against their rivals. In Ontario, particularly, some conclusive battles were fought on Hudson Bay and on Lakes Ontario and Erie. All the important cities established on the Ottawa, the St. Lawrence, and the Great Lakes—Kingston, Toronto, Niagara Falls, and Windsor—were originally founded by Frenchmen. From 1760 on, the English came and occupied the Ontario sector, then part of the province of Quebec.

The arrival of the Loyalists in 1783 is a turning point in the history of Ontario. Those voluntary exiles did not have any predisposition to preserve relations between the old and the new British subjects. Inspired with an indestructible loyalty to England, how could they love the fellow countrymen of those Frenchmen who had propagated in the United States the revolutionary ideas which had led the Americans to throw overboard the lawful government of London, of those Frenchmen who had come to the United States to fight in the rebels' ranks? On the other hand, around 1800, parents who could afford it used to send their children to schools in Lower Canada "where they acquired the French language and manners."[1]

Meanwhile the few Frenchmen who had remained on the shores of Lakes Ontario and Erie were completely destitute. They had occupied

[1]"Col. John Clark Memoirs" in *Ontario Historical Society, Papers and Records*, vol. VII (Toronto, 1906), p. 185.

the country for 150 years, but in a nomadic fashion. They were mostly interested in the fur trade. They may claim to have established a few short-lived missions; some martyrs sealed with their blood the conquest of this rugged territory; a few soldiers remained around the débris of the destroyed forts, but, ruined by war, they were left with only the worthless notes which the French troops had used to buy their supplies. Poor, scattered in very small numbers, they grimly witnessed the incoming tide of the Loyalists, of the immigrants, and of the wealthy English merchants. The courage of the discoverers, the sufferings of the missionaries, the efforts of the traders, together with the heroism of the soldiers, had not succeeded in securing for the French any stronghold on the upper St. Lawrence. The Constitutional Act of 1791, which detached Ontario from Quebec, was in a way a confirmation of this state of things.

It seemed that this separation would isolate and drown the French element of the new province. On the contrary, the government, assembled in Newark, issued as one of its first decrees a measure aimed at the protection of the French-speaking citizens: "Such Acts as have already passed or may hereafter pass the Legislature of this Province shall be translated into the French language for the benefit of the inhabitants of the Western district of this province and other French settlers who may come to reside within the province."[2] This text constitutes the Magna Carta of the rights of the French language in Ontario. It was published freely, without any restraint; it is the act of consecration, lucid and generous, of bilingualism in the territory then known as Upper Canada. At that time the important appointment of Commander of the Lake Ontario navy was given to a French Canadian, Jean-Baptiste Bouchette. The great majority of his crew were of French origin.

The sympathies of the Ontarians of those days were expressed anew on the occasion of the arrival in Kingston and Newark of the French Royalists exiled by the Revolution and led by Count de Puisaye. Governor Simcoe himself wished them a hearty welcome: "It is gratifying to know that the chief inhabitants of Upper Canada are those banished from the United States for manifesting that same attachment to their king which characterises all loyal Frenchmen who suffer from exile. It will be a consolation to those coming to settle Upper Canada to find people sympathetic to them."[3] If the perseverance of the French

[2]*Journals of the Legislative Assembly of Upper Canada, 1792–1804* (Toronto, 1911), p. 23.

[3]J. Edmond Roy, éd., *Rapport sur les Archives de France relatives à l'histoire du Canada* (Ottawa, 1911), Simcoe to Abbé Desjardins.

Royalists had been equal to that of the English Loyalists, the composition of the Ontario population might well have been different.

Under the Union the government sat in Kingston, where the first Speaker of the House in 1841 was a French Canadian, Augustin Cuvillier. It was in Kingston, in Ontario, that Louis-Hyppolite Lafontaine delivered his famous speech on the rights of the French language and succeeded in making both languages official. It should also be remembered that Lafontaine, defeated in Quebec, was re-elected in York.

Even though the present period witnesses some acts of intolerance, it is marked by links of undeniable sympathy. In any case, Ontarians of either English or French origin are both British and Canadian subjects, and they dress, eat, and live so much in the same fashion that, from a mere look at them, it is impossible to distinguish one from another.

II

However, there are some differences, and the most striking one is undoubtedly of a demographic nature. It would be interesting to determine the proportions of the various elements of the Ontario population at the time of the Treaty of Paris in 1763, in the year of the arrival of the Loyalists in 1783, and at the date of the creation of the province of Ontario in 1791. Unfortunately the necessary information is not available. The first census showing ethnic origins was taken only in 1851. For a total population of 952,002 it gives 26,417 Franco-Ontarians. In 1861, they were 6,870 more. It is impossible to locate their whereabouts with accuracy, but it is certain that the French element was by that time overflowing from the Quebec border between the Ottawa and the St. Lawrence, that it constituted quite a homogeneous group in the Essex peninsula in the vicinity of the former Detroit trading post, and that the rest of it was scattered mostly on the shores of the Ottawa and the St. Lawrence rivers. Lafontaine, a French-Canadian town on Georgian Bay, was about twenty years old at that time.

The movement of French-Canadian colonization in Ontario had begun after the insurrection of 1837–8, when Quebec was hit by a serious economic depression. In order to check the tide of migration across the United States border, the bishops encouraged colonization in Canada as a patriotic and religious enterprise. In 1850, Vicar General Macdonell was sent to the session of the legislature in Toronto to represent the bishops and to keep an eye on the interests of religion; he was to obtain from the government the funds required for colonization and the construction of roads between the towns and the settlement areas.

In 1871, the total population of Ontario was 1,620,851, of which 439,429 were of English and 75,383 of French origin. This last group had almost tripled in twenty years.

It was in those days that the famous colonizer, the Curé Labelle, appeared on the Canadian scene. His aims were great. In Ontario he looked towards the north via the Ottawa Valley. In that sector he advocated the extension of the railroad from Montreal to Témiscamingue and its junction with the western system, also the construction of a branch line to Hudson Bay. Because of the absence of other means of communication the Ottawa remained the route of penetration. In the Curé Labelle's mind a railroad would favour the establishment of many parishes as far as Winnipeg and Hudson Bay and would help to prevent emigration to the United States. His plans gained the sympathy of prominent writers in France; Rameau de Saint-Père and Onésime Reclus highly favoured his project to establish more French Canadians and French-speaking European settlers in the Ottawa Valley and to expand in the direction of the northwest. In 1883 the Curé Labelle wrote to Father Filion in Manitoba: "Have no cause of alarm; I am going toward the North West with my settlers of the Rouge [River] region [north of Montreal]. Those two rivers, mine and yours, which have the same name of 'Rouge' are bound to join some day. We are slowly advancing in the direction of the splendid and fertile lands of the Hudson Bay region. Once there we shall shake hands."[4]

The project was great but had very small chance of success. France was concentrating her interests on her North African colonies and did not care about Canada and especially about Ontario. Belgium and Switzerland did not have any important surplus population. On the other hand, for obvious reasons, English immigration to Ontario has always been considerable. Nevertheless the failure of Labelle's plan was not complete, as appears from Table I.

The other natural route of communication, the St. Lawrence River, did not have its propagandist. Consequently it was far less popular among the French Canadians. As was the case in the Ottawa Valley, they overflowed from the Quebec border into the counties of Glengarry and Stormont. They developed normally in the areas where the cession of Canada in 1763 had left them, that is to say in the vicinity of the Niagara and Essex peninsulas and of Toronto, formerly a French trading post and in those days sporadically the seat of the provincial and Canadian governments. On the other hand, the British immigrants

[4]Abbé Elie Auclair, *Le Curé Labelle* (Montréal, 1933), p. 183.

TABLE I

French Population by Groups of Counties, Ontario, Three Census Years

	1931		1941		1951		
	Total	Fr. origin	Total	Fr. origin	Total	Fr. origin	Fr. speech
*Ottawa River**							
Prescott	24,596	9,921	25,261	20,506	25,576	21,215	21,236
Russell	18,487	7,506	17,448	13,988	17,666	14,470	14,435
Carleton	170,040	22,929	202,520	61,002	242,247	70,997	63,118
Renfrew	52,227	3,846	54,720	8,312	66,717	10,531	4,677
Nipissing	41,207	10,206	43,315	21,467	50,517	23,999	21,435
Sudbury	58,251	13,042	80,815	31,661	109,519	44,683	39,843
Cochrane	58,033	12,627	80,730	32,744	83,850	39,569	37,509
Algoma	46,444	3,642	52,002	7,746	64,496	10,858	6,436
Thunder Bay	65,118	1,743	85,200	5,256	105,367	8,759	4,958
Kenora	21,946	822	33,372	2,116	39,212	3,046	1,676
Rainy River	17,359	923	19,132	1,979	22,132	2,382	1,242
Timiskaming	37,043	4,131	50,604	11,488	50,016	13,909	11,634
*St. Lawrence**							
Glengarry	18,666	4,831	18,732	10,121	17,702	10,055	8,533
Stormont	32,524	6,597	40,905	18,567	48,458	23,599	18,245
Dundas	16,098	636	16,210	1,464	15,818	1,468	670
Grenville	16,327	480	15,989	1,081	17,045	1,256	456
Leeds	35,157	978	36,042	2,079	38,831	2,514	869
Frontenac	45,756	1,158	53,717	3,203	66,099	4,307	1,260
Lennox-Addington	18,883	316	18,469	521	19,544	719	66
Hastings	58,846	1,827	63,322	4,175	74,298	4,755	1,017
Prince Edward	16,693	119	16,750	438	18,559	576	120
Northumberland	31,452	355	30,786	768	33,482	1,017	167
Durham	25,782	71	25,215	211	30,115	530	165
Ontario	59,667	423	65,718	2,277	87,088	2,359	772
York	856,955	6,624	951,549	20,319	1,176,622	33,252	13,784
Peel	28,156	53	31,539	339	55,673	1,354	488
Halton	26,558	127	28,515	429	44,003	876	293
Wentworth	190,019	1,481	206,721	4,556	266,083	8,286	3,583
Lincoln	54,199	613	65,066	1,950	89,366	3,722	1,814
Welland	82,731	1,515	93,836	4,360	123,233	10,411	7,754
Haldimand	21,428	178	21,854	483	24,138	547	115
Norfolk	31,359	323	35,611	716	42,708	994	326
Elgin	43,436	282	46,150	761	59,518	1,434	521
Kent	62,865	7,243	66,346	8,152	79,128	9,642	5,028
Essex	159,780	33,039	174,230	38,174	217,150	47,565	29,656
*Central**							
Brant	53,476	299	56,695	779	78,857	1,723	644
Bruce	42,286	369	41,680	764	41,311	615	41
Dufferin	14,892	20	14,075	59	14,566	125	25
Grey	57,699	293	57,160	682	58,960	847	103
Haliburton	5,997	76	6,695	170	7,760	256	34
Huron	45,180	546	43,742	1,183	49,280	1,792	913
Lambton	54,674	1,605	56,925	1,911	74,960	4,996	2,719
Lanark	32,856	620	33,143	1,134	35,601	1,601	387
Manitoulin	10,734	226	10,841	547	11,214	515	111
Middlesex	118,241	596	127,166	2,120	162,139	3,665	1,143
Muskoka	20,985	526	21,835	1,184	24,713	1,528	633
Oxford	47,825	275	50,974	890	58,673	1,204	326
Parry Sound	25,900	1,347	30,083	3,550	27,371	2,811	1,319
Perth	51,392	406	49,694	1,069	52,584	1,080	148
Peterborough	43,958	598	47,392	1,476	60,789	2,259	450
Simcoe	83,667	4,227	87,057	9,145	106,482	11,421	7,435
Victoria	25,844	205	25,934	583	27,127	626	98
Waterloo	89,852	838	98,720	2,901	126,123	3,671	1,040
Wellington	58,164	480	59,453	1,234	66,930	1,284	335

*Counties by geographical order in each section.

came most willingly into those areas where they found the sea and the trade which it promotes.

As far as the central counties are concerned it must be noted that Lambton touches the Essex peninsula. Simcoe and York constitute part of a line linking Lake Ontario to Georgian Bay. Other regions contain only a few islets of French population which are isolated.

As Table I shows, the increase in the French-Canadian population has been quite constant. Since 1871 the number of Franco-Ontarians has increased sixfold, and they now constitute 10.3 per cent of the total population. However, it must be noted that the Franco-Ontarians do not all speak French, especially in the centre of the province where fewer bilingual schools are to be found. Out of a total of nearly half a million of French origin, only 75 per cent have kept their language.[5] They are like a pygmy facing a giant.

In 1951 the Ontarians born in Quebec numbered 154,134. Most of them were settled in Carleton (29,553), York (24,322), Cochrane (14,795), Sudbury (8,164), Welland (6,126), Timiskaming (5,442), and Essex (5,323). Nearly two-thirds of them lived in the towns (111,644), the remainder (42,490) in the country. The census of that year showed that the group that is French in origin is about as much rural as it is urban, while the British element is nearly three times more urban than rural. Here are the ten Ontario cities which have the greatest number of citizens of French origin: Ottawa, 57,399; Windsor, 22,007; Toronto, 21,865; Sudbury, 16,060; Timmins, 11,493; Eastview, 9,002; Cornwall, 7,973; Hamilton, 6,771; North Bay, 4,931; Sault Ste Marie, 4,122.

Most Ontarians of English origin, who have arrived more recently in greater number from the British Isles, have had no reason to detach themselves from what they still consider the motherland. No revolution, no deep change in government has come to break the bonds of loyalty which tie them to their old country. The "New Canadians" who settle in Ontario become Anglo-Ontarian, except by blood, by the second generation. Ontarians of French origin come mostly from Quebec; they have long forgotten their relation to Europe, particularly after the French Revolution.

III

The contacts between these two different ethnic groups—the French and the English in Ontario—cause some social reactions which are rather difficult to analyse. Man is himself a very complex animal.

[5]These figures are taken from different Canadian decennial censuses. See also *Le Droit,* May 28, 1955.

He is influenced by his family, his home town, his province, his country; he changes under the influence of his studies, his reading, his profession; he behaves in accordance with different systems of principles, creeds, dogmas, and sentiments; he varies with places, climate, centuries; from his birth to his death he suffers thousands of either favourable or unfavourable accidents which form and transform his character to such an extent that the constant individual is *rara avis.*

Homogeneity is still less apparent when men belong to the different groupings which we call English- and French-speaking. In the first category the English, whether born in Ontario, England, the United States, or other countries of the Commonwealth, are usually jumbled all together, as if they were totally similar. Also included under the same label are the Welsh, the Northern Irish, the Southern Irish, and the Scotch. But these are quite different. Among those from the British Isles we can find distinctions between the Londoners, the Southerners, the Northerners, and so on. Things are not otherwise on the French side. Often immigrants from St. Malo, Bordeaux, Marseille, and Paris hardly spoke a common language. Those who came over during the century of Louis XIV undoubtedly differed from those who lived in France in the days of Voltaire and the Encyclopaedists, the Revolution, or any of the four Republics. Among the Franco-Ontarians, the rural and the urban dwellers, the Quebecers and the Montrealers, those from Gaspé, Beauce, the Saguenay, and the Eastern Townships should not be classified in the same social units. And in all those groups of whatever social origin there are distinctions: there are Orangemen, Loyalists, Nationalists, Catholics, Anglicans, Presbyterians, Baptists, Methodists; doctors, lawyers, teachers, manufacturers, merchants, and labourers. These are not merely logical categories, but indications of social differences which foster a variety of customs, habits, and often deeply rooted prejudices.

There are therefore many varied types of Ontarian, not just one. Very broadly speaking, it migh be said that Anglo-Ontarians are more readily attracted by practical rather than hypothetical speculations. Carved out of dynamic material they are realistic planners. They dig and bore the ground and the underground, build plants, and establish their economy much more on industry and commerce than on agriculture. They also have that care for order, control, and uniformity which assures the success of financial enterprises but which, from a social point of view, tends sometimes to annihilate individuality and to level personality. Among them success in life is bound to develop a superiority complex. Naturally inclined to action, they try to make others believe in their formula of happiness, by which the value of an individual is measured by the number of dollars he has succeeded in accumulating. Having had the good fortune to be born English, some of them have absolute faith in the billions of dollars and the millions of individuals of their universal community. Those who are not caught by that pride of strength and that ambition of domination, who resist that temptation of the spirit, are the more to be esteemed.

These inherited concepts and characteristics explain the various ways in which some Anglo-Ontarians understand their relations with Franco-Ontarians. For a number of them, Canada is still a British country and Ontario an English province. This little group constitutes an extreme wing. At the other pole is to be found another minority: university teachers, business organizers, and some politicians who not only accept the existence of ethnic and cultural differences, but also endeavour to improve relations with the other group. This element is recruited mostly from among the intellectual élite of Ontario. Finally there is the centre bloc which gathers up the moderates, whose rule of life is to live and let live. They achieve a superficial understanding of the problem, not very solid and not at all exacting, which varies from latent enmity to impersonal sympathy. This is the kingdom of "mind your own business" ruled by Mr. "I-could-not-care-less." They will appreciate, and at times admire, the qualities of a French neighbour; and they are happy to live side by side with him as long as they do not have to learn his tongue, practise his religion, or see the Dionnes' legendary fecundity spread to a point where it might jeopardize the ethnic equilibrium of the province. They smile, and justly so, when threatened by Toynbee's strange prediction: "I suspect that the coming people in the Americas may be the French Canadian."[6] Would it ever be possible for about eight million to take the lead over two hundred and twenty million? The weak French-Canadian lamb will take a long time to establish domination over both the British lion and the American eagle.

That does not prevent the lamb from guarding itself against the danger of an inferiority complex. By temperament the Frenchman is much more inclined to think than to act. As one must mingle with the crowd to act, one must retreat from it to think. This social concept is directly opposed to that of the Englishman, who must belong to a group, a club, a society, or a community. The Frenchman will set up barriers, walls, fences, and gates everywhere in protection of his private life, his home, and his family, the first exclusive social col-

[6] *World Review*, 1949.

lectivity. He will often elude indiscreet questions by saying "This is a family matter" and will wash his dirty clothes at home. All that touches the individual and the family is sacred. The only social grouping which he favours is the parish association, and he does so much more in a religious than in a collective spirit. He has no gregarious institutions; he is not attracted by clubs. Many Frenchmen are positively hostile to such regimented collectivities.

His liking for reflection and analysis easily inclines the Frenchman to pessimism, especially when the situation in which he finds himself carries more inconveniences than advantages. Continuous investigation of misdeeds is not very comforting, especially when the remedies proposed seldom have a chance of being adopted. If the Franco-Ontarian were not inclined by temperament to retire within himself or his group, he would be swallowed up in a milieu in which it is psychologically difficult for him to manifest his real personality.

On the other hand, the French Canadian in Ontario is far less impressed than the one in Quebec by what psychologists call misoneism, that is, a sort of dislike for all novelty; and he does not as deeply detest all that Péguy, Bernanos, and many other French writers before them have stigmatized: the world of money, machinery, and material progress. In that respect, he stands about midway between the average Frenchman and Englishman.

Individualistic, his aim is to become a free man in the city and in the church. But like other Frenchmen he still dreams of absolutism; he expects leaders and directives in politics as well as in religion. Analysing his situation and his own feelings he never tries to conceal his faults, but he will seldom allow anybody to tell him about them. In this touchy sensitivity everybody will recognize the French temperament.

To characterize the Franco-Ontarians we could group them by professions: the intellectuals, the business men, the farmers, and the artisans. We could also divide them according to temperament: the optimists, the resigned, the indifferent, the reactionaries, and the chauvinists. We believe they can more justly be observed in their milieux. In the case of Ontario there do not exist yet such works as Miner's *St. Denis: A French-Canadian Parish* or E. C. Hughes's *French Canada in Transition.* Either the University of Chicago has not yet taken any interest in our province or, and this we can forgive easily, it continues to ignore the presence of French groups in Ontario.

There are three different milieux. First, the organized French community. Whether this group is formed in the city or the country it is homogeneous; parish life is intensive; school organization functions smoothly. The people have a happy existence under the direction of a priest, a mayor, a school board, and sometimes an M.P. of French origin. They are well adapted. They have no history.

The second milieu is bi-ethnic, bicultural, and bilingual. Within this group the people of French extraction have created their own educational and religious institutions. It is a strong group, conscious of its responsibilities and capable of maintaining its distinctiveness. It is often more impulsive because it always feels the spur of contingencies, difficulties, resistance, and movement. When well organized this group lives intensively.

The third category counts only a small proportion of French Canadians, scattered over wide areas in the country or disseminated to the four corners of a large city. They are lost without their own schools and churches. Their sensitiveness slowly hardens under the rigour of isolation, of estrangement, and of the change in language and customs. The difficulties of the present make them forget the past; they develop a certain shyness of comportment and expression which hinders them from blooming to capacity. This milieu is certainly not fit for the embittered, the unsatisfied, the misanthropic, the sentimental, the dreamer, and the theoretician. They have number, language, and success lined up against them.

It is estimated that 85 per cent of the Franco-Ontarians live in the first and second surroundings. They are highly organized. School boards, teachers, and inspectors, farmers, youth, parents, families, translators, and many other groups are formed into associations under the shield of the Association canadienne-française d'Education d'Ontario. One daily newspaper, *Le Droit*, and many weeklies, the more outstanding being *La Feuille d'érable* (Tecumseh), *L'Ami du peuple* (Sudbury), and *Le Moniteur* (Hawkesbury), have a considerable influence. Some radio and television stations now broadcast a few programmes in French, more particularly in the Ottawa, Timmins, and Sudbury areas.

In the political field the two elements have conceded each other the most complete freedom in electing whomever they wish. The Toronto legislature has five French-speaking members, and about ten others represent quite considerable elements of French origin. A minister of French extraction is appointed to the cabinet to take in hand the interests of that one-tenth of the Ontario population. The selection of the cabinet at Queen's Park is made in proportion to the number of members elected to the legislature rather than of the population in the province. In the provincial bureaucracy it is the Department of Education that has the greatest number of bilingual civil servants. The problem has not yet arisen in other departments.

In Ottawa the Franco-Ontarians are in a fairly good position. They are numerous in the various branches of the federal government. They have two ministers, seven members of Parliament, two senators, and, in the province, seven judges.

This short outline of the main characteristics of the two more important ethnic groups of Ontario might make one believe that on the whole the Anglo-Ontarian is an extrovert who blossoms with great ease, and the Franco-Ontarian an introvert who needs a nearly perfect climate of security to reach the stage of full bloom.

Like all other peoples, the people of Ontario are made up of body and soul. Even though the parts of the body and the qualities of the soul are not necessarily uniform among the series of individuals who constitute the provincial type, they do not present such contradictions as to look like merely juxtaposed and disparate limbs. In the United States, one may fear that the gap between the white and Negro elements will never be filled. There is no such segregation in Ontario. The English and the French attract one another, even if only by their opposite characteristics.

IV

The more serious causes of friction and even conflict are in the educational field. The school question has kept much ink flowing and absorbed a great quantity of energy.

There are two types of schools in Ontario: the public and the separate. The two systems enjoy complete equality on the constitutional, legal, and pedagogic levels. The teaching of the French language, under certain conditions, has always been accepted since the province came into existence. One of the clearest texts in this respect was a letter from the Ontario Minister of Education addressed to the school trustees of Charlottenburgh in Glengarry County: "I have the honour to state . . . that as the French is the recognized language of the country as well as the English, it is quite proper and lawful for the trustees to allow both languages to be taught in their schools to children whose parents may desire them to learn both. . . ."[7] In 1913, Regulation XVII standardized education throughout the province; but

[7]Egerton Ryerson, April 24, 1857, cited by C. B. Sissons, *Bilingual Schools in Canada* (Toronto, 1917), p. 27.

the report of the Merchant-Scott-Côté Commission of 1927 recognized the rights of the first occupant and recommended the acceptance of certain linguistic and cultural differences. All the schools are now submitted to the same examinations, and teaching in bilingual schools is supervised by qualified bilingual inspectors. In 1945 the Hope Commission made another attempt to suppress both bilingual and Catholic schools for the sake of uniformity of teaching, strangely enough in the name of democratic liberties. The Ontario government never applied its recommendations.

Once liberated from those threats the bilingual institutions have never stopped progressing, especially in recent years. In 1951 they numbered 556, with 1,630 classrooms, 14 inspectors, and 54,558 pupils. The secondary schools, not including the private institutions, the convents, and academies, gave instruction to more than 4,000 students. The colleges of Sudbury, Ottawa (Rideau, Bruyère, La Salle), Cornwall, Hearst, and Timmins have already reached distinction. Higher education progresses with giant strides at Ottawa University with the creation of the new faculties of medicine, law, and engineering and striking progress in the faculties of arts and philosophy. In Ottawa also a bilingual normal school trains competent bilingual teachers and inspectors. The contest in French organized in Ontario by a prominent member of the Department of Education, Dr. Robert Gauthier, creates lively emulation by the glory and the rewards it brings to the winners.

However, earthly happiness is relative. From a financial point of view the separate schools are still behind the public schools. Money, that stimulus required for the advancement of teaching, is badly lacking in the schools supported by the Catholics of the province. In practice separate schools do not receive their share of the taxes of corporations and public utilities, and of certain succession duties. Consequently a student in a public school receives about one-third more than his counterpart in a separate school; he therefore enjoys better facilities, buildings, and accommodation; his teachers have higher salaries. There is an inequality of advantage and sacrifice among the children and the parents who must make up to a certain extent for the difference in treatment.

Other differences appear in the linguistic field. Among the Anglo-Ontarians, those who can speak only English vary along a quite extensive range. There is the arrogant character who asserts: "This is an English province; talk white." There is the unsuccessful student who admits politely: "I am sorry, I don't understand French." There is the practical person who gives a useful bit of advice: "Why don't you learn to speak better English?" There is the salesman who does not want to lose a customer: "With your English and my French we can get along." There is the diplomat who tries to adjust the conflict: "I would like to do as well in French as you do in English."

In the French group there are three linguistic types: those who speak English fluently, those who cannot carry on a conversation beyond simple subjects; and those who do not speak English at all. Of these three sorts, the first alone can succeed, sometimes so much so that they lose their national characteristics only to acquire others. We have then a strange product: a French Canadian who abides instinctively by the law, who takes no interest in political meetings and activities, who does not constantly call for help from his *curé,* who coldly drives his car, eats a sandwich for lunch, minds his own business, and speaks well of his neighbour. He spells his name O'Dett (for Audette) or Delaney (for Chapdelaine). He is an exception. Most Franco-Ontarians are reluctant to adopt an American or English way of life; they put up a kind of unarmed resistance and they use a battle vocabulary. The words *défense*, *attaque*, *victoire*, *défaite*, *retraite*, *conquête*, *perte*, *château-fort*, *forteresse*, *bastion*, *retranchements*, *négociations*, and so forth, are often spoken or written about ethnic relations.

But words do not kill. A more important question related to education is that of the teaching of a second language. It is the core of the Canadian problem of bilingualism and biculturalism. Let us first recognize the irrationality of integral bilingualism. By the term "bilingual" we mean a good knowledge of one's mother tongue and the ability to express oneself fluently in a second one. In this respect the non-isolated Franco-Ontarians are the best off in the whole country. They learn both languages concurrently, and with greater efficiency the better are the teachers. They have their official institutions at the elementary, secondary, and university levels. They are happy and proud of that achievement.

Their English-speaking fellow citizens are not as well provided for. In most of their schools the teaching of French is poorly conceived and backward. Eighty-two per cent of the students have had French taught in English. It is a subject on the curriculum which has to be seen but not necessarily heard. The high school pupils study complete treatises on the use of the subjunctive and the imperfect indicative; they know exactly where to place the adjective and the adverb. They can render in English all the French texts with the aid of translations circulated from year to year. French, that

> harmonieux langage
> Idiome de l'amour, si doux qu'à le parler
> Les femmes sur la lèvre en gardent un sourire,
>
> —MUSSET

becomes a dead language which provokes more grimaces than smiles. It is inconceivable that such a living tongue should foster such general boredom and discourage all goodwill. After studying French for five years without being able to speak a word of it, the student is disgusted with the language and consequently with all those who speak it. He is frustrated and has the feeling of having failed to learn something; therefore he abandons for life the disappointing project.

It is time that we should review our concept of the teaching of languages in the light of our national and international obligations. It is obvious that an English-speaking labourer, say from Sharbot Lake, and a French-speaking one from Ile d'Orléans can both earn their living without knowing a second language as long as they are satisfied to remain labourers and never travel out of their villages. On the other hand, should a young man desire to become a politician, a diplomat, an administrator, a salesman, a civil servant, a teacher, an actor, or a singer, to adopt a profession or join the army, to work on the railroad, in the post office, on television or radio, he will have to use a second language. With both French and English one can travel all over the world with enjoyment and profit. No more frontiers; one is free from the fear of not being understood. He who knows only his mother tongue lacks one element of human life, a means of communication, appreciation, and comprehension. He who cannot learn a second language lacks the liberating force of achievement.

The unilingual person, very naturally, tries to explain his failure by pretending that after all a second language is not indispensable and often adopts a negative attitude, completely losing sight of respect for other people's rights, of the intellectual advantages of an acquired discipline, of the practical utility of an instrument of instruction. Reducing the study of a second language to a question of sentiment and politics indicates not only a narrow-minded but a biased conception of the problem. For all Canadians it is today a matter of reason. Lord Beaverbrook, who spent the last part of his life in the most British of all countries, was taking lessons in French in 1953, when he was seventy-four. As he said: "There are . . . certain branches of education which many youths consider unnecessary for a business career. Foremost among these are mathematics and foreign languages. . . ." And he had this to add, aiming at a country we know well: "I regret that my business career was shaped on a continent which speaks only one language for commercial purposes from the Arctic Circle to the Gulf of Mexico. If a man can properly appraise the value of something he does not possess, I would place knowledge of languages high in the list of acquirements for success."[8]

The first recommendation is to start the study of languages at a much younger age. The greatest neurologists, including Dr. Wilder Penfield of Montreal, have clearly established the advantage of beginning the study of a second language in kindergarten, that is to say at the age of five or six. At that stage the ear is very sensitive, memory is fresh and quick, and prejudices are still non-existent. The second tongue must be mastered before the age of twelve.

Strangely enough, it is in the United States that the movement for renovation in the teaching of languages is more highly developed. Many experiments have been conducted; those of Dr. James A. Grew of Andover, Massachusetts, have been most successful. French is so well taught from Grade III in that small city's grammar school that its influence is felt outside; the parents themselves are asking to take lessons. Dr. Grew believes that oral teaching should continue from the third through the sixth grade, followed by textbook study, so that students can enter college already bilingual.[9]

To start the study of a second language at an early age is clearly the ideal. Four or five years of sound study should enable the student to attain in turn the following objectives: first, hearing and understanding; second, speaking; third, reading; fourth, writing. Then, at high school, he should be able to read books and occasionally listen to lectures in that language. At college or university he should be competent to do extensive reading in history, literature, the social and other sciences in the original, and to understand films and plays. The stress should not be placed on book knowledge before speaking knowledge, on grammar and *belles-lettres* rather than on everyday common conversation, on translation rather than discussion.

The most progressive institutions endeavour to adapt the traditional pattern to meet a reasonable modern standard. In that respect Ontario seems to be ahead of the other English-speaking provinces. More

[8]*Publications of the Modern Language Association of America* (*P.M.L.A.*), vol. XXII (Dec. 1953).

[9]On findings at Andover, see *P.M.L.A.*, vol. XIV (Dec. 1955).

teachers take special courses in French. Some language laboratories are in existence, but a more extensive use of radio and television facilities should be encouraged. In France the Department of Education has supported the creation of a television studio to prepare school programmes. In thirty-five states the Americans are using television to teach languages with less effort and better results than with the orthodox classroom method. On the other hand, most Ontario universities have organized summer courses and some, Toronto and Western for instance, have founded schools in areas where the language being studied is spoken. Such courses would be even more profitable for younger students. There also exists 'Les Visites interprovinciales' organized some twenty years ago by Mr. J. H. Biggar of Upper Canada College. There are student exchanges sponsored by the Alliance canadienne. There are some public schools where the teaching of French is started in Grade III. Among the educated class there are more parents who wish their children to begin the study of the second language at an earlier age than is officially prescribed. Trends like this prove that the question of language by itself is not insoluble, and some reforms would bring a happy *rapprochement* between the two groups.

We are still far from bilingualism. But the situation would improve if the Ontarians of French origin were given the full means of keeping their mother tongue. We see that in 1931 they had kept their language more easily in the country (115,389 out of 138,297) than in the towns (120,997 out of 161,435). In 1941 they numbered in all 373,990. Of that total, 88,685 spoke English only, 60,483 French only, and 224,646 were bilingual. On the other hand, 93,821 of English origin spoke French. In 1951 those figures have increased (see Table II).

TABLE II

ONTARIO ENGLISH AND FRENCH POPULATION BY ORIGIN AND LANGUAGE

	Total		Rural		Urban	
Language	English	French	English	French	English	French
English only	3,016,744	133,120	856,594	40,437	2,160,150	92,683
French only	961	74,925	386	45,117	575	29,808
English and French	64,137	269,597	12,086	88,379	52,051	181,218
Neither language	29	22	12	11	50	13

From the table it appears that more townsfolk than country people of French origin have forgotten their language. Similarly more English-speaking people proportionally speak French in the country than in the towns. Nevertheless a most striking fact is that almost 200,000 Anglo-Ontarians speak French. They constitute 200,000 separate pieces of evidence of the possibility of bilingualism among the people of English descent.

The question of culture, considered by many superior minds as the main *terrain d'entente* between English- and French-speaking Canadians, is intimately linked with the problems of languages and here again teaching plays an important role.

The Anglo-American system of education greatly differs from the French one. The English students, because of certain options, can specialize at an early stage of their studies and thus eliminate many subjects, such as philosophy and even history, that are considered indispensable in the French system. These subjects however are usually compulsory for English-speaking students who intend to take up a liberal profession. They receive all their instruction in their mother tongue, and most of the time even without going out of their milieu. Consequently they acquire a unilingual and uni-ethnic culture. Except for some allusions from their teachers, they have few reasons to believe that any other culture besides their own does exist, or that, if it does, it can be of any great importance since it has not so far reached them. For them there are two worlds: the English world and the non-English one. Only travelling and reading can open their eyes. They would then come to realize that besides Maupassant's tales and Zola's novels there is another civilization and a culture which manifests itself in their very neighbourhood.

By tradition the French element insists more on general culture, on the humanities and the liberal arts. The students are directed towards intellectual and aesthetic pleasures, and under favourable conditions they will take an early interest in the theatre, painting and music. On the other hand, the education of the young Franco-Ontarian is more pragmatic than that of his compatriot from Quebec, who spends months and even years analysing Cicero's and Demosthenes' speeches, Aeschyles' tragedies, enjoying the divine verses of Virgil; he is much more attracted by ancient pastoral life than by the economic struggle. In Ontario the pupil has to devote much more time to mathematics, physics, and chemistry. The programmes lead more rapidly to specialization, to practice rather than theory, to synthesis rather than analysis. But the institutions which the young Franco-Ontarian has attended up to now have been a little behind their time, and it is only since 1927 that they have been able to get in step with other institutions.

The University of Ottawa, where he terminates his studies, is just starting a big expansion programme. So, within a few years we shall be able to see at work young men of French intellectual character trained in bilingual institutions of an English type. At all levels this would mean the integration of the two cultures and the experiences should prove most interesting to follow.

In general, the contemporary student does not quibble any longer about the sympathy or antipathy of Murray, Carleton, and Durham for the French. He takes a keener interest in the characteristics of the various epochs, costumes, family traditions, and creeds. It is the study of the past with all its richness and artistic productions. It is an endeavour to revive the attitudes and the memories of the days gone by, to use that heritage instead of fighting about it.

Both the Anglo- and the Franco-Ontarians have a share in a culture which has had centuries of experience. It is by making that culture a personal possession—each group in its own milieu—and by allowing it to develop, grow, and produce, that they will contribute to their mutual enrichment. It would be an impoverishment to be reduced to one language, one painting, one literature, one culture. It is the hour of joint realization in arts, letters, and sciences. Diversity does not restrict the audience but on the contrary stirs up sound emulation.

Ottawa, a bilingual and bi-ethnic city, produces some of the best Canadian painters, actors, and writers. The two races work in peace for the edification and expansion of a national civilization of which the city wishes to be the prototype. Stratford is a manifestation of another kind where the two elements join in an artistic communion, like the pilgrims of yore who would stop at Saint-Jacques-de-Compostelle or Rome. It is in Toronto that many singers of both origins have been launched upon their careers.

Thus the educational problem is not insuperable if each party concerned makes a genuine effort to overcome the obstacles which impede a complete solution.

V

Lastly, cultural relations between the two main ethnic groups in Ontario are dominated by a factor which has a bearing on most human actions; it is related to beliefs which are deeply rooted in men's consciences and to convictions which are based on dogmas and supernatural guidance.

As far as religion is concerned, Ontario lives in a relative peace and

TABLE III

POPULATION OF ONTARIO BY RELIGION AND ORIGIN, 1951

Religion	British	French	Other
United Church	1,127,568	24,756	168,042
Catholic	394,961	417,570	329,609
Church of England	833,658	16,825	85,519
Presbyterian	390,529	6,348	42,195
Baptist	172,818	4,361	35,288
Lutheran	16,199	1,379	118,003
Others	146,186	6,438	259,290
TOTAL	3,081,919	477,677	1,037,946

freedom of creeds. More than twenty different religions are practised, the main ones being indicated in Table III.

The largest denominations in Ontario are the United Church of Canada and the Roman Catholic Church, each with well over one million members. Among the Catholics the strongest element is of French origin. It constitutes the greatest part of that ethnic group. However, 60,107 of the French do not profess the Catholic faith. If it is considered that 136,175 Ontarians of French origin do not speak French any longer, it could be estimated that more than half of those who lost their mother language changed their faith. It would therefore be more than half true to say that language is the guardian of faith.

This question has its full significance when we examine the relations between French-speaking Catholics, mostly French Canadians, and English-speaking Catholics, half of them Irish. These two groups are bound by their religious precepts to exercise charity toward their neighbours but their relations with each other are not always friendly. It has been often said that "they mix as comfortably as fire and water" because of a clash of interests which does not occur between each of these two groups and other religious denominations. They are partners when they insist on their rights to separate schools, but they are divided over the means of getting full financial assistance. The English-speaking Catholics would like French-speaking Catholics to cease demanding that their language be taught in their schools, because this claim might provoke the ill will of the authorities and endanger the law authorizing separate schools. Actually, the bilingual separate school differs in its programme and set-up from the monolingual separate school; it has its own teachers, inspectors, and sometimes school trustees. It is a division within an already separated organization—the two kinds of separate school are types of the same category. Furthermore, besides their own schools, the French-speaking Catholics claim their own church where the divine ministry can be exercised in the language in which they learnt their prayers. When they form a separate congregation they are said to weaken the parish and sometimes the diocese. Is it then to be much wondered that some bishops and some parish priests are opposed secretly or openly to such a division of strength? It is so natural to seek to increase rather than decrease one's own forces. This split is even aggravated by the alliances with the American Catholics on the one hand and the Quebec French-speaking Catholics on the other. The question of separate religious practices, complicated by technical and administrative differences within the separate school system, brings about serious clashes, as it did in Bishop Fallon's day, and stirring divisions such as that of the Oblate Fathers in Ottawa.

Historically, however, the Irish Canadians and the French Canadians have many reasons for helping each other, and they do in many instances. Their ethnic and religious existence has often been endangered. From the Tudor reign to the French Revolution Irish priests used to get their training in France. In Canada, English-speaking clerics long went to Quebec and Montreal for their classical and ecclesiastical education. In the middle of the nineteenth century when the Irish were starved and persecuted out of their country, a great number came to Canada where they met with a devastating plague. It was on the shores of the St. Lawrence River that they were taken care of and comforted. Lastly, to foster good relations between the flock and its pastors, the spiritual leader of the Catholic Church had to issue a directive which binds all the ecclesiastics of both languages: "We urge all priests engaged in the sacred ministry to become thoroughly conversant in the knowledge and use of the two languages and, discarding all motives of rivalry, to adopt one or the other according to the requirements of the faithful. . . ."[10] This rule has certainly not been fully applied as yet in all communities.

Relations between Catholics and other religious denominations are normally good as long as no discussions of fundamental beliefs arise to disturb them. A compromise based on a sense of truly Christian toleration has even in some instances allowed the use of each other's premises for worship.[11]

[10]Benedict XI, to the bishops of Canada, Sept. 8, 1916.

[11]A. H. Young, *The Parish Register of Kingston* (Kingston, 1921), p. 18.

VI

The discussion of the reactions created by the combination of very unequal parts of two bi-ethnic and bilinguistic national elements in the Ontario test-tube allows us to arrive at the following three possible solutions: domination, coexistence, co-operation.

The Attorney General of the Province of Quebec, Baron Francis Maseres, 200 years ago believed that French Canadians could be assimilated. He described the process as "the melting down of the French nation into the English in point of language, affections, religion and laws, which is so much to be wished for and which . . . a generation or two may perhaps effect if proper measures are taken for that purpose. . . .[12] This prediction now appears to be false, not only for the Quebec majority but also for minorities of all the other provinces. The reason is that a civilized race does not easily accept domination or absorption by another people; ethnic feelings seem to obey the same law as gases—to every action there is an equal and opposite reaction. On the other hand, in Ontario, the majority did not want to apply the rule that might is right and to force French-speaking immigrants to remain in Quebec or become anglicized. What would have been the use of destroying a people which is a partner in Canadian Confederation, and then having to support it and take care of its débris?

A state of coexistence would indicate that the mixture of the two elements had not succeeded; there would be a mere juxtaposition, a legal intercourse between the two bodies but no sharing; exhortations to avoid separation or divorce, but no sincere union. But peoples would thus endure their destinies enchained one to the other like convicts, unknown one to the other, unacquainted with each other's aspirations, paralysed in their most legitimate feelings, unable to face each other, to shake hands and to help one another. Coexistence is better than assimilation, but is it to live a really happy life to glare constantly at each other?

The third attitude, almost uniform throughout the province, is the deliberate acceptance of co-operation for the well-being and prosperity of the whole Ontario population by the development of the cultural resources of each group; it is for both groups the approval of a social (not national) contract based on accepted differences in history, in education, in religion. It is not a fusion or a confusion, but the joint development and progress of the two groups. Bi-ethnicalism and bi-

[12] A. Shortt and A. G. Doughty, eds., *Documents Relating to the Constitutional History of Canada, 1759–1791* (Ottawa, 1918), vol. I, p. 267.

culturalism mean a pooling of interest which does not entail unity of feelings but a balance of thought and action, harmony of the whole in a diversity of parts. As long as both ethnic and cultural forces converge from different points to the same end, we have the ideal individual and national equilibrium. The danger is that one should try to prevail over the other, thus disrupting the free action of the pair.

When considering the Ontarian bi-ethnic adventure without any optical illusions, it has to be realized that owing to the numerical and financial differences between the two groups, the situation of the smaller is extremely difficult. Optimism with its rosy view, and pessimism with its dark outlook on the future, are equally forbidden.

1956

Les Rapports ethniques dans les provinces maritimes

R.P. RENÉ BAUDRY, c.s.c.

Archiviste, Université Saint-Joseph

L'HISTOIRE AGIT souvent au rebours de la raison. Tandis que l'Amérique offrait tant d'espace inoccupé, les peuples européens semblent avoir voulu accaparer chacun pour soi toute la côte atlantique, et gaspillèrent longtemps leurs forces en guerres inutiles. Une solution toute simple, penserait M. de la Palice, eût été de partager les zones d'influence, et de vivre en paix chacun de son côté. Quoi que nous pensions de la situation actuelle, nous ne pouvons refaire le passé. Heureuse impuissance, car si nous pouvions rebâtir l'histoire du Canada, nous la construirions probablement encore plus mal. La plus élémentaire sagesse nous conseille donc d'accepter sans rechigner notre composition ethnique très complexe, et d'en tirer parti. L'exemple de nations comme la Grande-Bretagne, la Belgique et la Suisse, nous montre que des populations diverses peuvent habiter un même pays, et que cette variété, loin de nuire à leur progrès, les enrichit par l'apport de qualités diverses. A condition évidemment que ces peuples ne passent pas leur temps à se quereller, et puissent développer librement leurs vertus complémentaires.

* * *

De toutes les régions du Canada, les provinces maritimes ont connu les premières le plus de mélanges ethniques. Dès les années 1500, on voit des Anglais, des Portugais, des Espagnols et des Français se rencontrer en voyages de découverte et en expéditions de pêche sur les bancs de Terre-Neuve, dans le Golfe-Saint-Laurent ou sur le littoral de la Nouvelle-Ecosse. Si ce voisinage donna souvent lieu à des pirateries et destructions réciproques, en plusieurs occasions des groupes anglais et français vécurent ensemble sans trop de difficultés. Tels, les colons écossais laissés à Port-Royal par Alexander en 1632, et les familles demeurées sous l'occupation anglaise, de 1654 à 1667 et de 1713 à 1749. La lutte pour la suprématie en Amérique du Nord atteignit, aux Maritimes, un dénouement tragique avant la Guerre de Sept Ans, quand Lawrence et son conseil prirent l'initiative brutale d'expulser la population acadienne. Cette mesure barbare divise, comme un coup d'épée, l'histoire de cette région en deux périodes, et le souvenir de cet événement y plane encore comme une ombre funèbre. Lawrence croyait avoir résolu définitivement le problème, mais il avait compté sans la ténacité des Acadiens. Pendant que de nouveaux colons repeuplaient lentement ces provinces, plusieurs centaines de proscrits, sortis des prisons ou rentrés de l'exil, revinrent dans leur ancien pays. Les arrivées massives des Loyalistes, puis de colons écossais et irlandais, formèrent une majorité anglophone. Mais une minorité française continua de s'y développer, et constitue aujourd'hui un groupe important.

En chiffres approximatifs, l'élément français compte pour environ 400,000 dans les quatre provinces maritimes. Le bloc principal de 300,000 forme 40 pour cent de la population du Nouveau-Brunswick et se concentre dans l'isthme de Shédiac, le long du Golfe, et dans la partie supérieure de la rivière Saint-Jean. Soixante-quinze mille se répartissent aux deux extrémités de la Nouvelle-Ecosse : au nord, dans la région de Margaree et Chéticamp, au Cap-Breton, et aux Iles Madame, et au sud, à la Baie-Sainte-Marie. Environ 15,000 demeurent à l'Ile-du-Prince-Edouard. Une migration tardive (1848–50), provenant des Iles-de-la-Madeleine, en a poussé quelques milliers sur la côte ouest de Terre-Neuve, à la Baie-Saint-Georges. Un bon nombre habitent aussi les régions voisines du Nouveau-Brunswick, la Gaspésie et les Iles-de-la-Madeleine.

Bien qu'il y ait eu dans les régions limitrophes, Madawaska et Gaspésie, des échanges avec la population de Québec, la majorité de ces « Français » descend des colons de l'ancienne Acadie. C'est véritablement une résurgence du vieux peuple acadien, le premier colonisateur de ces régions. L'origine de plusieurs familles remonte aux colons amenés par Razilly, de 1632 à 1635, quelques-unes même aux compagnons des Biencourt et Latour. L'origine précise de ces premières recrues n'a pas encore été étudiée de façon complète; mais on sait qu'elles venaient plutôt du centre de la France et de la Bretagne, tandis que la population du Saint-Laurent venait principalement de Normandie. L'éloignement du Canada central a contribué ensuite à maintenir et accentuer les différences. Ils se rapprochent de leurs frères du Québec par des affinités profondes, d'origine, de langue et de religion, mais ils en diffèrent par plusieurs particularités de langue, de coutumes et de mentalité, qui leur donnent un caractère distinctif.

Ce groupe a gardé dans son ensemble, aux Maritimes, son existence propre, et n'a pas été assimilé. S'il éprouve déperdition dans les milieux où il forme une faible minorité, comme à l'Ile-du-Prince-Edouard et au Cap-Breton, par contre il se maintient assez bien, et son importance numérique et son organisation progressent au sud de la Nouvelle-Ecosse et au Nouveau-Brunswick. Il possède son clergé, ses congrégations religieuses, ses maisons d'éducation, ses associations, ses journaux et ses postes de radio.

Leurs sentiments à l'égard de leurs concitoyens de langue anglaise sont assez complexes. Le souvenir de l'expulsion, et de maints autres griefs, laisse en eux un pénible sentiment de rancœur et de méfiance qui les pousse à se replier un peu sur eux-mêmes et à faire groupe à part. Ils sont cependant de nature pacifique et n'entretiennent aucune idée de représailles. Ils comprennent que leurs concitoyens actuels ne peuvent être tenus responsables des erreurs passées, et ils ne demandent qu'à vivre en paix avec eux, en gardant leurs libertés essentielles. Ils sont prêts à prendre leurs responsabilités et jouer leur rôle dans la vie des provinces et du pays, ainsi qu'ils l'ont déjà prouvé par la participation à deux guerres. Plusieurs gestes de justice, de générosité, ou simplement de courtoisie, comme l'intervention d'Haliburton dans l'abolition du Serment du Test, la lettre pastorale de Mgr Walsh, et l'allocution française de la Reine lors de sa visite à Moncton, ont su toucher leurs cœurs, et contribué à leur redonner confiance.

* * *

En fait les conflits inter-ethniques aux Maritimes sont beaucoup moins fréquents que les antécédents historiques nous porteraient à le croire. Il n'y a pas eu, dans ces provinces, de graves crises comme l'insurrection de 1837 dans Québec et l'affaire Riel au Manitoba. Cependant, les relations entre les divers groupes ont donné lieu à quelques difficultés auxquelles on n'a pas encore trouvé de solutions pleinement satisfaisantes.

La mésentente la plus grave s'est produite au sujet des questions scolaires. La loi Tupper, en Nouvelle-Ecosse, et la loi de 1871, au Nouveau-Brunswick, imitées quelques années après par l'Ile-du-Prince-Edouard, établissaient des écoles publiques, neutres et unilingues, c'est-à-dire anglaises. Ces lois soulevèrent de vives oppositions dans les deux premières provinces, et la maladresse intransigeante de quelques fonctionnaires provoqua même au Nouveau-Brunswick des actes de violence qui causèrent quelques pertes de vies. Quoique l'application de ces lois ait été adoucie et rendue tolérable par des amendements successifs, leur principe fondamental demeure, rejetant hors de l'école tout enseignement confessionnel, et n'accordant au français qu'une part très secondaire. Par réaction, les clergés catholique et protestant ont établi en plusieurs endroits des universités, collèges et couvents indépendants. Bien que l'enseignement y soit souvent de haute qualité, la plupart de ces maisons ne reçoivent aucune subvention publique, et leur maintien impose de lourds sacrifices aux parents et aux organismes qui les soutiennent. Le Nouveau-Brunswick a corrigé partiellement cette situation en accordant, en ces dernières années, des octrois à toutes ses universités.

Les mêmes lois établissaient aussi l'anglais comme seule langue officielle à l'école. Elles imposaient ainsi à l'élément français un double obstacle. Les instituteurs de langue français recevaient leur formation et devaient enseigner uniquement en anglais; les écoliers acadiens devaient étudier des manuels, recevoir des explications et passer des examens dans cette langue, qui souvent ne leur était pas familière. Beaucoup n'y comprenaient rien et quittaient tôt l'école ou subissaient un retard considérable. Des concessions graduelles ont été accordées pour remédier à cette situation illogique : manuels français, usage du français dans les classes inférieures, quelques cours de français à l'Ecole normale, cours d'été, etc. Une attitude très libérale prévaut actuellement dans les gouvernements de Nouvelle-Ecosse et du Nouveau-Brunswick. Mais le traitement accordé à la langue française, dans l'ensemble de l'enseignement aux Maritimes, est encore loin d'être équitable.

La seule solution vraiment adéquate consisterait dans la franche reconnaissance du bilinguisme dans l'enseignement; c'est-à-dire que la langue française puisse s'enseigner librement partout où vivent des groupes français suffisants, et que les instituteurs de cette langue reçoivent une formation adaptée. Nous concédons volontiers que cet objectif ne peut se réaliser du jour au lendemain, et que son application dans les milieux mixtes posera et pose déjà plusieurs problèmes d'ordre pratique. Leur réglement exigera beaucoup de bonne volonté de la part des deux groupes. Nous croyons que l'établissement d'une section d'Ecole normale bilingue au Nouveau-Brunswick, que pourraient aussi fréquenter les instituteurs des autres provinces, contribuerait puisamment à régler ce problème, en formant un personnel spécialisé. Le nœud de cette question consiste surtout en questions de méthodes et d'organisation, et relève avant tout des pédagogues et des comités d'étude. Le Nouveau-Brunswick, qui a la plus forte minorité française, se doit de prendre l'initiative en ce domaine. Puisque cette province a déjà su résoudre un problème plus grave, en améliorant la situation financière de ses écoles, nous avons confiance qu'elle saura aussi résoudre celui du bilinguisme.

* * *

Une autre question controversée, qui revient périodiquement dans les journaux, est celle de la représentation aux Assemblées législatives et dans les emplois publics. La minorité se plaint de n'avoir pas un nombre de représentants, députés ou fonctionnaires, proportionné au chiffre de sa population. Tous s'accordent à reconnaître le principe démocratique de la représentation proportionnelle, et il revient aux corps responsables d'étudier la justesse de ces réclamations. Un rajustement partiel a déjà accordé aux Acadiens du Nouveau-Brunswick quelques députés de plus, et l'on compte quelques titulaires de langue française – très peu, il est vrai – dans les hauts postes des divers gouvernements. Qu'on nous permettre à ce propos une remarque tout-à-fait générale.

Dans toute saine administration, privée ou publique, l'intérêt même de l'entreprise et l'intérêt public exigent que l'on confie les postes aux candidats les plus compétents. Il est habituellement possible, avec un peu de bonne volonté, de concilier ce souci de la compétence avec la juste représentation des divers groupes. L'élément français des provinces maritimes a déjà fourni des hommes de valeur à la politique et à l'administration; mentionnons seulement les noms du Sénateur Poirier, du Juge P.-A. Landry et de l'Hon. Pierre Veniot. Il en compte encore dans les deux partis politiques et dans les diverses professions. On ne peut féliciter les gouvernements, quand il s'agit de choisir des titulaires français à des postes officiels, de choisir toujours les meilleurs candidats. Il arrive assez souvent que l'on considère le dossier politique ou la complaisance plutôt que la valeur de l'homme. Cet esprit de parti dans les nominations va d'abord contre le propre intérêt des partis. Ils trouveraient en effet grand avantage, pour leur propre réputation et l'efficacité de leurs mesures, à recruter dans leurs rangs et choisir comme représentants les meilleurs candidats disponibles. C'est aussi une grave injustice envers l'élément français. Quand un groupe forme une majorité, il peut se pérmettre la faiblesse de quelques médiocrités. Mais quand il constitue une minorité, on doit mettre en vedette ses meilleurs hommes. Autrement, cette représentation n'est qu'un trompe-l'œil, et ces fantoches ne peuvent jouer aucun rôle efficace, ni pour leur groupe, ni pour leur province, ni pour le pays.

La différence de religion n'a guère causé jusqu'ici de difficultés dans les provinces maritimes. Quoique la presque totalité des Acadiens pratique le catholicisme et que la majorité anglophone adhère au protestantisme, le comportement chrétien, dans la plupart des questions morales et sociales, se ressemble chez les deux groupes. Il existe bien quelques vieux préjugés tenaces, issus des persécutions religieuses, mais ils tendent à disparaître. Le présence aux Maritimes d'un fort groupe d'Ecossais et d'Irlandais catholiques contribue à atténuer les divergences. On a bien vu quelques prédicants fanatiques essayer de soulever l'animosité, mais leur haine maladive n'a pas provoqué de contagion. Au contraire, Catholiques et Protestants s'entendent souvent dans les questions d'éducation et collaborent souvent dans des œuvres à portée sociale.

Des frictions, fait assez étonnant, se sont plutôt produites à l'intérieur du catholicisme, entre clergé et fidèles de langues différentes. Mais ces différends relèvent des autorités religieuses et se règlent par voie de représentations à la hiérarchie. S'il existe encore des centres où la population française n'a pas de clergé francophone, elle a obtenu des évêques dans les régions où elle constitue la majorité. Dans les paroisses mixtes, la nomination d'un clergé bilingue et, dans les grandes villes, la création de paroisses nationales, devraient résoudre les dernières difficultés. Les religions, et particulièrement le catholicisme, loin d'être un sujet de division, peuvent aider à créer un terrain d'entente.

A part les causes générales de dissentiment, que nous avons énumérées plus haut, il en surgit parfois d'accidentelles, causées le plus souvent par des maladresses, des ambitions personnelles ou des oppositions d'intérêts. Chaque groupe possède aussi un petit nombre d'esprits violents et agressifs, toujours prêts à partir en guerre. De telles gens constituent un danger.

• • •

L'ensemble de la population veut la paix. C'est pourquoi on évite plutôt les discussions, et l'on cherche à s'entendre. Il existe d'ailleurs de nombreuses raisons de rapprochement. L'histoire de chacun des groupes qui peuplent les Maritimes, Acadiens, Loyalistes, Ecossais et Irlandais, a souvent été la même. Tous ont été persécutés, ont dû quitter leurs pays et ont souffert pour leur attachement à leur religion et à leur patrie. Ce trait commun devrait les amener à une grande tolérance et à la sympathie réciproque.

Les intérêts particuliers de chaque groupe coïncident souvent avec ceux des autres groupes. Les grands magasins ont une bonne clientèle française. Des ouvriers français travaillent dans les entreprises anglaises. Les professionnels des deux langues, médecins, dentistes et avocats, ont une clientèle hétérogène. Tous ont aussi en commun les intérêts supérieurs de leurs provinces et du pays. Les provinces maritimes souffrent, à l'intérieur de la Confédération canadienne, d'une grave infériorité économique, à cause de leurs ressources restreintes et de leur situation excentrique. Cette situation provoque un courant d'émigration vers le Canada central et vers les Etats-Unis, qui prive cette région de ses meilleurs éléments humains. Agriculture, pêcheries, forêts et industries ont grand besoin d'être développées et organisées de façon scientifique. L'industrie locale requiert encouragement, pour lutter contre la cherté des transports. Beaucoup reste à faire aussi pour améliorer la santé et l'hygiène publiques, l'éducation et l'organisation des bibliothèques, développer les lettres et les arts. Les provinces maritimes ont donc besoin des talents et des énergies de tous leurs citoyens, pour régler leurs problèmes et se développer en harmonie avec le reste du Canada. Elles doivent éviter tout gaspillage de forces, en supprimant les occasions de conflits intérieurs, et en assurant une coopération constructive de tous.

• • •

Dans ce but, il est urgent de faire disparaître les préjugés dans la masse du peuple, en favorisant la compréhension et l'estime réciproques. Ce travail doit commencer à l'école, par une étude objective de l'histoire du Canada, surtout des questions cruciales comme la dispersion des Acadiens et l'immigration des Loyalistes, puis par une étude sérieuse des deux langues et des deux littératures.

Journalistes, écrivains et conférenciers de la radio peuvent aussi exercer une direction en ce sens sur l'opinion publique. Plusieurs bons esprits ont employé leurs talents et leur influence à favoriser la compréhension et l'estime mutuelles, et leur action a produit d'excellents résultats. On peut bien différer d'opinion sur des sujets contestés, mais aucune bonne raison n'exige de confier nos disputes à l'imprimerie ou aux ondes, pour les répercuter et les amplifier. Il est bien difficile de conserver, dans les discussions publiques, la sérénité et le détachement nécessaires pour empécher les débats de dégénérer en tournois littéraires ou en invectives. Mieux valent assurément, dans l'intérêt de la vérité et de la concorde, les échanges de vues et les discussions amicales, loin des feux de la rampe.

Des organismes comme les chambres de commerce et les clubs, des sociétés comme les Chevaliers de Colomb, les associations professionnelles d'avocats, de médecins ou de techniciens divers, peuvent aussi offrir d'excellents terrains de rencontre. Dans ces groupements on ne discute ordinairement que des questions d'ordre technique ou d'aide mutuelle. Il est possible à tous de s'entendre sur ces sujets. Quand il existe des problèmes particuliers, comme dans les Coopératives, les Caisses populaires et les associations d'instituteurs, il peut résulter des avantages de la formation de sections distinctes réunies sous une même direction générale.

Rien n'empêche assurément les groupes religieux ou ethniques de former leurs propres associations nationales et patriotiques. Il importe cependant, dans l'intérêt général, de ne pas donner à ces groupements un esprit agressif ou extrémiste, et de leur garder un caractère constructif et pondéré. Quand la nécessité impose de prendre des mesures de protection ou de défense, il importe d'agir sans haine et veiller à ne pas léser les droits des autres en défendant les siens.

Les meilleurs ouvriers de l'entente nationale, ce sont les personnalités dirigeantes dans les divers domaines, membres de l'élite qui occupent des positions-clefs et influencent la vie publique : chefs religieux et politiques, hauts fonctionnaires, officiers municipaux, hommes d'affaires, universitaires, professeurs, etc. Ces personnes, par les postes qu'elles occupent et l'influence qu'elles exercent, peuvent jouer un rôle décisif en vue d'éviter les heurts ou apaiser les conflits. Des hommes intelligents, et bien renseignés, à l'esprit souple, capables de comprendre le point de vue des autres et de discuter posément, sont les intermédiaires tout désignés pour servir d'agents de liaison, et jouer le rôle de catalyseurs dans l'unité nationale.

Il suffit parfois d'un simple fonctionnaire aux idées étroites pour compliquer les questions les plus simples, et mettre la guerre dans un paisible village. Par contre il suffit souvent d'une seule personne conciliante pour détendre une situation. L'amitié de T. C. Haliburton et de l'abbé Sigogne nous a laissé sur ce point un grand exemple. Des rencontres organisées dans les provinces maritimes entre des hommes politiques et universitaires des divers groupes ethniques, de langues et de provinces différentes, ont déjà produit dans le passé d'excellents résultats, à commencer par la Confédération canadienne elle-même.

Il y aurait tout avantage à multiplier des contacts de ce genre, afin de parvenir à l'entente la plus complète et la plus durable, celle des esprits.

* * *

En somme, si l'accord absolu n'existe pas encore aux provinces maritimes, on s'efforce d'y parvenir. Nous croyons pouvoir dire que les rapports, dans l'ensemble, s'inspirent d'une loyale cordialité et qu'un effort de conciliation préside aux échanges.

Chaque groupe a déjà apporté sa contribution au développement de ces provinces. Tout en voulant garder leurs qualités distinctives, les descendants d'Ecossais, d'Irlandais, de Loyalistes et d'Acadiens s'unissent à vouloir le progrès de leurs quatre provinces solidaires, et l'intérêt général du Canada. L'harmonie entre ces sentiments et entre ces citoyens est sûrement réalisable. Le cas de la Grande-Bretagne, où Ecossais, Irlandais et Gallois gardent leurs mentalités propres, illustre cette possibilité. Mais les événements nous montrent aussi que cette harmonie est précaire, et qu'il faut constamment veiller à la défendre.

1955

Biculturalism in the Maritime Provinces

HUGH THORBURN

Department of Political and Economic Science, Queen's University

THE MARITIMES, of all the regions of Canada, is the one wherein the country's two great cultural groups are most evenly represented. In fact the Maritimes come near to constituting a microcosm of the country as a whole. The people of British origin constitute about two-thirds of the population of the area, and those of French origin about one-quarter. As in Canada as a whole we find the bulk of the French-speaking people concentrated in one area—the North Shore, or north-eastern counties of New Brunswick—and the other third or so scattered through the rest of the region. Thus in New Brunswick about 40 per cent of the population is of French origin in contrast to Nova Scotia and Prince Edward Island with only 15 per cent and 11 per cent respectively.

Moreover the 90,000 people of French descent in Nova Scotia and Prince Edward Island are scattered among the English-speaking majority. In only three out of the twenty-one counties do they constitute over 40 per cent of the population. The other eighteen counties range from 26 per cent to 2 per cent French by origin. The French settlements in Nova Scotia are in the two counties of Digby and Yarmouth at the easternmost extremity of the province, and in Richmond in southeastern Cape Breton. There are some 15,000 of them in Prince Edward Island, mostly in Prince County. Consequently their position in these two provinces is a much weaker one than in New Brunswick, where they make up a large, concentrated, and fairly homogeneous community; so it is in New Brunswick that the new Acadia is growing up with vigour and self-confidence, whereas in the other two provinces the erosion of assimilation is threatening the very existence of the French community.

The overwhelming majority of the French-speaking people of the Maritimes are Acadians, as distinct from French Canadians.[1] Only in the two New Brunswick counties of Madawaska and Restigouche which border on the province of Quebec are the French Canadians a significant group. Elsewhere the overwhelming majority are the descendants of the French settlers of the colony of Acadia which included Nova Scotia, southern New Brunswick, and Prince Edward Island. They have had a history which differs markedly from that of their neighbours in Quebec, and which in many ways accounts for their distinctive culture. Their forefathers came from the Poitou-Saintonge area of the Bay of Biscay coast of France, and settled along the shore of the Bay of Fundy and the Minas Basin. From the first, therefore, they came from a different part of France from the French Canadians and were a separate colony throughout the period of French rule.

Moreover their history after the period of settlement has been entirely different from that of their French-Canadian cousins. During the colonial period they were passed back and forth between Britain and France repeatedly. Thus they soon developed a feeling of indifference to their European connection, and a desire to be treated as neutrals in the struggle for empire. However, their numbers were small, so they could do little to direct their destiny when two giants were at war in their midst. "Their role was to be that of the football in an international match."[2] The bitterest blow of all, of course, was when they were dispossessed of their lands and chattels and scattered among the British colonies of the Atlantic seaboard in 1755. This expulsion shattered their community and exposed them to privation and hardship that to this day make the Acadians see themselves as martyrs. Most of them trekked back to Acadia and settled in isolated areas remote from British control. Many went up the Saint John River; others settled along the shore of the Gulf of St. Lawrence; and still others found their way past their old homes in the Annapolis Valley to the easternmost extremity of Nova Scotia. In these isolated retreats they tried to re-establish their communities, but were not a factor of real importance as far as the British settlers were concerned for at least a century.

After the Acadians had been disposed of, British settlements spread

[1]Throughout this essay the local nomenclature is followed, that is, the term "French Canadian" is applied to the French community that originates in Quebec, as distinguished from the Acadians, the descendants of the French people who first settled in what are now the maritime provinces.

[2]J. B. Brebner, *New England's Outpost: Acadia before the Conquest of Canada* (New York: Columbia University Press, 1927), p. 133.

widely throughout the Maritimes. New Englanders, along with Scots, English, Irish, and some Europeans built up thriving communities in these colonies. Well before Confederation their economies came to maturity as lumbering, shipbuilding, trading, and agricultural communities with a vigorous pioneer spirit and a rising standard of living. But it was a period of prosperity and expansion that the British enjoyed virtually alone. The Acadians lived in the backwoods on a subsistence level, and were economically insignificant; but their numbers were growing rapidly.

From 1881 to 1951 the proportion of the population of French origin in the Maritimes increased from 12 per cent to 23 per cent, and in New Brunswick from 17 per cent to 38 per cent. Numerically its increase is even more impressive: from 108,605 in 1881 to 286,868 in 1951. Thus today the French-speaking population is a factor to be reckoned with in the Maritimes, although, of course, its position in New Brunswick is stronger than in the other two provinces.

The population of French descent is overwhelmingly rural,[3] whereas that of British descent is over half urban in the two mainland provinces. Therefore it is not surprising that the educational attainment of the French-speaking population is lower than that of the English. Table I sets out the difference in years of schooling between the two groups.

Clearly then the educational attainment of the population of French origin is very considerably below that of the population of British

TABLE I

YEARS OF SCHOOLING BY ORIGIN FOR THE MARITIME PROVINCES*

	British %	French %
Never attended	5	13
Attendance from:		
1–4 years	6	18
5–8	40	48
9–12	43	19
13–16	5	1
17+	1	1

*Based on data in Census of Canada, 1951, vol. II, Table 52. The percentages shown are percentages of the total population over five years of age that is not attending school.

[3]Over 70 per cent in New Brunswick and Prince Edward Island and 50 per cent in Nova Scotia.

origin. In fact almost 80 per cent of the French-speaking population has less than eight years of schooling, whereas just over 50 per cent of the English-speaking is in this category. This represents a greater difference between the two groups than their rural–urban ratio would account for; so it must be related to their occupations or to a complex of cultural factors.

TABLE II

MALE LABOUR FORCE OF THE MARITIME PROVINCES SHOWING OCCUPATIONAL GROUP AND RACIAL ORIGIN IN PERCENTAGES*

	French origin		British origin	
	%		%	
Primary industries				
Agriculture	20		18	
Forestry and logging	13		5	
Fishing and trapping	6		4	
Mining, quarrying, and oil wells	3	42	6	33
Manufacturing		19		17
Service occupations				
Service	9		16	
Electricity, gas, water	1		1	
Transportation, storage, communication	9	19	10	27
Trade		8		12
Finance, insurance, real estate				1
Construction		9		8
Not stated		2		2

*Computed from Census of Canada, 1951, vol. IV, Table 20.

Table II shows the racial origin of the male labour force of the Maritimes by occupational group. As can be seen in the table the population of French origin is more concentrated in the primary industries than is the population of British origin. This is especially noticeable in forestry and logging. The service occupations, on the other hand, attract much larger proportions of persons of British origin. This is also true of trade and of finance, insurance, and real estate. The population of French origin in the Maritimes is largely rural, and tends to be engaged in manual occupations more than does the population of British origin. Moreover the average educational attainment of the French-speaking Maritimers is lower than that of their English-speaking neighbours.

Since the "white collar" occupations and the professions tend to be dominated by English-speaking people, considerable numbers of

French-speaking persons adopt the English language and culture to gain entry to business and the professions. This applies particularly in the overwhelmingly English-speaking counties. In twenty-two of the thirty-six counties in the Maritimes, less than 11 per cent of the population is French by origin (see Figure 1). In twenty of these counties,

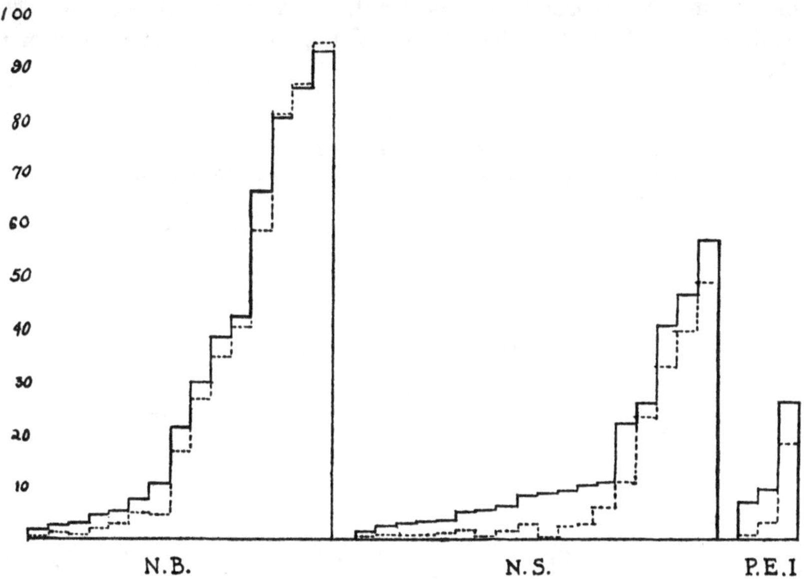

FIGURE 1. Population French by ethnic origin (solid lines) contrasted with population French by mother tongue (broken lines), in percentages, 1951, by counties.

the percentage of the population whose mother tongue is French is less than half the percentage of the population whose ethnic origin is French. Thus we could say that over half the population of the counties has become assimilated into the English-speaking community. On the other hand, in the three New Brunswick counties whose populations are over 80 per cent French in origin, we find a slightly larger percentage French by mother tongue than by origin. In these three counties the dominant culture is French, so the English are led to adopt the French language there. In the other eleven mixed counties (11 to 80 per cent French by origin) those of French origin outnumber those whose mother tongue is French. So, except for Madawaska, Gloucester, and Kent counties in northern New Brunswick, the dominant culture in the Maritimes is the English-speaking one, and there is an observable tendency for the French-speaking people to adopt the English language and culture. This tendency is much more prevalent in Prince Edward Island and Nova Scotia than in New Brunswick. Indeed, only 81 per cent of those persons who are French by origin speak French as their mother tongue in the Maritimes. This is mainly the result of two conditions: the fact that the English-speaking culture is the dominant one in thirty-three out of the thirty-six counties, and that it is the culture of the business and professional classes.

TABLE III

NUMBER AND PERCENTAGE OF PERSONS FRENCH BY ORIGIN AND BY MOTHER TONGUE, MARITIME PROVINCES, 1921–51*

	By origin		By mother tongue	
Year	Number	%	Number	%
1951	286,868	23	232,532	19
1941	244,993	22	209,890	19
1931	206,590	20	182,540	18
1921	189,701	19	132,115†	17

*Based on data from the censuses of 1921, 1931, 1941, and 1951.

†Population ten years of age and over only.

Table III shows that the Maritime population of French origin is increasing, both in numbers and in percentage of the total population. However, those whose mother tongue is French are increasing in *numbers* only; their percentage of the total population is almost constant through the four census years. The reason is that the higher rate of natural increase of the population of French origin is offset by its rate of assimilation into the English-speaking population.

However, this process is working out differently in New Brunswick from the other two provinces. The French culture in New Brunswick is winning on all fronts, as can be seen in Table IV. However, in Nova Scotia and Prince Edward Island, the trend is toward the assimilation of the people of French origin, as can be seen by comparing the percentages by origin with those by mother tongue. The English culture is gradually assimilating the French in Nova Scotia and Prince Edward Island, but in New Brunswick the position of the French culture is becoming continuously stronger.

The areas where the French people are concentrated and form the majority behave quite differently in politics from the rest of the

TABLE IV

PERCENTAGE OF PERSONS FRENCH BY ORIGIN AND MOTHER TONGUE, 1921–51*

Year	N.B. Origin	N.B. Mother tongue	N.S. Origin	N.S. Mother tongue	P.E.I. Origin	P.E.I. Mother tongue
1951	38	36	12	6	15	9
1941	36	35	12	7	16	11
1931	34	33	11	8	15	12
1921	31	29	11	10	14	13

*Based on data from censuses of 1921, 1931, 1941, and 1951.

Maritime community. As a minority in the area, they have felt the need to coalesce behind one party to make their weight felt. The party of their choice has been the Liberal party since about 1917. The greater the proportion of French- speaking people in a county, the larger is its Liberal vote likely to be. This is particularly noticeable in the three overwhelmingly French-speaking counties of Madawaska, Gloucester, and Kent in New Brunswick. These have been the real Liberal strongholds of the province, usually returning Liberal candidates with absolute majorities of 60 or 70 per cent.[4] Moreover, because their federal member is almost always French-speaking, they are the only safely French seats in the Maritimes. Each county also, of course, sends several members to the Legislative Assembly, and it is interesting to notice the difference between predominantly French-Canadian Madawaska and Acadian Gloucester and Kent. Madawaska gives more votes to French-speaking candidates, if indeed any English-speaking candidates run at all. The Acadian counties on the other hand consistently give more votes to the English-speaking candidates. The reason is that the Acadians vote the ticket; that is to say, they vote for all the candidates of one party. The English-speaking minority, on the other hand, tends to vote for English-speaking candidates only, thus giving them more votes. This acquiescent attitude of the Acadians is

[4]In the electoral success of the Conservatives in New Brunswick which occurred after this paper was written, Madawaska, which has a substantial French-Canadian admixture, went Conservative, but the Acadian counties of Kent and Gloucester remained loyal to the Liberals. In the federal elections of 1957 and 1958 the Liberal percentages were, respectively: in Restigouche-Madawaska, 45 and 42; in Gloucester, 58 and 53, and in Kent, 58 and 55. In provincial politics the constancy of Acadian support for the Liberals contrasts with the variations of Madawaska. In the elections of 1952, 1956, and 1960 the Liberal percentages were, respectively: in Kent, 57, 56, and 62; in Gloucester 59, 60, and 65; and in Madawaska 44, 41, 56.

typical. They are aware of their growing strength and realize that as their numbers grow, so must their influence. But they will not take any step that might spur the English-speaking majority to retaliation. They are mild and patient, displaying none of the militancy of their French-Canadian cousins.

The relations between the two cultures in the Maritimes are different from those existing in the rest of Canada, because the Acadians are so unlike the French Canadians of the rest of the country. The whole Acadian history is one of a weak and helpless people buffeted about by mighty forces that they could not hope to control. Their survival has depended on their tenacity and zeal for their own language, religion, and culture, and on their will to live a simple rural existence apart from their English-speaking neighbours. They have never been remote from the English in distance, yet culturally they have remained distinct. This separateness is traceable to the basic loyalty they feel to church and language—a loyalty which has been sustained by a simple, static, rural culture, different enough from the English to make rapid assimilation difficult, yet compatible enough with the English to prevent serious friction that might lead to strife. Relations between the two cultures have been fairly amicable, each tending to go its own way. The Acadians have allowed political and economic life to be dominated by the English not because they prefer this situation, but because their history has taught them to be mild and unobtrusive in their relations with the English majority. Moreover, since they are predominantly rural they tend to be scattered, disorganized, poor, and relatively uneducated. Thus there is no basis for that militantly nationalistic feeling which is so characteristic of the French Canadians in urban Quebec, although in Moncton, where urbanization and industrialization are starting to appear among the Acadians, we notice the beginnings of a similar spirit of nationalism. This is apparent in the columns of *L'Evangéline* and in the activities of la Société de l'Assomption. However, the response to this nationalistic appeal is faint in the rural areas where the bulk of the Acadian population lives.

An impressive characteristic of the Maritimes is the high degree of mutual toleration that exists between the two cultural groups, especially in New Brunswick where they have been living side by side for nearly two centuries. Each group is reconciled to the permanent existence of the other in the area; therefore each accepts the other for what it is. Even the functions of government are shared by the two societies. In the mixed counties there is a tacit understanding that the county's seats in the legislature will be shared fairly equitably between the two cultures. Each party presents a slate of candidates representing the major groups living in the county. Generally we find the English-speaking people over-represented on this list, owing largely to the fact that the French-speaking population is growing about eleven times as rapidly as the English-speaking, and there is always a lag between population ratios and political representation. Naturally there is some disappointment manifest among the English-speaking people at the decline of their representation although they are still so firmly in the saddle as not to feel seriously threatened.

In the Maritimes, unlike the rest of the country, political attention tends to be focused on economic problems and local improvements, so relations between the two cultures are not permitted to create issues to divide the voters. Maritimers of both British and French origin are at one in regretting the relative economic decline that their region has been undergoing since the time of Confederation. The effects of this change, especially in New Brunswick, have been to induce large numbers of the English-speaking population to migrate west and south, creating a vacuum into which many Acadians have been drawn. The percentage of persons of French origin has increased in every county in New Brunswick without exception since 1901. Therefore, the long-term trend in this province appears to be leading to a situation where the French-speaking population will be in the majority in the next quarter of a century or so. This of course might well make the Acadian culture the dominant one in the province. The race then is between the higher birth rate of the Acadians and the rate at which they are being absorbed into the English community. In New Brunswick the French culture is winning; but in Nova Scotia and Prince Edward Island, the English is gradually assimilating the French.

1955

The Franco-Americans of New England

GEORGE F. THERIAULT

Department of Sociology and Anthropology, Dartmouth College

OUTSIDE THE PROVINCE OF QUEBEC the largest concentration of people of French-Canadian origin in the New World is found in New England. It is an impressively large concentration, the best estimates placing its numbers somewhere between 900 thousand and one million. The Franco-Americans of New England thus constitute more than one in six of the French-Canadian stock on this continent. On the basis of numbers alone, therefore, they are of considerable importance in any study of French-Canadian society and its culture.

They are of far greater interest and importance, however, when their collective experience in the United States is viewed in the perspective of their response and adaptation, over a period of time extending back nearly a century, to the many-faceted challenges of life and living in an industrial civilization. In the current period of dynamic growth, industrialization, and urbanization in Canada few questions have more far-reaching import for the future of both English-speaking and French-speaking Canadians than this: What happens in the course of time to the traditional French-Canadian way of life, its values, institutions, and customs, when it is transplanted from the isolated rural, parochial, village setting to which it is indigenous to the dynamism of a highly industrialized urban milieu, and is exposed year in and year out for several generations to the ceaseless pressures and influences of a culture embodying in so many respects values antithetical to its own?

Recent studies[1] by Canadian scholars in many fields have reported highly interesting variations in the answers the Canadian scene is producing, and will produce increasingly in the years ahead, to this

[1]See particularly J.-C. Falardeau, éd., *Essais sur le Québec contemporain* (Québec: Presses Universitaires Laval, 1953).

truly fundamental question. While the dissimilarities between the American and Canadian settings prevent the drawing of precise analogues, the similarities are so numerous and in certain basic sociological respects so crucial that the Franco-American experience has considerable value for comparative purposes.

In the pages that follow I shall outline as fully as a short chapter permits the more important historical, ecological, and institutional features of Franco-American life in New England. In doing so I shall concentrate rather more upon what is implicit in the first than in the second word in the expression "Franco-American," since our primary interest lies in what has happened in the United States to the French-Canadian heritage of the Franco-American.

It is well for us to have in mind at the outset that the central motif of the Franco-American experiment has been that of combining elements drawn from the past and the present, from different societies and their cultures, from widely disparate traditions, ideals, and philosophies into a viable whole. It has been, in short, an ambitious attempt to put into practice and to carry forward a particular kind of cultural pluralism. Contemporary leaders of *la survivance* in New England recognize this clearly. A manifesto adopted upon the occasion of the celebration of the centennial of the founding of the first Franco-American parish described Franco-American life in these words: "Upon the spiritual plane, the Franco-Americans are Roman Catholics; upon the temporal plane, they are American citizens; finally they are by tradition, language, and spirit French; the whole being co-ordinated and combined in such a manner as to produce a way of life without a parallel in this country."[2]

For a minority group living within a larger society dedicated to ends different from its own to embark on and to hold to such a course is at best a precarious enterprise. Its members find themselves oriented at one and the same time to several different cultural worlds. They are subject to both internal tensions and the pull of conflicting interests in their relations with the peoples and institutions of the larger environment that people living in a more centrally integrated society are spared. From a sociological point of view it is not the failure of such undertakings that is surprising but rather the extent and duration of their successful life. On the American scene, which has seen in the past century and a half the testing of the experiments in survival of so

[2]*Notre Vie franco-américaine*, manifesto adopted at the Franco-American centennial celebration held at Worcester, Mass., May 28–9, 1949 (Boston, 1949), p. 8.

many minority groups, only the Spanish Americans of the Southwest have approached the degree of success of the Franco-Americans of New England.

To discover the extent of and the more important reasons for the measure of success they have achieved is the task to which we now address ourselves.

II

Evidence of *la Franco-Américanie* in New England is unobtrusive but catches the eye of the interested observer. It is most in evidence in the older textile centres, large and small, that were by far the most common goal of emigrating French Canadians in the nineteenth century. From 1865 onward, except in periods of economic stagnation, "the mills" beckoned with jobs, in good times with hundreds and thousands of jobs, that provided the immigrant with an economic foothold in the new land.

Today, nearly four generations later, these cities offer abundant testimony to the vitality and achievement of this hardy *habitant* stock. From Main Street to the neighbourhood grocery, stores bear such names as Gagnon, Lucier, Avard, Ouellette, Thibodeau. The shingles of lawyers and doctors display such names as Morin, Perreault, Menard. Signs and newspaper advertisements publicize such business enterprises as Lacroix, coal dealer; Marcotte, milkman; LeFebvre, radio and television service. In 1955 as in 1880, of course, Franco-American names are common on the employment rolls of textile, shoe, and paper industries. They are also found today in large numbers in industries that are relative newcomers to New England, plastics, electrical appliances, and other diversified industries. Within these firms their names are found all the way from unskilled and semi-skilled jobs to management positions, although their representation at the management level is still smaller than their numbers and long residence in the community would seem to call for. They are, in short, a prominent enough element in these New England industrial centres, alongside the Irish, who preceded them by a generation, and the Poles, Lithuanians, Greeks, Italians, and other south and central European peoples who came into these cities in the 1890's and the early years of this century.

Evidences that the Franco-Americans constitute a sub-community within the larger community are also found. Nearly all these cities have areas within them that both Franco-Americans and other residents generally regard as French. In the nineteenth century these were often spoken of as *p'tits Canadas*, Frenchville, and so on. More often, among the Franco-Americans themselves, these areas were and are known and spoken of by their parish names, St. Louis de Gonzague, Enfant Jésus, St. François-Xavier. While the churches, invariably large, with tall spires topped by the Roman Catholic cross, could not in these cities have the undisputed prominence against the skyline of their antecedents in the villages of Quebec, they have been none the less the nerve-centres of Franco-American life. Clustered around the church are the *presbytère*, the parochial schools—usually separate schools for boys and girls—the nuns' convent, the brothers' home. In the larger communities, parish-built and operated hospitals and orphanages are not uncommon.

These are the most prominent, but not the only, institutional features of the Franco-American sub-community. On the principal streets of these Franco-American areas men's clubs are prominent, with such names as Les Racquetteurs, Club Montcalm, Club Gagnon. In the larger centres a French-language newspaper such as *L'Action, Le Travailleur, L'Impartial* appears weekly. Insurance and mutual aid societies, as well as political organization at the ward level, are organized along ethnic lines. Each year in some of the larger centres symbolic recognition is accorded *la Franco-Américanie* by special observances, parades, masses, and so forth, on June 24, which is "la fête de St. Jean-Baptiste."

Such are some of the outward evidences of *la Franco-Américanie*. They are, as we have noted, unobtrusive features of the New England scene, taken for granted by both the Franco-Americans and their fellow citizens. Behind this public façade lies the much less readily observable, less easily measurable, massive but elusive reality of the Franco-American way of life. Questions about it abound; answers, firm answers, are hard to come by. How far has assimilation into the main stream of American life gone? How many defections from the faith have the three generations of life in the predominantly Protestant, secularly oriented United States brought about? How has the goal of bilingualism fared; what has happened to "la belle langue française?" Just what is the extent of interaction, co-operation, and mutuality of action and interests with French Canada?

These questions, and many others that spring to mind about the Franco-Americans, are not easily answered. Let us first identify and place *la Franco-Américanie* precisely. In speaking of it in the old textile centres we have only identified it with the type of cities with which the Franco-Americans are most commonly associated; where perhaps the experiment in survival has been most successful, but which collectively cannot even come close to accounting for the whereabouts and cultural life of the estimated 900 thousand to one million Americans of French-Canadian stock.

We need first to grasp the distribution of this population in the whole of New England, to sketch in the broad outlines of their regional ecology. We are handicapped by the fact that the United States census covers only the first two generations, whereas the third and fourth generations are vitally important for our purposes. Precise statistics are not available, but reasonably accurate estimates can be made. For our purposes it will only be important to delineate the most general demographic characteristics of *la Franco-Américanie.*

The Franco-Americans are by no means evenly distributed in New England; this fact is of crucial importance in understanding *la survivance.* They are found in appreciable numbers in predominantly rural states such as Maine and Vermont, and they have a considerable representation in such rural and "small town" occupations as logging, paper milling, and dairy and potato farming, but they are essentially and primarily an urban group. Massachusetts, heavily industrialized and urban, has more than twice as many Franco-Americans as Maine, which ranks second among the New England states in the number of Franco-Americans in its population. There follow in descending order New Hampshire, in third place, then Rhode Island, Connecticut, and Vermont.

The rural-urban distribution of Franco-American stock within these states attests to the essentially urban character of *la Franco-Américanie.* In Massachusetts the percentage of Franco-American stock of urban residence is 91; in Rhode Island it is even higher, 94. In New Hampshire it is 77; Connecticut, 68; Maine, 63; and Vermont, 38. A reasonable generalization from these figures[3] and other data would appear to be that four out of five Franco-Americans live in an urban environment.

Perhaps the most accurate index, from a sociological point of view, of the scope and character of *la Franco-Américanie* is provided by the numbers and location of parishes that have appreciable numbers of Franco-Americans on their parish rolls. Table I presents concisely the distribution of the Franco-Americans in the parochial structure of the Roman Catholic Church in New England, and at the same time sug-

[3]L. E. Truesdell, *The Canadian Born in the United States* (New Haven: Yale University Press, 1943), Table 32, p. 83.

TABLE I

FRANCO-AMERICAN PARISHES IN NEW ENGLAND, 1949*

Diocese	Total R.C.	Fr.-Am. nat'l parishes†	Fr.-Am. mixed‡	Mixed§	Total Fr.-Am.	%
Boston, Mass.	351	30	—	24	54	15.3
Burlington, Vt.	81	6	25	16	47	59.0
Fall River, Mass.	96	19	4	2	25	26.0
Hartford, Conn.	321	7	16	12	35	10.9
Manchester, N.H.	93	20	19	30	69	74.1
Portland, Me.	132	37	29	25	91	68.9
Providence, R.I.	130	18	10	8	36	27.6
Springfield, Mass.	212	41	4	25	70	33.0
TOTAL	1,416	178	107	142	427	30.1

*Comité d'Orientation franco-américaine, "Notre Vie franco-américaine" from a *Mémoire* presenting the principal statistics concerning *la Franco-Américanie* in New England (Boston, 1949), p. 21.

†A parish in which the priest(s) is Franco-American, and such duties as preaching, confession, and the prayers in which the congregation participates are conducted in French.

‡A parish in which the clergy and the majority of the parishioners are Franco-American, but where the priest is required to preach in both French and English, for the benefit of those parishioners who are not Franco-American.

§A parish in which the Franco-Americans constitute an appreciable proportion of the parishioners, but are not in the majority, in which the clergy is rarely Franco-American, and in which services may or may not be conducted in French as well as in English.

gests clearly the degree of concentration of the Franco-American population.

These data reveal that the Franco-Americans constitute practically the entire body of communicants in 178 parishes, and are in the majority in 107 other parishes. In at least 285 Roman Catholic parishes in New England, therefore, very sizable ecological groupings of Franco-Americans exist. It seems reasonable to assume further that in an appreciable percentage of the mixed parishes, numbering in all 142, Franco-American groupings of some size are also found. It would appear reasonable to estimate that 275 of the Catholic parishes in New England have Franco-American populations of 1,000 or more. These parishes may quite properly be regarded as the nerve-centres of the Franco-American experiment in survival.

Another view of these concentrations of population may be obtained from the comparative numbers of Franco-Americans in the cities of New England. Exact statistics are not available, but close approximations may be made that are adequate for the purpose of outlining the scope of *la Franco-Américanie*. The largest urban concentrations of Franco-Americans range from 30,000 to 40,000 persons. Woonsocket,

Rhode Island, Fall River, Massachusetts, and Manchester, New Hampshire, are in this category. Ranging from 20,000 to 30,000 are such communities as New Bedford, Lowell, and Worcester, in Massachusetts, and Lewiston, in Maine. A considerable number of communities fall in the 10,000 to 20,000 range; representative of these are Biddeford, Maine; Fitchburg, Haverhill, and Lawrence, Massachusetts; Nashua, New Hampshire; and Pawtucket and Central Falls, Rhode Island. A larger number of communities are found in the 5,000 to 10,000 range, including Auburn, Maine, Burlington, Vermont, and West Warwick, Rhode Island, as representative of such communities. Communities with Franco-American groups of from 1,000 to 5,000 are very numerous.[4]

III

The precise specification of the conditions necessary for the survival of a minority society and its culture within a larger, dominant society is a difficult task. It is perhaps especially difficult when the larger society is the United States, huge, amorphous, dynamic; characterized by tension, conflict, and ambivalence at numerous points; at once tolerant and intolerant of multiplicity; exerting pressures for conformity while simultaneously creating conditions that permit diversity.

The interaction of like-minded persons in some numbers is the fundamental requirement of all societies. A minority society is no exception to this basic sociological dictum. This basic condition was met in the case of *la Franco-Américanie*. The existence of relatively compact sub-communities of Franco-Americans in the industrial cities and towns of New England, organized in parishes that in their churches, schools, and associations gave explicit expression to the central values of their culture, the Roman Catholic faith, and the French language, provided the *sine qua non* of social interaction and regular, formal, institutionalized cultural expression.

Other factors tended to facilitate and enhance interaction and culture-building activities, notably the timing of immigration into these sub-communities and the socio-economic homogeneity of the Franco-American population during the early decades of their development. Franco-American immigration into the United States has been a

[4]The estimates in this paragraph are based on data given in *Sixteenth Census, 1940: Population, Nativity and Parentage of the White Population, Mother Tongue, by Nativity, Parentage, Country of Origin and Age, for States and Large Cities* (Washington, D.C., 1943), a special study tabulating a 5 per cent sample of the 1940 census returns, regarded by census officials as accurate within 10 per cent of the figures of the complete returns.

markedly wave-like phenomenon. Prior to the Civil War, people of French-Canadian origin in New England were few; still fewer came with the intention of becoming, or remaining as, permanent residents; many were migratory seasonal workers. In the late 1860's the boom in the cotton mills led to the first large-scale influx. In Nashua, New Hampshire, a community the writer has studied intensively, the Franco-American population jumped from fewer than 200 in 1869 to over 2,000 in 1872. The severe depression of the seventies, beginning in 1873, brought an abrupt end to immigration. The upswing of business in 1879 and the boom of the early eighties brought another wave of Franco-Americans into the community, swelling their total number to nearly 5,000. Immigration was again heavy in the early 1890's. After 1895 immigration tended to be more continuous, but on a smaller scale, less marked by heavy swells, except for the boom years of the 1920's. Return migration to Canada has been small. Only in the severe and long depression of the 1930's, and then only for two or three years, did the numbers leaving the United States for Canada exceed the numbers entering. In the past twenty years, comparatively few French Canadians have come to New England; and few have returned to Canada.

The wave-like pattern of migration, in the writer's opinion, had much to do with the successful establishment and maintenance of *la Franco-Américanie* in New England. The simultaneous arrival in New England's cities of large numbers of like-minded French Canadians, sharing a strong tradition, similar status as poor, unskilled, uneducated wage workers, and similar problems of finding jobs, homes for large families, and learning how to get along as French-speaking Catholics in a dominantly English-speaking Protestant environment created the necessary conditions for the prompt establishment of a minority sub-society.

The combined effect of the simultaneous arrival of large numbers and socio-economic homogeneity was to quickly bring into existence compact neighbourhoods of Franco-Americans in the cold-water flat and tenement districts clustered around the huge textile mills and shoe factories in dozens of New England industrial cities and towns.

The proximity of the mother country was and is an important factor influencing the lives and cultural destinies of Franco-Americans that, of all the immigrant groups in the United States, they share only with the Spanish Americans of the southwest. However nostalgic the Polish immigrant might feel about his childhood in a peasant village, he had made and knew that he had made an irrevocable commitment in coming to a new and vastly different land. He had turned his face on the past, made a clean and definitive break with it; he and his children looked to the future and a new life.

Not so the Franco-American. If he did not like the United States he could return to Canada. He could look forward to visiting the home country. He could maintain his ties with relatives and friends by correspondence. From time to time many of them joined him. There was much correspondence back and forth across the border, and a surprising amount of visiting back and forth even in the early years when economic resources were slender indeed. Canada as a source of leadership was very important. Priests, nuns, brothers came to lead the way in the reconstruction in New England of the parish, with its church, its schools, perhaps even its orphanages and hospitals—the parish that was the essential cornerstone of Franco-American society and the matrix within which Franco-American culture could be nurtured and sustained. Soon doctors, journalists, other professional men, trained in Canada, could follow and help play an important part in rounding out a viable structure of associational, fraternal, and community life. It is worthy of note that, once established, these Franco-American subcommunities recruited some of their religious and lay leaders from Franco-American youth of both sexes who were sent to Canada for their higher education.

IV

The social and institutional framework within which *la survivance* was achieved is of such importance that the manner and the order of its creation are worthy of note. For this purpose its development in a representative community may perhaps best suggest the general pattern. Nashua, New Hampshire,[5] is one of the larger centres of Franco-American settlement. Today some 17,000 of its total population of 34,000, or 50 per cent, are of French-Canadian origin. This particular community is therefore in the middle range of Franco-American centres, considerably smaller than the largest, which runs up to 40,000, considerably larger than the many cities and towns whose Franco-American populations run from 1,000 to 10,000. Nashua, by virtue of the size of its Franco-American population, must be regarded as one in which the necessary conditions for the creation and maintenance of the social framework for *la survivance* were unusually favourable. How

[5]The author's study of this community is reported in "The Franco-Americans in Nashua, New Hampshire: An Experiment in Survival," unpublished Ph.D. dissertation, Harvard University, 1951.

survival was achieved, and the time-table that was followed, are therefore especially interesting.

French Canadians were a little later in beginning their migration to Nashua than they were in coming to some other New England centres. In 1865 the local directory listed only thirty-one definitely or probably French-Canadian names. That number increased slowly until 1869, then, reflecting the first huge wave of migration, mounted steeply from 1870 to 1873, to approximately 2,200.

No time was lost in establishing a parish of their own. The Irish, who preceded the French Canadians by fifteen years or so, established the first Roman Catholic church in Nashua in the 1850's—the Church of the Immaculate Conception. The early French-Canadian settlers attended that church. In 1871 a separate parish, St. Louis de Gonzague, was created. In November of that year, Rev. J. B. H. V. Milette came from Canada to begin a long and extraordinarily successful pastorate, and in 1873 a large new church was dedicated.

The period that followed, through the remainder of the nineteenth and the early years of the twentieth century, was one that can only be described as of remarkable vitality and vigorous leadership. Writing of the parallel growth of Franco-American parishes throughout New England during this period, Mason Wade spoke of the movement as "an extraordinary effort, which is matched by no other ethnic group in the United States," and its leaders as "extraordinary men."[6] We can do no more than outline the dimensions of this achievement, in one community, and note certain considerations that heighten its stature.

Father Milette's parishioners were, almost without exception, newly arrived day labourers, without special skills. The great majority worked at wages averaging a dollar a day in the huge textile mills of the Nashua Manufacturing Company. Their families were large. They spoke little English and they had had but a few years of poor schooling in inadequate country and village schools. In the space of a generation these people were to invest over a million dollars, at nineteenth-century values, in the property Father Milette led them in building.

In 1875, two years after the church was dedicated, the parish acquired a *presbytère*, and in 1879 a cemetery was purchased. The parish grew rapidly: by 1883 its census showed 3,368 souls and 604 families. In that year, the church being almost paid for, the first convent was built, the Sœurs de Sainte-Croix came from Canada, and the first parochial school was opened.

[6]"The French Parish and Survivance in Nineteenth Century New England," *Catholic Historical Review*, vol. XXXVI, no. 2 (July 1950), p. 176.

In 1885 the parish was divided and Nashua's second Franco-American parish, St. François-Xavier, came into being with 663 communicants on its rolls. The division did not slow down the growth of St. Louis de Gonzague, however. In 1887 the church was improved. Two years later the boys' school was built. In 1891 a new *presbytère* was constructed. In the same year the boys' school was enlarged and the Frères du Sacré-Cœur came from Canada to take charge. The older parish had by 1890 regained the numbers of parishioners it had lost with the establishment of the new parish. In the early 1890's it grew rapidly; the parish census in 1893 reported 5,621 souls. In 1895 the residence of the brothers was built. In 1896 the church was enlarged. In 1897 a large new school of twenty-one classrooms was built. In 1906 a new boys' school was built. From 1901 to 1903 an orphanage with accommodations for 200 children was constructed, and the Sœurs de Charité came from Montreal to manage it. In 1907 Father Milette crowned his work by building one of the largest hospitals in the state, with 118 beds, which was also placed in the charge of the Sœurs de Charité.

In 1909 St. Louis de Gonzague was again divided and Nashua's third Franco-American parish, Enfant Jésus, was established. Developments similar to those traced above for the original parish, with the exception of hospital and orphanage, occurred in both of the new parishes. In 1910, Nashua's Franco-American population had increased to at least 8,555, or 33 per cent of the community's total population of 26,005.

In the traditional rural French-Canadian society the parish had been, in effect, the community, the all-embracing matrix within which farm, family, social relations had each had their appointed places. So now in the New England textile centre, *pari passu* with the wave-like influx of French Canadians, this social matrix was reconstituted.

The tall spires of Gothic churches rose in the densely peopled tenement districts clustered around the textile mills. In their shadows parochial schools were built, as quickly as possible, and, however great the strain on the parish's resources, the *presbytère*, a *couvent* for the nuns and a home for the brothers who came from Canada to teach French as well as English to the young and to see to it that the three R's were learned within a system of basic values in which religion had the central place. It is worthy of note that the Franco-Americans were much more assiduous in the building and staffing of bilingual parochial schools than were other immigrant Roman Catholic groups. In Nashua, as has already been noted, the Irish preceded the

Franco-Americans by about fifteen years. In the middle 1850's their numbers in the community were already 2,000 and they built their first church, but twenty-five years passed before they built a parochial school. In the larger Franco-American parishes vigorous leadership could cap this basic parish structure with a hospital and an orphanage, as Father Milette did at St. Louis de Gonzague in Nashua.

With the establishment of the parish, the building and staffing of churches and parochial schools, the cornerstone of *la survivance* was laid. The basic goal of retaining the identity of the Franco-Americans as a group was visualized by their leaders as attainable through the three crucially important institutions of the church, the school, and the home. The long experience of the French Canadians as a minority group disposed them to believe that if these three institutions, closely integrated one with the other, could be formed into havens of refuge impenetrable by outside influences, where the Catholic faith, the French language, and French-Canadian culture were cherished and nurtured, they could thrive, even in the midst of an alien and mildly hostile milieu.

It is well to note how in a community like Nashua (and there were many other cities and towns in which the pattern was duplicated), circumstances favoured in a more general way the attainment of this goal. As we have seen, by 1910 the community as a whole was one-third Franco-American. The implications are far-reaching. When such an appreciable percentage of a community's population speaks French, work and business feel the impact. It becomes "good business" for a Main Street store or bank to have clerks and tellers who can also speak it. French will be heard spoken by workmen on construction jobs, in factories, anywhere where men are associated in work.

Sections of the community, particularly in the thickly settled tenement districts hard by the mills and factories, became after 1871–2 almost exclusively French-speaking neighbourhoods. Thus the ordinary social interaction of everyday life in play groups, neighbourly relations, sports, and friendship lent effective support to the major institutional church, school, and home, in perpetuating French-Canadian culture. The fact that in the formative years, from 1870 to 1900, the Franco-American population was undifferentiated in economic and social status was a potent factor in shaping a homogeneous ethnic sub-community.

This solid community base for a Franco-American way of life likewise provided opportunities for further institutional elaboration and development. Voluntary associations of diverse kinds quickly developed. Parochial associations, charitable societies, societies supporting religious missions in foreign lands, and religious associations serving purely social functions for men, women, and children were formed. Non-parochial but church-sponsored mutual aid societies, burial societies, insurance societies, athletic and fraternal societies were formed. Such large Franco-American sub-communities attracted lay professional men from Canada, especially doctors and journalists. In Nashua a French-language newspaper, *L'Impartial*, still in existence, was launched in 1898.

The Franco-American experiment in survival in New England reveals many continuities in values, attitudes, institutions, and community ecological patterns from 1870 to the present day. Nevertheless, certain characteristics and tendencies clearly differentiate the earlier from the later periods. The assignment of specific dates to these periods is necessarily arbitrary, but if the caution is borne in mind that the dates used below are intended only as generally suggestive, their use has a certain convenience.

The period reviewed in the foregoing pages, extending from 1870 to 1910, was clearly one of most vigorous growth and institutional development. It included the late years of the nineteenth century when thirty years of economic depression in Canada spurred the wave-like movements of population into New England, which, by contrast to Canada, alternately experienced boom years of prosperity and sharp recessions. In the Franco-American sub-communities in New England these were the years in which the traditional parishes were constructed in the New England environment. This task was advanced with great vigour by a number of outstanding priests, of whom Father Milette in Nashua was an illustrious example. These were years in which both the clergy and their parishioners stood firmly united and adamant in their claim for the development of national parishes. In the centres of relatively large groupings of Franco-Americans the hierarchy of the Roman Catholic Church made no attempt to oppose the desires of the Franco-Americans for "their own" churches and schools in which the French language enjoyed a status equal to that of English, or for "their own" priests.

In secular life this period in Franco-American society was characterized by the dominant role of the immigrant, who was learning English as a second language but was much more at home in French. Economically *la Franco-Américanie* during these years was undifferentiated. It was a society of wage workers, largely unskilled and poorly educated. Fresh from the rural parishes of the province of

Quebec, these new Americans were prepared to adapt themselves to conditions in New England as they found them, particularly as regards work, but they were so numerous and lived so compactly together that there could be no question of making basic cultural choices. They were French, deeply Catholic, profoundly attached to the ethos that was their heritage.

The period that followed, roughly identified as the years from 1910 to 1930, was different in many respects from the first. Immigration from Canada was on a sharply reduced scale except for a few boom years in the twenties, but was fairly continuous, and returnees to Canada were few. The natural rate of increase was high. By 1920, Nashua's Franco-American population had risen to 10,420, or 36.7 per cent of the total population of 28,379, and by 1930 it had reached 12,683, or 40.3 per cent of the total population of 31,463. The sub-communities and their institutions continued to expand. Voluntary associations developed and grew stronger.

The prominent role of the first generation immigrant continued in so far as the traditional institutional activities were concerned, but new features made their appearance. Increasingly the new generation born in the United States, with no personal experience of French Canada, made itself felt. This generation was naturally and truly bilingual, having learned French at home, at church, and in the parochial schools, from friends and cliques, and in athletic and other social activities; and having learned English from the varied, omnipresent, ambient influence of life in an American community. Economic differentiation appeared. Semi-skilled and highly skilled workers developed. White-collar jobs in clerical, sales, and secretarial work came to be filled by the sons and daughters of immigrants. An emergent middle class composed largely of small business entrepreneurs, storekeepers, bakers, milkmen, real estate men, politicians, and office-holders came into existence. A sprinkling of professional men, doctors, and lawyers appeared.

Ecologically, this socio-economic differentiation expressed itself in the emergence, usually on the periphery of the densely populated tenement districts, of lower middle-class and middle-class residential areas, of which the most prominent architectural features in that period were the two- or four-family apartment building and the single and duplex family type of home in a somewhat less congested neighbourhood.

This was the period of the coming of age politically of the Franco-Americans, and their assumption of an increasingly prominent role in local and state politics. Local political leadership developed and found expression, first in naturalization campaigns, and later in the organization and consolidation of political action. Typically, local politics became a subject of lively interest, especially for rising, ambitious young men whose interests it served; and identification with their ethnic group played a most prominent role in this development.

Religious leadership tended to change in character. Parishes grew in numbers of communicants, and became institutionally stronger, but the dynamism of the earlier years was replaced by a spirit that seemed to stand principally for consolidation and the maintenance of close identification with the group. Struggles within the Church and in the press reflected a strong insistence upon the rights of Franco-Americans to run their own affairs in their own "national" parishes. Vigour, assertiveness, and some independence were manifest. The tendency away from the earlier dynamism, however, is perhaps best expressed symbolically in the fact that the *curés* who replaced the founders in large urban Franco-American parishes were priests approaching the end of their career, who, as rewards for long service in smaller parishes, were given secure posts where they were *inamovible* (had tenure for life) and would spend the remainder of their days in prestige and comfort, with the services of several curates as assistants. Since these appointments were in the hands of the hierarchy of the Church, it appears likely that the absence of vigorous leadership in the "national" parishes reflected a basic policy of not encouraging the further development of such parishes.

The third period, from 1930 to the middle 1950's is a more difficult one to evaluate in detail, but it also clearly revealed new trends, the most central and important of which was a sharply increased rate of loss to the minority sub-community of appreciable numbers of individuals of Franco-American background. In the writer's study of Nashua, whose population had grown to 34,666 by 1950, great care was taken to estimate this loss as closely as possible, but only the general findings and some indications of the factors at work can be presented here. Two methods were used to arrive at a close estimate of the percentage made up by people of Franco-American background. A complete tally was made of the ethnic identification of the voters on the community's checklists, and an independent tally was made by using a zoning map and city directory and identifying the residents on an evenly distributed sample of streets in each zone. These two checks independently arrived at a percentage just short of 50 for the proportion of the total population that was Franco-American in origin. It is interesting to compare this percentage with that arrived at in another local study made in 1936 which found that the Franco-American ethnic stock constituted 45.5 per cent of the total population.

Both in total numbers—approximately 17,000—and in percentage of the community's total population, the element that was Franco-American in origin in 1950 represented a considerable increase over the 12,638 found in 1930. However, if we take parochial school registrations in Franco-American parishes as the best single index of identification with the sub-community, we find that they are only very slightly larger in 1950 than in 1930. Our studies indicated that no more than 13,000 of the estimated total of 17,000 could be regarded in the early 1950's as being closely identified with the Franco-American sub-society. Other evidence tends also to support the general conclusion that this sub-community has at best held its own during these years.

Moreover, certain qualitative changes in the "cultural climate" of the sub-community during these years seem to indicate a steady erosion of values, traditions, and institutions that were firmly held to in the past and a steady strengthening of the factors and influences making for assimilation into the general American culture in the future. Let us examine some of these changes.

In the mid-fifties we are confronted by a population in *la Franco-Américanie* that is in large part three generations and, in increasing numbers, four generations removed from French Canada. Economic differentiation into the varied strata of the working, middle, and upper classes has proceeded apace and brought marked changes in residence, outlook, attitudes, associational affiliations, and cultural values. Even at the lowest levels the habits of life of the community today present the sharpest contrast to those of twenty years ago. Full employment and high levels of prosperity, in spite of the sharp economic readjustments that had to be made in this as in other New England communities by the shift away from textiles to electric appliances and other new industries, have wrought basic changes that tend in the aggregate to weaken the ethnic sub-community.

Specifically, these post-war years have brought military service, more and better automobiles, travel, and television, and participation in other aspects of American mass culture on a larger scale; substantial changes in the ecological distribution of the population away from ethnic concentration toward zonal patterns differentiated on the basis of socio-economic status in the community; and increased intermarriage among members of different ethnic stocks. These changes have not only loosened the bonds that traditionally bound Franco-Americans together in a mutuality of interests, but have also set in train innumerable intangible influences shaping individual destinies in the social and cultural multiplicities that characterize a contemporary American community

If we examine the influences at work within the institutional structure of the Franco-American sub-society, as represented in a community which we should again note carefully was one in which the conditions for the experiment in survival were exceptionally propitious, we find little basis for optimism about the prospects for the future. The national parish as the social matrix for Franco-American *survivance* and the French language so closely identified with both sacred and profane activities are the critical features. If they survive, *la Franco-Américanie* survives; if they pass from the scene, little of any significance of "notre héritage" will remain. Their prospects therefore deserve special attention.

In order to understand what is happening to the Franco-American parish in New England in the middle of the twentieth century certain basic background information is indispensable. Of crucial importance is the policy of the American Roman Catholic Church concerning the so-called national parishes. At the Catholic Congress of Baltimore in 1889, when the issue of national parishes assumed great importance because of the swelling tide of Catholic immigrants from south and central Europe, the official policy of the American Church was set in these terms: that "national societies, as such, have no place in the Church of this country; after the manner of this congress, they should be Catholic and American."[7] Since that time they have been tolerated, regarded basically as a temporary expedient, but they have not been encouraged.

It is especially significant that in recent years the hierarchy of the Church has begun to exert marked pressure upon the traditional Franco-American parishes. In contrast to the indirect methods followed in the middle period, such as the appointment of *curés* who by reason of age and length of service could be expected to pursue a more or less passive course, a number of positive steps have been taken to force changes in the direction of making these parishes conform to the basic policy of the Church. It is reasonable to assume that these steps are not being taken without a careful reading of the opportunities, even the necessities, created by internal changes in the habits of language and the interests and values of the Franco-American

[7]Wade, "The French Parish," p. 185.

parishioners. Pressures have been exerted to bring the curricula of the parochial schools more closely in line with the standards of the public schools in non-religious subjects. The amount of time allotted to instruction in the French language has been reduced and that allotted to English increased. Prayers must be learned in English, as well as French. English is more frequently heard in church.

The implementation of a policy aimed at reducing bilingualism is not new. It has always been in effect in mixed parishes, and in smaller communities where, although the Franco-Americans might be heavily in the majority, they did not constitute a large or powerful enough community to maintain their "rights" effectively. This has been a lively issue among Franco-Americans from the earliest days of their settlement in New England. What is new is the direct implementation of this policy in the large parishes in centres of heavy concentrations of Franco-Americans—centres such as Nashua and Manchester, New Hampshire, Woonsocket, Rhode Island, and Worcester, Massachusetts. Strident voices of protest are still heard, but popular support for the cries of anguish that appear in the Franco-American press is lacking. The fact that support from the Church is also lacking can be taken to mean only one thing—that the time is ripe for the hierarchy to press for an active start at the process of changing the national parishes into English-language, American-Catholic churches and schools.

Outside of the churches and schools in the everyday life of Franco-Americans, habits of language give every appearance of being in a highly unstable state. Over-all evaluations and predictions are difficult to make, but such indications as one finds do not present a hopeful prospect for the future of French as a language in everyday use. One should not, of course, under-estimate the vitality of a language that is still being used extensively in community centres of the size of the Franco-American community in Nashua. Neither, on the other hand, should one be blind to what appears to be going on.

It is still possible for members of the older generation to transact business, pray, read newspapers, and converse with their neighbours exclusively in French. One may still find individuals who have lived in these communities forty or fifty years without having learned English. When, however, one listens to middle-aged persons, youth, and little children, the speech is very different. It is not uncommon to find among the middle aged an easy and rapid alternating use of French and English words and phrases with no apparent awareness of switching from one language to another. Such instability in habits of language is not likely to last. Among the young, English tends to be the language in use. French may be understood, and frequently is, but it is much less frequently used. Very often one finds a marked reluctance to speak French.

In the course of the writer's field work in 1950 and 1951 a *fête champêtre* was held in the largest of the Franco-American parishes to raise funds. The title was a misnomer, because this was no more nor less than a small carnival, with booths, merry-go-round, and so on. Held in the parish grounds, literally in the shadow of the church, the carnival was well attended. The writer strolled through the dense crowds for several hours on two evenings and was struck by the marked use of English. French was heard only occasionally, and very rarely indeed from children and young people talking among themselves. Older people sometimes spoke French, sometimes called to their children in French. About half the time the children answered them in English.

It would be rash indeed to predict that the French language will not be heard in communities such as Nashua in ten or even twenty-five years. There are still first and second generation Franco-Americans, among whom the habits and tendencies of bilingualism and biculturalism are and will continue to be fairly strong. The massive inertia of the compact Franco-American neighbourhoods that characterize Franco-American sub-communities of the size of Nashua will doubtless retard and partially hold off the varied influences making for more complete assimilation.

Will the traditional rallying cry of the Franco-Americans, "Qui perd sa langue, perd sa foi," become reality in the not-so-distant future? This eventuality appears unlikely in so far as the majority is concerned. Substantial losses have been and probably will continue to be suffered by the Church. But the measures taken by the Church to counter this threat are impressive. Throughout the history of this Franco-American experiment the "Irish" parish in the community has been available to those who desired to become part of it, either because of intermarriage with Catholics of other national backgrounds or because of changes in habits of language; many have availed themselves of this opportunity in the past. Two new Roman Catholic parishes have been established in the last few years that have carefully avoided identification with one ethnic group. A Roman Catholic college has been established in the community. Several convents that take day students as well as boarders are now available both in the community and within easy commuting distance. For several years there has been much talk of the establishing Roman Catholic secondary schools. If this should happen, the proportion of the community's school population enrolled in the parochial schools—45 per cent at present—would rise to a substantial majority.

The evidence appears to be substantial that the central institutional structure of *la Franco-Américanie*, even in comparatively large centres such as Nashua, is showing increasing signs of weakening. The evidence points to further weakening in the future. This process is unlikely to be reversed; it is equally unlikely that it will be slowed. On the contrary, it will very probably be more rapid in the next twenty-five years than it has been in the past generation. That is not to say that it will be fast, however. Ways of life, deeply cherished institutions, religion and language, are too centrally in the grain of a people to change rapidly.

Whatever the future holds in store for the Franco-Americans of New England, their eighty years' long experiment in survival in the midst of a society and culture as kinetic as that of the United States is no inconsiderable testimony to the vitality and staying power of "notre héritage."

1955

V. CONCLUSIONS

V. EPILOGUE

Conclusions

MASON WADE
Director, Canadian Studies Program
University of Rochester

THE FIRST CONCLUSION to which the reader of these essays must come is that the English-Canadian and French-Canadian mentalities remain very different, and probably will continue so, despite the rapid growth of a common Canadianism. Since 1945, relations between French and English Canadians have become better than ever before, although the period opened with a sharp division between the two groups over the conscription question, a division which many thought would take as long to heal as that of 1918. But in the post-war period there has been much co-operation and adjustment between the two groups, though little synthesis except in the fields of law and labour, where administrative and economic necessities have favoured a closer *rapprochement*. Perhaps in no instance is the difference of mentality more marked than in the basic one of religion and philosophy. Father Régis' essay suggests, however, that French Catholics have a greater understanding of English Protestantism than is commonly thought, and also perhaps a more oecumenical outlook than their Protestant compatriots. President Kirkconnell's contribution indicates that it is not the French Catholics who are now preoccupied with *survivance*, but the English Protestants, who are still moved by the old distrust of Catholicism, despite the waning of the bitter sectarianism of the nineteenth century. The basic philosophic difference remains, reflected in sometimes curious fashions in the economic world and in the labour movement.

The outlooks of French and English Canadians reflect this basic differentiation, though both are clearly trying hard to understand and accept the other's point of view. In recent years the French Canadian has become more interested in and knowledgeable about economic and scientific matters, but his basic outlook remains humanistic. His mind tends to have a theoretical and metaphysical bent, while his English compatriot's tendency is toward the pragmatic and the practical. Each admits, grudgingly or not, that the other has greater talents in some respects. There is the French myth that only *les Anglais* can manage great business enterprises, while the English yield the cultural and creative palm, not to mention the linguistic one, to the French. Because of the increasingly close liaison between the English and French universities, and more bilingualism, it is probable that these differences of outlook will not be as marked in the future as they have been in the past. In any case there certainly will be a greater understanding by each of the other point of view, and less intransigence about accepting it as a fact of Canadian life. The French Canadian knows that in the nature of things he cannot go it alone in North America today; the English Canadian now accepts the fact that Canada must be both French and English if it is not to become American. The Massey Report and the action taken upon it by both the St. Laurent and Diefenbaker governments reflect this new acceptance of Canada's biculturalism as a national asset rather than a liability.

Some other old myths are shattered by the demographic studies in this volume. As birth rates level out under the impact of urbanization and the French and English family become more similar, much irrational folk-fear of the other group will disappear. Such studies make it clear that there has been no conspiracy by one group to swamp the other, no *revanche des berceaux* on the one hand, or calculated efforts to offset the formerly higher French birth rate by massive English-speaking immigration. It turns out, on close examination, to be a matter of different cultural traditions and different ways of life. And as the two ways of life draw closer together under the powerful forces of urbanization and industrialization, the differences tend to disappear. The language barrier becomes less significant when the way of life is much the same. Some differences will doubtless remain: the French-Canadian family will probably always remain a stronger social unit because of powerful cultural traditions. Early marriage, with the prompt formation of new families, will probably also remain more typical of French Canada than of English Canada. And it is doubtful whether *la créature* will become, or want to become, as emancipated from domestic concerns as the English-speaking career woman. Here again different basic social values are reflected.

Some of the most interesting conclusions of this symposium emerge from the essays on the outlying French groups who live beyond Quebec's borders. The French-Canadian fact—*le fait français dans l'Amérique du Nord*—can no longer be regarded as confined to that province, when French Canadians are found in considerable numbers in every province. But the old English racial fear of a vast French conspiracy to take over Canada should fade away with the realization that each of these outlying groups has its own ideology, which is perhaps closer to the prevailing regional one than to that of the French Canadian of Quebec. It has long been recognized that French Canadians and Acadians are very different, and frequently do not get along as well with each other as they do with English Canadians. These essays make it clear that there are many other instances of such profound differences among French-speaking Canadians, not to mention the Franco-Americans. The story of the latter indicates that French-Canadian cultural survival is not dependent upon the special rights and privileges which the French Canadian enjoys by law and custom in Quebec, and to a lesser degree in the rest of Canada. This people's vitality and will to live as a distinct entity can triumph over unfavourable environmental conditions.

If, then, as the record would indicate, *survivance* is assured, perhaps French Canadians in the future can devote more of their energy to a creative collaboration with their English compatriots, rather than wasting it in a resistance which is no longer necessary to assure cultural survival. There are many signs in present-day Canada that this shift is taking place. French Canadians are playing a larger role than ever before in the national life of Canada, both at home and abroad, while holding their own in Quebec, where for the first time they are distinguishing themselves in business, industry, and applied science, the fields which they formerly renounced, for lack of proper training, to English Canadians and others who were better equipped to deal with the technical problems of an increasingly complicated economy.

To answer some of the questions posed at the beginning of this volume, it would appear that there is much co-operation and adjustment between English and French in Canada today, although some ancient and deep-rooted misunderstandings remain. There is little evidence of serious friction and conflict. The Canadian compromise is being extended into many new areas, with the mutual recognition that both English and French Canadians have much to offer to enrich the Canadian pattern. There is a new confidence between the groups. The Editor can report that he received full co-operation from all the contributors, and that there were no difficulties arising out of cultural differences. All were eager to participate as usefully as possible in the common enterprise; none stood upon their rights or dignity and refused to budge from prepared positions at the Editor's request.

It is this writer's conviction that such frank joint examinations of French and English attitudes can do much to increase mutual understanding. As he concludes this volume, he would urge that another such book, concerned with the more humanistic aspects of biculturalism, might be even more valuable than this in achieving the goal of mutual understanding. For Canadians show a growing realization that it is cultural differences, rather than political or economic ones, which set peoples apart. Once more St. Augustine's wise observation should be cited: "A nation is an association of reasonable beings united in a peaceful sharing of the things they cherish; therefore, to determine the quality of a nation, you must consider what these things are."

1958

Index

www.ingramcontent.com/pod-product-compliance
Lightning Source LLC
LaVergne TN
LVHW010447080826
844660LV00027B/1228

* 9 7 8 1 4 8 7 5 8 5 5 1 8 *